o|s Ordnance Survey

C000131431

STREET

Cheshire

Contents

III *Key to map symbols*

IV *Key to map pages*

VI *Administrative and post code boundaries*

1 *Street maps*

237 *Extra-large-scale map of Chester town centre*

238 *Town maps*

    238 *Altrincham*
    239 *Cheadle and Gatley*
    240 *Stockport*
    241 *Hyde*
    241 *Romiley*
    242 *Sale*
    242 *Stalybridge*

243 *Index of hospitals, railway stations, schools, shopping centres, street names and universities*

PHILIP'S

First edition published 1995
First colour edition published 1998
Reprinted in 1999, 2000 by

George Philip Ltd, a division of
Octopus Publishing Group Ltd
2-4 Heron Quays, London E14 4JP

ISBN 0-540-07509-4 (pocket)

© Crown copyright 1998
© George Philip Ltd 1998

To the best of the Publishers' knowledge, the information in this
atlas was correct at the time of going to press. No responsibility
can be accepted for any errors or their consequences.

The representation in this atlas of a road, track or path is no
evidence of the existence of a right of way.

**The mapping between pages 1 and 237 (inclusive) in this
atlas is derived from Ordnance Survey® Large Scale and
Landranger® mapping; pages 238-242 (inclusive) are derived
from Ordnance Survey® OSCAR® and Land-Line® data, and
Landranger® mapping.**

Ordnance Survey, OSCAR, Land-line and Landranger are
registered trade marks of Ordnance Survey, the national
mapping agency of Great Britain.

Printed and bound in Spain by Cayfosa

Digital Data

The exceptionally high-quality mapping
found in this book is available as
digital data in TIFF format, which is
easily convertible to other bit-mapped
(raster) image formats.

The index is also available in digital
form as a standard database table.
It contains all the details found in the
printed index together with the
National Grid reference for the map
square in which each entry is named
and feature codes for places of
interest in eight categories such as
education and health.

For further information and to discuss
your requirements, please contact
Philip's on 020 7531 8440 or
george.philip@philips-maps.co.uk

	British Rail station
	Metrolink station
	Underground station
D	Docklands Light Railway station
M	Tyne and Wear Metro
	Private railway station
	Bus, coach station
◆	Ambulance station
◆	Coastguard station
◆	Fire station
◆	Police station
✚	Accident and Emergency entrance to hospital
H	Hospital
+	Church, place of worship
i	Information centre (open all year)
P **P&R**	Parking, Park and Ride
PO	Post Office
	Important buildings, schools, colleges, universities and hospitals

Motorway (with junction number)

Primary route (dual carriageway and single)

A road (dual carriageway and single)

B road (dual carriageway and single)

Minor road (dual carriageway and single)

Other minor road

Road under construction

Pedestrianised area

County and Unitary Authority boundaries

Railway

Tramway, miniature railway

Rural track, private road or narrow road in urban area

Gate or obstruction to traffic (restrictions may not apply at all times or to all vehicles)

Path, bridleway, byway open to all traffic, road used as a public path

The representation in this atlas of a road, track or path is no evidence of the existence of a right of way

Adjoining page indicators

The map area within the pink band is shown at a larger scale on the page indicated by the red block and arrow

Prim Sch	Important buildings, schools, colleges, universities and hospitals
River Medway	Water name
	Stream
	River or canal (minor and major)
	Water
	Tidal water
	Woods
	Houses
House	Non-Roman antiquity
VILLA	Roman antiquity

Acad	**Academy**	Mon	**Monument**
Cemy	**Cemetery**	Mus	**Museum**
C Ctr	**Civic Centre**	Obsy	**Observatory**
CH	**Club House**	Pal	**Royal Palace**
Coll	**College**	PH	**Public House**
Ent	**Enterprise**	Recn Gd	**Recreation Ground**
Ex H	**Exhibition Hall**	Resr	**Reservoir**
Ind Est	**Industrial Estate**	Ret Pk	**Retail Park**
Inst	**Institute**	Sch	**School**
Ct	**Law Court**	Sh Ctr	**Shopping Centre**
L Ctr	**Leisure Centre**	Sta	**Station**
LC	**Level Crossing**	TH	**Town Hall/House**
Liby	**Library**	Trad Est	**Trading Estate**
Mkt	**Market**	Univ	**University**
Meml	**Memorial**	YH	**Youth Hostel**

■ The dark grey border on the inside edge of some pages indicates that the mapping does not continue onto the adjacent page

■ The small numbers around the edges of the maps identify the 1 kilometre National Grid lines

The scale of the maps is 3.92 cm to 1 km (2½ inches to 1 mile)

0	¼	½	¾	1 mile
0	250m 500m 750m	1 kilometre		

The scale of the map on page numbered in red is 7.84 cm to 1 km (5 inches to 1 mile)

0	220 yards	440 yards	660 yards	½ mile
0	125m 250m	375m	½ kilometre	

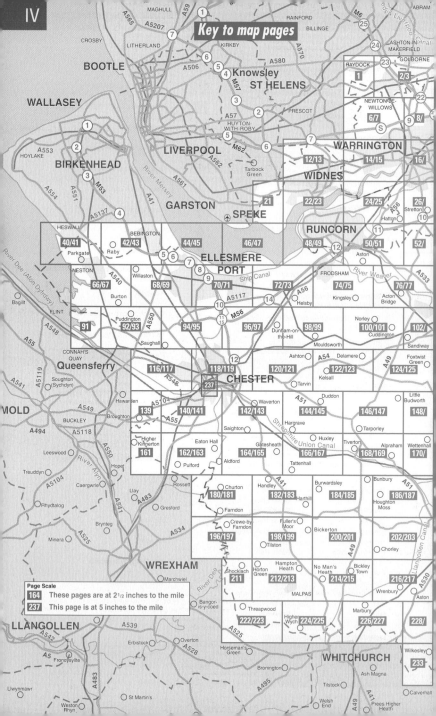

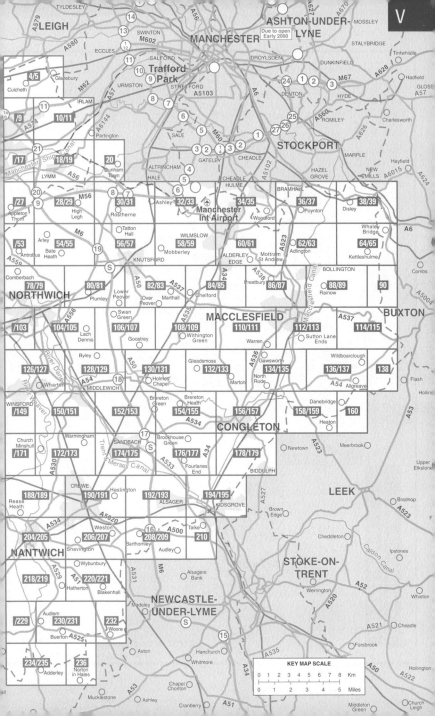

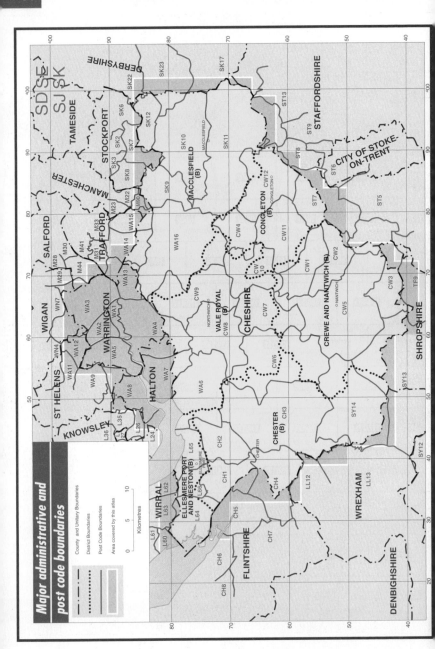

Major administrative and post code boundaries

	County and Unitary Boundaries
	District Boundaries
	Post Code Boundaries
	Area covered by this atlas

Kilometres

0   5   10

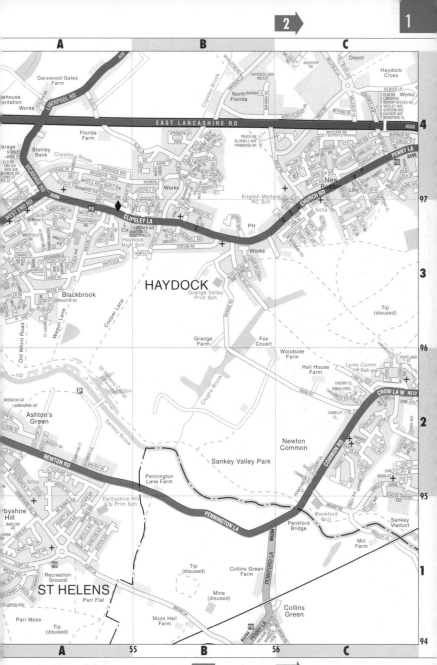

NEWTON-LE-WILLOWS

Haydock Cross
Old Boston Trad Est
Old Boston
Hotel
Haydock Park
Lady Hill Plantation
White Door Covert
White Door Dam
Race Course
EAST LANCASHIRE RD
Fox Covert
Dean Dam
Haydock Park Farm
Dean Dam Farm
Ellam's Rough
Ellam's Brook
Newton-Haydock Bridge
WOODLANDS IND EST
Lawson's Farm
Hollows Bridge
Haydock Park Golf Course
CH
Millingford Brook
ASHTON RD
Newton-le-Willows High Sch
Maritime
Newton Bank Sch
Valley View
Newton Lake
Tip (dis)
VISTA RD
CROW LA W
CROW LA E
Liby
HIGH ST
CHURCH ST
SOUTHWORTH RD
St Peter's CE Prim Sch
NEWTON-LE-WILLOWS
Wargrave
Newton-le-Willows Sta
Stone Crossing
Earlestown
Earlestown Station
Works
THE CROSSINGS
Sankey Brook
Newton Community
Cemy
Newton Brook
WINWICK RD
Newton Park Farm
Wargrave House Sch
LEAMINGTON AVE
St Helens Canal (dis)
OLD HEY WLK
Works
Red Bank
Red Bank Ave
New Hey Farm

1. ALPINE ST
2. SCEPTRE CL
3. LORD ST
4. GRAFTON ST
5. GRANT ST
6. BACK BOOTH ST
7. BACK LAWRENCE ST
8. WELLINGTON GDNS

1. HOUGHTON ST
2. HOUGHTON CL
3. DERBY CL

1. REDBANK CL
2. SAPPER CL
3. TONSTONE AVE
4. LAPWING CL
5. SUNNYBANK CL
6. GREENFIELDS CL

1. PRINCES ST
2. DUKE ST

A580
A599
B5209
A572
A49

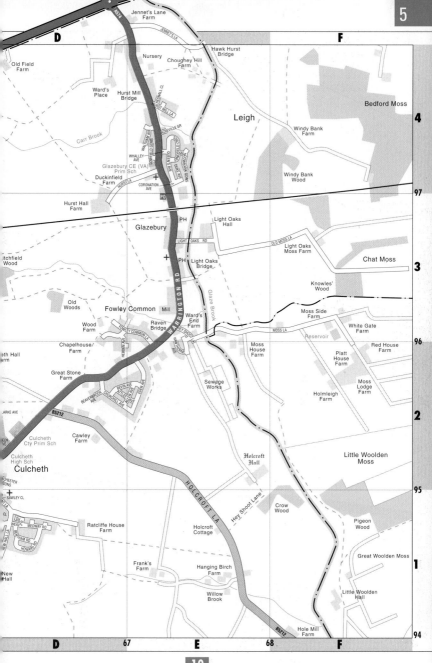

Old Field Farm

Jennet's Lane Farm

Nursery

Choughey Hill Farm

Hawk Hurst Bridge

Ward's Place

Hurst Mill Bridge

Bedford Moss

Leigh

Windy Bank Farm

Carr Brook

Glazebury CE (VA) Prim Sch

Duckinfield Farm

Windy Bank Wood

CORONATION AVE

PO

Hurst Hall Farm

97

PH

Light Oaks Hall

Glazebury

LIGHT OAKS RD

OLD MOSS LA

Light Oaks Moss Farm

itchfield Wood

Chat Moss

PH

Light Oaks Bridge

WARRINGTON RD

Knowles' Wood

3

Old Woods

Fowley Common

Mill

Glaze Brook

Moss Side Farm

MOSS LA

Wood Farm

Raven Bridge

Ward's End Farm

White Gate Farm

Reservoir

Chapelhouse Farm

th Hall arm

Moss House Farm

Red House Farm

96

Great Stone Farm

Platt House Farm

Sewage Works

Moss Lodge Farm

BS212

Holmleigh Farm

2

Cawley Farm

Culcheth Cty Prim Sch

Culcheth High Sch

Little Woolden Moss

Culcheth

95

SAWLEY CL

MEDWAY RD

Ratcliffe House Farm

HOLCROFT LA

Holcroft Hall

Hey Shoot Lane

Crow Wood

Pigeon Wood

Holcroft Cottage

New Hall

Frank's Farm

Hanging Birch Farm

Great Woolden Moss

1

Willow Brook

Little Woolden Hall

BS212

Hole Mill Farm

94

D   67   E   68   F

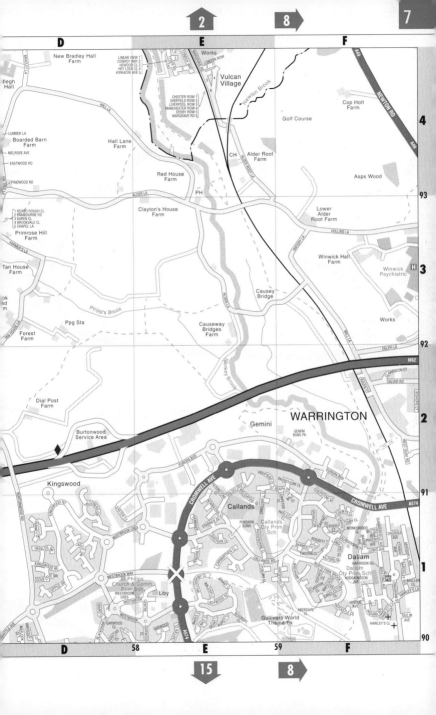

D   E   F

New Bradley Hall Farm

LINEAR VIEW 1
CONROY WAY 2
HEYWOOD CL 3
HEY LOCK CL 4
KIRKACRE AVE 5

Works

Vulcan Village

Newton Brook

Cop Holt Farm

4

dleigh Hall

LUMBER LA

Boarded Barn Farm

MELROSE AVE

EASTWOOD RD

PINEWOOD RD

Hall Lane Farm

CHESTER ROW 1
SHEFFIELD ROW 2
LIVERPOOL ROW 3
MANCHESTER ROW 4
DERBY ROW 5
WARGRAVE RD 6

Golf Course

Alder Root Farm

Asps Wood

CH

Red House Farm

PH

Lower Alder Root Farm

93

1 ROXBO ROUGH CL
2 CAMBOURNE RD
3 KAREN CL
4 BROOKVALE CL
5 CHAPEL LA

Clayton's House Farm

HOLLINS LA

FARMER'S LA

Primrose Hill Farm

Winwick Hall Farm

Winwick Psychiatric

H

Tan House Farm

Phipp's Brook

Causey Bridge

3

ok ad m

Ppg Sta

Causeway Bridges Farm

Works

Forest Farm

DELPH LA

92

Dial Post Farm

M62

CLARENDON CT
CALVER RD

Burtonwood Service Area

WARRINGTON

Gemini

GEMINI BSNS PK

BISHOPS CT

WEST DRAY

2

Kingswood

CROMWELL AVE

Callands

EUROPA BLVD

ST ASAPH CL

CROMWELL AVE   A574

91

Callands Cty Prim Sch

PENSARN GDNS

Dallam

HARRISON SQ
Dallam
Cty Prim Sch
HODGKINSON AVE

PO

1

WESTBROOK CRES

St Philips Church & Comm Prim Sch

Liby

WESTBROOK CRES

Gullivers World Theme Pk

ABERDARE CL

HAWLEY'S CL

TAYLIN AVE

HINDLE AVE

GARWOOD CL

ASTA

90

D   58   E   59   F

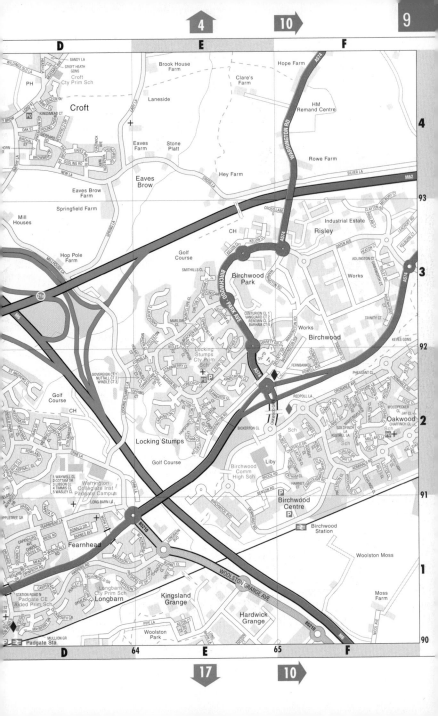

IRLAM

Cadishead Moss

Woolden View Farm

Great Woolden Hall Farm

Rose Bank Farm
Ryefield Farm

Lower Stanley Bank Farm

Higher Stanley Bank Farm

Ash Farm

Chat Moss

Rose Farm

Astley Road Farm
Irlam & Cadishead Comm High Sch

Irlam Sta

Glazebrook Exchange Sidings

Glazebrook

Glazebrook Inn

Glazebrook Sta

Brush Farm

DAM HEAD LA

GLAZEBROOK LA

BANK ST

Cadishead

Sewage Works

Lea Brook Farm

Mount Pleasant Farm

Tar Distillery

Our Lady of Lourdes RC Prim Sch

Manchester Ship Canal

Cadishead or Glazebrook Bridge

Cemy

PH

Hollinfare

eveland's Farm

Hollins Green

Brook Farm

Millbank Hall Farm

Millbank Hall

Sewage Works

Coroners Wood

Woodlands Inf Sch

Red Brook

Partington

Ortonbrook Prim Sch

Warburton High Level Bridge

WARBURTON BRIDGE

PARK RD

Warburton Park

Rye Park House

Heathlands Farm

Lighthouse Poultry Farm

Mosslane Farm

The Willows

Liby

MOSS LA

1 DAMSON WLK
2 ALMOND WLK
3 POPULAR WLK
4 LONG WLK
5 LIME WLK
6 HOLLY WLK
7 HAZEL WLK
8 GREEN WLK
9 GARDEN WLK
10 FIELD WLK
11 MEADOW WLK
12 HAWTHORN WLK
13 BOX WLK
14 MAY WLK
15 CONIFER WLK
16 SNOWBERRY WLK
17 LILAC WLK
18 ELDERBERRY WLK
19 ROSE WLK
20 THISTLE WLK
21 HEATHER WLK
22 IVY WLK
23 CHESTNUT WLK
24 CHERRY WLK
25 MIDDLE LA
26 YEW WLK
27 ROWAN WLK
28 LAVENDER WLK
29 FORSYTHIA WLK
30 BLACKTHORN WLK
31 THORN WLK
32 LABELIA WLK
33 LAUREL WLK
34 MAGNOLIA CL
35 IRIS WLK
36 FOXGLOVE WLK
37 SAFFRON WLK
38 ASTER WLK
39 JASMINE WLK
40 ROSEMARY WLK
41 MALLOW WLK
42 CAMAMILE WLK
43 BARBERRY WLK
44 ELM CL
45 WINTERGREEN WLK
46 BEECH CL
47 CHARLDOR WLK
48 WOODRUFF WLK
49 COLUMBINE WLK
50 CLOUDBERRY WLK
51 SHELDON CL
52 HANKINSON CL

D 70 E 71 F

4

93

3

92

2

91

1

90

D E F

4

89

3

88

2

87

1

86

WARRINGTON RD

Union Bank Farm Cottage

Old Brook Hall

Bold Bridge

Tibb's Cross Farm

Nursery Farm

Bold Heath

CH

Golf Course

Bank Head

Bridge Farm

BOLD CROSS

WARRINGTON RD A57

Griffin Inn (PH)

Works

Cranshaw Hall

Glebe Farm

Willow Farm

LUNT'S HEATH RD

Club

Lunt's Bridge Farm

Lunt Bridge

Garden Centre

Works

Mill Green Farm

South Lane Farm

Lunts Heath

SOUTH LA A5080

Boundary Farm

DERBY RD

Works

Barrow's Green

Abbey Farm

Works

Farnworth

WIDNES

Moorfield Cty Prim Sch

1 LAMPORT CL
2 FAIRBURN CL
3 ELTHAM WLK
4 BELGRAVE CL
5 SHEVINGTON WLK
6 SOMERFORD WLK
7 CHALGRAVE CL
8 SHELTON CL

Crematorium

Cemetery

Sch

Fairfield Cty High Sch

Pp Ho

Clock Lane Farm

Victoria Park

Bishops Way

Selwyn Cl

1 LARCHWAY
2 HAWTHORN AVE

WIDNES RD

WIDNES RD A562

Appleton

Crow Wood

Brookfields Sch

DANS RD

Shell Green

1 RABY CL
2 HADFIELD CL
3 KINGHAM CL
4 WILSON CL

Works

HALTON VIEW RD

1 TAYLOR ST
2 CLIFFE ST
3 HERIFF ST

PO

Sch

1 ASHFORD WAY
2 MELVILLE CL
3 KINGHAM CL
4 WILSON CL

Works

Power Station

Halton View

LEIGH AVE

DEACON RD

FIDDLER'S FERRY RD

D 52 E 53 F

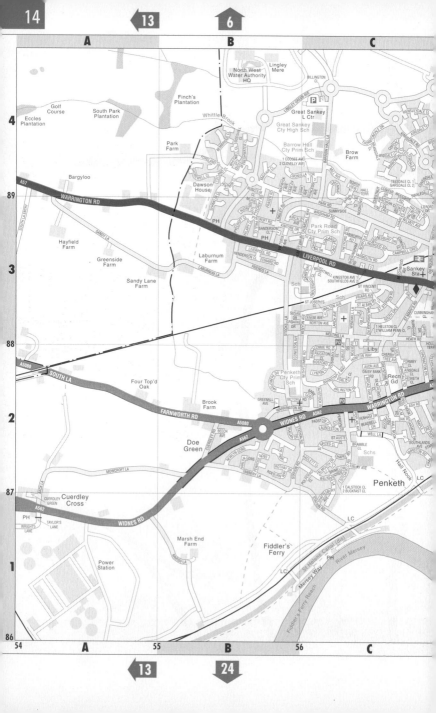

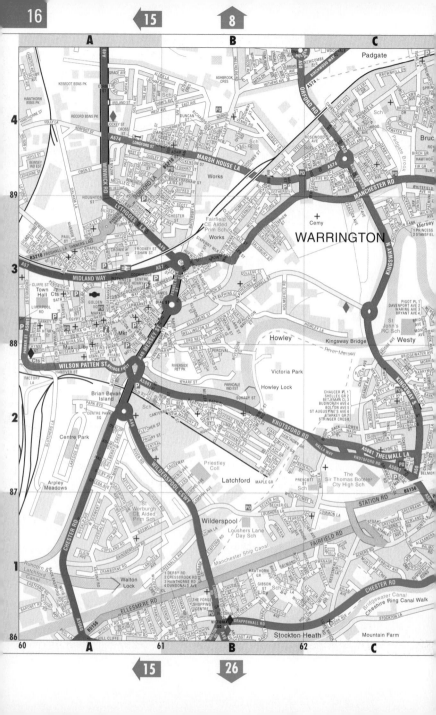

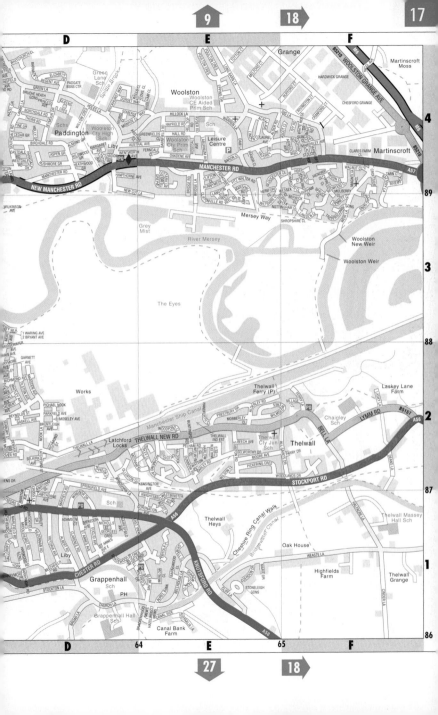

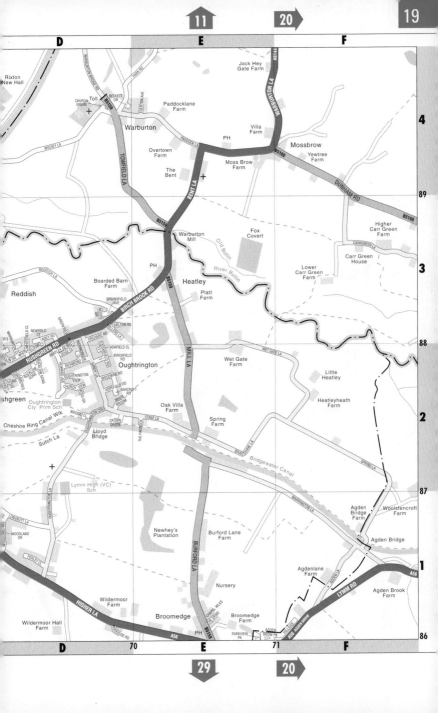

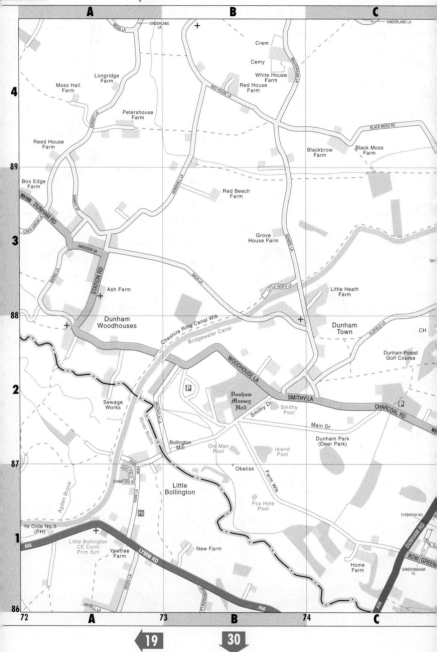

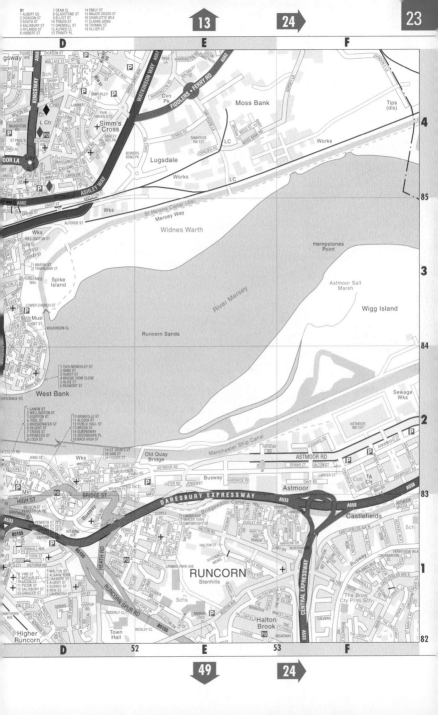

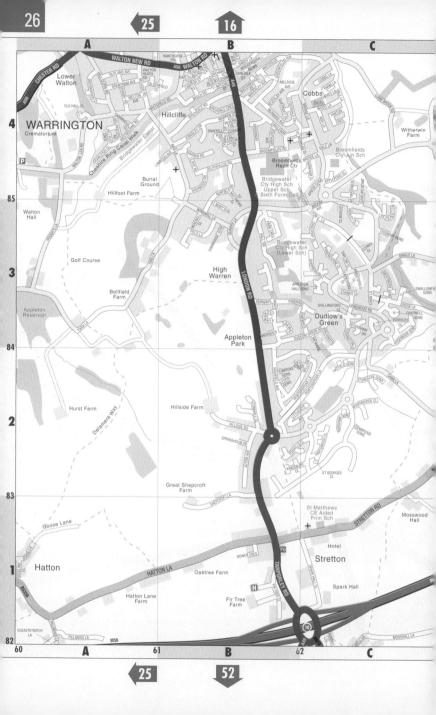

D   E   F

A50
KNUTSFORD RD
Massey Brook

CROSS LA

CLIFF LA

4

ULL LA

BROAD LA

Whitehouse
Farm

enhall
eys

Dairy
Farm

Yew Tree
Farm

Clifflane
Farm

85

A50

B5356

Reddish Hall
Farm

CARTRIDGE LA

right's
Green

GRAPPENHALL LA

Appleton

LUMB BROOK LA   NEW LA

Bradley
Hall

3

B5356

Appleton Thorn
Trading Estate

GREEN LA

P

ASHLEIGH RD

THORNTREE

CHIPPING

YEW TREE LA

Booth's
Farm

Barleycastle
Farm

Tan House
Farm

84

M56

Thorn Inn
(PH)

PARK LANE CL

VILLAGE LA

BARLEYCASTLE LA

Greenlane
Farm

+

STRETTON LN

STRETTON RD

HM Young
Offender Institution

BARLEYCASTLE
TRAD EST

Appleton
Thorn

PO

SCRETTON GREEN
DISTRIBUTION PARK

SWINE YARD LA

2

Cross
Farm

HANCE
CL

MOSS RD

BURLEY
LA

Ofd
Farm

AXLE FIELD

AMBERLEIGH CL

BARLEY
CASTLE CL

Appleton Thorn
Cty Prim Sch

PEPPER ST

Sewage
Works

Airfield
(disused)

83

Appleton Moss

Burleyheyes

New
Farm

1

Stretton Moss

REED RD

Fairbank
Farm

Laurel
Farm

REEDGATE LA

Reedgate
Farm

MOSSHALL LA

Moss
Hall

Whitley Reed

82

D   E   F

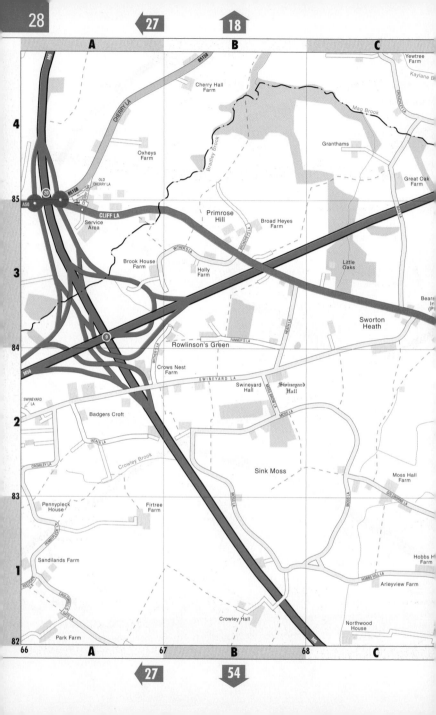

ALTRINCHAM

Ashley Heath

River Bollin

Coppice Farm

ool Bank Farm

Bow Green Farm

The Priory

Sewage Works

Dairy House Farm

ASHLEY RD

4

85

Ryecroft Farm

Ashley Hall

M56

CASTLE MILL LA

Tanyard Farm

3

Briddon Weir Farm

Birkin House

Ashley Sta

Ashley

HOUGH GREEN

EGERTON MOSS

Ashley CE Contr Prim Sch

BACK LA

QUAY LA

Stock Farm

Hough Green Farm

84

Birkin Farm

LAMB LA

MOOR LA

Shaw Green Farm

MARSH LA

BIRKINHEATH LA

ASHLEY RD

Twiss's Wood

Arden House

2

Lower House Farm

Birtles Farm

Ward's Plantation

Sugar Brook Farm

83

Rabbit Warren

Primrose Hill Farm

Sugar Brook

BREACH HOUSE LA

Tatton Park

Tatton Mere Brook

Birkin Brook

Mobberley Brook

1

Deer Enclosure

Kell House Farm

PECKFORTON LA

82

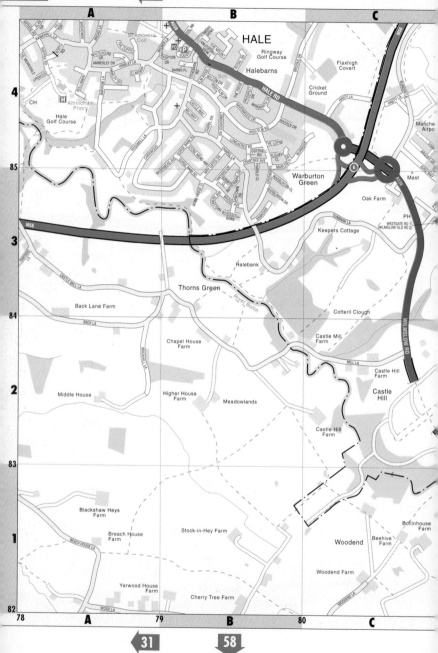

A   **B**   **C**

Wall Bank Farm

Dingle Farm

BEAUMARIS CRES
SKIPTON
Hazel Grove High Sch
PENRHYN CRES

1 AINSDALE CL
2 PRINCESS WLK
3 CHEVIN GDNS
4 HILLSIDE CL

Sch

Lady Brook

Norbury House Farm

JACKSON'S LA

A5143

CHARNWOOD CRES

CHARNWOOD CRES

DEAN LA

A5134

FIVEWAYS PAR

HAZEL GROVE

Denbigh Farm

WINSFIELD RD
SUDBURY RD
RIPLEY CL

Further Dairyground

WENTWORTH DR

POWNALL AVE

MACCLESFIELD RD

A523

ALDERLEY CL

MILL LA

ASHBOURNE CL

DARLEY RD

Norbu Hall

CAPESTHORNE CL
CAPESTHORNE RD

Dairyground

Millhill Bridge

Norbury Brook

Towers Farm

4

85

Barlowfold

Serpentine Wood

Mill Hill Farm

LOWER PARK RD

WOODFORD RD

ANGLESEY DR

3

Golf Course

Birch Hall

Hill Green Farm

Park House Farm

Phillip's Bridge

LONDON RD N

Poynton Lake

Poynton Park

TOWERS CL

Resr

Distaff Farm

LOWER PARK RD

Lower Park Road

Lower Park Lodge

GLASTONBURY DR
NEWSTEAD
NEATH CL
ABBOTSBURY CL

HARTLAND CL
SELBY
BUCKFAST CL

Prince's Incline

MILLSTONE DR

Tov Fa

84

TEWKESBURY CL
BYLANDS CLO
LAMBOURN CL

DEVA CL

Poynton Station

WAYSIDE DR

CHESTER RD

MILTON DR

OAK GR
OAK GR

WOODSIDE LA

Lady's Incline

KINGSWOOD

Poynton

Prince's Incline

2

A5149

WEST PARK RD
QUILL CL

BALLARD CRES

WIDGEON CL
PETREL CL
GREBE
PUFFIN AVE
FULMAR CL

Lostock Hall City Prim Sch

Wigwam Wood

Poynton Brook

WINDSOR

A5149

FOUNTAIN CL

Liby
Civic Hall
SCHOOL LA
SCHOOL CL

PARK LA

Hockley

WOBURN

Nursery

GROSVENOR DR

ARLINGTON DR

QUEENSWAY

SPRINGHAM

GEORGE'S RD W
GEORGE'S RD E

BROOKSIDE AVE

CLUMBER

Schs

ALDER AVE

CHERRY TREE AVE

83

Upper Swineseye Farm

Lostockhall Farm

LOSTOCK RD

Midway

MARLEY RD

Sch

CURZON RD

KETTLESHULME WAY
SUTTON RD
ADLINGTON

Poynton City High Sch

GAWSWORTH

BRIDLE WAY

Woodford Aerodrome

Industrial Estate

HOPE GREEN WAY

FIRST AVE

Sprink Farm

ALDERLEY CL
WINCLE

Work

1

Shirdfold Farm

Hope Green Farm

LONDON RD

ADLINGTON PARK

SECOND AVE

Industrial Estate

Clayton Greaves Farm

WOOD LA

82

Hope Green

Hope Lane

Brookside Farm

HOPE LA

90   **A**   **91**   **B**   **92**   **C**

D   E   F

1 CRANLEIGH DR
2 BIRCH TREE AVE

Golf Course
Oxhey Farm

Shores Farm

CAPESTHORNE RD

Ashley Sons
Hotel
Middlewood View

High Lane

BUXTON RD

Disley Tunnel

GRASSMERE CRES
Lomber Hey Farm

Sewage Works

High Lane Prim Sch
Liby

4

Long Plantation

Parkgate Farm

LC

Norbury Hollow

BRIDGFIELD CL

WOODSIDE DR

CAPESTHORNE RD
CORNWALL CL
SCARLET RD

HARTINGTON RD

MANIFOLD DR

85

Middlewood Station (lower)

Middlewood

New House Farm

Middle Wood

Norbury Brook

1 BEECH RD
2 ELM RD
3 HADDON CL
4 HARDWICK CL

Brookside Prim Sch

Brookside Farm

3

Rabbit Burrow Farm

Prince's Wood

Pool House Farm

Cheshire Ring Canal Walk

Macclesfield Canal

Ryles Wood

Beechfield

Golf Course

CH

St Elmo Park

CARLTON RD

Middlewood Way

Middlecale Farm

84

Petre Bank

TOWERS RD

Works

ANSON RD

Newtown

GREEN

Boar's Head (PH)

Towing Path

Barlow House Farm

Marine Ville Mooring

Platt Wood

2

Higher Poynton

Springbank Farm

PO

Hilltop Farm

Platt Wood Farm

Hockley

COPPICE RD

Coppiceside

Elm Wood

83

1 EATON CL
2 BOSLEY DR
3 KETTLESHULME WAY
4 SUTTON RD
5 WARFORD AVE
6 WINCLE AVE

Accomodation

DICKENS LA
Wardsend Bridge

Poynton Coppice

Poynton Brook

SHRIGLEY RD

Caravan Site

Hagg Farm

Ben's Wood

Haresteads Farm

Windgather

1

Wardsend

NARROW LA

Yewtree Farm

Wood Lane End Old Farm

YEW TREE LA

Throstlenest Farm

Green Farm

Lyme Park Knott

30 LA W

Mitchell Fold

82

D   94   E   95   F

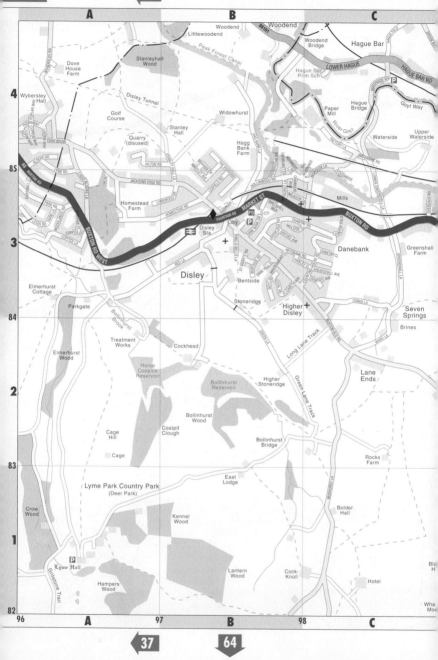

Woodend
Littlewoodend
Woodend
B6101
Woodend
Bridge
Hague Bar
Stanleyhall
Wood
LOWER HAGUE
Hague Bar
Prim Sch
Peak Forest Canal
Dove
House
Farm
Hague Bar Rd
Wybersley
Hall
Disley Tunnel
P
Golf
Course
Widowhurst
Paper
Mill
Hague
Bridge
Goyt Way
River Goyt
FACTORY LA
Waterside
Upper
Waterside
Stanley
Hall
Quarry
(disused)
Hagg
Bank
Farm
BUXTON RD
Mills
HILTON RD
JACKSONS EDGE RD
Homestead
Farm
LYMEWOOD RD
HOMESTEAD RD
MARKET ST
Lib
P
Buxton Rd
Danebank
Greenshall
Farm
Disley
Sta
Disley
Bentside
CHANTRY CL
BUXTON RD WEST
RED LA
KING-O-BELLS LA
Stoneridge
Higher
Disley
CORKS LA
Elmerhurst
Cottage
Seven
Springs
Parkgate
Bollinhurst Brook
Treatment
Works
Cockhead
Long Lane Track
Brines
Elmerhurst
Wood
Horse
Coppice
Reservoir
Higher
Stoneridge
Green Lane Track
Lane
Ends
Bollinhurst
Reservoir
Bollinhurst
Wood
Cage
Hill
Coalpit
Clough
Bollinhurst
Bridge
Rocks
Farm
Cage
Lyme Park Country Park
(Deer Park)
East
Lodge
Crow
Wood
Kennel
Wood
Bolder
Hall
P
Lyme Hall
Gritstone Trail
Hampers
Wood
Lantern
Wood
Cock-
Knoll
Hotel
Bla
H
Wha
Mo

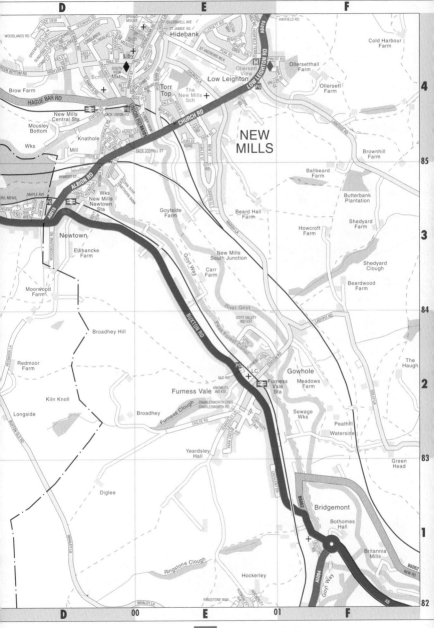

A **B** **C**

4

81

3

80

2

79

1

78

Sewage
Works

DEE SIDE

ARGET RD

PIPER'S
RD

WARREN
AVE

BROAD LA

MOSTYN AV

BANKS RD

THE MOORINGS

WITTERING LA

BROOMLANDS

FEATHER LA

PENSBY
RD

A540

CASTLE DR

Heather
Lane

Herberts
La

THE
HERMITAGE

Wirral Way

CHURCH
FARM
CT

PO

Brow
La

Park West

MAGAZINE LA

BROMLEY
CL

MANORS LA

SEABANK RD

RIVERBANK RD

WOODBURN
DR

HESWALL

COTTAGE DR WEST

COTTAGE DR EAST

River Dee

Gayton Sands

A B C

Clatterbridge

Thornton
Manor

Wirral
Manor
House

New
Rocklands

4

Grange
Farm

THORNTON COMMON RD

Willows
Farm

The
Foxes

Hesketh
Grange

Thornton
Hough
C'ty Prim

**Thornton
Hough**

B5136

81

Lodge Farm

RABY MERE RD

Raby Hall
Farm

OXFORD DR

P

Raby
Vale

3

Thornton
Farm

Four Lanes End

RABY MERE RD

RABY HALL RD

B5136

Hillyard
Farm

80

THE CROSSWAY

Raby

PH

Yew Tree
House

Willowbrow
Farm

Hargrave Hall
Farm

2

WILLOW LA

Hargrave
Cottages

BENTY HEATH LA

Upland's Farm

Cherry Farm

WILLOWBROW RD

Re
Ho
Fa

79

Leawood

The Red
Farm

1

Sch

Hinderton
Hall

Roseleae

The Old

Mill Lane
Farm

CHESTER HIGH RD

A540

BIRKENHEAD RD

The
Lydiate

MILL LA

QUARRY RD

B5151

WHITEGATES
CRES

MEADOW LA

78

HINDERTON
RD

HINDERTON LA

B5134

HANNS HALL RD

B5133

30 31 32

A B C

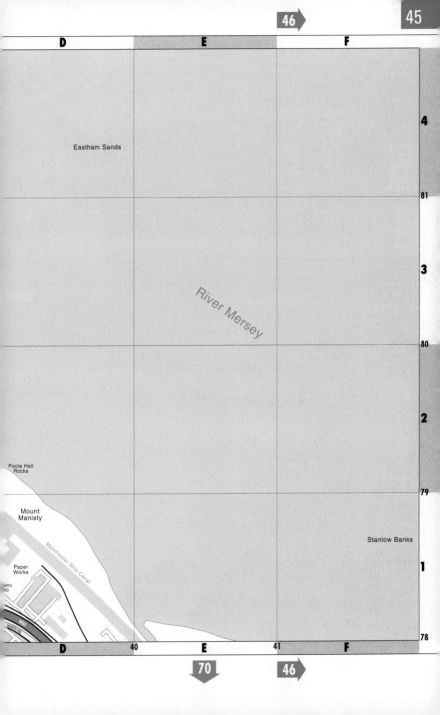

D E F

4

81

3

River Mersey

80

2

79

Eastham Sands

Poole Hall
Rocks

Mount
Manisty

Manchester Ship Canal

Stanlow Banks

Paper
Works

RTH
RD

M53

1

D 40 E 41 F 78

45

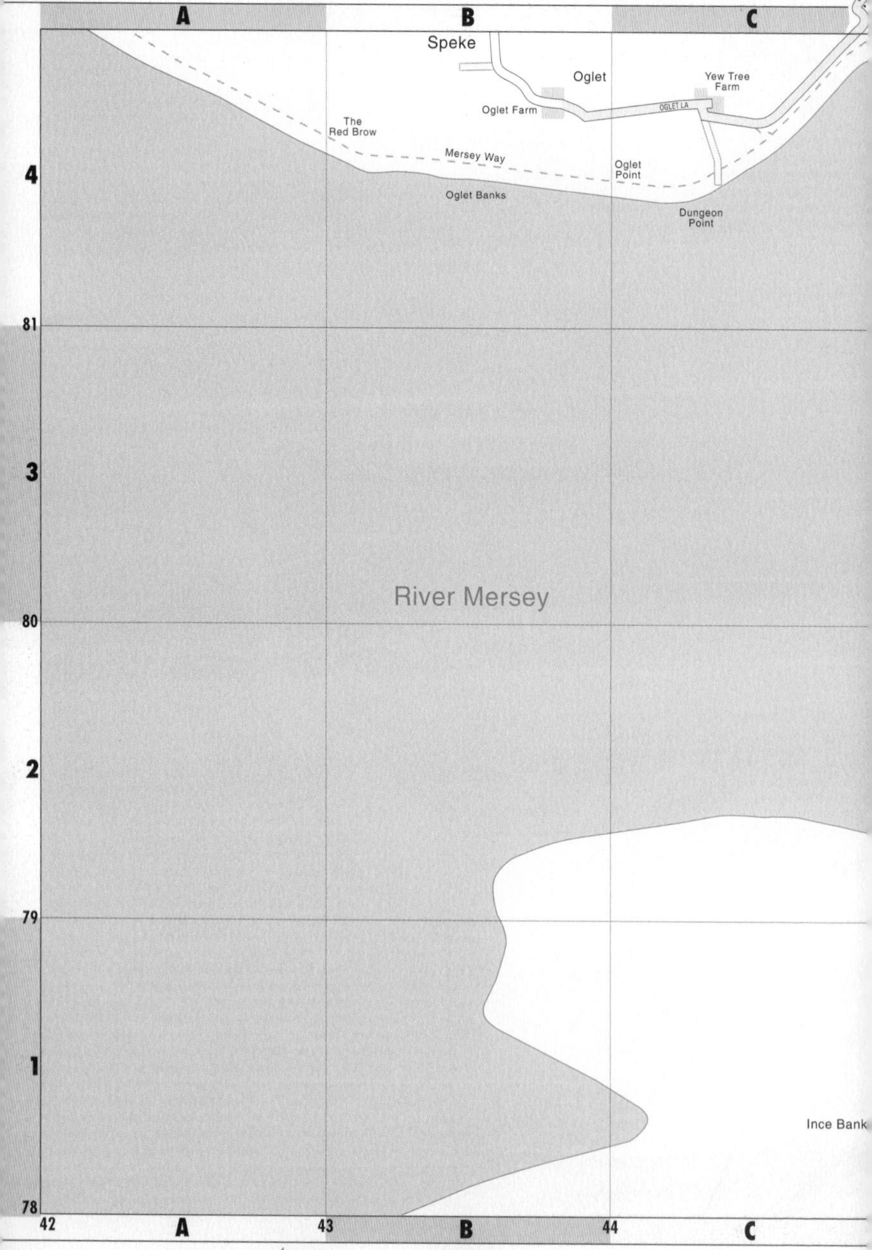
A
B
C
Speke
Oglet
Yew Tree Farm
Oglet Farm
OGLET LA
The Red Brow
Mersey Way
Oglet Point
Oglet Banks
Dungeon Point
4
81
3
River Mersey
80
2
79
1
Ince Bank
78
42
A
43
B
44
C

45
71

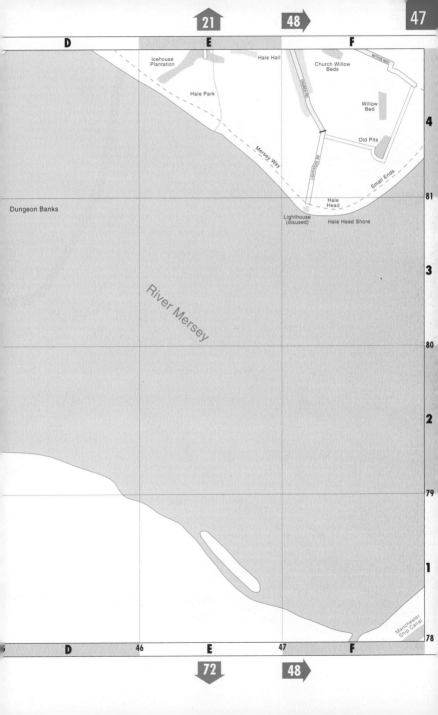

D E F

Icehouse Plantation
Hale Hall
Church Willow Beds
Hale Park
Willow Bed
Old Pits
WITHIN WAY
CHURCH RD
LIGHTHOUSE RD
Mersey Way
Small Ends

4

81

Dungeon Banks
Hale Head
Lighthouse (disused)
Hale Head Shore

River Mersey

3

80

2

79

1

Manchester Ship Canal

78

River Mersey

Docks

Works

Recn
Gd

Beacon Hill

Runcorn Hill
(Public Park)

BEACON HILL RD
CUNNINGHAM DR
HALE VIEW
HILL SIDE AVE
CAMERON AVE
HAZEL AVE
PERRIN AVE

Weston
Mersey
Locks

Swing
Bridge

CLARKS TERR
BEACON HILL
VIEW

POST OFFICE LA
WEST RD

BAKER RD

ST LEONARD ST
SYDNEY
ST

VOSSE LA

MATHER AVE

WESTON PT

WESTON POINT EXPRESSWAY

SANDY LA

LANCASTER AVE

ROSIDE CRES

Weston
Point
Cty Prim
Sch

LC

Weston
Point

LC

COMPANY'S CL 1
MONTPELIER AVE 2
LAMBSICKLE CL 3

Sewage
Works

COLLIER'S
ROW

CHESHYRE ST
LA

BARKS LA

WESTON
CT

Weston

APLETON CL
CRESTA DR

LAMBSICKLE
TILDESLEY CL

Works

Works

Weaver
Sluices

Weaver Navigation

Manchester Ship Canal

Runcorn & Weston Canal (disused)

Weston Marsh
Lock

River Weaver

Frodsham Score

Manchester Ship Canal

Frodsham Marsh
Farm

ALDER LA

Frodsham Marsh

BROOK FURLONG

Canal Deposit Dump

Jetties

MOORDITCH LA

TANNERS LA

MOORDITCH LA

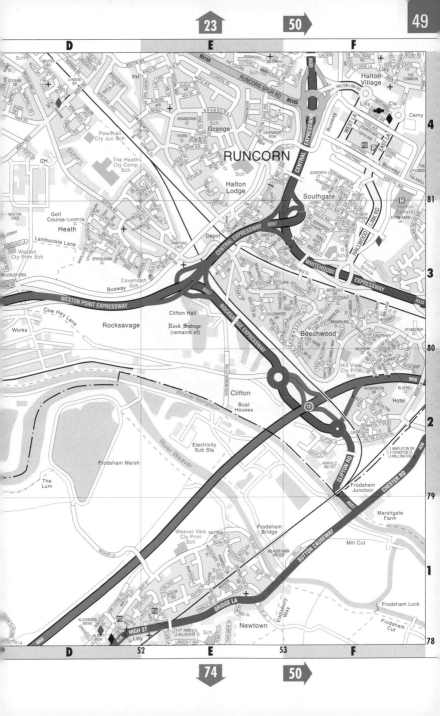

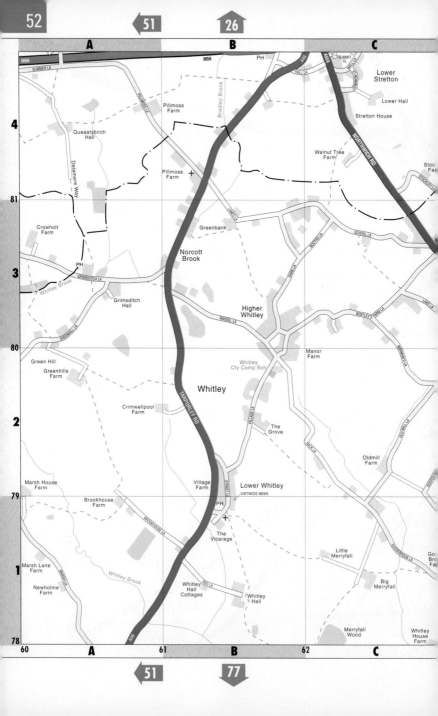

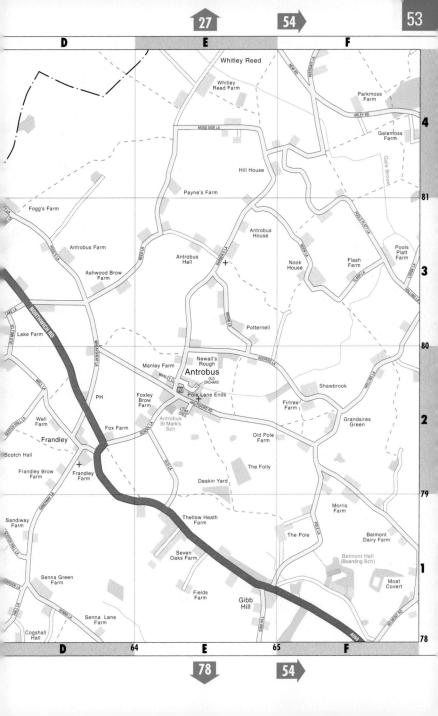

D E F

4

81

3

80

2

79

1

78

Whitley Reed

Whitley Reed Farm

Parkmoss Farm

ARLEY RD

Galemoss Farm

Gale Brook

MOSS SIDE LA

NEW RD

HEATHGATE LA

POOLE PLATT LA

Hill House

Payne's Farm

Fogg's Farm

BELL LA

DOGS LA

Antrobus Farm

Antrobus House

Antrobus Hall

REED LA

WARE LA

Ashwood Brow Farm

Nook House

BOOK LA

Flash Farm

FLASH LA

Pools Platt Farm

LODGE LA

REGENT LA

NORTHWICH RD

LAKE LA

OLD HALL LA

Lake Farm

BROW LA

Potternell

WARFINGTON LA

BELL LA

Manley Farm

MANLEY LA

Newall's Rough

Antrobus

OLD ORCHARD

KEEPERS LA

Shawbrook

MILL SIDE LA

PH

Foxley Brow Farm

Pole Lane Ends

PO

KNUTSFORD RD

Firtree Farm

Grandsires Green

Well Farm

Fox Farm

Antrobus St Mark's Sch

LONG LEES

FLAT LA

SCHOOL LA

Old Pole Farm

SCOTCH HALL LA

Frandley

Scotch Hall

Frandley Brow Farm

Frandley Farm

The Folly

Deakin Yard

POLE LA

Morris Farm

Sandiway Farm

SANDIWAY LA

Thellow Heath Farm

The Pole

Belmont Dairy Farm

SCOTCH HALL LA

TABLEY LA

Senna Green Farm

Seven Oaks Farm

Belmont Hall (Boarding Sch)

Moat Covert

BELMONT RD

Senna Lane Farm

SENNA LA

Fields Farm

Gibb Hill

GIBB HILL LA

A559

Cogshall Hall

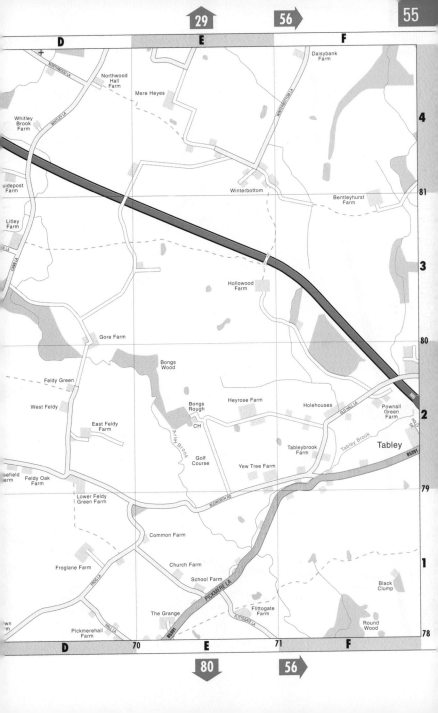

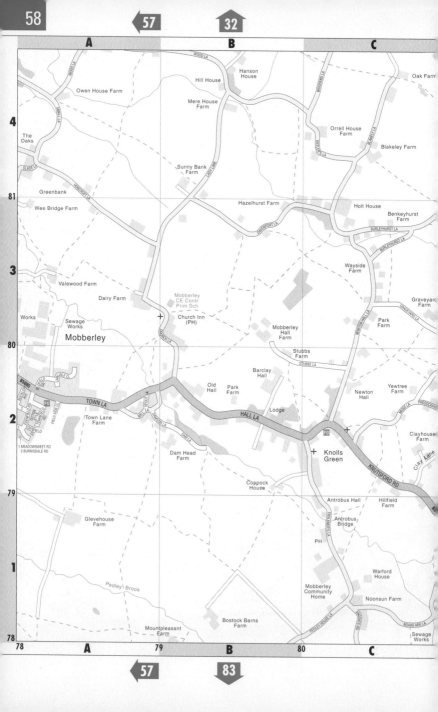

A   **B**   **C**

WOOD LA

Hanson
House

Hill House

Oak Farm

Owen House Farm

WOOD LA

Mere House
Farm

4

Orrell House
Farm

Blakeley Farm

The
Oaks

Sunny Bank
Farm

SLADE LA

81

Greenbank

Hazelhurst Farm

Holt House

Benkeyhurst
Farm

Wee Bridge Farm

BURLEYHURST LA

BURLEYHURST LA

Wayside
Farm

3

Valewood Farm

Dairy Farm

Mobberley
CE Contr
Prim Sch

Graveyard
Farm

Park
Farm

Works

Sewage
Works

Church Inn
(PH)

Mobberley
Hall
Farm

80

Mobberley

Stubbs
Farm

STUBBS LA

CARLISLE CL

Barclay
Hall

Old
Hall

Park
Farm

Newton
Hall

Yewtree
Farm

TOWN LA

FIELD BREK CL

2

Town Lane
Farm

Lodge

HALL LA

Clayhouse
Farm

Clay Lane

1 MEADOWSWEET RD
2 BURNISDALE RD

Dam Head
Farm

Knolls
Green

KNUTSFORD RD

79

Coppock
House

Antrobus Hall

Hillfield
Farm

Glevehouse
Farm

Antrobus
Bridge

PH

1

Warford
House

Pedley Brook

Mobberley
Community
Home

Noonsun Farm

Bostock Barns
Farm

Mountpleasant
Farm

Sewage
Works

78

78   **A**   **79**   **B**   **80**   **C**

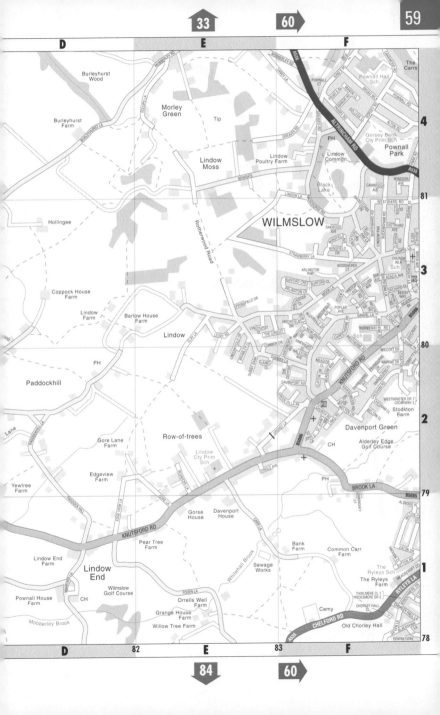

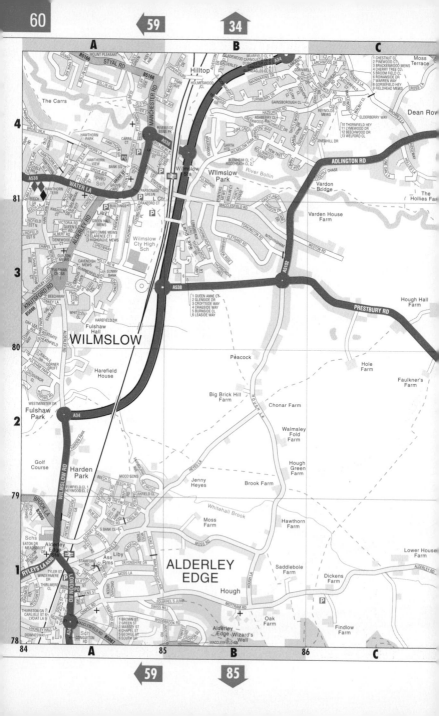

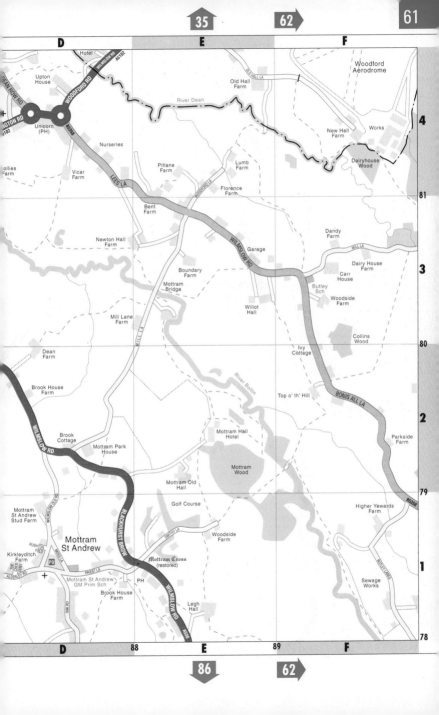

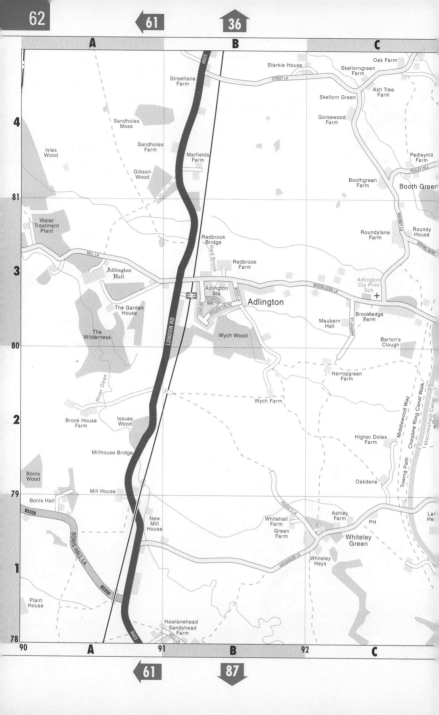

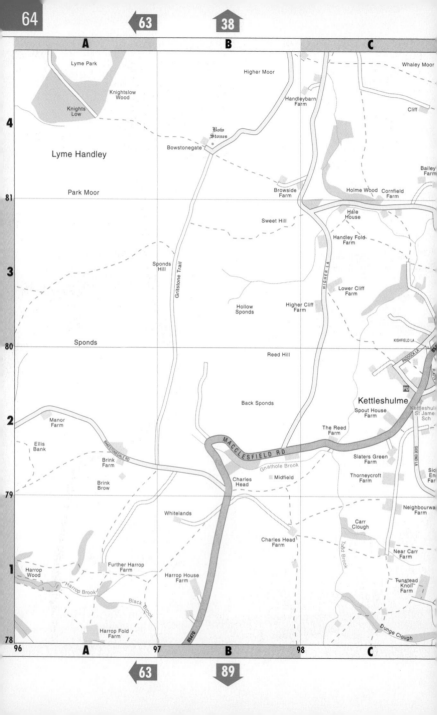

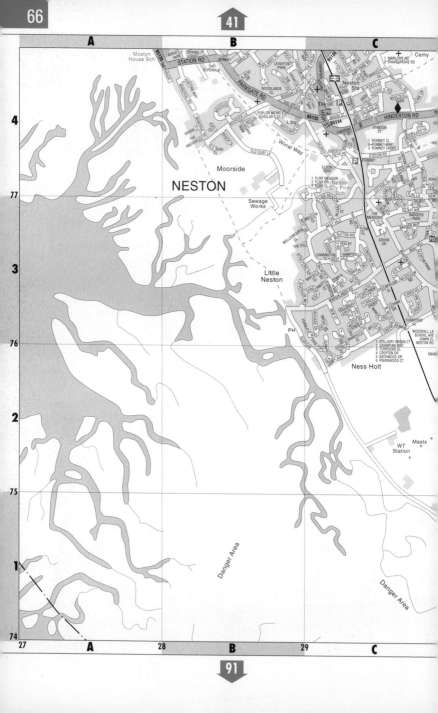

NESTON

Moorside

Little
Neston

Sewage
Works

Wirral Way

STATION RD

PARKGATE RD

Mostyn
House Sch

Neston
Sta

HINDERTON RD

Ness Holt

Danger Area

Danger Area

WT
Station

Masts

D E F

HINDERTON LA
HINDERTON RD
A540
B5134
B5133
HANNS HALL RD
WHITEGATES CRES
MEADOW CFT
MEADOW CL
WILLASTON CE Contr Prim Sch
NESTON RD
Liby
ELM GREEN
B5151
Hanns Hall Farm
LYDIATE LA
Ness Acre La
BROAD LAKE
CHESTER FARM
Picnic Area
Wood Park
Leahurst University of Liverpool Veterinary Field Sta
HAOLOW LA
4
Windle Hill
Wirral Country Park
Wirral Way
CHESTER HIGH RD
HADLOW RD
B5151
77
Heathfield
Willaston Grange
SANDY LA
ASHTREE
WOODFALL LA
Woodfall City Inf & Jun Sch
Ness Wood
MILL LA
Errington's Plantation
3
LABURNUM FARM CL
Mill Farm
FLASHES LA
Haddon Hall Farm
Shotwick Brook
A540
76
SMITHY DL
NAB LA
Orchard House
Haddon Hayes
Haddon Hall Farm
HADDON LA
Heath Farm
WOOD END LA
Visitor Centre
The Univ of Liverpool Botanic Gdns
Mickwell Brow
Friends Hall
Haddon Wood
2
NESTON RD
Dunstan Farm
75
SNIDALL LA
Fiddleston Plantation
MUGHOUSE LA
WOOD LA
Burton Wood
HADDON RD
VICARAGE LA
PRIESTWAY LA
1
STATION RD
Burton Marsh Farm
Hampston Well (disused)
MILL LA
THE RAKE
THE VILLAGE
Burton
Burton Bishop Wilson CE Aided Prim Sch
Burton Point Farm
Burton Manor Coll
74

D 31 E 32 F

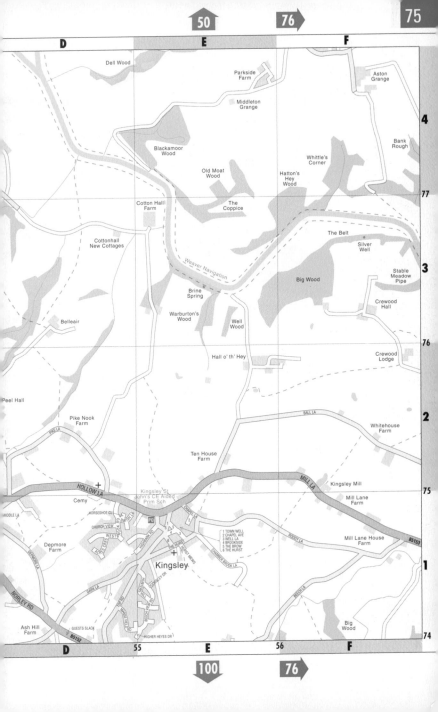

D
E
F

Dell Wood

Parkside Farm

Aston Grange

Middleton Grange

4

Bank Rough

Blackamoor Wood

Old Moat Wood

Whittle's Corner

Hatton's Hey Wood

77

Cotton Hall Farm

The Coppice

Cottonhall New Cottages

The Belt

Silver Well

Weaver Navigation

Big Wood

Stable Meadow Pipe

3

Belleair

Brine Spring

Crewood Hall

Warburton's Wood

Well Wood

76

Hall o' th' Hey

Crewood Lodge

Peel Hall

Pike Nook Farm

BALL LA

Whitehouse Farm

2

PIKE LA

Ten House Farm

MILL LA

Kingsley Mill

HOLLOW LA

Kingsley St John's CE Aided Prim Sch

Mill Lane Farm

75

Cemy

MIDDLE LA

HORSESHOE CL

CHURCH VIEW

WEST E

PO

CHAPEL LA

RODDY LA

Mill Lane House Farm

B5153

Depmore Farm

1 TOWN WELL
2 CHAPEL AVE
3 WELL LA
4 BROOKSIDE
5 THE BROW
6 THE HURST

CHINDLE BROOK LA

Kingsley

1

NORLEY RD

DARK LA

BEECH LA

Big Wood

Ash Hill Farm

B5152

GUESTS SLACK

HIGHER HEYES DR

74

D
E
F

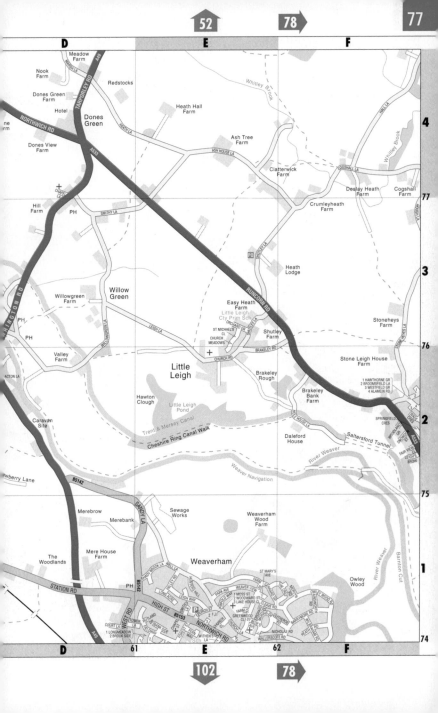

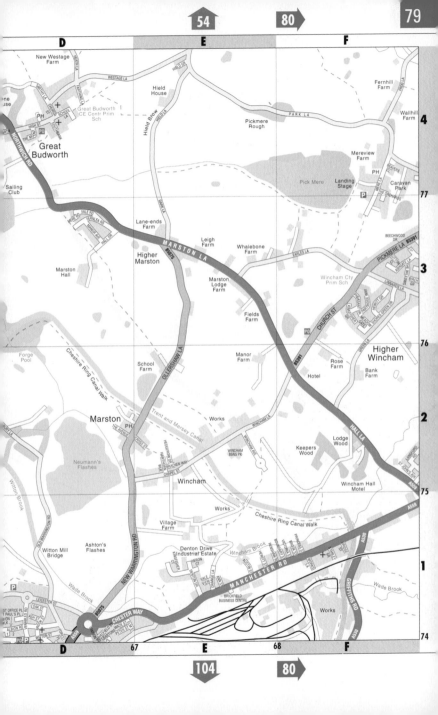

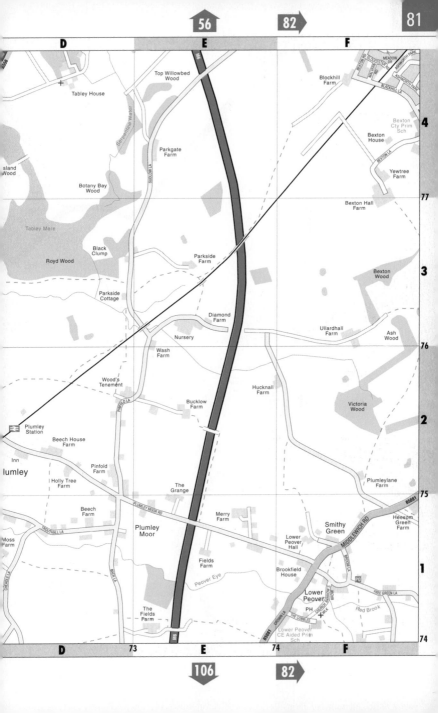

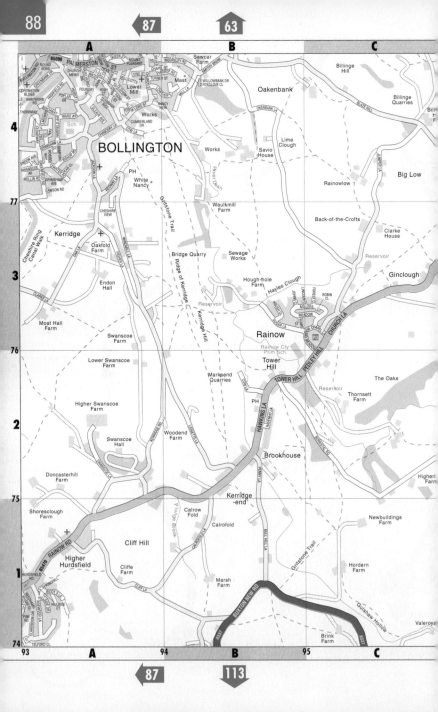

D
E
F

New Hey Farm
Blackbrook Bridge
Summer Close
Dunge Farm

Withinlow Farm
Moss-side Brook
Hollowcowhey Farm

4

Broad Moss
Green Booth

PH
Saddle Cote
Green Stock

77

Paddock Knoll Farm
MACCLESFIELD RD

Pike Low
BANK LA
Cook Hill
Fox Hill

Wimberry Moss
Blue Boar Farm
Saltersford Hall

3

Dawson Barn Farm
SMITH LA
Todd Brook

Waggonshaw Brow
Buxter Stoops Farm
Howlersknowl

Common Barn
Nab End

76

Yearns Low
Redmoor Brow

Works
Redmoor

2

BERRISTALL RD
P
Picnic Site
King's Clough

Ely Brow
Lamaload Reservoir
Eaves Farm
Andrew's Edge

75

Wickinford Farm
Brock Low

Lower Ballgreave Farm

1

Higher Ballgreave Farm

The Laches

74

D
97
E
98
F

A
B
C

Browtop
Farm

Wks

Oldfield

Hadgel Brook

4

Ladbitch
Wood

Hoo Moor

Goyt Valley

Fernilee Reservoir

77

Goyt Forest

P

Calfhay
Wood

Pymchair
Farm

Pym Chair

3

The Street

Oldgate
Nick

Jep Clough

76

Cats Tor

Withinleach
Moor

Picnic
Area

Buns
Cob

Sailing
Club

2

Foxlow Edge

Erwood Reservoir

Thursbitch

75

Errwood
Hall

Picnic
Area

Forest
Trail

The Tors

Shooter's Clough

1

River Goyt

Wild M

Stake
Side

74

99
A
00
B
01
C

LONG HILL

A 5004

B 5054

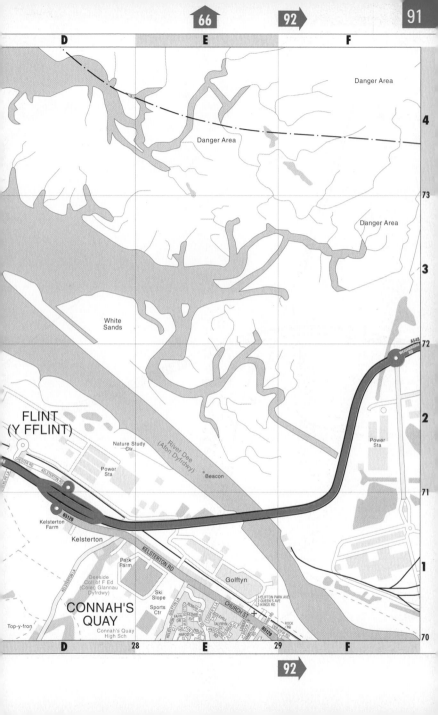

Danger Area

Danger Area

Danger Area

White
Sands

A548
WEPRE BROOK RD

FLINT
(Y FFLINT)

Nature Study
Ctr.

Power
Sta

River Dee
(Afon Dyfrdwy)

Beacon

Power
Sta

CHESTER RD

KELSTERTON RD

B5129

Kelsterton
Farm

Kelsterton

Park
Farm

KELSTERTON RD

Golftyn

1 CLIFTON PARK AVE
2 QUEEN'S AVE
3 KINGS RD

Deeside
Coll of F Ed
(Coleg, Glannau
Dyfrdwy)

Ski
Slope

Sports
Ctr

CHURCH ST

B5129

ROCK
RD

CONNAH'S
QUAY

Top-y-fron

Connah's Quay
High Sch

Puddington

PUDDINGTON LA

Old
Hall

Puddingt
Hall

The
Mere

Marsh
Covert

Barn
Farm

Burton Point

Danger Area

4

73

Rifle Range

Platts
Covert

Reservoir

3

Danger Area

72 A548 WEIGHBRIDGE RD

LC

Works

LC

SHOTWICK RD

2

Works

71

DEESIDE
IND EST
(PARC DIWYDIANNOL
GLANNAU DYFRDWY)

FOURTH AVE

SECOND AVE

Works

LC

LC

1

LC

LC

Birkenhead
Junction

FOURTH AVE

FIRST AVE

FIFTH AVE

THIRD AVE

SECOND AVE

PARKWAY

70

30 A **31** B **32** C

A **B** **C**

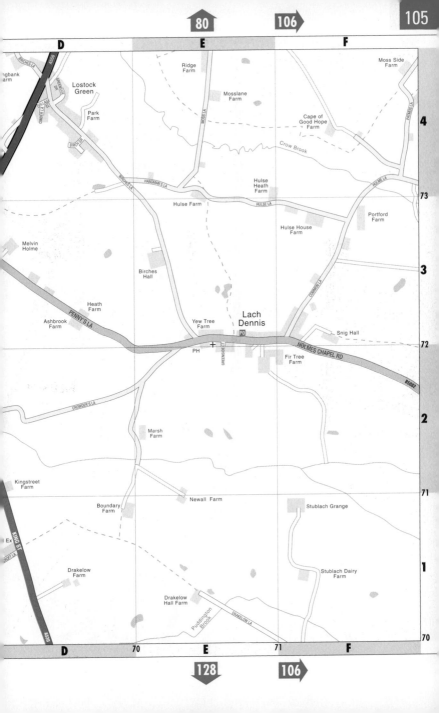

D E F

Moss Side
Farm

Ridge
Farm

ngbank
arm

Lostock
Green

Mosslane
Farm

Park
Farm

Cape of
Good Hope
Farm

4

Crow Brook

73

HANGMAN'S LA

Hulse Farm

Hulse
Heath
Farm

HULSE LA

Portford
Farm

Melvin
Holme

Hulse House
Farm

Birches
Hall

3

PENNY'S LA

Heath
Farm

Yew Tree
Farm

Lach
Dennis

Snig Hall

Ashbrook
Farm

72

PO

PH

HOLMES CHAPEL RD

Fir Tree
Farm

CROWDER'S LA

B5082

Marsh
Farm

2

Kingstreet
Farm

71

Newall Farm

Boundary
Farm

Stublach Grange

KING ST

Ex

Drakelow
Farm

Stublach Dairy
Farm

1

Drakelow
Hall Farm

Puddington Brook

DRAKELOW LA

A530

70

D 70 E 71 F

105

81

A **B** **C**

Cheadle Farm

New Farm

Back Lanes Farm

Backlane Farm

Millgate Farm

4

Crown Lane Farm

Parkside Farm

Foxce

Crown Inn (PH)

Mill Bank Farm

Swan Green

Yewtree Farm

Peover Eye

Heath Farm

Springfield

Birch Farm

73

Hulme Covert

Bradshaw Brook

Springbank Farm

Bradshaw House

Hea Fa

Graybrook Farm

3

Hulme Hall

Bradshawbrook Farm

Chapel Farm

Old Mill Farm

Townfield Farm

MIDDLEWICH RD

72

Hulme Hall La

Washlone Farm

Hole Lane

Hole House

Hole House Wood

Mote

Highfield House

Allostock Hall

Axon's Smithy Farm

Allostock

Brookhouse Farm

2

Chapel House Farm

LONDON RD

Three Greyhounds (PH)

Widow's Home Farm

Sculshaw Green Farm

HOLMES CHAPEL RD

Shakerley Mere

Caravan Park

71

Chestnut House Farm

Sandhole Farm

The Croft

Woodlands Farm

Newpla Wood

Rudheath Woods

1

Stubloch Farm

Works

King's Lane Farm

NORTHWICH RD

NEWPLATT LA

Earnshaw House Farm

Warrington Common

70

A **B** **C**

72 73 74

105

129

A

Bagbrook
Wood
Bridge
Wood
Bagbrook
Bridge
Bagbrook
Farm
Home Farm
North Lodge
Cranshawes
Park
Plantation
73
Capesthorne Park
Capesthorne
Hall
East
Lodge
3
Boathouse
Covert
72
Fanshawe
Redes Mere
Redesmere
Farm
2
NURSERY LA
Picnic
Site
Siddington
71
SIDDINGTON
BANK
B5392
Meadow
Bank
Siddington Hall
Farm
1
Horse
Wood
70
84
A
85

CONGLETON RD

MILL LA

FANSHAWE LA

REDESMERE LA

B

Birtles Hill
Farm
A537
Birtles
Bridge
CHELFORD RD
Ley Plantation
Marlheath
Farm
Lingards
Farm
Lodge
Farm
Henbury
Moss
Sycamore
Farm
FANSHAWE LA
Hills Green
Farm
Hazelwall
Wood
PEXHILL RD
Simon's
Wood
Simonswood
Buck's Hill
Snape Brook
Ettily Wood
B
85

C

Pale Farm
BIRTLES LA
Pale
Lodge
Big Wood
Henbury
Hall
The
Cave
Smithy
Wood
Henbury
Smithy
SCHOOL LA
Huntley
Wood
Sandbach
Farm
Bearhurst
Farm
Henbury Moss
Farm
Fanshawe Brook
Hazelwall
B53
Thorneycroft
Farm
Siddington
Manor
Thorneycroft
Pools
Keepers
Cottages
Pyethorn
Wood
Walkershe
Henshaw Hall
Farm
Heskey
Wood
Hammerpool
Wood
Moss Wood
Ranker's
Ford
MARL LA
C

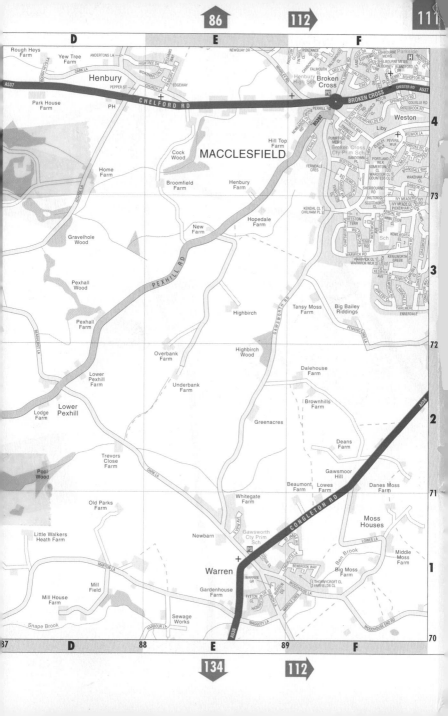

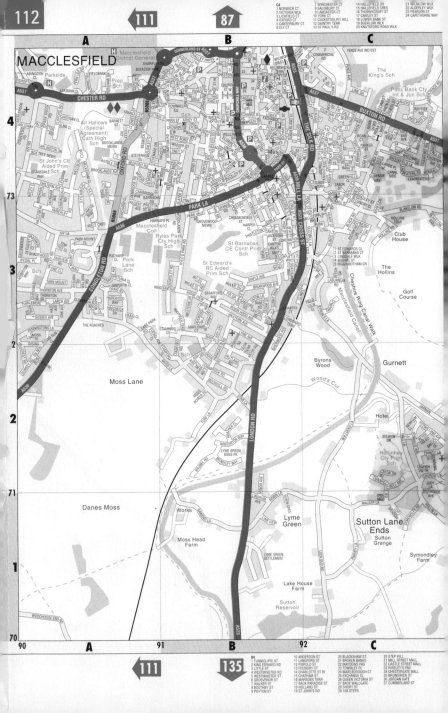

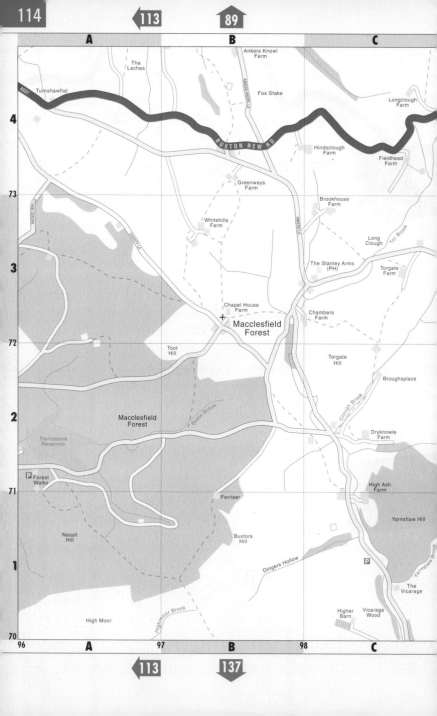

D E F

Shining Tor

Stake Side

Buxton

Goytsclough
Quarry

P

River Goyt

Goyt's Moss

4

73

BUXTON NEW RD

Stake
Farm

Stake Clough

Deep Clough

Goyt's Clough

Ravens Low

3

Foxhole Hollow

Jacob's
Cabin

t Hollow

Mast
Cat and Fiddle
(PH)

72

Derbyshire
Bridge

The
Scaurs

Cuckoo
Rocks

2

A537

n Gutter

71

Tinkerspit Gutter

Correction Brook

Whetstone
Ridge

A54

1

Danebower
Hollow

Cheshire
Knowl

Danebower
Quarries

Danethorn
Hollow

Dane Bower

A54

70

D 00 E 01 F

A B C

4

69

3

68

2

67

1

66

33 A 34 B 35 C

Camp

WELSH RD
A548
A550
A5480

Old Marsh
Farm

Bridge Farm

DEVA
BSNS PK

Seahill
Farm

A548

RIVERSIDE PK

Willow Farm

Brookfield
Farm

Station
Cottages

MANOR RD

Home
Farm

SEALAND RD

BARTHOLOMEWS CT

North
Green

South
Green

East Green

Waterloo Farm

Sealand

Church
Farm

Sealand Manor

Shooting
School

Deeside Cottages

Engineer
Park

River Row
Cottages

Deeside House

Sealand Nursery

ST IVES
PK

Works

BERNSDALE

Works

CLAIR
AVE

River Dee (Afon Dyfrdwy)

PRINCE WILLIAM AVE

Wood Farm

Sandycroft

Bridge Inn
(PH)

Hawarden

CHESTER RD

The Beeches

Cop House
Farm

Rake Cottages

B5129

B5129

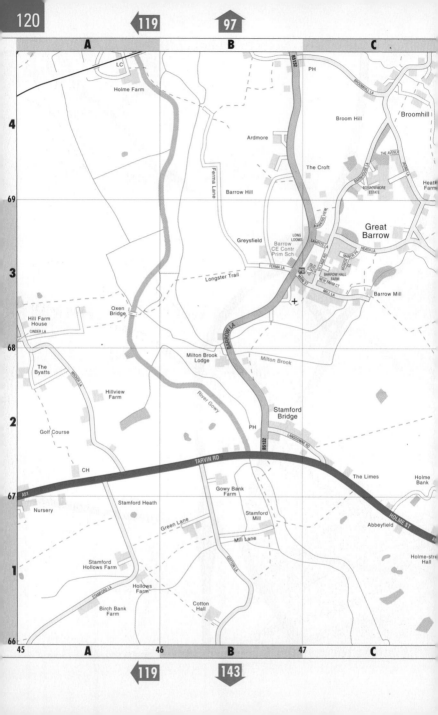

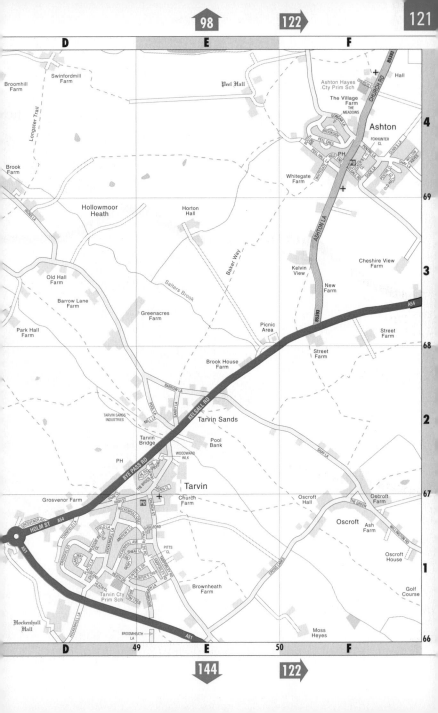

123
101

A   **B**   **C**

Crown Farm

Cheshire
Kennels

4

CHESTER RD

A556

Massey's
Lodge

Reeki Hole

Oakmere

Kennel Lane

FARM RD

69

Nunsmere

Shemmy
Moss

A556

Hogshead
Wood

Fourways Sand Quarry

Nunsmere
Hall

Abbotsmoss
Wood

Waste
Farm

3

Folly
Farm

Horse Training Ground

Abbotsmoss
Hall

TARPORLEY RD

Keeper's
Cottage

Abbots Moss

68

Polo Ground

Oak Mere

SHAY'S LA

Corner
Farm

Greenlands

Spring
Farm

Shaw's
Farm

Shay's
Farm

A54

2

Cabbage Hall
(PH)

Shay's Lane Brook

Sandymere
Plantation

Sandybrow

Stonehouse
Farm

Common Side

LONGSTONE LA

67

Sandymere
House

Shrewsbury Arms
(PH)

Butts
Farm

Sandymere
House

Moss Hall
Farm

Rosebank
Farm

Oaktree
Farm

Burslem Cottage
Farm

1

Heathfield

BEECH RD

SHOW LA

Sunnybank
Farm

WHITEHALL LA

PARK RD

Sandiford
Lodge

Polo
Ground

Picnic
Area

White
hall

Poolhead
Farm

SADLERS LA

MOSSPIT LA

CROOK RD

B5152 STOCK LA

A49

66

57   **A**   **58**   **B**   **59**   **C**

123
147

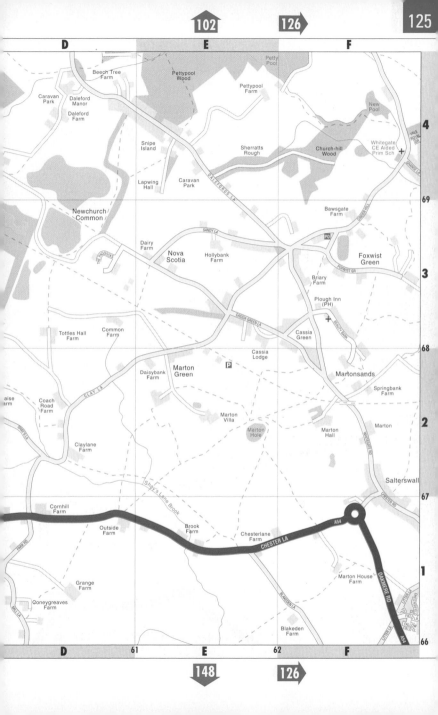

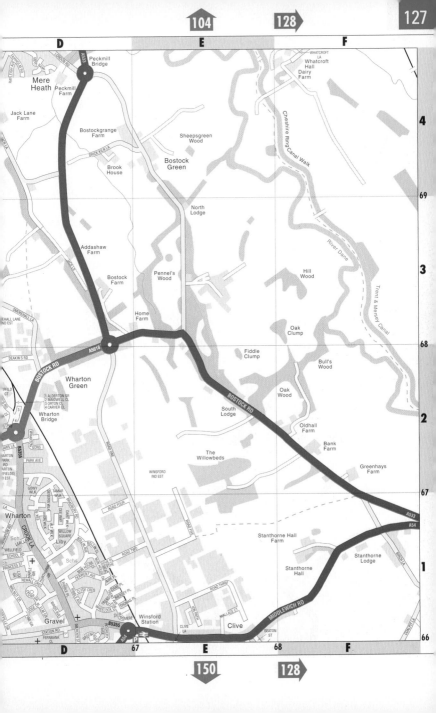

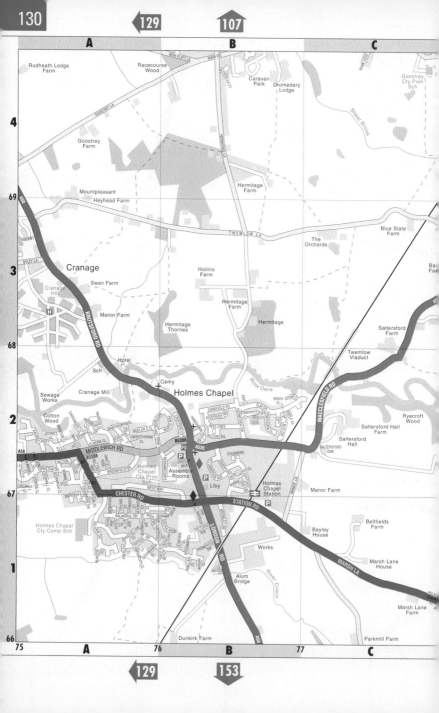

110
134

D
E
F

4

BLACKDEN LA

Sandbank
Farm

Northwood
Farm

Marton Brook

Toll Bar
Farm

Higher Gorsley
Farm

Holly Bank
Farm

Crabtree Moss
Farm

Crabmoss

Tidnock Wood

Marton
Gate
Farm

Martonheath

Pikelow
Farm

69

Lower Gorsley
Green Farm

Mere
Farm

Martonheath
Wood

Bank Farm

CONGLETON RD

Marton & District
CE Aided Prim
Sch

Great Tidnock
Farm

3

DAVENPORT LA

SCHOOL LA

Chapel Brook

High Wood

Marton

PH

Bunce
Lane
Farm

Church
Farm

68

Higher
Mutlow

BUNCE LA

Chapel Bridge

Mutlow
Farm

Black
Wood

Bruce Lane
Farm

Marton Hall

COCKSMOSS RD

Cocksmoss
Wood

Cocks Moss
Cottage

Moss
Bank

2

Cocks Moss
Farm

MARTON LA

67

ove House
Farm

Jack Field's
Farm

Brickyard
Farm

Gorsey Moor
Farm

Fields
Farm

1

Sandhole
Farm

A34

66

D
85
E
86
F

156
134

A   **B**   **C**

Mill End Farm

The Mount

New Hall Farm

4

Tidnock Wood

The Mollards

Gawsworth

Gawsworth Hall

Harrington Arms (Inn)

Harrington Hill Farm

Parkhouse

69

Gandys Brook

Gandysbrook

Butty Moss

Highlane

Shellow Wood

3

Yewtree Farm

CONGLETON RD

Foxbrook Farm

SHELLOW LA

Shellow Farm

Little Tidnock

68

Pastures

Dighills Farm

Rodegreen

Dobford

Dob Ford Bridge

Walle Woo

Dighill Brook

2

New Pastures

PEXHALL RD

Manor House

Bell Farm

The Grange

Hotel

Rodeheath

Manor Farm

67

MORTON LA

MACCLESFIELD RD

Bramhall Hill Farm

The Daintry Hall Prep Sch

PARK D

1

Rode Heath

Cloud View Farm

North Rode

Co e Brook

BANK LA

66

White House Farm

A536

Bank Farm

CHURCH LA

Rode Hall Farm

Ethel's Green Farm

A54

87   **A**   **88**   **B**   **89**   **C**

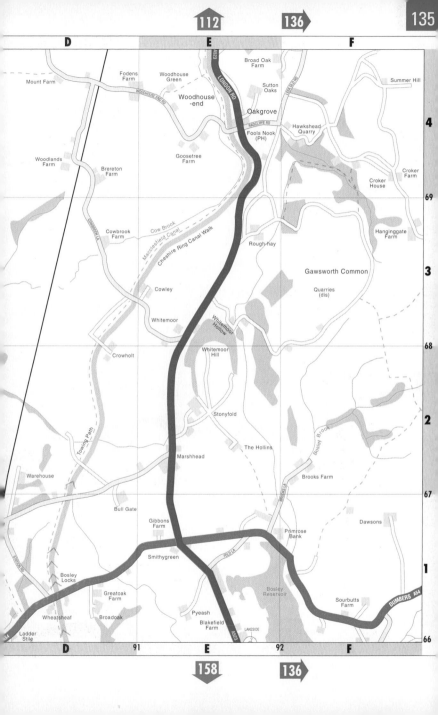

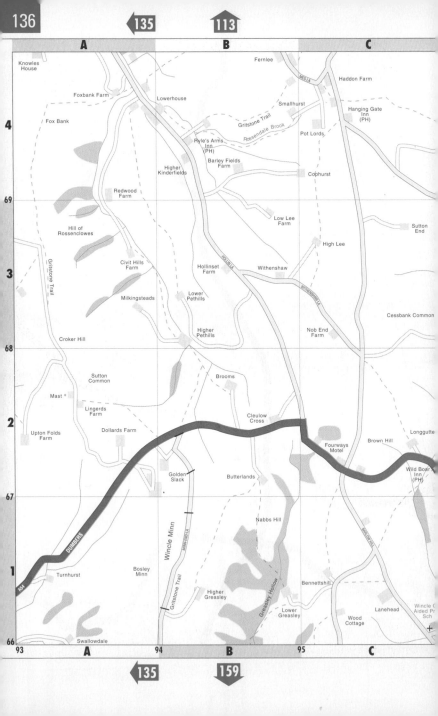

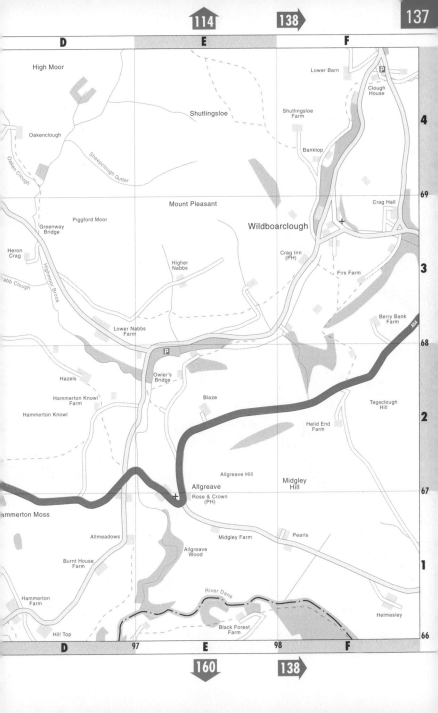

High Moor

Lower Barn

Clough House

Shutlingsloe Farm

Shutlingsloe

4

Oakenclough

Banktop

Oaken Clough

Sheepclough Gutter

69

Mount Pleasant

Crag Hall

Piggford Moor

Wildboarclough

Greenway Bridge

Crag Inn (PH)

Heron Crag

Higher Nabbs

Firs Farm

3

abb Clough

Highmoor Brook

Berry Bank Farm

A54

Lower Nabbs Farm

68

Hazels

Owler's Bridge

Blaze

Tagsclough Hill

Hammerton Knowl Farm

Hammerton Knowl

Helid End Farm

2

Allgreave Hill

Midgley Hill

Allgreave

67

Rose & Crown (PH)

ammerton Moss

Allmeadows

Midgley Farm

Pearls

Allgreave Wood

Burnt House Farm

1

Hammerton Farm

River Dane

Helmesley

Hill Top

Black Forest Farm

66

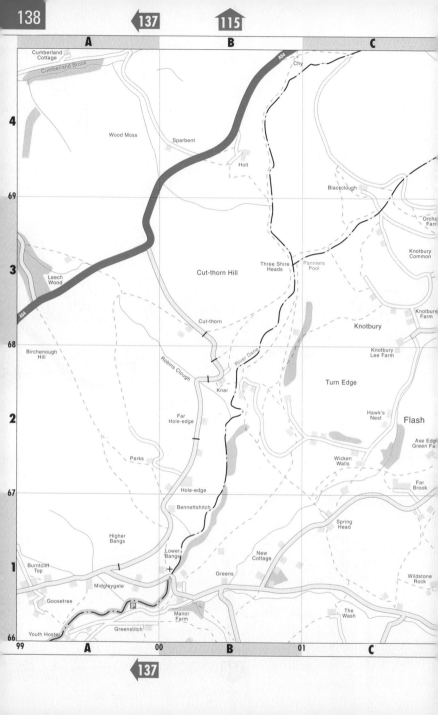

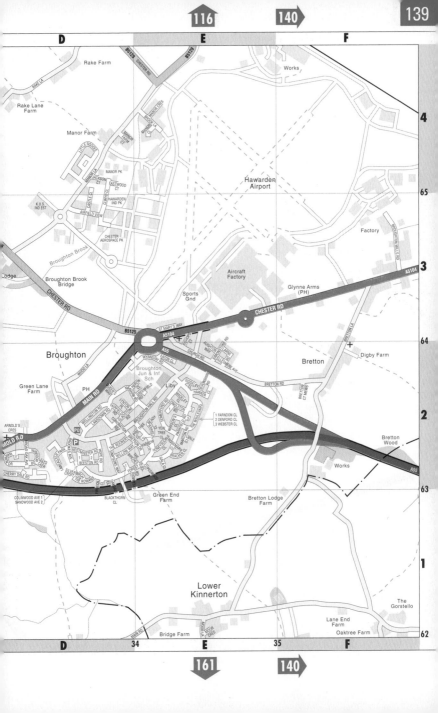

A   B   C

HOCKENHILL LA

Baker Way

Platts Lane

PLATTS LA

Broom Bank

Sheaf Farm

CROSS LANES

BROOMBANK LA

AST TARPORLEY RD

TARPORLEY RD

Duddon Hall

Old Moss

4

Duddon Heath

Cross Lanes Farm

Old Moss Farm

OLD MOSS LA

Moss Lane Farm

The Moss

Warren House Farm

MILL LA

65

RYECROFT LA

Duddon Heath

A5

Smithy Farm

DUDDON HOOK LA

Stapleford Hall

GILL LA

BROOKHOUSE LA

3

Ford Farm

Brookhouse Farm

Burton

64

Burton Hall

River Gowy

Waterless Brook

2

Upper Brookhouse Farm

Waterless Wood

MARTIN'S LA

Upper Brereton Park Farm

PARK LA

63

Brereton Park Farm

Lane End Farm

CY MILL RD

LEADGATE LA

1

Hargrave Hall

Leadgate Farm

Church Farm

Hargrave

+

Mill Lane Farm

MILL LA

Lower Huxley Hall

RD

62

Hargrave Farm

Southley Brook

48   A   49   B   50   C

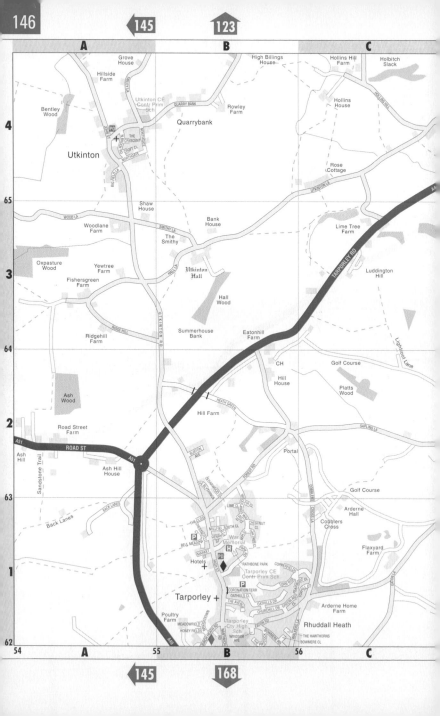

D E F

124
148

A49

PH

STABLE LA

Cotebrook

Tom's Hole

TARPORLEY RD

PO

HIGHLANDS RD

Little Budworth
Country Park

COACH RD

WHITHALL LA

PARK RD

Budworth
Pool

BELL LA

Egerton Arms
(PH)

PIERS LA

Little Budworth

4

OULTON MILL LA

Mill Covert

Hill Top
Farm

VICARAGE LA

BOOTS RD

TOWNSFIELD DR

YEW TREE CL.

WELL LA

UTKINTON LA

Mill
Pond

Park Place
Farm

65

Alvanley Arms
(PH)

Picnic Area

P

Home Farm

BEECH LA

Brownhill

BROWNHILL RD

OULTON PARK LA

Oulton
House

Oulton
Park

Lower
Farm

3

EATON LA

Beechlane
Farm

Garner
House

Rushton

Motor Racing Circuit

Hazelhurst
Covert

Oulton Lake

Moss Hall
Farm

DIGLAKE LA

64

Red Lion
(PH)

Parkwall
Farm

Withey
Bed

KNIGHT LA

2

LIGHTFOOT LA

Eaton

Eaton
Farm

Hunt's
Hill

Old
Lanes

MAN VILLA
(rems of)

SAPLING LA

WHALLEY DR

LOWER LA

YEW TREE CT

PO

BELVAL LA

EDGEWELL LA

Eaton Cty
Prim Sch

HICKHURST LA

Oak Tree
Farm

63

Oultonlowe
Farm

Boothouse
Farm

Philo
House

MILL LA

WHITEHERONS LA

Winterford
Farm

THE HALL LA

Philo
Gorse

1

Oxheys

62

D 58 E 59 F

169
148

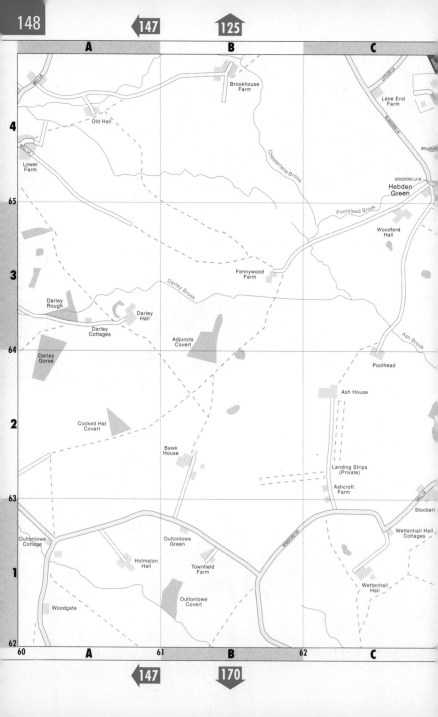

147
125

A   **B**   **C**

Brookhouse Farm

Lane End Farm

4

Old Hall

Chesterlane Brook

WOODFORD LA W

Lower Farm

Hebden Green

65

Poolstead Brook

Woodford Hall

3

Fennywood Farm

Darley Brook

Darley Rough

Darley Hall

Darley Cottages

Ash Brook

Adjuncts Covert

64

Darley Gorse

Poolhead

Ash House

2

Cocked Hat Covert

Bawk House

Landing Strips (Private)

Ashcroft Farm

63

Stockerl

Oultonlowe Cottage

Oultonlowe Green

Wettenhall Hall Cottages

WROXOLL RD

1

Holmston Hall

Townfield Farm

Wettenhall Hall

Woodgate

Oultonlowe Covert

62

60   **A**   **61**   **B**   **62**   **C**

147
170

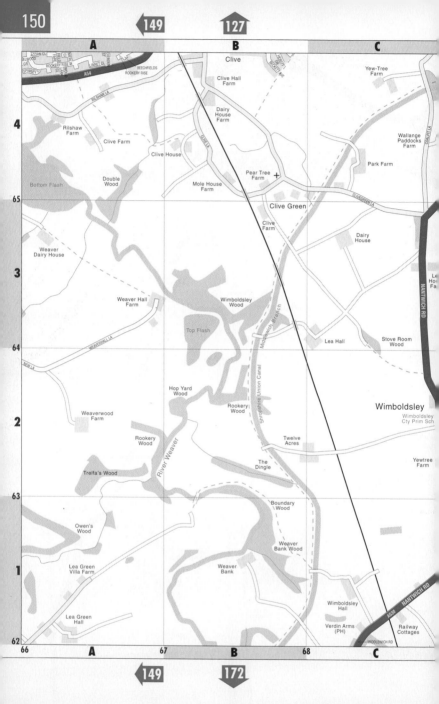

D E F

130

154

4

Allan Brook
Farm

Brereton
Pool

MILL LA

Park
House
Lodge

Blackberry
Covert

BRERETON LA

Court House
Farm

oresbarrow
Lodge

DOG LA

LONDON RD A50

65

Pewit
Farm

Pewit
Covert

BACK LA

Dog Lane
Farm

Dairyhouse
Farm

Sanderson's Brook

Fox
Covert

3

Brereton
Green

Backlane
Farm

Brereton
CE Aided
Prim Sch

NEWCASTLE RD N

WINDS LA

Whitening
House

SCHOOL LA

ST OSWALD'S

Foxcovert
Farm

64

School
Farm

Duke's Oak
Farm

RECTORY CT

A5022

NEWCASTLE RD

WALNUT TREE LA

Walnut Tree
Farm

Green
Farm

BRINDLEY LA

2

Holmleas
Farm

A50

Bradwall
Green

Chesworth
Farm

Brown Edge
Farm

63

Bradwall
Manor

Wellbank
Farm

Brindley Grange
Farm

Bradwall
House

Small Brook

Brindley Green
Farm

Springbank
Farm

Brindley
Green

1

Denman
Wood

Smallbrook

BRADWALL RD

Taxmere

Fields
Farm

Arclid
Sand Pit

Motel

A5022 HOLMES CHAPEL RD

Brickhouse
Farm

62

D 76 E 77 F

175

154

Ladder
Stile

A54

Lower House
Farm

Bosley

St Mary's
CE Contr
Sch

PH

Chutch
Farm

PH

Bosley
Reservoir

Chaff Hall
Farm

Highfield
House

Aqueduct

Kiln Hill
Farm

Conduit

Macclesfield Canal

Cheshire Ring Canal Walk

TUNSTALL RD

Lowerworks
Mill

65

BENNETTS LA

SMITH LA

Milt House
Farm

Woodside
Farm

Wood Flour
Mills

Greenfields
Farm

Cemy

Cemy

3

Toftgreen
Farm

Key Green
Farms

High Bent
Farm

64

Cloudwood End
Farm

Raven's
Clough

FOXLEA LA

Quarry
(dis)

Hillside
Farm

The Cloud

Cloud Side

Staffordshire Way

Mow Cop Trail

Peck's
House

2

Cloud
Plantation

Holmlea

Lee

63

Ravensclough Brook

Wood Common
Farm

Woodhouse
Green

Ditchway
Farm

BEARDROW LA

1

Oulton

Cloud Park
Farm

The Bridestones

Willowshaw
Farm

62

DIAL LA

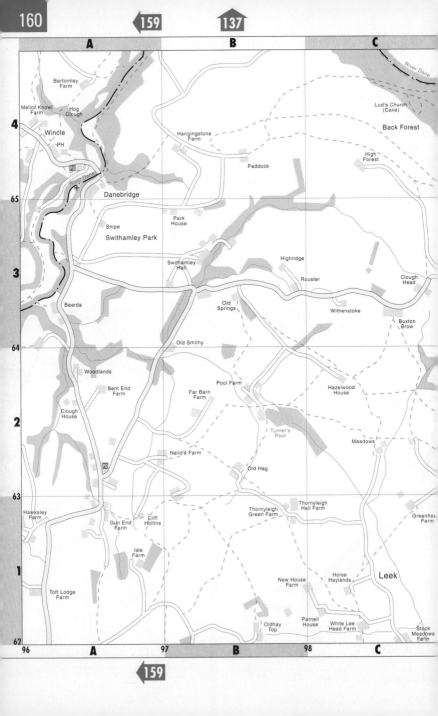

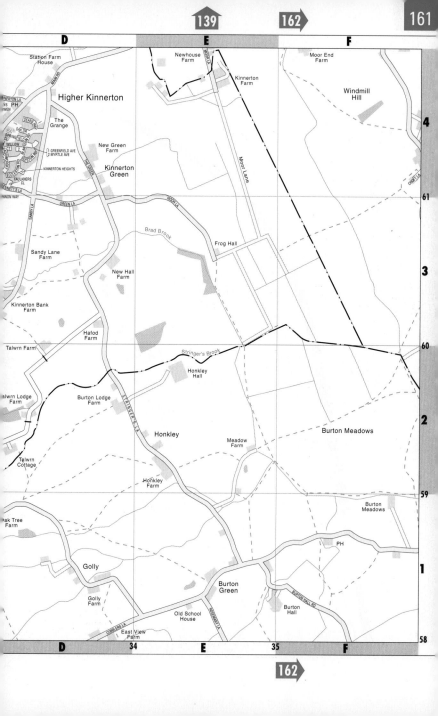

161

140

A B C

Black Wood

Belgrave Bridge

Balderton Drive

Greenwalls

4 Dodleston Hall

Dodleston CE Contr Prim Sch

Dodleston

Balderton Drive

Belgrave Farr

Belgrave Aven

Belgrave Cottages

Belgrave Lodge

61 CROFT LA

MALLORY WY

CHURCH

CASTLE WY

BELGRAVE CL

Belgrave

Moat Farm

FLOOR LA

3 Dodleston Lane Farm

Oldfields Farm

Works

WREXHAM RD

Cuckoo's Nest

STRAIGHT MILE

The Elms

60 Meadow House Farm

The Elms

Moorfield Cottages

The Manor

Lyndale Farm

DODLESTON LA

2 Pulford Crossing

Pulford

59 ROMANS FI

CASTLE

FAIRMEADOW

OLD LA

Pulford Approach

Broadoak

CASTLE HILL Hotel

Pulford Brook

Broadoak Farm

Pulford Bridge

Brookside Farm

1 LC

Cam-yr-Alyn Farm

Collynie

CHESTER RD

Sewage Works

Lavister

B5445

ROSSETT PK

Llyndir Hall Hotel

58 36 A 37 B 38 C

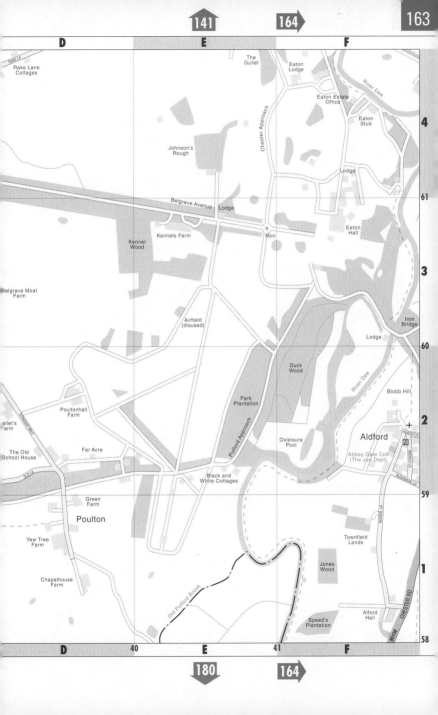

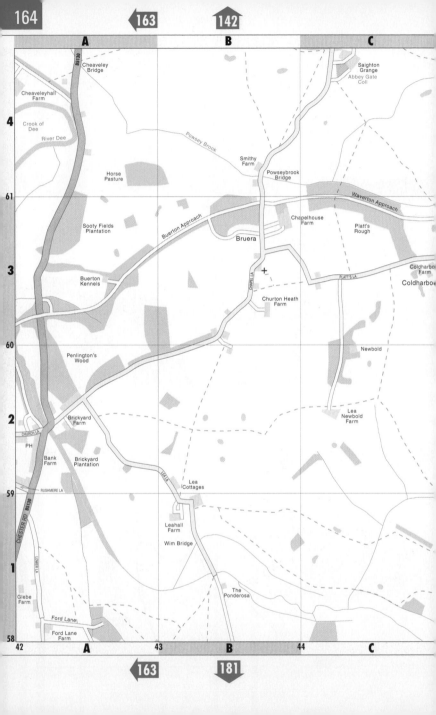

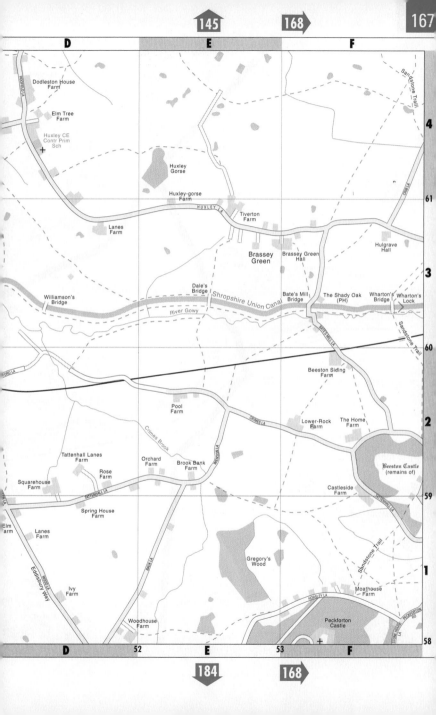

D
E
F

4

Sandstone Trail

Dodleston House Farm

Elm Tree Farm

Huxley CE Contr Prim Sch

Huxley Gorse

61

Huxley-gorse Farm

HUXLEY LA

Tiverton Farm

Lanes Farm

Brassey Green

Brassey Green Hall

Hulgrave Hall

3

Williamson's Bridge

Dale's Bridge

Shropshire Union Canal

Bate's Mill Bridge

The Shady Oak (PH)

Wharton's Bridge

Wharton's Lock

River Gowy

Sandstone Trail

60

STAFFORD LA

Beeston Siding Farm

BATES MILL LA

Pool Farm

Crimes Brook

CRIMES LA

Lower-Rock Farm

The Home Farm

2

Tattenhall Lanes Farm

Orchard Farm

Brook Bank Farm

RICKORN LA

Beeston Castle (remains of)

Squarehouse Farm

Rose Farm

TATTENHALL LA

Castleside Farm

59

TATTENHALL LA

Elm Farm

Lanes Farm

Spring House Farm

RICK LA

BROOK LA

Eddisbury Way

WOODS LA

Gregory's Wood

Sandstone Trail

1

Ivy Farm

Moathouse Farm

HORSLEY LA

STONE HOUSE LA

PECKFORTON RD

Woodhouse Farm

Peckforton Castle

58

D
52
E
53
F

A

B

C

4

61

3

60

2

59

1

58

Birch Heath Farm

Redhill Cottages

BIRCH HEATH RD

Birch Heath

CRIB LA

SPRING HILL

THE MEWS

WARREN WAY

Sch

NANTWICH RD

DALE HEY WEST

WALKERS LA
BOWMERE RD

RUE DE RIVIER

HEATH WAY

BROOK RD

BROADFIELD

CROSS LA

Springfield Farm

Ferney Lees

PADSMEAD

Sandstone Trail

Brook Farm Sch

Wettenhall Brook

Sewage Works

Tilston Lodge

Tiresford

Four Lane Ends

NANTWICH RD

Tilstone Fearnall

Town Fields

The Red Fox (PH)

Brookside

Tiverton Hall

HUXLEY LA

TOWNFIELD LA

DALE

The Old Court House

A49 EAST

Fishpond Farm

Hand Green

Tiverton

PO

+

Bank Farm

+

Tilstone House

TILSTONE PADDOCKS

A49

Beeston-brook

Beeston Iron Lock

River Gowy

Shropshire Union Canal

Beeston Stone Lock

VALE RD

Cattle Market

PH

Tilstone Bank Farm

Tilstone Bank

Beeston Hall

DEAN BANK

Mill Farm

Tilstone Lock

Castlegate Farm

Sandstone Trail

P

Deanbank Cottages

Hotel

Beeston

TATTENHALL LA

BROXTON RD

Brook Farm

Beeston Gate Farm

River Gowy

Priestland

Nursery

Higher Bunbury

BOWE'S GATE RD

CASTLE LA

Cem

BERRY'S LA

WYCH RD

VICARAGE LA

Willis's Wood

Beeston Moss

Heath Farm

DODDS LA

A49

White House

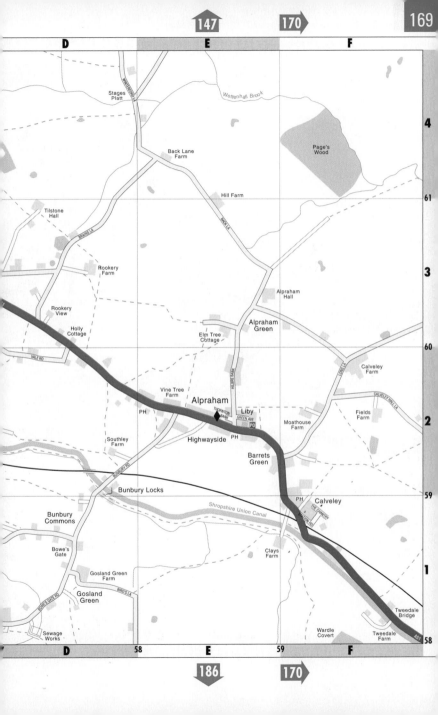

D
E
F

4

61

3

60

2

59

1

58

Stages Platt

Wettenhall Brook

Back Lane Farm

Page's Wood

Hill Farm

Tilstone Hall

BEANS LA

BACK LA

WHITEFORD LA

Rookery Farm

Alpraham Hall

Rookery View

Alpraham Green

Holly Cottage

Elm Tree Cottage

VALE RD

Calveley Farm

LONG LA

HELENS BANK

CALVELEY MILL LA

Vine Tree Farm

Alpraham

Liby

GREEN AVE

PO

PH

Fields Farm

Moathouse Farm

Southley Farm

Highwayside

PH

Barrets Green

BUNBURY RD

Bunbury Locks

Shropshire Union Canal

PH

Calveley

THE CHANTRY

STATION RD

Bunbury Commons

Bowe's Gate

Clays Farm

Gosland Green Farm

BIRD'S LA

BOWE'S GATE RD

Gosland Green

Sewage Works

Wardle Covert

Tweedale Farm

Tweedale Bridge

A51

D
E
F

58
59

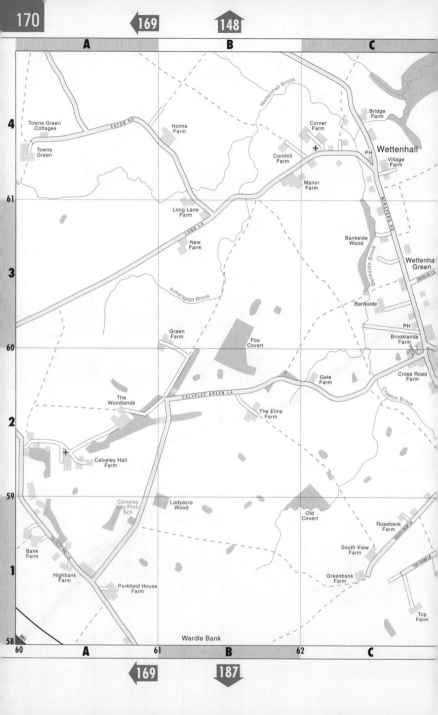

A B C

4

Towns Green Cottages

EATON RD

Holme Farm

Wettenhall Brook

Corner Farm

Bridge Farm

Towns Green

PH Wettenhall

Cornhill Farm

Village Farm

61

Long Lane Farm

LONG LA

Manor Farm

WINSFORD RD

New Farm

Bankside Wood

Ankersplatt Brook

Bankside Brook

Wettenha Green

DOUGLAS LA

3

Bankside

Green Farm

Fox Covert

PH

Brooklands Farm

60

Cross Road Farm

The Woodlands

CALVELEY GREEN LA

Gale Farm

Cowton Brook

The Elms Farm

2

Calveley Hall Farm

59

Calveley Cty Prim Sch

Ladyacre Wood

Old Covert

Rosebank Farm

SOUTH VIEW LA

South View Farm

TOP FARM LA

Bank Farm

CALVELEY HALL LA

1

Highbank Farm

Parkfield House Farm

Greenbank Farm

Top Farm

58

AST

Wardle Bank

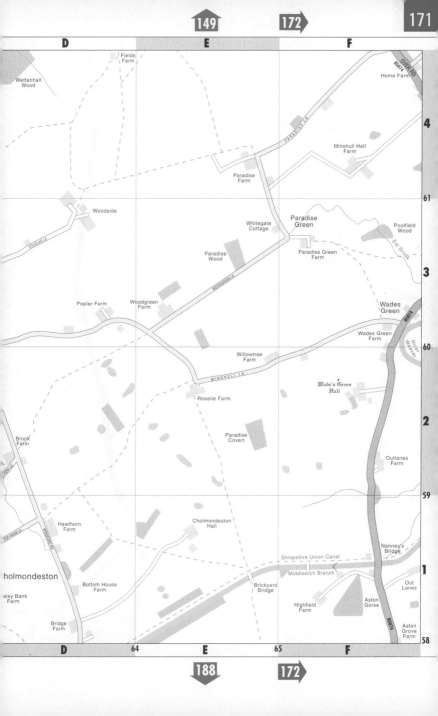

D
E
F

Fields
Farm

Wettenhall
Wood

OVER RD
B5074

Home Farm

PARADISE LA

4

Minshull Hall
Farm

61

Woodside

DOUGLAS LA

Whitegate
Cottage

Paradise
Green

Paradise
Farm

Poolfield
Wood

Eel Brook

Paradise
Wood

Paradise Green
Farm

3

Poplar Farm

Woodgreen
Farm

WOODGREEN LA

Wades
Green

B5074

Wades Green
Farm

River Weaver

60

Willowtree
Farm

MINSHULL LA

Rosalie Farm

Wade's Green
Hall

2

Paradise
Covert

Outlanes
Farm

Brook
Farm

OVER LA

59

TOP FARM LA

Hawthorn
Farm

REEDING RD

Cholmondeston
Hall

Nanney's
Bridge

1

holmondeston

Bottom House
Farm

Shropshire Union Canal

Middlewich Branch

Out
Lanes

aisy Bank
Farm

Brickyard
Bridge

Aston
Gorse

Bridge
Farm

Highfield
Farm

Aston
Grove
Farm

B5074

58

D
64
E
65
F

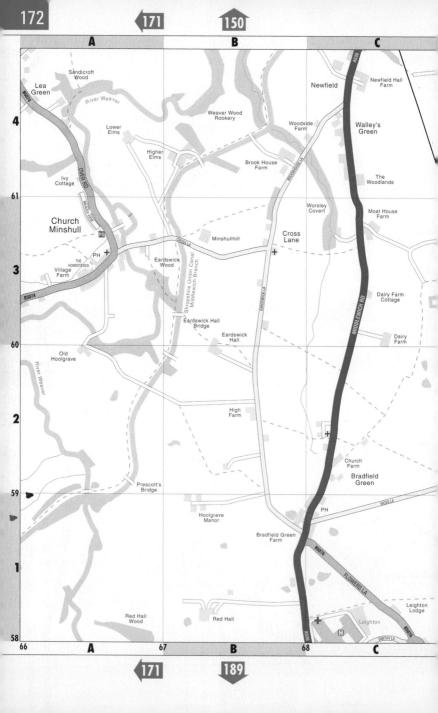

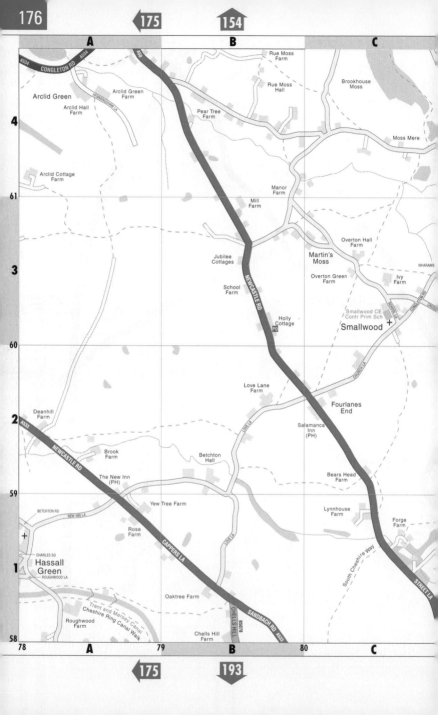

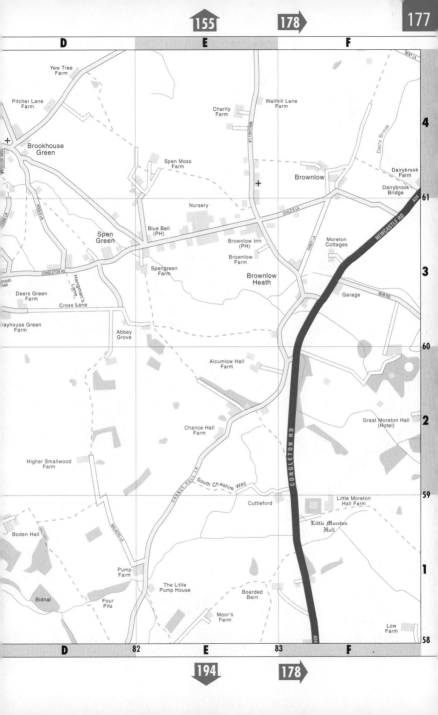

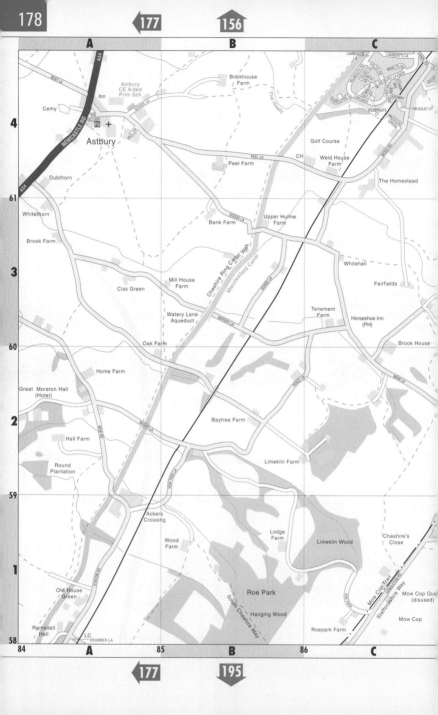

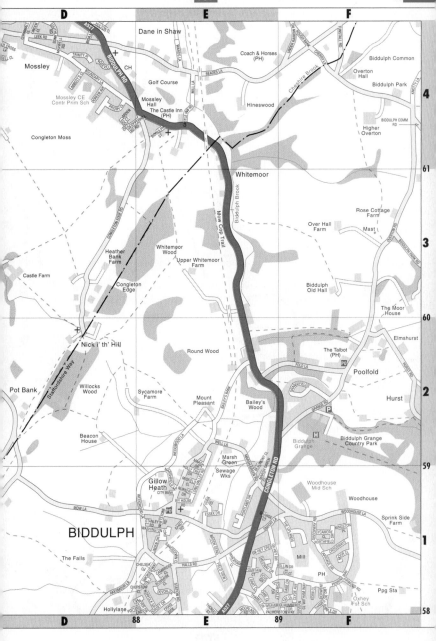

163

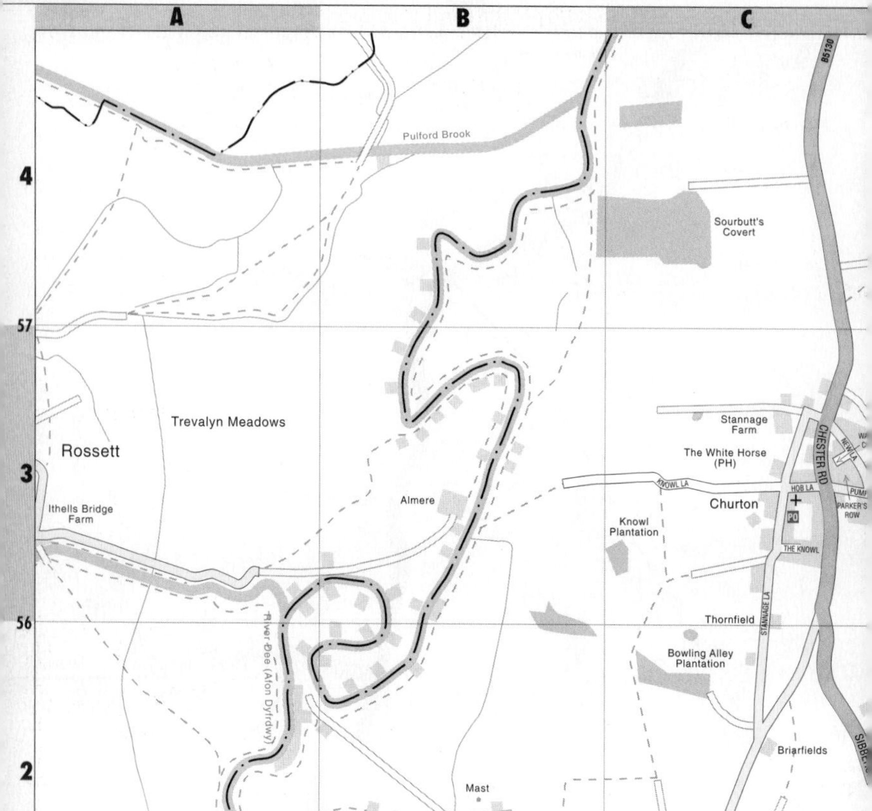

A
B
C
4
57
3
56
2
55
1
54
39
40
41
Pulford Brook
B5130
Sourbutt's Covert
Trevalyn Meadows
Rossett
Stannage Farm
The White Horse (PH)
CHESTER RD
KNOWL LA
HOB LA
Churton
PARKER'S ROW
THE KNOWL
Ithells Bridge Farm
Almere
Knowl Plantation
River Dee (Afon Dyfrdwy)
Thornfield
STANNAGE LA
Bowling Alley Plantation
Briarfields
Mast
Barnston's Monument
BREWERY LA
TOWNFIELD LA
Farndon Cty Prim Sch
Farndon
CHURTON RD
OLD SCHOOL CL
SPEED'S WAY
TOWNFIELD
DEE CRES
RIVER LA
DEE VIEW
PH
HIGH ST
LLOYD CL
BARNSTON CT
MILL FIELD CL
GREENWAY
NIGHTINGALE CL
CHURCH LA
CHURCH CT
Earndon or Holt Bridge
RECTORY CL
LIME TREE DR
BARTON RD
HERON CL
QUARRY HILL
PARKER DR
PARKER AVE
QUARRY DR
PARKER DR S
ORCHARD GR
MEADOW CL
CREWE LA
Plas Devon
Devon Brook
Works
Brook Lawn
B5102
FIELDS
WHITEGATE
CAERLLEW
GREEN ST
BRIDGE ST
QUAKERS WAY
Cemy
LABURNUM WAY
THE GARDENS
CHURCH ST
VICARAGE CT
Esp Hill
P
PO

196

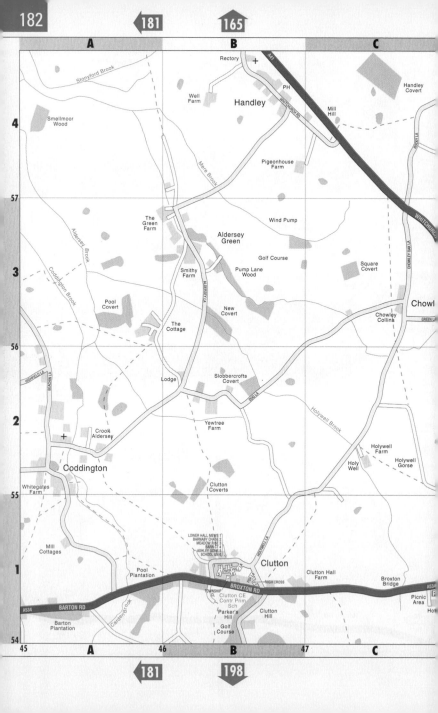

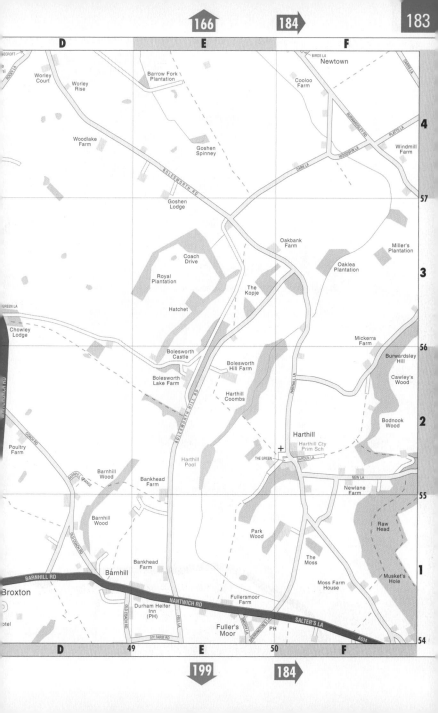

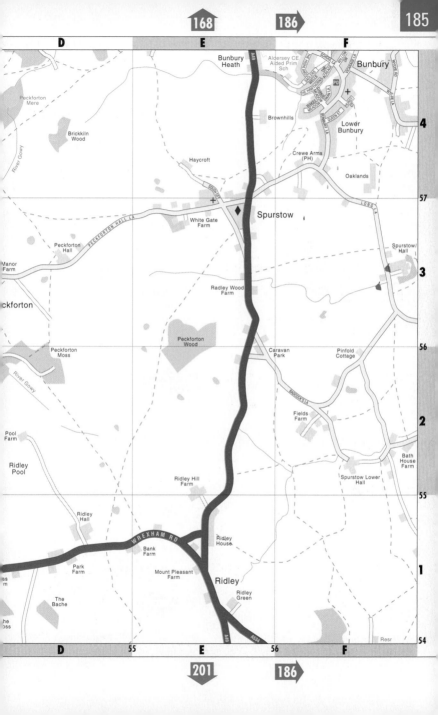

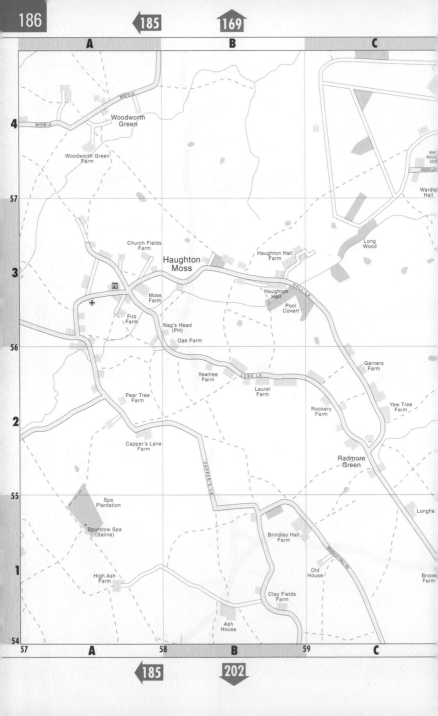

D E F

4

Wardle Hall Bridge
NANTWICH RD
Humble Bee Bank Cottages
Hill's Gorse
adio scope
Wardle Bridge Farm
WARDLE INDUSTRIAL ESTATE
Green-lane Farm
GREEN LA
Wardle
Wardle Old Hall
Rutters Bridge
Shropshire Union Canal
Middlewich Branch
Sandhole Bridge
Benyon's Bridge
Crossbanks Farm

57

The Poplars Farm
Barbridge Junction
Bar Bridge
Jolly Tar (PH)
PO
Works
Barbridge
BANKSIDE CL
Stoke Bank
Bullsgreen Farm
MILL LN
CHESTER RD
CHAPEL ROW
The Barbridge Inn
STOKEHALL LN
Stoke Hall Farm
Stoke Hall
The Rookery
Bremilow's Bridge
Stokehall Bridge

3

Clatterdishes Farm
Verona
Shropshire Union Canal
Vicker's Bridge

56

Stoke Manor
Yew Tree Farm

Little Bachehouse Covert
Little Bache House
Hurleston Reservoir
Hurleston Junction

2

Radmore Covert
Bachehouse Covert
Works
Hurleston Bridge

55

Bache House
Bachehouse Bridge
Corners Bridge
Bachehouse Pool
Park Farm
New Farm

1

Martin's Bridge
Lee's Bridge
A51

54

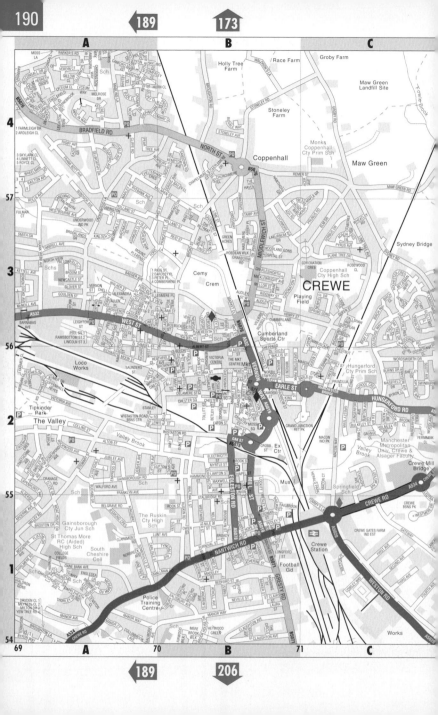

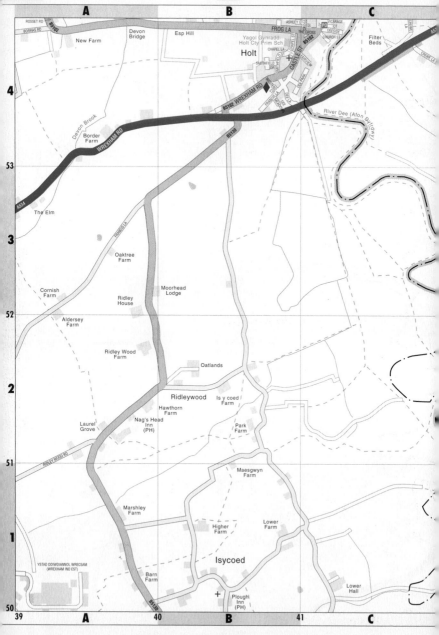

181
198

D
E
F

4

Rowley Hill
Farm

eadow View

Tom Irohs'
Rough

Crewe-by-
Farndon

Lodge Farm

Wetreins Green
Farm

Stretton
Lower Hall

53

Crewe
Hall

Kingslee

Wetreins
Green

WETREINS LA

The
Wetreins

Stretton Hall

Stretton
Old
Hall

ewe Hall

Stretton

3

Mrs Leche's
Gorse

Crewe
Gorse

The
Wetreins

Crewe Farm

52

Caldecott Farm

Caldecott Green

River Dee (Afon Dyfrdwy)

Caldecott
Hall

Grafton
New Covert

2

Castletown

51

Caldecott
Farm

Castletown Bridge

River Dee (Afon Dyfrdwy)

Castletown
Rough

CASTLETOWN LA

Lords
Fields

1

Chestnuts

CHURCH RD

50

D
43
E
44
F

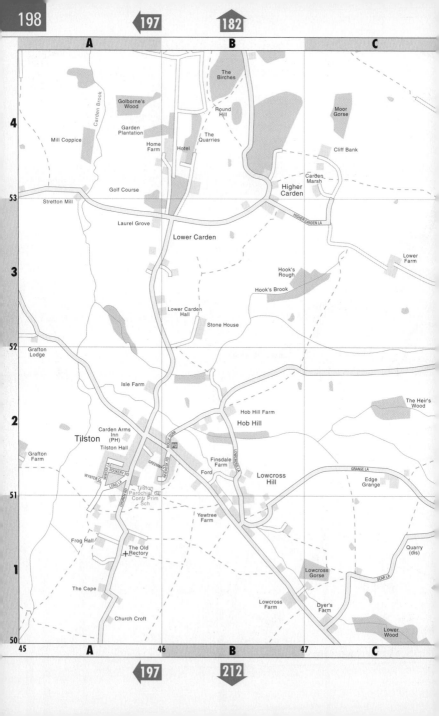

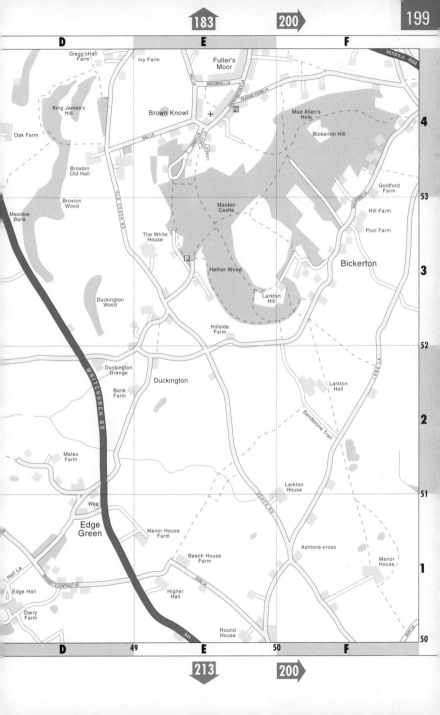

199
184

A   B   C

WREXHAM RD
A534

Gallantry
Bank

Bickerton
Farm

Gallantry-bank
Farm

Bulkeley
Hall

Walnut -Tree
Farm

Manor
Farm

CHOLMONDELEY LA

Bulkeleyhay

4

Yewtree
Farm

Townsend
Farm

LONG LA

Bickerton CE
Contr Prim Sch

53

Bickerton
Hall

Fields
Farm

Manor
Farm

Gate House
Farm

3

Egerton
Green

Green
Farm

Yew Tree
Farm

Bankhouse
Farm

Oak Tree
Farm

52

Egerton
Farm

Park
House

Bickley Brook

Scotch
Farm

2

Castle
Hill

Cholmondele
Castle

Castle
Farm

PO

Cholmondeley
Castle Gardens

Egerton
Cottages

51

Egerton
Hall

1

Hampton
Grange

Egerton Bank
Farm

DIRT LA

Hetherson Green
Farm

Cross Lanes
Farm

Red Hall

GROTSWORTH LA

50

51   A   52   B   53   C

199
214

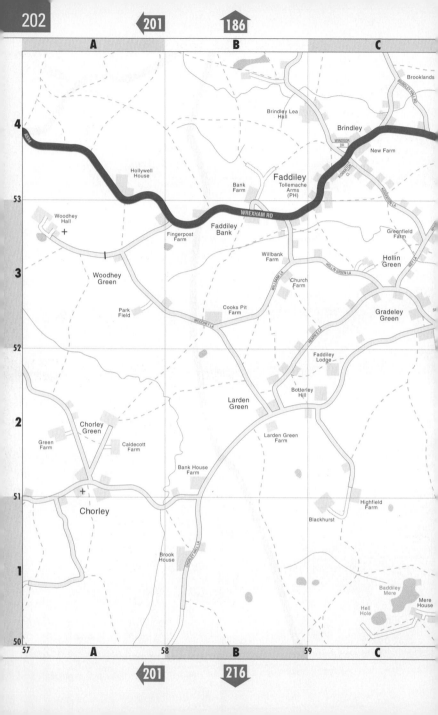

201
186

A   B   C

4

Brooklands

Brindley Lea
Hall

Brindley

New Farm

Hollywell
House

Faddiley

Bank
Farm

Tollemache
Arms
(PH)

53

WREXHAM RD

Woodhey
Hall

Faddiley
Bank

Greenfield
Farm

Fingerpost
Farm

Willbank
Farm

Hollin
Green

3

Woodhey
Green

Church
Farm

HOLLIN GREEN LA

Park
Field

Cooks Pit
Farm

Gradeley
Green

WOODHEY LA

WILLIAMS LA

DEANS LA

SF

52

Faddiley
Lodge

Botterley
Hill

Larden
Green

2

Chorley
Green

Green
Farm

Caldecott
Farm

Larden Green
Farm

Bank House
Farm

Chorley

Highfield
Farm

51

Blackhurst

Brook
House

DOCKET HILL LA

Baddiley
Mere

1

Mere
House

Hell
Hole

50
57   A   58   B   59   C

201
216

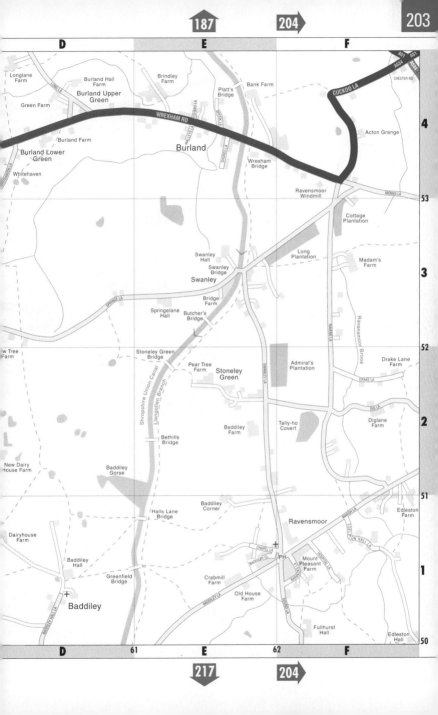

187
204

D   **E**   **F**

Longlane
Farm

Burland Hall
Farm

Brindley
Farm

Platt's
Bridge

Bank Farm

CHESTER RD

CUCKOO LA

A51
A534

Burland Upper
Green

Green Farm

WREXHAM RD

Acton Grange

Burland Farm

LONG LA

Burland

MONKS LA

Burland Lower
Green

Wrexham
Bridge

53

Whitehaven

Ravensmoor
Windmill

Cottage
Plantation

Long
Plantation

Madam's
Farm

Swanley
Hall

Swanley
Bridge

3

Swanley

SPRINGE LA

Bridge
Farm

Ravensmoor Brook

Springelane
Hall

Butcher's
Bridge

52

Stoneley Green
Bridge

Pear Tree
Farm

Stoneley
Green

Admiral's
Plantation

DRAKE LA

Drake Lane
Farm

w Tree
Farm

Shropshire Union Canal

Llangollen Branch

SWANLEY LA

NANTES LA

Tree
Farm

Baddiley
Farm

Tally-ho
Covert

DIG LA

Diglane
Farm

2

Bethills
Bridge

Baddiley
Gorse

New Dairy
House Farm

Halls Lane
Bridge

Baddiley
Corner

Ravensmoor

MARSH LA

Edleston
Farm

51

Dairyhouse
Farm

Baddiley
Hall

Greenfield
Bridge

CHAPEL LA

BADDILEY CL

PH

Mount
Pleasant
Farm

HOSPITAL LA

ACTON HALL LA

1

Baddiley

Crabmill
Farm

BADDILEY LA

Old House
Farm

SOUND LA

Fullhurst
Hall

Edleston
Hall

50

D   61   **E**   62   **F**

217
204

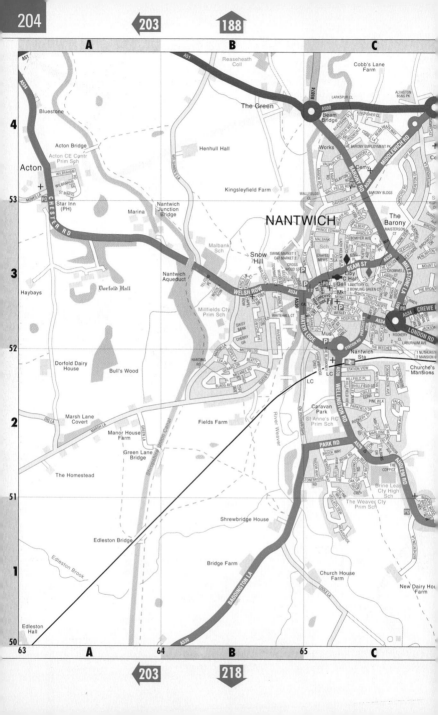

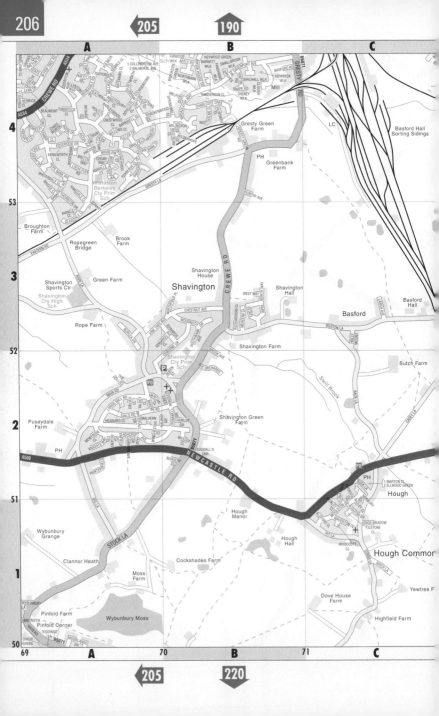

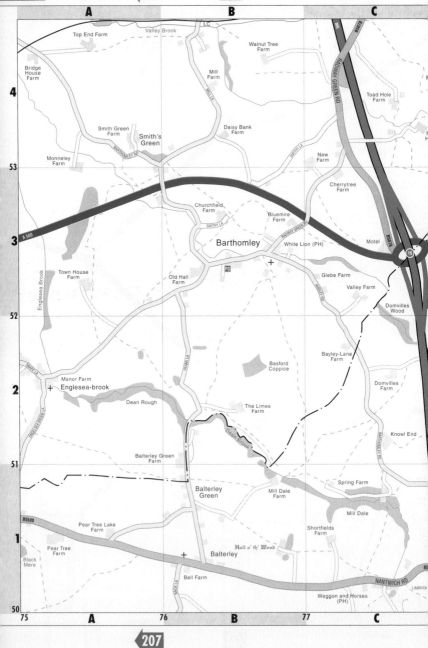

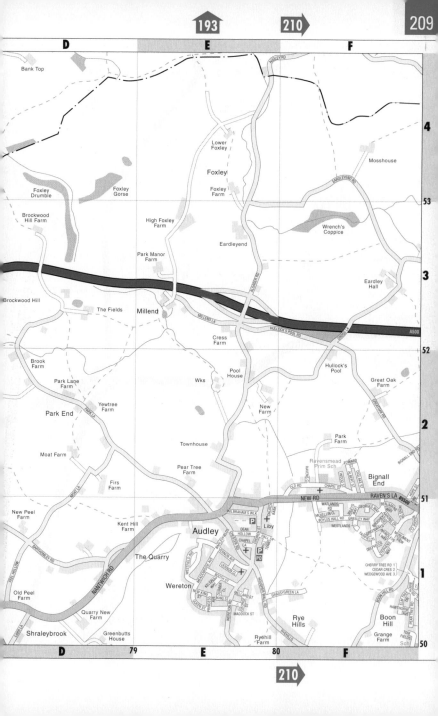

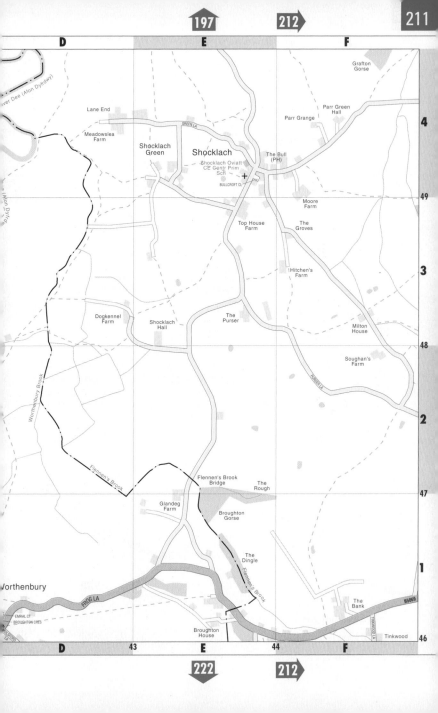

D   **E**   **F**

Grafton Gorse

River Dee (Afon Dyfrdwy)

Lane End

Parr Green Hall

Parr Grange

4

Meadowslea Farm

GREEN LA

Shocklach Green

Shocklach

The Bull (PH)

Afon Dyfrdwy

Shocklach Oviatt CE Contr Prim Sch

BULLCROFT CL

49

Moore Farm

Top House Farm

The Groves

3

Hitchen's Farm

Dogkennel Farm

Shocklach Hall

The Purser

Milton House

48

Worthenbury Brook

Soughan's Farm

RUSSIA LA

2

Flennen's Brook

Flennen's Brook Bridge

The Rough

47

Glandeg Farm

Broughton Gorse

The Dingle

Flennen's Brook

1

Worthenbury

FROG LA

The Bank

B5069

EMRAL CT

BROUGHTON CRES

Broughton House

Tinkwood

TINKWOOD LA

46

D   43   **E**   44   **F**

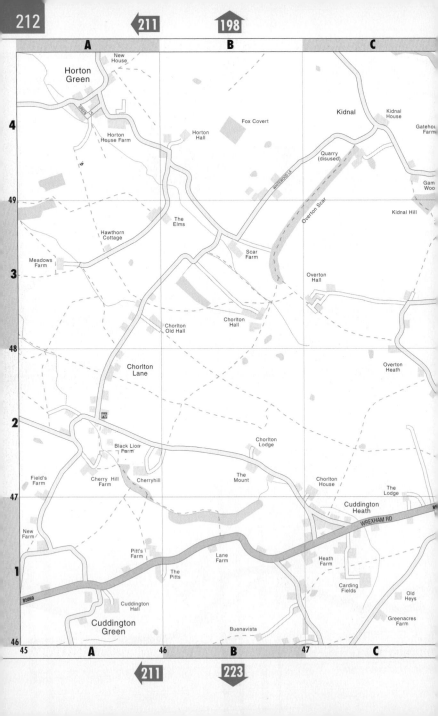

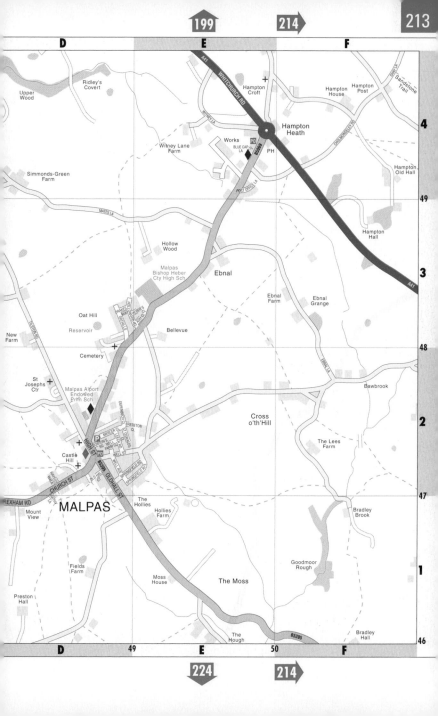

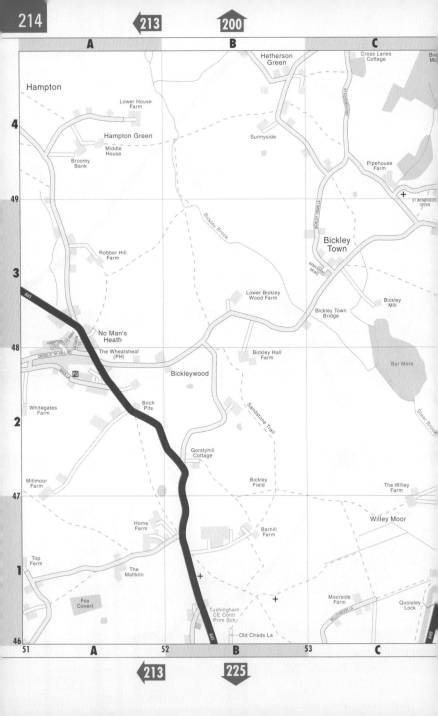

A B C

Hetherson
Green

Cross Lanes
Cottage

Bre
Mo

Hampton

Lower House
Farm

4

Hampton Green

Sunnyside

Pipehouse
Farm

Middle
House

St WENFREDE
GREEN

Broomy
Bank

49

Bickley Brook

Robber Hill
Farm

Bickley
Town

3

A41

Bickley
Mill

BANK FARM
MEWS

Lower Bickley
Wood Farm

Bickley Town
Bridge

No Man's
Heath

48

HAMPTON
CRES

The Wheatsheaf
(PH)

Bickley Hall
Farm

Bar Mere

CROSS O TH HILL RD

BUCK LA PO

Bickleywood

Sheer Brook

Whitegates
Farm

Birch
Pits

Sandstone Trail

2

Gorstyhill
Cottage

Millmoor
Farm

Bickley
Field

The Willey
Farm

47

Home
Farm

Willey Moor

Barhill
Farm

Top
Farm

1

The
Maltkiln

Fox
Covert

Moorside
Farm

Quoisley
Lock

Tushingham
CE Contr
Prim Sch

WILLEYMOOR LA

A41

A49

46

Old Chads La

51 A 52 B 53 C

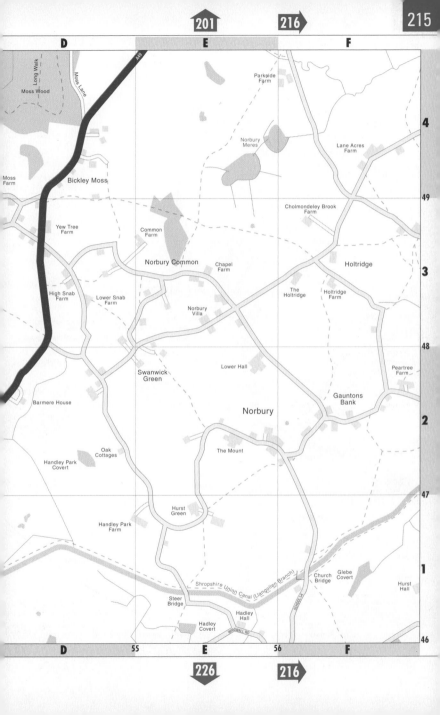

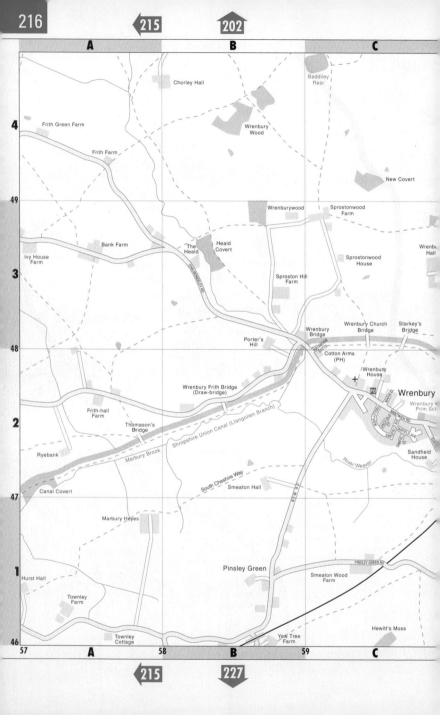

215
202

A **B** **C**

4

Frith Green Farm

Chorley Hall

Baddiley
Resr

Wrenbury
Wood

New Covert

Frith Farm

49

Wrenburywood

Sprostonwood
Farm

Ivy House
Farm

Bank Farm

The
Heald

Heald
Covert

Sprostonwood
House

Wrenbu
Hall

3

Sproston Hill
Farm

Wrenbury
Bridge

Wrenbury Church
Bridge

Starkey's
Bridge

Porter's
Hill

48

Cotton Arms
(PH)

Wrenbury
House

Wrenbury
Frith Bridge
(Draw-bridge)

Wrenbury

Wrenbury
Prim Sch

2

Frith-hall
Farm

Thomason's
Bridge

Shropshire Union Canal (Llangollen Branch)

Sandfield
House

Ryebank

Marbury Brook

River Weaver

Canal Covert

South Cheshire Way

Smeaton Hall

47

Marbury Heyes

NEW RD

Pinsley Green

PINSLEY GREEN RD

1

Hurst Hall

Smeaton Wood
Farm

Townley
Farm

Hewitt's Moss

46

Townley
Cottage

Yew Tree
Farm

57 **A** 58 **B** 59 **C**

215
227

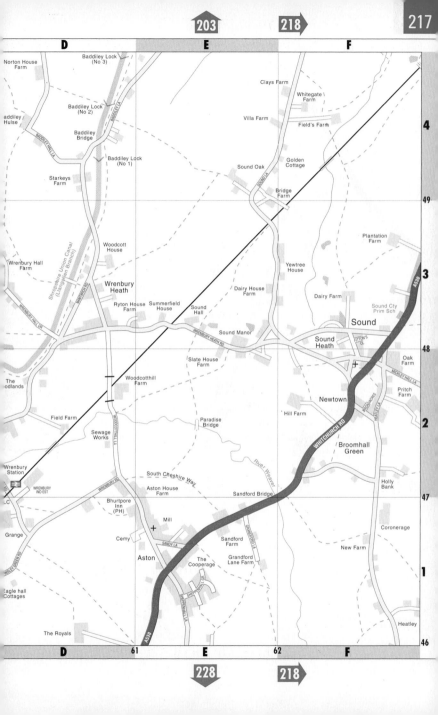

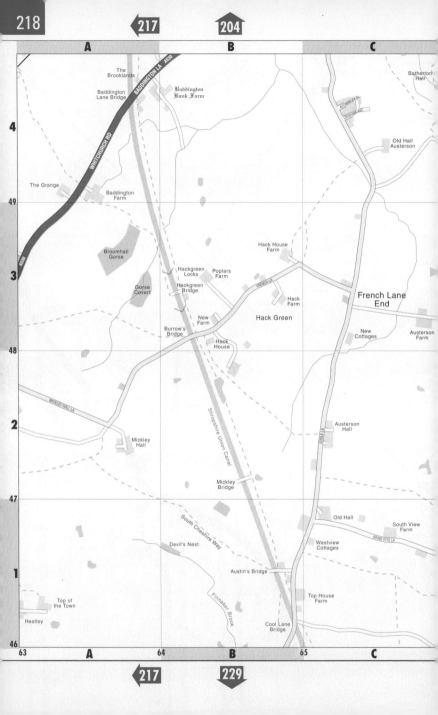

217
204

A B C

4

49

3

48

2

47

1

46

63 A 64 B 65 C

WHITCHURCH RD

A530

BADDINGTON LA A530

The Brooklands

Baddington Lane Bridge

Baddington Bank Farm

Batherton Hall

ATCHERLEY CL

CRUSHAM AVE

Old Hall Austerson

The Grange

Baddington Farm

Broomhall Gorse

Gorse Covert

Hackgreen Locks

Hackgreen Bridge

Poplars Farm

Hack House Farm

FRENCH LA

Hack Farm

French Lane End

New Cottages

Austerson Farm

Burrow's Bridge

New Farm

Hack House

Hack Green

MICKLEY HALL LA

Mickley Hall

Shropshire Union Canal

Austerson Hall

COOLE LA

Old Hall

South View Farm

BRINE PITS LA

Westview Cottages

South Cheshire Way

Devil's Nest

Mickley Bridge

Austin's Bridge

Finnaker Brook

Cool Lane Bridge

Top House Farm

Top of the Town

Heatley

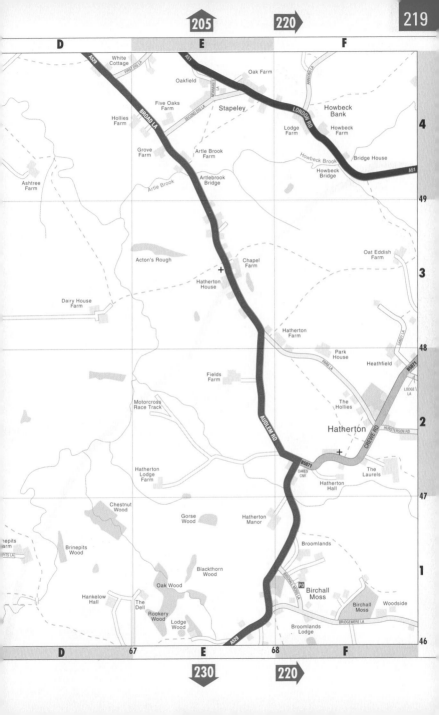

D E F

4

49

3

48

2

47

1

46

White Cottage
FROST DALE LA
A529
BROAD LA
A51
Oakfield
Oak Farm
Five Oaks Farm
NEWMANS LA
SECOND DIG LA
Stapeley
LONDON RD
ARNANS LA
Howbeck Bank
Hollies Farm
Lodge Farm
Howbeck Farm
Grove Farm
Artle Brook Farm
Bridge House
Howbeck Brook
Artlebrook Bridge
Artle Brook
Howbeck Bridge
A51
Ashtree Farm
Oat Eddish Farm
Acton's Rough
Chapel Farm
Hatherton House
Dairy House Farm
Hatherton Farm
Park House
Heathfield
B5071
CANOL LA
PARK LA
LODGE LA
Fields Farm
Motorcross Race Track
The Hollies
AUDLEM RD
Hatherton
CREWE RD
HUNSTERSON RD
Hatherton Lodge Farm
B5071
OAKES CNR
The Laurels
Chestnut Wood
Hatherton Hall
Gorse Wood
Hatherton Manor
Brinepits Wood
Broomlands
Blackthorn Wood
epits arm
PITS LA
Oak Wood
BIRCHALL MOSS LA
PO
Birchall Moss
Hankelow Hall
The Dell
Rookery Wood
Lodge Wood
A529
Broomlands Lodge
Birchall Moss
Woodside
BRIDGEMERE LA
D 67 E 68 F

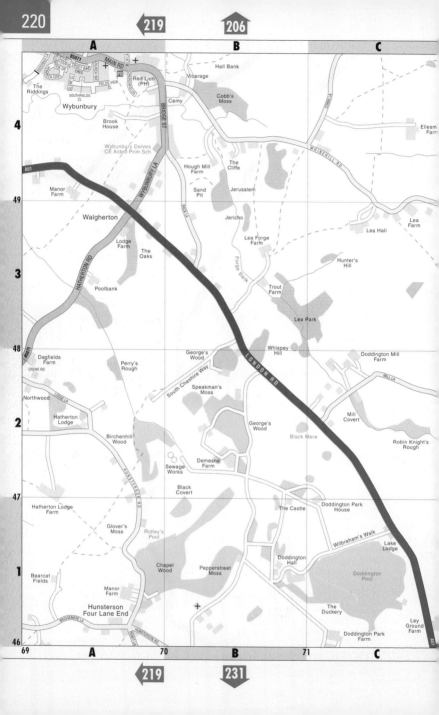

A B C

4

Wybunbury

The Riddings

SOUTHFIELDS CL

B5071 MAIN RD

Red Lion (PH)

Hall Bank

Vicarage

Cobb's Moss

Cemy

Brook House

Wybunbury Delves CE Aided Prim Sch

BRIDGE ST

COBBS LA

WRINEHILL RD

Ellesm Farm

Manor Farm

49

Hough Mill Farm

The Cliffe

Sand Pit

Jerusalem

WYBUNBURY LA

A51

Lea Farm

Walgherton

Jericho

Lea Hall

Lodge Farm

The Oaks

Lea Forge Farm

Forge Bank

Hunter's Hill

3

HATHERTON RD

Poolbank

Trout Farm

Lea Park

Dagfields Farm

48

CREWE RD

B5071

George's Wood

Whispey Hill

Doddington Mill Farm

Perry's Rough

South Cheshire Way

LONDON RD

MILL LA

Northwood

Speakman's Moss

Mill Covert

2

Hatherton Lodge

LOGGE LA

Birchenhill Wood

George's Wood

Black Mere

Robin Knight's Rough

Sewage Works

Demesne Farm

47

Hatherton Lodge Farm

Black Covert

The Castle

Doddington Park House

HUNSTERSON RD

Glover's Moss

Ridley's Pool

Wilbraham's Walk

Lake Lodge

Chapel Wood

Pepperstreet Moss

Doddington Hall

Doddington Pool

1

Bearcat Fields

Manor Farm

The Duckery

Ley Ground Farm

Hunsterson Four Lane End

BRIDGEMERE LA

HUNSTERSON RD

FINLA

Doddington Park Farm

A51

46

69 A 70 B 71 C

West Heath

The Elms

Betley

The Anchorage

Doddlespool Hall

4

Doddlespool Farm

Buddileigh

Elmer Riddings

The Slum

49

Half Moon Farm

Gonsley Green Farm

Betley Common

BROADHILL RD

Oak Tree Farm

COMMON LA

3

Gonsley Cottages

lakenhall Moss

Green Valley Farm

Coppice Bank

Manor Farm

Lower Den Farm

48

Betley Mere

DEN LA

Higher Den Farm

Den Bridge

Cracow Moss

West View

Blakenhall

New Farm

Fog Cottages

2

MILL LA

Yew Tree Farm

Ash Tree Farm

Hayes Farm

Dairy Farm

Blakenhall Farm

Bunkers Hill

47

Shaw's Rough

Ash Coppice

Randilow Farmhouse

1

Checkley Brook

Grange Farm

Checkley Brook Farm

The Coppice

Yew Tree Farm

Checkley Bridge

Checkley Hall

CHECKLEY LA

Checkley

Little Meadow

46

Swill Brook

Mere Gutter

WEBBUTT LA

A531

Wood Farm

Powys Sch

MILSFORD LA

Emral Brook

Caenant Wood

Middle Wood Farm

Wych Brook

Upper Wood Farm

CROFT LA

BARN RD

BOUNDARY LA

SANDY LA

DOD LA

BACK LA

Topwood Farm

Upper Threapwood

Windmill (disused)

Threapwood

GREAVES LA

Lower Threapwood

Turpinford Bridge

Mulsford

Sarn Farm

Sarn Bridge

PH

Greaves Wood

Mulsford Cottage Farm

Caelica Farm

Tallarn Green

WARWAY

PO

Emral Stud

Cae-li-cae

Lower Tallarngreen Farm

Talwrn Green Prim Sch

ELX VIEW

Mulsford Hall

Whalebone Cottage

Fields Farm

Tallarn Green Bridge

The Pools

Whalebone Farm

Oak Farm

Pandy Farm

Pandy Bridge

Burton's Wood

The Fields

Trowstree Villa

Trowstree

Pandy

A525

Plassey

Willington Cross

Roger's Rough

Willington

HALGHTON LA

Halghton Lane Farm

Rook Lane

Buck Farm

Charity Farm

Cherrytree Farm

Neil Peter's Lane

Penley

DARTMORE

A525

Bowen's Hall

Cal Lane

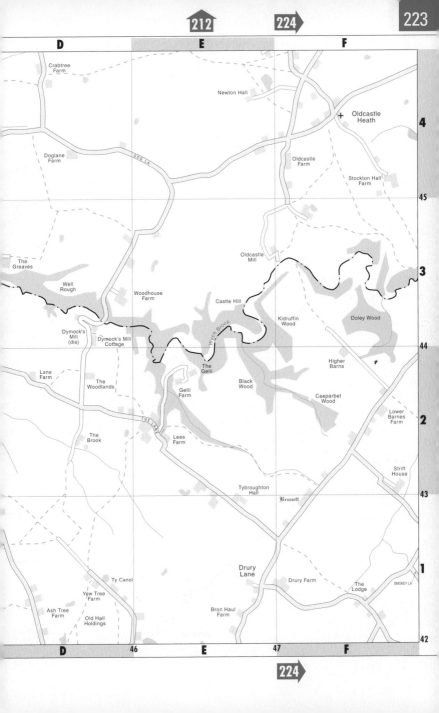

D E F

Crabtree
Farm

Newton Hall

Oldcastle
Heath

4

Doglane
Farm

DOG LA

Oldcastle
Farm

45

Stockton Hall
Farm

The
Greaves

Oldcastle
Mill

3

Well
Rough

Woodhouse
Farm

Castle Hill

Kidruffin
Wood

Doley Wood

Wych Brook

Dymock's
Mill
(dis)

Dymock's Mill
Cottage

The
Gelli

Higher
Barns

44

Lane
Farm

The
Woodlands

Gelli
Farm

Black
Wood

Caeparbet
Wood

Lower
Barnes
Farm

2

THE LANE

The
Brook

Lees
Farm

Strift
House

Tybroughton
Hall

Brunett

43

Drury
Lane

Drury Farm

The
Lodge

1

SMOKEY LA

Ty Canol

Yew Tree
Farm

Bron Haul
Farm

Ash Tree
Farm

Old Hall
Holdings

D 46 E 47 F

42

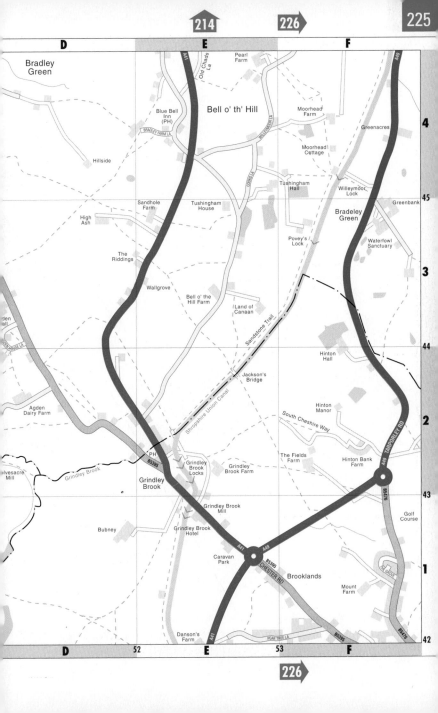

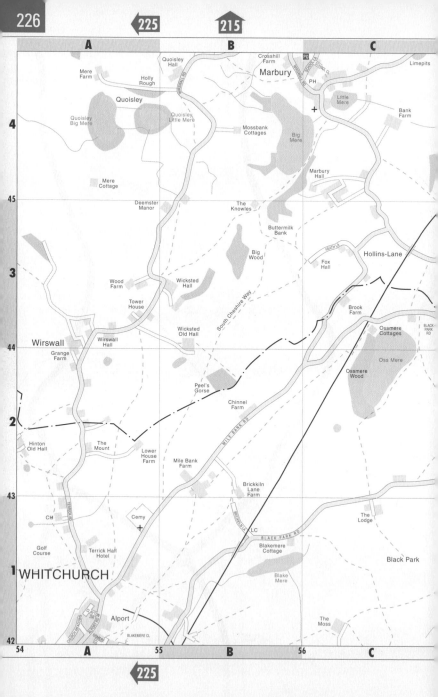

A   B   C

4

45

3

44

Wirswall

2

43

1 WHITCHURCH

42
54   55   56

A   B   C

Mere
Farm

Holly
Rough

Quoisley
Hall

Crosshill
Farm

Marbury

PO

PH

Limepits

Quoisley

Quoisley
Big Mere

Quoisley
Little Mere

Little
Mere

Bank
Farm

Mossbank
Cottages

Big
Mere

Mere
Cottage

Deemster
Manor

The
Knowles

Marbury
Hall

Buttermilk
Bank

Big
Wood

HEATH LA

Fox
Hall

Hollins-Lane

Wood
Farm

Wicksted
Hall

South Cheshire Way

Brook
Farm

Ossmere
Cottages

BLACK
PARK
RD

Tower
House

Wirswall
Hall

Wicksted
Old Hall

Oss Mere

Grange
Farm

Ossmere
Wood

Peel's
Gorse

Chinnel
Farm

Hinton
Old Hall

The
Mount

Lower
House
Farm

Mile Bank
Farm

MILE BANK RD

Brickkiln
Lane
Farm

CM

Cemy

The
Lodge

Golf
Course

Terrick Hall
Hotel

BLACK PARK RD

LC

Blakemere
Cottage

Black Park

Blake
Mere

Alport

The
Moss

BLAKEMERE CL

D   **E**   **F**

Marley Moss

Poole
Hook

LC

Marley Green

Marley
Hall

Adamley
Pool

4

Marley Hall
Covert

Poole
Gorse

45

Grange
Farm

Poole's
Riding Wood

Big Wood

Duckbay
Island

● Monument

Hollyhurst

Brankelow
Moss

Summerhouse
Island

Comber Mere

Long Walk
Covert

3

Hollyhurst
Wood

Brankelow
Folly

Combermere
Abbey

Combermere Park

Larder
Wood

44

Cocked Hat

Blackpark
Farm

BLACK PARK RD

The Stews

Bridge
Plantation

Stonelodge
Wood

A530 WHITCHURCH RD

2

Steel's
Rough
Plantation

43

Combermere
Cottage

Wood Farm

Shropshire Gate
Farm

Bank Acres
Farm

Old Woodhouse

Lower Lodge

Martin's
Ash

Broadoak
Farm

SHROPSHIRE LA

Shropshire Lane
Farm

Ancient
Briton
(PH)

1

New Woodhouse

Bank
Farm

A525

D   58   **E**   59   **F**

42

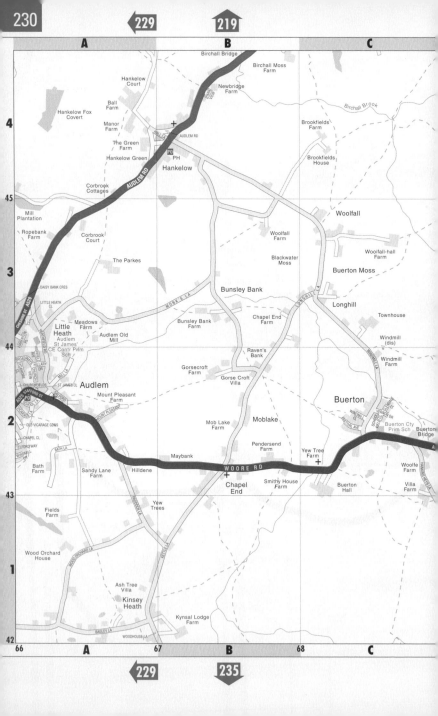

D
E
F

Foxes Bank Farm

Vic

A51 LONDON RD

Villa Farm

HUNTERSONS RD

Bridgemere

Whittaker's Green Farm

Greenfields Farm

Bridgemere CE Aided Prim Sch

4

Bridgemere Hall

Brown Moss Farm

Maltkiln Farm

Parrah Green

Ford

Brown Moss

Bridgemere Wildlife Park

Beech Meadow Farm

45

The Hollies

PINFOLD

Woodend

Pewit Hall Cottages

Prince Hill

Wheel Green

3

Pewit Hall

The Hollins Farm

Berrington's Oak Cottage

Acorn Coppice

44

New Farm

Birchall Brook

Parkfields

Lea's Wood

Admirals Gorse

Buerton Farm

2

South View Farm

Harrow's Wood

Three Brooks

Millhay Wood

WOORE RD

43

Manor Farm

Choriton Green Farm

The Grange

Fields Farm

Sandy Ford Farm

Gorsey Bank Farm

Gorsey Bank

AUDLEM RD

A525

Sandyford Bridge

Three Wells

Crab Wood

NANTWICH RD A534

1

College Fields

Canridden Wood

42

D
70
E
71
F

D E F

Square
Covert

Dodcott
Grange

Wilkesley
Covert

4

Withymoor
Cottage

Wilkesley

Manor
Farm

HEYWOOD
LA

41

Withymoor
Farm

Dodcott Brook

GOMORLA

Blackhurst
Farm

Lower
Morrey

Middle Morrey
Cottages

3

Middle
Morrey

Cheshire
Fields

40

Briar Hill
Farm

The
Dingle

Higher
Morrey

Dairy
House

The
Oaks

field
Hall

2

Wall Plantation

Shavington Wood
Farm

Snakes
Plantation

39

Calverhall

Shavington Park

Cloverley
Dale

1

Fatfarm
Covert

Corra Common
Farm

38

Corra Common

D 61 E 62 F

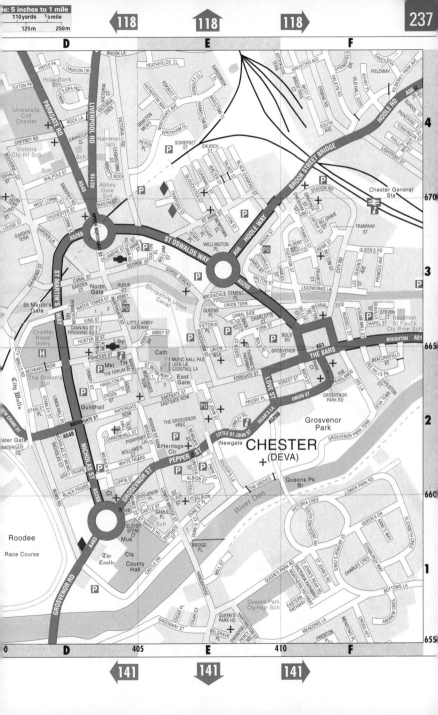

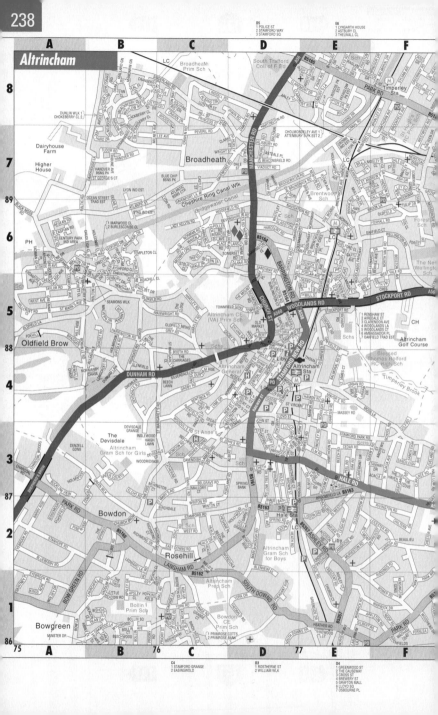

Cheadle & Gatley

Stockport

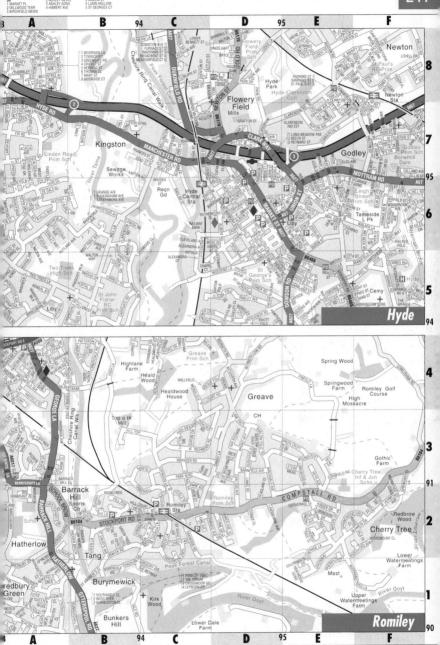

Hyde

Romiley

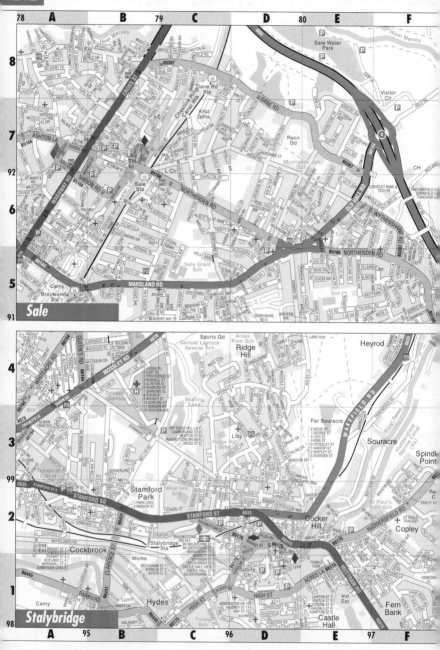

Street names are listed alphabetically and show the locality, the Postcode District, the page number and a reference to the square in which the name falls on the map page

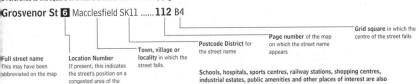

Grosvenor St **6** Macclesfield SK11 ...... **112** B4

Grid square in which the centre of the street falls

Page number of the map on which the street name appears

Postcode District for the street name

Town, village or locality in which the street falls.

Location Number
If present, this indicates the street's position on a congested area of the map instead of the name

Full street name
This may have been abbreviated on the map

Schools, hospitals, sports centres, railway stations, shopping centres, industrial estates, public amenities and other places of interest are also listed.

Abbreviations used in the index

App **Approach**
Arc **Arcade**
Ave **Avenue**
Bvd **Boulevard**
Bldgs **Buildings**
Bsns Pk **Business Park**
Bsns Ctr **Business Centre**
Bglws **Bungalows**
Cswy **Causeway**
Ctr **Centre**
Cir **Circus**

Cl **Close**
Comm **Common**
Cnr **Corner**
Cotts **Cottages**
Ct **Court**
Ctyd **Courtyard**
Cres **Crescent**
Dr **Drive**
Dro **Drove**
E **East**
Emb **Embankment**

Ent **Enterprise**
Espl **Esplanade**
Est **Estate**
Gdns **Gardens**
Gn **Green**
Gr **Grove**
Hts **Heights**
Ho **House**
Ind Est **Industrial Estate**
Intc **Interchange**
Junc **Junction**

La **Lane**
N **North**
Orch **Orchard**
Par **Parade**
Pk **Park**
Pas **Passage**
Pl **Place**
Prec **Precinct**
Prom **Promenade**
Ret Pk **Retail Park**
Rd **Road**

Rdbt **Roundabout**
S **South**
Sq **Square**
Strs **Stairs**
Stps **Steps**
St **Street, Saint**
Terr **Terrace**
Trad Est **Trading Estate**
Wlk **Walk**
W **West**
Yd **Yard**

Town and village index

Acton 204 A4
Acton Bridge 76 C2
Adderley 235 D2
Adlington 62 B3
Alderley Edge 60 B1
Aldford 163 F2
Allostock 106 C2
Alpraham 169 E2
Alsager 193 F3
Altrincham 31 E4
Altrincham 238
Alvanley 73 E1
Antrobus 53 E2
Appleton 27 D3
Ashley 31 F3
Ashton 121 F4
Astbury 178 A4
Aston 217 E1
Audlem 230 A2
Audley 209 E1
Backford 95 D2
Barbridge 187 E3
Barnton 78 B2
Bartholmey 208 B3
Barton 181 F1
Bate Heath 54 C2
Bebington 43 F3
Beeston 168 A1
Bell o' th' Hill 225 E4
Betley 221 F3
Bickerton 199 F3
Bickley Town 214 C3
Biddulph 179 D1
Blacon 117 F2
Blakenhall 221 D2
Bold Heath 13 F4
Bollington 88 A4
Bosley 158 B4
Bradwall Green 153 D2
Bramhall 35 F4
Brereton Green 153 F3
Bridgemere 231 F4
Broughton 139 D2
Brown Knowl 199 E4
Broxton 183 D1
Buerton 230 C2
Bulkeley 184 C1
Bunbury 185 F4
Burland 203 E4
Burton 67 E1
Burtonwood 6 C3
Burwardsley 184 A3
Buxton 115 F4

Capenhurst 94 A4
Cheadle 34 B4
Cheadle 239
Cheadle Hulme 35 D4
Chelford 84 A1
Chester 118 C1
Cholmondeston 171 D1
Chowley 182 C3
Christleton 142 C4
Church Minshull 172 A3
Clutton 182 B1
Coddington 182 A2
Comberbach 78 B4
Congleton 157 D2
Connah's Quay 91 D1
Cranage 130 A3
Crewe 190 C3
Croft 9 D4
Cronton 12 B3
Crowton 76 B1
Cuddington 101 F2
Culcheth 5 D2
Daresbury 25 D1
Davenham 104 A1
Delamere 123 E3
Disley 38 B3
Dodleston 162 A4
Duddon 145 D3
Dunham Town 20 C2
Dunham-on-the-Hill 97 F3
Dutton 51 E1
Eaton 147 D2
Eccleston 141 E1
Edge Green 199 D1
Ellesmere Port 70 A4
Elton 72 B2
Faddiley 202 B3
Farndon 180 C1
Frodsham 74 B4
Gatley 239
Gawsworth 5 E3
Goldborne 3 E3
Goostrey 107 E1
Great Barrow 120 C3
Great Budworth 79 D4
Great Sankey 15 D3
Guilden Sutton 119 F3
Hale 21 E1
Hale (G Manchester) 32 B4
Halewood 21 D4
Hampton 214 A4
Handley 182 B4
Hargrave 144 A1

Hartford 103 E3
Harthill 183 F2
Haslington 191 F3
Hassall Green 176 A1
Hatherton 219 F2
Hatton 26 A1
Hawarden 116 A1
Haydock 1 B3
Hazel Grove 36 B4
Helsby 73 E2
Henbury 111 D4
Heswall 40 C3
High Lane 37 F4
High Legh 29 D3
Higher Kinnerton 161 D4
Higher Walton 26 A4
Higher Wincham 79 F2
Hollins Green 11 D1
Holmes Chapel 130 B2
Holt 196 B4
Hough Common 206 C1
Huntington 142 A3
Huxley 166 C4
Hyde 241
Isycoed 196 B1
Kelsall 122 B2
Kettleshulme 64 C2
Kidsgrove 195 D1
Kingsley 75 E1
Knutsford 57 D2
Lach Dennis 105 E3
Lawton-gate 194 A2
Ledsham 68 C1
Leigh 5 E4
Lindow End 59 D1
Little Bollington 20 B1
Little Budworth 147 F4
Little Leigh 77 E2
Lostock 80 B1
Lower Peover 81 E1
Lymm 18 C2
Macclesfield 112 A4
Macclesfield Forest 114 B3
Malpas 213 D1
Manley 99 D2
Marbury 226 B4
Marston 79 D2
Marton 133 D3
Mere 56 A4
Mickle Trafford 119 F4
Middlewich 128 B1
Milton Green 165 E1

Mobberley 58 A3
Mollington 94 C1
Moore 25 D3
Mottram St Andrew 61 D1
Mouldsworth 98 C1
Moulton 126 C4
Mow Cop 195 E4
Nantwich 204 C3
Neston 66 B4
Nether Alderley 85 D3
New Mills 39 E4
Newcastle-under-Lyme .. 210 B1
Newton-le-Willows 2 B2
Norley 100 C3
Northwich 103 E4
Norton in Hales 236 B1
Oakmere 124 A4
Ollerton 82 C3
Packmoor 195 F1
Partington 11 F1
Peckforton 185 D3
Penketh 14 C2
Pickmere 80 A4
Picton 96 B2
Plumley 81 D2
Pott Shrigley 63 E2
Poulton 163 D1
Poynton 36 C2
Prestbury 87 D4
Preston on the Hill 51 D3
Puddington 92 C4
Pulford 162 B2
Rainow 88 B3
Ravensmoor 203 F1
Ridley 185 E1
Rode Heath 193 F4
Romiley 241
Rostherne 30 C2
Royal's Green 228 C1
Runcorn 49 E4
Saighton 142 C1
Sale 242
Sandbach 175 D3
Saughall 94 A1
Scholar Green 194 C3
Sealand 116 C3
Shavington 206 A3
Shocklach 211 E4
Shotwick 93 D2
Siddington 110 A2
Smallwood 176 C3
Sound 217 F3

Sproston Green 129 E1
Spurstow 185 E3
St Helens 1 A1
Stalybridge 242
Stanlow 71 D3
Stapeley 219 E4
Stoak 96 A4
Stockport 240
Stretton 26 C1
Styal 33 F2
Sutton 50 A1
Sutton Lane Ends 112 C1
Swettenham 131 F2
Tabley 55 F2
Tarporley 146 B1
Tarvin 121 E2
Tattenhall 166 A1
Thornton Hough 42 A4
Thornton-le-Moors 71 E4
Threapwood 222 C4
Tilston 198 A2
Tiverton 168 B3
Trafford 96 C3
Utkinton 146 A4
Warmingham 173 E4
Warren 111 E1
Warrington 16 C3
Waverton 143 D2
Weaverham 102 B4
Weston 207 E3
Wettenhall 170 C4
Whaley Bridge 65 E4
Whitchurch 226 A1
Whitegate 126 A4
Whitewell 224 B1
Whitley 52 B2
Widnes 22 C4
Willaston 68 A4
Willaston (nr Nantwich) 205 E3
Wilmslow 60 A3
Wimboldsley 150 C2
Wincle 160 A4
Winsford 126 C1
Winwick 8 A3
Wistaston 205 E4
Withington 109 D1
Woodford 35 E1
Woore 232 A1
Worleston 188 C3
Worthenbury 211 D1
Wrenbury 216 C2
Wybunbury 220 A4
Wythenshawe 33 E4

108 Steps 图 SK11 .... 112 B4
Aarons Dr ST7 .... 209 F1
Abbey Cl Altrincham WA14 .. 238 E1
　Croft WA3 .... 9 D4
　Whitegate CW8 .... 126 A4
　Widnes WA8 .... 22 B4
　Winsford CW7 .... 149 D4
Abbey Fields CW2 .... 205 E4
Abbey Gate Coll CH3 ...... 164 C4
Abbey Gate Coll
　(The Jun Dept) CH3 ...... 163 F2
Abbey Gate Sch CH2 ...... 237 D4
Abbey Gn CH1 .... 237 D3
Abbey Hey WA7 .... 50 B4
Abbey La Delamere CH8 .. 123 F3
　Hartford CW8 .... 103 D2
Abbey Pl CW1 .... 190 B3
Abbey Rd Cheadle SK8 .... 240 A1
　Goldborne WA3 .... 4 A1
　Haydock WA11 .... 1 C4
　Macclesfield SK10 .... 87 D1
　Sale M33 .... 242 A8
　Sandbach CW11 .... 174 C3
　Widnes WA8 .... 22 B4
Abbey Sq CH1 .... 237 D3
Abbey St CH1 .... 237 E3
Abbey Way CW7 .... 103 D2
Abbeyway N WA11 .... 2 A4
Abbeyway S WA12 .... 2 A4
Abbot's Dr CH2 .... 118 B2
Abbot's Grange CH2 .... 237 D4
Abbot's Nook CH2 .... 237 D4
Abbots Cl Macclesfield SK10 . 87 D1
　Sale M33 .... 242 D7
Abbots Keep CH2 .... 118 B2
Abbots Mews L65 .... 70 A3
Abbots Pk CH2 .... 118 B2
Abbots Way CW8 .... 103 D2
Abbotsbury Cl Poynton SK12 . 36 B3
　Shavington CW2 .... 206 A4
Abbotsfield Cl WA4 .... 26 C3
Abbotsford Gr WA14 .... 238 E8
Abbott's Cl CW12 .... 179 D4
Abbotts Cl Runcorn WA7 .. 49 D4
　Waverton CH3 .... 143 D3
Abbotts Dr CH3 .... 143 D3
Abbotts Way CW7 .... 126 A1
Aber Rd SK8 .... 240 A2
Abercrombie Ct M33 .... 242 D7
Aberdare Cl WA5 .... 7 F1
Aberdaron Dr CH1 .... 117 F2
Aberdeen Cl SK3 .... 240 D4
Aberdeen Gr SK3 .... 240 D4
Aberfeldy Cl CW4 .... 130 A1
Abingdon Ave WA1 .... 17 F4
Abingdon Cl SK11 .... 111 F4
Abingdon Cres CW4 .... 140 C3
Abingdon St OL6 .... 242 A2
Abingdon Cl CW1 .... 190 A3
Abingdon Rd M33 .... 242 C5
Abington Wlk WA7 .... 50 B3
Abstone Cl WA8 .... 17 E4
Acacia Ave Altrincham WA14 . 238 F3
　Denton M34 .... 241 A7
　Knutsford WA16 .... 56 C1
　Warrington WA1 .... 17 E4
　Widnes WA8 .... 13 A3
　Wilmslow SK9 .... 59 F3
Acacia Cl CH2 .... 72 B2
Acacia Cres CW1 .... 190 C3
Acacia Dr Altrincham WA14 . 238 F3
　Ellesmere Port L65 .... 69 F1
　Sandbach CW11 .... 174 C4
Acacia Gdns ST7 .... 195 E2
Acacia Gr 4 Reddish SK5 . 240 F8
　Runcorn WA7 .... 49 E4
Acacia St WA12 .... 1 C2
Academy St WA1 .... 16 A3
Academy Way WA1 .... 16 A3
Acer Ave CW7 .... 190 C4
Achilles Ave WA2 .... 8 A1
Ack La E SK7 .... 35 E3
Ack La W SK7 .... 35 E3
Ackerley Cl WA2 .... 8 C2
Ackers La WA4 .... 16 C1
Ackers Rd WA4 .... 16 C1
Ackersley Ct SK8 .... 35 D3
Ackerson Ct SK8 .... 239 E5
Acorn Bank Cl CW2 .... 206 A4
Acorn Bsns Ctr SK4 .... 240 D5
Acorn Cl Cuddington CH8 . 101 F1
　Winsford CW7 .... 150 A4
Acorn Dr L65 .... 70 A1
Acorn La CW12 .... 157 F2
Acorn St WA12 .... 2 B2
Acorn Terr SK22 .... 39 D3
Acre La Bebington L62 ..... 43 E4
　Cheadle Hulme SK7 .... 35 E3
　Heswall L60 .... 41 E4
Acre Rd L66 .... 69 E3
Acre St SK6 .... 241 B2
Acreage The Bunbury CW6 . 185 F4
　Goostrey CW4 .... 107 F1
Acrefield Ave SK4 .... 240 B8
Acrefield Rd WA8 .... 12 A1
Acres La WA6 .... 75 D1
Acres La Chester CH2 ..... 118 B4
　Stalybridge SK15 .... 242 E1
Acres Rd SK8 .... 239 A5
Acreville Gr WA3 .... 5 D4
Acton Ave M22 .... 46 B2
Acton Bridge Sta CW8 ..... 76 C1
Acton CE Contr Prim Sch
　CW5 .... 204 A4
Acton Cl WA11 .... 1 B3

Acton La CW8 .... 76 C2
Acton Pl SK11 .... 111 F4
Acton Rd Burtonwood WA5 .. 6 C2
　Crewe CW2 .... 189 E3
Acton Way ST7 .... 193 E3
Adam Ave L66 .... 69 E2
Adam Cl L66 .... 69 E2
Adams St WA2 .... 16 B4
Adams Cl Newton-le-W WA12 . 2 B1
　Poynton SK12 .... 36 C1
Adams Hill WA16 .... 57 D1
Adamson St WA4 .... 17 D1
Adaston Ave L62 .... 43 F2
Adcroft St SK1 .... 240 F3
Adder Hill CH3 .... 142 A4
Adderly Cl WA7 .... 23 E1
Addingham Ave WA8 .... 22 B4
Addingham Cl WA8 .... 22 B4
Addison Cl CW2 .... 205 F4
Addison Rd WA15 .... 238 E2
Addison Sq WA8 .... 13 D1
Adela Rd WA7 .... 22 C1
Adelaide Rd Blacon CH1 . 117 E2
　Bramhall SK7 .... 35 F3
　Stockport SK3 .... 240 D4
Adelaide St CW1 .... 190 B3
Adey Rd WA13 .... 19 D3
Adfalent La L64 .... 68 A4
Adlington Cl SK12 .... 36 C1
Adlington Ct WA3 .... 9 F3
Adlington Cty Prim Sch
　SK10 .... 62 C3
Adlington Dr
　Northwich CW9 .... 104 A3
　Sandbach CW11 .... 175 E4
Adlington Pk SK10 .... 36 B1
Adlington Rd Bollington SK10 63 D1
　Crewe CW2 .... 189 F2
　Runcorn WA7 .... 24 D2
　Wilmslow SK9 .... 60 C4
Adlington St SK11 .... 112 B4
Adlington Sta SK10 .... 62 B3
Adlington Wlk SK1 .... 240 E5
Admirals Rd WA3 .... 9 F4
Adshall Rd SK8 .... 240 A1
Adswood Gr SK3 .... 240 D2
Adswood La E SK2 .... 240 F2
Adswood La W SK3 & SK2 240 F2
Adswood Prim Sch SK2 .. 240 F2
Adswood Rd SK3 & SK8 . 240 E2
Adswood Terr SK3 .... 240 E2
Adwell Cl WA3 .... 4 A4
Aegean Rd WA14 .... 238 A6
Afton WA8 .... 12 A1
Agden Brow WA13 .... 19 F1
Agden Brow Pk WA13 ...... 29 E4
Agden House La SY13 .... 225 E3
Agden La
　Little Bollington WA13, WA14 . 29 F4
　Lymm WA13 .... 19 F1
Agden Park La WA13 .... 29 E4
Agecroft Rd Northwich CW9 104 B4
　Romiley SK6 .... 241 A1
Aikman Cl WA3 .... 4 A3
Ainscough Rd WA3 .... 4 A3
Ainsdale Cl Bebington L63 . 43 E3
　Bramhall SK7 .... 36 A4
　Penketh WA5 .... 14 C2
Ainsdale Dr SK8 .... 239 B1
Ainsworth La CW8 .... 76 A2
Ainsworth Rd WA5 .... 77 F1
Aintree Gr Ellesmere Port L66 69 E2
　Stockport SK3 .... 240 E1
Airdrie Cl L62 .... 43 E2
Aire WA8 .... 12 A1
Aire Cl L65 .... 70 A4
Aire Pl CW7 .... 127 D1
Airedale Cl Cheadle SK8 . 239 C6
　Great Sankey WA5 .... 14 C4
Airedale Ct WA14 .... 238 C3
Airfield View CH4 .... 139 D3
Aitchison Rd CW9 .... 80 A1
Ajax Ave WA2 .... 8 A1
Akesmoor La Biddulph ST6 . 179 D1
　Kidsgrove ST7 .... 195 F4
Alamein Cres WA2 .... 8 A1
Alamein Dr Romiley SK6 .. 241 F2
　Winsford CW7 .... 149 E4
Alamein Rd Barnton CW8 .. 78 A2
　Chester CH2 .... 95 D1
Alan Dr WA15 .... 32 A4
Alan Rd SK4 .... 240 B8
Alan St CW9 .... 104 A4
Alandale Rd SK3 .... 240 C3
Alban Ret Pk WA2 .... 8 A1
Alban St CW1 .... 190 B3
Albany Cres WA13 .... 18 B2
Albany Gdns L66 .... 69 E4
Albany Gr WA13 .... 18 B2
Albany Rd Bramhall SK7 .. 35 F2
　Lymm WA13 .... 18 B2
　Wilmslow SK9 .... 59 F3
Albany Terr WA7 .... 23 D1
Albert Cl WA14 .... 238 D4
Albert Dr Neston L64 .... 66 B4
　Lymm WA13 .... 18 C2
Albert Pl Altrincham WA14 . 238 D5
　Congleton CW12 .... 156 C1
　Northwich CW9 .... 104 A4
Albert Rd Altrincham WA14 . 238 E5
　Bollington SK10 .... 87 F4
　Hyde SK14 .... 241 D6
　Manchester SK4 .... 240 A7
　Sale M33 .... 242 C6
　Warrington WA4 .... 17 D1
　Widnes WA8 .... 13 D1
　Wilmslow SK9 .... 60 A3

Albert Rd E WA15 .... 238 E3
Albert Row WA6 .... 49 D1
Albert Sq Altrincham WA14 . 238 D3
　Stalybridge SK15 .... 242 C1
　🚊 Widnes WA8 .... 23 D4
Albert St Audley ST7 .... 209 F2
　Chester CH2 .... 237 F3
　Crewe CW1 .... 190 B3
　Hyde SK14 .... 241 D6
　Irlam M44 .... 11 F3
　Knutsford WA16 .... 56 C1
　Macclesfield SK11 .... 112 B4
　Nantwich CW5 .... 204 C3
　Runcorn WA7 .... 23 D1
　Stockport SK3 .... 240 D5
　Winsford CW7 .... 126 B1
Alberta St SK1 .... 240 F4
Albion Cl SK4 .... 240 E7
Albion Gdns SK15 .... 242 C1
Albion Gr M33 .... 242 A6
Albion Pl CH4 .... 237 E1
Albion Rd New Mills SK22 . 39 D3
　Northwich CW9 .... 79 D1
　Stockton SK4 .... 237 F2
　Crewe CW2 .... 190 B1
　Hyde SK14 .... 241 D6
　Sale M33 .... 242 B6
　Stalybridge SK15 .... 242 C2
Albion Trad Est OL6 .... 242 A3
Albion Wlk CW9 .... 79 D1
Albury Cl WA11 .... 1 B4
Alcester Ave SK3 .... 239 F7
Alcester Rd SK8 .... 239 B4
Alcock St WA7 .... 23 D2
Aldcliffe WA3 .... 3 F4
Alder Ave Poynton SK12 .. 36 C2
　Widnes WA8 .... 13 A3
Alder Cres WA2 .... 16 B4
Alder Dr L66 .... 69 F1
Alder Gr Chester CH2 ...... 119 D2
　Denton M34 .... 241 A7
　Stockport SK3 .... 240 C4
Alder La Burtonwood WA12 .. 7 E4
　Cronton WA8 .... 12 A3
　Frodsham WA6 .... 48 B2
　Warrington WA2 .... 8 B1
　Winwick WA12 .... 7 E4
Alder Rd Cheadle SK8 .... 239 E5
　Goldborne WA3 .... 3 F4
　Warrington WA1 .... 17 E4
　Weaverham CW8 .... 102 B4
Alder Rise SK23 .... 65 E4
Alder Root La WA2 .... 7 E4
Alder St WA12 .... 2 B2
Alder Wood Ave L24 .... 21 D2
Alderbank Rd WA5 .... 15 D3
Alderdale Dr SK6 .... 59 F3
Alderdale Rd L24 .... 21 D2
Aldergate Ave WA7 .... 50 B4
Alderhay La ST7 .... 195 E3
Alderley Ave WA3 .... 3 E4
Alderley Cl Hazel Grove SK7 . 36 C4
　Poynton SK12 .... 36 C1
　Sandbach CW11 .... 175 E4
Alderley Edge
　City Prim Sch SK9 .... 60 A1
Alderley Edge Golf Course
　SK9 .... 59 F2
Alderley Edge Sta SK9 ..... 60 A1
Alderley Lodge SK9 .... 60 A3
Alderley Rd Chelford SK10 . 84 B2
　Mottram St Andrew SK10 60 C1
　Northwich CW9 .... 103 F4
　Prestbury SK10 .... 86 C2
　Warrington WA4 .... 17 E2
　Wilmslow SK9 .... 60 A3
Alderley Wlk 图 SK11 ...... 112 C4
Alderly Pl CH1 .... 117 F3
Alderney Cl
　Ellesmere Port L65 .... 70 B1
　Macclesfield SK11 .... 111 F4
Alders Rd SK6 .... 38 A4
Alders Way SK10 .... 86 C3
Aldersey CE Aided
　Prim Sch CW6 .... 185 F4
Aldersey Cl Runcorn WA7 . 24 B1
　Saughall CH1 .... 94 A1
Aldersey La
　Coddington CH3 .... 182 B3
　Handley CH3 .... 182 B3
Aldersey Rd CW2 .... 190 A1
Aldersgate SK2 .... 240 F1
Aldersgate Dr L24 .... 21 D3
Aldersgate Rd SK8 .... 35 E3
Aldersgreen Ave SK6 .... 37 F4
Alderton Gr CW7 .... 127 D2
Alderwood Ave SK4 .... 240 A5
Aldewood Cl WA3 .... 4 A3
Aldford Cl Bebington L63 . 43 D3
　Hough Common CW2 ...... 206 C1
Aldford Pl SK9 .... 59 F1
Aldford Rd CH2 .... 118 C3
Aldford Way CW7 .... 126 B1
Aldgate L65 .... 70 A3
Aldington Dr CW10 .... 151 E3
Aldridge Dr WA5 .... 6 C4
Aldwych Dr WA8 .... 12 A2
Alexander Dr WA8 .... 22 B4
Alexander Gr WA7 .... 23 E1
Alexandra Ave SK14 .... 241 C6
Alexandra Cl SK3 .... 240 C2
Alexandra Ct WA8 .... 22 B4
Alexandra Cres CW1 ...... 190 A4
Alexandra Hospl The SK8 239 D6
Alexandra Ind Est WA8 ... 22 A4
Alexandra Mews WA9 ...... 49 D1
Alexandra Park Inf Sch
　SK3 .... 240 C3
Alexandra Pl CW1 .... 190 A3

Alexandra Rd
　Dukinfield M34 .... 241 A8
　Manchester SK4 .... 240 C7
　Middlewich CW10 .... 151 E3
　Sale M33 .... 242 D5
　Warrington WA4 .... 16 B1
　Warrington, Stockton Heath .. 16 B1
Alexandra Sq 图 CW7 .... 149 D4
Alexandra St
　Ashton-u-L OL6 .... 242 A4
　Ellesmere Port L65 .... 70 B4
　Hyde SK14 .... 241 C5
　Newton-le-W WA12 .... 2 A2
　Widnes WA8 .... 23 D4
　Winsford CW7 .... 126 B1
Alforde St Widnes WA8 .... 23 D3
Alfred Cl 🚊 WA8 .... 23 D4
Alfred Rd Goldborne WA3 .. 4 A4
　Haydock WA11 .... 1 A4
Alfred St Ashton-u-L OL6 . 242 A4
　Denton SK14 .... 241 C7
　Irlam M44 .... 11 F3
　Newton-le-W WA12 .... 2 C2
　Northwich CW8 .... 103 F3
　Widnes WA8 .... 23 D4
Alger St OL6 .... 242 A4
Algernon St Warrington WA1 16 B3
　Warrington, Stockton Heath ..
Algreave Rd SK3 .... 240 A4
Alice Ct WA8 .... 23 D2
Alice St M33 .... 242 D6
Alison Ct SK4 .... 240 B7
Alison St SK10 .... 87 F1
Alistair Dr L63 .... 43 E3
All Hallows
　(Special Agreement)
　Cath High Sch SK11 .... 112 A4
All Saints CE Prim Sch
　SK4 .... 240 D7
All Saints Dr WA4 .... 17 F2
All Saints Parish Church
　CE
　SK4 .... 23 D2
All Saints' Rd SK4 .... 240 E8
All Saints Upton CE Contr
　Prim Sch WA8 .... 12 A2
All Saints Way WA13 .... 18 B4
Alladale Cl WA8 .... 12 A2
Allanson Rd CH3 .... 143 D2
Allans Cl L64 .... 66 C4
Allansford Ave CH3 .... 143 D2
Allcard St WA5 .... 15 F4
Allen Ave WA3 .... 5 D2
Allen Dr CW9 .... 103 F1
Allen Pl CW1 .... 190 A3
Allen Rd WA7 .... 48 B4
Allen St Bollington SK10 ... 88 A4
　Macclesfield SK11 .... 112 C4
　Warrington WA2 .... 16 A3
Allenby Rd M44 .... 11 E2
Allendale WA7 .... 50 A3
Allerby Way WA3 .... 3 F4
Allerton Rd WA8 .... 13 D1
Allgreave Cl CW10 .... 151 E3
Allington La CH4 .... 141 F4
Allington Pl CH4 .... 141 F4
Allotment Rd M44 .... 11 E3
Allport La L62 .... 43 E4
Allport Rd L62 .... 43 E4
Allports The L62 .... 43 E4
Allumbrook Ave CW4 ...... 130 B2
Allysum Ct WA7 .... 49 F2
Alma Ave CW1 .... 190 B3
Alma Cl Macclesfield SK11 112 A4
　Scholar Green ST7 .... 194 C4
Alma La SK9 .... 60 A4
Alma Rd SK7 .... 37 D4
Alma St Chester CH2 ...... 118 C1
　Newton-le-W WA12 .... 2 A2
　Stalybridge SK15 .... 242 D2
Almeda Rd L24 .... 21 D2
Almer Dr WA5 .... 15 E3
Almond Ave Crewe CW1 .. 190 C3
　Runcorn WA7 .... 49 E4
　Widnes WA8 .... 22 B4
Almond Gr Warrington WA1 . 17 D4
　Widnes WA8 .... 22 B4
Almond Pl ST5 .... 210 C1
Almond Tree Cl L24 .... 21 F1
Almond Wlk M31 .... 11 E1
Alnwick Dr L65 .... 70 B1
Alpass Ave WA2 .... 16 A4
Alpine St WA12 .... 2 A2
Alport Rd SY13 .... 226 A1
Alpraham Cres CH2 .... 118 C3
Alric Wlk M22 .... 33 F4
Alsager Rd Audley ST7 .... 209 E3
　Haslington CW11 .... 192 B4
　Hassall Green CW11 ...... 192 B4
Alsager Sch ST7 .... 193 D2
Alsager St ST7 .... 193 F2
Alsfeld Way SK22 .... 39 D4
Alstone Dr WA14 .... 238 A6
Alt WA8 .... 12 A1
Alt Wlk CW7 .... 127 D1
Alton Dr SK10 .... 87 F2
Alton Rd SK9 .... 59 F4
Alton St CW2 .... 190 A2
Altrincham CE (VA)
　Prim Sch
　WA14 .... 238 D5
Altrincham General Hospl
　WA14 .... 238 D5
Altrincham Golf Course
　WA15 .... 238 F5

Altrincham Gram Sch
　for Boys WA14 .... 238 D
Altrincham Gram Sch
　for Girls Altrincham WA14 . 238 C
　Altrincham WA14 .... 238 C
Altrincham Prep Sch
　WA14 .... 238 D
Altrincham Priory Hospl
　WA15 .... 32 A
Altrincham Rd Styal SK9 .. 33 E
　Wilmslow SK9 .... 33 E
Altrincham Sta WA15 ...... 238 E
Alum Cl CW4 .... 130 B
Alun Cres CH4 .... 140 C
Alundale Rd CW7 .... 126 B
Alvanley Cl SK11 .... 240 C
Alvanley Cty Prim Sch WA4 73 E
Alvanley Dr WA6 .... 73 E
Alvanley Rd
　Ellesmere Port L66 .... 69 F
　Helsby WA6 .... 73 E
Alvanley Rise CW9 .... 104 A
Alvanley Terr WA6 .... 74 A
Alvanley View CW7 .... 72 A
Alvanley Way L66 .... 69 F
Alvaston Ave SK4 .... 240 B
Alvaston Bsns Pk CW5 .. 204 C
Alvaston Rd CW5 .... 204 C
Alvaston Wlk CW2 .... 189 F
Alverton Cl WA8 .... 22 B
Alveston Ct M33 .... 32 C
Alveston Dr SK9 .... 34 B
Alvis Rd CH5 .... 116 A
Alwyn Gdns CH2 .... 118 B
Alyn Rd CH2 .... 96 C
Alyndale Rd CH4 .... 140 B
Ambassador Pl WA15 .... 238 E
Amberleigh Cl WA4 .... 27 D
Amberley Dr WA15 .... 32 A
Amberley Rd SK11 .... 112 A
Ambleside Chester CH2 . 119 D
　Stalybridge SK15 .... 242 D
Ambleside Cres WA2 .... 8 B
Ambleside Cl CW12 .... 155 F
Ambleside Rd L65 .... 70 B
Ambourne Cl WA8 .... 12 A
Ambrose Cl CW1 .... 190 C
Amelia Cl WA8 .... 12 A
Amelia St 图 Hyde SK14 . 241 E
　Warrington WA2 .... 16 B
Amersham Cl SK10 .... 87 E
Amis Gr WA3 .... 3 E
Amy St CW2 .... 190 B
Anchor Cl WA7 .... 50 A
Anchorage The Neston L64 . 66 B
　Waverton CH3 .... 143 D
Ancoats Rd SK9, WA16 .. 83 F
Anderson Cl Crewe CW1 . 191 D
　Warrington WA3 .... 9 C
Anderson Ct L62 .... 43 E
Anderson St 🚊 SK11 ..... 112 A
Anderson St 图 CW2 .... 34 B
Andertons La SK10 .... 86 A
Andover Cl WA2 .... 1 C
Andover Rd WA11 .... 1 C
Andrew Cl WA8 .... 22 B
Andrew Cres CH4 .... 237 F
Andrew Gr SK10 .... 113 D
Andrew La SK6 .... 37 F
Andrew St Hyde SK14 .... 241 F
　Stockport SK3 .... 240 D
Andrew's Cl CH3 .... 121 D
Andrew's Wlk L60 .... 41 D
Anfield Mews SK8 .... 239 F
Anfield Rd Cheadle SK8 .. 239 F
　Sale M33 .... 242 C
Angel St M34 .... 241 A
Anglesea Ave SK2 .... 240 F
Anglesey Cl L65 .... 70 B
Anglesey Dr SK12 .... 36 C
Anglesey Gr SK8 .... 240 A
Anglesey Water SK12 ...... 36 C
Angus Rd L63 .... 43 E
Angus Wlk SK10 .... 86 C
Ankers Knowl La
　SK11, SK10 .... 114 B
Ankers La SK11 .... 114 B
Ann Cl L66 .... 69 E
Ann St Denton SK14 .... 241 C
　Northwich CW9 .... 79 D
　Reddish SK5 .... 240 E
　Runcorn WA7 .... 23 D
Ann St W WA8 .... 23 D
Annable Rd M44 .... 11 F
Annan Ct WA12 .... 157 D
Anne Ct ST7 .... 210 B
Anne's Way CH4 .... 237 F
Annette Ave WA12 .... 2 A
Annie St WA2 .... 16 B
Annions La CW5 .... 205 F
Annis Cl SK9 .... 60 A
Annis Rd SK9 .... 60 A
Ansdell Rd WA8 .... 13 E
Ansley Gr SK4 .... 240 B
Anson Cl Bramhall SK7 .... 35 F
　Warrington WA2 .... 8 C
Anson Rd Poynton SK12 .. 37 D
　Wilmslow SK9 .... 34 C
Anthony Dr CW1 .... 126 C
Anthony's Way L60 .... 41 D
Antons Ct L26 .... 21 D
Antons Rd L26 .... 21 D
Antony Rd WA4 .... 16 A
Antrim Cl WA11 .... 1 B
Antrim Dr L66 .... 69 F

:trim Rd WA2 .... 8 A1
:trobus St CW12 .... 156 B2
:trobus St Mark's Sch
CW9 .... 53 E2
:wil Cl CH1 .... 94 A1
ple Market St CW9 .... 103 F4
ple Tree St L24 .... 21 F1
ple Tree Gr CH1 .... 94 C4
pleby Cl
Macclesfield SK11 .... 111 F3
Stockport SK3 .... 240 D5
Widnes WA8 .... 22 B7
pleby Rd Gatley SK8 ...... 239 B4
Warrington WA2 .... 8 B4
plecroft ST5 .... 210 C1
plecross Cl WA3 .... 10 A3
pledale Dr CH1 .... 95 D4
plefield CW8 .... 103 E4
pleford Cl WA4 .... 26 C4
pleton Cl CW12 .... 178 C4
pleton Dr L65 .... 70 B4
pleton Hall Gdns WA4 ... 26 C3
pleton Mews WA13 .... 18 B2
pleton Rd
Altrincham WA15 .... 238 F1
Chester CH2 .... 118 C3
Widnes WA8 .... 13 D1
pleton St Northwich CW8 .. 78 B1
Widnes WA8 .... 23 D4
pleton Thorn Cty
Prim Sch WA4 .... 27 E3
pleton Thorn Trad Est
WA4 .... 27 E3
pleton Village WA8 .... 13 D1
pleton Wlk **15** SK9 .... 34 B1
plefare Gr WA2 .... 8 C1
pleyards La CH4 .... 141 F4
prentice La SK9 .... 33 F2
pril Rise SK10 .... 87 F1
pron Rd M90 .... 33 E3
psley Cl WA14 .... 238 B1
psley St WA14 .... 238 B1
sagon Ct WA7 .... 24 A6
sagon Gn CH4 .... 117 F3
an Cl L24 .... 21 F1
:bour Cl Macclesfield SK10 .. 87 E2
Northwich CW9 .... 104 B4
:bour Cres SK10 .... 87 E2
:bour Mews SK10 .... 87 E2
:bour St ST7 .... 210 B3
:bourhay St SK10 .... 87 F1
:bury Ave SK3 .... 240 A3
:bury La WA2 .... 8 B3
:cade The
Ellesmere Port L65 .... 70 A3
Northwich CW9 .... 103 F4
:cher Ave WA4 .... 16 C1
:cl Church CW9 .... 78 B2
:chers Way Blacon CH1 .. 118 A2
Ellesmere Port L65 .... 70 A3
:clid Cl **12** SK9 .... 34 C1
:clid Hospl CW11 .... 154 A1
:den Ave WA5 .... 208 A4
:den St
Cheadle SK8 .... 34 B4
:den Cl CH3 .... 121 E2
:arvin CH3 .... 10 A3
Warrington WA3 .... 10 A3
:den Ct CW12 .... 179 D4
:den Dr L64 .... 66 C3
:den St SK2 .... 39 E4
:den Wlk SK1 .... 240 E5
:denbrook Rise SK10 ...... 86 C3
:dern Gr SK1 .... 240 F4
:dern Lea WA6 .... 73 E2
:derne Ave CW7 .... 190 A1
:dleigh Cl CW1 .... 189 F4
:gosy Dr WA15 .... 232 D4
:gyll Ave Bebington L62 .. 43 E2
Chester CH4 .... 141 D4
:gyll Cl SK10 .... 87 D1
:gyll St SK8 .... 239 F5
:gyll St SK8 .... 242 B3
:kenshaw Rd WA3 .... 9 D4
:kenstone Cl WA8 .... 12 B1
:kle Ave SK9 .... 34 C2
:klow Dr L24 .... 21 E1
:kwright Cl CW7 .... 149 D4
:kwright Ct WA7 .... 23 F2
:kwright Rd WA7 .... 23 F2
:ley Ave WA4 .... 26 B4
:ley Cl Alsager ST7 .... 193 E2
:altrincham WA14 .... 238 D8
Chester CH2 .... 118 C3
:Macclesfield SK11 .... 112 A4
:ley Cty Prim Sch CW9 .. 54 C3
:ley Dr WA8 .... 12 A1
:ley End WA6 .... 29 E2
:ley Hall CW9 .... 54 B3
:ley Mere Cl SK8 .... 239 B3
:ley Mossend La CW9 .... 54 B1
:ley PI CW2 .... 206 A4
:ley Rd Antrobus CW9 .... 54 A4
:ppleton CW9 .... 27 E1
:Northwich CW9 .... 104 B4
:lies Cl SK13 .... 242 C4
:lies St CH3 .... 242 A4
:lies Prim Sch SK13 ..... 242 C4
:lies St OL6 .... 242 A4
:lington Ave WA3 .... 241 A6
:ington Cl CW2 .... 206 B4
:ington Dr SK9 .... 59 F3
:ington Dr Goldborne WA3 .. 4 B4
:Macclesfield SK11 .... 112 A4
:enketh WA5 .... 14 C2
:oynton SK12 .... 36 B2
:ington Rd SK8 .... 239 C4
:ington Way SK9 .... 59 F3

Armadale Cl SK3 .... 240 F1
Armett St SK11 .... 112 B4
Armitage Rd WA14 .... 238 D3
Armitstead Rd CW14 ..... 174 C2
Armour Ave WA2 .... 8 A1
Armoury St SK3 .... 240 E4
Armstrong Cl Audlem CW3 .. 229 F2
Warrington WA3 .... 9 E2
Armthorpe Dr L66 .... 69 E3
Arncliffe Dr WA8 .... 6 C3
Arndale WA7 .... 49 F3
Arnesby Ave M33 .... 242 E7
Arnfield Rd SK3 .... 240 D1
Arnham Cl WA4 .... 26 B4
Arnhem Way CH3 .... 142 A3
Arnold Pl WA8 .... 22 B4
Arnold St Nantwich CW5 . 204 C3
Stockport SK3 .... 240 E3
Arnold's Cres CH4 .... 139 D2
Arnside Ave
Congleton CW12 .... 156 A1
Haydock WA11 .... 1 C4
Arnside Cl Gatley SK8 .... 239 B4
High Lane SK6 .... 37 F4
Winsford CW7 .... 126 B1
Arnside Dr SK14 .... 241 C8
Arnside Rd Sale M33 ...... 242 B8
Arncroft Rd WA13 .... 16 A1
Arpley Rd WA1 .... 16 A2
Arpley St WA1 .... 16 A2
Arradon Ct CH2 .... 118 C3
Arran Ave
Ellesmere Port L65 .... 70 B1
Sale M33 .... 242 C5
Arran Cl
Holmes Chapel CW4 ...... 130 B1
Warrington WA2 .... 9 D1
Arran Dr WA6 .... 74 A3
Arrivals Way M90 .... 33 D4
Arron Pl CW2 .... 189 E2
Arrowcroft Rd CH3 .... 119 F3
Arrowsmith Dr ST7 .... 193 D2
Arrowsmith Rd WA11 ..... 1 C4
Arthill La WA14 .... 20 A1
Arthog Dr WA15 .... 31 F4
Arthog Rd WA15 .... 31 F4
Arthur Ave L65 .... 70 B1
Arthur St Blacon CH1 ..... 118 A1
Crewe CW2 .... 190 B1
Hyde SK14 .... 241 C5
Lostock CW9 .... 80 A1
Runcorn CW9 .... 23 D1
Warrington WA1 .... 16 A3
Artists La SK10 .... 85 E4
Artle Rd CW2 .... 206 B4
Arundel Ave SK7 .... 36 B4
Arundel Cl Knutsford WA16 .. 57 F1
Wistaston CW2 .... 205 F4
Arundel Cl L65 .... 70 C2
Arundel Rd SK8 .... 35 D3
Arundel St OL6 .... 242 B3
Arundell Cl WA5 .... 6 C3
Ascot Dr WA7 .... 49 D3
Ascot Ave WA7 .... 49 D3
Ascot Cl Congleton CW12 .. 156 B2
Macclesfield SK10 .... 87 E2
Warrington, Grappenhall WA4 17 E1
Ascot Dr L66 .... 69 F2
Ash Ave Altrincham WA14 .. 238 A5
Cheadle SK8 .... 239 E5
Irlam M44 .... 11 E3
Newton-le-W WA12 .... 2 B2
Ash Cl Ellesmere Port L66 .. 69 F1
Holmes Chapel CW4 ..... 130 B4
Malpas SY14 .... 213 E3
Tarporley CW6 .... 146 B1
Ash Gr Altrincham WA15 . 238 F7
Altrincham, Rosehill WA14 . 238 C1
Cheadle SK8 .... 34 A4
Chester CH4 .... 141 D3
Congleton CW12 .... 156 A2
Ellesmere Port L66 .... 69 E3
Goldborne WA3 .... 3 D4
Knutsford WA16 .... 57 E1
Macclesfield SK11 .... 112 B2
Middlewich CW10 .... 151 E4
Nantwich CW5 .... 204 C2
Rode Heath ST7 .... 193 F4
Runcorn WA7 .... 49 E4
Stalybridge SK15 .... 242 C3
Warrington WA4 .... 16 B2
Weaverham CW8 .... 102 C4
Widnes WA8 .... 22 B4
Wilmslow SK9 .... 59 F5
Ash Grove Cty Prim Sch
SK11 .... 112 B2
Ash Hay La CH2 .... 96 B1
Ash House La CW8 .... 76 B4
Ash La Appleton WA4 .... 26 C4
Widnes L26, WA8 .... 22 A4
Ash Lawn Ct CH2 .... 118 B2
Ash Priors WA8 .... 12 B2
Ash Rd Crewe CW1 .... 190 B3
Cuddington CW8 .... 101 F1
Elton CH2 .... 72 B2
Haydock WA11 .... 1 C4
Hollins Green WA3 .... 11 D1
Lymm WA13 .... 18 D3
Partington M31 .... 11 F2
Penketh WA5 .... 14 C2
Poynton SK12 .... 36 C2
Winwick WA2 .... 8 A3
Ash St Northwich CW9 .... 79 D1
Stockport SK4 .... 240 B4
Ash Terr SK11 .... 112 B2
Ash Way L60 .... 41 D3

Ashbank CW9 .... 104 B4
Ashberry Cl SK9 .... 60 B8
Ashberry Dr WA9 .... 27 D3
Ashbourne Ave
Cheadle SK8 .... 239 F6
Runcorn WA7 .... 49 D3
Ashbourne Cl CH1 .... 94 C4
Ashbourne Dr SK6 .... 37 F3
Ashbourne Mews SK11 ... 111 F4
Ashbourne Rd
Great Sankey WA5 .... 15 D3
Hazel Grove SK7 .... 36 C4
Ashbrook Ave WA7 .... 49 E2
Ashbrook Cl SK8 .... 239 B1
Ashbrook Cres WA2 ...... 16 B4
Ashbrook Dr SK10 .... 87 D3
Ashbrook Rd Bollington SK10 87 F4
Nether Alderley SK10 ... 85 F3
Ashburn Gr SK4 .... 240 D7
Ashburn Rd SK4 .... 240 D7
Ashburton Rd SK3 .... 240 E1
Ashbury Cl WA7 .... 24 B1
Ashbury Dr WA11 .... 1 B4
Ashby Dr **13** CW11 .... 174 B3
Ashby Pl CW2 .... 237 F4
Ashcombe Cl SK8 .... 239 B3
Ashcroft Ave CW2 .... 206 A4
Ashcroft Rd WA13 .... 19 D2
Ashdale Cl ST7 .... 193 E3
Ashdale Dr SK8 .... 239 B2
Ashdend Cty Prim Sch SK9 59 F3
Ashdene Rd SK9 .... 59 F3
Ashdown La WA3 .... 10 A3
Ashdown Rd
Manchester SK4 .... 240 C7
Ollerton WA16 .... 82 C3
Ashenhurst Rd ST7 .... 193 F2
Ashenough Rd ST7 .... 210 B3
Ashfield Cl WA13 .... 19 D2
Ashfield Cres Bebington L62 .. 43 E4
Blacon CH1 .... 117 E3
Cheadle SK8 .... 239 D6
Ashfield Dr SK10 .... 87 D1
Ashford Rd SK9 .... 60 A2
Ashford Way WA8 .... 13 D1
Ashgate La CH2 .... 96 A1
Ashgrove CW7 .... 149 E4
Ashlands Frodsham WA6 .. 74 B4
Sale M33 .... 242 A7
Ashlea Dr CW5 .... 205 F3
Ashleigh Cl CH4 .... 140 C3
Ashley CE Contr
Prim Sch WA15 .... 31 F4
Ashley Cl Hassington CW1 .. 191 E3
Warrington WA4 .... 17 E2
Ashley Ct Altrincham WA15 .. 238 E1
Holt LL13 .... 196 B4
Ashley Dr
Cheadle Hulme SK7 ...... 35 E3
Marple SK6 .... 103 D3
Ashley Gdns Clutton CH3 .. 182 B1
High Lane SK6 .... 37 E4
13 Hyde SK14 .... 241 E5
Ashley Grange CW7 ...... 103 F2
Ashley Mews **2** SK14 ... 241 E5
Ashley Mill La WA14 ..... 31 E4
Ashley Mill Rd N WA14 . 31 F4
Ashley Rd Altrincham WA15 . 238 E2
Ashley WA15 .... 31 F4
Mere WA16 .... 56 B4
Newborne WA14 .... 31 E2
Runcorn WA7 .... 23 E1
Wilmslow SK9 .... 60 A5
Ashley Ret Pk WA8 .... 23 D4
Ashley Sch WA8 .... 12 B3
Ashley St SK14 .... 241 E8
Ashley Sta WA15 .... 31 F3
Ashley Way W WA8 .... 22 C4
Ashley Way W WA8 .... 22 C4
Ashmall SK14 .... 240 B7
Ashmead Cl ST7 .... 193 F2
Ashmead Mews ST7 ...... 193 F2
Ashmore Ave SK3 .... 239 F7
Ashmore Cl
Middlewich CW10 .... 151 E3
Warrington WA3 .... 10 A4
Ashmore's La ST7 .... 193 E2
Ashmuir Cl Blacon CH1 .. 117 F3
Crewe CW1 .... 190 A3
Ashness Dr SK7 .... 35 F4
Ashridge St WA7 .... 22 C2
Ashton Ave
Altrincham WA14 .... 238 E6
Macclesfield SK10 .... 86 B1
Ashton Cl Bebington L62 . 43 E4
Congleton CW12 .... 157 D1
Frodsham WA6 .... 49 E1
Middlewich CW10 .... 151 F3
Runcorn CW9 .... 48 C3
Ashton Dr WA6 .... 49 E1
Ashton Hayes Cty
Prim Sch CH3 .... 121 F4
Ashton La Ashton CH3 ... 121 F3
Sale M33 .... 242 A7
Ashton Rd Hyde SK14 ... 241 E8
Manley WA6 .... 99 F2
Newton-le-W WA12 ...... 2 B3
Norley WA6 .... 100 A2

Ashton St WA2 .... 16 A3
Ashton's Green Sch WA9 . 1 A2
Ashton-under-Lyne
Sixth Form Coll OL6 ..... 242 B3
Ashtree Cl Neston L64 .... 67 D4
Prestbury SK10 .... 87 E4
Ashtree Croft L64 .... 68 A4
Ashtree Dr L64 .... 68 A4
Ashtree Farm Ct L64 ..... 68 A4
Ashurst Dr SK3 & SK8 .. 240 B1
Ashville Ct CW2 .... 206 A4
Ashville Ind Est WA7 .... 49 F2
Ashville Rd WA7 .... 49 F2
Ashwood WA1 .... 31 D4
Ashwood Ave Goldborne WA3 . 3 E4
Warrington WA1 .... 16 C4
Ashwood Cl Barnton CW8 . 78 A2
Ellesmere Port L66 .... 69 C1
Ashwood Cres CW8 ...... 78 A2
Ashwood Ct CH2 .... 119 D2
Ashwood La CW2 .... 96 A3
Ashwood Rd SK12 .... 38 B3
Ashworth Cl WA14 .... 238 B1
Ashworth Pk WA16 .... 81 F4
Askerbank La SK11 .... 159 D1
Askett Cl WA11 .... 1 B4
Askrigg Ave L66 .... 69 D3
Aspen Cl Ellesmere Port L66 . 69 F1
Heswall L60 .... 41 E4
Kidsgrove ST7 .... 195 F2
Stockport SK4 .... 240 A5
Aspen Gn M34 .... 241 A6
Aspen Gr Saughall CH1 .. 117 D4
Warrington WA1 .... 16 C4
Aspen Way Chester CH2 . 119 D2
High Lane SK6 .... 38 A4
Aspen Wood SK14 .... 241 F7
Aspens The
Cuddington CW8 .... 101 E3
Gatley SK8 .... 239 A6
Aspinall Cl WA2 .... 9 D2
Aspull Cl WA3 .... 9 E2
Asquith Cl CW1 .... 191 E3
Asshetom Wlk L24 .... 21 F1
Astbury CE Aided
Prim Sch CW12 .... 178 A4
Astbury Cl
2 Altrincham WA15 ... 238 E6
Goldborne WA3 .... 4 A4
Kidsgrove ST7 .... 195 E2
Astbury Dr CW8 .... 78 A2
Astbury Lane Ends CW12 . 178 C3
Astbury St WA7 .... 22 C2
Aster Cres WA7 .... 49 F3
Aster Rd WA11 .... 1 A4
Astle Cl WA11 .... 84 A2
Astle Ct WA11 .... 84 A2
Astley Cl Warrington WA4 . 16 A2
Widnes WA8 .... 12 B2
Astley Gr SK15 .... 242 C3
Astley La WA16 .... 30 B1
Astley St Hyde SK14 ..... 241 C8
Stockport SK3 & SK4 .... 240 E5
Neston L64 .... 66 C3
Avon Ct ST7 .... 193 E3
Avon Dr Congleton CW12 . 156 C1
Crewe CW1 .... 191 D3
Avon Rd Altrincham WA15 . 31 F4
Cheadle SK8 .... 34 B4
Culcheth WA3 .... 5 D1
Avon St WA5 .... 240 E3
Avon Wlk CW7 .... 127 D1
Avondale L65 .... 70 A1
Avondale Ave L62 .... 43 F3
Avondale Dr WA8 .... 12 A1
Avondale Rd Haydock WA11 . 1 A4
Stockport SK3 .... 240 C4
Avondale Sch SK3 .... 240 B3
Avonlea Cl CH4 .... 140 C3
Avonside Way SK11 ..... 112 B3
Avro Way SK3 .... 32 C4
Axminster Wlk SK7 ...... 35 F4
Aycliffe Wlk **3** WA8 .... 13 E1
Aylesbury Cl
Ellesmere Port L66 ...... 69 E2
Macclesfield SK10 .... 87 D1
Aylesby Cl WA16 .... 57 D1
Aylsham Cl WA8 .... 12 B2
Aylwin Dr M33 .... 242 C5
Ayreshire Way CW12 .... 157 D1
Aysgarth Ave CH2 .... 118 D2
Aysgarth Ave Cheadle SK8 . 239 C6
Romiley SK6 .... 241 D4
Ashford Cl WA14 .... 238 B6
Azalea Gr WA7 .... 49 F2

Babage Rd CH5 .... 116 A3
Babbacombe Rd WA5 ... 14 C2
Bache Ave CH2 .... 118 B3
Bache Dr CH2 .... 118 B3
Bache Hall Est CH2 ..... 118 B3
Bache Sta CH2 .... 118 B3
Bachefield Ave CH3 ..... 142 A3
Bachelor's La CH3 .... 142 A4
Back Adcroft St **4** SK1 . 240 F3
Back Booth St WA12 .... 2 A2
Back Bridge St WA12 ... 2 A2
Back Brook Pl WA4 ...... 16 C2
Back Crosland Terr WA6 . 73 D1
Back Cross La CW12 .... 179 D4
Back Eastford Rd WA4 . 16 A1
Back Edisbury Rd
Macclesfield SK11 .... 113 A1
Rainow SK10 .... 113 E4

Back Forshaw St WA2 .... 16 B4
Back Heathcote St ST7 ... 195 D1
Back High St WA7 .... 23 D2
Back Jodrell St SK22 .... 39 D4
Back La Alpraham CW6 ..... 169 E3
  Alvanley WA6
  Antrobus CW9 .... 54 B4
  Ashley WA15 .... 32 A2
  Bate Heath CW9 .... 54 B4
  Beeston CW9 .... 167 E1
  Betley CW2 .... 208 B1
  Brereton Green CW11 ...... 153 E3
  Burtonwood WA5 .... 6 B4
  Congleton CW12 .... 156 A2
  Duddon CW6 .... 145 D3
  Dunham Town WA14 .... 20 B3
  High Legh WA14 .... 29 F3
  No Man's Heath SY14 ..... 214 A2
  Penketh WA8 .... 14 A2
  Peover WA16 .... 106 A4
  Plumley WA16 .... 81 D1
  Radnor CW12 .... 155 F3
  Shavington CW2 .... 206 C2
  Threapwood SY14 .... 222 C4
  Whitley WA4 .... 52 C2
  Wybunbury CW5 .... 220 B3
Back Lane Ave WA6 .... 146 A1
Back Lawrence St WA12 ..... 2 A2
Back Legh St WA12 .... 2 A2
Back Market St WA12 .... 49 E4
Back Massie St SK8 .... 239 D6
Back Paradise St [1] SK11 .. 112 B4
Back Park St CW12 .... 156 C1
Back Queen St CH1 .... 237 E3
Back River St CW12 .... 156 B2
Back Union St SK22 .... 39 E4
Back Wallgate [2] SK11 ...... 112 B4
Back Water St [3] SK4 ...... 240 F6
Backford CI WA7 .... 50 B3
Backford Gdns CH1 .... 94 C4
Badbury CI WA11 .... 1 B4
Badcock's La CW6 .... 185 F2
Baddeley CI SK3 .... 240 D1
Baddeley CI CW5 .... 203 E1
Baddiley Hall La CW5 .... 217 D4
Baddiley La CW5 .... 203 E1
Baddington La CW5 .... 204 B1
Badger Ave CW1 .... 190 A3
Badger Bait L64 .... 66 C3
Badger CI WA7 .... 50 A3
Badger Rd Macclesfield SK10 . 87 E1
  Prestbury SK10 .... 87 D4
Badgers CI Christleton CH3 . 142 C4
  Frodsham WA6 CH1 .... 94 C4
  Winsford CW7 .... 126 A1
Badgers Pk L64 .... 66 C3
Badgers Set CW8 .... 101 E3
Badgers Wlk CW7 .... 95 F1
Badgers Wood CW2 .... 205 F4
Badgersrake La
  Ellesmere Port L64 .... 68 C3
  Ledsham L66 .... 68 B2
  Puddington L66 .... 68 B2
Bag La Crowton CW8 .... 101 F4
  Cuddington CW8 .... 101 F4
  Norley WA6 .... 101 D3
Bagley La CW3 .... 230 A1
Bagmere CI
  Brereton Green CW11 ...... 153 F2
  Sandbach CW11 .... 174 C4
Bagmere La CW11 .... 154 A3
Bagnall CI WA5 .... 15 E3
Bagot Ave WA5
Bagstock Ave SK12 .... 36 C1
Baguley Ave WA8 .... 22 A3
Baguley Cres SK3 .... 240 D2
Baguley La M33 .... 242 E5
Baguley Rd M33 .... 242 E6
Bahama CI WA11 .... 1 B4
Bahama Rd WA11 .... 1 B4
Bailey Ave L65 .... 69 F3
Bailey CI CW5 .... 190 B4
Bailey Cres
  Congleton CW12 .... 157 D2
  Sandbach CW11 .... 175 E3
Bailey Ct ST7 .... 193 F2
Bailey La M31 .... 11 F2
Bailey Wlk WA13 .... 31 E4
Bailey's Bank ST6 .... 179 E2
Baileys La L24 .... 21 D3
Baileys CI WA8 .... 13 D3
Baileys La L20 .... 21 D4
Bainbridge Ave WA3 .... 3 F4
Baines Ave M44 .... 11 F4
Baker Dr L66 .... 69 F2
Baker Rd WA7 .... 48 B4
Baker St Macclesfield SK11 . 112 B4
  Stalybridge SK15 .... 242 E1
  Stockport SK4 .... 240 E7
Baker's Ct CW7 .... 126 C1
Baker's La CW7 .... 126 C1
Bakers PI WA2 .... 16 A4
Bakestondale Rd SK10 ..... 63 F2
Bakestonedale Rd SK10 . 64 A2
Bakewell CI CH1 .... 94 C4
Bakewell Rd
  Burtonwood WA5 .... 7 D4
  Hazel Grove SK7 .... 36 C4
Bakewell St SK3 .... 240 D3
Bala CI WA5 .... 7 F1
Balcary Ave WA4 .... 17 E2
Baldon Cres ST7 .... 193 E3
Balfour CI CW1 .... 191 E2
Balfour Rd WA8 .... 238 D7
Balham CI WA8 .... 13 D2

Balharry Ave WA11 .... 1 C4
Ball La Bollington SK10 .... 87 E3
  Crowton WA6 .... 75 F2
Ballantyne La WA5 .... 75 F2
Ballater Cres CH3 .... 119 D1
Ballater Dr WA2 .... 8 C2
Balliol CI Romiley SK6 .... 241 C4
  Sutton Lane Ends SK11 .... 112 C2
Balmoral Ave Crewe CW2 .. 190 A1
  Northwich CW9 .... 104 A3
Balmoral CI Knutsford WA16 . 57 D3
  Winsford CW7 .... 126 B2
Balmoral Cres SK10 .... 87 F1
Balmoral Dr
  Altrincham WA14 .... 238 F8
  Helsby WA6 .... 73 D2
  High Lane SK6 .... 37 F4
  Holmes Chapel CW4 .... 130 A1
  Poynton SK12 .... 36 B2
  Stalybridge SK15 .... 242 D3
Balmoral Gdns L65 .... 70 B2
Balmoral Pk CH1 .... 118 A2
Balmoral Rd
  Altrincham WA15 .... 238 F8
  Manchester SK4 .... 240 A7
  Warrington WA4 .... 16 C1
  Widnes WA8 .... 12 C2
Balmoral Way SK9 .... 34 A1
Baltic Rd WA14 .... 238 A6
Bamber Ave WA3 .... 242 E5
Bamburgh Ct L65 .... 70 C2
Bamford CI Cheadle SK8 ..... 34 B4
  Runcorn WA7 .... 49 E4
Bamford St
  Macclesfield SK10 .... 87 F1
  Stockport SK1 .... 240 F4
Banastre Dr WA12 .... 2 C2
Banbury CI SK10 .... 87 F1
Banbury Dr
  Altrincham WA14 .... 238 E8
  Great Sankey WA5 .... 15 E3
Banbury St Kidsgrove ST7 .. 194 B1
  Stockport SK1 .... 240 F5
Bancroft CH8 .... 76 C2
Bancroft Rd WA8 .... 13 E1
Bandon CI L24 .... 21 E1
Banff Ave L63 .... 43 E3
Bangor CI CH1 .... 94 C4
Bangor St SK8 .... 239 F6
Bangor St
  Ashton-u-L OL6 & SK15 ... 242 B2
  Reddish SK5 .... 240 F8
Bank CI Chester CH2 .... 118 C3
  Macclesfield SK11 .... 112 C4
  Neston L64 .... 67 D3
Bank Coole La CW5 .... 228 C3
Bank Farm Mews SY14 ... 214 C3
Bank Gdns WA5 .... 14 C2
Bank House La Helsby WA6 . 73 E2
  Smallwood CW11 .... 177 D3
  Smallwood CW11 .... 177 D4
Bank La Eaton CW12 .... 134 B1
  Rainow SK10 .... 89 E3
Bank Mews WA5 .... 73 E2
Bank Rd Connah's Quay CH5 . 91 E1
  Romiley SK6 .... 241 A3
Bank Side CW8 .... 77 E1
Bank Sq SK9 .... 60 A4
Bank St Cheadle SK8 .... 239 E6
  Congleton CW12 .... 156 C1
  Goldborne WA3 .... 3 D4
  Hollins Green WA3 .... 11 D3
  Hyde SK14 .... 241 D7
  Kidsgrove ST7 .... 195 E2
  Newton-le-W WA12 .... 1 C2
  Sale M33 .... 242 C7
  Warrington WA1 .... 16 A3
  Widnes WA8 .... 23 D2
Bank The ST7 .... 195 D4
Bankes' La WA7 .... 48 C3
Bankfield Ave Irlam M44 ..... 11 E3
  Stockport SK4 .... 240 C5
  Wistaston CW2 .... 206 A4
Bankfield Rd Cheadle SK8 . 239 F1
  Widnes WA8 .... 12 B1
Bankfield St CW8 .... 240 E8
Bankfield Trad Est SK5 .... 240 E8
Bankfields Dr L62 .... 44 A3
Bankhall La WA15 .... 31 F4
Bankhall St WA3 .... 240 A6
Banklands CW4 .... 66 C3
Bankhouse Dr CW12 .... 157 D2
Banklands CW4 .... 11 E3
Banks CI CW11 .... 156 B2
Banks Cres WA4 .... 16 C2
Banks Rd L60 .... 40 B4
Banks View CW4 .... 107 F1
Bankside Altrincham WA15 ... 32 B3
  Warrington WA4 .... 50 C4
Bankside CI Barbridge CW5 . 187 E3
  Wilmslow SK9 .... 34 B1
Bankside CI Alsager ST7 ... 193 F3
  Manchester SK4 .... 240 A6
Bankside Rd M20 .... 239 B7
Banky Fields CW12 .... 156 B4
Bann St SK3 .... 240 E3
Bannister Dr SK8 .... 239 F2
Bannister St L24 .... 21 D3
Barbauld St WA1 .... 16 A3
Barber Dr ST7 .... 194 C4
Barber St SK11 .... 112 C3
Barber's La Antrobus CW9 .. 53 E3
  Northwich CW8 .... 103 F4
Barberry CI WA14 .... 238 B7
Barberry Wlk M31 .... 11 F1
Barbondale CI WA5 .... 14 C4
Barbridge Rd ST5 .... 210 B1

Barcheston Rd SK8 .... 239 C4
Barclay Rd SK12 .... 36 C1
Bardell CI SK12 .... 36 B1
Bardsey CI L65 .... 70 B1
Bardsley Ave WA5 .... 7 F1
Bardsley Cl WA3 .... 240 D7
Barford CI WA5
Barford Dr Goldborne WA3 .... 4 A4
  Wilmslow SK9 .... 34 B1
Barford Grange L66 .... 68 B4
Barham Ct WA3
Barington Dr WA7 .... 50 C4
Baristow CI CH2 .... 237 E4
Bark St CW12 .... 156 C1
Barker Gr Crewe CW2 .... 190 B1
Nantwich CW5 .... 204 C3
Barker's Hollow Rd WA4 .... 51 D3
Barker's La M33 .... 242 A6
Barkhill Rd CH2 .... 119 D4
Barley Ave WA4 .... 17 E2
Barley Castle CI WA4 .... 27 D2
Barley Croft Alsager ST7 ... 193 F1
  Cheadle SK8 .... 239 F1
  Chester CH3 .... 142 A4
Barley Dr SK7 .... 35 F4
Barley Mow CI L66 .... 69 E1
Barley Way WA4 .... 17 E2
Barleycastle La WA4, CW9 .. 27 E2
Barleycastle Trad Est WA4 . 27 E2
Barleycroft Terr ST7 .... 194 C4
Barlow Fold ST7 .... 209 E1
Barlowood CW2 CW2 .... 206 A4
Barlow Dr CW7 .... 148 C4
Barlow Fold SK14 .... 241 D3
Barlow Fold Rd SK6 .... 241 D3
Barlow Gr WA9
Barlow Hill SK11 .... 136 C1
Barlow Rd Altrincham WA14 . 238 B7
  Moulton CW9 .... 126 C4
  Wilmslow SK9 .... 34 A1
Barlow Way CW11 .... 175 D4
Barmouth CI WA5
Barn Croft WA6 .... 73 E2
Barn Croft Rd L26 .... 21 D4
Barn Ct CH3 .... 182 B1
Barn La WA3
Barn Meadow CW6 .... 7 E4
Barn Rd Congleton CW12 .. 156 B2
  Threapwood SY14 .... 222 B4
Barn St WA8 .... 2 A2
Barnabas Ave CW1 .... 189 F3
Barnaby Chase CH3 .... 182 B1
Barnaby Rd SK12 .... 36 B1
Barnack CI WA1 .... 41 D1
Barnacre Dr L64 .... 43 D1
Barnard Ave WA5 .... 16 A2
Barnard CI SK11 .... 111 F3
Barnard St WA5 .... 15 E2
Barnbridge CI ST7 .... 194 C4
Barnbrook CI CW7 .... 126 A1
Barncroft WA7 .... 50 B4
Barncroft SK11 .... 86 A2
Barnes CI CW11 .... 175 D3
Barnes Ave Manchester SK4 . 240 A6
  Warrington WA2 .... 9 D1
Barnes CI Blacon CH1 .... 117 F3
  Great Sankey WA5 .... 14 C4
  Haslington CW1 .... 191 E2
  Widnes WA8 .... 13 E1
Barnes Hospl SK8 .... 239 C6
Barnes Rd WA8 .... 13 E1
Barneston Rd WA8 .... 13 E1
Barnett Ave WA12 .... 2 C1
Barnett St SK11 .... 112 A4
Barnett Wlk CW2 .... 206 B4
Barnfield CH3 .... 166 A1
Barnfield Ave Romiley SK6 . 241 D3
  Runcorn WA7 .... 50 B2
Barnfield CI L66 .... 69 E1
Barnfield Rd Bollington SK10 . 87 F3
  Warrington WA1 .... 17 E4
Barngate Rd M22 .... 239 A6
Barnham CI WA3 .... 3 D4
Barnhill Farm Cotts SY14 . 214 B1
Barnhill Grange CH3 .... 183 D2
Barnhill Rd CH3 .... 183 D1
Barnhouse La CH3 .... 98 A1
Barns La WA13 .... 20 A3
Barns PI WA15 .... 32 B4
Barnsia Way
  Macclesfield SK10 .... 87 E2
  Moulton CW9 .... 126 C4
Barnstaple Way WA5 .... 14 C2
Barnston CI CH1 .... 118 A2
Barnston Prim Sch L60 ..... 41 E4
Barnston Rd L60 .... 41 D4
Barnston Towers CI L60 ... 41 E4
Barnswood WA14 .... 17 E1
Barnton CI WA3
Barnton City Inf Sch CW8 . 78 A1
Barnton City Jun Sch CW8 . 78 A2
Barnwell Ave WA3 .... 4 B2
Baron CI WA1 .... 17 E4
Baron Ct WA1 .... 22 B4
Baronet Rd WA4 .... 16 A1
Baronia PI CW5 .... 204 C3
Barons Quay Rd CW9 .... 78 C1
Barons Rd CW2 .... 206 A2
Barony Bldgs CW5 .... 204 C3
Barony CI CW5 .... 204 C3
Barony Employment Pk The
  CW5 .... 204 C4
Barony Rd CW5 .... 204 C3
Barony Terr CW5 .... 204 C3
Barrack Hill SK6 .... 240 C4
Barrack Hill CI SK6 .... 241 A2

Barrack CI SK6 .... 241 A3
Barrack Hill Prim Sch SK6 241 A2
Barracks La
  Buckley CH3 .... 184 B3
  Macclesfield SK10 .... 112 C4
  Ravensmoor CW5 .... 203 F1
Barracks Sq SK11 .... 112 A3
Barrastitch La CW8 .... 101 F3
Barratt CI ST7 .... 193 F2
Barrel Well Hill CH2 .... 118 C1
Barrie Gdns ST7 .... 210 B4
Barrington CI WA14 .... 238 D6
Barrington Rd WA14 .... 238 D5
Barrow Ave WA4 .... 8 B1
Barrow CE
  Contr Prim Sch CH3 .... 120 B3
Barrow Hall Cty Prim Sch
  WA5 .... 14 C4
Barrow Hall Farm CW3 ..... 187 D4
Barrow Hall La WA5 .... 14 C4
Barrow La Altrincham WA15 . 32 A4
  Great Barrow CH3 .... 120 B3
Barrow Rd Altrincham WA15 . 32 A4
  Newton-le-W WA3 .... 3 E1
Barrow Meadow SK8 .... 34 C4
Barrow's Brow WA16 .... 81 F1
Barrow's Green La WA8 .... 13 F2
Barrow's Row WA8 .... 13 D2
Barrowdale Rd WA3 .... 3 D4
Barrows CI CW1 .... 190 A4
Barrule CI WA7 .... 26 B4
Barry Rise L63 .... 43 D3
Barry St WA4 .... 16 B2
Barrymore Ave WA4 .... 16 C2
Barrymore Cres CW9 .... 79 B4
Barrymore CI WA4 .... 17 D1
Barrymore Rd Runcorn WA7 . 49 D4
  Warrington WA4 .... 17 D1
  Weaverham CW8 .... 77 F4
Barrymore Way L63 .... 43 D3
Barrymore Cres WA4 .... 8 A2
Barshaw Gdns WA4 .... 26 C2
Barston Ave L65 .... 69 F3
Bartartine Way CW4 .... 141 E3
Bartholomew CE
  Prim Sch CW5 .... 216 C3
Bartholomews Ct CW2 .... 189 E2
Bartholomey Rd
  Audley ST7 .... 209 D1
  Barthomley CW2 .... 208 A4
  Betley CW2 .... 208 C2
Barton Ave WA4 .... 17 D1
Barton CI Runcorn WA7 ...... 50 B4
  Wilmslow SK9 .... 34 B1
Barton Fold SK14 .... 241 D5
Barton Rd Barton SY14 .... 181 E1
  Congleton CW12 .... 156 C2
  Macclesfield SK11 .... 112 B3
Barton St Goldborne WA3 .... 3 D4
  Macclesfield SK11 .... 112 B3
Barton Stad CW7 .... 79 D1
Bartons PI CW9 .... 79 D1
Barwick PI M33 .... 242 A4
Barwood Ave ST7 .... 194 A3
Basford CI WA3
Basford Way CW7 .... 126 A1
Basil St SK4 .... 240 E7
Basildon CI L65 .... 41 D3
Baskervyle CI L60 .... 41 D3
Baskervyle Rd L60 .... 41 D3
Baslow Dr SK8 .... 34 B4
Bate's Mill La
  Beeston CW6 .... 167 F3
  Tiverton CW6 .... 167 F3
Bateman Rd CW9 .... 80 A1
Batemill Rd Congleton CW12 . 156 B4
Batemill La
  Peover WA16, SK11 .... 108 B3
  Whipbottom WA16, SK11 . 108 B3
Bates La WA6 .... 73 E2
Bath Cres SK8 .... 35 D3
Bath La CW7 .... 230 A2
Bath PI WA14 .... 238 D2
Bath St Altrincham WA14 . 238 D2
  Chester CH1 .... 237 F2
  Sandbach CW11 .... 175 E3
  Warrington WA1 .... 16 A3
Batherton CI WA8 .... 23 D4
Batherton La CW5 .... 204 C2
Battersby La CW1 .... 66 C3
Battersby La WA1 .... 16 B3
Battersea Rd SK4 .... 240 A6
Battery La WA1 .... 191 E3
Battersby La WA1 .... 17 F4
Battery La WA1 .... 17 F4
Bawtry Rd WA2 .... 8 C1
Baxter CI WA7 .... 50 B3
Baxter Cl WA7 .... 242 B6
Baxter St L65 .... 15 F3
Baycliffe WA13 .... 18 B1
Baycliffe CI WA7 .... 50 C2
Bayley St ST5 .... 242 C1
Bayswater CI WA7 .... 24 C4
Baytree Ave M34 .... 241 A6
Baytree CI L66 .... 69 F1
Baytree CI L26 .... 21 D4
Baywill CI WA7 .... 50 C2
Beach Gr CW8 .... 103 F3
Beach House La WA16 .... 32 A1
Beach Rd Hartford CW8 .... 103 D3
  Northwich CW8 .... 103 D3
Beachin La CH3 .... 143 D2
Beacon Hill View WA7 .... 48 B4
Beacon La L60 .... 41 D4
Beacon Rd SK6 .... 241 A1
Beaconsfield Cres WA8 .... 13 D2

Beaconsfield Gr WA8 .... 13 D2
Beaconsfield Rd
  Altrincham WA14 .... 238 D5
  Runcorn WA7 .... 22 C4
  Widnes WA8 .... 13 C2
Beaconsfield St CH2 .... 237 A3
Beadnall Dr WA5 .... 14 C4
Beaford Dr M22 .... 33 B4
Beagle Point CW7 .... 126 A2
Beagle Wlk M22 .... 33 B3
Beam Heath Way CW5 ..... 204 C4
Beam St CW5 .... 204 C3
Beamont Cty Schs WA2 .... 16 B3
Beamont St WA8 .... 23 D2
Beard Cres SK22 .... 39 E4
Beardsmore Dr WA3 .... 3 F4
Bearhurst La SK11 .... 111 C1
Bearstone Rd
  Norton in Hales TF9 .... 236 C4
  Woore TF9 .... 236 C4
Beasley CI L66 .... 68 C3
Beatrice Ave SK8 .... 239 F2
Beatty Ave WA2 .... 16 B4
Beatty Dr CW7 .... 157 E1
Beatty Rd CW5 .... 204 B4
Beaufort Ave WA33 .... 242 A6
Beaufort Chase SK9 .... 34 C1
Beaufort CI
  Alderley Edge SK9 .... 60 A4
  Great Sankey WA5 .... 15 D3
  Runcorn WA7 .... 24 C1
  Wilmslow SK9 .... 32 A1
Beaufort Rd
  Ashton-u-L OL6 .... 242 C1
  Nantwich CW5 .... 204 A4
Beaufort St WA5 .... 15 A4
Beaulieu WA15 .... 238 C4
Beaulieu Ave CW7 .... 126 A2
Beaumaris Cres SK7 .... 36 A4
Beaumaris Dr L65 .... 70 A2
Beaumont CI Biddulph ST6 . 179 A4
  Chester CH4 .... 140 C1
  Prestbury SK10 .... 87 D4
  Wistaston CW2 .... 205 F3
Beauty Bank
  Ellesmere Port CW7 .... 125 D2
  Winsford CW7 .... 149 D3
Beaver Ctr The CW9 .... 103 F4
Beaverbrook Ave WA3 .... 5 D4
Beavers CI WA18 .... 79 D4
Bebbington Dr M33 .... 242 A6
Bebington Rd L66 .... 69 F3
Becconsall CI CW3 .... 190 A1
Becconsall Dr CW1 .... 190 A1
Bechers WA8 .... 12 A4
Beck La SK10 .... 88 D4
Beckenham Gr [3] CW7 ..... 149 F1
Beckett Ave CW7 .... 150 A1
Beckett Dr WA13 .... 18 C1
Beckett's La CH3 .... 142 C4
Becket CH3 .... 142 C4
Beconfree Ave M34 .... 241 A6
Bedells La SK9
Bedford Ave
  Ellesmere Port L65 .... 70 A2
  Hyde SK14 .... 241 A6
Bedford Ave E L65 .... 70 A2
Bedford CI CW2 .... 190 C1
Bedford Gdns CW7 .... 149 F1
Bedford Grn M31 .... 11 F1
Bedford PI WA7 .... 22 B4
Bedford PI CW2 .... 190 C1
Bedford Rd Kidsgrove ST7 . 195 D2
  Macclesfield SK11 .... 112 C4
Bedford Rise CW7 .... 149 F1
Bedford St Crewe CW2 .... 190 C1
  Warrington WA4 .... 16 A1
Bedward Row CH1 .... 237 A2
Beech Ave Culcheth WA3 .... 5 D4
  Frodsham WA6 .... 74 A4
  Gatley SK8 .... 239 A4
  Goldborne WA3 .... 3 F4
  Haydock WA11 .... 1 D4
  Mobberley WA16 .... 57 F4
  Penketh WA5 .... 14 C4
  Rode Heath ST7 .... 193 A2
  Stockport SK2 & SK3 .... 240 D1
  Warrington WA4 .... 17 D1
Beech CI Alderley Edge SK9 . 60 A2
  Congleton CW12 .... 156 A2
  Cuddington CW8 .... 101 F3
  Newton-le-W WA12 .... 2 A2
  Ollerton WA16 .... 82 B2
  Partington M31 .... 11 F1
Beech Cotts SK9 .... 85 A3
Beech Cres SK12 .... 36 B3
Beech Ct
  Chester CH2 .... 119 A2
  Crewe CW1 .... 190 C1
  Ellesmere Port CH1 .... 95 F4
  Lymm WA13 .... 18 C1
  Macclesfield SK11 .... 112 C4
  Sandbach CW11 .... 175 E3
  Warrington, Latchford WA4 . 16 A1
  Warrington, Padgate WA1 . 17 A2
  Weaverham CW8 .... 102 A4
  Wilmslow SK9 .... 60 A2
  Winsford CW7 .... 149 D3
Beech Dr Ball SK10 .... 87 D4
Beech Hall Sch SK10 .... 87 D4
Beech Hey La CH64 .... 43 D1
Beech Heyes CI CW8 .... 102 A4
Beech Heyes Dr CW8 .... 102 A4

eech La Barnton CW8 ... 78 A2
Eaton CW6 ... 147 D3
Macclesfield SK10 ... 87 E1
Norley WA6 ... 75 F1
Romiley SK6 ... 241 C2
Wilmslow SK9 ... 60 A3
eech Lawn WA14 ... 238 C4
eech Rd Alderley Edge SK9 . 60 A2
Altrincham WA15 ... 238 E3
Common Side CW6 ... 124 B1
Heswall L60 ... 41 E4
High Lane SK6 ... 37 F4
Sale M33 ... 49 E4
Stockport SK2 & SK3 ... 240 D6
Sutton WA7 ... 50 A2
Warrington WA4 ... 65 F4
Whaley Bridge SK23 ... 65 F4
eech Rise Crowton CW8 ... 76 A1
Crowton CW8 ... 76 B1
Whaley Bridge SK23 ... 65 E3
eech St Hyde SK14 ... 241 D7
eech St W CW1 ... 190 B2
eech Tree Cl CW5 ... 205 E3
eech View Rd WA6 ... 75 F1
eechcroft Ave CW2 ... 206 A4
eechcroft Dr L65 ... 70 A1
eeches The
Altrincham WA14 ... 238 C2
Chester CH2 ... 119 D3
Helsby WA6 ... 73 F2
Nantwich CW5 ... 204 C3
eechfield
Altrincham WA15 ... 238 C3
Moulton CW9 ... 126 C3
eechfield Ave SK9 ... 59 F3
eechfield Cl L60 ... 41 D4
eechfield Dr CW10 ... 128 A1
eechfield Gdns CW8 ... 103 D3
eechfield Rd
Alderley Edge SK9 ... 85 D3
Cheadle Hulme SK8 ... 35 D4
Ellesmere Port L65 ... 70 A3
Stockport SK3 ... 240 F1
Warrington WA4 ... 17 D3
eechfields CW7 ... 150 A4
eechlands Ave CH3 ... 119 D1
eechmill Dr WA3 ... 4 C2
eechmoore WA4 ... 25 D3
eechmuir CH1 ... 117 F2
eechtree Farm Cl WA16 . 29 E4
eechtree La WA13 ... 29 D4
eechurst Rd SK8 ... 240 B1
eechway Bollington SK10 . 88 A4
Chester CH2 ... 118 B3
High Lane SK6 ... 37 F4
Wilmslow SK9 ... 60 A3
eechways WA4 ... 26 B3
eechways Dr L64 ... 66 B4
eechwood
Altrincham WA14 ... 238 B1
Knutsford WA16 ... 57 E1
eechwood Ave
Great Sankey WA5 ... 14 C3
Hartford CW8 ... 103 D3
Newton-le-W WA12 ... 2 B2
5 Reddish SK5 ... 240 F8
Romiley SK6 ... 241 D2
Stalybridge SK15 ... 242 F4
Warrington WA1 ... 16 C4
eechwood Cty Prim Sch
Crewe CW1 ... 190 B3
Runcorn WA7 ... 49 F1
eechwood Dr Alsager ST7 193 D2
Eaton (nr Congleton) CW12 . 156 C4
Ellesmere Port L66 ... 69 E1
Higher Wincham CW9 ... 79 F3
Wilmslow SK9 ... 60 C4
eechwood Gr SK8 ... 35 D3
eechwood La
Culcheth WA3 ... 4 B2
Stalybridge SK15 ... 242 F4
eechwood Mews SK10 ... 87 E1
eechwood Rd
Bebington L62 ... 43 E4
Broughton CH4 ... 140 C3
eecroft Cl WA5 ... 7 E1
eeley St SK14 ... 241 E6
eeston Ave WA15 ... 238 F6
eeston Brook SK10 ... 88 A4
eeston Castle CW6 ... 167 F2
eeston Cl Bollington SK10 .. 63 E1
Holmes Chapel CW4 ... 130 A2
Middlewich CW10 ... 151 E3
Warrington WA3 ... 9 E2
eeston Ct WA7 ... 24 B2
eeston Dr Alsager ST7 193 E2
Knutsford WA16 ... 82 A4
Winsford CW7 ... 149 E4
eeston Gn L66 ... 69 F3
eeston Gr SK3 ... 240 E1
eeston Mount SK10 ... 63 E1
eeston Rd Broughton CH4 139 D2
Higher Kinnerton CH4 ... 161 D4
Wilmslow SK9 ... 34 B3
eeston St CW8 ... 103 F4
eeston Terr SK11 ... 111 F3
eeston View CW4 ... 141 F4
eggarman's La WA16 ... 82 A4
elfry Rd WA11 ... 1 C4
elfry Cl SK7 ... 60 B4
elfry Dr SK10 ... 87 E2
elgrave Ave Kingsmere ST7 . 193 E3
Broughton CH4 ... 140 C3
Congleton CW12 ... 156 B2
Warrington WA1 ... 16 C4

Belgrave Cl Dodleston CH4 . 162 A3
Goldborne WN7 ... 4 B4
Widnes WA8 ... 13 F2
Belgrave Cty Inf Sch CH4 . 162 A3
Belgrave Dr L65 ... 69 F3
Belgrave Pl CH4 ... 237 E1
Belgrave Rd
Altrincham WA14 ... 238 C3
Chester CH3 ... 142 A4
Crewe CW2 ... 190 A1
Irlam M44 ... 11 E3
Macclesfield SK11 ... 112 A2
Northwich CW9 ... 104 A2
Sale M33 ... 242 A6
Belgrave St CH2 ... 237 F3
Belgravia Gdns WA15 ... 31 F4
Bell Ave WA11 ... 112 C2
Bell House Rd WA8 ... 13 E1
Bell La WA7 ... 17 F2
Bell Meadow Cl CW6 ... 146 B1
Bellaport Rd TF9 ... 236 A2
Bellard Dr CH2 ... 119 D2
Belldale Cl SK4 ... 240 A6
Belle Vue Terr CW1 ... 175 D3
Bellemonte Rd WA6 ... 74 B3
Belleville Ave M22 ... 33 F4
Bellhouse La
Higher Walton WA4 ... 25 E4
Warrington WA4 ... 17 E1
Bellingham Dr WA7 ... 24 B4
Bellsfield Cl WA13 ... 18 C1
Bellvue La CH3 ... 119 F2
Belmont Ave
Macclesfield SK10 ... 88 A1
Sandbach CW11 ... 175 D4
Warrington WA4 ... 16 C4
Belmont Cl SK4 ... 240 E7
Belmont Cres WA5 ... 15 D3
Belmont Hall
(Boarding Sch) CW9 ... 53 F1
Belmont Rd
Altrincham WA15 ... 238 E2
Bramhall SK7 ... 35 F3
Gatley SK8 ... 239 B6
Great Budworth CW9 ... 53 F1
Northwich CW9 ... 104 B4
Sale M33 ... 242 A8
Widnes WA8 ... 13 E1
Belmont St SK4 ... 240 E7
Belmont Way SK4 ... 240 E7
Belvedere Cl WA6 ... 49 E1
Belvedere Dr CH1 ... 117 F2
Belvedere Rd WA12 ... 2 A3
Belvedere Terr ST7 ... 193 F4
Belvoir Rd Warrington WA4 .. 26 A4
Widnes WA8 ... 13 D1
Bembridge Cl
Great Sankey WA5 ... 14 B4
Widnes WA8 ... 12 C2
Bembridge Ct CW10 ... 151 F4
Bemrose Ave WA14 ... 238 C6
Ben Nevis Dr L65 ... 69 F3
Benbow Cl M33 ... 242 B7
Benbrook Gr 5 SK9 ... 34 B1
Benbrook Way SK11 ... 111 F1
Bendee Ave L64 ... 67 D4
Bendee Rd L64 ... 67 D4
Bengal St SK4 ... 240 E4
Benja Fold SK7 ... 35 D3
Benjamins Way ST7 ... 209 F1
Bennet Cl L64 ... 68 A4
Bennet Rd CW9 ... 104 B3
Bennett Ave WA1 ... 16 C3
Bennett Cl 4 SK3 ... 240 A4
Bennett St Stalybridge SK15 242 D1
5 Stockport SK4 ... 240 A4
Warrington WA1 ... 16 A3
Bennett's La
Higher Kinnerton CH4 ... 161 D4
Widnes WA8 ... 13 F1
Bennetts La SK11 ... 158 C3
Benson Rd WA3 ... 9 E2
Benson Wlk 6 SK9 ... 34 B1
Bent La Astbury CW12 ... 178 A4
Crowton CW8 ... 101 E4
Culcheth WA3 ... 5 D1
Partington WA3 ... 19 E4
Bentham Ave WA2 ... 8 B2
Bentham Rd WA3 ... 5 D1
Bentinck Rd WA14 ... 238 C6
Bentinck St WA7 ... 22 C2
Bentley Dr CW9 ... 191 D3
Bentley Gr CW7 ... 149 E3
Bentley's Farm La WA4 ... 52 C3
Bentleys The SK5 ... 240 F7
Bentley St WA12 ... 118 B2
Bent Field La SK9 ... 38 B3
Benty Heath La
Thornton Hough L64 ... 42 C2
Willaston L64 ... 43 D2
Beresford St WA1 ... 16 C4
Berisford Cl WA15 ... 238 E7
Berkeley Ave ST7 ... 193 E3
Berkeley Cl Goldborne WA3 ... 4 B4
Hyde SK14 ... 241 D5
Berkeley Cres Hyde SK14 ... 241 D5
Wistaston CW2 ... 206 A4
Berkeley Ct WA7 ... 24 B2
Berkeley Rise CW7 ... 149 D4
Berkley Dr CH4 ... 141 E3
Berkshire Cl SK10 ... 86 C1
Berkshire Dr
Congleton CW12 ... 156 B2
Irlam M44 ... 11 E3
Warrington WA1 ... 17 F4
Berlin Rd SK3 ... 240 D2
Bernard Ave WA4 ... 26 B4

Bernisdale Rd WA16 ... 57 F2
Bernsdale Cl CH5 ... 116 A2
Berristal Rd SK10 ... 88 C2
Berry Cl Ellesmere Port L66 ... 69 E2
Wilmslow SK9 ... 60 A3
Berry Dr L66 ... 69 E2
Berry Rd WA8 ... 22 B3
Berrycroft La L66 ... 241 A3
Berrystead CW8 ... 103 D2
Bertram St
Newton-le-W WA12 ... 2 A2
Sale M33 ... 242 E6
Berwick Ave L62 ... 43 F2
Berwick Cl Macclesfield SK10 86 C1
Warrington WA1 ... 17 F3
Berwick Ct CW4 ... 130 A1
Berwick Gdns L66 ... 69 D3
Berwick La L66 ... 69 D3
Berwick Rd L66 ... 69 D3
Berwyn Ave SK8 ... 240 B1
Berwyn Cl L66 ... 69 D3
Berwyn Gr WA9 ... 1 A2
Bessancourt CW4 ... 130 B2
Bessemer Rd WA4 ... 11 F3
Beswick St SK11 ... 112 A4
Beswicks La Lindow End SK9 . 59 E2
Norton in Hales TF9 ... 236 B1
Beswicks Rd CW8 ... 78 C1
Betchton Cres CW11 ... 175 E4
Betchton Rd CW11 ... 175 F1
Betchworth Cres WA7 ... 49 E3
Betchworth Way SK10 ... 87 E2
Bethesda Spec Sch SK8 ... 239 D2
Betjeman Cl WA4 ... 16 C2
Betjeman Way CW1 ... 190 C3
Betley Cl CW9 ... 104 A3
Betley St CW1 ... 190 B2
Betleymere Rd SK8 ... 239 F4
Bettisfield Dr WA3 ... 9 D4
Bettisfield Ave L62 ... 43 E3
Betty's La CW6 ... 168 B1
Bevan Ave ST7 ... 210 C3
Bevan Cl WA5 ... 15 D2
Beverley Ave Appleton WA4 . 26 B4
Denton M34 ... 241 A6
Beverley Dr L60 ... 41 D3
Beverley Rd WA5 ... 15 E3
Beverley Way
Ellesmere Port L66 ... 69 D4
Macclesfield SK10 ... 87 E2
Bevin Ave WA3 ... 5 D2
Bevyl Rd L64 ... 41 D1
Bewley Ct CH3 ... 142 A4
Bewsey Farm Cl WA5 ... 15 E1
Bewsey Ind Est WA2 ... 16 A4
Bewsey Rd WA5 ... 15 F3
Bewsey St WA2 ... 16 A3
Bexhill Ave
Altrincham WA15 ... 238 F6
Warrington WA2 ... 8 C1
Bexington Dr CW1 ... 190 A4
Bexton La WA16 ... 82 A4
Bexton Rd WA16 ... 56 C1
Bexton Rd WA16 ... 82 A4
Bibby Ave WA1 ... 16 C3
Bibby St WA7 ... 193 F4
Bickerton Ave WA6 ... 74 B4
Bickerton Rd WA14 ... 238 B6
Bickerton Way L66 ... 69 D4
Bickley Cl
Hough Common CW2 ... 206 C1
Runcorn WA7 ... 23 E1
Warrington WA2 ... 8 C2
Bickley Town La SY14 ... 214 C3
Bicknell Cl WA5 ... 15 D4
Bida La CW12 ... 179 D4
Biddulph Common Rd
CW12 ... 179 D4
Biddulph Grange Gdns
ST8 ... 179 F2
Biddulph Grange Ctry Pk
ST8 ... 179 F2
Bignall End Rd ST7 ... 210 A2
Billington Ave WA12 ... 2 B3
Billington Cl WA5 ... 14 C4
Billington Rd WA8 ... 12 A2
Bilson Dr SK3 ... 240 B3
Bilton Cl WA8 ... 13 F1
Bilton Way CW1 ... 189 F3
Biddy's La SK10 ... 88 A1
Bingswood Ave SK23 ... 65 F4
Bingswood Ind Est SK23 ... 65 F4
Bingswood Rd SK23 ... 65 F4
Binney Rd CW9 ... 104 A4
Binns St SK15 ... 242 C1
Binyon Way CW1 ... 191 D2
Birch Ave Alsager ST7 ... 193 F1
Crewe CW1 ... 190 C3
Irlam M44 ... 11 E3
Macclesfield SK10 ... 87 D1
5 Manchester SK4 ... 240 B8

Birch Ave continued
Romiley SK6 ... 241 D2
Sale M33 ... 242 B5
Warrington WA2 ... 8 A2
Wilmslow SK9 ... 59 F3
Winsford CW7 ... 127 D1
Birch Brook Rd WA13 ... 19 D3
Birch Cl Crewe CW1 ... 190 C3
Holmes Chapel CW4 ... 130 B2
Birch Cres WA1 ... 1 C2
Birch Ct CW12 ... 155 F2
Birch Fold CW4 ... 107 D3
Birch Gdns CW1 ... 175 E3
Birch Gr Ellesmere Port L66 ... 70 A1
Higher Wincham CW9 ... 79 F3
Knutsford WA16 ... 57 E1
Lostock CW9 ... 105 D1
Warrington, Bruche WA1 ... 16 C4
Warrington, Latchford WA4 ... 16 B2
Birch Heath La CH3 ... 142 C4
Birch Heath Rd CW6 ... 168 B4
Birch House Rd ST5 ... 210 B1
Birch La
Hough Common CW2 ... 206 C1
Winsford CW10 ... 127 F1
Chester CH4 ... 140 C3
Winsford CW10 ... 127 F1
Gatley SK8 ... 239 A5
Haydock WA11 ... 1 C4
Partington M31 ... 11 E2
Poynton SK12 ... 36 C1
Runcorn WA7 ... 49 D2
Warrington WA2 ... 8 B2
Bittern Gr SK10 ... 87 D1
Bk Adcroft St SK1 ... 240 F3
Bk Grosvenor St SK15 ... 242 D1
Birch Tree Cl WA4 ... 238 C1
Birch Tree Ct CH2 ... 237 F4
Birch Tree La Antrobus WA4 . 53 D3
Goostrey CW4 ... 107 E1
The Bank ST7 ... 195 D4
Birch Tree Rd WA5 ... 15 F1
Birch Way SK10 ... 86 D2
Birchall Ave WA3 ... 4 C2
Birchall Moss La CW5 ... 219 F1
Birchall St WA3 ... 9 D4
Birchall Wlk CW2 ... 206 B4
Birchdale WA1 ... 238 C2
Birchdale Ave SK8 ... 239 B2
Birchdale Cres WA4 ... 26 B4
Birchdale Rd Appleton WA4 . 26 B4
Warrington WA1 ... 17 D4
Birchen Rd L26 ... 21 D4
Birchenwood Rd ST7 ... 195 F1
Birches Cl L60 ... 41 D4
Birches Croft Dr SK10 ... 86 C1
Birches La Lach Dennis CW9 105 D4
Lostock CW9 ... 105 D4
Birches The Broughton CH4 . 139 D2
Crewe CW2 ... 206 B4
Neston L64 ... 41 F1
Birches Way ST7 ... 195 D1
Birchfield Ave
Rode Heath ST7 ... 193 F4
Warrington WA5 ... 13 D1
Birchfield Mews 3 SK4 ... 240 A6
Birchfield Rd Cheadle SK3 . 240 A3
Great Sankey WA5 ... 15 D3
Lymm WA13 ... 19 D2
Warrington WA4 ... 26 C3
Birchfields WA15 ... 238 F1
Birchgate Cl SK10 ... 86 C1
Birchin Cl CW5 ... 205 D3
Birchin La CW5 ... 205 D3
Birchinall Cl SK11 ... 112 A4
Birchmuir CH1 ... 117 F2
Birchmuir Cl CW1 ... 190 A3
Birchvale Ave SK6 ... 241 D3
Birchway Bollington SK10 ... 88 A4
Cheadle Hulme SK7 ... 35 E4
Heswall L60 ... 41 E3
High Lane SK6 ... 37 F4
Birchways WA4 ... 26 C3
Birchwood Bvd WA3 ... 9 E1
Birchwood Grange Hospl
Prim Sch WA3 ... 9 F2
Birchwood Cl
Ellesmere Port L66 ... 69 E1
Elton CH2 ... 72 B2
Stockport SK4 ... 240 A5
Birchwood
Comm High Sch WA3 ... 9 E2
Birchwood Dr
Nantwich CW5 ... 204 C3
Peover WA16 ... 106 B4
Wilmslow SK9 ... 60 B4
Birchwood Park Ave WA3 ... 9 E3
Birchwood Sta WA3 ... 9 F1
Bird Hall La SK3 & SK8 ... 240 B2
Bird Hall Rd SK8 ... 240 A2
Bird's La CW6 ... 186 A4
Birds La L60 ... 166 C1
Birdwell Dr WA5 ... 15 D3
Birdsdale Ave L63 ... 43 E3
Birkdale Cl Bramhall SK7 ... 35 F4
Macclesfield SK10 ... 87 E2
Birkdale Ct CW7 ... 104 A4
Birkdale Dr SK8 ... 239 A5
Birkdale Rd Penketh WA5 ... 14 C2
Widnes WA8 ... 13 D3
Birkenhead Rd L64 ... 42 C1
Birkenheath Rd CW5 ... 205 D3
Birkin Cl WA16 ... 57 E2
Birkinheath La WA14 ... 31 D2
Birley Cl WA15 ... 238 F7
Birley St WA12 ... 2 A3
Birstall St ST7 ... 49 E4

Birtles Cl Cheadle SK8 ... 240 A1
Sandbach CW11 ... 175 E4
Birtles La SK10 ... 85 F1
Birtles Rd SK10 ... 86 B1
Birtles Way 8 SK9 ... 34 B3
Birtlespool Rd SK8 ... 239 F4
Birtley Cl WA8 ... 12 A1
Birtwistle Rd CW9 ... 104 B3
Bishop Rd SK10 ... 88 A4
Bishop Reeves Rd WA11 ... 1 C4
Bishop Rd Sutton ... 118 C2
Bishop's Cl Cheadle SK8 ... 240 A1
Kidsgrove ST7 ... 210 B4
Bishopdale Cl WA5 ... 14 C4
Bishopgate St CW9 ... 103 F2
Bishops (Blue Coat)
CE (Aided) High Sch
CH3 ... 142 A4
Bishops Cl WA14 ... 238 B1
Bishops Ct Broughton CH4 .. 139 E2
Warrington WA2 ... 7 F2
Bishops Gdns L65 ... 70 A3
Bishops Way WA8 ... 13 E2
Bishops Wood CW5 ... 204 C1
Bishopsfield Ct CH2 ... 118 C2
Bishopton Dr SK11 ... 111 F4
Bispham Rd WA5 ... 15 D2
Bittern Cl Poynton SK12 ... 36 A2
Runcorn WA7 ... 50 B4
Warrington WA2 ... 8 B2
Bittern Gr SK10 ... 87 D1
Black Diamond St CH2 ... 237 E4
Black Firs Cty Prim Sch
CW12 ... 155 F2
Black Firs La CW12 ... 155 F2
Black Friars CW1 ... 237 D2
Black La SK10 ... 87 F1
Black Lion La L66 ... 69 E3
Black Moss Rd WA14 ... 20 C4
Black Park Rd SY13 ... 226 B1
Black Rd SK11 ... 112 C4
Blackacres Cl CW11 ... 174 C3
Blackberry Cl WA14 ... 238 B8
Blackboards La L66 ... 69 D1
Blackbrook Cl WA8 ... 12 B2
Blackbrooke Ave WA2 ... 6 C1
Blackburn Cl WA3 ... 3 F4
Blackburne Ave WA8 ... 22 A3
Blackburne Cl WA2 ... 9 E1
Blackcroft Ave CW8 ... 78 A1
Blackden La Goostrey CW4 108 A4
Siddington SK11 ... 132 C4
Blackden Wlk 9 SK9 ... 34 B1
Blackdown Cl L66 ... 69 D3
Blackeys La L64 ... 66 C4
Blackhill La WA16 ... 81 F4
Blackhurst Brow SK10 ... 61 D1
Blackhurst St WA1 ... 16 A3
Blackledge Cl WA5 ... 9 D2
Blackshaw Cl CW12 ... 157 D1
Blackshaw Dr WA5 ... 7 D1
Blackshaw La 3 SK9 ... 59 F1
Blackshaw St
20 Macclesfield SK11 ... 112 B4
4 Stockport SK3 ... 240 E4
Blackthorn Cl
Broughton CH4 ... 139 D2
Huntington CH3 ... 142 A3
Blackthorn Pl ST7 ... 210 C1
Blackthorn Wlk M31 ... 11 E1
Blackthorne Ave WA5 ... 15 D4
Blackwell Cl CW10 ... 151 E3
Blackwood Ave L64 ... 118 A3
Blacon Cty High Sch CH1 . 117 E2
Blacon Cty Inf Sch CH1
CH1 ... 117 F3
Blacon Hall Rd CH1 ... 117 F3
Blacon Point Rd CH1 ... 117 F2
Blagg Ave CW5 ... 204 B2
Blair Cl SK7 ... 36 B4
Blair Dr WA8 ... 12 C2
Blairgowrie Dr SK10 ... 87 D2
Blaizefield Cl CW3 ... 232 B1
Blake Cl Blacon CH1 ... 117 F3
Wistaston CW2 ... 189 F1
Blake La CW8 ... 102 A1
Blakeacre Rd L26 ... 21 D3
Blakeden La CW7 ... 148 C4
Blakelely Cl L63 ... 43 D3
Blakeley Cl L63 ... 43 D3
Blakeley Dene L63 ... 43 D3
Blakeley Rd L63 ... 43 D3
Blakelow Bank SK11 ... 112 C4
Blakelow Cl CW10 ... 151 D4
Blakelow Cres CW5 ... 205 F2
Blakelow La L63 ... 58 C4
Blakelow Rd SK11 ... 112 C4
Blakemere Ave M33 ... 242 E5
Blakemere Cl CW11 ... 226 A1
Blakemere Ct L65 ... 70 B4
Blakemere Dr CW9 ... 103 F2
Blakemere Way CW11 ... 174 C4
Blandford Cl SK13 ... 242 D2
Blandford Dr SK11 ... 111 F4
Blandford Rd
Great Sankey WA5 ... 15 D3
Stockport SK4 ... 240 C6
Blandford St SK15 ... 242 D2

Blankney The CW5 .... 204 C2
Blantern Rd CH4 .... 161 D4
Blantyre St WA7 .... 22 C2
Blazon Cl SK3 .... 240 F1
Blaze Hill SK10 .... 88 C4
Bleasdale Rd CW1 .... 173 D1
Bleeding Wolf La ST7 .... 194 C3
Blenheim Cl
  Altrincham WA14 .... 238 D2
  Davenham CW9 .... 103 F2
  Macclesfield SK10 .... 87 D1
  Poynton SK12 .... 36 C2
  Warrington WA2 .... 8 C1
  Wilmslow SK9 .... 60 B4
  Wistaston CW2 .... 205 F4
Blenheim Ct ST7 .... 193 E3
Blenheim Gdns CW7 .... 149 E4
Blessed Thomas Holford
  RC High Sch WA15 .... 238 C4
Blossom Ave
  Cheadle Hulme SK8 .... 35 D1
  Wilmslow SK9 .... 35 D1
Blossoms St 5 SK2 .... 240 F3
Blue Cap La SY14 .... 213 E4
Blue Chip Bsns Pk WA14 ... 238 C7
Blue Hatch WA6 .... 74 B4
Bluebell Ave WA11 .... 1 C4
Bluebell Cl Huntington CH3 . 142 A3
  Macclesfield SK10 .... 87 E2
  Northwich CW8 .... 78 C1
Bluebell Ct WA7 .... 49 F2
Bluebell Gr SK8 .... 239 D4
Bluebell La SK10 .... 87 E2
Bluebell Mews SK10 .... 87 E2
Blueberry Rd WA14 .... 238 A2
Bluecoat St WA2 .... 16 A4
Blundell Rd WA8 .... 22 B4
Blyth Cl Macclesfield SK10 . 86 C1
  Runcorn WA7 .... 50 B3
Blyth Rd L63 .... 43 E4
Blythe Ave
  Cheadle Hulme SK7 .... 35 E3
  Congleton CW12 .... 156 A1
  Widnes WA8 .... 13 D3
Blythe Pl CW7 .... 127 D1
Blythings The CW6 .... 146 B2
Board St SK10 .... 242 A4
Boardman St SK14 .... 241 D6
Boat Stage WA13 .... 18 C2
Boathorse Rd ST7 .... 210 C4
Boathouse La L64 .... 41 E2
Bob's La M44 .... 11 E2
Boddens Hill Rd SK4 .... 240 A5
Boden St SK11 .... 112 B4
Bodiam Ct L65 .... 70 C1
Bodmin Ave SK10 .... 86 C1
Bodmin Cl WA7 .... 50 A3
Bodmin Dr SK7 .... 35 F4
Bodnant Cl CW1 .... 190 A4
Bold Cross WA8 .... 13 F4
Bold Ind Est WA8 .... 13 F4
Bold La Bold Heath WA5 .... 6 B4
  Burtonwood WA5 .... 6 B4
Bold PI CH1 .... 237 E3
Bold Sq CH1 .... 237 F3
Bold St Altrincham WA14 ... 238 D3
  Haslington CW1 .... 191 E2
  Runcorn WA7 .... 23 D2
  Sandbach CW11 .... 175 D3
  Warrington WA1 .... 16 A3
  Widnes WA8 .... 23 D4
Bolesworth Hill Rd CH3 .... 183 E2
Bolesworth Rd Broxton CH3 183 E4
  Chester CH2 .... 118 C3
  Tattenhall CH3 .... 183 E4
Boleyn Cl CH1 .... 117 F3
Boleyn Ct WA7 .... 24 B2
Boleynwood Ct SK9 .... 34 A1
Bolland's Ct CH1 .... 237 D2
Bollin Ave Altrincham WA14 238 B1
  Winsford CW7 .... 127 D1
Bollin Cl Alsager ST7 .... 192 C2
  Culcheth WA3 .... 5 D1
  Lymm WA13 .... 19 D2
  Sandbach CW11 .... 174 C4
  Winsford CW7 .... 127 D1
Bollin Cross Sch SK9 .... 34 A1
Bollin Ct Altrincham WA14 . 238 B1
  Wilmslow SK9 .... 60 B8
Bollin Dr Altrincham WA14 . 238 E8
  Congleton CW12 .... 156 C1
  Lymm WA13 .... 19 D2
Bollin Gr SK6 .... 179 F1
Bollin Hill SK9 .... 60 A4
Bollin Mews SK10 .... 86 C4
Bollin Prim Sch WA14 ...... 238 B1
Bollin Sq WA14 .... 238 B1
Bollin Way SK10 .... 87 D3
Bollin Wlk SK9 .... 60 A4
Bollinbarn SK10 .... 87 D1
Bollinbarn Dr SK10 .... 87 D1
Bollinbrook CE Aided
  Prim Sch SK10 .... 87 D1
Bollinbrook Rd SK10 .... 87 D1
Bollington Ave CW9 .... 104 A3
Bollington Cross CE Contr
  Prim Sch SK10 .... 87 F4
Bollington La SK10 .... 84 C1
Bollington Rd SK10 .... 87 F4

Bollinway WA15 .... 32 A4
Bollinwood Chase SK9 .... 60 B4
Bolshaw Cty Prim Sch SK8 . 34 A4
Bolshaw Farm La SK9 .... 34 B3
Bolshaw Rd SK9 .... 34 B3
Bolton Ave
  Cheadle Hulme SK8 .... 35 D3
  Warrington WA4 .... 16 C2
Bolton Cl Goldborne WA3 ...... 4 A4
  Poynton SK12 .... 36 B2
Bolton Jun Sch WA4 .... 16 C2
Bombay Rd SK3 .... 240 C3
Bombay St SK3 .... 240 C3
Bomish La CW4, SK11 .... 108 B2
Bonar Cl SK3 .... 240 C4
Bonar Rd 5 SK3 .... 240 C4
Bond Cl WA5 .... 15 E2
Bond St Macclesfield SK11 . 112 B4
  Northwich CW8 .... 78 B1
  Stalybridge SK15 .... 242 D3
Bonis All La SK10 .... 61 F2
Bonville Chase WA14 .... 238 A4
Bonville Rd WA14 .... 238 A4
Boon Hill Rd ST7 .... 209 F1
Booth Ave Ashton CH3 ...... 121 F4
  Little Budworth CW6 .... 147 F4
  Sandbach CW11 .... 175 D3
Booth Bed La
  Allostock WA16 .... 107 D2
  Goostrey WA16 .... 107 D2
Booth Cl SK15 .... 242 C1
Booth La Middlewich CW10 . 151 F3
  Sandbach CW10 .... 151 F3
Booth Rd Altrincham WA14 238 C4
  Hartford CW8 .... 103 D2
  Sale M33 .... 242 B8
  Wilmslow SK9 .... 34 A1
Booth St Audley ST7 .... 209 E1
  Congleton CW12 .... 156 B1
  Hyde SK14 .... 241 E5
  Newton-le-W WA12 .... 2 A2
  Stockport SK3 .... 240 E3
  Warrington WA5 .... 15 F2
Booth's Hill Cl WA13 .... 18 B2
Booth's Hill Rd WA13 .... 18 B2
Booth's La WA13 .... 18 A1
Boothbank La WA14 .... 30 A3
Boothby St 8 SK11 .... 112 B4
Boothfields WA16 .... 57 C1
Booths La WA4 .... 26 C3
Boothsdale CW6 .... 122 B2
Boothsmere Cl CW11 ...... 174 C4
Border Rd L60 .... 41 D4
Border Way CH3 .... 119 E1
Bordon Rd SK3 .... 240 B3
Borganey Ct CH4 .... 162 B1
Borough Rd
  Altrincham WA15 .... 238 E4
  Congleton CW12 .... 156 C2
  Warrington WA5 .... 8 B1
  Winsford CW7 .... 126 B1
Borras Rd LL13 .... 196 A4
Borron Rd WA12 .... 2 A3
Borrowdale Ave Gatley SK8 239 B4
  Warrington WA2 .... 8 B2
Borrowdale Cl Crewe CW2 . 189 F2
  Frodsham WA6 .... 74 B4
Borrowdale Rd WA8 .... 22 B4
Borrowmore Est CH3 .... 120 C4
Bosden Cl SK9 .... 34 B3
Bosden Fold SK1 .... 240 F4
Bosley Cl Middlewich CW10 . 151 E3
  Wilmslow SK9 .... 34 B1
Bosley Dr SK12 .... 37 D2
Bosley St SK3 .... 240 A4
Bosley View CW12 .... 157 D1
Bostock Gn L65 .... 69 F3
Bostock Rd
  Macclesfield SK11 .... 111 F4
  Moulton CW10 .... 127 E2
  Winsford CW7 .... 127 D2
Bostock St WA5 .... 15 F3
Boston Ave WA7 .... 23 E1
Boston Cl Cheadle Hulme SK7 35 E4
  Culcheth WA3 .... 4 C2
Boston St SK14 .... 241 E6
Boswell Ave WA4 .... 16 A1
Botteler Ave WA5 .... 15 D3
Bottom St SK14 .... 241 F7
Bottoms La CH4 .... 237 F1
Boughey Rd ST7 .... 210 A4
Boughton CH2 .... 118 C1
Boughton Heath Cty
  Prim Sch CH3 .... 142 A4
Boughton Hill Ave CH3 ..... 119 D1
Boughton Hill Dr CH3 .... 119 D1
Boughton St Paul's Cty
  Inf Sch CH2 .... 237 F3
Boulderstone Rd SK15 ..... 242 D4
Boulevard The
  Broughton CH4 .... 139 E2
  Ellesmere Port L65 .... 69 F2
Boulton Cl CW11 .... 175 E2
Boundary Ct SK8 .... 239 C5
Boundary La Chester CH4 . 140 C3
  Congleton CW12 .... 179 D4
  Heswall L60 .... 41 D3
  Peover WA16 .... 108 B4
  Siddington SK11 .... 132 C4
  Threapwood SY14 .... 222 C4
Boundary La N CW8 .... 101 F1
Boundary La S CW8 .... 101 F1
Boundary Pk L64 .... 66 B4
Boundary Rd SK8 .... 240 A2
Boundary St Northwich CW7 . 79 F1
  Warrington WA1 .... 16 C4
Boundary Terr SK9 .... 33 F3
Bourne Ave WA3 .... 3 E4
Bourne Rd ST7 .... 194 C3

Bourne St Mow Cop ST7 ... 195 E4
  Reddish WA8 .... 240 E8
  Wilmslow SK9 .... 59 F3
Bournemouth Cl WA7 .... 50 B3
Bournville Ave SK4 .... 240 E8
Bourton Cl ST2 .... 237 D4
Boverton Cl WA5 .... 7 F1
Bow Green Rd WA14 .... 238 A1
Bow La WA14 .... 31 D4
Bow St SK3 .... 240 C4
Bowden Cl Congleton CW12 156 A2
  Culcheth WA3 .... 4 C2
  Warrington WA1 .... 16 C4
Bowden Cres SK2 .... 39 E4
Bowden Dr CW9 .... 104 B4
Bowden View La WA16 .... 29 F1
Bowdon CE Aided
  Prim Sch WA14 .... 238 C1
Bowdon Prep Sch WA14 .. 238 C2
Bowdon Rd WA14 .... 238 C3
Bowdon Rise WA14 .... 238 D2
Bowe's Gate Rd CW6 .... 169 D1
Bowen Cl Bramhall SK7 ..... 35 F3
  Widnes WA8 .... 12 B2
Bowen Cooke Ave CW1 ... 190 A3
Bower Ave SK4 .... 240 C6
Bower Cres WA4 .... 26 B1
Bower Gr SK15 .... 242 F2
Bower Rd Altrincham WA15 . 238 F1
  Heswall L60 .... 41 E4
Bower St WA8 .... 13 E1
Bowerfield Ave SK7 .... 36 B4
Bowerfield Cres SK7 .... 36 C4
Bowerfold La SK4 .... 240 D6
Bowers Bsns Pk WA8 ...... 23 D4
Bowery Ave SK8 .... 34 C3
Bowfell Cl L63 .... 43 E2
Bowfell Gr WA5 .... 14 B4
Bowker St SK14 .... 241 E7
Bowkers Cft CW11 .... 191 F4
Bowland Cl Runcorn WA7 ... 49 F3
  Warrington WA3 .... 10 A3
Bowland Ct CW1 .... 173 D1
Bowland Rise CW7 .... 149 D4
Bowling Green Ct
  Nantwich CW5 .... 204 C3
  Northwich CW8 .... 78 C1
Bowling Green St SK14 .... 241 D6
Bowman Ave WA4 .... 17 D3
Bowman Cres OL6 .... 242 A3
Bowmere Cl Biddulph ST6 .. 179 E1
  Tarporley CW6 .... 146 B1
Bowmere Dr CW7 .... 149 F4
Bowmere Rd CW6 .... 146 B1
Bowness Ave Bebington L63 . 43 E3
  Irlam M44 .... 11 E2
  Warrington WA2 .... 8 B1
  Winsford CW7 .... 126 B1
Bowness Cl CW4 .... 130 A2
Bowness Ct SW12 .... 156 A1
Bowness Rd CW2 .... 189 E2
Bowood Ct WA2 .... 8 A2
Bowring Cl WA5 .... 41 D1
Bowyer Ave CW5 .... 204 C3
Box La CW12 .... 155 F2
Box Tree Mews SK11 .... 112 A4
Box Wlk M31 .... 11 E1
Boxgrove Cl WA8 .... 13 D2
Boxmoor Cl CH4 .... 141 D3
Boydell Ave
  Warrington, Grappenhall WA4 17 D1
  Warrington, Westy WA4 ...... 16 C2
Boydell Way CH4 .... 162 A3
Boyle Ave WA2 .... 8 C1
Boyles Hall Rd ST7 .... 209 F1
Brabyns Ave SK6 .... 241 D3
Bracadale Dr SK3 .... 240 F1
Bracepeth Ct L65 .... 70 B2
Bracken Cl Broughton CH4 . 139 E2
  Macclesfield SK10 .... 86 C1
  Rode Heath ST7 .... 193 F4
  Warrington WA3 .... 9 E3
Bracken Way Barnton CW8 . 78 A2
  Comberbach CW9 .... 78 B4
  Frodsham WA6 .... 74 B3
  Higher Wincham CW9 .... 79 E2
  Knutsford WA16 .... 82 A4
Brackendale Elton CH2 .... 72 A2
Brackenlands CH3 .... 119 D1
Brackenlea Pl SK3 .... 240 D1
Brackenwood Cl CW2 ...... 206 A4
Brackenwood Dr SK8 ...... 239 E4
Brackenwood Mews
  Warrington WA4 .... 17 E1
  Widnes WA8 .... 12 C4
Brackley St Runcorn WA7 ... 22 C2
  Warrington WA4 .... 16 B1
Brackley St WA4 .... 16 B1
Bradburn Cl M44 .... 11 F4
Bradburn La CW8 .... 103 D3
Bradbury Ave WA14 .... 238 A5
Bradbury Gdns CW12 ...... 156 C1
Bradbury Rd CW7 .... 127 D1
Bradbury St SK14 .... 241 E5
Braddan Ave M33 .... 242 C5
Braddon Cl CW9 .... 103 F2
Bradeley Hall Rd CW1 ..... 191 E3
Bradeley Rd Haslington CW1 191 E3
  Haslington, Sydney CW1 ... 191 D3
Bradfield Rd CW1 .... 190 A4
Bradford Ave L63 .... 43 D2
Bradford Rd CW7 .... 126 A4
Bradford St CH4 .... 141 E4
Bradgate Ave SK8 .... 239 D1
Bradgate Rd WA14 .... 238 A5

Brading Wlk M22 .... 33 F4
Bradlegh Rd WA12 .... 2 A1
Bradley Bvd WA5 .... 15 D3
Bradley Cl Altrincham WA15 238 E7
  Middlewich CW10 .... 151 D4
Bradley Farm La SY13 ...... 225 E4
Bradley Fold SK15 .... 242 E2
Bradley La Burtonwood WA5 .. 2 A1
  Frodsham WA6 .... 74 B3
  Newton-le-W WA5, WA12 ... 1 C1
Bradley St SK11 .... 112 C3
Bradley Way WA8 .... 13 E1
Bradshaw Ave CH4 .... 140 A4
Bradshaw Hall Inf Sch SK8 239 E1
Bradshaw Hall Jun Sch
  SK8 .... 239 E1
Bradshaw Hall La SK8 .... 34 C4
Bradshaw La Lymm WA13 ... 19 E2
Bradshaw La 3 SK4 .... 240 D6
Bradshaw Lane Cty
  Prim Sch SK4 .... 17 D1
Bradshaw Pl CW12 .... 156 C1
Bradshaw St WA8 .... 13 D1
Bradwall Rd CW11 .... 175 D4
Bradwall St CW11 .... 175 D4
Bradwell Cl L65 .... 70 A2
Bradwell Dr SK8 .... 34 B4
Bradwell Gr CW12 .... 156 C2
Bradwell Rd Goldborne WA3 ... 3 F4
  Hazel Grove SK7 .... 36 C4
Bradwen Cl M34 .... 241 A5
Braemar Ave WA4 .... 104 B4
Braemar Cl
  Holmes Chapel CW4 .... 130 B1
  Warrington WA2 .... 9 D2
  Wistaston CW2 .... 205 F4
Braemar Ct L65 .... 70 C2
Braeside Cl
  Ellesmere Port L66 .... 69 E3
  Macclesfield SK11 .... 112 C3
Braham Cres M44 .... 11 E2
Braidwood Ave WA6 .... 57 E2
Brains La CW6 .... 169 D3
Braintree Rd M22 .... 33 F4
Braithwaite Cl WA7 .... 49 F3
Braithwaite Ct WA7 .... 49 E3
Brake Level ST7 .... 195 D4
Brake The ST7 .... 195 D4
Brake Village ST7 .... 195 D4
Brakeley Rd CW8 .... 77 E2
Bramall Cl CW11 .... 174 C4
Bramall St WA14 .... 241 D8
Bramble Cl Chester CH3 ... 142 A4
  Macclesfield SK10 .... 87 D1
  Penketh WA5 .... 14 C2
  Winsford CW7 .... 126 B2
Bramble Way WA7 .... 49 F2
Brambles The CW1 .... 191 D2
Brambling Cl WA3 .... 49 F3
Bramhall Cl Sale M33 .... 242 E5
  Winsford CW7 .... 126 A1
Bramhall Ctr The SK7 .... 35 F3
Bramhall Dr Bebington L62 . 43 F2
  Holmes Chapel CW4 .... 130 A2
Bramhall High Sch SK7 ..... 35 F4
Bramhall La SK2 & SK3 .... 240 F1
Bramhall La S SK7 .... 35 F4
Bramhall Park Golf Course
  SK7 .... 35 E4
Bramhall Rd CW2 .... 189 F1
Bramhall St WA5 .... 15 F3
Bramhall Sta SK7 .... 35 F3
Bramley Cl Bramhall SK7 ... 35 F3
  Ellesmere Port CH1 .... 94 C4
Bramley Cres WA4 .... 240 B5
Bramley Dr SK7 .... 35 F3
Bramley Rd SK7 .... 35 F3
Brampton Wlk WA6 .... 73 D1
Brampton Ave SK10 .... 87 D1
Brampton Ct WA9 .... 1 A2
Bramway Cheadle Hulme SK7 . 35 E4
  High Lane SK6 .... 37 F4
Branch Way WA11 .... 1 B3
Brancote Gdns L62 .... 43 E4
Branksome Dr SK8 .... 239 D1
Bransome Rd SK4 .... 240 E5
Bransdale Cl WA5 .... 14 C4
Bransdale Way SK11 .... 111 F4
Brantfield Ct WA2 .... 8 C1
Brantwood Rd Cheadle SK8 239 F1
  Manchester SK4 .... 240 C8
Brassey St CH3 .... 118 C1
Brassey Way CW5 .... 205 F3
Brassey's Contract Rd
  .... 199 D1
Brathay Cl WA2 .... 8 A2
Brathwaite Rd WA3 .... 4 A1
Brattswood Dr ST7 .... 194 A3
Bray Cl Cheadle SK8 .... 239 E2
  Crewe CW1 .... 190 C3
  Runcorn WA7 .... 49 F2
Bray Rd CH4 .... 140 C3
Braystan Gdns SK8 .... 239 B6
Bread St SK11 .... 112 B4
Breamar Cl CH3 .... 119 E2
Breck Rd WA8 .... 13 D1
Breck The L66 .... 69 F1
Brecon Ave SK8 .... 239 E1
Brecon Dr L66 .... 69 F1
Brecon Way CW2 .... 206 A4

Breconway CW7 149
Bredbury Gn SK6 241
Bredon Cl L66 69
Breezehill Cl L64 66
Breezehill Pk L64 66
Breezehill Rd L64 66
Brendon Ave WA2 8
Brendon Gr WA9 1
Brent Cl SK12 36
Brent Rd SK4 240
Brentfield WA8 12
Brentnall Cl WA5 15
Brentnall St 2 SK1 240
Brenton Ave M33 242
Bretland Dr CW8 34
Brentwood M33 242
Brentwood Ave
  Altrincham WA14 238
  Irlam M44 11
Brentwood Cl SK15 242
Brentwood Cres WA14 238
Brentwood Dr L66 69
Brentwood Rd CH1 117
Brentwood Sch WA11 238
Brereton CE Aided
  Prim Sch CW11 153
Brereton Cl
  Altrincham WA14 238
  Crewe CW2 189
  Malpas SY14 213
  Runcorn WA7 50
  Sandbach CW11 175
Brereton Ct
  Brereton Green CW12 154
  Cheadle SK8 239
Brereton Dr CW5 204
Brereton Gr M44 11
Brereton Hall Sch CW11 ... 154
Brereton Heath La CW12 ... 154
Brereton Heath Pk CW12 . 154
Brereton La
  Brereton Green CW11 153
  Sproston Green CW10 152
Brereton Rd Hartford CW8 . 103
  Wilmslow SK9 34
Bretland Dr CW8 34
Bretton Cl CH2 118
Bretton Ct Mews CH4 139
Bretton Dr CH4 139
Bretton La CH4 139
Bretton Rd CH4 139
Bretton Wlk M22 33
Brewery La CH3 180
Brewery St
  4 Altrincham WA14 238
  Stockport SK1 240
Brian Ave Warrington WA2 ... 9
  Warrington, Stockton Heath
  16
Briar Ave WA13 18
Briar Cl WA10 1
Briar Ct L64 41
Briar Dr L60 102
Briar Rd WA3 3
Briardale Cl CW2 205
Briardale Gdns L66 69
Briardale Rd
  Ellesmere Port L66 69
  Willaston L64 43
Briardene M34 241
Briarfield Ave WA4 12
Briarfield Rd
  Ellesmere Port L65 70
  Heswall L60 41
Briarlands Cl SK7 35
Briars Mount SK4 240
Briarstead Cl SK7 35
Briarswood ST7 195
Briarwood Ave
  Macclesfield SK11 112
  Widnes WA8 16
Brick Bank CW5 204
Brick Bank La WA16 107
Brick Kiln La CW10 127
Brick St Newton-le-W WA12 .. 1
  Warrington WA1 16
Brickfield Bsns Ctr CW9 ... 79
Brickfield La CH3 119
Brickhill La WA15 32
Brickhurst Way WA1 17
Brickiln La
  Dunham Town WA14 20
  Whitchurch SY13 226
Bricklin Row WA14 238
Bridal Cl SK7 35
Bridge Ave Altrincham WA15 . 32
  Warrington WA4 16
Bridge Ave E WA4 16
Bridge Cl Audley ST7 209
  Cuddington CW8 102
Bridge Ct Chester CH2 119
  Neston L64 66
Bridge Dr Cheadle SK8 239
  Christleton CH3 142
  Wilmslow SK9 34
Bridge End Dr SK10 87
Bridge End La SK10 87
Bridge Foot WA1 16
Bridge Gn SK10 87
Bridge Gr WA15 238
Bridge Hall Prim Sch SK3 240
Bridge La Appleton WA4 26
  Cuddington CW8 101
Bridge Lea WA6 49
Bridge Meadow L66 69
Bridge Pl CH4 237

dge Rd WA1 .... 17 E4
dge Row CW12 .... 156 C2
dge St Broughton CH4 ..... 140 B4
hester CH1 .... 237 E2
oldborne WA3 .... 3 D4
olt LL13 .... 180 C1
acclesfield SK11 .... 112 B4
eston L64 .... 66 C4
ewton-le-W WA12 .... 2 A2
orthwich CW9 .... 79 F1
uncorn WA7 .... 23 D2
alybridge SK15 .... 242 C1
ockport SK1 .... 240 F6
arrington WA1 .... 16 A3
haley Bridge SK23 .... 65 F4
ybunbury CW5 .... 220 B4
dge St Row CH1 .... 237 E2
dge Terr CH3 .... 119 D1
dge View Cl WA8 .... 23 D2
dgedown CW6 .... 146 B1
dgefield Ave SK9 .... 34 B1
dgefield St SK1 .... 240 E6
dgeman Rd CH1 .... 117 F2
dgeman WA5 .... 15 E2
dgemere CE Aided
rim SCh CW5 .... 231 F4
dgemere Cl CW11 .... 174 C4
dgemere Garden World
WA5 .... 232 A2
dgemere La CW5 .... 219 F1
dgemere Way CW9 .... 103 F2
dgend CH2 .... 97 D1
dgend Cl WA8 .... 12 B2
dges Rd L65 .... 70 C3
dgeside Dr WA6 .... 73 D2
dgestones CW12 .... 156 B1
dgewater Ave WA4 .... 16 C2
dgewater Cl Cheadle SK8 .. 34 B4
angleton CW12 .... 157 D1
dgewater Cty High Sch
ower Sch) WA4 .... 26 B3
dgewater Cty High Sch
pper Sch & Sixth Form
oll WA4 .... 26 B4
dgewater Dr CH3 .... 119 E1
dgewater Mews WA4 .... 26 B4
dgewater Pl CW7 .... 126 A1
dgewater Rd WA14 .... 238 D7
dgewater St Lymm WA13 ..18 C2
dgewater St 23 D1
ale M33 .... 242 B7
dgeway East WA7 .... 24 B1
dgeway West WA7 .... 24 B1
dgewood Dr L66 .... 69 E1
dgfield Cl SK6 .... 37 F4
dgeworth Gr ST5 .... 210 D1
dle Cl L62 .... 43 F4
dle Hey CW5 .... 204 C1
dle Pk L62 .... 43 F4
dle Rd Bebington L62 .... 43 F3
eave CW2 .... 190 A2
oodford SK7 .... 35 F1
dle Way Ellesmere Port L66 69 E2
oodford SK7 .... 35 F1
llemere Ct WA1 .... 16 C4
eedon Way L66 .... 69 D3
n Ave WA14 .... 238 E7
erley Cty Prim Sch CW1 190 B2
erley Rd CW12 .... 157 D1
erley St Crewe CW1 .... 190 B2
alybridge SK16 .... 242 A1
ers Cl WA2 .... 8 C2
eryhurst Rd ST7 .... 195 D2
gs Ave CW2 .... 190 B1
ght St Ashton-u-L OL6 ..... 242 A2
hton Cres SK11 .... 113 D2
hton Gr 1 Hyde SK14 .. 241 E5
ale M33 .... 242 B7
hton Rd SK4 .... 240 C5
hton Road Ind Est SK4 240 C5
hton St WA5 .... 15 F3
hts Ave ST7 .... 195 D1
htwell Cl WA13 .... 14 C3
nelow Cres WA5 .... 14 C2
nstage Cl L60 .... 41 E4
nstage La L60 .... 41 E4
nstage Rd L60 .... 41 E4
adley Ave Sale M33 .... 242 C8
arrington WA4 .... 16 C2
ershot CW7 .... 126 B1
dley Cl ST7 .... 194 C1
dley Gr 3 SK9 .... 34 C1
dley Hall Rd
rland CW5 .... 202 C4
ddley CW5 .... 186 C1
dley La WA11 .... 153 E2
dley Pk 1 CW11 .... 174 C4
dley Rd WA7 .... 23 F2
dley St WA1 .... 22 C2
dley Way
ngleton CW12 .... 157 D1
dley St 1 CW11 .... 112 B2
dleys Way ST7 .... 209 F1
ee Lees Cty High Sch
U5 .... 204 C2
ee Pits La CW5 .... 218 C1
ee Rd CW5 .... 204 C2
ell Dr M44 .... 11 F3
aksway SK3 .... 240 C6
aksway Trad Est 1 SK3 240 C4
aley Cl L62 .... 43 E3
alton Cl WA8 .... 22 C4
bane Cl SK7 .... 35 F3
bane Rd CH1 .... 117 E2
tol Ave WA7 .... 50 C3
tol Cl Blacon CH1 .... 117 F3
eadle SK8 .... 34 A4

Bristol Dr L66 .... 69 F1
Bristow Cl WA5 .... 15 D4
Britannia Rd WA3 .... 242 C7
Britannia Dr CW9 .... 104 C4
Brittania Gdns WA6 .... 73 D1
Brittania Rd WA6 .... 73 D1
Brixham Ave SK8 .... 34 C4
Brixham Wlk SK7 .... 35 F4
Broad Hey SK6 .... 241 D3
Broad La Altrincham WA15 .. 32 A4
Appleton WA4 .... 27 E4
Burtonwood WA5 .... 1 B1
Heswall L60 .... 40 B4
Holmes Chapel CW4 .... 129 F1
Sproston Green CW4 .... 129 F1
Stapeley CW5 .... 205 D1
Broad Oak Ave
Broughton CH4 .... 139 D2
Haydock WA11 .... 1 A3
Penketh WA5 .... 14 C2
Broad Oak La
Manchester M20 .... 239 B8
Manchester M20 .... 239 C8
Broad Oak Prim Sch M20 . 239 C8
Broad Rd M33 .... 242 D7
Broad St CW1 .... 190 B3
Broad Street Cty Inf Sch
CW1 .... 190 B3
Broad Wlk SK9 .... 59 F4
Broadacre CW9 .... 78 B3
Broadacres CW5 .... 217 F2
Broadbent Ave WA4 .... 16 C2
Broadbent St SK14 .... 241 D8
Broadcar Rd SK11 .... 113 C3
Broadfield Cl M34 .... 241 A6
Broadfields WA7 .... 50 B4
Broadheath Prim Sch
WA14 .... 238 C8
Broadheys La WA16 .... 28 B3
Broadhurst Ave
Culcheth WA3 .... 4 C1
Warrington WA5 .... 15 E2
Broadhurst La CW12 .... 156 B2
Broadhurst St SK3 .... 240 F3
Broadlake L64 .... 67 F4
Broadland Gdns L66 .... 69 F1
Broadland Rd L66 .... 69 F1
Broadleigh Way CW2 .... 206 B4
Broadley Ave WA3 .... 4 B4
Broadmead Chester CH4 ..119 E1
Heswall L60 .... 41 E4
Broadoak Comp Sch M31 .. 11 F1
Broadoak La High Legh WA16 29 E3
Mobberley WA16 .... 57 F3
Broadoaks Rd M33 .... 242 B7
Broadwalk SK10 .... 87 D3
Broadway Altrincham WA15 .. 32 A4
Barnton CW8 .... 78 A2
Cheadle SK8 .... 239 C4
Widnes WA8 .... 242 A7
Widnes WA8 .... 12 A1
Wilmslow SK9 .... 60 A3
Broadway Ave SK8 .... 239 D5
Broadway E CH2 .... 118 C3
Broadway The CW5 .... 204 C3
Broadway W CH2 .... 118 B3
Broadways CW3 .... 230 A2
Broadwood Cl SK6 .... 37 F4
Broady Ct CW2 .... 190 B1
Brock Gdns L24 .... 21 F1
Brock Rd WA3 .... 9 E2
Brockhurst St CW9 .... 104 A4
Brockhurst Way CW9 .... 104 A3
Brocklehurst Ave SK10 .... 87 F1
Brocklehurst Cl SK11 .... 112 C4
Brocklehurst Dr SK10 .... 87 D4
Brocklehurst Way SK10 ..... 87 E2
Brockway E CH3 .... 166 A1
Brockway W CH3 .... 166 A1
Brockwell Cl 2 CW7 .... 149 D4
Brodie Cl CH2 .... 95 E1
Brogden Ave WA3 .... 4 C2
Brogden Gr SK8 .... 239 B5
Brogden Gr M33 .... 242 A5
Brogden Terr M33 .... 242 B5
Broken Banks 21 SK11 .. 112 B4
Broken Cross SK11 .... 111 F4
Broken Cross Cty Prim Sch
SK11 .... 111 F4
Brokencross Pl CW9 .... 104 A4
Bromborough Golf Course
L63 .... 43 D3
Bromborough Rake Sta L62 43 D4
Bromborough Sta L63 .... 43 E3
Bromborough Village Rd
L62 .... 43 F4
Bromleigh Ave SK8 .... 239 B6
Bromley Ave WA3 .... 4 B4
Bromley Cl Crewe CW1 .. 189 F4
Heswall L60 .... 40 C4
Warrington WA2 .... 8 C2
Bromley Dr CW4 .... 130 B1
Bromley Rd
Congleton CW12 .... 156 C2
Macclesfield SK10 .... 111 F4
Brompton Gdns WA5 .... 15 F4
Brompton Rd SK4 .... 240 A6
Brompton Way L66 .... 69 F1
Bronington Ave L62 .... 43 D3
Brook Acre Cty Prim Sch
WA2 .... 8 C1
Brook Ave Altrincham WA15 238 E6
Shavington, Stoke Heath
CW2 .... 206 B3
Warrington, Stockton Heath
WA4 .... 16 C3
Warrington, Westy WA4 .... 16 C3
Wilmslow SK9 .... 34 B2
Brook Bottom Rd SK22 .... 39 D4

Brook Cl Altrincham WA15 238 E6
Crewe CW1 .... 190 C2
Crewe CW1 .... 12 B3
Brook Ct CW11 .... 175 D3
Brook Dr Cheadle Hulme SK8 . 35 D4
Great Sankey WA5 .... 15 D3
Kelsall CW6 .... 122 B2
Brook End WA9 .... 1 A1
Brook Farm Sch CW6 ..... 168 B4
Brook Furlong WA6 .... 48 C1
Brook Gdns ST6 .... 179 E1
Brook Hey L64 .... 41 D1
Brook House Dr CW2 .... 206 B4
Brook La Altrincham WA15 .. 238 E6
Broughton CH5 .... 139 E4
Burland CW5 .... 203 E4
Chester CH2 .... 118 C2
Knutsford WA16 .... 57 D1
Warrington WA3 .... 18 A4
Wilmslow SK9 .... 59 F2
Brook Lane Ind Est CW10 . 151 E4
Brook Lodge SK8 .... 239 D4
Brook Pl WA4 .... 16 C2
Brook Rd Cheadle SK8 ..... 239 D6
Ellesmere Port L66 .... 69 E3
Lymm WA13 .... 18 B2
Warrington WA5 .... 14 C2
Brook Side CW8 .... 102 B4
Brook St Cheadle SK8 .... 239 F6
Chester CH2 .... 237 E3
Congleton CW12 .... 156 C2
Crewe CW2 .... 190 B2
Golborne WA3 .... 3 D4
Hyde SK14 .... 241 E7
Knutsford WA16 .... 57 D1
Macclesfield SK10 .... 87 E1
Macclesfield SK11 .... 112 B4
Macclesfield SK11 .... 112 C4
Neston L64 .... 66 C4
Northwich CW9 .... 79 D1
Northwich CW9 .... 79 F1
Runcorn WA7 .... 23 D1
Sale M33 .... 242 C7
Widnes WA8 .... 13 D1
Brook Street Bridge CH2 .. 237 F4
Brook Terr CW11 .... 175 D2
Brook Way Great Sankey WA5 15 D3
Nantwich CW5 .... 204 C2
Brook Well L64 .... 66 C4
Brookdale WA8 .... 12 A2
Brookdale Ave Denton M34 241 B6
Knutsford WA16 .... 57 E1
Brookdale Pl CH1 .... 237 E3
Brookdale Way CH3 .... 143 D3
Brooke Ave CH2 .... 118 B4
Brooke Dr SK9 .... 34 B2
Brooke Way 11 SK9 .... 34 B2
Brookes Ave CW4 .... 139 D2
Brookfield CW1 .... 191 E3
Brookfield Ave
Altrincham WA15 .... 238 F8
Poynton SK12 .... 36 B2
Romiley SK6 .... 241 A4
Runcorn WA7 .... 23 F1
Brookfield Cl Lymm WA13 .. 18 B2
Tarporley CW6 .... 168 B4
Brookfield Cres
Cheadle SK8 .... 239 D4
Goostrey CW4 .... 107 F1
Brookfield Dr Alsager ST7 .. 193 E3
Chester CH2 .... 118 C2
Holmes Chapel CW4 .... 130 A2
Brookfield Gr OL6 .... 242 A2
Brookfield La SK11 .... 112 C4
Brookfield Park WA4 .... 27 D1
Brookfield Rd Cheadle SK8 . 239 E5
Comberbach CW9 .... 78 B4
Culcheth WA3 .... 4 B2
Brookfield St WA12 .... 2 A2
Brookfields SK8 .... 34 B4
Brookhead Dr SK8 .... 240 A2
Brookhead Jun Sch SK8 . 239 F5
Brookhouse La
Church Minshull CW10 ..... 172 B4
Congleton CW12 .... 157 E1
Duddon CH3 .... 144 B3
Whitley WA4 .... 52 A1
Brookhouse Rd Alsager ST7 193 E2
Brookhurst Ave L63 .... 43 E3
Brookhurst Cl L63 .... 43 E3
Brookhurst Prim Sch L62 ... 43 E3
Brookhurst Rd L63 .... 43 E3
Brookkash Rd M22 .... 34 A4
Brookland Ave CW2 .... 205 E4
Brookland Dr CW11 .... 175 F3
Brookland La WA9 .... 1 A1
Brookland St WA1 .... 16 C4
Brooklands Ave SK11 .... 112 A4
Brooklands Cres M33 .... 242 B5
Brooklands Dr
Goostrey CW4 .... 107 F1
Northwich CW9 .... 104 A2
Brooklands Gr CW1 .... 190 A3
Brooklands Mews SK11 ..... 112 A4
Brooklands Rd
Congleton CW12 .... 155 F1
Neston L64 .... 41 E1
Sandbach SK3 .... 242 A5
Brooklands Station App
M33 .... 242 B5
Brookledge La SK10 .... 62 C3
Brookln Pl SK8 .... 239 D6
Brooklyn Cres SK8 .... 239 D5

Brooklyn Dr
Ellesmere Port L65 .... 69 F3
Lymm WA13 .... 18 C2
Brooklyn Rd SK8 .... 239 D5
Brooklyn St CW2 .... 190 B1
Brookmere Cl CW11 .... 174 C4
Brooks Ave SK14 .... 241 E5
Brooks Dr WA15 .... 32 B4
Brooks La Bosley SK11 ..... 135 F1
Middlewich CW10 .... 128 B1
Brooks St SK1 .... 240 F3
Brookside Ashton CH3 .... 121 F4
Chester CH4 .... 142 A4
Cuddington CW8 .... 101 E4
Kingsley WA6 .... 75 E1
Brookside Ave
Great Sankey WA5 .... 15 D2
Haydock WA11 .... 1 B4
Poynton SK12 .... 36 D2
Sutton Lane Ends SK11 ..... 112 C1
Warrington WA4 .... 16 B1
Brookside Cl Cheadle SK8 .. 239 D4
Haydock WA11 .... 1 B4
Brookside Ct SK10 .... 87 D1
Brookside Cty Inf Sch L66 .. 69 E2
Brookside Gn CW2 .... 206 B4
Brookside La SK6 .... 37 F4
Brookside Prim Sch SK6 ... 37 F4
Brookside Rd
Congleton CW12 .... 156 B2
Gatley SK8 .... 239 A6
Brookside Terr CW2 .... 237 F4
Brookside View WA11 .... 1 A4
Brookside Way WA11 .... 1 A4
Brookvale Ave N WA7 .... 50 A3
Brookvale Ave S WA7 .... 50 A3
Brookvale Cl WA5 .... 6 C2
Brookvale Cty Comp Sch
WA7 .... 50 B3
Brookvale Cty Inf Sch WA7 . 50 A3
Brookvale Cty Jun Sch WA7 50 A3
Brookway WA15 .... 238 F7
Brookway La WA9 .... 1 A1
Brookwood Cl WA4 .... 26 C3
Broom Cres CH4 .... 121 D1
Broom Field Cl SK9 .... 60 C4
Broom La WA16 .... 29 D1
Broom Rd Altrincham WA15 . 238 E3
Partington M31 .... 11 D4
Broom St CW1 .... 190 A3
Broom's La CW6 .... 122 B3
Broome Ct WA7 .... 50 A3
Broomehouse Ave M44 .... 11 F4
Broomfield Cl SK11 .... 84 A2
Broomfield La WA15 .... 238 E3
Broomfield Rd SK4 .... 240 C8
Broomfields Cty Jun Sch
WA4 .... 26 C4
Broomfields Rd WA4 .... 26 B4
Broomfields Recn Ctr WA4 . 26 B4
Broomgrove La M34 .... 241 A8
Broomheath La
Duddon CH3 .... 144 B4
Tarvin CH3 .... 121 E1
Tarvin, Broom Bank CH3 ..... 144 B4
Broomhill La
Brown Knowl CH3 .... 199 E4
Great Barrow CH3 .... 120 C4
Broomlands L60 .... 40 C4
Broomsfield La CW8 .... 78 A2
Broomville Ave M33 .... 242 B6
Broseley Ave WA3 .... 4 B2
Broseley La WA3 .... 4 B3
Brotherton Cl L62 .... 43 E4
Brough St W SK11 .... 112 B4
Brougham St SK15 .... 242 C1
Broughton Ave WA3 .... 3 D4
Broughton Cres SY14 .... 211 D1
Broughton Hall Rd CH4 .. 139 E2
Broughton Jun & Inf Sch
CH4 .... 139 E2
Broughton La CW2 .... 189 F1
Broughton Mills Rd CH4 ... 139 F3
Broughton Rd Adlington SK10 62 B3
Crewe CW1 .... 190 B4
Reddish SK5 .... 240 F8
Broughville Dr M20 .... 239 C8
Brow Cty Prim Sch The
WA7 .... 23 F1
Brow La Antrobus CW9 .... 53 E3
Heswall L60 .... 40 C4
Brow The WA6 .... 75 E1
Browmere Dr WA3 .... 9 D4
Brown Ave
Lawton-gate ST7 .... 194 A3
Nantwich CW5 .... 204 C2
Brown Heath Rd
Christleton CH3 .... 143 D3
Waverton CH3 .... 143 D3
Brown La SK8 .... 239 B1
Brown Lees Cl CW2 .... 190 A1
Brown Lees Rd ST7 .... 195 F3
Brown St Alderley Edge SK9 . 60 A1
Altrincham WA14 .... 238 D3
Congleton CW12 .... 156 C2
Macclesfield SK11 .... 112 B4
Sandbach CW11 .... 240 E6
Widnes WA8 .... 23 E4
Brown's La Chester CH4 .. 141 E4
Wilmslow SK9 .... 60 C4
Brownbill Dr WA1 .... 16 C4
Brownhills Rd CW6 .... 147 E3
Browning Ave WA8 .... 22 C4
Browning Cl Blacon CH1 .. 117 F2
11 Sandbach CW11 .... 174 B3
Browning Dr L65 .... 69 F2
Browning Gn L65 .... 69 F2

Browning Gr ST7 .... 210 B4
Browning St CW1 .... 190 B2
Browning Way CW7 .... 149 D4
Brownlow Cl SK12 .... 36 C1
Broxton Ave CW10 .... 151 E3
Broxton Cl SK12 .... 12 B2
Broxton Dr CW2 .... 190 A1
Broxton Rd Broxton CH3 ... 182 B1
Clutton CH3 .... 182 B1
Ellesmere Port L66 .... 69 F3
Bruce Ave WA2 .... 8 B1
Bruce Cres L63 .... 43 E3
Bruce Dr L66 .... 69 E2
Bruche Ave WA1 .... 16 C4
Bruche Cty Inf Sch WA1 ... 17 D4
Bruche Cty Jun Sch WA1 ... 17 D4
Bruche Dr WA1 .... 16 C4
Bruche Heath Gdns WA1 ... 17 D4
Bruen The CH3 .... 121 E2
Bruera Rd L65 .... 70 A1
Brunel Rd SK11 .... 112 B2
Brunner Bsns Ctr CW8 ..... 78 B1
Brunner Gr CW5 .... 205 D3
Brunner Rd WA8 .... 22 C3
Brunswick Cres L66 .... 69 F2
Brunswick Hill SK11 .... 112 B4
Brunswick Rd
Altrincham WA14 .... 238 D7
Newton-le-W WA12 .... 1 C2
Brunswick St
3 Macclesfield SK11 .... 112 B4
St Helens WA9 .... 1 A2
Brunswick Terr SK11 .... 112 B4
Bruntleigh Ave WA4 .... 17 D2
Bruntwood Ave WA8 .... 239 A1
Bruntwood La Cheadle SK8 . 239 E1
Cheadle SK8 .... 239 E1
Bruntwood Prim Sch SK8 . 239 E2
Brussels Rd SK3 .... 240 D2
Bryant Ave WA4 .... 16 C3
Bryce St SK14 .... 241 D8
Brymau Four Est CH4 .... 140 B4
Brymau One Est CH4 .... 140 C4
Brymau Three Est CH4 ..... 140 B4
Brymau Two Est CH4 .... 140 C4
Brynlow Dr CW10 .... 151 D4
Brynmore Dr SK11 .... 112 C4
Brynn St WA8 .... 23 D4
Brynton Cl SK10 .... 87 E1
Brynton Rd SK10 .... 87 E1
Buchan Cl WA5 .... 15 D4
Buchan Gr CW2 .... 190 A2
Buck La CW2 .... 206 C2
Buckbean Way CW4 .... 107 F1
Buckden Way SK11 .... 112 B4
Buckfast Ave WA11 .... 2 A4
Buckfast Cl
Cheadle Hulme SK8 .... 35 D3
Macclesfield SK10 .... 87 E1
Penketh WA5 .... 14 C2
Poynton SK12 .... 36 B3
Buckfast Way CW10 .... 128 A1
Buckingham Ave
Chester CH3 .... 119 D1
Denton M34 .... 241 B6
Widnes WA8 .... 13 D2
Buckingham Cl CW2 .... 205 F4
Buckingham Dr
Davenham CW9 .... 103 F2
Great Sankey WA5 .... 15 E2
Knutsford WA16 .... 57 D1
Winsford CW7 .... 149 E4
Buckingham Rd
Ellesmere Port L65 .... 70 B1
Irlam M44 .... 11 E3
Poynton SK12 .... 36 B2
Stalybridge SK15 .... 242 D3
Wilmslow SK9 .... 59 F3
Buckingham Rd W SK4 ..... 240 A8
Buckingham Way SK2 .... 240 F2
Buckland Cl WA8 .... 22 B4
Buckland Gr SK7 .... 36 C4
Buckley Cl CW10 .... 128 C4
Buckley Cl CW10 .... 151 D4
Buckley Dr SK6 .... 241 A1
Buckley St
Macclesfield SK11 .... 112 B4
Newton-le-W WA12 .... 16 A3
Bucklow Ave
Mobberley WA16 .... 58 A2
Partington M31 .... 11 F2
Bucklow Gdns WA13 .... 19 D2
Bucklow Gr CW14 .... 238 A3
Bucklow Wlk 10 SK11 .... 112 C4
Bucklowhill La WA16 .... 30 A2
Buckton St WA1 .... 16 B4
Bude Cl Alsager ST7 .... 193 D2
Bramhall SK7 .... 35 F4
Crewe CW1 .... 190 A4
Bude Rd WA8 .... 12 C2
Budworth Ave
Warrington WA4 .... 16 C2
Widnes WA8 .... 12 B1
Budworth Cl Runcorn WA7 .. 49 E4
Sandbach CW11 .... 174 C4
Budworth Heath La CW9 .... 54 B1
Budworth La
Comberbach CW9 .... 78 C4
Great Budworth CW9 .... 78 C4
Budworth Rd
Bate Heath CW9 .... 54 C1
Ellesmere Port L66 .... 69 F1
Sale M33 .... 242 E5
Tabley WA16 .... 55 E1

Budworth Wlk SK9 34 C1
Buerton Cty Prim Sch
  CW3 230 C2
Buffs La L60 41 D4
Buggen La L64 66 B4
Buglawton Cty Prim Sch
  CW12 157 D2
Buglawton Hall Sch CW12 157 E3
Buglawton Ind Est CW12 156 C2
Builovas Rd L64 41 F1
Bulkeley Rd Cheadle SK8 239 C6
  Poynton SK12 36 C2
  Wilmslow SK9 34 B2
Bulkeley St Chester CH1 119 D1
  Stockport SK3 240 D4
Bull Hill L64 66 C3
Bull Hill La SK10 88 B1
Bull Ring CW9 103 F4
Bull Ring The CW10 128 B1
Bullcroft Cl SY14 211 E4
Bullock St SK2 240 F3
Bullocks House Rd ST7 195 F2
Bullocks La
  Macclesfield SK11 112 C2
  Sutton Lane Ends SK11 112 C2
Bumper's La CH1 117 F1
Bumpers Cl
  Middlewich CW10 151 E3
  Northwich CW9 104 A3
  Stoak CH2 96 A4
Bunbury Dr WA7 49 E3
Bunbury Gn L65 70 B1
Bunbury La CW6 185 F4
Bunbury Rd L65 169 E2
Bunce La SK11 133 D2
Bunce St CH4 237 D1
Bungalow Rd WA12 2 C1
Bunham Cl ST7 193 E2
Bunkershill Rd SK6 241 B1
Buntingford Rd WA4 17 E2
Bunts La CW12 156 C1
Burdett Rd L66 69 F1
Burfield Dr WA4 26 B4
Burford Ave SK7 35 E3
Burford Cl SK9 59 F3
Burford Cres SK9 59 F3
Burford La WA13 19 E1
Burgamot La CW9 78 B4
Burges St CH2 118 C2
Burgess Ave WA4 16 A1
Burgess Dr CH1 117 D3
Burgess Pl CW8 103 F4
Burgess St SK10 112 C4
Burjen Way CW1 190 A3
Burkhardt Dr WA12 2 C2
Burkitt St SK14 241 E6
Burland Cl WA7 22 C1
Burland Ct CW7 126 A1
Burland Rd ST5 210 B1
Burlea Cl CW2 189 F3
Burlea Dr CW2 206 A3
Burlescombe Cl WA14 238 B6
Burley Ct SK4 240 C6
Burley La WA4 27 E2
Burleyhurst La WA16 58 C3
Burlington Cl WA14 238 D5
Burlington Rd WA14 238 D5
Burnell Rd L65 70 C2
Burnet Cl WA2 9 E1
Burnfell WA3 3 F4
Burnham Cl Cheadle SK8 239 F2
  Culcheth WA3 4 C2
  Penketh WA5 14 C3
  Widnes WA8 12 B2
Burnham Rd CH4 140 C3
Burns Ave SK8 239 F6
Burns Cl Ellesmere Port L66 69 F2
  Rode Heath ST7 193 F4
Burns Cres WA8 22 C4
Burns Dr CW1 190 C2
Burns Gr WA2 8 B1
Burns Rd CW12 157 D1
Burns Way CH1 117 F3
Burnsall Ave WA3 3 F4
Burnside WA15 32 B4
Burnside Ave WA4 16 B1
Burnside Cl SK9 60 B3
Burnside Rd SK8 239 B5
Burnt Acre SK11 84 A2
Burrant Rd M22 33 E4
Burrough Cl WA3 9 F2
Burrows Hill CW8 103 D4
Burrows St WA11 1 A3
Burrows The CW8 101 C3
Burscough Way WA8 22 A3
Burslam St CW12 156 C1
Burton Ave CW6 146 B2
Burton Bishop Wilson CE
  Aided Prim Sch L64 67 E1
Burton Cl Culcheth WA3 4 C2
  Widnes WA8 12 C2
Burton Dr SK12 36 B2
Burton Gn L66 69 E2
Burton Gr CW1 190 B2
Burton Hall Rd LL12 161 F1
Burton La CW6 144 C3
Burton Manor Coll L64 67 E1
  Neston L64 66 C3
  Warrington WA2 8 B1
Burton St SK4 240 E7
Burton Wlk SK4 240 E7
Burtonwood Cty Prim Sch
  WA5 6 C4

Burtonwood Rd
  Burtonwood WA5 7 D1
  Great Sankey WA5 15 D4
Burtonwood Service Area
  WA5 7 D2
Burwardsley Rd CH3 166 B1
Bury St SK5 240 F7
Bush Rd Christleton CH3 142 C4
  Widnes WA8 22 C3
Bushell Cl L64 66 C4
Bushell Rd L64 66 C4
Bushway L60 40 B4
Butler Way CW5 204 C2
Butley Cl Macclesfield SK10 87 E2
  Middlewich CW10 151 E4
Butley Lanes SK10 61 F1
Butley Sch SK10 61 F3
Butter Ave WA5 7 F1
Butterbache Rd CH3 142 A3
Buttercup Cl CH3 142 A3
Buttercup Dr SK3 240 D1
Buttermarket St WA1 16 A3
Buttermere Ave
  Ellesmere Port L65 70 B2
  Warrington WA2 8 B2
Buttermere Cl WA6 74 B4
Buttermere Ct CW12 156 A1
Buttermere Dr
  Altrincham WA15 32 B3
  Crewe CW1 173 D1
Buttermere Gr WA7 49 E3
Buttermere Rd Gatley SK8 239 B3
  Partington M31 11 F2
  Winsford CW7 126 B1
Butterton La Crewe CW1 192 B1
  Haslington CW1 192 B1
Button Field CW8 126 A4
Butts The Alsager ST7 193 E2
  Runcorn WA7 23 F1
Buxton Ave CW1 190 C2
Buxton Cl WA5 15 D4
Buxton New Rd
  Macclesfield Forest SK11 114 B4
  Rainow SK10 88 B1
Buxton Old Rd
  Congleton CW12 157 D2
  Disley SK12 38 C2
  Macclesfield SK10 113 E4
  Rainow SK10 113 E4
Buxton Rd
  Congleton CW12 157 E3
  Disley SK12 38 C3
  Hazel Grove SK7 37 E4
  High Lane SK6 37 E4
  Macclesfield SK10 112 C4
  New Mills SK23 39 E2
  Whaley Bridge SK23 39 E2
Buxton Rd W WA12 38 A3
Buxton St SK8 239 A5
Bye Pass Rd CH3 121 D2
Bye Pass The CH3 119 F1
Byland Ave SK8 35 D3
Bylands Cl SK12 36 B2
Byley Cty Prim Sch CW10 129 D4
Byley La Cranage CW10 129 E3
  Middlewich CW10 128 C2
  Sproston Green CW10 128 C2
Byley Way CW7 126 A1
Byng Ave M44 11 E2
Byrom St WA14 238 D3
Byron Cl Blacon CH1 117 F3
  Crewe CW1 190 C2
  Middlewich CW10 151 E3
  Rode Heath ST7 193 F4
Byron Ct WA2 8 B1
Byron Dr SK8 239 F6
Byron St WA7 23 D1
Byron Way CW2 190 A1
Byron's La SK11 112 C3
Byrons St SK11 112 B3
Bythom Cl CH3 142 C4

Cabot Cl WA5 7 E1
Cabot Pl SK5 240 F8
Cabul Cl WA2 16 B4
Cadished Inf Sch M44 11 E3
Cadished Jun Sch M44 11 F3
Cadnant Cl CH1 117 E2
Cadshaw Cl WA3 9 E3
Caerleon Cl CW7 149 D4
Caerllew LL13 180 C1
Caernarvon Ave CW7 149 D4
Caernarvon Cl WA7 23 F1
Caernarvon Ct L65 70 B1
Caernarvon Rd CW2 205 F4
Caesars Cl WA7 23 F1
Cairns Cres CH1 117 E2
Cairo St WA1 16 A3
Caister Way CW7 149 E4
Caithness Cl WA7 23 D1
Calamine St WA13 112 C3
Calcutta Rd SK3 240 C3
Calday Gr WA11 1 A4
Caldbeck Ave Sale M33 242 E7
  Warrington WA2 8 B1
Caldene Terr SK23 65 F4
Calder Ave CW1 191 D3
Calder Cl Bollington SK10 87 F4
  Poynton SK12 36 B1
  Widnes WA8 12 C2
Calder Way L66 69 E3
Calderfield Cl WA4 26 A4
Caldicott Ave L62 43 E4
Caldicott Cl CW7 149 E4
Caldwell Rd WA4 26 A4
Caldwell's Gate La CW9 54 A4
Caldy Cl CW2 118 B3
Caldy Dr L66 69 E2

Caldy Rd Alsager ST7 193 E2
  Wilmslow SK9 34 B2
Caldy Valley Rd
  Chester CH3 142 A4
  Huntington CH3 142 A4
Caldy Way CW7 126 A1
Cale Gn SK2 240 F2
Cale Green Prim Sch SK3 240 F2
Cale St SK2 240 F2
Calland Ave SK14 241 D7
Callands Cty Prim Sch WA5 7 F1
Callands Rd WA1 7 E1
Calmington La WA7 24 C2
Calrofold Dr ST5 210 B1
Calrofold La SK10 88 B1
Calstock Cl WA5 14 C2
Calveley Ave L62 43 F2
Calveley Cty Prim Sch
  CW6 170 A1
Calveley Green La
  Alpraham CW6, CW7 170 B2
  Wettenhall CW6, CW7 170 B2
Calveley Hall La CW6 170 A1
Calver Rd WA2 8 A2
Calver Wlk SK8 239 E1
Calverley Cl SK9 60 B4
Calverly Cl WA7 50 B3
Calverly Rd SK8 240 A1
Calvers WA7 23 F1
Camamile Wlk M31 11 F1
Camberley Cl SK7 36 A4
Camborne Ave SK10 111 F4
Camborne Cl WA7 50 B3
Cambourne Cl CW12 178 C4
Cambourne Rd WA5 6 C3
Cambrai Ave WA4 16 B1
Cambrian Ave CH3 119 D1
Cambrian Cl L66 69 D3
Cambrian Rd SK3 240 C4
Cambrian Way CW7 149 D4
Cambridge Ave
  Macclesfield SK11 112 A4
  Wilmslow SK9 59 F4
  Winsford CW7 126 A1
Cambridge Cl Biddulph ST6 179 E1
  Warrington WA4 26 A4
Cambridge Gdns
  Appleton WA4 26 B3
  Helsby WA6 73 E2
Cambridge Rd
  Altrincham WA15 238 E2
  Bebington L62 43 F4
  Chester CH2 118 C3
  Ellesmere Port L65 70 B3
  Gatley SK8 239 B5
  Macclesfield SK11 112 A4
Cambridge Road Cty
  Prim Sch L65 70 B3
Cambridge St Runcorn WA7 23 E1
  Stalybridge SK15 242 D2
  Widnes WA8 23 D4
Camden Cl WA7 24 A1
Camden Rd L65 70 A3
Camden St CW1 190 B2
Camelot Cl WA12 1 C2
Camelot Gr WA7 206 B2
Camelot Way WA7 50 A4
Cameron Ave Runcorn WA7 48 C4
  Shavington CW2 206 A2
Cameron Ct WA2 8 A2
Cameron Rd WA8 23 D4
Camm St CW2 190 B1
Campbell Ave WA7 49 D4
Campbell Cl
  Congleton CW12 157 D2
  Haslington CW1 191 E2
  Macclesfield SK10 87 D1
Campbell Cres WA5 14 C3
Campden Way SK9 34 B2
Campion Cl Huntington CH3 142 A3
  Warrington WA3 9 E3
Campsey Ash WA8 12 C2
Camsley La CW7 149 E3
Camsley La WA13 18 A2
Canaan WA3 4 A4
Canada Cl WA2 9 D1
Canadian Ave CH2 119 D2
Canal Bridge Ent Pk CH1 118 A3
Canal Cotts WA7 70 B4
Canal Rd Altrincham WA14 238 E8
  Congleton CW12 156 C1
Canal Reach WA7 24 B1
Canal Side Appleton WA4 17 E1
  Barnton CW8 78 A1
  Chester CH1 118 C1
  Chester CH2 237 F3
  Macclesfield SK11 112 C4
  Moore WA4 25 E3
  Preston on the Hill WA4 50 C3
  Runcorn WA7 48 B4
Canal St Chester CH1 237 D3
  Congleton CW12 156 C1
  Hyde SK14 241 C7
  Macclesfield SK11 112 C4
  Newton-le-W WA12 1 C2
  Runcorn WA7 23 D1
  Stalybridge SK15 242 D1
  Stockport SK1 240 F4
  Whaley Bridge SK23 65 F4
Canal Terr CW10 151 F4
Canalside L65 70 B3
Canberra Ave WA3 8 B2
Canberra Rd SK7 35 F3
Canberra Sq WA2 8 A3
Canberra Way CH1 117 E2
Candelan Way WA16 29 E2
Candle La CW3 232 A1
Candleston Cl WA5 7 F1

Canford Cl Crewe CW1 190 A4
  Great Sankey WA5 15 E3
Canley Cl SK1 240 F4
Cann La Appleton WA4 26 C2
  Bate Heath CW9 55 D3
Cannel Ct WA7 50 A3
Cannell St WA5 15 E2
Canning St Chester CH1 237 D3
  Warrington WA1 1 A3
Cannock Cl CH1 94 C4
Cannock Dr SK4 240 A6
Cannon St L65 70 A3
Cannon Way CH4 161 D4
Canon Gr WA7 238 B1
Canon St WA7 24 A2
Canon Wilson Cl WA11 1 B3
Canons Rd WA5 15 E3
Canterbury Cl CH1 94 C4
Canterbury Rd 🅑 SK10 112 C4
Canterbury Rd Blacon CH1 117 F3
  Widnes WA8 22 B4
Canterbury St WA4 16 B2
Cantley Cl WA7 49 E3
Canton Pl CH8 103 E4
Canton St SK11 112 B3
Canton Wlks SK11 112 B3
Canute Pl WA16 57 D1
Capeland Cl CH3 140 C3
Capenhurst Ave
  Crewe CW2 190 A2
  Warrington WA2 9 D1
Capenhurst CE Contr
  Prim Sch CH1 94 A4
Capenhurst Gdns L66 69 E1
Capenhurst Grange Sch L66 69 F1
Capenhurst La
  Capenhurst CH1 94 A4
  Ellesmere Port L65 70 A2
Capenhurst Sta CH1 69 A4
Capesthorne Cl Alsager ST7 193 E2
  Davenham CW9 103 F2
  Hazel Grove SK7 36 C4
  Holmes Chapel CW4 130 A2
  Sandbach CW11 175 E4
Capesthorne Hall SK11 110 A3
Capesthorne Rd
  Crewe CW2 189 F2
  Hazel Grove SK7 36 C4
  High Lane SK6 37 F4
  Warrington WA2 8 C1
  Wavertoin CH3 143 D3
  Wilmslow SK9 59 F3
Capethorne Way 🅧 SK11 112 C4
Capitol Wlk CW12 156 B1
Capper Cl ST7 195 D1
Capper's La Faddiley CW6 186 B2
  Spurstow CW6 186 B2
Cappers La CW11 176 B1
Carden Cl WA3 9 E2
Cardenbrook Gr 🅑 SK9 34 B1
Cardeston Cl WA7 49 F2
Cardiff Cl CH1 94 C4
Cardigan Cl
  Macclesfield SK11 112 A4
  Warrington WA5 7 E1
Carey St WA8 13 D1
Carisbrook Ave SK10 87 E1
Carisbrook Dr CW7 149 E4
Carisbrooke Cl CW2 205 F4
Carleton Rd SK12 37 E2
Carlett Bvd L62 43 F4
Carlett Park Coll of Tech
  L62 44 A4
Carlile St SK3 240 E4
Carlingford Cl SK3 240 E1
Carlingford Rd WA4 26 A4
Carlisle Cl Macclesfield SK11 112 A4
  Mobberley WA16 58 A2
  Romiley SK6 241 A1
  Winsford CW7 126 A1
Carlisle Dr WA14 238 E8
Carlisle Rd CH1 117 F3
Carlisle St Alderley Edge SK9 60 A1
  Crewe CW7 190 A1
  Warrington WA4 26 B4
Carlow Cl L24 21 E1
Carlton Ave Broughton CH4 140 B3
  Cheadle SK8 239 F3
  Cheadle Hulme SK7 35 E3
  Romiley SK6 241 D2
  Runcorn WA7 23 E1
  Wilmslow SK9 34 B1
Carlton Cl
  Mickle Trafford CH2 119 F4
  Neston L64 41 E1
Carlton Cres L66 69 F4
Carlton Dr M22 & SK8 239 A6
Carlton Pl CH2 119 D2
Carlton Rd Lymm WA13 19 D3
  Manchester SK4 240 A6
  Northwich CW9 104 A4
  Sale M33 242 A8
Carlton St Warrington WA4 26 B4
  Widnes WA8 23 D4
Carlton Way WA3 11 E3
Carlyle Cl ST7 193 F4
Carlyle Cres L66 69 F2
Carlyn Ave M33 242 D6
Carmarthen Cl
  Warrington WA5 7 E1
  Winsford CW7 149 E4
Carmel Cl CH1 117 E2
Carmel St WA8 13 D2
Carmel Mews SK4 240 A6
Carmenna Dr SK7 35 F4
Carmichael St M31 11 F2
Carmichael Cl M31 11 F2

Carnegie Cl SK10 8
Carnforth Dr M33 24
Carnoustie Cl SK9 6
Carnoustie Dr Gatley SK8 23
  Macclesfield SK10 8
Carnoustie Gr WA11
Carol Dr L60
Carol St WA4
Caroline St
  Ashton-u-L OL6 24
  Irlam M44
  Stalybridge SK15 24
  Stockport SK3 24
  Widnes WA8 24
Carpenter Gr WA2
Carr Brow SK6 3
Carr La Audley ST7 20
  Goldborne WA3
  Hale WA8, L24
  Lindow End SK9 5
  Widnes WA8, L24
Carr St ST7 19
Carr Wood Ave SK7 3
Carrgate Rd M34 24
Carrgreen La WA13
Carriage Dr Biddulph ST6 17
  Frodsham WA6
Carriages The WA14 23
Carrick Dr L65 7
Carrick Rd CH4 14
Carrington Way WA4
Carrington Way CW1 19
Carroll Dr CW2 20
Carrs Ave SK3 & SK8 24
Carrs Ct SK9 6
Carrs La CH3 16
Carrs Rd SK8 2
Carrwood Altrincham WA15 3
  Knutsford WA16 5
Carrwood Rd SK9 5
Carsdale Rd M22
Carter Ave CW6 17
Carter La CW11 17
Carter St Chester CH2 23
  Stalybridge SK15 24
Cartier Cl WA5 1
Cartledge Cl CW8 10
Cartmel Ave WA2
Cartmel Cl Gatley SK8 23
  Holmes Chapel CW4 13
  Macclesfield SK10 8
  Warrington WA5
  Winsford CW7 12
Cartmel Dr L66 6
Cartmell Cl WA7 4
Cartridge La WA4 2
Cartwright Rd CW1 19
Cartwright St Runcorn WA7 2
  Warrington WA3
Carver Cl WA7 12
Carver Rd WA11 24
Case Rd WA11
Casey La CW2 20
Cashmere Rd SK3 24
Caspian Rd WA14 23
Cassia Green La CW7 12
Cassley Rd L24 2
Casson St CW1 19
Castle Bank CW8 10
Castle Cl Broughton CH4 13
  Kelsall CW6 12
  Pulford CH4 16
Castle Croft Rd CH4 14
Castle Ct CW8 10
Castle Dr Chester CH4 23
  Ellesmere Port L65 7
  Heswall L60 4
Castle Gn WA5
Castle Hall Cl SK15 24
Castle Hall Ct SK15 24
Castle Hall View SK15 24
Castle Hill Newton-le-W WA12
  Prestbury SK10 8
  Pulford CH4 16
Castle Hill Ct SK10
Castle Inn Rd CW12 17
Castle Mill La WA15 3
Castle Prim Sch ST7 19
Castle Rd Kidsgrove ST7 19
  Runcorn WA7
Castle Rise Prestbury SK10 8
  Runcorn WA7 2
Castle St Chester CH4 23
  Crewe CW1 19
  Holt LL13 19
  Hyde SK14 24
  Macclesfield SK11 11
  Nantwich CW5
  Northwich CW8 10
  Stalybridge SK15 24
  Stockport SK3 24
  Stockport SK3 24
  Widnes WA8 11
Castle St Mall 🅧 SK11 11
Castle View Cty Prim Sch
  WA7
Castle Way Altrincham WA15 3
  Dodleston CH4
Castle Yard SK1 24
Castlefields Ave E WA7 16
Castlefields Ave N WA7 2
Castlefields Ave S WA7 2
Castleford Dr SK10 8
Castlegate SK10 8
Castlegate Mews SK10
Castlemead Wlk CW9 10
Castlemere Dr CW1 19

astleton Dr SK6 ...... 37 F3
astleton St WA14 ...... 238 C7
astletown Cl SK10 ...... 87 E2
astletown La CH3 ...... 197 E1
astleview Rd ST7 ...... 195 D2
atchpenny La SK11 ...... 108 C2
ateford Cl WA8 ...... 12 B1
atford Gn L24 ...... 21 D2
atfoss Cl WA7 ...... 8 C1
athcart Gn CH3 ...... 119 F3
athedral Church of Christ
& the Blessed Virgin Mary
CH1 ...... 237 E2
atherine Rd WA14 ...... 238 C3
atherine St Chester CH1 .. 118 A1
Crewe CW2 ...... 190 B1
Hyde SK14 ...... 241 D2
Macclesfield SK11 ...... 112 B4
Warrington WA5 ...... 15 F4
Warrington WA2 ...... 16 A4
Widnes WA8 ...... 23 D4
atherine Way WA12 ...... 2 A1
atterall Ave WA2 ...... 8 B1
aughall Rd CH2 ...... 95 F1
aunce Ave Goldborne WA3 .. 3 A4
Haydock WA11 ...... 1 A3
auseway Ave WA4 ...... 16 B2
auseway The 2 WA14 .. 238 D4
avalier Dr CH2 ...... 117 F3
avan Cl SK4 ...... 239 F7
avell Dr L65 ...... 70 A2
avendish Cl
Great Sankey WA5 ...... 15 E4
Macclesfield SK10 ...... 87 E2
8 Winsford CW7 ...... 149 D4
avendish Cres ST7 ...... 193 E3
avendish Farm Rd WA7 .. 49 D3
avendish Gdns L65 ...... 70 A2
avendish Mews SK9 ...... 60 A3
avendish Rd
Altrincham WA14 ...... 238 C3
Chester CH4 ...... 141 D3
Crewe CW2 ...... 189 F3
Hazel Grove SK7 ...... 36 C4
avendish Sch WA7 ...... 49 E3
avendish St 4 WA7 ...... 22 C1
aversham CH WA4 ...... 26 C3
awdor Dr CH3 ...... 119 D1
awdor St Runcorn WA7 .. 22 C2
Warrington WA4 ...... 26 B4
awfield Ave WA8 ...... 4 E2
awley Ave WA8 ...... 12 C1
awley St
7 Macclesfield SK11 .. 112 C4
Runcorn WA7 ...... 23 D1
awood Cl L66 ...... 69 E3
awthorne Ave WA4 ...... 17 D1
axton Cl Ellesmere Port L66 .. 69 F2
Widnes WA8 ...... 12 B2
ecil Rd WA15 ...... 238 E2
ecil Rigby Cl WA7 ...... 175 D3
ecil St Chester CH3 ...... 119 F1
Stalybridge SK15 ...... 242 E1
edab Rd L65 ...... 70 B3
edar Ave Alsager ST7 ...... 193 E2
Altrincham WA14 ...... 238 C4
Connah's Quay CH5 ...... 91 E1
Deeside Ind Est CH5 ...... 116 A4
Ellesmere Port L66 ...... 69 E3
Goldborne WA3 ...... 3 F4
Kidsgrove ST7 ...... 194 B1
Runcorn WA7 ...... 49 E4
Sutton WA7 ...... 50 A2
Widnes WA8 ...... 13 D1
edar Cl Holmes Chapel CW4 130 B2
Lostock CW9 ...... 80 A2
Middlewich CW10 ...... 151 F3
Poynton SK12 ...... 36 C2
Sandbach CW11 ...... 175 E3
edar Cres Audley ST7 ...... 209 F1
Newton-le-W WA12 ...... 2 B1
edar Ct Alsager ST7 ...... 193 F2
Congleton CW12 ...... 178 C4
Croft WA3 ...... 4 C1
Willaston (nr Nantwich)
CW5 ...... 205 E3
edar Dr Barnton CW8 ...... 78 A2
Chester CH2 ...... 119 D2
edar Gr Chester CH2 ...... 119 D2
Haydock WA11 ...... 1 C4
Macclesfield SK11 ...... 112 B3
Nantwich CW5 ...... 205 D3
Neston L64 ...... 66 C4
Warrington, Latchford WA4 .. 16 B2
Warrington, Paddington WA1 .. 17 D4
Winsford CW7 ...... 127 D1
edar Mews CH1 ...... 117 F2
edar Pk CH3 ...... 119 E1
edar Rd Altrincham WA15 .. 238 E2
Gatley SK8 ...... 239 A5
Great Sankey WA5 ...... 14 B4
Newcastle-u-L ST5 ...... 210 B1
Partington M31 ...... 11 F1
Widnes WA8 ...... 19 D2
edars The ST7 ...... 193 E2
edarway Heswall L60 ...... 41 D3
Wilmslow SK9 ...... 59 F3
edarways WA4 ...... 26 B3
edarwood CW6 ...... 101 E3
edarwood Ave SK4 ...... 240 A5
edarwood Cl CH4 ...... 146 B2
elandine Cl CH3 ...... 142 A4
elyn Cres CH4 ...... 140 B3

Cement Pl CH2 ...... 237 E3
Cemetery Rd CW2 ...... 207 D3
Cemlyn Cl CH1 ...... 117 F2
Central Ave
Ellesmere Port L65 ...... 70 B2
Warrington WA2 ...... 16 B4
Warrington, Latchford WA4 .. 16 A2
Central Dr Barnton CW8 ...... 78 A2
Cheadle SK8 ...... 34 B4
Nantwich CW5 ...... 204 C3
Romiley SK6 ...... 241 C3
Central Expressway WA7 ...... 49 F4
Central Gr CW7 ...... 104 B4
Central Rd Northwich CW9 .. 104 B4
Partington M31 ...... 11 F2
Central St ST7 ...... 195 D3
Central Trad Est CH4 ...... 140 C4
Central Way
Altrincham WA14 ...... 238 D4
Newton-le-W WA12 ...... 2 C1
Centre Ct ST7 ...... 193 F2
Centre Park Sq WA1 ...... 16 A2
Centurion Cl WA3 ...... 9 E2
Centurion Row WA7 ...... 23 F1
Century Park Ind Area
WA14 ...... 238 A6
Chadkirk Rd SK6 ...... 241 C3
Chads Gn CW5 ...... 206 A1
Chadvil Rd SK8 ...... 239 C5
Chadwick Ave Croft WA3 .. 9 D4
Warrington WA4 ...... 16 C1
Chadwick Ct SK9 ...... 34 B1
Chadwick Rd
Middlewich CW10 ...... 151 E3
Runcorn WA7 ...... 23 F2
Chadwick St
Ashton-u-L OL6 ...... 242 B2
8 Stockport SK1 ...... 240 F4
Chadwick Terr SK10 ...... 87 F1
Chaffinch Cl
Congleton CW12 ...... 156 C1
Warrington WA3 ...... 9 F2
Chaffinch Way CW7 ...... 149 E3
Chaigley Rd WA4 ...... 17 F2
Chain Maker's Row CH4 .. 140 C4
Chalfield Ave L60 ...... 69 E3
Chalfield Cl
Ellesmere Port L66 ...... 69 E3
Wistaston CW2 ...... 206 A4
Chalfont Cl WA4 ...... 26 C3
Chalgrave Cl WA8 ...... 13 F2
Chalkwell Dr L60 ...... 41 E4
Challinor St CH3 ...... 119 D1
Chalmondeley Rd CW5 .. 216 A3
Chamber Brook La WA6 .. 75 E1
Chambers St CW7 ...... 190 B1
Chance Hall La
Astbury CW12 ...... 177 E2
Scholar Green CW12 ...... 177 E2
Chancel La WA5 ...... 60 A4
Chancery La Alsager ST7 .. 193 D2
Bollington SK10 ...... 88 A4
Chandley St SK8 ...... 239 D6
Chandos Cl CH4 ...... 141 F3
Change La L64 ...... 66 C4
Channel The CH1 ...... 95 D2
Chantler Ave WA4 ...... 16 C2
Chantry Ave CH8 ...... 103 D2
Chantry Cl SK12 ...... 38 C3
Chantry Ct Blacon CH1 ...... 117 F1
Crewe CW1 ...... 190 B2
Macclesfield SK11 ...... 112 B3
Chantry Fold SK12 ...... 38 C3
Chantry Rd SK12 ...... 38 B3
Chantry The CW6 ...... 169 F1
Chantry Wlk L60 ...... 41 D3
Chapel Ave WA6 ...... 75 E1
Chapel Bank ST7 ...... 195 E3
Chapel Cl Audlem CW3 .. 229 F2
Cholmondeston CW7 ...... 170 C2
Comberbach CW9 ...... 78 B4
Ellesmere Port L65 ...... 70 B2
Mount Pleasant ST7 ...... 195 D3
Saughall CH1 ...... 94 A1
Waverton CH3 ...... 143 D3
Chapel Cross Rd WA2 ...... 9 D1
Chapel Ct Altrincham WA14 238 D4
Chelford SK11 ...... 84 A2
Hyde SK14 ...... 241 C5
Northwich CW9 ...... 103 F4
Chapel Dr WA15 ...... 32 B4
Chapel Gn SK10 ...... 63 F4
Chapel House La L64 ...... 93 D4
Chapel La Acton Bridge CW8 .. 76 C2
Alford CH3 ...... 164 B3
Allostock WA16 ...... 106 C2
Altrincham WA15 ...... 32 B4
Appleton WA4 ...... 27 D2
Audley ST7 ...... 209 E1
Burtonwood WA5 ...... 6 C3
Chester CH3 ...... 119 D1
Crewe CW1 ...... 173 E1
Cronton WA8 ...... 12 C4
Duddon WA6 ...... 100 A2
Hollins Green WA3 ...... 10 C1
Holt LL13 ...... 196 B4
Kingsley WA6 ...... 75 E1
Manley WA6 ...... 98 C2
Mere WA16 ...... 30 A2
Milton Green CH3 ...... 165 D1
Moulton CW9 ...... 126 C4
Norton in Hales TF9 ...... 236 B1
Partington M31 ...... 11 F1
Rainow SK10 ...... 88 C3
Ravensmoor CW5 ...... 203 E1
Rode Heath ST7 ...... 193 F4

Chapel La continued
Threapwood SY14 ...... 222 C4
Warrington WA4 ...... 26 B4
Wilmslow SK9 ...... 60 A3
Withington SK11 ...... 109 E1
Chapel Mews
Ellesmere Port L65 ...... 70 A2
Nantwich CW5 ...... 204 C3
Chapel Rd Alderley Edge SK9 .. 60 A1
Ollerton WA16 ...... 82 C3
Penketh WA5 ...... 14 C2
Saighton CH3 ...... 164 B3
Sale M33 ...... 242 B7
Whaley Bridge SK23 ...... 65 F3
Winsford CW7 ...... 126 C1
Chapel Row Barbridge CW5 187 E3
Northwich CW9 ...... 204 B3
Chapel St Alderley Edge SK9 .. 60 A1
Audley ST7 ...... 209 F2
Bollington SK10 ...... 88 A4
Cheadle SK8 ...... 239 D5
Chester CH2 ...... 237 F3
Congleton CW12 ...... 156 B1
Crewe CW2 ...... 190 B2
Haydock WA11 ...... 1 C3
Higher Wincham CW9 ...... 79 E2
Holt LL13 ...... 196 B4
Hyde SK14 ...... 241 D6
Kidsgrove ST7 ...... 194 B1
Macclesfield SK11 ...... 112 B3
Moulton CW9 ...... 126 C4
Mount Pleasant ST7 ...... 195 D3
New Mills SK22 ...... 39 D3
Newton-le-W WA12 ...... 2 A2
Northwich CW9 ...... 103 F4
Sandbach CW11 ...... 175 D3
Sandbach, Wheelock CW11 .. 175 D3
Stalybridge SK15 ...... 242 D2
Weaverham CW8 ...... 77 E1
Whaley Bridge SK23 ...... 65 F4
Widnes WA8 ...... 23 D4
Chapel Wlks
Cheadle Hulme SK8 ...... 35 D3
Lymm WA13 ...... 19 D3
Chapel Yd WA2 ...... 16 A3
Chapelfields WA6 ...... 74 A4
Chapelmere Cl CW11 ...... 174 C4
Chapelmere Ct CW1 ...... 190 B4
Chapman Cl WA8 ...... 12 B2
Charcoal Rd WA14 ...... 31 F2
Charcoal Woods WA14 ...238 A3
Charity La SK11 ...... 114 A3
Charlcote Cres CW2 ...... 206 B4
Charlecote Rd SK12 ...... 36 C2
Charles Ave Davenham CW9 103 F2
Great Sankey WA5 ...... 14 B4
Charles Cres CH4 ...... 237 F1
Charles Price Gdns L65 .. 70 B3
Charles Rd CH2 ...... 95 E1
Charles Sq CW11 ...... 175 F1
Charles St Chester CH2 ...... 237 E3
Chester, Hoole Pk CH2 ...... 118 C2
Crewe CW1 ...... 190 B2
Irlam M44 ...... 11 F3
Widnes WA8 ...... 23 D4
Charlesworth Cres SK23 .. 39 E2
Charlesworth Ct 2 WA11 . 175 E3
Charlesworth Rd SK23 ...... 39 E2
Charlesworth St
8 Stockport SK1 ...... 240 F3
Charlock Sq WA14 ...... 238 B8
Charlook Wlk M31 ...... 11 F1
Charlotte Ct CH1 ...... 237 E3
Charlotte St Cheadle SK8 .. 239 D5
Chester CH1 ...... 118 A1
Macclesfield SK11 ...... 112 B4
Charlotte St W 14 SK11 ... 112 B4
Charlotte Wlk 16 WA8 ...... 23 D4
Charlton Cl WA7 ...... 50 A4
Charlton Dr M33 ...... 242 C6
Charlton St
Macclesfield SK11 ...... 112 B4
Warrington WA4 ...... 16 C2
Charminster Cl WA5 ...... 15 D3
Charnock Ave WA12 ...... 1 C2
Charnock Rd WA3 ...... 4 C2
Charnwood ST7 ...... 195 D1
Charnwood Cl
Macclesfield SK10 ...... 87 D1
Warrington WA3 ...... 10 A3
Charnwood Cres SK7 ...... 36 B4
Charter Ave WA2 ...... 8 A4
Charter Cres L66 ...... 69 F2
Charter Rd
Altrincham WA15 ...... 238 E4
Bollington SK10 ...... 88 A4
Charter Way SK10 ...... 87 F2
Charterhall Dr CH2 ...... 118 C1
Chartwell Pk CW11 ...... 175 D2
Chase Dr L66 ...... 69 F1
Chase The L63 ...... 43 E3
Chase Way L66 ...... 69 F1
Chasefield WA14 ...... 238 A3
Chaser Ct CH1 ...... 117 F2
Chasewater CW7 ...... 126 C2
Chatburn Ct WA3 ...... 4 C1
Chatfield Dr WA3 ...... 9 F2
Chatham St
15 Macclesfield SK11 .. 112 B4
Stockport SK3 ...... 240 D4
Warrington WA1 ...... 191 E3
Chatswood Ave SK2 ...... 240 C4
Chatsworth Ave
Culcheth WA3 ...... 4 C2
Macclesfield SK11 ...... 111 F3

Chatsworth Cl
Ellesmere Port L66 ...... 69 E3
Wistaston CW2 ...... 206 C4
Chatsworth Dr Chester CH2 119 D3
Congleton CW12 ...... 156 A2
Widnes WA8 ...... 12 B2
Chatsworth Rd
Hazel Grove SK7 ...... 36 C4
High Lane SK6 ...... 37 F3
Wilmslow SK9 ...... 59 F2
Chatteris Rd WA7 ...... 24 B1
Chatterton Dr WA7 ...... 50 C4
Chatwell Gdns WA4 ...... 26 C3
Chaucer Cl CH1 ...... 117 F3
Chaucer Pl WA4 ...... 16 C2
Chaucer St WA7 ...... 23 D1
Cheadle
SK8 ...... 34 B4
Cheadle Heath Jun & Inf
Sch SK3 ...... 240 A3
Cheadle Hulme High Sch
SK8 ...... 35 D4
Cheadle Hulme Sch SK8 .. 35 D4
Cheadle La Peover WA16 .. 106 A4
Cheadle Old Rd SK3 ...... 240 C3
Cheadle Prep Sch SK8 ...... 34 B4
Cheadle Prim Sch SK8 .. 239 D6
Cheadle RC Inf Sch SK8 . 239 E2
Cheadle RC Jun Sch SK8 . 239 E2
Cheadle Rd SK8 ...... 239 F3
Cheadle Royal Hospl SK8 . 239 C2
Cheam Rd WA15 ...... 238 F8
Cheapside SK14 ...... 241 E7
Checkley Dr ST6 ...... 179 E1
Checkley La CW3 ...... 221 F1
Checkley Rd ST5 ...... 210 B1
Chedlee Dr SK8 ...... 34 C4
Chedworth Dr WA8 ...... 12 B2
Cheerbrook Rd CW5 ...... 205 F2
Cheese Hill La CW7 ...... 101 D2
Chelford Ave WA3 ...... 3 E4
Chelford Cl
Altrincham WA15 ...... 238 E6
Blacon CH1 ...... 117 F1
Chelford Ct 2 SK8 ...... 34 C3
Chelford Gr SK3 ...... 240 D1
Chelford La WA16 ...... 83 E1
Chelford Rd
Chelford SK10, SK11 ...... 84 B1
Chelford, Marthall WA16 .. 83 E2
Henbury SK10 ...... 110 C4
Macclesfield SK11 ...... 111 E4
Nether Alderley SK9 ...... 84 B4
Nether Alderley, Monks Heath
SK9 ...... 85 D1
Prestbury SK10 ...... 86 B3
Radnor CW12 ...... 155 F3
Wilmslow SK9 ...... 34 B3
Chelford Sta SK11 ...... 84 A1
Chell Cl WA3 ...... 190 A3
Chells Hill CW11 ...... 176 B1
Chelmsford Rd SK3 ...... 240 C4
Chelsea Cl ST6 ...... 179 E1
Chelston Dr WA9 ...... 34 B3
Cheltenham Cl WA5 ...... 15 D4
Cheltenham Cres
Crewe CW1 ...... 190 A4
Runcorn WA7 ...... 49 D3
Cheltenham Dr M33 ...... 242 C6
Cheltenham Rd
Blessed SK3 ...... 240 A3
Ellesmere Port L65 ...... 70 B2
Chemical St WA12 ...... 2 A2
Cheney Wlk CW2 ...... 206 B4
Chepstow Cl Biddulph ST6 .. 179 E1
Winsford CW7 ...... 149 E4
Cherington Cl SK9 ...... 34 C2
Cherington Cres SK11 ...... 112 A4
Cherington Rd SK8 ...... 239 C4
Cherinton Ave M33 ...... 242 C7
Cheriton Way CW2 ...... 206 A4
Cherry Bank CW5 ...... 204 C2
Cherry Bank Gdns CW6 .. 184 C3
Cherry Blossom Rd WA7 .. 49 F2
Cherry Cl Newcastle-u-L ST5 210 B1
Newton-le-W WA12 ...... 1 C2
Willaston L64 ...... 67 E4
Cherry Cnr WA13 ...... 28 A4
Cherry Cres L66 ...... 149 E4
Cherry Ct M33 ...... 242 A6
Cherry Dale Rd CH4 ...... 139 D2
Cherry Gr
Ellesmere Port L66 ...... 70 A1
Nantwich CW5 ...... 204 B3
Cherry Grove Cty Prim
Sch CH3 ...... 119 D1
Cherry Grove Rd CH3 ...... 119 D1
Cherry La Congleton CW12 .. 179 F4
Cuddington CW8 ...... 101 F1
Lawton Heath ST7 ...... 193 F3
Lymm WA13 ...... 28 A4
Weaverham CW8 ...... 102 B4
Cherry Rd CH3 ...... 119 D1
Cherry Tree Ave
Barnton CW8 ...... 78 A2
Lawton-gate ST7 ...... 194 A3
Lymm WA13 ...... 18 B1
Penketh WA5 ...... 14 C2
Poynton SK12 ...... 36 C2
Runcorn WA7 ...... 49 E4
Cherry Tree Cl Hale L24 .. 21 F1
Haydock WA11 ...... 1 A3
Poynton SK12 ...... 36 C2
Wilmslow SK9 ...... 60 C4

Cherry Tree Inf Sch SK6 .. 241 E3
Cherry Tree Jun Sch SK6 .. 241 E2
Cherry Tree La
Romiley SK6 ...... 241 E3
Woore CW3 ...... 232 B1
Cherry Tree Rd Audley ST7 . 209 F1
Crewe CW1 ...... 190 C3
Goldborne WA3 ...... 3 F4
Newcastle-u-L ST5 ...... 210 C1
Cherry Wlk
Cheadle Hulme SK7 ...... 35 E4
Partington M31 ...... 11 E1
Peover WA16 ...... 106 B4
Cherrycroft SK6 ...... 241 E1
Cherryfields Rd SK11 ...... 111 F4
Cherrysutton WA8 ...... 12 A2
Cherrywood Cres CW8 ...... 78 A2
Cherwell Cl
Cheadle Hulme SK8 ...... 35 D4
Warrington WA2 ...... 8 B1
Cheryl Ct CW8 ...... 102 A2
Cheryl Dr WA8 ...... 13 E1
Chesford Grange WA1 ...... 17 F4
Chesham Cl SK9 ...... 59 F2
Chesham Pl WA14 ...... 238 C2
Chesham Rd SK9 ...... 59 F2
Cheshire Cl WA12 ...... 2 C2
Cheshire Oaks Outlet
Village L65 ...... 70 C1
Cheshire St CW3 ...... 229 F2
Cheshire View SK10 ...... 88 A3
Cheshire Workshops CH3 . 184 B3
Cheshyre Dr WA7 ...... 23 F1
Cheshyre's La WA7 ...... 48 C4
Chessington La WA4 ...... 26 C3
Chest Nut Cl CW6 ...... 146 B1
Chester Aerospace Pk
CH4 ...... 139 D3
Chester Ave
Altrincham WA15 ...... 238 F2
Goldborne WA3 ...... 3 E4
Chester Bsns Pk CH4 ...... 141 D2
Chester Catholic (Voluntary
Aided) High Sch CH4 ..141 E3
Chester Cl Irlam M44 ...... 11 E3
Kidsgrove ST7 ...... 210 C4
Runcorn WA7 ...... 24 A1
14 Wilmslow SK9 ...... 34 C1
Chester Gates CH1 ...... 94 B3
Chester General Sta CH2 . 237 F3
Chester High Rd L64 ...... 67 E4
Chester La CW7 ...... 125 E1
Chester New Rd WA4 ...... 25 F4
Chester Rd Acton CW5 ...... 204 A3
Audley ST7 ...... 209 E1
Barbridge CW5 ...... 187 E3
Broughton CH4 ...... 139 E3
Churton CH3 ...... 180 C3
Daresbury WA4 ...... 25 D1
Delamere CW6, CW8 ...... 123 E3
Ellesmere Port L65 ...... 70 A1
Ellesmere Port, Great Sutton
L66 ...... 69 E2
Flint CH6 ...... 91 D2
Frodsham WA6 ...... 74 A4
Gatesheath CH3 ...... 165 F3
Hartford CW8 ...... 102 C2
Hartford, Greenbank CW8 .. 103 D3
Hawarden CH5 ...... 116 A1
Hazel Grove SK7 ...... 36 B4
Heswall L60 ...... 41 E3
Higher Walton WA4 ...... 25 E3
Holmes Chapel CW4 ...... 130 A1
Huntington CH3 ...... 142 A3
Kelsall CW6 ...... 122 B3
Kidsgrove ST7 ...... 210 B4
Knutsford WA16 ...... 56 A3
Lavister LL12 ...... 162 B1
Macclesfield SK11 ...... 112 A4
Mere WA16 ...... 56 A3
Middlewich CW10 ...... 128 A1
Neston L64 ...... 66 B4
Northwich CW8 ...... 103 E3
Oakmere CW8 ...... 124 A4
Plumley WA16 ...... 80 C3
Poynton SK12 ...... 36 B2
Rostherne WA16 ...... 30 B3
Runcorn WA7 ...... 50 D2
Sutton WA7 ...... 50 A2
Tabley WA16 ...... 56 A1
Tattenhall CH3 ...... 166 A1
Warrington WA4 ...... 17 D1
Weaverham CW8 ...... 102 B3
Whitchurch SY13 ...... 225 E1
Winsford CW7 ...... 125 F1
Woodford SK12 ...... 36 B2
Chester Retail Pk CH1 ...... 118 A2
Chester Row WA12 ...... 7 F4
Chester Royal Infmy CH1 . 237 D3
Chester Sq CW1 ...... 190 B2
Chester St Chester CH4 ...... 140 C4
Crewe CW1 ...... 190 B2
Stockport SK3 ...... 240 D5
Warrington WA1 ...... 16 A4
Widnes WA8 ...... 13 D1
Chester Way CW9 ...... 104 A4
Chester West Employment
Pk CH1 ...... 117 F1
Chester Wlks SK6 ...... 241 A1
Chester Zoological Gdns
CH2 ...... 95 F1
Chesterfield Cl CW7 ...... 125 F1
Chesterfield Gr OL6 ...... 242 A3
Chesterfield Rd L62 ...... 43 E2

Chestergate
Macclesfield SK11 .... 112 B4
Stockport SK3 .... 240 E5
Chestergate Mall 24 SK11 .. 112 B4
Chesterton Cl CW10 .... 151 F3
Chesterton Dr CW2 .... 189 F1
Chesterton Rd 10 CW1 ...... 174 B3
Chestnut Ave Cheadle SK8 .. 239 E5
   Ellesmere Port L66 .... 69 F1
   Great Sankey WA5 .... 14 B4
   Irlam M44 .... 11 E3
   Macclesfield SK10 .... 87 F1
   Rode Heath ST7 .... 193 F4
   Shavington CW2 .... 206 B3
   Widnes WA8 .... 13 D1
Chestnut Cl Chester CH2 .... 119 D2
   Cuddington CW8 .... 101 F1
   Middlewich CW10 .... 128 A1
   Tarporley CW6 .... 146 B1
   Wilmslow SK9 .... 60 C4
Chestnut Ct CW6 .... 146 B1
Chestnut Dr
   Congleton CW12 .... 156 A2
   Holmes Chapel CW4 .... 130 B2
   Poynton SK12 .... 36 C2
Chestnut Gr Barnton CW8 .... 78 A2
   Bebington L62 .... 43 E4
   Crewe CW1 .... 190 C3
   Goldborne WA3 .... 3 F4
   Newcastle-u-L ST5 .... 210 C1
   Winsford CW7 .... 149 E4
Chestnut La WA6 .... 73 F2
Chestnut Lodge Sch WA8 .... 12 C1
Chestnut Villas SK4 .... 240 C6
Chestnut Wlk M31 .... 11 E1
Chesworth Fold SK1 .... 240 F4
Chetham Ct WA2 .... 8 A2
Chetton Dr WA7 .... 50 C4
Chetwode Mews WA4 .... 52 B1
Chetwode St CW1 .... 190 B3
Chetwood Dr WA8 .... 12 C2
Cheveley Cl SK10 .... 87 E1
Chevin Gdns SK7 .... 36 A4
Cheviot Ave Cheadle SK8 .... 239 F2
   Warrington WA2 .... 8 A2
Cheviot Cl
   Ellesmere Port L66 .... 69 D3
   Stockport SK4 .... 240 D7
Cheviot Cl CW7 .... 149 D4
Chevithorne Cl WA14 .... 238 B5
Chevron Cl CH1 .... 117 F2
Chevron Hey CH1 .... 117 F2
Chevron Pl WA14 .... 238 D7
Cheyne Wlk CW5 .... 204 C2
Cheyney Rd Blacon CH1 .... 118 A2
   Chester CH1 .... 118 A2
Chicago Ave M90 .... 33 D4
Chichester Cl WA7 .... 50 B4
Chichester Rd SK6 .... 241 C2
Chichester St CH1 .... 237 D3
Chidlow Cl
   Hough Common CW2 .... 206 C2
   Widnes WA8 .... 23 D3
Child's La CW12 .... 177 F3
Childer Cres L66 .... 69 D4
Childer Gdns L66 .... 69 C4
Childer Thornton Cty Prim
   Sch L66 .... 69 D4
Childwall Ct L66 .... 69 F4
Childwall Gdns L66 .... 69 F4
Childwall Rd L66 .... 69 F4
Chilham Cl CW7 .... 149 E4
Chilham Pl SK11 .... 111 F3
Chilington Ave WA8 .... 22 B4
Chillingham Cl CW10 .... 128 B1
Chiltern Ave Cheadle SK8 .. 239 F2
   Macclesfield SK11 .... 112 A4
   Warrington WA2 .... 8 A2
Chiltern Cl Chester CH4 .... 141 D3
   Cuddington CW8 .... 102 A1
Chiltern Cres WA2 .... 8 A2
Chiltern Dr WA5 .... 238 F2
Chiltern Pl WA2 .... 8 A2
Chiltern Rd Culcheth WA3 .... 4 C2
   St Helens WA9 .... 1 A2
   Warrington WA2 .... 8 A2
Chiltern Way CW7 .... 149 D4
Chilton Dr L66 .... 69 D3
Chilworth Cl CW2 .... 206 B1
China La WA4 .... 16 B1
Chines The CW8 .... 101 E3
Chinley Cl Manchester SK4 .. 240 F7
   Sale M33 .... 242 D5
Chippingdall Cl WA5 .... 15 E3
Chipstead Cl CW8 .... 103 D2
Chirk Cl CH2 .... 118 C3
Chirk Pl CW7 .... 126 A1
Chirton Cl WA11 .... 1 B4
Chisledon Cl WA11 .... 4 A4
Chiswick Cl WA7 .... 50 B4
Chiswick Gdns WA4 .... 26 C3
Chokeberry Cl WA14 .... 238 B8
Chollerton Cl WA16 .... 29 E2
Cholmondeley Ave WA4 .... 238 E8
Cholmondeley Castle
   Gdns SY14 .... 200 C4
Cholmondeley La SY14 .... 200 C4
Cholmondeley Rd
   Ellesmere Port L65 .... 69 F1
   Hampton SY14 .... 213 F4
   Runcorn WA7 .... 49 E2
Cholmondeley St WA8 .... 23 D2
Cholmondely St SK11 ...... 112 B3
Chomlea WA14 .... 238 B4
Chorley Hall Cl SK9 .... 59 F1

Chorley Hall La
   Alderley Edge SK9 .... 60 A1
   Chorley CW5 .... 202 B1
Chorley St WA2 .... 16 A3
Chorley's La WA8 .... 13 F2
Chorlton Cl WA7 .... 24 B1
Chorlton Dr SK8 .... 239 E6
Chorlton La CW2 .... 207 D1
Chowley Oak La CH3 .... 182 C3
Chrimes Dr CW8 .... 103 E3
Christ Church CE Aided
   Prim Sch L65 .... 70 A1
Christ The King RC Prim
   Sch L62 .... 43 F4
Christchurch Ave CW2 ...... 190 A1
Christie Cl L66 .... 44 A1
Christie St WA8 .... 13 E1
Christleton Ave CW2 .... 189 E3
Christleton Ct WA7 .... 24 B2
Christleton Cty High Sch
   CH3 .... 142 C4
Christleton Cty Prim Sch
   CH3 .... 142 C4
Christleton Dr L66 .... 69 F3
Christleton Rd CH3 .... 119 D1
Christleton Sports Ctr
   CH3 .... 142 C4
Christleton Way 11 SK9 .... 34 B3
Christopher Dr L62 .... 44 A3
Chudleigh Cl WA14 .... 238 B6
Church Ave SK9 .... 34 A1
Church Bank Audlem ST7 .. 209 E1
   Tattenhall CH3 .... 166 A1
Church Bk SK23 .... 65 E4
Church Brow
   Altrincham WA14 .... 238 B2
   Hyde SK14 .... 241 D5
Church Cl CW8 .... 77 E1
Church College Cl CH1 .... 118 A2
Church Coppenhall Cty
   Jun Sch CW1 .... 190 A3
Church Croft CH4 .... 162 A3
Church Ct Altrincham WA15 . 238 D1
   Ashton CH3 .... 121 F4
   Farndon CH3 .... 180 C1
Church Dr WA2 .... 9 D1
Church End L24 .... 21 E1
Church Farm Ct Heswall L60 40 C4
   Willaston L64 .... 67 F4
Church Fields TF9 .... 236 B1
Church Gn WA13 .... 19 D4
Church Hall Cl CH1 .... 117 F2
Church Hill WA16 .... 57 D1
Church La Aldford CH3 ...... 163 F2
   Appleton WA4 .... 17 D1
   Backford CH1 .... 95 D2
   Bebington L62 .... 44 A2
   Chester CH2 .... 118 B4
   Culcheth WA3 .... 4 C2
   Eaton CW12 .... 134 C1
   Ellesmere Port L66 .... 69 E2
   Elton WA6 .... 72 B1
   Farndon CH3 .... 180 C1
   Goldborne WA3 .... 3 F4
   Guilden Sutton CH3 .... 119 F3
   Henbury SK11 .... 111 E4
   Kidsgrove ST7 .... 195 F4
   Mobberley WA16 .... 58 B3
   Nantwich CW5 .... 204 C3
   Neston L64 .... 66 C4
   New Mills SK22 .... 39 E4
   Rainow SK10 .... 88 C3
   Romiley SK6 .... 241 C2
   Sandbach CW11 .... 175 F4
   Scholar Green ST7 .... 194 B4
   Smallwood CW11 .... 176 C2
   Stoak CH2 .... 96 A4
   Sutton Lane Ends SK11 .... 112 C2
   Warren SK11 .... 134 B4
   Weaverham CW8 .... 77 E1
   Wistaston CW2 .... 205 F4
   Woodford SK7 .... 35 E1
Church Lawton Gate Cty
   Prim Sch ST7 .... 194 A3
Church Manor SK4 .... 240 B8
Church Mead CH3 .... 181 D3
Church Meadow
   Hyde SK14 .... 241 C7
   Norton in Hales TF9 .... 236 B1
Church Meadow Gdns
   SK14 .... 241 C7
Church Meadow La L60 .... 40 C4
Church Meadows
   Little Leigh CW8 .... 77 E3
   Whitchurch SY13 .... 226 A1
Church Mews
   Bollington SK10 .... 88 A4
   Knutsford WA16 .... 57 D1
Church Par L65 .... 70 B3
Church Rd Alsager ST7 ...... 193 E2
   Ashton CH3 .... 121 F4
   Barnton CW8 .... 78 A1
   Broughton CH4 .... 139 E2
   Burwardsley CH3 .... 184 A3
   Cheadle Hulme SK8 .... 35 D4
   Eccleston CH4 .... 141 F1
   Frodsham WA6 .... 74 B4
   Gatley M22 & SK8 .... 239 A5
   Hale L24 .... 47 F4
   Halewood L26 .... 21 D4
   Haydock WA11 .... 1 C4
   Little Leigh CW8 .... 77 E2
   Lymm WA13 .... 18 E1
   New Mills SK22 .... 39 E4
   Northwich CW8, CW9 ...... 103 F1
   Sale M33 .... 242 D6
   Saughall CH1 .... 94 A1
   Shocklach CH3 .... 197 E1

Church Rd continued
   Stockport SK4 .... 240 E6
   Thornton Hough L63 .... 42 A3
   Tilston SY14 .... 198 A2
   Wilmslow, Davenport Green
   SK9 .... 59 F2
   Wilmslow, Handforth SK9 .. 34 B2
   Worleston CW5 .... 188 B3
Church Rd E M33 .... 242 D6
Church Rd W M33 .... 242 D6
Church St Altrincham WA14 238 D5
   Audley ST7 .... 210 A1
   Bollington SK10 .... 88 A4
   Cheadle SK8 .... 239 D6
   Chester CH1 .... 237 E4
   Connah's Quay CH5 .... 91 E1
   Davenham CW9 .... 104 A2
   Ellesmere Port L65 .... 70 B3
   Farndon CH3 .... 180 C1
   Frodsham WA6 .... 74 A4
   Great Budworth CW9 .... 79 D4
   Higher Wincham CW9 ...... 79 F3
   Holt LL13 .... 180 C1
   Hyde SK14 .... 241 D5
   Kelsall CW6 .... 122 B2
   Kidsgrove, Butt Lane ST7 ... 194 B1
   Kidsgrove, The Rookery ST7 195 D2
   Macclesfield SK11 .... 112 B4
   Malpas SY14 .... 213 D2
   Moulton CW9 .... 126 C4
   Mount Pleasant ST7 .... 195 E3
   Newton-le-W WA12 .... 2 C2
   Runcorn WA7 .... 23 D2
   Sandbach CW11 .... 175 E3
   Stalybridge SK15 .... 242 D2
   Stockport SK4 .... 240 E7
   Tarvin CH3 .... 121 E1
   Warrington WA1 .... 16 B3
   Weaverham CW8 .... 77 E1
   Widnes WA8 .... 23 D3
   Wilmslow SK9 .... 60 A4
   Winsford CW7 .... 126 C1
Church St N CW6 .... 122 B3
Church St W SK11 .... 112 B4
Church Terr 10 SK9 .... 34 B2
Church View Audlem CW3 . 230 A2
   Hyde SK14 .... 241 D5
   Kingsley WA6 .... 75 D1
   Knutsford WA16 .... 57 D1
   Lower Peover WA16 .... 81 F1
   Northwich CW9 .... 104 A4
   Stalybridge SK15 .... 242 D3
   Wilmslow SK9 .... 59 F3
Church Wlks CH3 .... 142 C4
Church Wood View WA13 .. 18 C2
Church Way Blacon CH1 .... 117 F3
   Wybunbury CW5 .... 220 A4
Church Wk WA7 .... 50 A4
Church Wlk
   Holmes Chapel CW4 .... 130 B2
   Knutsford WA16 .... 57 D1
   Lower Peover WA16 .... 81 F1
   Northwich CW9 .... 104 A4
   Stalybridge SK15 .... 242 D3
   Wilmslow SK9 .... 59 F3
Church's Mansions CW5 .. 204 C2
Churchfield Rd WA6 .... 74 B4
Churchfields
   Altrincham WA14 .... 238 B1
   Audlem CW3 .... 230 A2
   Barnton CW8 .... 78 A2
   Croft WA3 .... 9 D4
   Cuddington CW8 .... 102 A1
   Helsby WA6 .... 73 E2
   Knutsford WA16 .... 57 E1
   Widnes WA8 .... 13 D3
   Wybunbury CW5 .... 220 A4
Churchgate SK1 .... 240 F5
Churchill Ave WA3 .... 5 D2
Churchill Cl CW12 .... 156 A2
Churchill Dr CW6 .... 146 B1
Churchill Parkway CW7 .... 149 E4
Churchill Rd WA14 .... 238 D7
Churchill St SK4 .... 240 D7
Churchill Way
   Macclesfield SK11 .... 112 B4
   Neston L64 .... 66 C4
Churchley Cl SK3 .... 240 A2
Churchley Rd SK3 .... 240 A3
Churchmere Cl CW1 .... 190 B4
Churchside SK11 .... 112 B4
Churchside Wlk CH4 .... 140 C4
Churchward Cl CH1 .... 118 B2
Churchway Alvanley WA6 .. 73 E1
   Macclesfield SK10 .... 86 C1
Churchway Rd L24 .... 21 D1
Churchyard Side CW5 .... 204 C3
Churton Cl Davenham CW9 . 103 F2
   Hough Common CW2 ...... 206 C2
Churton Rd Chester CH3 .. 119 D1
   Farndon CH3 .... 180 C1
Churton St CH3 .... 119 D1
Cicely Mill La WA16 .... 30 B2
Cinder Cl CH3 .... 119 F3
Cinder Hill CW7 .... 125 F3
Cinder Hill La ST7 .... 194 C4
Cinder La Appleton WA4 .... 17 F1
   Guilden Sutton CH3 .... 119 F3
   Lostock CW9 .... 105 D4
   Peover WA16 .... 108 B4
   Worleston CW5 .... 188 B1
Cinnamon Brow WA2 .... 8 C2
Cinnamon Brow CE Aided
   Prim Sch WA2 .... 8 C2
Cinnamon La WA2 .... 8 C2
Cinnamon La N WA2 .... 8 C2
Circle Ave CW5 .... 205 F3

Circle The Crewe CW2 ...... 190 B1
   Mere WA16 .... 30 B1
Circuit The
   Alderley Edge SK9 .... 60 A2
   Cheadle, Handforth Green
   SK8 .... 34 B4
   Stockport SK3 .... 240 C2
   Wilmslow SK9 .... 59 E3
Circular Dr CH4 .... 140 C2
City Bank ST6 .... 179 E1
City Rd CW2 .... 237 F3
City Walls Rd CH1 .... 237 D2
Civic Way Ellesmere Port L65 .. 70 A2
   Middlewich CW10 .... 128 B1
Clair Ave CH5 .... 116 A2
Claire Pl CW7 .... 149 E4
Clamhunger La WA16 ...... 56 A4
Clamley Ct L24 .... 21 D2
Clap Gate Cres WA8 .... 22 A3
Clap Gates Cres WA5 .... 15 F4
Clap Gate Rd WA5 .... 15 F4
Clare Ave Chester CH2 .... 119 D2
   Wilmslow SK9 .... 34 B2
Clare Dr Ellesmere Port L65 .. 70 A1
   Macclesfield SK10 .... 87 E2
   Wistaston CW2 .... 189 F1
Clare Rd SK5 .... 240 F8
Clare St Kidsgrove ST7 .... 195 F2
   Mount Pleasant ST7 .... 195 E3
Claremont Ave
   Altrincham WA14 .... 238 E8
   Widnes WA8 .... 13 E2
Claremont Cl CW9 .... 103 F2
Claremont Dr
   Altrincham WA14 .... 238 E8
   Widnes WA8 .... 13 D2
Claremont Gr WA15 .... 238 E3
Claremont Rd
   Cheadle Hulme SK8 .... 35 D4
   Crewe CW2 .... 190 A1
   Culcheth WA3 .... 4 B2
   Runcorn WA7 .... 23 D3
   Sale M33 .... 242 B7
Claremount CT OL6 .... 242 B4
Clarence Ave Chester CH3 . 119 D1
   Widnes WA8 .... 13 D2
Clarence Cl SK9 .... 60 A3
Clarence Gr CW1 .... 190 A3
Clarence Rd
   Altrincham WA15 .... 238 F3
   Bollington SK10 .... 63 D1
   Warrington WA4 .... 17 D1
Clarence St Hyde SK14 .... 241 E8
   Newton-le-W WA12 .... 1 C2
   Runcorn WA7 .... 22 C2
Stalybridge
   OL6 & SK15 & SK16 .... 242 B1
   Warrington WA1 .... 16 C4
Clarence Terr
   Bollington SK10 .... 63 D1
   Runcorn WA7 .... 23 D2
Clarendon Ave
   Altrincham WA15 .... 238 E5
   Manchester SK4 .... 240 B7
Clarendon Cl Chester CH4 . 141 F3
   Runcorn WA7 .... 50 B4
Clarendon Cres WA2 .... 242 D7
Clarendon Ct WA2 .... 7 F2
Clarendon Dr SK10 .... 88 A1
Clarendon Ind Est SK14 .. 241 E7
Clarendon Pl SK14 .... 241 E6
Clarendon Rd Denton SK14 . 241 B6
   Hyde SK14 .... 241 E2
   Irlam M44 .... 11 F4
   Sale M33 .... 242 D6
Clarendon St Hyde SK14 .. 241 D7
   Macclesfield SK10 .... 240 F7
Clares Farm Cl WA1 .... 17 F4
Clark Way SK14 .... 241 D7
Clarke Ave Culcheth WA3 .... 5 D2
   Warrington WA4 .... 16 B1
Clarke Gdns 17 WA8 .... 23 D4
Clarke La Bollington SK10 .. 87 F3
   Langley SK11 .... 113 E2
Clarke St WA14 .... 238 D7
Clarke Terr SK11 .... 112 B3
Clarkson Terr SK4 .... 240 E7
Clarks Terr WA7 .... 48 B4
Clary Meadow CW8 .... 78 C1
Clatterbridge Hospl L63 .. 42 B4
Clatterbridge Rd L63 .... 42 B4
Claude St WA1 .... 16 B1
Claughton Ave CW2 .... 190 B1
Claverton Cl WA7 .... 49 D3
Clay Heys SK11 .... 84 A2
Clay La Burtonwood WA5 ...... 6 C3
   Haslington CW11 .... 174 A1
   Marton Green CW7 .... 125 D2
   Peover WA16 .... 108 A4
   Wilmslow, Handforth SK9 .. 34 B3
   Wilmslow, Lindow SK9 ...... 59 E3
Claydon Gdns WA3 .... 10 C1
Clayhill Gn L66 .... 69 E4
Clayhill Light Ind Pk L64 .. 41 F3
Claypit Rd CH4 .... 141 D3
Claypitts La CH3 .... 142 C3
Clayton Av CW12 .... 157 D3
Clayton Ave WA3 .... 3 F4
Clayton Cres Runcorn WA7 .. 22 C1
   Widnes WA8 .... 12 C1
Clayton Dr SY13 .... 226 A1
Clayton Rd WA3 .... 9 F3
Clayton's Row CW5 .... 204 C4
Clayton-by-pass CW12 .... 156 B2
Cleaver Rd CW8 .... 77 E1
Cleaver Rd CH1 .... 117 F2
Cledford Cres CW10 .... 151 F3

Cledford Cty Inf & Jun
   Sch CW10 .... 151 F3
Cledford La CW10 .... 151 F3
Cleethorpes Rd WA7 .... 50 B4
Cleeve Way SK8 .... 35 D4
Cleeves Cl WA1 .... 16 B4
Clegg Pl OL6 .... 242 A2
Clegg St SK11 .... 112 C4
Clegge St WA2 .... 16 A4
Cleggs Cl CH3 .... 142 A4
Clelland St WA4 .... 16 C1
Clement St SK14 .... 240 F4
Clemley Cl CW6 .... 122 B3
Clerewood Ave SK8 .... 34 C4
Clevedon Cl SK11 .... 112 A4
Cleveland Ave SK14 .... 241 C6
Cleveland Dr
   Ellesmere Port L66 .... 69 D3
   Goldborne WA3 .... 3 E4
Cleveland Rd
   Altrincham WA15 .... 238 F3
   Manchester SK4 .... 240 A8
   Warrington WA2 .... 8 A2
Cleveland Way CW7 .... 149 D3
Cleveleys Ave Gatley SK8 . 239 A5
   Widnes WA8 .... 13 D3
Cleveleys Rd WA5 .... 15 D3
Cleves Cl CH1 .... 117 E3
Cliff Gr SK4
Cliff La Acton Bridge CW8 .... 76 C2
   Appleton WA4 .... 17 D1
   Lymm WA16 .... 28 A4
   Macclesfield SK10 .... 88 A4
   Rainow SK10 .... 88 A4
Cliff Rd Acton Bridge CW8 .... 76 C1
   Wilmslow SK9 .... 60 A4
Cliff Side SK9 .... 60 A4
Cliff View WA6 .... 74 A2
Cliffbrook Gr 8 SK9 .... 34 B3
Cliffe Rd Appleton WA4 .... 26 B3
   Crewe CW1 .... 190 A4
   Neston L64 .... 66 C4
Cliffe St Warrington WA1 .... 16 A4
   Widnes WA8 .... 13 F1
Cliffmere Cl SK8 .... 239 F2
Clifford Dr CH4 .... 140 C1
Clifford Gr CW1 .... 191 F3
Clifford Pl CW7 .... 149 E4
Clifford Rd
   Macclesfield SK11 .... 112 A4
   Penketh WA5 .... 15 D2
   Poynton SK12 .... 36 B4
   Wilmslow SK9 .... 59 F4
Clifton Ave
   Altrincham WA15 .... 238 F3
   Bebington L62 .... 43 F4
   Crewe CW2 .... 190 A2
   Culcheth WA3 .... 4 C2
   Gatley SK8 .... 239 A5
Clifton Cl WA1 .... 17 E1
Clifton Cres WA6 .... 49 D3
Clifton Dr Blacon CH1 ...... 117 F2
   Gatley M22 .... 8 B8
   Gatley, Heald Green SK8 .. 239 A5
   Northwich CW9 .... 104 A2
   Wilmslow SK9 .... 59 F4
Clifton Gdns L65 .... 70 B1
Clifton La WA7 .... 49 E2
Clifton Park Ave CH5 .... 91 E1
Clifton Rd Manchester SK4 . 240 A7
   Runcorn WA7 .... 49 E1
   Runcorn, Heath WA7 .... 49 D1
   Sale M33 .... 242 B7
   Warrington WA1 .... 17 E1
Clifton St Alderley Edge SK9 . 60 A1
   Crewe CW2 .... 190 A2
   Warrington WA4 .... 16 B1
Cliftonville Rd WA1 .... 17 D1
Clincton Cl WA8 .... 22 A4
Clincton View WA8 .... 22 A4
Clinton Av CW12
Clinton St L26 .... 22 C4
Clipsley Cres WA11 .... 1 A4
Clipsley La WA11 .... 1 A3
Clitheroe Rd CW8 .... 77 F1
Clive Ave WA2 .... 8 B2
Clive La WA7 .... 150 C4
Cliveden Rd CH4 .... 140 C2
Clivegreen La CW10 .... 150 C4
Clock Face Rd WA8 .... 13 C3
Cloisters The Cheadle SK8 . 240 A2
   Sale M33 .... 242 C7
Cloonberry Ave L60 .... 40 C2
Cloud The CW12 .... 158 A2
Cloud View CW12 .... 157 D3
Cloudberry Wlk M31 .... 11 E1
Clough Ave Warrington WA2 . 8 A2
   Wilmslow SK9 .... 34 A1
Clough Bank SK10 .... 87 F1
Clough Fold Rd SK14 ...... 241 D1
Clough Hall Dr ST7 .... 210 C4
Clough Hall Rd ST7 .... 210 C4
Clough Hall Sch The ST7 . 194 C1
Clough La CW8 .... 103 D3
Clough Rd CW2 .... 126 C4
Clough The WA7 .... 50 B4
Clough Wlk CW2 .... 206 A6
Cloughside SK12 .... 38 C4
Cloughwood Sch CW8 .... 103 D4

ovelly Ave WA5 ... 14 C4
ovelly Gr WA7 ... 50 B3
over Ave Frodsham WA6 ... 74 B4
  Stockport SK3 ... 240 D1
over Ct WA7 ... 50 A3
over Dr CW7 ... 126 B2
over La CW4 ... 140 C3
over Pl CW4 ... 140 C3
over Rd SK6 ... 241 E3
overdale CW8 ... 103 E4
overdale Rd SK11 ... 112 A3
overfield WA7 ... 50 B4
overfield Gdns L66 ... 69 E4
overfields CW1 ... 190 C3
lowes Ave ST7 ... 193 F1
lowes St SK11 ... 112 A4
lumber Cl SK12 ... 36 C2
lumber La CW5 ... 204 C4
lutton CE Contr Prim
  Sch CH3 ... 182 B1
lwyd Ave SK3 ... 240 D3
lwyd Cl CW7 ... 139 D3
lwyd Way L66 ... 69 D3
lyde Ave S16 ... 179 F1
lyde Cres CW7 ... 127 D1
lyde Gr CW7 ... 190 A2
lyde Rd SK3 ... 240 C3
lydesdale L65 ... 70 A2
lydesdale Ave CW1 ... 190 A2
lydesdale Rd WA4 ... 26 B4
oach Rd Bickerton SY14 ... 199 E1
  Chowley CH3 ... 183 D2
  Edge Green SY14 ... 199 E1
  Hampton SY14 ... 199 F1
  Little Budworth CW6 ... 147 E4
oachway SK10 ... 86 C4
oalbrookdale Rd L64 ... 41 F1
oalpit Hill ST7 ... 210 B4
oalpit La Langley SK11 ... 113 E3
  Mollington CH1 ... 94 B2
  Winsford CW10 ... 127 F1
oare St SK10 ... 87 E1
oastguard La L64 ... 41 D1
ob Hall La WA6 ... 98 B3
ob Moor Rd
  Kidsgrove ST7 ... 195 D2
  Lawton-gate ST7 ... 195 D2
obal Ct WA6 ... 74 A4
obb's La CW5 ... 204 C4
obbett's Way SK9 ... 59 F2
obblers Cross La CW6 ... 146 C1
obblers La LL12 ... 161 D1
obbles The Chester CH4 ... 141 E4
  Cuddington CW8 ... 101 E2
  Lower Peover WA16 ... 81 F1
obbs Cty Inf Sch The
  WA4 ... 26 C4
obbs La Appleton WA4 ... 26 C4
  Hough Common CW2 ... 206 C1
obden St
  Ashton-u-L OL6 ... 242 A2
  Newton-le-W WA12 ... 2 B2
  Warrington WA1 ... 16 A3
ock Hall La SK11 ... 113 E2
ock La WA6 ... 78 C4
ocker Hill SK15 ... 242 E2
ockhedge Ctr WA1 ... 16 A3
ockhedge La WA1 ... 16 B2
ockhedge Way WA1 ... 16 A3
ockington Cl CW9 ... 104 A2
ocklade La L24 ... 21 E4
ockpit La CW9 ... 102 A1
ocksheadhey Rd SK10 ... 63 E1
ocksmoss Rd SK11 ... 133 E2
oe La WA14 ... 30 B4
oerdon Dr WA4 ... 17 E1
ogshall La Comberbach CW9 78 A4
  Little Leigh CW9 ... 77 F4
  Northwich CW9 ... 78 B3
olborne Ave SK6 ... 241 C2
olborne St WA12 ... 2 B2
olchester Pl SK4 ... 240 C7
olchester Sq CH4 ... 140 C3
oldmoss Dr CW11 ... 175 E2
oldstream Cl WA2 ... 8 C2
ole Ave WA12 ... 2 B2
ole Ave (or Law
  Christleton Hall CH3 ... 142 B4
ollege Rd ST7 ... 193 D3
ollege View CH5 ... 91 E1
ollege of Law
  Hassall Green CW11 ... 175 E3
  Sandbach CW11 ... 175 E3
olleys La Nantwich CW2 ... 205 E4
  Willaston (nr Nantwich)
  CW2 ... 205 E4
ollier St WA7 ... 22 C2
ollier's Row WA7 ... 48 C4
olliers La CW1 ... 54 C1
olliery Green Cl L64 ... 66 C3
olliery Green L64 ... 66 C3
olliery Green Dr L64 ... 66 C3
ollin St WA5 ... 15 F3

Collinbrook Ave CW2 ... 190 A1
Collingham Gn L66 ... 69 D3
Collingham Way CW7 ... 126 B1
Collingtree Ave CW7 ... 127 D2
Collingwood Cl
  Macclesfield SK10 ... 87 D1
  Poynton SK12 ... 37 D2
Collingwood Rd WA12 ... 2 A2
Collins Green Rd WA5 ... 1 C3
Collins St CW2 ... 190 A2
Collinson Ct WA6 ... 74 A4
Colmere Cl L65 ... 70 B4
Colne Rd WA8 ... 6 C3
Colshaw Cty Prim Sch SK9 34 B1
Colshaw La SK11 ... 109 F1
Colshaw Wlk SK9 ... 34 B1
Coltsfoot Dr WA14 ... 238 B8
Columbine Cl
  Huntington CH3 ... 142 A3
  Widnes WA8 ... 12 A2
Columbine Wlk M31 ... 11 F1
Colveley Way CW7 ... 126 A1
Colville Ct WA2 ... 8 A2
Colville Rd SK11 ... 111 F4
Colwick Ave WA14 ... 238 E6
Colwyn Cl ... 7 F1
Colwyn Rd Bramhall SK7 ... 35 F4
  Sale M33 ... 239 E1
Comber Way M31 ... 82 A4
Comberbach Cty Prim Sch
  CW9 ... 78 B4
Combermere Cl SK8 ... 239 F4
Combermere Pl CW1 ... 190 A3
Combermere Dr CW9 ... 104 B3
Combs Cl SK22 ... 39 D4
Comer Terr WA3 ... 242 A6
Commercial Ave SK8 ... 34 C3
Commercial Brow SK14 ... 241 E8
Commercial Rd SK10 ... 112 C4
Commercial St SK11 ... 241 E7
Common Farm La SK11 ... 83 F1
Common La Betley CW3 ... 221 F3
  Chelford SK11 ... 83 F1
  Culcheth WA3 ... 4 C2
  Duddon CW6 ... 145 D4
  Kelsall CW6 ... 122 B2
  Lach Dennis CW9 ... 105 F3
  Stretton WA4 ... 52 C4
  Tarvin CH3 ... 122 B2
  Warrington WA4 ... 16 C1
  Waverton CH3 ... 143 D2
Common Rd WA12 ... 1 C2
Common The WA7 ... 49 E4
Commonhall St CH1 ... 237 D2
Commons Mill CW11 ... 175 D4
Commons The CW11 ... 175 D3
Commonside WA6 ... 73 F1
Commonwealth Cl CW7 149 E3
Company's Cl WA7 ... 48 C3
Compass Cl WA7 ... 50 B3
Compstall Rd SK6 ... 241 E2
Compton Cl WA11 ... 1 B4
Compton Pl Chester CH4 ... 141 D3
  Ellesmere Port L65 ... 70 A3
Compton St SK15 ... 242 E1
Concord Pl WA2 ... 8 B1
Conery Cl WA6 ... 73 E2
Coney Gr WA7 ... 50 A3
Coneymead SK15 ... 242 D4
Congleton Cl SK9 ... 85 D4
Congleton Edge Rd CW12 179 D3
Congleton La
  Siddington SK11 ... 109 E3
  Withington SK11 ... 109 E3
Congleton Rd
  Alderley Edge SK10 ... 85 D3
  Astbury CW12 ... 178 B2
  Biddulph ST6 ... 179 E1
  Biddulph, Mow Cop CW12 . 178 C1
  Broughton CH4 ... 139 E2
  Kidsgrove ST7 ... 194 B1
  Macclesfield SK11 ... 112 A3
  Marton SK11 ... 133 D3
  Nether Alderley SK10 ... 85 D3
  Sandbach CW11 ... 175 D4
  Scholar Green CW12 ... 177 F2
  Siddington SK11 ... 110 A3
  Smallwood CW11 ... 177 D3
  Smallwood, Arclid Green
  CW11 ... 176 A4
  Warren SK11 ... 111 F1
Congleton Rd N
  Lawton-gate ST7 ... 194 C3
  Scholar Green ST7 ... 194 C3
Congleton Rd S ST7 ... 194 B2
Congleton Sta CW12 ... 157 D1
Congleton War Memorial
  Hospl CW12 ... 156 C1
Conifer Cl CH1 ... 95 D4
Conifer Gr WA5 ... 14 C4
Conifer Wlk M31 ... 11 E1
Conifers The ST7 ... 193 D2
Coniston Ave
  Bebington L63 ... 43 E2
  Congleton CW12 ... 155 F1
  Dukinfield SK14 ... 241 C8
  Penketh WA5 ... 14 B2
  Winsford CW7 ... 126 B1
Coniston Cl Hooton L66 ... 44 A1
  Nantwich CW5 ... 205 D3
  Runcorn WA7 ... 49 E3
Coniston Dr Frodsham WA6 . 74 B4
  Holmes Chapel CW4 ... 130 A2
  Stalybridge SK15 ... 242 D3
  Wilmslow SK9 ... 34 B2

Coniston Rd Chester CH2 . 118 C3
  Gatley SK8 ... 239 B5
  High Lane SK6 ... 37 E4
  Neston L64 ... 66 C3
  Partington M31 ... 11 F4
Coniston Way SK11 ... 111 F3
Connah's Quay High Sch
  CH5 ... 91 E1
Connaught Ave WA1 ... 16 C4
Connaught Cl SK9 ... 60 A6
Connaught Dr WA12 ... 2 B1
Conroy Way WA12 ... 7 E4
Consort Pl WA14 ... 238 E3
Constable Dr SK9 ... 60 C4
Constables Cl WA7 ... 24 A1
Constance Rd M31 ... 11 F4
Constance Way WA8 ... 23 D3
Convamore Rd SK7 ... 35 E4
Conway Ave Irlam M44 ... 11 F4
  Warrington WA5 ... 7 F1
  Winsford CW7 ... 149 E4
Conway Cl Broughton CH4 . 139 E2
  Crewe CW1 ... 190 B4
  Great Sankey WA5 ... 14 C3
  Knutsford WA16 ... 82 A4
Conway Cres SK10 ... 87 F1
Conway Ct L65 ... 70 B2
Conway Dr Newton-le-W WA12 2 C2
  Stalybridge SK15 ... 242 D3
Conway Rd Cheadle SK8 ... 239 E2
  Sale M33 ... 242 D5
Conway St WA5 ... 240 E8
Coogee Ave WA5 ... 14 C4
Cook Ave WA11 ... 1 C4
Cook St Ellesmere Port L65 ... 70 B3
  Stockport SK3 ... 240 E5
Cooke's La CW9 ... 104 C3
Cooks La SY13 ... 225 E4
Cooksmere La CW11 ... 175 D4
Coole La
  French Lane End CW5 ... 218 C2
  Newhall CW5 ... 229 E3
Coombe Dr WA7 ... 49 D4
Coombe Park L66 ... 69 E3
Coombes Ave SK14 ... 241 D8
Coombes Cl SK14 ... 87 F3
Cooper Ave
  Newton-le-W WA12 ... 1 C2
  Warrington WA2 ... 8 A1
Cooper La WA11 ... 1 B3
Cooper St Congleton CW12 . 156 C2
  Runcorn WA7 ... 23 D2
  Stockport SK1 ... 240 F3
  Widnes WA8 ... 23 D2
Cooper's Ch CH3 ... 142 A4
Cooper's La CH5 ... 91 E1
Coopers Opening CW11 ... 175 D4
Cop Meadow SK11 ... 112 C1
Copage Dr SK6 ... 241 A4
Cope Ave CW5 ... 204 E2
Copeland Dr WA7 ... 49 F3
Copeland Rd WA4 ... 16 A1
Copes La CW5 ... 204 B2
Copgrove Cl CW4 ... 139 E2
Copperas Wlk M22 ... 33 F4
Copley Ave SK15 ... 242 F2
Copley Park Mews SK15 ... 242 F2
Coppenhall Cty High Sch
  CW1 ... 190 C3
Coppenhall Gr CW2 ... 190 A2
Coppenhall Heyes CW2 ... 190 A2
Coppenhall La CW2 ... 189 E2
Copper Beach Cl CH4 ... 139 E2
Copper St SK11 ... 112 C3
Copper Wood CW8 ... 101 F3
Copperfield Cl WA3 ... 9 E3
Copperfield Rd
  Cheadle Hulme SK8 ... 35 D3
  Poynton SK12 ... 36 B1
Copperfields Tarporley CW6 146 B1
  Wilmslow SK9 ... 60 B4
Coppermill Rd CW12 ... 178 C1
Coppermine La SY14 ... 184 A1
Coppice CW8 ... 101 E3
Coppice Cl Disley SK12 ... 38 A3
  Romiley SK6 ... 241 B4
  Runcorn WA7 ... 24 A1
  Willaston (nr Nantwich)
  CW5 ... 205 E3
Coppice Dr Disley SK12 ... 38 A3
  Middlewich CW10 ... 151 F3
Coppice Gn WA5 ... 7 D1
Coppice Gr WA16 ... 57 D2
Coppice La SK12 ... 38 A3
Coppice Rd
  Haslington CW1 ... 192 A4
  Kidsgrove ST7 ... 210 B4
  Poynton SK12 ... 37 D2
  Willaston (nr Nantwich)
  CW5 ... 205 E3
Coppice Rise SK11 ... 112 B3
Coppice The
  Altrincham WA15 ... 32 A4
  Nantwich CW5 ... 204 C2
  Sandbach CW11 ... 174 C4
  Whaley Bridge SK23 ... 65 F3
Coppice Way SK9 ... 34 C2
Coppins Cl Chester CH1 ... 119 D1
  Helsby WA6 ... 73 D2
Coppins The Warrington WA2 . 8 B1
  Wilmslow SK9 ... 59 F2
Copse The Altrincham WA15 . 32 B4
  Neston L64 ... 66 C4
  Runcorn WA7 ... 50 A3
Copthorne Cl CW3 ... 156 C1
Copthorne Dr CW3 ... 229 F2
Corbet Ave WA2 ... 16 A4
Corbet Dr TF9 ... 235 D2

Corbet St WA2 ... 16 A4
Corcoran Dr SK6 ... 241 F2
Cordale Cl WA1 ... 14 C4
Corfe Way CW7 ... 149 E4
Coridor Rd L65 ... 71 D3
Corkland Cl OL6 ... 242 B2
Corkland St OL6 ... 242 B2
Corks La SK12 ... 38 C3
Corley Ave SK5 ... 239 F7
Cormorant Cl CW1 ... 190 C2
Cormorant Dr WA7 ... 22 C1
Cornbrook Rd SK11 ... 112 B2
Corner Croft SK9 ... 60 A2
Corner Ct SK8 ... 239 F6
Cornerhouse La WA8 ... 12 B2
Corners The CW8 ... 102 C3
Cornfield Cl
  Ellesmere Port L66 ... 69 F1
  Macclesfield SK10 ... 87 E2
  Sale M33 ... 242 F5
Cornfield Rd SK8 ... 241 E3
Cornforth Way WA8 ... 12 C2
Cornhill Cl STS ... 210 B1
Cornish Cl M22 ... 33 E4
Cornishway M22 ... 33 E4
Cornishway Ind Est M22 ... 33 E4
Cornubia Rd WA8 ... 23 D1
Cornwall Ave WA7 ... 24 A2
Cornwall Cl
  Congleton CW12 ... 157 D1
  High Lane SK6 ... 37 F4
  Macclesfield SK10 ... 87 D3
  Runcorn WA7 ... 24 A2
Cornwall Cl CW1 ... 190 A3
Cornwall Rd Cheadle SK8 ... 34 A4
  Chester CH2 ... 118 B4
  Irlam M44 ... 11 E3
  Widnes WA8 ... 13 D2
Cornwall St Chester CH2 ... 237 E4
  Warrington WA1 ... 16 C4
Cornwell Cl SK9 ... 60 C1
Corona Ave SK14 ... 241 E7
Coronation Ave
  Alsager ST7 ... 193 D2
  Glazebury WA3 ... 5 E4
  Hyde SK14 ... 241 E5
  Warrington WA4 ... 17 E1
  Winsford CW7 ... 126 C1
Coronation Bldgs SK10 ... 88 A4
Coronation Cres
  Crewe CW1 ... 190 C3
  Kidsgrove ST7 ... 194 C1
  Sandbach CW11 ... 175 D3
Coronation Dr
  Frodsham WA6 ... 49 E1
  Haydock WA11 ... 2 A4
  Newton-le-W WA12 ... 2 C1
  Penketh WA5 ... 14 C2
  Widnes WA8 ... 22 A4
Coronation Gr CW8 ... 78 A3
Coronation Rd
  Broughton CH4 ... 139 D2
  Congleton CW12 ... 156 C2
  Ellesmere Port L65 ... 70 B2
  Middlewich CW10 ... 151 E3
  Runcorn, Higher Runcorn
  WA7 ... 23 D1
  Runcorn, Preston Brook WA7 . 50 C3
Coronation St Chester CH4 . 140 C4
  Crewe CW1 ... 190 B3
  Macclesfield SK11 ... 112 B3
  Reddish SK5 ... 240 E8
Coronation Terr CW6 ... 146 B1
Coroner's La WA8 ... 12 C3
Coronet Ave CW9 ... 103 F2
Coronet Way WA8 ... 22 A4
Corporation St Hyde SK14 . 241 D6
  Stalybridge SK15 ... 242 D1
  Stockport SK1 ... 240 F5
Correction Brow SK12 ... 37 E3
Corstons La L64 ... 67 D3
Corwen Cl WA5 ... 7 F1
Cossack Ave WA2 ... 8 A1
Cotebrook Dr CH2 ... 118 B3
Cotebrook Rd CW9 ... 104 B4
Cotes Pl CH1 ... 117 F2
Cotesmore Dr L60 ... 41 E4
Cotgreaves Cl CH4 ... 141 D3
Cotswold Ave CH4 ... 3 E3
Cotswold Cl Chester CH2 ... 118 C3
  Cuddington CW8 ... 102 A1
  Macclesfield SK10 ... 86 C1
Cotswold Gr WA9 ... 1 A2
Cotswold Stockport SK4 240 D7
  Warrington WA2 ... 8 C2
Cotswold Way CW7 ... 149 D4
Cotswold Cl Bebington L63 ... 43 E3
  Neston L64 ... 66 C4
Cottage Dr East L60 ... 40 C3
Cottage Dr West L60 ... 40 C3
Cottage La Heswall L60 ... 40 C3
  Macclesfield SK10 ... 112 C4
Cottage Rd SK11 ... 112 A4
Cottam Dr WA2 ... 9 D2
Cotterdale Cl WA5 ... 14 C4
Cotterill WA7 ... 49 E4
Cotterill Dr WA1 ... 17 E4
Cotterill St CW2 ... 190 B1
Cottesmore Gdns WA15 ... 32 B4
Cotton La Duddon CW6 ... 145 E4
  Sandbach CW11 ... 175 D2
Cotton Tree St SK3 & SK4 . 240 E5
Cottonwood Dr ST7 ... 195 F2
Cottrell Rd WA15 ... 32 B4
Coulton Rd WA8 ... 13 F2
Counce Ave WA12 ... 2 B1

Countess Ave SK8 ... 34 C3
Countess Cl SK11 ... 111 F4
Countess of Chester
  Hospl CH2 ... 118 A3
Countess Rd SK11 ... 112 A4
Countess St SK11 ... 242 A2
Countess Way CH2 ... 118 B2
Counting House Rd SK12 ... 38 C3
County Ave OL6 ... 242 B4
Courier Row SK10 ... 87 F4
Court La CW8 ... 77 D1
Court The CW7 ... 156 A2
Courtney Gn SK9 ... 34 B1
Courtney Pl WA14 ... 238 A1
Courtney Rd CW4 ... 140 C2
Cousens Way CH1 ... 118 A2
Cove The WA15 ... 238 F3
Covent Garden ID SK1 ... 240 F5
Coventry Ave Cheadle SK3 . 239 F7
  Ellesmere Port CH1 ... 94 C4
Coverdale Cl WA5 ... 14 B4
Covert Cl CW7 ... 149 D4
Covert Gdns ST7 ... 210 B4
Covert Rise CH3 ... 166 A1
Covington Pl SK9 ... 60 A3
Cow La Ashley WA15 ... 31 F3
  Bollington SK10 ... 88 A4
  Hargrave CH3 ... 144 A1
  Macclesfield SK11 ... 112 B3
  Norley WA6 ... 101 D3
  Rainow SK10 ... 88 B2
  Sale M33 ... 242 E7
Cowanway WA8 ... 12 C3
Cowbrook La SK11 ... 113 E3
Cowdell St WA2 ... 16 A4
Cowfields CW5 ... 204 C3
Cowhey Cl CH4 ... 141 D3
Cowley Way CW1 ... 190 C1
Cowlishaw Rd SK14 & SK6 . 241 A4
Cowthorne Ct CW7 ... 206 A4
Cowthorne Dr CH3 ... 143 D2
Coyt Rd SK23 ... 65 F3
Crab La WA2 ... 9 D2
Crabmill Dr CW11 ... 174 C4
Crabmill La Norley WA6 ... 100 C3
  Warmingham CW1 ... 173 F4
Crabtree Ave
  Altrincham WA15 ... 32 B4
  Disley SK12 ... 38 C3
Crabtree Fold WA7 ... 50 B4
Crabtree Gr CW1 ... 190 C3
Crabtree La WA13 ... 29 D3
Crabwall Pl CH1 ... 117 F3
Crackley Bank Prim Sch
  ST5 ... 210 C1
Cragside Way SK9 ... 60 B3
Craig Cl Macclesfield SK11 . 112 A3
  Stockport SK4 ... 240 B5
Craig Dr SK23 ... 65 F3
Craig Gdns L66 ... 69 F4
Craig Rd Congleton CW12 . 156 C2
  Macclesfield SK11 ... 112 A3
  Stockport SK4 ... 240 B5
Craig Wlk ST7 ... 193 F1
Craigleigh Gr L62 ... 43 F2
Craigside ST5 ... 179 E1
Craithe Rd CH1 ... 119 D1
Crampton Dr WA15 ... 32 B4
Cranage Cl WA7 ... 49 E4
Cranage Hill Hospl CW4 ... 130 A3
Cranage Rd CW2 ... 190 A2
Cranage Way ID SK8 ... 34 B3
Cranberry Cl WA14 ... 238 B8
Cranberry Cty Inf & Jun
  Sch ST7 ... 193 D2
Cranberry Dr ST5 ... 210 B1
Cranberry La ST7 ... 193 D2
Cranberry Moss La ST7 ... 193 D2
Cranberry Rd M31 ... 11 F2
Cranborne Rd Crewe CW1 ... 190 A4
Cranbourne Cl SK4 ... 240 B8
Cranbourne Rd SK4 ... 240 B8
Crandon Dr M20 ... 239 C8
Cranebrook Cl CW1 ... 190 A4
Cranfield Dr ST7 ... 193 D2
Cranford Ave
  Knutsford WA16 ... 56 C1
  Macclesfield SK11 ... 112 C4
  Sale M33 ... 242 C8
Cranford Cl L62 ... 43 F2
Cranford Ct Chester CH4 ... 141 D3
  Warrington WA4 ... 17 F4
Cranford Mews ST7 ... 193 D2
Cranford Rd SK9 ... 34 A1
Cranham Ave WA3 ... 3 F4
Cranleigh Cl WA4 ... 26 A4
Cranleigh Cres CH1 ... 118 A2
Cranleigh Dr Cheadle SK8 . 239 F6
  Hazel Grove SK7 ... 37 D4
  Sale M33 ... 242 A7
Cranmere Cl CW9 ... 104 A2
Cranshaw La WA8 ... 13 D3
Cranston Dr
  Manchester M20 ... 239 B8
  Sale M33 ... 239 B8
Cranswick Gn L66 ... 69 E3
Crantock Dr SK8 ... 34 B4
Cranwell Ave WA3 ... 4 C2
Cranworth St SK15 ... 242 E1
Crauford Rd CW12 ... 157 D4
Craven Ave WA3 ... 3 F2
Craven Dr WA14 ... 238 C8

Craven Rd WA14 .... 238 C7
Craven Terr M33 .... 242 C6
Crawford Ave WA4 .... 12 A1
Crawford Pl WA7 .... 49 D3
Crawford St OL6 .... 242 A2
Crawford's Wlk CH2 .... 118 C2
Crawley Ave WA1 .... 17 A2
Crayford Ave CW12 .... 157 D3
Crediton Cl WA14 .... 238 B6
Cresanne Cl CW10 .... 151 E4
Crescent Dr Helsby WA6 ... 73 D2
   Whaley Bridge SK23 ...... 39 E1
Crescent Rd SK4 .... 239 C6
Crescent Pk SK4 .... 240 C6
Crescent Rd
   Alderley Edge SK9 .... 60 A1
   Altrincham WA15 .... 238 E1
   Altrincham, Oldfield Brow
   WA14 .... 238 A5
   Cheadle SK8 .... 239 C6
   Congleton CW12 .... 156 B1
   Cranage CW4 .... 129 F3
   Ellesmere Port L65 .... 70 B3
   Rostherne WA16 .... 30 A2
Crescent The
   Altrincham WA15 .... 238 F7
   Altrincham, Oldfield Brow
   WA14 .... 238 A5
   Cheadle SK8 .... 239 D6
   Chester CH2 .... 118 B2
   Congleton CW12 .... 156 B1
   Ellesmere Port L65 .... 69 F3
   Hartford CW8 .... 103 D3
   Lymm WA13 .... 18 C1
   Macclesfield SK10 .... 87 F1
   Middlewich CW10 .... 128 A1
   Mottram St Andrew SK10 . 61 D1
   Nantwich CW5 .... 204 C3
   New Mills SK22 .... 39 D4
   Northwich CW8, CW9 ..... 103 F3
   Rostherne WA16 .... 30 A2
   Utkinton CW6 .... 146 A4
   Weaverham CW8 .... 77 F1
Cressbrook Rd WA4 .... 26 B4
Cressington Gdns L65 ...... 70 B3
Cresswell Ave
   New Mills SK22 .... 39 E4
   Newcastle-u-L ST5 .... 210 B1
Cresswell Cl WA5 .... 7 F1
Cresswell St SK22 .... 39 E4
Cresta Dr WA7 .... 48 C3
Crestwood Cl CW2 .... 206 A4
Crew Ave SK10 .... 87 F1
Crew Bsns Pk SK17 .... 193 F2
Crewe Gates Farm Ind Est
   CW1 .... 190 C1
Crewe Golf Course CW1 . 191 F1
Crewe Green Ave CW1 .... 191 E2
Crewe Green Rd CW1 ..... 191 D2
Crewe Hill La CH3 .... 197 D3
Crewe La CH3 .... 180 C1
Crewe La S CH3 .... 190 C4
Crewe Rd Alsager ST7 .... 193 D2
   Crewe CW1 .... 190 C1
   Haslington CW1 .... 191 E3
   Hatherton CW5 .... 219 F2
   Nantwich CW5 .... 205 E3
   Sandbach CW11 .... 175 D2
   Shavington CW2 .... 206 B3
   Willaston (nr Nantwich)
   CW5 .... 205 E3
   Wistaston CW5 .... 205 E3
Crewe St Chester CH2 .... 237 F3
   Crewe CW1 .... 190 B2
Crewe Sta CW1 .... 190 C1
Crewood Common Rd
   CW8 .... 76 A2
Crib La CW6 .... 168 A4
Criccieth Ct L65 .... 70 B1
Criccieth Rd SK3 .... 240 A3
Cricket St M34 .... 241 A8
Cricket's La OL6 .... 242 A3
Criftin Cl L66 .... 69 E1
Crimes La CH3, CW6 ..... 167 E2
Cringle Dr SK8 .... 239 C3
Crisham Ave CW5 .... 218 C4
Critchley Cl SK14 .... 241 F5
Critchley Rd L24 .... 21 D2
Croasdale Dr WA7 .... 49 F3
Crocus St CW8 .... 78 A2
Croesmere Dr L66 .... 69 E1
Croft Cl Altrincham WA15 . 32 B3
   Utkinton CW6 .... 146 A4
   Waverton CH3 .... 143 D3
Croft La L65 .... 70 C2
Croft Prim Sch WA3 .... 9 D4
Croft Heath Gdns WA3 .... 9 D4
Croft La Doddleston CH4 . 162 A4
   Knutsford WA16 .... 82 A4
Croft Rd SK9 .... 59 F2
Croft St Goldborne WA3 .... 3 D4
   Hyde SK14 .... 241 D6
   Stalybridge SK15 .... 242 E2
   Widnes WA8 .... 23 D3
Croft The Chester CH4 ... 118 B3
   Runcorn WA7 .... 23 F1
Croften Dr L64 .... 66 C3
Crofters Cl
   Ellesmere Port L66 .... 69 F1
   Wistaston CW2 .... 206 A4
Crofters Ct CW4 .... 130 B2
Crofters Grn SK9 .... 59 F1
Crofters Heath L66 .... 69 F1
Crofters Lea CW8 .... 103 E4

Crofters Pk CH5 .... 116 A2
Crofters The WA3 .... 242 F5
Crofters Way CH1 .... 116 C4
Crofton Cl WA4 .... 27 E3
Crofton Gdns WA3 .... 4 C2
Crofton Rd WA7 .... 22 C1
Croftside WA1 .... 17 F4
Croftside Way SK9 .... 60 B3
Croftsway L60 .... 40 B4
Cromer Dr CW1 .... 190 A4
Cromer Rd Cheadle SK8 . 239 E6
   Sale M33 .... 242 C5
Cromford Ct SK23 .... 65 F3
Cromford Mews SK23 .... 65 F3
Cromley Rd SK6 .... 37 F3
Crompton Rd SK11 .... 112 A4
Crompton St OL6 .... 242 B4
Cromwell Ave Gatley SK8 . 239 A6
   Great Sankey WA5 .... 15 D4
   Warrington WA5 .... 7 E2
Cromwell Ave S WA5 ...... 15 E2
Cromwell Ct Irlam M44 ... 11 F4
   Nantwich CW5 .... 204 C3
Cromwell Dr CW2 .... 206 B2
Cromwell Rd
   Cheadle Hulme SK7 .... 35 E3
   Ellesmere Port L65 .... 70 B3
   Irlam M44 .... 11 F4
   Northwich CW8 .... 103 F4
Cromwell St
   Stockport SK4 .... 240 D7
   Widnes WA8 .... 23 D3
Cronkinson Ave CW5 ..... 204 C2
Cronkinson Oak CW5 ..... 204 C2
Cronton CE Sch WA8 ...... 12 B3
Cronton La WA8 .... 12 C3
Cronton Park Ave WA8 .. 12 B3
Cronton Park Cl WA8 ..... 12 B3
Cronton Rd WA8 .... 12 B3
Cronulla Dr WA5 .... 14 B4
Crook La CW7 .... 127 D1
Crook St Chester CH1 .... 237 D2
   Hyde SK14 .... 241 E6
Crooked La CH3 .... 145 E2
Crookedyard Rd SK11 ... 113 F4
Crookenden Cl CH2 .... 95 E1
Crookenden Rd CH2 .... 95 E1
Croppers Rd WA2 .... 8 C2
Crosby Ave WA1 .... 16 A4
Crosby Gr L64 .... 66 C3
Crosby St SK2 .... 240 F3
Crosfield St WA1 .... 16 A3
Cross Gn CH3 .... 143 D3
Cross Gr WA15 .... 238 F8
Cross Hey CH4 .... 237 F1
Cross La Audley ST7 ...... 209 F3
   Church Minshull CW1 ..... 172 B3
   Congleton CW12 .... 157 D1
   Croft WA3 .... 9 D4
   Frodsham WA6 .... 73 D4
   Haslington CW1 .... 191 F4
   Middlewich CW10 .... 151 E3
   Neston L64 .... 66 C3
   Newton-le-W WA12 .... 2 A2
   Sandbach CW11 .... 175 E3
   Smallwood CW11 .... 176 C3
   Swettenham CW12 .... 131 F2
   Warrington WA4 .... 17 D2
   Wilmslow SK9 .... 60 C4
Cross La E M31 .... 11 F1
Cross La W M31 .... 11 F1
Cross Lanes
   Tarvin, Old Moss CH3 .... 144 B4
   Tarvin, Oscroft CH3 ...... 121 C1
Cross O' Th' Hill Rd SY14 . 214 A2
Cross Rd Cheadle SK8 ..... 34 A4
   Haslington CW1 .... 191 E2
Cross St Alsager ST7 ..... 193 E2
   Altrincham WA14 .... 238 D4
   Barnton CW8 .... 78 A2
   Chester CH2 .... 118 C1
   Congleton CW12 .... 156 B2
   Crewe CW1 .... 190 B2
   Goldborne WA3 .... 3 D4
   Haslington CW1 .... 191 E2
   Hyde SK14 .... 196 C4
   Hyde SK14 .... 241 D6
   Marston CW9 .... 79 E2
   Neston L64 .... 66 C4
   New Mills SK22 .... 39 E4
   Runcorn WA7 .... 23 D2
   Sale M32 & M33 .... 242 B8
   Warrington WA2 .... 16 A4
   Widnes WA8 .... 13 E1
Cross The Holt LL13 ...... 196 C4
   Lymm WA13 .... 18 C2
Cross Wood St SK15 ...... 204 B3
Crossall St SK11 .... 112 B4
Crossdale Rd L62 .... 43 E3
Crossfield Ave WA3 .... 4 C1
Crossfield Ct Denton M34 . 241 A6
   Stalybridge SK15 .... 242 D1
Crossfield Rd
   Bollington SK10 .... 87 F3
   Wilmslow SK9 .... 34 B2
Crossfields CH3 .... 121 D1
Crossings The WA12 .... 2 B2
Crossland Terr WA6 .... 73 D1
Crosslands
   Congleton CW12 .... 157 D1
   Haslington CW1 .... 191 E2
Crossledge CW12 .... 156 A2
Crossley Ave L66 .... 69 F3
Crossley Cres CH2 .... 119 C3
Crossley Dr L60 .... 40 B4
Crossley East Hospl WA6 . 99 E4
Crossley Rd M33 .... 242 A8

Crossley St
   Stalybridge SK15 .... 242 C2
   Warrington WA1 .... 16 B3
Crossmoor Cres SK6 ...... 241 C1
Crossmoor Gr SK6 .... 241 C2
Crossway Bramhall SK7 .... 35 F3
   Crewe CW1 .... 190 B3
   Widnes WA8 .... 22 B4
Crossway The L63 .... 42 B2
Crossways ST6 .... 179 F1
Crossways Rd ST7 .... 194 A2
Crosswaithe Ave L62 ...... 43 F2
Croston Cl
   Alderley Edge SK9 .... 60 B1
   Widnes WA8 .... 12 B2
Crotia Ave CW7 .... 207 D3
Crouch La CW12 .... 157 E2
Crouchley Hall Mews WA13 . 18 C1
Crouchley La WA13 .... 18 C1
Croughton Ct L66 .... 69 F4
Croughton Rd
   Ellesmere Port L66 .... 69 F4
   Stoak CH2 .... 96 A4
   Stoak, Croughton CH2 .... 95 F3
Crow Gdns WA12 .... 2 A2
Crow La E WA12 .... 2 B2
Crow La W WA12 .... 2 A2
Crow Wood Pl WA8 .... 13 F2
Crowbrook Gr SK9 .... 34 B1
Crowder's La CW7 .... 105 D2
Crowland Gdns SK8 .... 35 D3
Crowley La CW9 .... 28 A4
Crown Ave WA8 .... 22 A4
Crown Bank CW11 .... 175 D3
Crown Bank Cres ST7 .... 210 B3
Crown Ctyd CW3 .... 229 F2
Crown Fields Cl WA12 ...... 2 A3
Crown Gate WA7 .... 49 F4
Crown Gn WA13 .... 19 D2
Crown Ind Est WA14 ..... 238 C7
Crown La WA16 .... 106 B4
Crown Park Dr WA12 .... 2 A2
Crown Passages WA15 . 238 E2
Crown St Newton-le-W WA12 . 2 A2
   Northwich CW8 .... 103 F4
   Warrington WA1 .... 16 A3
Crown St W SK11 .... 112 B4
Crownest La WA4 .... 26 A4
Croxton Christ Church CE
   Aided Prim Sch CW8 .... 76 A1
Crowton View WA6 .... 101 D3
Croxton La CW10 .... 128 A2
Croxton Way CW8 .... 103 D2
Croyde Rd L24 .... 21 D2
Crum Hill CW9 .... 104 A4
Crummock Rd SK8 .... 239 B3
Cryers La Elton CH2 .... 72 A1
   Thornton-le-M CH2 .... 96 C4
Cty High Sch Leftwich The
   CW9 .... 104 A4
Cuckoo La Acton CW5 .... 203 F4
   Neston L64 .... 67 E4
Cuckstoolpit Hill SK11 . 112 C4
Cuddington Cres SK3 .... 240 D2
Cuddington Cty Prim Sch
   CW8 .... 101 F1
Cuddington Gn L66 .... 69 F4
Cuddington Sta CW8 ..... 102 A2
Cuddington Way SK9 .... 34 B3
Cuerdley Gn WA5 .... 14 A1
Cuerdley Rd WA5 .... 14 B2
Culbin Cl WA3 .... 10 A3
Culcheth Cty Prim Sch 5 D2
   Culcheth Hall Prep Sch
   WA14 .... 238 D3
Culcheth High Sch WA3 .... 4 C1
Culcheth Hill WA3 .... 4 C2
Culcheth Rd WA14 .... 238 D3
Cullen Cl WA7 .... 24 B1
Culland St CW2 .... 190 B1
Cullen Rd WA7 .... 48 B4
Culver Rd L63 .... 43 E2
Cumber Cl SK9 .... 59 E2
Cumber Dr SK9 .... 59 E3
Cumber La SK9 .... 59 E2
Cumberland Ave Irlam M44 . 11 E3
   Nantwich CW5 .... 204 C3
Cumberland Cl Crewe CW1 . 190 B3
   Kidsgrove ST7 .... 210 C4
Cumberland Cres WA11 .... 1 A3
Cumberland Dr
   Altrincham WA14 .... 31 D4
   Bollington SK10 .... 88 A4
Cumberland Gr L66 .... 69 E2
Cumberland Rd
   Congleton CW12 .... 156 A3
   Partington M31 .... 11 F1
   Warrington WA5 .... 15 D2
Cumberland Sports Ctr
   CW1 .... 190 B3
Cumberland St
   [SK] Macclesfield SK11 . 112 B4
   Stalybridge SK15 .... 242 C2
   Warrington WA4 .... 16 B2
Cumbermere Dr CW9 .... 174 C4
Cumbers La SK9 .... 60 A1
Cumbers Dr SK9 .... 67 D3
Cumbrae Dr L65 .... 70 B1
Cuncliffe Cl WA7 .... 50 A4
Cuncliffe Dr WA3 .... 242 C5
Cundiff Ct SK11 .... 112 C3
Cundy St SK14 .... 241 E8
Cunliffe Ave WA12 .... 2 A3
Cunliffe St Dukinfield SK14 . 241 C8
   Stockport SK3 .... 240 C4
Cunningham Cl WA5 ...... 14 B4

Cunningham Dr
   Bebington L63 .... 43 E4
   Runcorn WA7 .... 22 C1
   Wythenshawe M22 .... 34 A4
Cunningham Rd WA8 .... 22 B4
Cuppin St CH1 .... 237 D2
Curlender Way L24 .... 21 F1
Curlew Cl Goldborne WA3 . 3 E4
   Winsford CW7 .... 149 E3
Curlew Gr WA3 .... 9 F2
Curlew Rd WA7 .... 50 A4
Currier La OL6 .... 242 A2
Curtis Rd SK4 .... 240 D6
Curzon Ave CW7 .... 193 E3
Curzon Cl WA1 .... 141 D4
Curzon Dr CW7 .... 126 C1
Curzon Mews L60 .... 60 A3
Curzon Pk N CH4 .... 141 D4
Curzon Pk S CH4 .... 141 D4
Curzon Rd
   Ashton-u-L OL6 .... 242 A4
   Cheadle SK8 .... 34 A4
   Poynton SK12 .... 36 C1
   Sale M33 .... 242 B7
Curzon St Chester CH4 . 140 C4
   [G] Runcorn WA7 .... 22 C1
Cuthbert Rd SK8 .... 239 E6
Cygnet Cl L66 .... 69 E2
Cyman Cl CH1 .... 117 E2
Cymbal Ct SK5 .... 240 F7
Cynthia Ave WA1 .... 17 D4
Cynthia Rd WA7 .... 22 C1
Cypress Ave
   Ellesmere Port L66 .... 69 F1
   Widnes WA8 .... 13 D1
Cypress Cl Stockport SK3 . 240 C4
   Warrington WA1 .... 17 F4
Cypress Gr Denton M34 .. 241 A7
   Runcorn WA7 .... 49 F4
Cyprus Way SK6 .... 38 A4
Cyril Bell Cl WA13 .... 18 C2
Cyril St WA2 .... 16 A4

Daffodil Cl WA7 .... 13 F2
Dagnall Ave WA5 .... 7 F1
Daintry Hall Prep Sch The
   CW12 .... 134 B1
Daintry St SK11 .... 112 C4
Daintry Terr **[R]** SK11 . 112 C4
Dairy Farm Cl WA13 ...... 18 C2
Dairy House La
   Cheadle Hulme SK7 .... 35 D2
   Wilmslow SK7 .... 35 D2
Dairy House Rd SK8 .... 35 D3
Dairy House Way CW2 .. 189 F1
Dairyground Cl SK7 .... 35 F4
Dairyground Rd SK7 .... 35 F4
Dairyhouse La WA14 ..... 238 B7
Dairylands Rd ST7 .... 193 F2
Daisy Ave WA12 .... 2 B1
Daisy Bank SK9 .... 204 B3
Daisy Bank Cres CW3 ... 229 F3
Daisy Bank La Anderton CW8 . 78 B2
   Gatley SK8 .... 239 A1
Daisy Bank Mill Cl WA3 .... 4 C2
Daisy Bank Rd Lymm WA13 . 18 B2
   Penketh WA5 .... 14 C2
Daisy St SK1 & SK2 .... 240 F3
Daisy Way SK6 .... 37 F4
Daisybank Dr
   Congleton CW12 .... 156 B2
   Sandbach CW11 .... 175 E3
Daisyhill Cl M33 .... 242 E6
Dalby Cl WA3 .... 10 A3
Dalby Ct CW9 .... 104 C3
Dale Ave Bebington L62 .... 43 E4
   Bramhall SK7 .... 35 F3
   Ellesmere Port L66 .... 69 E3
Dale Cl Warrington WA5 .. 15 F2
Dale Cres SK14 .... 224 E4
Dale Ct SK9 .... 151 E4
Dale Dr Chester CH2 ..... 118 B4
   Ellesmere Port L65 .... 69 F3
Dale Gdns L65 .... 70 A2
Dale Gr Altrincham WA15 . 238 F7
   Congleton CW12 .... 157 D1
   Irlam M44 .... 11 F4
Dale Head Rd SK10 .... 86 C2
Dale Hey L66 .... 43 F1
Dale House Fold SK12 .... 37 D2
Dale La WA4 .... 26 C4
Dale Rd Bebington L62 .... 43 E3
   Goldborne WA3 .... 3 D4
   New Mills SK22 .... 39 D4
Dale Sq WA14 .... 238 D7
Dale St Altrincham WA14 . 238 D4
   Chester CH3 .... 119 D1
   Macclesfield SK11 .... 112 C4
   Runcorn WA7 .... 23 D1
   Stockport SK1 .... 240 D3
Dale The Great Sankey WA5 . 14 C3
   Neston L64 .... 66 C4
   Tiverton WA6 .... 168 B3
Dale Valley WA12 .... 9 C2
Dale's Sq CW9 .... 103 F3
Dalebrook Ct SK4 .... 240 C5
Dalecroft WA6 .... 72 C1
Dalefords La
   Cuddington CW8 .... 102 A1
   Kingsley WA6 .... 125 E4
Dales Green Rd ST7 ...... 195 E3
Dalesford Cl SK11 .... 111 F4
Dalesford Cres SK11 ..... 111 F4
Daleside CH2 .... 118 B4
Daleway Rd L60 .... 40 C4

Dalewood Cres CH2 .... 72 A4
Dalham La WA2 .... 16 A4
Dallam Cty Prim Sch WA5 . 7 F3
Dalmahoy Cl CW7 .... 126 B1
Dalston Dr SK7 .... 35 E4
Dalton Bank WA1 .... 16 B4
Dalton Cl CH1 .... 117 E4
Dalton Ct Runcorn WA7 . 23 E3
   Sandbach CW11 .... 174 C1
Dalton Gr SK4 .... 240 C6
Dalton St Runcorn WA7 . 23 E3
   Sale M33 .... 242 C6
Dalton Way CW10 .... 128 B1
Dalveen Dr WA15 .... 238 F1
Dalwood Cl WA7 .... 50 C4
   Hollins Green WA3 .... 11 D1
   Mobberley WA16 .... 58 A1
   Warrington WA1 .... 17 F4
Dame Hollow SK8 .... 34 B1
Damery Ct SK7 .... 35 F4
Damery Rd SK7 .... 35 F4
Damhead La CH4 .... 141 A4
Damian Dr WA12 .... 2 A2
Dams La WA16 .... 106 B1
Damson La WA16 .... 58 A4
Damson Wlk M31 .... 11 F1
Danby Cl Hyde SK14 ..... 241 E8
   Runcorn WA7 .... 49 F4
Danby Rd SK14 .... 241 E8
Dane Ave Cheadle SK3 .. 240 A4
   Partington M31 .... 11 F1
Dane Bank Ave
   Congleton CW12 .... 156 C2
   Crewe CW2 .... 190 A2
Dane Bank Dr SK12 .... 38 A4
Dane Bank Rd CW9 ...... 104 A4
Dane Cl Alsager ST7 ...... 193 D1
   Sandbach CW11 .... 174 C1
Dane Dr Biddulph ST6 ... 179 F1
   Wilmslow SK9 .... 60 B4
Dane Gdns ST7 .... 195 E4
Dane Gr CH2 .... 119 F4
Dane Hill Cl SK12 .... 38 B4
Dane Pl CW7 .... 127 D3
Dane Rd M31 .... 242 D6
Dane Road Sta M33 .... 242 C6
Danebank Ave CW12 ..... 156 B4
   Middlewich CW10 .... 156 A4
   Wilmslow SK9 .... 103 F1
Dane Valley Cty High Sch
   CW12 .... 156 C1
Danebank Rd WA13 .... 18 B4
Danebank Rd E WA13 ..... 18 B4
Danefield Ct SK8 .... 34 A4
Danefield Rd
   Holmes Chapel CW4 ...... 130 B4
   Northwich CW9 .... 104 A4
   Sale M33 .... 242 C6
Danes Sq SK11 .... 112 B4
Danesbury Rise SK8 ...... 239 D3
Danescroft WA8 .... 12 A2
Danesford Cl CW2 .... 206 C4
Daneside Bsns Pk CW12 . 156 C2
Danesway M31 .... 11 F1
Daniel Adamson Ave M31 . 11 E1
Daniel Cl WA3 .... 10 A3
Daniel's La SK1 .... 240 E4
Daniell Way CW1 .... 142 A4
Dans Rd WA8 .... 13 F1
Danwood Cl M34 .... 241 A8
Dappleheath Rd CW2 .... 190 A4
Darent Rd WA11 .... 1 A4
Daresbury Ave WA15 ..... 238 E2
Daresbury Cl
   Holmes Chapel CW4 ...... 130 B4
   Sale M33 .... 242 F7
   Stockport SK3 .... 240 D2
Daresbury Cty Prim Sch
   WA4 .... 25 D3
Daresbury Expressway
   Daresbury WA4 .... 25 D1
   Runcorn WA7 .... 24 B3
Daresbury La WA4 .... 25 E2
Dargle Rd M33 .... 242 B6
Darian Ave WA22 .... 33 E1
Dark Ash La
   Ashton CH3, WA6 .... 99 D3
   Manley CH3, WA6 .... 99 D3
Dark La Henbury SK11 ... 111 D2
   Kingsley WA6 .... 75 D2
   Marston CW9 .... 79 E1
   Old Woodhouse SY13 .... 227 D2
   Tattenhall CH3 .... 183 F4
   Warren SK11 .... 111 E1
   Warren SK11 .... 111 E1
   Whitley WA4 .... 52 B1
Darkie Meadow CH5 ...... 116 A3
Darland La CH4 .... 162 B3
Darley Ave Crewe CW2 . 190 A3
   Gatley SK8 .... 239 B4
Warrington WA2 .... 8 A4
Darley Cl WA8 .... 12 A3
Darley Rd SK7 .... 36 C2
Darley St SK1 .... 240 F3
Darleydale Dr L62 .... 43 F3
Darlington Ave CW1 ...... 189 F1
Darlington Cres CH1 ...... 94 A2
Darlington St M34 .... 128 B3
Darnaway Cl WA3 .... 10 A3
Darnhall School La CW7 . 149 C1
Darnton Rd OL6 & SK15 . 242 B3
Dart Cl Alsager ST7 ...... 193 D2
   Biddulph ST6 .... 179 E1
Dart Wlk CW7 .... 127 D3
Dartnall Cl SK12 .... 38 A3

...win Gr SK7 35 F3
...win Rd CH1 117 E2
...win Street Cty Prim
....ch CW8 103 F4
...yl Rd L60 41 D4
...en Ave WA3 9 E1
...ancey CI CH2 95 F1
...ehall Ave SK9 60 A6
...en Cty Prim Sch CW12 156 C1
...ven Rd CW12 156 C1
...renham Ave WA1 16 C4
...renham Cres CW2 190 A2
...renham Ct CW9 104 A2
...renham Rd
...avenham CW9 104 C2
...ch Dennis CW9 104 C2
■ Wilmslow SK9 34 B2
...renham Way CW10 151 E3
...enport Ave Crewe CW2 206 B4
...antwich CW5 204 C4
...arrington WA1 16 C3
...ilmslow SK9 59 F2
...enport CI CW11 175 E4
...enport La
...trincham WA14 238 C7
...enton Green CW11 154 B1
...macron SK11 132 C3
...obberley WA16 58 B3
...enport Rd
...trincham WA14 238 C7
...eswall L60 40 C4
...venport Row WA7 49 E4
...venport St
...ngleton CW12 156 B1
...rewe CW1 190 B3
...acclesfield SK11 112 C4
...enport Sta SK3 240 F1
...vey La SK9 60 A4
...reylands SK9 60 B4
...vid CI M34 241 A5
...vid Lewis Manchester
...pileptic Colony The SK9 84 A3
...vid Rd WA13 18 B2
...vid St Denton M34 241 A6
...orthwich CW8 103 F4
...rid's Ave WA5 15 D3
...ridson Ave CW12 157 D3
...ries Ave Cheadle SK9 34 A3
...ewton-le-W WA12 2 B2
...arrington WA4 16 C2
...ries CI WA8 23 D2
...ries Way WA13 18 B2
...ries CI ST7 193 F2
...ry Rd WA7 23 F2
...y Bank SK3 240 E5
...wlish Ave SK8 34 C4
...wlish CI Bramhall SK7 35 F4
...ollins Green WA3 11 D2
...vulish La 67 D3
...en Gdns L65 70 A2
...wpool CI CH2 118 B3
...wpool Dr L62 43 E4
...wson Dr CW2 237 D4
...wson Rd
...trincham WA14 238 D8
...ollington SK10 88 A4
...eadle SK8 34 B4
...acclesfield SK11 111 F4
...wson St WA4 241 E5
...vstone Rd L60 41 D4
...ylesford CI SK8 239 D4
...ylesford Cres SK8 239 D4
...ylesford Rd SK8 239 D4
...Lacy Row WA7 24 A1
...acon CI Altrincham WA14 238 B1
...roft WA3 9 D4
...acon Rd WA8 13 D1
...acon Trad Est WA12 2 A1
...adman's La CW5 205 D1
...akin's Rd CW7 127 D2
...al Sq SK14 241 E6
...al St SK14 241 E6
...an Bank CW6 168 B2
...an CI Bollington SK10 88 A4
...arrington M31 11 F2
...ndrach CW11 174 C4
■ Widnes WA8 23 D4
...ilmslow SK9 34 B1
...an Cres WA2 8 A1
...an Ct SK10 88 A3
...an Dr Altrincham WA14 238 B1
...ilmslow SK9 34 B1
...an Hollow ST7 209 E1
...an La SK7 36 C4
...an Meadow WA12 2 B2
...an Pk SY14 214 A3
...an Rd Goldborne WA3 4 A4
...tam M44 11 F3
...ilmslow SK9 34 C2
...an Row Cty Jun Sch SK9 34 C1
...an Row Rd SK9 34 B1
...an St Middlewich CW10 128 B1
...orthwich CW9 104 B4
...alybridge SK15 242 D1
...idnes WA8 23 D4
...rrinsford CW7 126 C1
...an Valley Cty Prim Sch
...K10 87 F4
...an's La ST5 210 B1
...ane Ave SK8 239 F5
...anery CI CW12 118 B2
...anery Way SK1 240 F6
...ans CI Chester CH2 118 B3
...arvin CH3 121 D1
...ans La Barthomley CW2 208 B2
...andbach CW11 174 C3
...arrington WA4 17 F2

Deans Rd L65 70 C2
Deans Way
Higher Kinnerton CH4 161 D4
Tarvin CH3 121 D1
Dearnsgate L65 70 A3
Deansgate La
WA14 & WA15 238 E7
Deansway WA8 22 B4
Deanwater CI WA3 9 E2
Deanwater Ct SK8 34 B4
Deanway SK9 34 B1
Dearden St SK15 242 D2
Dearnford Ave L62 43 E3
Dearnford CI L62 43 E3
Debra CI L66 69 E2
Debra Rd L66 69 E2
Dee Banks CH4 141 D4
Dee Banks Sch CH4 142 A4
Dee CI Biddulph ST6 179 F1
Kidsgrove ST7 210 C4
Sandbach CW11 174 C4
Dee Cres CH3 180 C1
Dee Fords Ave CH3 119 D1
Dee Hills Pk CH2 237 C3
Dee La Chester CH1 237 F2
Holt LL13 196 B4
Dee Meadows LL13 196 B4
Dee Park CI L60 41 D3
Dee Park Rd L60 41 D3
Dee Pk LL13 196 B4
Dee Point Cty Prim Sch
CH1 117 E2
Dee Side L60 40 B4
Dee View CH3 180 C1
Dee View Rd
Connah's Quay CH5 91 E1
Heswall L60 40 C4
Dee Way CW7 127 D1
Deepdale WA8 12 C2
Deer Park Ct WA7 49 F3
Deerwood CI
Ellesmere Port L66 69 E4
Macclesfield SK10 88 A6
Deerwood Cres L66 69 E4
Deeside Ellesmere Port L65 70 A2
Holt LL13 196 B4
Deeside CI L65 70 A1
Deeside Coll of F Ed (Coleg
Glannau Dyfrdwy) CH5 91 E1
Deeside Cres CH1 116 C3
Deeside Ind Est (Parc
Ddiwydiannol Glannau
Dyfrdwy) CH5 93 D1
Deeside La CH1 116 C2
Deirdre Ave WA8 13 D1
Delafield CI WA2 8 A4
Delamer Rd WA14 238 C3
Delamere Ave Bebington L62 43 F2
Ellesmere Port L66 69 F3
Goldborne WA3 3 F3
Sale M33 242 E5
Widnes WA8 12 B1
Delamere CE Contr Prim
Sch CW6 123 E3
Delamere CI Bebington L62 43 F2
Sandbach CW11 174 C4
Delamere Ct Alsager CW12 192 C2
Bebington L62 43 F2
Delamere Dr
Ellesmere Port L66 69 F3
Macclesfield SK10 87 D3
Delamere Forest Sch WA6 100 B2
Delamere Gn L66 69 F3
Delamere Park Way E CW8 101 E3
Delamere Park Way W
CW8 101 E3
Delamere Rd Ashton CH1 99 D1
Congleton CW12 155 F2
Gatley SK8 239 B5
Nantwich CW5 204 C2
Norley WA6 100 C3
Wilmslow SK9 34 C2
Delamere Rise CW7 126 A1
Delamere St Chester CH1 237 D3
Crewe CW1 190 B2
Warrington WA5 15 F3
Winsford CW7 126 A1
Delamere Sta CW8 100 A1
Delamore's Acre L64 68 A4
Delavor CI L60 40 C4
Delavor Rd L60 40 C4
Delenty Dr WA3 9 F2
Delery Dr WA1 16 C4
Delford Rd WA16 82 B4
Delfur Rd SK7 35 F4
Dell Rd M44 11 E4
Dell CI L63 43 D3
Dell Dr WA2 9 D1
Della La L60 41 D4
Dell The Cuddington CW8 101 E3
Guilden Sutton CH3 119 F5
Warrington WA5 122 B2
Delmar Rd WA16 57 D1
Delph La Daresbury WA4 25 D1
Warrington WA2 8 C3
Winwick WA2 8 C3
Winwick WA2 8 C4
Delphield WA7 50 B4
Delphfields Rd WA4 26 B4
Delphside ST7 209 F1
Delta Ct CH4 140 A3
Delvine CI WA3 15 F4
Delves CI CW2 206 A2
Delves Wlk WA8 142 A4
Delvine Dr CH2 118 B3
Demage CI L66 69 E2
Demage La Backford CH1 94 C2
Chester CH2 95 D2

Demage La S CH2 118 B4
Demesne CI SK15 242 F1
Demesne Cres SK15 242 F1
Demesne St WA5 15 F2
Demmings Inf Sch SK8 239 F5
Demmings Rd SK8 239 F5
Den La CW3 221 E2
Denbigh CI Hazel Grove SK7 36 B4
Helsby WA6 73 D1
Denbigh Cres CW10 151 E4
Denbigh Ct L65 70 A4
Denbigh Dr CW7 149 D4
Denbigh Gdns L65 70 B2
Denbigh St Chester CH1 118 A2
Stockport SK4 240 D7
Denbury Ave WA4 16 C1
Denbury Dr WA14 238 B5
Denby La SK4 240 D8
Dene Ave WA12 1 C2
Dene Ct SK4 240 C6
Dene Dr CW7 149 E4
Denehurst Park Way CW8 101 E3
Denesgate CW7 149 E4
Deneside CW1 190 B3
Deneway Cheadle Hulme SK7 35 E4
High Lane SK6 37 D4
Stockport SK4 240 C6
Deneway CI SK4 240 C6
Deneway Mews SK4 240 C6
Denewood CI SK9 60 A3
Denford CI CH4 139 F2
Denford PI ST7 193 E3
Denhall CI CH2 118 C3
Denhall La L64 67 D1
Denham Ave WA5 15 D3
Denham Dr SK7 35 E4
Denholm Rd M20 239 C8
Denise Ave WA5 14 C2
Denison Rd SK7 36 C4
Denmark Rd M33 242 B8
Denmark St WA14 238 D4
Dennett CI WA1 17 F3
Dennis Dr CH4 141 D3
Dennis Rd WA8 23 E4
Dennison Rd SK8 34 A2
Densham Ave WA2 8 A1
Denston CI CW2 190 A1
Denstone Dr CH4 141 D2
Dentdale WA8 22 B4
Dentith Dr CH1 117 F3
Denton CI CW7 126 B1
Denton Dr CW9 79 E1
Denton Drive Ind Est CW9 79 E1
Denton St WA8 13 E1
Denver Ave CW2 190 A2
Denzell Gdns WA14 238 A3
Denpebech CI SY14 213 D2
Deplach Rd SK8 239 D5
Depmore La WA6 75 D1
Deramore CI L66 242 B3
Derby CI Irlam M44 11 E3
Neston L64 66 C2
Newton-le-W WA12 2 A3
Derby Ct M33 242 C5
Derby Dr WA1 16 C4
Derby PI CH2 118 C2
Derby Range SK4 240 B8
Derby Rd Ashton-u-L OL6 242 A3
Goldborne WA3 3 C4
Hyde SK14 241 E8
Kidsgrove ST7 210 B4
Manchester SK4 240 C8
Warrington WA4 16 B1
Widnes WA8 13 E2
Derby Row WA12 1 C4
Derby St Altrincham WA14 238 E5
Congleton CW12 156 B2
Crewe CW1 190 A3
Newton-le-W WA12 2 A2
Stockport SK3 240 D4
Derbyshire Hill Cty Prim
Sch WA9 1 A1
Derbyshire Hill Rd WA9 1 A1
Derbyshire Rd
Partington M31 11 E1
Poynton SK12 37 E3
Sale M33 242 C6
Derbyshire Rd S M33 242 D5
Derek Ave WA2 8 C1
Derrington Ave CW2 190 B2
Derwen Rd SK3 240 E3
Derwen Sch CH4 161 D4
Derwent Ave CW7 127 D1
Derwent CI Alsager ST7 193 D2
Culcheth WA3 5 D1
Holmes Chapel CW4 130 A2
Macclesfield SK11 112 A3
Partington M31 11 F2
Willaston (nr Nantwich)
CW5 205 D5
Derwent Cres ST7 195 E1
Derwent Dr Biddulph ST6 179 F1
Cheadle Hulme SK7 35 E3
Congleton CW12 156 C1
Hooton L66 44 A3
Wilmslow SK9 34 B3
Derwent Rd Chester CH2 118 D3
High Lane SK6 37 F4
Warrington WA4 16 A1
Widnes WA8 12 B3
Desoto Rd WA8 22 C3
Desoto Rd E WA8 22 C3
Desoto Rd W WA8 22 C3
Deva Ave CH4 140 B3
Deva Bsns Pk CH5 116 A4

Deva CI SK12 36 A2
Deva Ct CH2 118 C1
Deva La CH3 118 B3
Deva Link CH1 118 A2
Deva Rd CW2 189 E2
Deva Stad (Chester City
FC) CH1 117 F1
Deva Terr CH2 237 F2
Devisdale Grange WA14 238 B3
Devisdale Rd WA14 238 B4
Devon Ave WA3 4 A1
Devon Gr ST6 179 F2
Devon PI Congleton CW12 156 C2
Widnes WA8 13 D2
Devon Rd Chester CH2 118 C3
Irlam M44 11 E3
Partington M31 11 F1
Devonshire Dr SK9 60 A1
Devonshire Gdns WA12 2 B1
Devonshire PI Chester CH4 141 F4
Runcorn WA7 23 D1
Devonshire Rd
Altrincham WA14 238 D6
Broughton CH4 139 E2
Hazel Grove SK7 36 C4
Manchester SK4 240 B7
Warrington WA1 16 C4
Dewar CI WA7 23 F2
Dewes St CH1 190 A3
Dewhurst Rd WA3 9 E1
Dexter Way CW10 128 B1
Dial La CW12 158 A1
Dial Rd WA15 32 B4
Dial St WA1 16 B3
Diamond CI L64 242 A4
Diamond St OL6 242 A4
Dibbins Gn L63 43 D4
Dibbinsdale Rd L63 43 D4
Dickens CI
Cheadle Hulme SK8 35 D3
■ Sandbach CW11 174 B3
Dickens La SK12 36 C1
Dickenson St WA2 16 B4
Dickinson CI WA11 1 C4
Dickson CI WA8 23 D4
Dickson St ■ WA8 23 D4
Dicksons Dr CH2 118 B2
Didsbury Rd SK4 240 B6
Dierden St CW7 127 D1
Dierdens Terr CW10 128 B1
Dig La Acton CW5 203 F2
Frodsham WA6 74 A4
Ravensmoor CW5 203 F2
Shavington CW2 206 A2
Digkake St ST7 209 F2
Diglee Rd SK23 39 F2
Dinas CI CH1 117 E2
Dingle Ave Denton M34 241 B6
Lindow End SK9 59 E2
Newton-le-W WA12 1 C1
Dingle Bank CH4 141 E4
Dingle Bank CI WA13 18 C2
Dingle CI Macclesfield SK10 87 D2
Romiley SK6 241 D2
Dingle Cty Prim Sch The
CW1 191 E3
Dingle La Appleton WA4 26 C3
Kelsall CW6 122 C3
Sandbach CW11 175 D5
Winsford CW7 126 B1
Dingle The Barnton CW8 76 A2
Haslington CW1 191 E3
Warrington WA1 18 C2
Dingle Way CW8 101 F3
Dingle Wlk CW7 126 B1
Dinglebrook Gr ■ SK9 34 C1
Dingleway WA4 26 B4
Dinmor Rd M22 33 F4
Dirty La WA14 31 E2
Disley Cty Prim Sch SK12 38 B3
Disley Sta SK12 38 B3
Ditchfield La WA16 29 E2
Ditchfield PI WA8 22 A4
Ditchfield Rd Penketh WA5 14 C2
Widnes WA8 22 A4
Ditton CE Contr Prim Sch
WA8 12 A1
Ditton CE Prim Sch WA8 12 B1
Ditton Rd Widnes WA8 23 E1
Widnes, Ditton Marsh WA8 22 B3
Dixon Ave WA12 2 A3
Dixon CI WA11 2 A4
Dixon Ct SK8 239 D5
Dixon Dr SK11 84 A2
Dixon Rd Congleton CW12 157 D2
Denton M34 241 A6
Dixon St Ashton-u-L OL6 242 A4
Irlam M44 11 E3
Warrington WA1 16 A3
Dobb Hedge CI WA15 32 B7
Dobell's Rd CW9 103 F3
Dobers La Frodsham WA6 74 B2
Kingsley WA6 74 B2
Dobson's Sq SY14 213 D2
Dock Rd Northwich CW9 103 F4
Widnes WA8 23 D3
Widnes, Ditton Marsh WA8 22 C2
Dock St Ellesmere Port L65 70 B4
Widnes WA8 23 D3
Dock Yard Rd L65 70 C3
Dodd's Green La SY13 228 A2
Dodd's La Appleton WA4 27 D3
Bradley Green ST7 224 C1
Doddington CI CW11 175 E4
Doddington Rd CW2 190 B1
Dodds La CW12 156 C2
Doddswood Dr CW12 156 C2
Dodge Hill SK1 & SK4 240 E6

Dodgsley Dr WA6 75 E1
Dodleston CE Contr Prim
Sch CH4 162 A4
Dodleston La
Dodleston CH4 162 B2
Pulford CH4 162 B2
Doe's Meadow Rd L63 43 D4
Doeford CI WA3 4 C3
Dog La Brereton Green CW11 153 F4
Chowley CH3 182 B3
Coddington CH3 182 B2
Nantwich CW5 204 C3
Threapwood SY14 223 E4
Dogmore La CW6 147 E2
Dolly La SK23 39 F2
Dolphin Cres L66 69 F1
Dolphin Ct CH4 141 D4
Dombey Rd SK12 36 B1
Domestic App M90 33 E4
Domville CI WA13 18 C2
Don Wlk L65 70 A3
Donagh CI SK10 86 C1
Donald Ave SK14 241 F5
Donkey La SK9 60 A3
Donne PI CH1 117 F3
Donnington Ave CW8 239 F6
Donnington Way CW4 140 C4
Dooley's Grig SK11 108 C1
Dooley's La SK9 33 E1
Dorac Ave SK8 34 B4
Dorchester CI WA9 60 B4
Dorchester Pk WA7 24 C2
Dorchester Rd Chester CH4 140 C3
Great Sankey WA5 15 E3
Dorchester Way
Burtonwood WA5 6 C3
Macclesfield SK10 87 E2
Doreen Ave CW12 179 D4
Doreold Dr CW5 204 B3
Dorfold St CH1 190 B2
Dorfold Way CH2 118 A4
Doric Ave WA6 74 B4
Dorin Park Sch CH2 118 B3
Doris Rd SK3 240 C4
Dormer CI CH3 143 D3
Dorney CI WA4 26 C3
Dornoch Ct CW4 130 A1
Dorothea St WA2 16 B4
Dorric Way CW1 190 B4
Dorrington CI WA7 50 B4
Dorrington Rd SK3 240 A3
Dorrit CI SK12 36 C1
Dorset Ave SK8 240 C1
Dorset CI CW12 156 C2
Dorset Ct CH4 17 D1
Dorset Dr ST8 50 A3
Dorset Dr ST6 179 F1
Dorset PI Chester CH2 119 D3
Kidsgrove ST7 195 D1
Dorset Rd Altrincham WA14 238 B5
Chester CH2 118 B4
Irlam M44 11 E3
Dorset St WA8 242 A2
Dorset Way WA1 17 D4
Dorset Wlk SK10 86 C1
Douglas Ave WA9 6 A3
Douglas CI Hartford CW8 103 E3
Widnes WA8 13 F2
Douglas La CH2 171 D3
Douglas PI CH4 140 C3
Douglas St
Ashton-u-L OL6 242 A3
Hyde SK14 241 E6
Doune Ct L65 70 B2
Dounrey CI WA2 9 D1
Douthwaite Dr SK6 241 D3
Dove Bank Prim Sch ST7 195 D1
Dove CI Ellesmere Port L65 70 A4
Helsby WA6 73 D3
Sandbach CW11 175 D4
Warrington WA3 9 F2
Dove Cote SK6 179 E1
Dove PI CW7 127 D1
Dovecot Bsns & Tech Pk
M33 242 F6
Dovecote CI CW2 206 A4
Dovedale CI Bebington L62 43 F3
Congleton CW12 157 D2
High Lane SK6 37 F4
Warrington WA2 8 C2
Dovedale Ct WA8 12 C3
Dover CI Runcorn WA7 50 C3
Dover Ct L65 70 B1
Dover Dr Ellesmere Port L65 70 B1
Winsford CW7 149 D4
Dover Rd Chester CH4 141 D3
Warrington WA5 87 F1
Widnes WA8 17 D2
Dovesmead Rd L60 41 E4
Doveston Rd M33 242 B8
Doward St WA8 13 E1
Downes CI SK10 87 D1
Downesway WA6 59 F1
Downham Ave WA3 4 C1
Downham Dr L60 41 D2
Downham PI CH1 117 F2
Downham Rd S L60 40 C2
Downing CI SK11 112 C2
Downs Dr WA14 238 E8
Downs End WA16 57 E1
Downs The
Altrincham WA14 238 D3
Cheadle SK8 239 D3
Cuddington CW8 101 E3

Downsfield Rd CH4 .... 141 D3
Downside WA8 .... 12 A2
Downswood Ct CH2 .... 118 B2
Downswood Dr CH2 .... 118 B2
Downway La WA9 .... 1 A1
Dowson Rd SK14 .... 241 E5
Dragon Yd WA8 .... 13 D2
Dragon's La CW11 .... 152 A1
Drake Ave M44 .... 11 F3
Drake Cl WA5 .... 7 E1
Drake Ct SK5 .... 240 E8
Drake La Acton CW5 ...... 203 F2
Ravensmoor CW5 .... 203 F2
Drake Rd Altrincham WA14 . 238 B8
Neston L64 .... 41 F1
Drakelow La
Lach Dennis CW10 .... 128 C4
Middlewich CW10 .... 128 C4
Drakes Way SY14 .... 213 D3
Draycott Dr SK8 .... 60 A3
Draycott Dr ST5 .... 210 B1
Drayton Ave SK8 .... 34 A4
Drayton Cl Runcorn WA7 ... 22 C1
Wilmslow SK9 .... 34 B1
Drayton Cres CW1 .... 190 C3
Drayton Manor M20 .... 239 B8
Drenfell Rd ST7 .... 194 C4
Drill Field Rd CW9 .... 103 F4
Drive A CH5 .... 93 D1
Drive B CH5 .... 93 D1
Drive C CH5 .... 93 D1
Drive The Altrincham WA15 . 32 B4
Macclesfield CW4 .... 130 B1
Lymm WA13 .... 19 E1
Drome Rd CH5 .... 93 D2
Drovers Way CW11 .... 175 D3
Drumber La ST7 .... 195 D4
Drumber The CW7 .... 126 B1
Drumble Field SK11 .... 84 A2
Drummond Ave L66 .... 69 E2
Drummond Ct WA8 .... 13 E1
Drummond Way SK11 ...... 86 C1
Druridge Dr WA5 .... 14 C2
Drury Cl CW1 .... 190 C3
Drury La Knutsford WA16 .. 57 D1
Warmingham CW1 .... 173 E2
Dryden Ave SK8 .... 239 F6
Dryden Cl CW2 .... 190 A1
Dryden Pl WA2 .... 8 B1
Dryhurst Dr SK12 .... 38 B3
Dryhurst La SK12 .... 38 B3
Dublin Croft L66 .... 69 F1
Duchy Rd CW1 .... 190 A4
Duchy St SK3 .... 240 D3
Duck La CH3 .... 121 F4
Duckworth Gr WA7 .... 9 D1
Duddon Cl Dunham CW9 . 103 F2
Duddon CW6 .... 145 D3
Duddon Hook La CW6 .... 144 C3
Duddon Rd CW6 .... 145 D3
Duddon St Peter's CE
Contr Prim Sch CW6 .... 145 D3
Dudleston Rd L66 .... 69 D3
Dudley Ave WA7 .... 23 E1
Dudley Cres L62 .... 44 A2
Dudley Rd Ellesmere Port L65 . 70 A3
Irlam M44 .... 11 E2
Sale M33 .... 242 C8
Dudley St WA2 .... 16 A4
Dudley Wlk SK11 .... 111 F4
Dudlow Green Rd WA4 ... 26 C3
Dutton Wlk M22 .... 33 F4
Duke Ave Cheadle Hulme SK8 . 34 C3
Glazebury WA3 .... 5 E4
Duke St Alderley Edge SK9 . 60 A1
Chester CH4 .... 237 E1
Congleton CW12 .... 156 B1
Crewe CW2 .... 190 B2
Macclesfield SK11 .... 112 B4
Newton-le-W WA12 .... 2 A2
Stalybridge SK15 .... 242 C1
[8] Stockport SK1 .... 240 F5
Duke's Cres CW11 .... 175 D4
Duke's Ct CH4 .... 237 E1
Dukes Way CW9 .... 103 F2
Dukesway CH2 .... 118 C4
Dukinfield Rd SK14 .... 241 C8
Dulas Ct CH2 .... 118 B4
Dulverton Ave CH3 .... 119 E1
Dumbah La SK10 .... 87 E3
Dumbers SK11 .... 136 A1
Dunbar Cl
Connah's Quay CH5 .... 91 E1
Ellesmere Port L66 .... 69 E3
Holmes Chapel CW4 ...... 130 B2
Dunblane Ave SK4 .... 240 D6
Duncan Ave
Newton-le-W WA12 .... 2 B3
Runcorn WA7 .... 23 E1
Duncan St WA2 .... 16 B4
Duncansby Cres WA5 ..... 14 C3
Duncansby Dr L63 .... 43 E2
Dundalk La WA8 .... 22 B4
Dundalk Rd WA8 .... 22 C4
Dundee Cl WA2 .... 8 C2
Dundee Ct L65 .... 70 C2
Dundonald Ave WA4 .... 16 B1
Dundonald Rd SK8 .... 35 D4
Dundonald St SK2 .... 240 F2
Dundrennan Cl SK12 ...... 36 B3
Dunecroft M34 .... 241 A8
Dunham Cl Bebington L62 . 43 F2
Sandbach CW11 .... 175 E3
Dunham Cres CW2 .... 206 A4
Dunham Ct WA6 .... 97 F3

Dunham Forest Golf Course
WA14 .... 20 C2
Dunham Lawn WA14 ...... 238 B4
Dunham Massey Hall WA14 . 20 B2
Dunham Pk WA14 .... 20 C2
Dunham Rd
Altrincham WA14 .... 238 B4
Northwich CW9 .... 104 A2
Partington WA13 .... 19 F4
Wilmslow SK9 .... 34 B3
Dunham Rise WA14 .... 238 C4
Dunham Way CH2 .... 118 C3
Dunham-on-Hill Cty Prim
Sch WA6 .... 97 F3
Dunkirk Ave CW7 .... 149 E4
Dunkirk Dr L65 .... 70 A1
Dunkirk La Capenhurst CH1 . 94 B4
Dukinfield SK14 .... 241 B8
Ellesmere Port L65 .... 70 A1
Dunley Cl WA3 .... 10 A3
Dunlin Ave WA12 .... 2 B2
Dunlin Cl Poynton SK12 ... 36 A2
Runcorn WA7 .... 49 F3
Warrington WA2 .... 8 C2
Dunlin Wlk WA14 .... 238 B8
Dunlop St WA4 .... 16 C1
Dunmore Cl CW10 .... 151 E4
Dunmore Rd WA11 .... 1 B4
Dunmore Rd
Ellesmere Port L66 .... 69 D3
Gatley SK8 .... 239 B6
Dunnow Rd WA4 .... 17 E2
Dunn's La CH3 .... 121 F4
Dunnock Cl WA2 .... 6 C2
Dunnock Gr WA3 .... 9 F2
Dunnocksfold Rd ST7 .... 193 D2
Dunnockswood ST7 ...... 193 D2
Dunollie Rd M33 .... 242 E5
Dunoon Cl CW4 .... 130 A1
Dunraven Rd L64 .... 67 D4
Dunscar Cl WA3 .... 9 E3
Dunsford WA8 .... 12 B2
Dunsmore CI WA11 .... 1 B4
Dunstan La L64 .... 67 F2
Dunstan Cl CW9 .... 104 A2
Dunster Ave L60 .... 41 D4
Dunster Rd SK10 .... 87 F1
Dunwood Dr ST7 .... 193 E3
Durban Ave CH3 .... 142 B4
Durber Cl ST7 .... 209 E1
Durham Cl
Macclesfield SK10 .... 86 C1
Romiley SK6 .... 241 A1
Warrington WA1 .... 17 F4
Durham Ct L65 .... 70 C2
Durham Dr CW7 .... 149 E3
Durham Gr M44 .... 11 E3
Durham Rd Blacon CH1 . 117 F3
Widnes WA8 .... 13 D2
Durkston Cl WA8 .... 12 B1
Durrell Way WA3 .... 3 F4
Dutton Cl CW5 .... 204 C2
Dutton Gn L65 .... 70 C2
Dutton La CW8 .... 101 E3
Duxford Cl WA2 .... 8 C2
Dyar Terr CW8 .... 78 B1
Dyberth Rd CH1 .... 117 E2
Dye House La SK22 .... 39 E4
Dye La SK6 .... 241 B2
Dyer St WA3 .... 2 C4
Dyers Cl WA13 .... 19 D2
Dyers La WA13 .... 19 D2
Dykin Cl WA8 .... 13 F2
Dykin Rd WA8 .... 13 F2
Dysart St SK1 .... 240 F3
Dyserth Gr [2] SK8 .... 34 C3
Dystelegh Rd SK12 .... 38 B3

Eadie Gr CW1 .... 190 A4
Eaglaisway SK10 .... 86 C1
Eagland Pl CW12 .... 156 C2
Eagle Brow WA13 .... 18 B2
Eagle La L66 .... 69 E4
Eagles Way WA7 .... 49 F3
Eaglesfield CW8 .... 103 E2
Earles La
Higher Wincham CW9 ...... 79 F3
Marston CW9 .... 79 F3
Ealing Rd WA5 .... 15 D3
Eanleywood La WA7 .... 50 B4
Eardley Cl CW2 .... 156 C2
Eardley Pl CW1 .... 190 A3
Eardleyend Rd ST7 .... 209 F4
Eardswick Cl WA3 .... 237 E4
Eardswick La CW1 .... 172 B3
Eardswick Rd CW10 ...... 151 E3
Earle's La CW6 .... 122 B3
Earls La
Higher Wincham CW9 ...... 79 F3
Marston CW9 .... 79 F3
Earls St SK15 .... 242 C7
Earls Oak CH2 .... 118 B4
Earls Rd CW2 .... 206 A2
Earls Way Davenham CW9 . 103 F2
Runcorn WA7 .... 49 F3
Earlston Ct CH2 .... 237 F2

Earlsway Chester CH4 .... 141 D4
Macclesfield SK11 .... 111 F4
Earndale WA8 .... 13 D3
Easby Cl Cheadle Hulme SK8 . 35 D3
Poynton SK12 .... 36 B2
Easenhall Cl WA1 .... 13 E3
Easingwold [2] WA14 .... 238 C8
East Ave Bollington SK10 . 87 F4
Cheadle SK8 .... 34 B4
Great Sankey WA5 .... 15 D2
Northwich CW9 .... 104 B3
Stalybridge SK15 .... 242 D3
Warrington WA4 .... 16 B4
Weston CW2 .... 207 E3
East Ct ST7 .... 193 F2
East Dam Wood Rd L24 . 21 D1
East Downs Rd
Altrincham WA14 .... 238 C2
Cheadle SK8 .... 239 F2
East Dudley St CW7 ...... 126 C1
East Rd Halewood L24 .... 21 D2
East Rd Middlewich CW10 . 128 A1
Wythenshawe M90 .... 33 E4
East St Ashton-u-L OL6 ... 242 A4
Widnes WA8 .... 13 E1
East View WA4 .... 17 E1
Eastbury Cl WA8 .... 13 E3
Eastcott Cl CW12 .... 155 F2
Eastdale Pl WA14 .... 238 D7
Eastdale Rd WA1 .... 17 D4
Easter Ct WA5 .... 7 D1
Eastern Pathway CH4 .... 237 F1
Eastern Rd Shavington CW5 . 205 F3
Willaston (nr Nantwich)
CW5 .... 205 F3
Eastfields Gr CH1 .... 117 D4
Eastford Rd WA4 .... 16 A1
Eastgate Cl CW8 .... 130 B2
Eastgate Row CW1 .... 237 E2
Eastgate St CH1 .... 237 E2
Eastham Ctry Pk L62 ...... 44 A4
Eastham Glenburn Cty Inf
Sch L62 .... 43 F3
Eastham Rake Bebington L62 . 43 F2
Willaston L62 .... 43 F2
Eastham Rake Sta L62 ... 43 E2
Eastham Village Rd L62 . 44 A2
Easthope Rd WA3 .... 3 D4
Eastleigh Rd SK9 .... 239 B1
Easton Dr SK8 .... 240 A1
Eastward Ave SK9 .... 59 F3
Eastway Ellesmere Port L66 . 69 E4
Widnes WA8 .... 12 B1
Eastwood WA7 .... 24 B1
Eastwood Ave WA12 .... 2 C1
Eastwood Ct CW4 .... 139 D3
Eastwood Rd WA8 .... 6 C4
Eaton Ave CH4 .... 141 D4
Eaton Bank CW12 .... 156 C2
Eaton Bank Ind Est CW12 . 156 C2
Eaton Cl Broughton CH4 . 139 E2
Cheadle SK8 .... 239 F3
Poynton SK12 .... 37 D2
Sandbach CW11 .... 175 E4
Eaton Cres CW9 .... 103 F1
Eaton Cty Prim Sch CW6 . 147 D2
Eaton Dr Alderley Edge SK9 . 59 F1
Middlewich CW10 .... 151 D4
Eaton Gr CH4 .... 140 C3
Eaton La Davenham CW9 . 103 F1
Eaton CW6 .... 146 C1
Goostrey CW4 .... 107 E1
Macclesfield SK11 .... 112 B3
Tarporley CW6 .... 168 C4
Eaton Mews CH4 .... 141 D4
Eaton Rd Alsager ST7 .... 193 E2
Altrincham WA14 .... 238 C1
Chester CH4 .... 141 F2
Eccleston CH4 .... 141 F2
Sale M33 .... 242 A6
Tarporley CW6 .... 146 B1
Wettenhall CW7 .... 170 B4
Eaton St Crewe CW2 ...... 190 B2
Runcorn WA7 .... 23 D1
Eaton View CW9 .... 126 C4
Eaves Brow Rd WA3 .... 9 D4
Eaves Knoll Rd SK22 ...... 39 D4
Ebnal La SY14 .... 213 F2
Eccles Cl SK23 .... 65 E4
Eccles Rd SK23 .... 65 E4
Eccleston Ave Bebington L62 . 43 E4
Chester CH4 .... 141 E3
Ellesmere Port L65 .... 70 A4
Eccleston CE Aided Prim
Sch CH4 .... 141 F1
Eccleston Cl WA3 .... 9 E3
Eccleston Dr WA7 .... 23 E1
Eccleston Rd CH4 .... 161 D4
Eccleston Way [3] SK9 ... 34 B2
Eccups La SK9 .... 59 E4
Echo Cl CH4 .... 140 C3
Ecton Ave SK10 .... 113 D4
Ecton Cl CW7 .... 127 D2
Edale Cl Altrincham WA14 . 238 C1
Bebington L62 .... 43 F3
Cheadle SK8 .... 34 B4

Edale Dr CW6 .... 122 B3
Edbury Pl CH4 .... 141 E4
Eddisbury Cl SK11 .... 112 C4
Eddisbury Dr ST5 .... 210 B1
Eddisbury Hill CW8 .... 123 E4
Eddisbury Rd L66 .... 69 F1
Eddisbury Sq WA6 .... 74 A4
Eddisbury Terr SK11 ...... 112 C4
Eddisford Dr WA3 .... 4 B2
Edelsten St WA5 .... 15 F3
Edelston Hall La CW5 .... 203 F1
Eden Ave
Fowley Common WA3 .... 5 E2
High Lane SK6 .... 37 F4
Winsford CW7 .... 126 C1
Eden Cl Biddulph ST6 .... 179 F1
Ellesmere Port L66 .... 69 E3
Kidsgrove ST7 .... 195 D1
Wilmslow SK9 .... 59 F3
Eden Dr SK13 .... 87 F1
Eden Pl Cheadle SK8 ..... 239 D6
Edenbridge Gdns WA4 ... 26 C2
Edendale WA8 .... 12 A1
Edenfield Cl WA16 .... 58 A2
Edenfield Rd WA16 .... 58 A2
Edenhall Cl CW4 .... 130 A2
Edgar Cr CH4 .... 237 E1
Edgar Pl CH4 .... 237 E1
Edgars Dr WA2 .... 9 D1
Edge Gr CH2 .... 118 C1
Edge La SY14 .... 199 E1
Edge View La WA16 .... 59 D1
Edgecroft CH3 .... 166 A2
Edgehill Chase SK9 .... 60 C4
Edgeley Fold SK3 .... 240 C3
Edgeley Park (Stockport
County FC) SK3 .... 240 E3
Edgeley Rd SK3 .... 240 B3
Edgeley Road WA4 .... 238 A2
Edgerley La CW5 .... 181 D3
Edgerton Rd WA3 .... 3 F4
Edgeview Rd CW12 .... 179 D4
Edgeway Henbury SK11 . 111 E4
Wilmslow SK9 .... 60 A3
Edgewell La CW6 .... 147 D2
Edgewood Dr Bebington L62 . 43 E3
Wistaston CW2 .... 206 A4
Edgworth St WA2 .... 16 A3
Edinburgh Cl SK8 .... 239 F6
Edinburgh Cr L65 .... 70 B2
Edinburgh Dr
Macclesfield SK10 .... 87 D1
Romiley SK6 .... 241 C4
Edinburgh Pl CW12 .... 156 C1
Edinburgh Rd
Congleton CW12 .... 156 C1
Widnes WA8 .... 22 A4
Wistaston CW2 .... 205 F4
Edinburgh Way CH4 ...... 237 F1
Edison Rd WA7 .... 23 E2
Edith St WA7 .... 22 C4
Edleston Cty Prim Sch
CW2 .... 190 B2
Edleston Rd CW2 .... 190 B2
Edlestone Gr [3] SK9 ..... 34 C1
Edmund Cl SK4 .... 240 E8
Edna St Chester CH2 ..... 118 C2
Widnes WA8 .... 13 D1
Edward Gdns WA1 .... 17 F3
Edward St WA1 .... 14 B3
Edward St
Ashton-u-L OL6 .... 242 B2
Audley ST7 .... 209 F2
Crewe CW2 .... 190 B1
Ellesmere Port L65 .... 70 B4
Haydock WA11 .... 1 A3
Hyde SK14 .... 241 C7
Macclesfield SK11 .... 112 A4
Northwich CW9 .... 104 B4
Sale M33 .... 242 C6
Stockport SK1 .... 240 F4
Widnes WA8 .... 13 E1
Edwards Ave CW2 .... 206 B3
Edwards Cl CW2 .... 206 B3
Edwards Rd CH4 .... 141 D3
Edwards Way Alsager ST7 . 193 F2
Widnes WA8 .... 22 B4
Edwin St WA8 .... 13 E1
Egdon Cl WA8 .... 12 B1
Egerton WA16 .... 29 E3
Egerton Ave Hartford CW8 . 103 D2
Partington WA13 .... 19 E4
Warrington WA1 .... 16 C4
Egerton Cty Prim Sch
WA16 .... 56 C1
Egerton Dr Chester CH2 . 118 B3
Sale M33 .... 242 B7
Egerton Moss WA15 .... 31 F3
Egerton Rd Blacon CH1 . 117 E3
Lymm WA13 .... 18 B3
Wilmslow SK9 .... 34 A1
Egerton Rd S SK4 .... 240 C8
Egerton Sq WA16 .... 57 D1
Egerton St Chester CH2 . 237 F3
Congleton CW12 .... 156 B1
Ellesmere Port L65 .... 70 B3
Runcorn WA7 .... 23 D2
Warrington, Howley WA1 .. 16 C3
Warrington, Stockton Heath
WA4 .... 16 B1
Egerton Street Sch CH2 . 237 F3
Egerton Wlk CH4 .... 162 A4
Eggbridge La CH3 .... 143 D3
Egremont Gr [2] SK3 ..... 240 B4
Egypt St Warrington WA1 . 16 A3
Widnes WA8 .... 22 C4

Eisenhower Cl WA5 .... 15?
Elaine Cl Ellesmere Port L66 . 69?
Widnes WA8 .... 13?
Elaine St WA1 .... 16?
Elanor Rd [2] CW11 ...... 174?
Elcho Rd WA14 .... 238?
Elcombe Ave WA3 .... 4?
Elder Dr CH4 .... 140?
Elderberry Way SK9 .... 60?
Elderberry Wlk M31 .... 11?
Eldon Rd Macclesfield SK11 . 111?
Stockport SK3 .... 240?
Eldon St WA1 .... 16?
Eldon Terr L64 .... 66?
Eleanor Cl CW1 .... 189?
Eleanor St
Ellesmere Port L65 .... ?
Widnes WA8 .... 22?
Electra Way CW1 .... 191?
Electricity St CW2 .... 190?
Elf Mill Cl SK3 .... 240?
Elgar Ave L62 .... 43?
Elgar Cl L65 .... 70?
Elgin Ave
Holmes Chapel CW4 ...... 130?
Macclesfield SK10 .... 87?
Warrington WA1 .... 16?
Elgin Cl CH3 .... 119?
Elgin Dr M33 .... 242?
Elgin St SK15 .... 242?
Elgol Cl SK3 .... 240?
Eliot Cl WA2 .... 191?
Eliza St M33 .... 242?
Elizabeth Ave Disley SK12 . 38?
Stockport SK1 .... 240?
Elizabeth Cres CH4 .... 237?
Elizabeth Ct CW6 .... 122?
Elizabeth Cres Kidsgrove ST7 . 210?
Stockport SK4 .... 240?
Elizabeth Dr WA1 .... 17?
Elizabeth Rd Haydock WA11 . ?
Partington M31 .... ?
Elizabeth St
Congleton CW12 .... 156?
Crewe CW1 .... 190?
Hyde SK14 .... 241?
Macclesfield SK11 .... 112?
Elizabethan Way CW9 ... 104?
Elk View SY14 .... 222?
Elkan Cl WA8 .... 13?
Elkan Rd WA8 .... ?
Ella Gr WA16 .... 57?
Elland Dr L66 .... 69?
Ellen Brook Rd M22 .... 33?
Ellen St Stockport SK4 ... 240?
Warrington WA5 .... 15?
Ellerby Cl WA7 .... 69?
Ellerton Ave WA5 .... 6?
Ellerton Cl WA8 .... 12?
Ellesmere Ave
Broughton CH4 .... 139?
Chester CH2 .... 118?
Ellesmere Cl CW11 .... 174?
Ellesmere Dr SK8 .... 240?
Ellesmere Port Cth
(Aided) High Sch L65 .... 70?
Ellesmere Port Hospl L65 . 70?
Ellesmere Port Sta L65 ... 70?
Ellesmere Port Stadium
The L65 .... ?
Ellesmere Rd
Altrincham WA14 .... 238?
Cheadle SK3 .... 240?
Culcheth WA3 .... ?
Northwich CW9 .... 104?
Warrington WA4 .... ?
Ellesmere Cl Runcorn WA7 . 23?
Warrington WA1 .... 16?
Ellesworth Cl WA5 .... 15?
Elliot St [3] WA8 .... 23?
Ellis St Crewe CW1 .... 190?
Hyde SK14 .... 241?
Widnes WA8 .... 22?
Ellison St
Warrington, Howley WA1 .. 16?
Warrington, Stockton Heath
WA4 .... 16?
Elloway Rd L24 .... 21?
Elmwood Gn CW2 .... 206?
Elm Ave Newton-le-W WA12 . ?
Widnes WA8 .... 13?
Elm Beds Rd SK12 .... 37?
Elm Cl L61 Partington M31 . ?
Poynton SK12 .... 36?
Tarporley CW6 .... 168?
Wistaston CW2 .... 205?
Elm Cres SK9 .... 60?
Elm Dr Crewe CW1 .... 190?
Holmes Chapel CW4 ...... 130?
Macclesfield SK11 .... 112?
Elm Gn L64 .... 42?
Elm Gr Alderley Edge SK9 . 60?
Alsager ST7 .... 193?
Broughton CH4 .... 140?
Ellesmere Port L66 .... 70?
Hyde SK14 .... 241?
Sale M33 .... 242?
Warrington WA1 .... 16?
Wilmslow SK9 .... 59?
Winsford CW7 .... 126?
Elm Rd Altrincham WA15 . 238?
Congleton CW12 .... 156?
Gatley SK8 .... ?
Haydock WA11 .... 1?
High Lane SK6 .... 37?

m Rd continued
Hollins Green WA3 .... 11 D1
Middlewich CW10 .... 151 E4
Penketh WA5 .... 14 C2
Runcorn WA7 .... 49 E4
Warrington WA2 .... 8 B2
Weaverham CW8 .... 102 B4
Willaston L64 .... 67 F4
m Rd S SK3 .... 240 A3
m Ridge Dr WA5 .... 32 B4
m Rise Frodsham WA6 .... 74 B4
Prestbury SK10 .... 86 C3
m Sq CH4 .... 140 C3
m St Ellesmere Port L65 ... 70 B4
Northwich CW9 .... 79 D1
m Tree Ave Lymm WA13 ... 18 B1
Warrington WA1 .... 16 C4
m Tree Cl CW7 .... 147 D2
m Tree Dr ST7 .... 209 F1
m Tree La CW11 .... 174 B4
m Tree Rd Goldborne WA3 .. 4 A1
Lymm WA13 .... 18 B1
mbridge Prim Sch WA15 .. 32 A4
mdale Ave SK6 .... 239 B2
mfield Cl SK9 .... 60 A1
mfield Rd
Alderley Edge SK9 .... 60 A2
Stockport SK3 .... 240 F1
m St 117 F2
more Cl
Holmes Chapel CW4 ...... 130 A2
Warrington WA1 .... 24 B1
ms The Goldborne WA3 ... 3 F4
Runcorn WA7 .... 22 C1
msleigh Rd SK8 .... 239 A2
mstead Cres CW1 .... 189 F4
mstead Rd SK11 .... 84 A2
msway Altrincham WA15 .. 32 A4
Bollington SK10 .... 88 A4
Cheadle Hulme SK7 .... 35 E4
High Lane SK6 .... 37 F3
mtree Dr SK4 .... 240 C6
mwood WA4 .... 26 A4
mwood Ave Chester CH2 .. 118 C2
Warrington WA1 .... 16 C4
mwood Cl SW7 .... 194 A2
mwood Gr CW7 .... 149 F4
mwood Rd CW8 .... 78 A2
nor Ave SK23 .... 65 F3
nsby Rd ST7 .... 193 F1
ston Ave WA12 .... 2 B3
strea Ave CH3 .... 119 D2
stree Gr SK3 .... 240 A6
sham Cl WA6 .... 35 F4
tham Wlk WA8 .... 13 F2
ton Cl Bebington L62 ..... 43 F2
Goldborne WA3 .... 4 A1
ton Crossings Rd CW1 ... 174 B3
ton Cty Prim Sch CH2 ... 72 A2
ton La Elton WA6 .... 72 C2
Haslington CW1 .... 174 B3
ton Lordship La WA6 .... 73 D4
ton Rd CW11 .... 174 B3
vington Cl WA7 .... 24 B1
worth Ave WA8 .... 13 D3
worth CE Contr Prim
Sch CW11 .... 174 C4
worth Hall Cty Prim Sch
CW11 .... 174 C4
worth Rd CW11 .... 174 C3
worth St CW11 .... 175 D4
wyn Cl WA5 .... 34 B2
wyn Dr L26 .... 21 D4
ly Cl CW1 .... 94 C4
y Ct SK10 .... 112 C4
mbassy Cl CH1 .... 117 E2
mbleton CH CW3 .... 230 A3
mbleton Ct WA7 .... 24 B1
mbridge Cswy SK10, SK17 .. 90 A3
merald Rd M22 .... 33 F4
mily Cl SK4 .... 240 A8
mily St SK8 .... 23 D4
mlyn Gr SK8 .... 240 A2
mmerdale Ave WA2 ...... 8 B2
mmett St CW8 .... 78 A2
mpress Dr Crewe CW2 ... 190 A2
Reddish SK4 .... 240 D8
mral Ct SY14 .... 211 D1
mslie Cl L64 .... 66 B4
nderby Rd CH1 .... 237 D3
ndon Av SK10 .... 88 A4
ndsleigh Cl CH2 .... 118 B4
ndsleigh Gdns CW2 ...... 118 B4
nfield Cl CW2 .... 206 A2
nfield Park Rd WA2 ...... 9 D2
nfield Rd L65 .... 70 A3
nglesea Brook La CW2 ... 208 A2
nglefield Ave CW4 .... 140 B3
nglefield Cl CW1 .... 190 A4
nglesea Gr CW2 .... 190 A1
nglish Martyrs RC Sch
WA11 .... 1 C4
nnerdale Chester CH2 ... 118 C3
Macclesfield SK11 .... 111 F3
nnerdale Ave L62 .... 43 F2
nnerdale Cl CW7 .... 126 B2
nnerdale Dr
Congleton CW12 .... 156 A1
Crewe CW1 .... 74 B4
nnerdale Rd Crewe CW2 .. 189 D2
Gatley SK8 .... 239 B3
Partington M31 .... 11 F2
Romiley SK6 .... 12 B3
nnerdale Terr SK15 ...... 242 D2

Ennis Cl L24 .... 21 E1
Enticott Rd M44 .... 11 E3
Enville Rd WA14 .... 238 C3
Enville St WA4 .... 17 E4
Epping Dr WA1 .... 17 E4
Epsom Ave SK9 .... 34 C2
Epsom Gdns WA4 .... 26 C4
Epworth Cl WA5 .... 6 C4
Era St M33 .... 242 B6
Eric Ave WA1 .... 16 C4
Eric St WA8 .... 13 E1
Erlesmere Ave M34 ...... 241 A8
Ermine Rd CH2 .... 237 E4
Ernest St Cheadle SK8 ... 239 C1
Crewe CW2 .... 190 B1
Errington Ave L65 .... 70 B3
Errwood Cl L24 .... 21 F1
Erskine Rd M31 .... 11 F1
Erwood St WA2 .... 16 A3
Esk Dale Cl CW7 .... 126 B1
Esk Rd CW7 .... 127 D1
Eskdale Ellesmere Port L65 .. 70 A2
Eskdale Ave
Cheadle Hulme SK7 .... 35 E3
Warrington WA2 .... 8 B2
Eskdale Cl Bebington L62 .. 43 F3
Runcorn WA7 .... 49 D2
Essex Ave SK6 .... 240 B4
Essex Cl CW12 .... 156 C3
Essex Dr Biddulph ST6 ... 179 E1
Kidsgrove ST7 .... 194 C1
Essex Gdns WA4 .... 26 C4
Essex Rd CH2 .... 119 D3
Esther St WA8 .... 13 D1
Esthers La CW8 .... 102 B4
Etchells Prim Sch SK8 ... 239 C1
Etchells Rd SK8 .... 239 D1
Etchells St SK1 .... 240 F5
Ethelda Dr CH2 .... 119 D3
Etherow Ave SK6 .... 241 E2
Etherow Cl CW11 .... 174 C4
Eton Dr L63 .... 41 F3
Eton Rd L65 .... 70 B2
Etterick Pk CH3 .... 119 D1
Ettiley Ave CW7 .... 174 B3
Euclid Ave WA4 .... 17 E4
Europa Bvd WA5 .... 7 F2
Europa Way Cheadle SK3 .. 240 B2
Ellesmere Port L65 .... 70 B3
Eustace St WA2 .... 16 A3
Eva Rd SK3 .... 240 A3
Eva St CW11 .... 174 B4
Evans Cl WA11 .... 1 C4
Evans Pl WA4 .... 16 C2
Evans St Ashton-u-L OL6 .. 242 A4
Crewe CW1 .... 190 B3
Evansleigh Dr CH5 .... 116 A2
Evelyn St WA5 .... 15 F2
Evelyn Street Cty Prim
Sch WA5 .... 15 F2
Everdon Cl CW7 .... 126 C2
Everest Cl L66 .... 69 F2
Everglade Cl SK11 .... 112 A3
Everite Rd WA8 .... 22 A4
Eversley WA8 .... 12 A1
Eversley Cl Appleton WA4 . 26 B3
Frodsham WA6 .... 74 B4
Eversley Ct CH2 .... 118 B2
Eversley Pk CH2 .... 118 B2
Evesham Ave WA4 .... 26 B3
Evesham Cl
Macclesfield SK10 .... 87 F2
Warrington WA4 .... 26 B3
Evesham Gr M33 .... 242 E6
Ewart St CH4 .... 140 A4
Ewloe Cl L65 .... 69 E3
Excalibur Cty Prim Sch
ST7 .... 193 F1
Excalibur Ind Est ST7 ... 193 F2
Excalibur Way WA1 .... 11 F4
Exchange Cl SK11 .... 112 B4
Exeter Cl SK8 .... 34 C4
Exeter Pl CH1 .... 117 F3
Exeter Rd L65 .... 70 B3
Exeter Wlk SK7 .... 35 F4
Exit Rd W M90 .... 33 D4
Exmouth Cres WA7 .... 50 C3
Exmouth Way WA5 .... 6 A3
Exton Pk CH2 .... 237 D4
Eyam Rd SK7 .... 36 C4
Eyebrook Rd WA14 ...... 238 A2

Factory La Disley SK12 ... 38 C4
Widnes WA8 .... 13 D2
Fairbourne Cl WA5 .... 6 C4
Newton-le-W WA12 ...... 2 A2
Fairfax Dr Runcorn WA7 . 23 E1
Wilmslow SK9 .... 59 F2
Fairfield Ave Cheadle SK8 . 239 F2
Ellesmere Port L65 .... 70 A1
Romiley SK6 .... 241 A4
Sandbach CW11 .... 175 D3
Fairfield CE Aided Prim
Sch WA1 .... 16 B3
Fairfield Cty High School
WA8 .... 13 D2
Fairfield Cty Inf Sch WA8 . 13 D1
Fairfield Cty Jun Sch WA8 . 13 D1
Fairfield Gdns WA4 .... 16 C1
Fairfield Rd Broughton CH4 . 139 D2
Chester CH2 .... 118 B3
Irlam M44 .... 11 E3
Northwich CW9 .... 104 A2
Warrington WA4 .... 16 C1
Fairfield St WA1 .... 16 B3
Fairfields ST7 .... 209 F1
Fairford Rd CH4 .... 140 C3
Fairford Way SK9 .... 60 B4
Fairhaven Cl Bramhall SK7 . 35 F4
Great Sankey WA5 .... 15 D2
Fairhaven Rd WA8 .... 13 E1
Fairhills Rd M44 .... 11 F4
Fairholme Rd CW7 .... 127 D4
Fairholme Ave L64 .... 43 D2
Fairholme Cl CH1 .... 94 A1
Fairholme Rd M44 .... 240 C7
Fairlawn SK4 .... 240 D7
Fairlawn Cl L63 .... 43 D3
Fairlea M34 .... 241 A6
Fairlie Cl SK8 .... 34 C4
Fairmile Dr M20 .... 239 C8
Fairoak La WA7 .... 50 C2
Fairoak La WA7 .... 50 C2
Fairview WA8 .... 22 A4
Fairview Ave Alsager ST7 . 193 F2
Weston CW2 .... 207 D3
Fairview Rd
Ellesmere Port L65 .... 70 A1
Macclesfield SK11 .... 112 A3
Fairway Cheadle Hulme SK7 . 35 E3
Gatley SK8 .... 239 B4
Hawarden CH5 .... 116 A1
Fairway The ST7 .... 193 E2
Fairways Appleton WA4 .. 26 B3
Frodsham WA6 .... 74 B4
Fairways Gr L66 .... 69 F4
Fairy La M33 .... 242 F6
Fairywell Cl SK9 .... 34 B1
Falcon Cl Middlewich CW10 . 151 E3
New Mills SK22 .... 39 E4
Winsford CW7 .... 149 E3
Falcon Dr CW1 .... 190 A4
Falcon Rd L66 .... 69 F2
Falcondale Rd WA4 ...... 8 A3
Falconers Gn WA5 .... 7 D1
Falcons Way WA7 .... 49 F3
Fallibroome Cl WA1 ...... 16 B2
Fallibroome High Sch
SK10 .... 86 C1
Fallibroome Rd SK11 .... 111 F4
Fallowfield WA7 .... 23 F1
Fallowfield Cl CW7 .... 125 F1
Fallowfield Ct CW1 .... 190 A3
Fallowfield Gr WA2 ...... 9 D1
Falls Gr SK8 .... 239 A3
Falmouth Cl SK10 .... 111 F4
Falmouth Dr WA5 .... 7 D4
Falmouth Pl WA7 .... 50 C3
Falmouth Rd
Congleton CW12 .... 178 C4
Crewe CW2 .... 190 A3
Falstone Cl WA3 .... 4 A4
Falstone Dr WA7 .... 50 C4
Fanner's La WA16 .... 28 B3
Fanny's Croft ST7 .... 193 E1
Fanshawe La SK11 .... 110 C3
Fanshawe Wlk CW2 ...... 206 B4
Far Ridings SK6 .... 241 D3
Faraday Rd
Ellesmere Port L65 .... 70 A2
Runcorn WA7 .... 23 E2
Faraday St WA3 .... 9 F2
Farams Rd ST7 .... 193 F4
Farbailey Cl CH4 .... 141 D3
Farfields Cl SK11 .... 111 F1
Faringdon Rd WA2 .... 8 A3
Farlands Dr M20 .... 239 B7
Farley Gr Ivl CW10 .... 151 D4
Farley Ct SK8 .... 239 F3
Farm Cl CW8 .... 77 E1
Farm Dr CH5 .... 91 E1
Farm La Appleton WA4 .. 26 C4
Disley SK12 .... 38 B3
Withington SK11 .... 108 C1
Farm Rd Northwich CW9 . 104 C4
Oakmere CW8 .... 124 A4
Weaverham CW8 .... 77 E1
Farm Way WA12 .... 2 C1
Farmdale Dr CH2 .... 72 A2
Farmer Cl CW2 .... 206 A3
Farmer St WA4 .... 240 E7
Farmer's La WA3 .... 7 D3
Farmers Heath L66 ...... 69 E1
Farmfield Dr SK10 .... 87 D3
Farmfields Rise CW3 .... 232 B1

Farmleigh Dr CW1 .... 189 F4
Farmleigh Gdns WA5 ... 15 E3
Farmstead Way L66 ...... 69 F1
Farndale Cl CW2 .... 206 A3
Farndon Cl Broughton CH4 . 139 E2
Cuddington CW8 .... 102 A2
Widnes WA8 .... 242 E5
Farndon Cty Prim Sch
CH3 .... 180 C1
Farndon Rd L66 .... 69 F3
Farne Cl CH2 .... 95 E4
Farnham Ave SK11 .... 112 A3
Farnham Cl Appleton WA4 . 26 C4
Cheadle Hulme SK8 ...... 35 D4
Farnhill WA7 .... 50 B4
Farnley Cl WA7 .... 24 B1
Farnworth CE Contr Prim
Sch WA8 .... 13 D2
Farnworth Cl WA8 .... 13 D2
Farnworth Rd WA5 .... 13 D2
Farr Hill Rd L60 .... 40 C4
Farr Hill Rd L60 .... 40 C4
Farr St WA3 .... 240 D4
Farrant St WA8 .... 13 D4
Farrell Ave M44 .... 26 B4
Farrell St WA1 .... 16 B3
Farriers Way CW7 .... 126 A1
Farthing La CW9 .... 79 D4
Farwood Cl SK10 .... 86 C1
Faulkner Dr CW10 .... 151 F3
Faulkner Cl WA5 .... 118 C2
Faulkner's La
Lindow End WA16 .... 58 C1
Mobberley WA16 .... 58 C1
Faulkners Cl CH4 .... 161 D4
Faulkners La CH3 .... 142 B4
Faulkners Way L64 .... 241 D5
Fawns Keep SK9 .... 60 B4
Fawns Leap CW8 .... 101 F3
Fearndown Way SK10 ... 87 E2
Fearnhead La WA2 .... 9 D1
Fearnley Way WA12 ..... 2 C1
Feather La L60 .... 40 C4
Feilden Ct CH1 .... 94 C1
Felix Rd CW8 .... 103 F4
Fellside Gm SK15 .... 242 D3
Felskirk Rd M22 .... 33 E4
Fence Ave SK10 .... 112 C4
Fence Ave Ind Est SK10 . 112 C4
Fence La CW12 .... 178 B2
Fenham Dr WA5 .... 14 C2
Fennel St WA1 .... 16 B3
Fenton Cl Congleton CW12 . 157 D1
Widnes WA8 .... 12 B2
Fenwick La WA7 .... 49 E3
Fenwick Rd L66 .... 69 F1
Ferguson Dr WA2 .... 8 B1
Ferma La CH3 .... 120 B3
Fern Ave WA12 .... 2 A1
Fern Bank SK15 .... 242 F1
Fern Cl WA3 .... 9 E2
Fern Cres Congleton CW12 . 157 D2
Stalybridge SK15 .... 242 F1
Fern Ct CW1 .... 190 C2
Fern Lea CW8 .... 77 E1
Fern Lea SK8 .... 239 B1
Fern Rd L65 .... 70 A1
Fern Way CW8 .... 77 E1
Fernacre M33 .... 242 C7
Fernally St WA4 .... 241 E6
Finlay Ave WA5 .... 14 C2
Fernbank Cl Crewe CW1 . 190 C2
Winsford CW7 .... 149 E4
Fernbank Rise SK10 ...... 88 A4
Fernbanckl WA3 .... 9 F2
Ferndale Ave CH2 .... 72 A2
Ferndale Cl Bold Heath WA8 . 13 F4
Sandbach CW11 .... 175 D3
Ferndale Cres WA7 ...... 49 F4
Ferndale Rd
Ellesmere Port L65 .... 70 A1
Warrington WA5 .... 14 C4
Weston CW2 .... 207 D3
Ferndale Cres SK11 ...... 111 F4
Fernhill Rd CW7 .... 149 E4
Fernhurst WA7 .... 49 E4
Fernilee Cty Inf Sch SK23 . 65 F2
Fernlea Rd Heswall L60 .. 41 D4
Fernlea St ST7 .... 209 D3
Fernleigh Cwm 103 E4
Ferns Way M34 .... 241 A6
Fernwood Gr SK9 .... 60 B4
Ferrers Rd WA4 .... 16 C1
Ferry Cl Bollington SK23 . 65 F2
Ferry La Sealand CH1 ... 117 E1
Warrington WA7 .... 23 F1
Ferry Rd L61 .... 44 A3
Ferrywerv Wlk WA7 ..... 23 F1
Festival Ave Buerton CW3 . 230 C2
Warrington WA1 .... 8 B1
Festival Cres WA2 .... 8 B1
Festival Dr St ST0 .... 85 F3
Festival Hill CW12 .... 156 C1
Festival Rd L65 .... 69 F3
Festival St WA7 .... 49 E4
Fiddler's Ferry Rd WA8 .. 13 E1
Fiddlers La CH1 .... 94 B1
Field Ave CW1 .... 189 F1
Field Cl Bollington SK10 . 87 F4
Cheadle Hulme SK8 ...... 35 E2
Northwich CW8 .... 103 E4
Tarvin CH3 .... 121 D1
Field Hey La L64 .... 43 D1
Field La Appleton WA4 ... 26 B3
Tarvin CH3 .... 121 D1
Tattenhall CH3 .... 166 A1
Wistaston CW2 .... 189 F1
Field Side Cl WA16 .... 58 C4
Field St WA3 .... 241 A6

Field View SK11 .... 179 E1
Field View SK11 .... 112 C3
Field Way ST7 .... 193 F2
Field Wlk WA1 .... 11 E1
Fieldbank SK11 .... 112 A4
Fieldfare Cl WA8 .... 13 D2
Fieldfare CW7 .... 150 A4
Fieldfare Cl WA3 .... 9 F4
Fieldgate WA8 .... 22 A4
Fieldhead Mews SK9 .... 60 C4
Fieldhead Rd SK9 .... 60 C4
Fieldhouse Row WA7 ... 49 E4
Fields Cl Alsager ST7 .... 36 C1
Fields Cl ST7 .... 193 F2
Fields Cres CW12 .... 156 B1
Fields Dr CW11 .... 175 D3
Fields Rd Alsager ST7 ... 193 F2
Congleton CW12 .... 178 C4
Haslington CW1 .... 191 F4
Fields The CW5 .... 205 E3
Fields View SY13 .... 228 B1
Fields View CW5 .... 220 A4
Fieldsend Dr WN7 .... 4 B4
Fieldside CW6 .... 145 D2
Fieldsway WA7 .... 49 D3
Fieldview Dr WA2 .... 8 B1
Fieldway Chester CH2 ... 118 C2
Ellesmere Port L66 .... 69 D4
Frodsham WA6 .... 74 B4
Saughall CH1 .... 94 A1
Weaverham CW8 .... 77 E1
Widnes WA8 .... 13 E1
Fife Rd WA1 .... 16 C4
Fifth Ave Kidsgrove ST7 . 194 C1
Runcorn WA7 .... 49 F4
Fiji St WA5 .... 15 F3
Filkin's La CH3 .... 119 D1
Finchale Gdns WA3 ...... 4 A4
Finchett Dr CH1 .... 118 A2
Finchley Rd WA15 .... 238 E3
Findlay Cl WA12 .... 2 A1
Finham Rd SK3 .... 240 D3
Finlay Ave WA5 .... 14 C2
Finlow Hill La SK10 ...... 85 F3
Finney Cl SK9 .... 34 B1
Finney Dr SK9 .... 34 B1
Finney Gr WA11 .... 1 C3
Finney La Cheadle SK8 .. 34 A4
Gatley SK8 .... 239 C1
Wythenshawe SK8 .... 34 A4
Finney's La CW10 .... 128 A1
Finningley Dr WA5 .... 8 C1
Finny Bank Rd M33 ...... 242 A8
Finsbury Park WA8 ...... 13 E3
Finsbury Wlk CW7 .... 149 D4
Fir Ave Bramhall SK7 .... 35 F4
Halewood L26 .... 21 D4
Fir Cl Halewood L26 ..... 21 D4
Newton CW7 .... 126 C2
Tarporley CW6 .... 146 B1
Fir Ct SK10 .... 86 C1
Fir Gr Macclesfield SK11 . 112 B3
Warrington WA1 .... 16 C4
Weaverham CW8 .... 102 A1
Fir La CW7 .... 102 A1
Fir Rd Bramhall SK7 ..... 35 F4
Denton M34 .... 241 A7
Fir St Irlam M44 .... 11 E3
Stockport SK4 .... 240 E6
Widnes WA8 .... 13 D1
Fir Tree Ave Chester CH4 . 141 D3
Goldborne WA3 .... 3 F4
Knutsford WA16 .... 82 B4
Fir Tree Cl WA4 .... 7 D4
Fir Tree La Burtonwood WA5 . 7 D4
Chester CH3 .... 119 F1
Fir Way L60 .... 41 D3
Firbank CH2 .... 72 B2
Firbank Cl WA7 .... 24 B1
Firbeck Cl Broughton CH4 . 139 D2
Congleton CW12 .... 155 F2
Firbeck Gdns CW2 .... 189 E2
Fircroft Cl SK8 .... 103 D4
Firfields Cres WA1 .... 237 D3
Firman Cl WA5 .... 15 D4
Firs Gr SK8 .... 239 A4
Firs La L26 .... 26 A3
Firs Rd SK8 .... 239 A4
Firs Sch The CH2 .... 118 B3
Firs The WA14 .... 238 B3
Fir Tree Ave Adlington SK10 . 36 B1
Crewe CW1 .... 190 C1
Deeside Ind Est CH5 .... 93 D1
Kidsgrove ST7 .... 194 C1
Sandbach CW11 .... 175 D3
First Dig La CW5 .... 219 E4
First Wood St CW5 .... 204 B3
Firswood Mount SK8 ... 239 A4
Firths Fields CW9 .... 103 F1
Firths Fields CW9 .... 103 F1
Firtree Ave WA1 .... 17 D4
Firtree Cl CW8 .... 78 A2
Firtree Gr CH1 .... 95 D4
Firvale Ave SK8 .... 239 B1
Firwood Rd ST6 .... 179 F1
Firwood Wlk CW2 .... 206 B4
Fisher Cl CH1 .... 117 F2
Fisher St WA7 .... 23 D2
Fishersfield Dr WA3 ..... 10 A3
Fishermans Cl CW11 ... 191 F4
Fishers La CW5 .... 203 E4
Fistral Ave SK8 .... 34 B4

Fitton St CW9 80 A1
Fitton's Cl CW5 217 F3
Fitz Cl SK10 87 E2
Fitz Cres SK10 87 E2
Fitz Walter Rd WA1 17 E4
Fitzherbert St WA2 16 B4
Fitzwilliam Ave SK11 112 C2
Fitzwilliam Wlk WA7 24 A1
Five Ashes Rd CH4 141 D3
Fiveways Par SK7 36 C4
Flacca Ct CH3 166 A1
Flag La Crewe CW1, CW2 190 B2
Neston L64 66 C4
Flag La N CH2 118 C4
Flag La S CH2 118 B4
Flamingo Cl CW1 189 F4
Flander Cl WA8 12 B1
Flash La Antrobus CW9 53 F3
Bollington SK10 87 E4
Flashes La L64 67 D3
Flat La Kelsall CW6 122 B2
Sandbach CW11 175 D3
Flatt La L65 70 A3
Flatts La SK23 64 C2
Flaxley Cl WA3 10 A3
Flaxmere Dr CH3 142 A4
Fleet La WA9 1 A1
Fleet St Ellesmere Port L65 70 A3
Hyde SK14 241 E7
Fleetwood Cl WA5 15 D2
Fleetwood Wlk WA7 50 B3
Fleming St L65 70 B3
Flemish Rd M34 241 B6
Flers Ave WA4 16 B2
Fletcher Dr SK6 37 F3
Fletcher Gr CW9 104 B3
Fletcher St Crewe CW1 190 A3
Stockport SK1 240 F5
Warrington WA4 16 A2
Fletchers La WA13 18 C2
Fletsand Rd SK9 60 B3
Flint Cl L64 66 C3
Flint Ct L65 70 B1
Flint Dr L64 66 C3
Flint Gr M44 11 E3
Flint Meadow L64 66 C4
Flint St Macclesfield SK11 112 C4
Stockport SK3 240 E3
Flittogate La WA16 80 C4
Flixton Dr CW2 190 A1
Florence Ct SK3 240 B2
Florence St Sale M33 242 B8
6 Stockport SK4 240 E6
Warrington WA4 16 B2
Florist St SK3 240 E3
Flower St CW8 103 F4
Flowers La CW1 172 C1
Flowery Field Prim Sch
SK14 241 D8
Fluin La WA6 74 B4
Foden Ave ST7 194 A2
Foden La Lindow End SK9 59 E1
Woodford SK7 35 E2
Foden St SK10 87 E1
Foden Wlk 11 SK9 34 B1
Fogg's La CW9, WA4 53 D3
Fol Hollow CW12 156 A1
Fold La Biddulph ST6 179 F2
Bosley SK11 135 E1
Fold The SK10 87 D4
Folden Cl L66 69 D3
Folds The L63 42 A3
Foley Wlk M22 33 F4
Folkestone Cl SK10 87 D1
Folkstone Way WA7 50 B4
Folly La WA5 15 F4
Forbes Cl WA3 9 F2
Forbes Pk SK7 35 E4
Ford Cl CW1 190 A3
Ford Ct CW7 149 E3
Ford La Crewe CW1 190 A3
Tattenhall CH3 166 C2
Ford St Stockport SK3 240 D5
Warrington WA1 16 B3
Ford's La SK7 35 E3
Fordington Rd WA5 15 D3
Fords La ST7 195 E3
Fordton L Ctr WA2 8 A2
Foregate St CH1 237 E2
Foreland Cl WA5 14 B4
Forest Ave CW4 107 E1
Forest Cl Cuddington CW8 101 F2
Rainow SK10 88 C3
Forest Dr Altrincham WA15 238 F6
Broughton CH4 139 D2
Forest Gate La CW6 122 C4
Forest Gdns M31 11 E2
Forest La WA6 100 B3
Forest Park Sch M33 242 A6
Forest Pl CW9 79 D1
Forest Rd Cuddington CW8 101 F2
Ellesmere Port L66 69 F4
Heswall L60 41 D4
Macclesfield SK11 113 F3
Tarporley CW6 146 B2
Winsford CW7 149 D4
Forest Sch WA15 238 F6
Forest St Chester CH1 237 F2
Weaverham CW8 102 B4
Forester Ave WA16 57 E1
Forester Dr SK15 242 D1
Foresters Cl WA6 101 D3
Forge Cl Cronton WA8 12 B3
Warren SK11 111 E1
Forge Fields CW11 174 C2
Forge La Congleton CW12 156 A2
Norton in Hales TF9 236 B1
Forge Rd Ellesmere Port L66 69 E3
Great Sankey WA5 14 C3
Whaley Bridge SK23 65 F4
Forge Sh Ctr The WA4 16 B1
Forge St CW1 190 B2
Forge Way CH4 140 C2
Formby Cl WA5 14 C2
Formby Dr SK8 34 A4
Forrest Dr SK11 113 E2
Forrest Rd M34 241 B5
Forshaw St WA2 16 B4
Forshaw's La WA5 6 C4
Forster Ave CW8 102 C4
Forster St WA2 16 A4
Forsythia Wlk M31 11 E1
Forty Acre La
Cranage CW4 131 E3
Swettenham CW4 131 E3
Forum The Chester CH1 237 D2
Romiley SK6 241 C2
Forwood Rd L62 43 E4
Foster St WA8 13 D1
Fosters Rd CW12 157 D3
Fothergill St WA1 16 B4
Fotheringay Ct L65 70 B1
Foulkes Ave CW1 189 F3
Foundary Bank CW12 156 C2
Foundry Ct 13 SK11 112 B4
Foundry La Sandbach CW11 174 B4
Scholar Green ST7 194 C4
Widnes WA8 22 B3
Foundry St Bollington SK10 88 A4
Newton-le-W WA12 2 A2
Warrington WA2 16 A3
Fountain Cl SK12 36 B2
Fountain Ct Biddulph ST6 179 E1
Winsford CW7 126 B1
Fountain La Davenham CW9 103 F1
Frodsham WA6 74 A4
Fountain Sq SK12 38 B3
Fountain St
Ashton-u-L OL6 242 B4
Congleton CW12 156 B1
Hyde SK14 241 F7
Macclesfield SK11 112 C4
Fountains Ave WA11 1 C4
Fountains Cl
Middlewich CW10 128 A1
Runcorn WA7 50 B3
Fountains Rd SK7 35 E3
Fountains Wlk WA3 4 A4
Four Lanes End CW2 207 F1
Fourseasons Cl CW2 206 A4
Fourth Ave Crewe CW1 190 C1
Deeside Ind Est CH5 92 C1
Kidsgrove ST7 194 C1
Runcorn WA7 49 F4
Fowey Cl SK10 86 B1
Fowler Rd CH1 117 E2
Fowler St SK10 87 E1
Fowlers Bench La CH3 184 B3
Fowley Common La WA3 5 E3
Fox Bank Ct SK3 240 D4
Fox Bench Cl SK7 35 E3
Fox Cl WA15 238 F6
Fox Cover CH3 119 F3
Fox Covert WA7 50 B4
Fox Covert La Picton CH2 96 A1
Stoak CH2 96 A1
Fox Gdns Kidsgrove ST7 210 B4
Lymm WA13 18 B2
Fox Gr WA16 57 E1
Fox Hill CW6 122 B2
Fox La Clutton CH3 182 B1
Waverton CH3 143 D3
Fox Lea CH1 117 D4
Fox St Congleton CW12 156 C2
Runcorn WA7 23 D1
Stockport SK3 240 D4
Warrington WA5 15 F3
Fox's Dr CH5 116 A3
Foxall Way L66 69 E1
Foxcote WA8 12 A1
Foxcover Rd L60 41 E4
Foxcovert La WA16 106 C4
Foxdale Ct WA4 26 B4
Foxes Fold CW8 78 C1
Foxes Hey CW8 101 E3
Foxes Wlk CH3 142 A4
Foxfield Cl WA2 8 C2
Foxfield La CW7 126 A1
Foxglove Cl Bollington SK10 88 B4
Huntington CH3 142 A3
Wistaston CW2 206 A4
Foxglove Ct WA6 74 B4
Foxglove Dr WA14 238 C8
Foxglove La SK15 242 D3
Foxglove Way L64 66 C3
Foxglove Wlk M31 11 F1
Foxhall Rd WA15 238 F6
Foxhill WA14 238 A5
Foxhill Ct CW6 146 C1
Foxhill Gr WA6 73 E2
Foxhills Cl WA4 26 B2
Foxholes Rd SK14 241 D5
Foxhunter Cl CH3 121 F4
Foxland Rd SK8 239 B4
Foxlea CW9 78 B4
Foxley Cl WA13 19 D1
Foxley Heath WA8 22 C4
Foxwist Cl CH2 237 E4
Foxwist Gr CW7 125 F3
Foxwood Dr WA16 108 A4
Frances Ave SK8 239 A6
Frances St Cheadle SK8 239 E6
Crewe CW2 190 B1
Frances St continued
Denton SK14 241 C7
Irlam M44 11 F3
Macclesfield SK11 112 A4
8 Stockport SK1 & SK3 240 E4
Frances St W SK14 241 C7
Francis Cl WA8 22 B4
Francis Ct CH2 237 F3
Francis La LL13 196 A3
Francis Rd Frodsham WA6 49 E1
Irlam M44 11 F4
Warrington WA4 16 B1
Francis St CH2 237 F3
Frank Bott Ave CW1 190 A4
Frank Perkins Way M44 11 F4
Frank St Hyde SK14 241 E6
Widnes WA8 13 E1
Frank Webb Ave CW1 190 A3
Franklin Cl WA5 15 E4
Fraser Ave M33 242 E5
Fraser Ct CH4 141 E4
Fraser Rd WA5 14 B3
Frawley Ave WA12 2 B3
Freckleton Cl WA5 15 D2
Frederick St
Ashton-u-L OL6 & SK15 242 B2
Warrington WA4 16 C2
Widnes WA8 23 D4
Fredric Pl WA7 23 D2
Free Green La WA16 107 D4
Freeman Ave OL6 242 A3
Freemantle St SK3 240 D4
French Ave SK15 242 F1
French La
French Lane End CW5 218 B3
Sound CW5 218 B3
French St
Ashton-u-L OL6 242 A4
Stalybridge SK15 242 F1
Widnes WA8 13 E1
Freshfield SK8 34 A4
Freshfield Ave SK14 241 D5
Freshfield Dr SK10 87 E2
Freshfields
Comberbach CW9 78 B4
Wistaston CW2 206 A4
Freshfields Dr WA2 9 E1
Freshmeadow La WA6 73 D1
Freshwater Cl WA5 14 B4
Friar's Cl SK9 59 F4
Friar's Rd M33 242 B6
Friars Cl Altrincham WA14 238 B1
Rainow SK10 88 B3
Friars Gate WA1 16 A2
Friars La WA1 16 A2
Friars Way SK10 86 C1
Frida Cres CW8 103 F3
Friends La WA5 14 B3
Friesian Gdns ST5 210 B1
Frieston Rd WA14 238 E8
Frith Ave CW8 123 E4
Frith Terr SK11 112 B2
Frobisher Pl SK5 240 E8
Frobisher Rd L64 66 C4
Froda Ave WA6 74 A4
Frodsham Ave SK4 240 C7
Frodsham CE Contr Prim
Sch WA6 74 A4
Frodsham Cty High Sch
WA6 74 A4
Frodsham Manor House
Cty Jun Sch WA6 49 E1
Frodsham Rd WA6 73 E1
Frodsham St Chester CH1 237 E3
Kelsall CW6 122 A3
Frodsham St Luke's RC
Aided Prim Sch WA6 74 A4
Frodsham Sta WA6 74 A4
Frodsham Way 5 SK9 34 C2
Frog La Handley CH3 165 F1
Holt LL13 196 A4
Milton Green CH3 165 F1
Pickmere WA16 55 D1
Tattenhall CH3 166 A1
Worthenbury SY14 211 D1
Froghall La
High Legh WA16 29 E4
Warrington WA2 16 A3
Frome Ct L65 70 A4
Front St CW11 175 E3
Frosts Mews L65 70 A3
Fryer Rd CW9 80 A2
Fuchsia Cl L66 69 F1
Fulbeck WA8 12 B1
Fulbeck Cl CW2 206 A4
Fulbrook Dr SK8 35 D3
Fuller Dr CW2 206 A4
Fullerton Rd Hartford CW8 103 D2
Manchester SK4 240 B6
Fulmar Cl SK12 36 A2
Fulmar Ct CW1 189 F4
Fulmards Cl SK9 60 B4
Fulshaw Ave SK9 60 A3
Fulshaw CE Contr Prim Sch
SK9 59 F3
Fulshaw Cross SK9 60 A3
Fulshaw Ct SK9 60 A3
Fulshaw Park S SK9 60 A2
Fulshaw Pk SK9 60 A3
Fulton Gr CW9 103 F1
Fulwood Gdns L66 69 E3
Fulwood Mews L66 69 E3
Fulwood Rd
Ellesmere Port L66 69 E3
Goldborne WA3 3 F4
Furber St CW1 190 B3
Furnace St SK14 241 C8
Furne Rd CH1 117 F2
Furness Cl
Holmes Chapel CW4 130 A2
Poynton SK12 36 B2
Winsford CW7 149 D4
Furness Ct WA7 24 C2
Furness Gr SK4 240 A5
Furness Lodge Cl SK23 39 E2
Furness Rd SK7 35 E3
Furness Row SK23 39 E2
Furness Vale Sta SK23 39 E2
Furnival St Crewe CW2 190 B1
Sandbach CW11 175 D4
Furrocks Cl L64 66 C3
Furrocks La L64 66 C3
Furrocks Way L64 66 C3
Furrows The CH1 94 C4
Fylde Ave SK8 34 B4
Fylde Rd SK4 240 A6
Fytton Cl SK11 111 E1

Gable Wlk SK9 60 A4
Gables Cl WA2 8 C2
Gables The ST7 193 E2
Gabriel Bank CW8 76 A1
Gadbrook Bsns Ctr CW9 104 B3
Gadbrook Pk CW9 104 B3
Gadbrook Rd CW9 104 B3
Gaddum Rd WA14 238 B1
Gail Ave SK4 240 D6
Gail Cl SK9 60 A1
Gainford Ave SK8 239 B4
Gainford Cl WA8 12 B2
Gainsborough Cl SK9 60 C4
Gainsborough Ct WA8 12 A1
Gainsborough Cty Inf Sch
CW2 190 A2
Gainsborough Cty Jun
Sch CW2 190 A1
Gainsborough Dr SK8 239 F6
Gainsborough Rd
Crewe CW2 190 A2
Warrington WA4 16 A1
Gair Rd SK5 240 F8
Gair St SK14 241 D8
Gairloch Cl WA2 8 C2
Gaisgill Ct WA8 12 B1
Gala Cl CH4 139 E2
Galbraith Cl CW12 156 B1
Gale Rd SK22 39 E4
Galion Way WA8 12 C2
Galleys Bank ST7 195 D2
Gallowsclough La
Norley WA6 100 C2
Oakmere WA6 100 C2
Galway Gr CW2 206 A2
Game St CW11 175 D2
Gamul Pl CH4 237 E1
Ganton Cl WA8 13 D2
Garden Ave CW7 126 A1
Garden Ct CH1 237 D3
Garden La Altrincham WA14 238 D5
Chester CH1 237 D3
Harthill CH3 183 F2
Garden Rd WA16 56 C2
Garden St Bollington SK10 87 F4
Congleton CW12 156 B2
Hyde SK14 241 E8
Macclesfield SK10 87 F1
Garden Terr Chester CH1 237 D3
Chester, Hoole Park CH2 118 C1
Garden Wlk M31 11 E1
Gardens The Holt LL13 180 C1
Sandbach CW11 175 D3
Gardner Ave WA11 1 B3
Garfit St CW10 128 B1
Garigill Cl WA8 13 E3
Garlick St SK14 241 F7
Garner Cl WA14 238 D2
Garner St WA2 16 B4
Garner's La SK3 240 E1
Garnets La WA8 22 A2
Garnett Ave WA4 17 D2
Garnett St SK1 240 F5
Garrett Field WA3 9 E3
Garrett Wlk SK3 240 C4
Garsdale Cl WA5 15 D4
Garside Ave WA3 3 E4
Garside St SK14 241 E5
Garston Cl SK4 240 C7
Garth Ave WA15 238 E6
Garth Dr CH2 118 B3
Garth Hts SK9 60 B4
Garth Rd L65 71 D3
Garton Dr WA3 3 F4
Garven Pl WA1 16 A3
Garwood Cl WA5 15 E4
Gas Rd SK11 112 B4
Gas St SK4 240 E5
Gaskell Ave Knutsford WA16 56 C1
Warrington WA4 17 D2
Gaskell Rd WA14 238 D6
Gaskell St WA4 16 B1
Gatcombe Mews SK9 60 A3
Gate Warth St WA5 15 E2
Gateacre Ct L66 69 F4
Gatefield St CW1 190 B2
Gatesheath Dr CH2 118 B4
Gatesheath La CH3 165 F3
Gateway CW1 190 C1
Gathill Cl SK8 239 F1
Gatley Gn SK8 239 A5
Gatley Golf Course SK8 239 A3
Gatley Prim Sch SK8 239 A5
Gatley Rd Cheadle SK8 239 C5
Sale M33 242 E5
Gatley Sta SK8 239 B5
Gaunts Way WA7 49 F3
Gavin Rd WA8 22 A4
Gawend La SK11 112
Gawer Pk CH2 118
Gawesworth Way 3 SK9 34 C
Gawsworth Ave CW2 189
Gawsworth Cl Alsager ST7 193
Bramhall SK7 35 F
Holmes Chapel CW4 130 A
Northwich CW9 104 A
Poynton SK12 36 C
Stockport SK3 240 D
Gawsworth Cty Prim Sch
SK11 111 E
Gawsworth Dr CW11 175 E
Gawsworth Hall SK11 134 C
Gawsworth Mews SK8 239 B
Gawsworth Rd
Ellesmere Port L66 69 F
Macclesfield SK11 111 E
Warren SK11 111 E
Gayhurst Ave WA2 8 C
Gaymoore Cl CH2 237 D
Gaynor Ave WA11 1 C
Gayton Cl CH2 118 C
Gayton Farm Rd L60 41 D
Gayton La L60 41 D
Gayton Parkway L60 41 D
Gayton Prim Sch L60 41 D
Gayton Rd L60 41 D
Gee St SK3 240 D
Gemini Bsns Pk WA5 7
Gemmull Cl CW3 229
General St WA1 16
Geneva Rd CW7 126
George Bates Cl ST7 193
George Kenyon Mews
CH4 140 C
George La SK6 241 A
George Rd WA5 15 E
George St Alderley Edge SK9 60 A
Altrincham WA14 238 D
Audley ST7 209 E
Barnton CW8 78 A
Chester CH1 237 D
Denton M34 241 A
Ellesmere Port L65 70 B
Knutsford WA16 57 D
Macclesfield SK11 112 B
Newton-le-W WA12 2 A
Sandbach CW11 174 C
Stalybridge SK15 242 D
Whaley Bridge SK23 65 F
Winsford CW7 126 C
George St W SK11 112 B
George VI Ave CW10 151 E
George VI Cl CW10 151 E
George's Cl SK12 36 C
George's La CW9 54 B
George's Rd Sale M33 242 B
Stockport SK4 240 D
George's Rd E SK12 36 C
George's Rd W SK12 36 C
George's Wlk CW11 175 D
Georges Cres WA4 17 D
Georges Way ST7 209 F
Gerard Dr CW5 204 E
Gerosa Ave WA2 8 A
Gerrard Ave
Ellesmere Port L66 69 E
Warrington WA5 15 F
Gerrard Dr CW8 77 E
Gerrard Rd WA3 9 D
Gerrard St
Stalybridge SK15 242 E
Widnes WA8 23 D
Gerrards Ave CH3 119 D
Giantswood La CW12 156 E
Gibb Hill CW9 53 E
Gibbon Dr CW9 80 A
Gibson Cres CW11 174 B
Gibson St
Warrington, Howley WA1 16 B
Warrington, Stockton Heath
WA4 16 B
Gibson Way WA14 238 C
Gibsons Rd SK4 240 B
Gig La WA1 17 F
Gigg La WA4 25 D
Gilbert Cl ST7 195 D
Gilbert Rd WA15 238 E
Gilbertbank SK6 241 B
Gilchrist Ave SK11 111 F
Gilchrist Rd M44 11 F
Gilderdale Cl WA3 10 A
Gill Bent Rd SK8 35 D
Gillan Cl WA7 50 B
Gillow Cl CW1 190 A
Gilmore St SK3 240 B
Giltbrook Cl WA8 12 C
Gilwell Cl WA4 17 E
Gingerbread La CW5 205 D
Girton Cl L65 70 B
Girton Rd L65 70 B
Girvin Dr L64 66 C
Glade The SK4 240 A
Gladewood Cl SK9 60 B
Gladstone Ave CH1 118 A
Gladstone Ct SK4 240 B
Gladstone Gr SK4 240 A
Gladstone Mews SK4 240 B
Gladstone Rd
Altrincham WA14 238 D
Broughton CH4 139 D
Chester CH1 118 A
Neston L64 66 C
Gladstone St Crewe CW1 190 B
Northwich CW8 103 F
Warrington WA2 16 A
8 Widnes WA8 23 D

ladstone St continued
allation (nr Nantwich)
CW5 .... 205 E3
Winsford CW7 .... 149 E4
adville Dr SK8 .... 240 A2
laisdale Cl CW2 .... 206 A3
lamis Cl Chester CH3 .... 119 D1
Wistaston CW2 .... 205 F4
lan Aber Pk CH4 .... 141 D4
landon Dr SK7 .... 35 E4
lanvor Rd SK3 .... 240 C4
lastonbury Ave
Cheadle Hulme SK7 .... 35 E3
Chester CH2 .... 118 B4
lastonbury Cl WA7 .... 24 C2
lastonbury Dr
Poynton SK12 .... 36 B3
laswen Gr SK5 .... 240 F8
lazebrook La WA3 .... 11 F2
lazebrook St WA3 .... 16 E3
lazebrook Sta WA3 .... 11 E3
lazebury CE (VA) Prim
Sch WA3 .... 5 E4
laziers La WA3 .... 4 A1
leadmere Rd WA4 .... 12 B1
leave Av SK10 .... 88 A4
leave Rd WA5 .... 6 C3
leave St M33 .... 242 B8
lebe Ave WA4 .... 17 E1
lebe Cl CW5 .... 220 A4
lebe Green Dr CW7 .... 149 E3
lebe La WA8 .... 13 D3
lebe Meadows CH2 .... 96 C1
lebe Rd WA8 .... 102 A2
lebe St ST7 .... 194 B1
lebe The WA7 .... 23 F1
lebecroft Av CH2 .... 72 A2
lebeland WA3 .... 4 C2
lebelands Rd
Knutsford WA16 .... 57 D1
Sale M33 .... 242 A8
lederway Rd L65 .... 70 C3
ledhall St SK15 .... 242 D2
len Aber Dr CH4 .... 140 C4
len Ave M33 .... 242 A8
len Cl WA13 .... 11 D1
len Rd L66 .... 69 E2
len The Blacon CH1 .... 117 F3
Runcorn WA7 .... 49 F3
lenathol Rd L66 .... 69 E2
lenbourne Pk SK7 .... 35 E3
lenburn Ave L62 .... 43 F2
lencoe Cl CW4 .... 130 B1
lencoe Rd L66 .... 69 E2
lencourse Rd WA8 .... 13 C2
lendale Av CH2 .... 72 A2
lendale Ave CH5 .... 116 A2
lendale Ct Buerton CW3 ..... 230 C2
Wistaston CW2 .... 189 E2
lendene Ave SK7 .... 35 E3
lendyke Rd L66 .... 69 E2
leneagles Cl Bramhall SK7 .. 36 A4
Chester CH2 .... 119 D2
Wilmslow SK9 .... 60 B4
leneagles Dr
Macclesfield WA11 .... 1 A3
Holmes Chapel WA16 .... 130 A1
Macclesfield SK10 .... 87 E2
Widnes WA8 .... 13 D1
Winsford CW7 .... 126 B1
leneagles Rd
Ellesmere Port L66 .... 69 E2
Gatley SK8 .... 239 C1
leneck Rd L66 .... 69 E2
lenfield WA14 .... 238 B4
lenfield Dr SK12 .... 36 B2
lenfield Rd SK4 .... 240 D8
lenholme Rd SK7 .... 35 E4
lenlea Dr M20 .... 239 B8
lenmaye Rd L66 .... 69 E2
lenmere Rd M20 .... 239 C8
lenn Pl WA8 .... 12 C1
lenorchy Cl CW4 .... 130 B1
lenside CH11 .... 117 E3
lenside Dr SK9 .... 60 B3
lent View SK15 .... 242 D4
lenthorn Gr M33 .... 242 B5
lenton Pk L64 .... 66 C3
lenville Way WA4 .... 241 A6
lenwood Cl L66 .... 69 E3
lenwood Gdns L66 .... 69 E3
leyve WA16 .... 29 E3
loucester Ave WA3 .... 3 D4
loucester Cl
Ellesmere Port CH1 .... 94 C4
Macclesfield SK10 .... 87 F2
Warrington WA1 .... 17 E4
loucester St Chester CH2 ... 237 E4
Kidsgrove ST7 .... 194 C1
Knutsford WA16 .... 81 F4
Poynton SK12 .... 36 B2
Widnes WA8 .... 13 D2
lover Rd WA3 .... 9 E2
lover St Crewe CW1 .... 190 A3
Newton-le-W WA12 .... 2 B2
lovers Loom CH5 .... 142 A4
loverstone Ct CH4 .... 237 E1
lyn Ave L62 .... 44 A3
loathland Way SK11 .... 112 B3
loddard Rd WA2 .... 8 C4
loddard St CW1 .... 190 A3
lodfrey St WA2 .... 16 B4

Godley Ct SK14 .... 241 F6
Godley Prim Sch SK14 .... 241 F7
Godley St SK14 .... 241 F8
Godscroft La WA6 .... 73 F3
Godshill Cl WA5 .... 14 B4
Godstall La CH1 .... 237 E2
Godstow WA7 .... 24 C2
Godward Rd SK22 .... 39 D4
Golborne Dale Rd WA3 .... 3 D2
Golborne Rd Goldborne WA3 . 3 E4
Winwick WA2 .... 8 A4
Golborne St WA1 .... 16 A3
Gold Triangle Complex
WA8 .... 22 A3
Goldborne All Saints RC
Sch WA3 .... 3 D4
Goldborne Cty Prim Sch
WA3 .... 3 D4
Goldborne La WA16 .... 28 C1
Goldcliffe Cl WA5 .... 7 E2
Goldcrest Cl Crewe CW1 .... 189 F4
Runcorn WA7 .... 49 F3
Winsford CW7 .... 149 E3
Golden Sq WA1 .... 16 A3
Goldfinch Cl CW12 .... 156 C1
Goldfinch La WA3 .... 9 F3
Goldford La SY14 .... 199 F3
Goldsmith Dr CW12 .... 174 B3
Goldsworth Cl WA15 .... 238 F3
Sale M33 .... 242 F6
Golftyn Dr CH5 .... 91 E1
Golftyn La CH5 .... 91 C1
Gongar La CH3 .... 98 A1
Gonsley Cl CW2 .... 237 E4
Gonville Ave SK11 .... 112 C2
Gooch Dr WA12 .... 2 B1
Goodall St SK11 .... 112 C4
Goodall's Cnr CW2 .... 206 B2
Goodier St M33 .... 242 A6
Goodrington Rd SK9 .... 34 C2
Goodwood Cl Barnton CW8 . 78 A2
Chester CH1 .... 118 A1
Goodwood Gr L66 .... 69 F2
Goose Gn WA14 .... 238 D4
Goose La WA4 .... 26 A1
Gooseberry La Kelsall CW6 122 C2
Runcorn WA7 .... 24 B1
Goosebrook Cl WA4 .... 78 B4
Goosebrook La WA4, CW9 .... 52 C1
Goosetrey Cl 10 SK9 .... 34 C1
Goostrey Cty Prim Sch
CW4 .... 130 C4
Goostrey Cty Prim Sch
(The Annexe) CW4 .... 130 F1
Goostrey La Cranage CW4 . 130 A4
Goostrey CW4 .... 130 D4
Goostrey Sta CW4 .... 131 D4
Gordon Ave Bebington L62 . 43 F4
Haydock WA11 .... 1 C4
Warrington WA1 .... 16 D2
Gordon La CH1 .... 95 D3
Gordon Rd M33 .... 242 B8
Gordon St
Ashton-u-L OL6 .... 242 A4
Hyde SK14 .... 241 E6
Stalybridge SK15 .... 242 E1
Stockport SK4 & SK5 .... 240 E7
Gore La SK9 .... 59 E1
Gorse Bank Rd WA15 .... 32 B4
Gorse Cl WA4 .... 101 D3
Gorse Covert Cty Prim Sch
WA3 .... 10 A3
Gorse Covert Rd WA3 .... 10 B3
Gorse Hall Cty Prim Sch
SK15 .... 242 C1
Gorse Hall Dr SK15 .... 242 C1
Gorse La CW12 .... 178 B3
Gorse Sq M31 .... 11 E2
Gorse Stacks CH1 .... 237 E3
Gorse The WA14 .... 31 D4
Gorse Way CH3 .... 142 A3
Gorsefield CH3 .... 166 A4
Gorsefield Cl L62 .... 43 E3
Gorsefield Cl L62 .... 43 E3
Gorsefield Hey SK9 .... 60 C4
Gorselands SK8 .... 35 D3
Gorsewood Rd WA7 .... 50 B3
Gorsey Bank Cres CW5 ..... 220 A4
Gorsey Bank Cty Prim Sch
SK9 .... 59 F4
Gorsey Bank Rd SK3 .... 240 B4
Gorsey Brow SK6 .... 241 A2
Gorsey La Altrincham WA14 238 B5
Bold Heath WA9 .... 6 B3
Partington WA13 .... 20 A4
Warrington WA3 .... 18 A4
Widnes WA8 .... 13 F1
Gorsey Mount St ▓ SK1 ... 240 F5
Gorsey Rd SK9 .... 59 F4
Gorseywell La WA7 .... 50 C3
Gorsley Cl CW10 .... 151 E3
Gorstage La CW8 .... 102 B4
Gorsthills Cty Prim Sch
L66 .... 69 E2
Gorston Wlk M22 .... 33 E4
Gorsty ferryhole La CW12 . 158 A1
Gosforth Cl WA4 .... 26 A1
Gosling Rd WA3 .... 9 F3
Gosling Cl WA4 .... 26 A1
Gosport Dr WA2 .... 8 C1
Goss St CH1 .... 237 D2
Gotherage Cl SK6 .... 241 E2
Gotherage La SK6 .... 241 E2
Gothic Cl SK6 .... 241 F2
Gothurst St WA8 .... 22 B4
Gough Ave WA2 .... 8 A1

Gough St SK3 .... 240 D5
Gough's La WA16 .... 82 B4
Goulden St Crewe CW1 ..... 190 A3
Warrington WA5 .... 15 F3
Goulders Ct WA5 .... 50 A3
Gover St SK14 .... 239 F2
Gowanhill Gdns WA16 .... 82 A4
Gowatt Rd Hyde SK14 .... 241 D5
Reddish SK4 .... 240 D8
Gower Cl Alsager ST7 .... 192 C2
Sandbach CW11 .... 174 C4
Gowey Cres CH3 .... 121 D1
Gowy Cl L66 .... 69 F4
Gowy Rd CH2 .... 96 C1
Gowy Wlk CW7 .... 127 D2
Goyt Pl SK23 .... 65 F4
Goyt Rd Disley SK12 .... 38 B3
New Mills SK22 .... 39 E3
Goyt Valley Ind Est SK23 .... 39 E2
Goyt View SK22 .... 39 D3
Goyt's La SK17 .... 90 C1
Grace Ave WA2 .... 16 A4
Grace Cl CW1 .... 191 E2
Gradwell St SK3 .... 240 D4
Grafton Mall 5 WA14 ...... 238 D4
Grafton Mews CH2 .... 237 E4
Grafton Rd L65 .... 70 B4
Grafton St Altrincham WA14 238 D4
Ashton-u-L OL6 .... 242 A2
Hyde SK14 .... 241 D7
Newton-le-W WA12 .... 2 A2
Reddish SK4 .... 240 E7
Graham Ave L66 .... 69 E3
Graham Cl WA8 .... 12 B1
Graham Dr Disley SK12 ...... 38 B3
Halewood L26 .... 21 D4
Graham Rd Blacon CH1 ..... 117 F2
Widnes WA8 .... 22 B4
Grainger's Rd CW9 .... 103 F3
Grammar School Rd
Lymm WA13 .... 18 C1
Neston L64 .... 66 C3
Grampian Way Bebington L62 43 F2
Neston L64 .... 66 C3
Winsford CW7 .... 149 D4
Granby Cl WA7 .... 50 B3
Granby Rd
Cheadle Hulme SK8 .... 35 D4
Warrington WA4 .... 26 A4
Grand Junction Ret Pk
CW1 .... 190 B2
Grandford La CW5 .... 217 E1
Grange Ave Barnton CW8 .... 78 A2
Cheadle SK8 & M19 .... 239 F3
Denton M34 .... 241 B6
Warrington WA4 .... 16 C2
Grange Cl Crewe CW1 .... 190 C2
Goldborne WA3 .... 3 E4
Sale SK9 .... 241 F5
Sandbach CW11 .... 174 C4
Grange Cres L66 .... 44 A1
Grange Ct Altrincham WA14 238 C1
Biddulph ST6 .... 179 C1
Grange Cty Comp Sch The
WA7 .... 23 E1
Grange Cty Inf Sch The
WA7 .... 23 E1
Grange Cty Jun Sch The
WA7 .... 23 E1
Grange Dr Hartford CW8 .... 103 D3
Penketh WA5 .... 14 C4
Thornton Hough L63 .... 42 A4
Widnes WA8 .... 12 B1
Grange Jun Sch The CW8 .. 103 D3
Grange La Edge Green SY14 198 C2
Tilston SY14 .... 198 C2
Weaverham CW8 .... 102 A4
Winsford CW7 .... 126 A2
Grange Lea CW10 .... 128 A1
Grange Park Ave
Cheadle SK8 .... 239 D5
Runcorn WA7 .... 23 D1
Wilmslow SK9 .... 60 A4
Grange Park Rd SK8 .... 239 D5
Grange Rd Altrincham WA14 238 C1
Ashton CH3 .... 99 D1
Barnton CW8 .... 78 A2
Biddulph ST6 .... 179 F2
Chester, Bache CH2 .... 118 B2
Cuddington SK8 .... 101 F1
Ellesmere Port L66 .... 70 B2
Haydock WA11 .... 1 B3
Hyde SK14 .... 241 F5
Macclesfield SK11 .... 112 B3
Northwich, Rudheath CW9 .. 104 B3
Runcorn WA7 .... 23 E1
Sale M33 .... 242 A6
Grange Rd N SK14 .... 241 F6
Grange Rd S SK14 .... 241 F5
Grange Sch The WA8 .... 103 D3
Grange The Hartford CW8 .. 103 D3
Hyde SK14 .... 241 F5
Grange Valley WA11 .... 1 B3
Grange Valley Prim Sch
WA11 .... 1 B3
Grange Way CW11 .... 174 C4
Grangebrook Dr CW7 .... 126 B2
Grangefields L66 .... 179 F2
Grangeland Dr WA10 .... 83 F2
Grangelands SK10 .... 86 C1
Grangemoor WA7 .... 24 B1
Grangeside CH2 .... 118 B4
Grangeway Runcorn WA7 .... 49 E4
Wilmslow SK9 .... 34 B2

Grangeway Ct WA7 .... 49 E4
Granston Cl WA5 .... 7 F1
Grant Cl WA5 .... 7 E1
Grant Rd WA5 .... 15 D3
Grant St WA12 .... 2 A2
Grantham Ave
Warrington WA1 .... 16 C4
Warrington, Lower Walton
WA4 .... 26 A4
Grantham Cl CW9 .... 104 B4
Grantham Rd SK4 .... 240 C6
Granville Dr L66 .... 69 D4
Granville Rd
Cheadle SK3 & SK8 .... 240 C1
Chester CH1 .... 118 A2
Northwich CW9 .... 104 A3
Warrington WA5 .... 59 F3
Granville Sq CW7 .... 149 F4
Granville St
Ashton-u-L OL6 .... 242 A2
Runcorn WA7 .... 23 D2
Warrington WA1 .... 16 B3
Winsford CW7 .... 149 F4
Grapes St SK11 .... 112 B4
Grappenhall CE Aided
Prim Sch WA4 .... 17 D1
Grappenhall Hall Sch WA4 . 27 F3
Grappenhall Rd
Ellesmere Port L65 .... 69 F2
Warrington WA4 .... 16 B1
Grasmere SK11 .... 111 F3
Grasmere Ave
Congleton CW12 .... 155 F1
Crewe CW2 .... 189 F3
Warrington WA2 .... 8 C2
Grasmere Cl
Stalybridge SK15 .... 242 D4
Winsford CW7 .... 126 B1
Grasmere Cres SK7 .... 35 F4
Grasmere Dr
Holmes Chapel WA16 .... 130 A2
Runcorn WA7 .... 49 E3
Grasmere Rd
Alderley Edge SK9 .... 60 A1
Chester CH2 .... 118 C3
Ellesmere Port L65 .... 70 B1
Frodsham WA6 .... 74 B4
Gatley SK8 .... 239 B3
Neston L64 .... 66 C3
Partington M31 .... 11 F2
Grason Ave SK9 .... 34 C2
Grasscroft Rd SK15 .... 242 D1
Grassfield Way WA16 .... 82 A4
Grassmere Cres SK6 .... 37 F4
Grassmoor Cl L62 .... 43 F4
Grassygreen La ST7 .... 209 F1
Gratrix La M33 .... 242 F5
Gratrix Rd L62 .... 43 E4
Gravel La SK9 .... 59 F3
Graveyard La WA16 .... 58 C3
Gray Ave WA11 .... 1 B3
Gray's Cl SY17 .... 195 D4
Graylag Cl WA7 .... 49 F3
Graysands Rd WA15 .... 238 F3
Greasby Dr L66 .... 69 F2
Great Ashfield WA8 .... 12 B2
Great Budworth CE Contr
Prim Sch CW9 .... 79 D4
Great Delph WA11 .... 1 B4
Great Egerton St
SK1 & SK4 .... 240 E6
Great King St SK14 .... 112 B4
Great Norbury St SK14 ..... 241 D6
Great Portwood St SK1 ..... 240 F6
Great Queen St SK11 .... 112 B4
Great Riding WA7 .... 50 B4
Great Sankey Cty High Sch
WA5 .... 14 C4
Great Sankey L Ctr WA5 ... 14 C4
Great Sankey Cty Prim Sch
WA5 .... 15 D3
Great Underbank SK1 .... 240 F5
Greatoak Rd ST7 .... 209 F2
Greave La CW6 .... 241 D4
Greave Fold SK6 .... 241 D4
Greave Prim Sch SK6 .... 241 D4
Greaves La SY14 .... 222 C4
Greaves Rd SK9 .... 59 F4
Grebe Cl Knutsford WA16 ... 57 D2
Poynton SK12 .... 36 A2
Greek St Runcorn WA7 .... 22 C2
Stockport SK1 & SK3 .... 240 F5
Green Acre Cl WA16 .... 82 A4
Green Ave Alpraham CW6 .. 169 E2
Barnton CW8 .... 78 A2
Davenham CW9 .... 103 F2
Green Bank Ctr CH1 .... 141 F3
Green Bridge Cl WA7 .... 24 A1
Green Cl SK8 .... 239 A6
Green Coppice WA7 .... 50 B4
Green Courts WA14 .... 238 B3
Green Croft SK6 .... 241 E1
Green Dr Alsager ST7 .... 193 E2
Wilmslow SK9 .... 34 B1
Green Gables Cl SK8 .... 239 B1
Green Hall Mews SK9 .... 60 A3
Green Hill St WA3 .... 242 A2
Green Hill Terr SK3 .... 240 D3
Green Jones Brow WA5 .... 6 C3
Green La Acton CW5 .... 204 A2
Alderley Edge SK9 .... 60 A1
Appleton WA4 .... 26 B4
Audlem CW3 .... 229 F1

Green La continued
Barbridge CW5 .... 187 D4
Bollington SK10 .... 63 D1
Burtonwood WA5 .... 6 C4
Chester CH5, CH4 .... 119 D2
Chester, Lache CH4 .... 140 C3
Chowley CH3 .... 182 C3
Davenham CW9 .... 103 F2
Disley SK12 .... 38 B2
Ellesmere Port CH1 .... 70 B2
Ellesmere Port, Sutton Green
L66 .... 69 E2
Higher Kinnerton CH4 .... 161 D3
Higher Wincham CW9 .... 79 F2
Horton Green SY14 .... 212 A4
Irlam M44 .... 11 F3
Kelsall CW6 .... 122 B2
Knutsford WA16 .... 56 B2
Lindow End SK9 .... 84 C4
Manchester SK4 .... 240 B7
Peover WA16 .... 83 E1
Picton CH2 .... 96 B2
Plumley WA16 .... 80 C3
Poynton SK12 .... 37 F2
Romiley SK6 .... 241 B2
Sandbach CH11 .... 173 F4
Saughall CH1 .... 117 E4
Shocklach SY14 .... 211 E4
Stockport SK4 .... 240 D6
Stockport, Heaton Norris
SK4 .... 240 C6
Warrington WA1 .... 17 D2
Widnes WA8 .... 22 C1
Willaston (nr Nantwich)
CW5 .... 205 D3
Wilmslow SK9 .... 60 A4
Winwick WA2 .... 8 A4
Green La Cl WA2 .... 8 A4
Green La E CH5 .... 116 B4
Green La W CH5 .... 141 D3
Green Lane Ind Est SK4 .... 240 D6
Green Lane Sch WA1 .... 17 D4
Green Meadows WA3 .... 7 F3
Green Oaks Path WA8 .... 23 E4
Green Oaks Way WA8 .... 23 E4
Green Pk CW8 .... 102 C4
Green Rd M31 .... 11 F2
Green St Alderley Edge SK9 . 60 A1
Holt L13 .... 180 C1
Hyde SK14 .... 241 E5
Knutsford WA16 .... 57 D1
Macclesfield SK11 .... 112 C4
Sandbach CW11 .... 175 D4
Stockport SK3 .... 240 F2
Warrington WA5 .... 15 F3
Green The Cheadle SK8 ...... 34 C4
Ellesmere Port L65 .... 70 A1
Hartford CW8 .... 103 D3
Harthill CH3 .... 183 F2
Higher Kinnerton CH4 .... 161 D4
Lawton-gate ST7 .... 194 A2
Middlewich CW10 .... 151 E3
Neston L64 .... 66 C3
Neston L64 .... 66 C3
Stockport SK4 .... 240 C6
Tarvin CH3 .... 121 F1
Thornton Hough L63 .... 42 B2
Wilmslow SK9 .... 34 C2
Green Tree Gdns SK6 .... 241 B2
Green View WA13 .... 19 D3
Green Villa Pk SK9 .... 59 F2
Green Way CH1 .... 94 A1
Green Wlk
Altrincham WA14 .... 238 B3
Cuddington SK8 .... 102 A2
Gatley SK8 .... 239 A6
Partington M31 .... 11 E1
Greenacre Dr L63 .... 43 E4
Greenacre Rd CH4 .... 140 C2
Greenacres Crewe CW1 ..... 190 B3
Duddon CW6 .... 145 D3
Frodsham WA6 .... 74 B3
Lymm WA13 .... 19 D2
Sandbach CW11 .... 175 D4
Greenacres Cl WA3 .... 4 A4
Greenacres Rd CW12 .... 155 F1
Greenall Ave WA5 .... 14 B2
Greenall Rd CW9 .... 104 A4
Greenalls Ave WA4 .... 16 B1
Greenbank Ave
Ellesmere Port L66 .... 69 E4
Gatley M22 .... 239 A5
Greenbank Cl WA5 .... 4 A4
Greenbank Dr SK10 .... 88 A4
Greenbank Gdns WA4 .... 16 C1
Greenbank La CH8 .... 103 E3
Greenbank Pk CW11 .... 175 D4
Greenbank Rd
Chester CH2 .... 119 D2
Gatley SK8 .... 239 A6
Greenbank Residential
Sch CW8 .... 103 E3
Greenbank Sta CW8 .... 103 E3
Greenbridge Rd WA7 .... 24 A1
Greencourts Bsns Pk
M22 .... 34 A4
Greendale Dr
Middlewich CW10 .... 151 D4
Newcastle-u-L ST5 .... 210 B1
Greendale La SK10 .... 86 B4
Greenfield Ave CH4 .... 161 D4

Greenfield Cl
New Mills SK22 .... 39 D4
Stockport SK3 .... 240 E2
Greenfield Cres CH3 .. 143 D3
Greenfield Gdns CH2 ...... 72 A2
Greenfield La
Chester CH2 .... 119 D3
Frodsham WA6 .... 49 F1
Greenfield Prim Sch
SK14 .... 241 D6
Greenfield Rd
Bollington SK10 .... 88 A4
Broughton CH4 .... 139 E2
Congleton CW12 .... 156 A2
Ellesmere Port L66 .... 69 D4
Waverton CH3 .... 143 D3
Greenfield St SK14 .... 241 D6
Greenfield Way CW8 .. 102 A2
Greenfields Chester CH2 .. 95 F1
Winsford CW7 .... 127 D1
Greenfields Ave
Appleton WA4 .... 26 B4
Bebington L62 .... 43 E4
Shavington CW2 .... 206 A2
Greenfields Cl Neston L64 .. 66 C3
Newton-le-W WA12 .... 2 B2
Warrington WA1 .... 17 E4
Greenfields Cres L62 .... 43 E4
Greenfields Croft L64 .... 66 C3
Greenfields Dr L64 .... 66 C3
Greenfields Rd ST7 .... 193 F2
Greengate Rd
Dukinfield M34 .... 241 A8
Lawton-gate ST7 .... 193 F3
Greengates Cres L64 .... 66 C3
Greenhalgh St SK4 .... 240 E6
Greenhill Ave M33 .... 242 A8
Greenhill La WA4 .... 52 A3
Greenhill Wlk SK12 .... 38 B3
Greenhills Cl SK11 .... 112 C4
Greenhouse Farm Rd
WA7 .... 50 A4
Greenhythe Rd SK9 .... 34 B3
Greenland Cl CW6 .... 146 B1
Greenlands CH3 .... 166 A2
Greenlaw Cl CW9 .... 104 A3
Greenlea Cl L65 .... 70 A1
Greenore Dr L24 .... 21 E1
Greensbridge La L26 .... 21 D4
Greenshall La SK12 .... 38 C3
Greenshank Cl WA12 .... 2 B2
Greenside SK4 .... 240 A5
Greenside Ave WA6 .... 74 B4
Greenside Ct CW9 .... 105 E3
Greenside Dr
Altrincham WA14 .... 238 E1
Lostock CW9 .... 105 D4
Greenside La CH1 .... 141 D4
Greenvale Dr SK8 .... 239 C6
Greenview Dr M20 .... 239 C8
Greenway Alsager ST7 .... 193 D3
Altrincham WA14 .... 238 A5
Appleton WA4 .... 26 B4
Cheadle Hulme SK7 .... 35 E3
Congleton CW12 .... 156 A2
Crewe CW1 .... 190 B4
Farndon CH3 .... 180 C1
Great Sankey WA5 .... 14 C4
Hyde SK14 .... 241 D5
Romiley SK6 .... 241 E1
Tilston SY14 .... 198 B2
Warrington WA1 .... 16 C4
Wilmslow SK9 .... 60 A3
Greenway St CH4 .... 237 E1
Greenway Wlk CW9 .... 104 B4
Greenways ST7 .... 209 F1
Greenwell Rd WA11 .... 1 B3
Greenwood Ave
Chester CH4 .... 141 E4
Congleton CW12 .... 156 C2
Greenwood Cl Croft WA3 .... 4 C1
Weaverham CW8 .... 77 E1
Greenwood Cres WA2 .... 8 C1
Greenwood Dr
Newton-le-W WA12 .... 2 B2
Wilmslow SK9 .... 60 B4
Greenwood Rd WA13 .... 18 C1
Greenwood St ■ WA14 .. 238 D4
Greg Ave SK10 .... 87 F4
Greg Mews SK9 .... 34 A1
Gregory Ave SK6 .... 241 C1
Gregory Cl WA5 .... 15 E4
Gregson Rd WA8 .... 13 E1
Grenfell Cl L64 .... 41 E1
Grenfell Pk L64 .... 41 E1
Grenfell St ■ WA8 .... 22 D3
Grenville Cl CW1 .... 191 E3
Grenville Cres L63 .... 43 E4
Grenville Rd L64 .... 41 F1
Grenville St SK3 .... 240 D4
Gresford Ave CW2 .... 237 F4
Gresford Cl WA5 .... 7 F1
Gresham Wlk SK4 .... 240 E7
Gresley Way ST7 .... 209 F1
Gresty Green Rd CW2 .. 206 B4

Gresty La CW2 .... 206 A4
Gresty Rd CW2 .... 190 B1
Gresty Road Football Gd
(Crewe Alexandra FC)
CW2 .... 190 B1
Gresty Terr CW1 .... 190 C2
Greta Ave SK3 .... 34 B3
Greville Dr CW7 .... 127 D1
Grey Cl SK6 .... 241 A4
Grey Friars CH1 .... 237 D2
Grey Rd WA14 .... 238 D3
Grey St Stalybridge SK15 .. 242 F1
Warrington WA1 .... 16 B3
Greyhound Park Rd
CH1 .... 117 F2
Greyhound Pk CH1 .... 118 A1
Greyhound Rd SK10 .... 86 A3
Greylands Rd M20 .... 239 C8
Greymarsh Dr SK12 .... 36 C1
Greymist Ave WA1 .... 17 E4
Greys Ct WA1 .... 9 F2
Greystoke Ave M33 .... 242 B5
Greystoke Dr SK9 .... 60 A1
Greystoke Rd SK10 .... 87 F1
Greystone Heath Sch
WA5 .... 14 C4
Greystone Pk CW1 .... 190 B2
Greystone Rd WA5 .... 14 C2
Greystones L66 .... 68 C3
Greystones Rd CH3 .... 119 E1
Grice St WA4 .... 16 B3
Griffin Cl Blacon CH1 .... 117 F3
Burtonwood WA5 .... 6 C3
New Mills SK22 .... 39 D3
Norton in Hales TF9 .... 236 B1
Griffin Mews WA8 .... 13 D2
Griffiths Dr CW9 .... 104 B3
Griffiths Rd Lostock CW9 .. 79 F1
Northwich CW9 .... 104 C4
Griffiths St WA4 .... 16 C2
Grig Pl ST7 .... 193 E3
Grimsditch La
Daresbury WA4 .... 52 A3
Whitley WA4 .... 52 A3
Grimshaw Ave SK10 .... 88 A4
Grimshaw Cl SK6 .... 241 A4
Grimshaw La SK10 .... 88 A4
Grindley Bank CH2 .... 119 F4
Grindley Gdns L65 .... 70 B1
Grisdale Ave WA2 .... 8 A2
Grisdale Cl WA7 .... 49 F3
Grisedale Rd L62 .... 43 E3
Grisedale Way SK11 .... 112 A3
Grizedale WA8 .... 12 C2
Grizedale Rd SK6 .... 241 B4
Groarke Dr WA5 .... 14 B3
Groby Pl WA14 .... 238 D5
Groby Rd Altrincham WA14 . 238 D4
Crewe CW1 .... 190 C4
Groby St SK15 .... 242 F1
Grosvenor Ave
Alsager ST7 .... 193 E3
Goldbourne WA3 .... 3 E4
Hartford CW8 .... 103 D2
Warrington WA1 .... 16 C4
Grosvenor Cl
Great Sankey WA5 .... 15 E3
Wilmslow SK9 .... 60 A2
Grosvenor Cres SK14 .. 241 C5
Grosvenor Ct Chester CH1 . 237 F2
Winsford CW7 .... 149 E4
Grosvenor Dr SK12 .... 36 B2
Grosvenor Gdns WA12 .. 2 C4
Grosvenor Nuffield Hospl
CH4 .... 141 E3
Grosvenor Pk Rd CH2 .. 237 F2
Grosvenor Pk Terr CH2 .. 237 F2
Grosvenor Pl CH4 .... 237 E1
Grosvenor Prec CH1 .. 237 E2
Grosvenor Rd
Altrincham WA14 .... 238 E5
Chester CH4 .... 141 E4
Congleton CW12 .... 156 A2
Haydock WA11 .... 1 A4
Hyde SK14 .... 241 D5
Manchester SK4 .... 240 B7
Tarvin CH3 .... 121 D1
Widnes WA8 .... 13 D2
Grosvenor Sq M33 .... 242 A6
Grosvenor St Chester CH1 . 237 D2
Crewe CW1 .... 190 A3
■ Macclesfield SK11 .. 112 B4
Runcorn WA7 .... 23 D2
Stalybridge SK15 .... 242 D1
■ Stockport SK3 .... 240 F4
Winsford CW7 .... 149 F4
Grotsworth La SY14 .. 214 C4
Grotto La WA16 .... 108 A4
Grounds St WA2 .... 16 A4
Grove Arc SK9 .... 60 A4
Grove Ave Chester CH3 .. 119 D2
Kidsgrove ST7 .... 194 C1
Lawton-gate ST7 .... 194 A2
Lostock CW9 .... 80 A2
Lymm WA13 .... 18 B2
Wilmslow SK9 .... 60 A2
Grove Cl CW7 .... 149 D4
Grove Cres CW3 .... 232 B1
Grove Ct Alsager ST7 .... 193 F2
Sale M33 .... 242 D6
Grove Gdns CH1 .... 119 F1
Grove La SK6 .... 35 D3
Grove Park Ave ST7 .. 194 A2
Grove Pk WA16 .... 57 D1
Grove Prim Sch The SK15 . 35 D4
Grove Rd Altrincham WA15 . 238 E3
Backford CH1 .... 94 C2
Grove Rise WA10 .... 18 C2

Grove St New Mills SK22 .. 39 D4
Runcorn WA7 .... 22 C2
Stalybridge SK16 .... 242 A1
Warrington WA4 .... 16 B2
Wilmslow SK9 .... 60 A4
Grove The
Cheadle Hulme SK8 .... 35 D3
Knutsford WA16 .... 57 E2
Lawton-gate ST7 .... 194 A2
Penketh WA5 .... 14 C2
Sale M33 .... 242 B5
Stockport SK3 .... 240 E3
Grovemount CW9 .... 103 F1
Groves The Chester CH1 .. 237 E2
Ellesmere Port CH1 .... 95 D4
GroveThe SY13 .... 225 F1
Grovewood Mews SK11 .. 112 B3
Grub La CW6 .... 122 B3
Grundy Cl WA8 .... 12 C2
Grundy St WA3 .... 3 D4
Guardian St WA5 .... 15 F3
Guernsey Cl Appleton WA4 .. 26 B4
Congleton CW12 .... 157 D1
Guernsey Dr L65 .... 70 B1
Guernsey Rd WA8 .... 13 F2
Guest St WA8 .... 23 D4
Guests Slack WA6 .... 100 A4
Guilden Gn CH3 .... 119 F1
Guilden Sutton CE Contr
Prim Sch CH2 .... 119 F3
Guilden Sutton La CH2 .. 119 E3
Guildford Ave SK8 .... 35 D3
Guildford Cl WA5 .... 15 E4
Guildford Rd CH4 .... 140 C3
Guillemot Cl CW1 .... 190 C3
Gull Cl SK12 .... 36 A2
Gullane Cl SK10 .... 87 D2
Gullet The CW5 .... 204 C3
Gullivers World Theme Pk
WA5 .... 7 E1
Gulls Way L60 .... 40 C4
Gunco La
Macclesfield SK11 .... 112 C3
Prestbury SK10 .... 87 E4
Gundy Rd SK9 .... 60 A2
Gunn Gr L64 .... 66 C4
Guttercroft CW1 .... 191 E3
Gutticar Rd WA8 .... 12 A1
Guy La Hargrave CH3 .... 143 E3
Waverton CH3 .... 143 E3
Guywood La SK6 .... 241 C3

Hackberry Cl WA14 .. 238 B8
Hacked Way La SK11 .. 113 F3
Haddon Cl
Alderley Edge SK9 .... 59 F1
High Lane SK6 .... 37 F4
Holmes Chapel CW4 .... 130 A2
Macclesfield SK11 .... 112 A3
Wistaston CW2 .... 206 A4
Haddon Dr WA8 .... 12 B2
Haddon Gr
Altrincham WA15 .... 238 F7
Sale M33 .... 242 A6
Haddon La L64 .... 67 E2
Haddon Rd Burton L64 .... 67 E1
Cheadle SK8 .... 34 B4
Hadfield Cl WA8 .... 13 F1
Hadfield St CW9 .... 79 D1
Hadleigh Cl WA5 .... 14 C2
Hadley Ave L62 .... 43 E4
Hadley Cl WA8 .... 13 F1
Hadlow Gr WA14 .... 6 F4
Hadlow Rd L64 .... 67 D3
Hadrian Dr CH1 .... 117 F3
Hadrian Way CW8 .... 102 A1
Hafod Blacon CH1 .... 117 E2
Hag Bank La SK12 .... 38 B4
Hague Bar Prim Sch SK22 . 38 C4
Hague Bar Rd SK22 .... 39 D4
Hague Fold SK22 .... 38 C4
Hague St SK6 .... 242 A4
Haig Ave Great Sankey WA5 . 15 D3
Irlam M44 .... 11 E2
Haig Ct SK10 .... 57 E2
Haig Rd Knutsford WA16 .. 57 E2
Widnes WA8 .... 13 D1
Haigh Lawn WA14 .... 238 B3
Hale Ave SK12 .... 36 B1
Hale Bank Rd WA8 .... 21 F3
Hale CE Contr Sch L24 .. 21 E1
Hale Ct WA8 .... 21 F3
Hale Gate Rd Hale L24 .. 21 F1
Widnes WA8 .... 22 A2
Hale Golf Course WA15 .. 32 A4
Hale Gr WA5 .... 15 D3
Hale Low Rd WA15 .... 238 F3
Hale Prep Sch WA15 .... 238 E3
Hale Rd Altrincham WA15 .. 32 B4
Hale L24 .... 21 D1
Manchester SK4 .... 240 C7
Widnes WA8 .... 22 B4
Hale Road Ind Est WA8 . 22 B3
Hale St WA2 .... 16 A4
Hale Sta WA14 .... 238 F2
Hale View WA7 .... 48 C4
Hale View Rd WA6 .... 73 E2
Halebank CE Contr Prim
Sch WA8 .... 22 A2
Halewood La Ends L26 .. 21 D4
Haley Rd N WA5 .... 6 C3
Haley Rd S WA5 .... 6 C3
Half St SK11 .... 112 B3
Halfacre La WA4 .... 25 F1
Halghton La SY13 .... 222 A1
Halifax Cl WA2 .... 8 B1
Halkett Cl CH4 .... 140 C3
Halkyn Rd CH2 .... 237 F4

Hall Ave
Altrincham WA15 .... 238 F7
Widnes WA8 .... 12 A1
Hall Cl SK10 .... 87 E2
Hall Dr Alsager ST7 .... 193 E2
Appleton WA4 .... 26 B3
Marston CW9 .... 79 D3
Willaston (nr Nantwich)
CW5 .... 205 E3
Hall Gr Cheadle SK8 .... 239 C6
Macclesfield SK10 .... 87 E2
Hall Hill SK10 .... 87 E2
Hall La Antrobus CW9 .... 53 D1
Audlem WA4 .... 230 A4
Bold Heath WA9 .... 6 A2
Brown Knowl CH3 .... 199 E4
Cronton WA8 .... 12 B4
Daresbury WA4 .... 25 E1
Haughton Moss CW6 .... 186 B3
Higher Wincham CW9 .... 79 F2
Kelsall CW6 .... 122 B3
Little Leigh CW9 .... 77 F4
Lostock CW9 .... 79 F2
Mobberley WA16 .... 58 B2
Partington M31 .... 11 F2
Pickmere WA16 .... 55 D1
Sandbach CW11 .... 174 A3
Stretton WA4 .... 52 C4
Sutton Lane Ends SK11 .. 112 C2
Utkinton CW6 .... 146 B3
Warmingham CW11 .... 173 F2
Winsford CW7 .... 149 D2
Hall La The CW6 .... 147 E1
Hall Meadow SK8 .... 239 E1
Hall Moss La SK7 .... 35 E2
Hall Nook WA5 .... 14 C2
Hall O'shaw St CW1 .... 190 C2
Hall Rd Altrincham WA14 .. 238 C1
Haydock WA11 .... 1 C4
Warrington WA1 .... 17 F4
Wilmslow SK9 .... 60 A4
Hall St Ashton-u-L OL6 .... 242 B2
Audley ST7 .... 209 E1
Cheadle SK8 .... 239 D6
Denton SK14 .... 241 B7
Macclesfield SK11 .... 112 B4
New Mills SK22 .... 39 D4
Warrington WA1 .... 16 B3
Hall Terr WA5 .... 14 C4
Hall Wood Ave WA11 .... 1 C4
Hall Wood Rd SK9 .... 34 C1
Halla Way WA1 .... 16 C2
Hallastone Rd WA6 .... 73 E2
Hallcroft M31 .... 11 F2
Hallcroft Pl WA4 .... 17 D1
Hallefield Cres SK11 .... 112 C4
Hallefield Dr ■ SK11 .. 112 C4
Hallefield Rd ■ SK11 .. 112 C4
Hallfield Dr CH2 .... 72 A4
Hallfield Park L66 .... 69 E2
Hallfields Rd Tarvin CH3 .. 121 E1
Warrington WA2 .... 16 B4
Hallgate Dr SK8 .... 239 A2
Hallgreen La CW12 .... 155 E4
Halliday Cl WA3 .... 9 F2
Halliwell's Brow WA16 .. 29 D2
Hallows Ave WA2 .... 16 B4
Hallows Dr CW6 .... 122 B2
Hallowsgate Ct CW6 .... 122 B2
Halls Rd Biddulph ST6 .... 179 E1
Mow Cop ST7 .... 195 E4
Hallsgreen La CH2 .... 96 C4
Hallshaw Ave CW1 .... 190 C3
Hallwood Cl WA7 .... 49 F3
Hallwood Dr L66 .... 68 B2
Hallwood Link Rd WA7 .. 49 F3
Hallwood Park Ave WA7 . 49 F3
Hallwood Park Cty Prim
Sch WA7 .... 49 F3
Halsall Ave WA2 .... 16 B4
Halsall Cl WA7 .... 50 B3
Halston Cl SK5 .... 240 F8
Halstone Ave SK9 .... 59 F2
Halton Brook Ave WA7 .. 23 E1
Halton Coll of F Ed WA8 . 23 D4
Halton Coll of F Ed
(Annexe) Runcorn WA7 .. 23 F2
Widnes WA8 .... 23 D4
Halton Cres L66 .... 69 F1
Halton Ct WA7 .... 23 E1
Halton Dr CW2 .... 206 C4
Halton General Hospl
WA7 .... 49 F3
Halton Link Rd WA7 .... 49 F4
Halton Lodge Ave WA7 . 49 F4
Halton Lodge Cty Prim Sch
WA7 .... 49 F4
Halton Rd Chester CH2 .. 118 C3
Ellesmere Port L66 .... 69 F1
Great Sankey WA5 .... 14 C4
Runcorn WA7 .... 23 E1
Halton St Haydock WA11 .. 1 C3
Hyde SK14 .... 241 F7
Halton St Mary's CE Aided
Prim Sch WA7 .... 50 A4
Halton Station Rd WA7 .. 49 F2
Halton View Rd WA8 .... 13 E1
Halton Way L66 .... 69 F1
Hamble Dr WA5 .... 15 D2
Hamble Way SK10 .... 86 C1
Hambledon Cl L66 .... 69 D2
Hambleton Cl WA8 .... 12 B2
Hambleton Rd SK8 .... 34 B4
Hambleton Way CW7 .. 149 D4
Hambletts Hollow WA6 . 100 C3

Hamilton Ave
Hawarden CH5 .... 116 A
Irlam M44 .... 11 E
Hamilton Cl
Haslington CW1 .... 191 E
Macclesfield SK10 .... 113 D
Neston L64 .... 41 D
Hamilton Cres SK14 .... 240 E
Hamilton Pl CH1 .... 237 D
Hamilton Rd
Connah's Quay CH5 .... 91 E
Lymm WA13 .... 18 F
Hamilton Sq SK4 .... 240 B
Hamilton St Chester CH2 .. 118 C
Stalybridge SK15 .... 242 C
Hammond Sch
Chester CH2 .... 237 D
Chester, Hoole Bank CH2 .. 119 D
Hammond St CW2 .... 190 D
Hamnet Cl WA3 .... 9 F
Hamnett St WA14 .... 241 D
Hamon Rd WA15 .... 238 F
Hampden Rd M33 .... 242 A
Hampshire Cl WA12 .. 156 B
Hampshire Rd M31 .... 11 E
Hampshire Wlk SK10 .... 86 C
Hampson Ave WA3 .... 4 C
Hampson Cres SK9 .... 34 B
Hampson St M33 .... 242 C
Hampstead Ct ■ CW7 .. 149 F
Hampton Cl Neston L64 .. 66 C
Widnes WA8 .... 13 D
Hampton Cres Neston L64 .. 66 C
No Man's Heath SY14 .... 214 A
Hampton Ct WA4 .... 26 C
Hampton Dr Cronton WA8 .. 12 B
Great Sankey WA5 .... 15 E
Hampton Gdns L65 .... 70 A
Hampton Gr SK8 .... 239 F
Hampton Rd Chester CH4 .. 140 C
Hampton St ■ SK9 .... 60 A
Hamsterley Cl WA3 .... 10 A
Hanbury Cl CW2 .... 206 A
Hancock Rd CW12 .... 156 C
Hand St SK11 .... 112 A
Handbridge CH4 .... 237 D
Handel Mews M33 .... 242 C
Handford Ave L62 .... 43 B
Handford Rd CH2 .... 118 C
Handforth La WA7 .... 17 E
Handforth Hall Cty Prim
Sch SK9 .... 34 B
Handforth La WA7 .... 49 F
Handforth Rd Crewe CW2 .. 189 F
Wilmslow SK9 .... 34 B
Handforth Sta SK9 .... 34 B
Handley Cl SK3 .... 240 C
Handley Hill CW7 .... 149 D
Handley St WA7 .... 149 D
Hankelow Cl Chester CH2 . 237 E
Middlewich CW10 .... 151 E
Hankey St WA7 .... 22 C
Hankins Heys La CW3 .. 231 D
Hankinson St M31 .... 11 F
Hanley Cl Disley SK12 .... 38 B
Widnes WA8 .... 12 B
Hanmer Ct WA7 .... 22 B
Hanns Hall Rd L64 .... 67 D
Hanover Bsns Pk WA14 .. 238 E
Hanover Dr CW7 .... 149 E
Hanover St WA7 .... 22 C
Hanover St
Stalybridge SK15 .... 242 C
Warrington WA1 .... 16 A
Hapsford Cl WA3 .... 9 F
Hapsford La
Dunham-on-t-H WA6 .... 97 F
Elton CH2 .... 72 B
Elton, Hapsford WA6 .... 72 C
Hapton Pl SK4 .... 240 E
Harbord St WA1 .... 16 C
Harbour Cl WA7 .... 50 B
Harbour La SK11 .... 111 E
Harbourn Wlk M22 .... 33 E
Harcourt Cl WA3 .... 9 A
Harcourt Rd
Altrincham WA14 .... 238 F
Sale M33 .... 242 A
Hardcastle Rd SK3 .... 240 D
Harden Pk SK9 .... 60 A
Harding Ave
Tattenhall CH3 .... 166 A
Warrington WA2 .... 8 C
Harding Rd Chester CH2 .. 118 A
Nantwich CW5 .... 204 E
Hardingswood Rd ST7 .. 194 C
Hardknott Rd L62 .... 43 D
Hardman Ave SK6 .... 241 A
Hardman St SK3 .... 240 D
Hardwick Cl SK6 .... 37 E
Hardwick Dr SK11 .... 112 A
Hardwick Grange WA1 .. 17 E
Hardwicke Rd SK12 .... 36 C
Hardy Cl Blacon CH1 .... 118 A
Hardy Rd WA13 .... 18 F
Hardy St Warrington WA2 .. 16 A
Hare La CH3 .... 119 E
Harebell Cl WA3 .... 9 E
Harebell Cl CH3 .... 142 A
Harebell St ST7 .... 195 F
Harecastle Ave ST7 .... 194 C
Harefield Dr SK9 .... 34 A

arefield Rd SK9 .... 34 C2
arehill Gdn SK10 .... 86 A3
arewood Ave L66 .... 69 E2
arewood Cl CW7 .... 126 A1
arewood Ct M33 .... 242 C5
arewood Way SK11 .... 112 A3
arfield Gdns L66 .... 69 E3
argrave Ave CW2 .... 189 F2
argrave Dr L66 .... 69 F3
argrave La L63 .... 42 C3
arington Cl WA5 .... 13 E1
argreaves Rd CW9 .... 104 B4
arington Cl CH2 .... 95 E1
arington Rd CH2 .... 118 B4
arlech Cl WA5 .... 7 F1
arlech Ct L65 .... 70 B2
arley Rd SK3 .... 242 C2
arley Way L65 .... 70 B2
arlow Cl WA4 .... 17 E2
arlyn Ave SK7 .... 35 F4
arlyn Gdns WA5 .... 14 B2
arm The L66 .... 69 E2
arold Rd WA11 .... 1 A3
arper Cl
  Ellesmere Port L66 .... 69 C2
  Macclesfield SK11 .... 112 B3
arper Gr CW17 .... 156 C2
arper St SK3 .... 240 E3
arpers Rd WA2 .... 9 D1
arpur Cres ST7 .... 193 D3
arraps Pl SK11 .... 112 A3
arrier Cl CW1 .... 189 F4
arriet St WA4 .... 11 F3
arrington Dr SK11 .... 111 E1
arrington Rd WA14 .... 238 B5
arris Cl CW1 .... 173 D1
arris Rd CW9 .... 80 A1
arris St WA8 .... 13 E1
arrisxehead La ST7 .... 195 E2
arrison Cl Allostock CW4 .... 107 D1
  Haydock WA11 .... 1 A3
arrison Gr CH5 .... 116 A2
arrison Sq WA5 .... 7 F1
arrison St
  Stalybridge SK15 .... 242 D2
  Stockport SK1 & SK2 .... 240 F3
  Widnes WA8 .... 22 A3
arrison Way WA12 .... 2 B2
arrisons Pl CW8 .... 103 F4
arrogate Cl Bebington L62 .... 43 E2
  Warrington WA5 .... 7 D1
arrogate Rd L62 .... 43 E2
arrop Rd Altrincham WA15 .... 238 F2
  Bollington SK10 .... 88 B4
  Runcorn WA7 .... 23 D1
arrop St SK15 .... 242 D2
arrow Cl Appleton WA4 .... 26 C3
  Crewe CW2 .... 190 A1
arrow Dr WA7 .... 23 F1
arrow Gr L62 .... 43 F4
arrow Rd L65 .... 70 B2
arrowgate Cl WA5 .... 15 D4
arrytown SK6 .... 241 A2
arrytown RC High Sch
  SK6 .... 241 A2
art Ave M33 .... 242 F5
art St WA14 .... 238 E5
artford Ave SK9 .... 59 F3
artford Bsns Ctr CW8 .... 102 C2
artford Cl CW11 .... 175 E4
artford Cty High Sch
  CW8 .... 103 E3
artford Cty Prim Sch
  CW8 .... 103 D2
artford Dr L65 .... 69 F2
artford Manor Cty Prim
  Sch CW8 .... 103 E3
artford Rd CW11 .... 103 F1
artford Sta CW8 .... 103 D2
artford Way CW1 .... 118 A1
arthill Cty Prim Sch CH3 .... 183 F2
arthill La CH3 .... 183 F2
arthill Rd Blacon CH1 .... 117 F3
  Burwardsley CH3 .... 184 A3
artington Dr SK7 .... 36 C4
artington Rd
  Altrincham WA14 .... 238 D8
  Bramhall SK7 .... 35 F4
  Cheadle SK8 .... 34 B4
  High Lane SK6 .... 37 F4
artington St CH4 .... 141 F4
artland Cl Poynton SK12 .... 36 B3
  Widnes WA8 .... 13 D3
artley Cl WA3 .... 3 D3
artley Gr SK10 .... 87 F4
artley Rd WA14 .... 238 C5
artley St WA9 .... 240 D4
artshead Ave SK15 .... 242 D3
artshead View SK14 .... 241 F5
artswood Cl
  Appleton WA4 .... 26 C2
  Dukinfield SK14 .... 241 A8
arty Rd WA11 .... 1 A3
arvard Cl WA4 .... 24 B1
arvard Cl WA2 .... 9 D2
arvest Cl CW9 .... 126 C4
arvest Rd SK10 .... 87 E2
arvey Ave Nantwich CW5 .... 205 D3
  Newton-le-W WA12 .... 1 C2
arvey La WA3 .... 3 D4
arvey Rd CW12 .... 157 D3
arvey St SK1 .... 240 F5
arvin Gr WA4 .... 241 A6
arwood Gdns WA4 .... 17 D1
arwood St CW2 .... 240 E7
aryngton Ave WA5 .... 15 F4
aseley Cl WA12 .... 2 C4
aslam Rd SK3 .... 240 E2

Haslemere Ave WA15 .... 32 B3
Haslemere Dr WA5 .... 14 B2
Haslemere Way CW1 .... 190 B3
Haslin Cres CH3 .... 142 B4
Haslington Cty Prim Sch
  CW1 .... 191 E2
Hassall Rd Alsager ST7 .... 193 D3
  Haslington CW11 .... 192 A4
  Hassall Green CW11 .... 192 A4
  Sandbach CW11 .... 175 D2
Hassall St SK15 .... 242 E1
Hassall Way SK8 .... 34 C3
Hastings Ave WA2 .... 8 A2
Hasty La Altrincham M90 .... 32 C4
  Wythenshawe WA15 .... 32 C4
Hatch Mere WA6 .... 100 B3
Hatchery Cl WA4 .... 27 D2
Hatchings The WA13 .... 18 C1
Hatchmere Cl
  Warrington WA5 .... 174 C4
  Warrington WA5 .... 15 F3
Hatchmere Dr CH3 .... 142 A4
Hatchmere Rd SK8 .... 239 F4
Hatfield Ct CW4 .... 130 A2
Hatfield Gdns WA4 .... 26 C2
Hathaway Cl SK8 .... 34 A4
Hathaway Rd WA3 .... 112 B3
Hatherlow SK6 .... 241 A1
Hatherlow Hts SK6 .... 241 A1
Hatherton Cl
  Davenham CW9 .... 103 F2
  Newcastle-u-L ST5 .... 210 B1
Hatherton Rd CW5 .... 220 A3
Hatherton Way CH2 .... 237 E4
Hatley La WA6 .... 73 F4
Hatter St CW12 .... 156 C2
Hatton Ave L62 .... 43 F2
Hatton La Appleton WA4 .... 26 A1
  Hatton WA4 .... 26 A1
  Northwich CW8 .... 103 E3
  Stretton WA4 .... 26 A1
Hatton Rd CH1 .... 117 F3
Hatton St Macclesfield SK11 .... 112 B4
  Stockport SK1 .... 240 E6
Haughton Hall Rd M34 .... 241 A7
Haughton St SK14 .... 241 C5
Havana La CW12 .... 157 D3
Havannah Cty Prim Sch
  CW12 .... 157 D3
Havannah La
  Congleton CW12 .... 156 C3
  St Helens WA9 .... 1 A2
Havannah St CW12 .... 156 C3
Haven The Altrincham WA15 .... 238 F3
  Crewe CW1 .... 190 B4
Havergal St **⁵** WA7 .... 22 C1
Havisham Cl WA3 .... 9 E3
Hawarden Gdns L65 .... 70 B1
Hawarden Ind Pk CH4 .... 139 D3
Hawarden Rd WA14 .... 238 D6
Haweswater Ave WA11 .... 173 D1
Haweswater Cl WA7 .... 50 A3
Haweswater Dr WA7 .... 126 B1
Hawick Cl L66 .... 69 D3
Hawk Dr WA5 .... 39 F4
Hawk St CW11 .... 175 D3
Hawke St SK15 .... 242 E1
Hawker Ct CH4 .... 139 E2
Hawkeshead Way CW7 .... 126 B1
Hawkins La SK10 .... 88 B2
Hawkins Rd L64 .... 41 F1
Hawks St WA8 .... 240 E8
Hawkins View CH3 .... 120 C3
Hawks St WA7 .... 49 F3
Hawks Way L60 .... 40 C4
Hawkshaw Cl WA3 .... 9 E2
Hawkshead Rd WA5 .... 6 C3
Hawkstone Gr WA6 .... 73 F4
Hawley Dr WA15 .... 32 A4
Hawley La WA15 .... 32 A4
Hawley's Cl WA5 .... 7 F1
Hawley's La WA2 .... 8 A1
Haworth Ave CW12 .... 157 D3
Haworth Cl SK11 .... 112 A3
Hawthorn Ave
  Altrincham WA15 .... 238 F8
  Nantwich CW5 .... 204 C3
  Newton-le-W WA12 .... 2 B2
  Runcorn WA7 .... 23 D1
  Widnes WA8 .... 13 D1
  Wilmslow SK9 .... 60 A4
Hawthorn Bank SK22 .... 39 D3
Hawthorn Cl
  Altrincham WA15 .... 238 F7
  Holmes Chapel CW4 .... 130 B2
  Winsford CW7 .... 126 B2
Hawthorn Dr WA11 .... 11 E3
Hawthorn Gdns ST7 .... 210 B4
Hawthorn Gr
  Cheadle Hulme SK7 .... 35 E3
  Crewe CW1 .... 190 B4
  High Lane SK6 .... 241 D5
  Manchester SK4 .... 240 B7
  Warrington WA4 .... 16 B2
  Wilmslow SK9 .... 60 A4
Hawthorn La
  Bebington L62 .... 43 E4
  Wilmslow SK9 .... 60 A4
  Wistaston CW7 .... 189 F1
Hawthorn Pk SK9 .... 60 A4
Hawthorn Rd
  Altrincham WA15 .... 238 E3
  Bollington SK10 .... 87 F4
  Chester CH4 .... 140 C3
  Christleton CH3 .... 142 C4
  Ellesmere Port L66 .... 69 E3
  Gatley SK8 .... 239 A5

Hawthorn Rd continued
  Neston L64 .... 41 E1
  Newcastle-u-L ST5 .... 210 C1
  Plumley WA16 .... 80 C2
  Weaverham CW8 .... 102 B4
Hawthorn Rise SK10 .... 86 C3
Hawthorn St SK9 .... 60 A3
Hawthorn Terr
  Manchester SK4 .... 240 B7
  Wilmslow SK9 .... 60 A3
Hawthorn View
  Deeside Ind Est CH5 .... 116 A4
  Wilmslow SK9 .... 60 A4
Hawthorn Villas CW4 .... 130 B2
Hawthorn Way SK10 .... 87 F1
Hawthorn Wlk
  Higher Wincham CW9 .... 79 E2
  Partington M31 .... 11 E1
  Warrington WA3 .... 9 E2
Hawthorne Ave Audley SK7 .... 209 F1
  Fowley Common WA3 .... 5 E2
  Great Sankey WA5 .... 15 D3
  Warrington WA3 .... 17 D4
Hawthorne Cl
  Congleton CW12 .... 156 A2
Hawthorne Dr
  Sandbach CW11 .... 175 D3
  Willaston L64 .... 43 D1
Hawthorne Gr Barnton CW8 .... 77 F2
  Poynton SK12 .... 37 E2
  Warrington WA4 .... 16 B1
  Warrington WA1 .... 16 C2
  Winsford CW7 .... 127 D1
Hawthorne Rd WA4 .... 26 B4
Hawthorne St WA12 .... 106 C3
Hawthorns The
  Bunbury CW6 .... 185 F4
  Ellesmere Port L66 .... 69 F4
  Northwich CW8 .... 103 E4
  Tarporley CW6 .... 146 B1
Hay Croft SK8 .... 34 C4
Haycastle Cl WA5 .... 7 F1
Haycroft Cl L66 .... 69 E1
Haydock Cl CH1 .... 118 A1
Haydock High Sch WA11 .... 1 B3
Haydock La WA11 .... 1 B4
Haydock Lane Ind Est
  WA11 .... 1 C4
Haydock Park Golf Course
  .... 2 C3
Haydock St
  Newton-le-W WA12 .... 2 A2
  Warrington WA2 .... 16 A3
Haye's Rd M44 .... 11 F3
Hayes Cres WA6 .... 49 E1
Hayes Dr CW8 .... 78 B2
Hayes Pk CH2 .... 237 D4
Hayfield Cl SK4 .... 241 A4
Hayfield Rd New Mills SK22 .... 39 E4
Hayfield Rd SK10 .... 87 D2
Haygarth Rd CW9 .... 79 E2
Hayle Cl SK10 .... 86 B1
Hayling Cl CW1 .... 190 A4
Haymakers Cl CH4 .... 140 C2
Haymakers Way CH1 .... 117 D4
Haymoor Green Rd CW5 .... 205 F2
Hayside Wlk SK14 .... 213 D2
Hayton St WA16 .... 56 C1
Haywood Cres WA7 .... 24 B1
Hazel Ave Cheadle SK8 .... 239 E5
  Haslington CW11 .... 192 A3
  Romiley SK6 .... 241 D2
  Sale M33 .... 242 A5
Hazel Cl Ellesmere Port L66 .... 69 F1
  Kidsgrove ST7 .... 195 D2
Hazel Dr Lymm WA13 .... 18 C1
  Poynton SK12 .... 36 C2
  Weaverham CW8 .... 102 B4
  Winsford CW7 .... 149 E4
  Wythenshawe M22 .... 34 A4
Hazel Gr Alsager ST7 .... 193 D3
  Crewe CW1 .... 190 B4
  Goldborne WA3 .... 3 D4
  Warrington WA1 .... 17 D4
Hazel Grove High Sch SK7 .... 36 B4
Hazel Rd Altrincham WA14 .... 238 D6
  Chester CH4 .... 140 C3
Hazel St WA1 .... 16 B4
Hazel Wlk M31 .... 11 E1
Hazelbadge Cl SK12 .... 36 B2
Hazelbadge Rd SK12 .... 36 B2
Hazelborough Cl WA3 .... 10 A3
Hazelcroft SK9 .... 85 D4
Hazelhurst Rd WA6 .... 74 B3
Hazelhurst Dr SK10 .... 88 A4
Hazelmere Cl CW8 .... 103 E3
Hazelshaw La CW11 .... 154 A2
Hazelwood Mews WA4 .... 17 E1
Hazelwood Rd
  Barnton WA15 .... 238 E2
  Barnton CW8 .... 78 A2
  Wilmslow SK9 .... 60 B4
Hazlemere Ave SK11 .... 112 A3
Headland Cl WA3 .... 3 F3
Headlands The CH2 .... 237 F2
Heald Cl WA13 .... 238 C2
Heald Cr WA14 .... 238 C2
Heald Gr SK8 .... 239 A1

Heald Green Sta M22 .... 34 A4
Heald Rd WA14 .... 238 C2
Heald St WA12 .... 1 C2
Healdwood Rd SK6 .... 241 C4
Healey Cl WA1 .... 190 A4
Hearn's La Burland CW5 .... 202 C3
  Faddiley CW5 .... 202 C3
Heary St SK11 .... 112 C3
Heath Ave
  Deeside Ind Est CH5 .... 175 F3
  Chester CH2 .... 118 C3
Heath Ave
  Rode Heath ST7 .... 193 F4
  Sandbach CW11 .... 175 F3
Heath Bank CH2 .... 119 E3
Heath Cl Chester CH3 .... 142 A4
  Sandbach CW11 .... 175 E3
  Tarvin CH3 .... 121 D1
Heath Cres SK3 & SK3 .... 240 F1
Heath Ct L66 .... 69 D3
Heath Dr Runcorn WA7 .... 49 D4
  Tarvin CH3 .... 121 D1
Heath End Rd ST7 .... 193 D3
Heath Gn CW6 .... 146 B2
Heath La Allostock WA16 .... 106 C3
  Chester CH3 .... 142 A4
  Croft WA3 .... 4 A1
  Ellesmere Port L66 .... 68 B4
  Goldborne WA3 .... 3 E3
  Great Barrow CH3 .... 120 C2
  Great Budworth CW9 .... 54 A1
  High Legh WA16 .... 28 B3
  Little Leigh WA4 .... 77 D4
  Marbury SY13 .... 226 C3
  Peover WA16 .... 106 C3
  Stoak CH2 .... 95 F4
  Willaston L66 .... 68 B4
Heath Rd
  Altrincham, Hale WA14 .... 238 D2
  Altrincham, Timperley WA15 .... 238 E8
  Bollington SK10 .... 87 F3
  Chester CH2 .... 118 B4
  Congleton CW12 .... 156 A1
  Penketh WA5 .... 14 C3
  Runcorn WA7 .... 22 C3
  Sandbach CW11 .... 175 E3
  Stockport SK3 & SK3 .... 240 F2
  Weaverham CW8 .... 77 F1
  Widnes WA8 .... 12 C1
Heath Rd S WA7 .... 48 C3
Heath St Crewe CW1 .... 190 B2
  Goldborne WA3 .... 3 D4
  Warrington WA4 .... 26 B4
Heath Terr CH2 .... 118 B4
Heath Way CW6 .... 168 B4
Heathbank Rd Cheadle SK8 .... 34 C4
  Stockport SK3 .... 240 B3
Heathbrook CW9 .... 104 C4
Heathcote Ave SK4 .... 240 C7
Heathcote Cl CH2 .... 118 B2
Heathcote Gdns
  Northwich CW9 .... 104 B4
  Romiley SK6 .... 241 E1
Heathcote St ST7 .... 195 D1
Heather Ave M44 .... 11 E3
Heather Brae WA12 .... 2 A2
Heather Cl
  Ellesmere Port L66 .... 69 F2
  Macclesfield SK11 .... 112 B2
  Runcorn WA7 .... 49 F2
  Warrington WA3 .... 9 E3
Heather Ct CH3 .... 142 A4
Heather Lea M34 .... 241 A6
Heather Rd WA14 .... 238 E1
Heather Wlk M31 .... 11 E1
Heatherfield Ct SK9 .... 60 C4
Heatherfield Pk SK9 .... 60 C4
Heatherfield Ave Crewe CW1 .... 190 B2
  Gatley SK8 .... 239 B5
Heathfield Cl
  Congleton CW12 .... 155 F2
  Nantwich CW5 .... 204 C3
  Sale M33 .... 242 F6
Heathfield Cty High Sch
  CW12 .... 155 F2
Heathfield Dr SK15 .... 210 B1
Heathfield Park WA4 .... 17 D2
Heathfield Pk WA8 .... 12 B2
Heathfield Rd Audlem CW3 .... 230 A3
  Ellesmere Port L66 .... 70 A3
  Stockport SK2 & SK3 .... 240 F2
Heathfield Sq WA16 .... 56 C1
Heathfields Cl CH2 .... 237 E4
Heathgate Ave L24 .... 21 D1
Heathland Terr SK3 .... 240 E3
Heathlands Rd L66 .... 69 D4
Heathmoor Ave WA3 .... 3 E4
Heaths La CW6 .... 123 E1
Heathside CW5 .... 204 C3
Heathside Park Rd SK3 .... 239 F7
Heathside Rd SK3 .... 240 A3
Heathview CW11 .... 174 C2
Heathview Cl WA8 .... 22 A3
Heathview Rd WA8 .... 22 A3
Heathway L60 .... 41 D4
Heathwood Dr ST7 .... 193 D3
Heathwood Gr WA1 .... 17 D4
Heatley Cl WA13 .... 19 D2
Heatley La CW5 .... 217 F2
Heatley Way SK9 .... 34 B2
Heaton Cl WA10 .... 151 E3
Heaton Ct Manchester SK4 .... 240 B8
  Warrington WA3 .... 9 D3
Heaton La SK4 .... 240 E5
Heaton Moor Rd SK4 .... 240 B8
Heaton Rd SK4 .... 240 C7

Heaton Sq CW7 .... 149 E4
Heaward Cl CW2 .... 206 A2
Hebden Ave
  Fowley Common WA3 .... 5 D2
  Romiley SK6 .... 241 A4
Hebden Green Sch CW7 .... 149 D4
Heber's Ct SY14 .... 213 E3
Hedge Hey WA7 .... 24 A1
Hedge Row SK10 .... 63 E1
Hedgerow Dr CW9 .... 79 F2
Hefferston Rise CW8 .... 102 A4
Heights The WA6 .... 73 E2
Helena Cl WA16 .... 57 E1
Helford St CW12 .... 156 B2
Helliar Wm CW4 .... 204 C1
Hellyar-Brook Rd ST7 .... 193 D2
Helmsdale Cl CW1 .... 190 A3
Helmsdale La WA5 .... 15 E3
Helmsley Cl WA5 .... 15 F4
Helsby Cl L62 .... 43 F2
Helsby Cty High Sch WA6 .... 73 D1
Helsby Horns Mill Cty Prim
  Sch WA6 .... 73 D1
Helsby Rd WA6 .... 73 E1
Helsby St WA1 .... 16 B3
Helsby Sta WA6 .... 73 D2
Helsby Way SK9 .... 34 B2
Helston Cl Bramhall SK7 .... 35 F4
  Penketh WA5 .... 14 C3
  Runcorn WA7 .... 50 A3
Helston Gr SK8 .... 34 B4
Helton Cl CW4 .... 130 A2
Hemlegh Vale WA6 .... 73 D1
Hemming St CW8 .... 78 B1
Hemmingshaw La CW11 .... 176 A4
Hemsworth Ave L66 .... 69 E3
Henbury Cl CW10 .... 151 E3
Henbury High Sch SK10 .... 111 F4
Henbury La SK8 .... 34 C3
Henbury Pl WA7 .... 49 D3
Henbury Rise SK11 .... 111 E4
Henderson Cl WA5 .... 14 B4
Henderson Rd WA8 .... 22 C4
Henderson St SK11 .... 112 B4
Hendham Dr WA14 .... 238 B5
Hendon Cl CW1 .... 190 C3
Henley Ave SK8 .... 34 A3
Henley Ave Cheadle SK8 .... 239 F7
  Irlam M44 .... 11 F3
Henley Cl Appleton WA4 .... 26 C3
  Neston L64 .... 66 C3
Henley Ct WA7 .... 23 E1
Henley Dr Altrincham WA15 .... 238 F7
  Winsford CW7 .... 126 C1
Henley Rd Chester CH4 .... 140 C3
  Neston L64 .... 66 C3
Henrietta St CW12 .... 156 B2
Henry Pl CH2 .... 237 E3
Henry St Crewe CW1 .... 190 B3
  Haslington CW1 .... 191 E2
  Hyde SK14 .... 241 D6
  Lymm WA13 .... 18 C2
  Tarporley CW6 .... 146 B3
  Warrington WA1 .... 16 A3
  Widnes WA8 .... 13 E1
Henry Wood Ct CH4 .... 140 C3
Henshall Ave WA4 .... 16 C2
Henshall Dr CW11 .... 175 E4
Henshall Hall Dr CW12 .... 157 D1
Henshall La WA14 .... 20 B3
Henshall Rd SK10 .... 87 F4
Henshall St CH2 .... 237 D4
Henshaw La CH1 .... 110 C1
Hepburn Cl WA3 .... 5 E2
Hepley Rd SK12 .... 37 D2
Herald Pk CW1 .... 190 C2
Heralds Cl WA8 .... 22 A4
Heralds Gn WA5 .... 7 D1
Herbert St Burtonwood WA5 .... 6 C2
  Congleton CW12 .... 156 C2
  Crewe CW1 .... 191 D3
  Dukinfield SK14 .... 241 A8
  Lostock CW9 .... 80 A1
  Stockport SK3 .... 240 D3
Herberts La L60 .... 40 C4
Herdman St CW7 .... 190 B1
Hereford Ave
  Ellesmere Port CH1 .... 94 C4
  Goldborne WA3 .... 3 D4
Hereford Cl
  Macclesfield SK10 .... 86 C1
  Warrington WA1 .... 17 E4
Hereford Dr SK9 .... 34 C2
Hereford Pl CH1 .... 118 A3
Hereford Rd M33 .... 242 B6
Hereford Way CW10 .... 128 B1
Hereward Rd CH3 .... 119 D1
Hermitage Ave SK6 .... 241 F2
Hermitage Cl CH1 .... 117 D4
Hermitage Cty Prim Sch
  CW4 .... 130 B2
Hermitage Dr CW4 .... 130 B2
Hermitage Gdns SK6 .... 241 F2
Hermitage Green La WA3 .... 3 D1
Hermitage La
  Cranage CW4 .... 130 B4
  Goostrey CW4 .... 130 B4
Hermitage Rd CH1 .... 117 D4
Hermitage The L60 .... 40 C4
Heron Cl Broughton CH4 .... 139 D3
  Farndon CH3 .... 180 C1
  Knutsford WA16 .... 57 D2
  Winsford CW7 .... 149 E3
Heron Cres CW1 .... 190 C3

Heron Ct Neston L64 .... 66 B4
Northwich CW9 .... 79 E1
Heron Dr SK12 .... 36 A2
Heron Pl CH2 .... 237 E4
Heron St SK3 .... 240 D3
Herons Way WA7 .... 24 C2
Herrick Cl CW7 .... 206 A4
Herries St OL6 .... 242 A4
Hertford Cl
  Congleton CW12 .... 156 C2
  Warrington WA1 .... 17 F4
Hertford Gr M44 .... 11 E3
Hesketh Cl WA5 .... 14 C2
Hesketh Croft CW1 .... 190 A4
Hesketh Dr CW9 .... 80 A2
Hesketh Meadow La WA3 ...... 3 F4
Hesketh Rd L24 .... 21 F1
Hesketh St SK4 .... 240 E7
Hesketh St N WA5 .... 15 E2
Hesnall Cl WA3 .... 5 E4
Hessle Dr L60 .... 40 C4
Heswall Ave WA3 .... 4 C4
Heswall Rd L66 .... 69 E2
Heswall Sta L60 .... 41 A4
Hewitt Dr CW7 .... 150 B4
Hewitt Gr CW9 .... 79 F3
Hewitt St Chester CH2 .... 118 C2
  Crewe CW2 .... 190 B1
  Northwich CW9 .... 79 F1
  Warrington WA4 .... 16 B2
Heywood Cl WA12 .... 7 E4
Hey Lock Cl WA12 .... 7 E4
Hey Shoot La WA3 .... 5 E3
Heybridge La SK10 .... 87 D3
Heyes Ave WA11 .... 1 A3
Heyes Dr WA13 .... 18 B1
Heyes Farm Rd SK11 .... 111 F4
Heyes La Alderley Edge SK9 .... 60 B2
  Appleton WA4 .... 26 C4
Heyes Pk CW8 .... 102 C2
Heyes Rd WA8 .... 22 B4
Heyeswood La CW8 .... 103 D2
Heyfield Park Rd L66 .... 69 D4
Heygarth Prim Sch L62 .... 43 F3
Heyes Ave Bebington L62 .... 43 E4
  Romiley SK6 .... 241 E3
Heys La SK6 .... 241 E3
Heys Prim Sch The OL6 ...... 242 A3
Heys Rd OL6 .... 242 A3
Heys The WA7 .... 23 F1
Heysbank Rd SK12 .... 38 B3
Heyscroft Rd SK4 .... 240 A6
Heysham Cl WA7 .... 50 B3
Heysoms Ave CW8 .... 103 E4
Heysoms Cl CW8 .... 103 E4
Heythrop Dr L60 .... 41 E4
Heywood Cl SK9 .... 60 A1
Heywood Gn CW2 .... 206 B4
Heywood Gr M33 .... 242 B8
Heywood La WA3 .... 234 B4
Heywood Rd
  Alderley Edge SK9 .... 60 A1
  Ellesmere Port L66 .... 69 E3
  Sale M33 .... 242 B5
Heywood St CW12 .... 156 B1
Heywoods Ridge CW3 .... 229 F2
Heywoods The CH2 .... 118 B2
Heyworth Ave SK6 .... 241 D3
Hibbert Cl SK14 .... 241 E5
Hibbert St New Mills SK22 ..... 39 D3
  ⑮ Widnes WA8 .... 23 D4
Hibel Rd SK10 .... 87 E1
Hickhurst La CW6 .... 147 E2
Hickmore Heys CH3 .... 119 F3
Hickory Cl WA1 .... 17 F4
Hickson St CW8 .... 78 A2
Hickton Dr WA14 .... 238 B6
Hidcote Cl CW2 .... 206 A4
Hield Gr CW9 .... 79 E4
Hield La CW9 .... 79 E4
Higginbotham Gn SK11 ...... 112 C3
High Bank WA14 .... 238 D5
High Bank Cl WA4 .... 26 C1
High Bank Rd SK14 .... 241 F7
High Bank Side SK1 .... 240 F5
High Bent Ave SK8 .... 35 D3
High Cross CH3 .... 182 B1
High Ct SK10 .... 88 A4
High Elm Dr WA15 .... 32 B4
High Elm Rd WA15 .... 32 B4
High Elms SK8 .... 35 D3
High Field WA14 .... 20 A1
High Gates Cl WA5 .... 15 E4
High Grove Rd SK8 .... 239 C5
High Hill Rd SK22 .... 39 E4
High La CW6 .... 241 B4
High Lane Prim Sch SK6 .... 37 F4
High Lea Rd SK22 .... 39 D4
High Lee SK8 .... 239 C5
High Legh Cty Prim Sch
  WA16 .... 29 E3
High Legh Rd WA13, WA16 ..... 29 F2
High Mdw WA8 .... 34 C4
High Meadows SK6 .... 241 E3
High St Altrincham WA14 .... 238 D4
  Audley ST7 .... 210 A1
  Bollington SK10 .... 88 A4
  Broughton CH4 .... 140 C4
  Cheadle SK8 .... 239 D6
  Congleton CW12 .... 156 B1
  Crewe CW2 .... 190 B2
  Duddon CW6 .... 145 E2
  Farndon CH3 .... 180 C1
  Frodsham WA6 .... 49 D1

High St continued
  Goldborne WA3 .... 3 D4
  Great Budworth CW9 .... 79 D4
  Hale L24 .... 21 E1
  Hyde SK14 .... 241 F7
  Kidsgrove, Harriseahead ST7 175 F3
  Kidsgrove, Newchapel ST7 ... 195 F1
  Kidsgrove, Talke ST7 .... 210 B3
  Kidsgrove, The Rookery
  ST7 .... 195 E2
  Macclesfield SK11 .... 112 B3
  Malpas SY14 .... 213 D2
  Mow Cop ST7 .... 195 E4
  Nantwich CW5 .... 204 C3
  Neston L64 .... 66 C4
  New Mills SK22 .... 39 E4
  Newton-le-W WA12 .... 2 B2
  Norley WA6 .... 100 C3
  Northwich CW8, CW9 .... 103 F4
  Runcorn WA7 .... 23 D1
  Sandbach CW11 .... 175 D3
  Stalybridge, Castle Hall
  SK15 .... 242 D1
  Stalybridge, Hydes
  SK15 & SK16 .... 242 C1
  Stockport SK1 .... 240 F5
  Tarporley CW6 .... 146 B1
  Tarvin CH3 .... 121 E1
  Tattenhall CH3 .... 166 A1
  Warrington WA1 .... 16 B3
  Weaverham CW8 .... 77 E1
  Winsford CW7 .... 126 A1
High View Helsby WA6 .... 73 E2
  Mount Pleasant ST7 .... 195 D3
Higham Ave WA5 .... 7 F1
Highbank Cl CW8 .... 78 A2
Highbank Dr M20 .... 239 B8
Highbank Rd
  Kingsley WA6 .... 75 E1
  Northwich CW8 .... 103 E4
Highcliffe Ave CH1 .... 118 A2
Highcroft Ave CW12 .... 156 C1
Highcroft Cl WA4 .... 26 C3
Higher Ash Rd ST7 .... 210 B4
Higher Ashton WA8 .... 12 C2
Higher Barlow Row SK1 .... 240 F4
Higher Bents La SK6 .... 241 A3
Higher Bury St SK4 .... 240 D6
Higher Carden La SY14 ..... 198 B3
Higher Downs
  Altrincham WA14 .... 238 C3
  Knutsford WA16 .... 57 E1
Higher Fence Rd SK10 .... 87 F1
Higher Ferry CH1 .... 140 A4
Higher Henry St SK14 .... 241 D5
Higher Heyes Dr WA6 .... 75 E1
Higher Hillgate SK1 & SK2 . 240 F4
Higher La Bollington SK10 .... 88 A3
  Dutton WA4 .... 51 E2
  Kettleshulme SK23 .... 64 C3
  Lymm WA13 .... 19 D1
Higher Rd Halewood L24 .... 21 D3
  Widnes WA8 .... 21 E3
Higher Tame St SK15 .... 242 E2
Highfield Elton CH2 .... 72 A2
  Prestbury SK10 .... 87 D3
  Sale M33 .... 242 C5
Highfield Ave
  Appleton WA4 .... 26 B2
  Audlem CW3 .... 230 A2
  Goldborne WA3 .... 2 C4
  Great Sankey WA5 .... 15 D3
  Kidsgrove ST7 .... 195 D1
  Lostock CW9 .... 80 A2
Highfield Cl L64 .... 66 C4
Highfield Cres
  Widnes WA8 .... 13 D1
  Wilmslow SK9 .... 34 B4
Highfield Cty Prim Sch
  CH1 .... 117 F2
Highfield Dr Lymm WA13 ..... 18 B1
  Macclesfield SK10 .... 87 D1
  Nantwich CW5 .... 205 D3
Highfield Est SK9 .... 34 B1
Highfield Gdns WA14 .... 241 F7
Highfield La
  Coddington CH3 .... 181 F2
  Winwick WA2 .... 8 A4
Highfield Parkway SK7 .... 35 E2
Highfield Pl CW8 .... 103 F4
Highfield Rd Blacon CH1 ... 117 E3
  Bollington SK10 .... 88 A4
  Cheadle SK8 .... 239 F1
  Congleton CW12 .... 156 C1
  Ellesmere Port L65 .... 70 A2
  Ellesmere Port, Little Sutton
  L66 .... 69 D3
  Lymm WA13 .... 18 B1
  Macclesfield SK11 .... 112 B4
  Neston L64 .... 66 C4
  Northwich CW8 .... 103 E4
  Poynton SK12 .... 36 A2
  Widnes WA8 .... 13 D1
Highfield Rd N L65 .... 70 B3
Highfield Sch L26 .... 21 D4
Highfield St ⑫ SK3 .... 240 C4
Highfield Terr SK22 .... 39 E4
Highfields SY13 .... 224 A1
Highfields Cty Prim Sch
  Alsager ST7 .... 193 E2
  Nantwich CW5 .... 204 C3
Highgate Cl CW1 .... 190 A4
Highgate Rd WA14 .... 238 B4
Highgrove Mews SK9 .... 60 A3
Highland Ave SK6 .... 241 A2
Highland Way WA16 .... 82 A4
Highlands Rd WA7 .... 48 C4
Highlands The CW6 .... 185 F4

Hightown Crewe CW1 .... 190 B2
  Middlewich CW10 .... 128 B1
  Sandbach CW11 .... 175 D3
Hightree Dr SK11 .... 112 A4
Highwood Rd WA4 .... 26 B4
Highfield Ave M33 .... 242 C5
Hignett Ave WA7 .... 1 A1
Hilary Ave SK8 .... 34 B4
Hilary Cl Chester CH3 .... 119 D1
  Great Sankey WA5 .... 14 B3
  Stockport SK4 .... 240 D6
  Widnes WA8 .... 13 F3
Hilary Rd Bebington L62 .... 43 F3
  Wythenshawe M22 .... 33 E4
Hilbre Bank CW6 .... 169 E2
Hilbre Dr L65 .... 70 B1
Hilda Ave SK8 .... 239 E5
Hilda Gr SK5 .... 240 F8
Hilda St ⑯ SK6 .... 241 A5
Hilden Rd WA2 .... 8 C1
Hill Cl L64 .... 67 D3
Hill Cliffe Rd WA4 .... 26 A4
Hill Court Mews SK6 .... 241 B2
Hill Crest Ave SK4 .... 240 A6
Hill Ct L64 .... 67 D3
Hill Dr SK9 .... 34 C2
Hill Farm Cl WA2 .... 8 C2
Hill Fields Cl CW12 .... 156 B2
Hill La Brown Knowl CH3 .... 199 E4
  Burwardsley CW6 .... 184 C3
  Peckforton CW6 .... 184 C3
Hill Rd CH4 .... 141 F1
Hill Rd N WA6 .... 73 E2
Hill Rd S WA6 .... 73 E2
Hill Rise
  Altrincham WA14 .... 238 A5
  Romiley SK6 .... 241 B2
Hill St Altrincham WA14 .... 238 C8
  Crewe CW1 .... 190 B2
  Macclesfield SK11 .... 112 B3
  Romiley SK6 .... 241 B2
  Runcorn WA7 .... 23 D1
  Sandbach CW11 .... 174 B4
  Winsford CW7 .... 126 C1
Hill Terr ST7 .... 209 E1
Hill The
  Hassall Green CW11 .... 175 E3
  Sandbach CW11 .... 175 E3
Hill Top Altrincham WA15 ..... 32 A4
  Barnton CW8 .... 78 A1
  Romiley SK6 .... 241 B3
Hill Top Ave
  Cheadle Hulme SK8 .... 35 D4
  Wilmslow SK9 .... 60 A4
  Winsford CW7 .... 126 B1
Hill Top La Heswall L60 .... 41 A4
  Neston L64 .... 67 D3
Hill Top Rd
  Dutton CW8 .... 76 C1
  Dutton WA4 .... 51 B1
  Warrington WA4 .... 16 C1
  Warrington, Woolston WA1 .. 17 D4
Hill Top Rise SK23 .... 65 E4
Hill View Bollington SK10 ..... 87 F4
  Marbury CW9 .... 79 B2
  Whaley Bridge SK23 .... 65 E4
  Widnes WA8 .... 12 C4
Hill View Ave WA6 .... 73 D1
Hill View Cty Prim Sch
  WA7 .... 24 A1
Hilary Ave CW12 .... 157 D1
Hilary Dr CW7 .... 230 A2
Hilary Rd ST7 .... 195 D2
Hillberry Cres WA4 .... 16 A2
Hillbre Ave WA5 .... 40 C3
Hillbre Way SK9 .... 34 B2
Hillbrook Rd SK7 .... 35 E3
Hillcourt Rd High Lane SK6 .. 37 F4
  Romiley SK6 .... 241 C4
Hillcrest CW12 .... 156 B2
Hillcrest Ave CW4 .... 130 A2
Hillcrest Dr Denton M34 ..... 241 A5
  Ellesmere Port L66 .... 69 D3
Hillcrest Gram Sch SK3 .... 240 F2
Hillcrest Rd
  Bollington SK10 .... 87 F4
  Ellesmere Port L66 .... 69 D3
  Kelsall CW6 .... 122 C3
  Warren SK11 .... 112 A2
Hillcroft Rd WA14 .... 238 A5
Hillfield Frodsham WA6 .... 74 A4
  Runcorn WA7 .... 50 B4
Hillfield Gdns CW5 .... 204 C2
Hillfield Pl CW5 .... 204 C2
Hillfield Rd L66 .... 69 E4
Hillfield View CW5 .... 204 C2
Hillfields CW12 .... 156 B2
Hillfoot Cres WA4 .... 26 A4
Hillfoot La WA6 .... 74 C2
Hillingden Ave L26 .... 21 D4
Hillington Rd SK3 .... 240 C4
Hillock La WA1 .... 17 E4
Hillsboro Ave WA6 .... 74 B4
Hillsdown Way L66 .... 69 E1
Hillside Lymm WA13 .... 19 F1
  Northwich CW8 .... 103 E4
Hillside Ave
  Newton-le-W WA12 .... 1 C1
  Runcorn WA7 .... 48 C4
Hillside Cl Bramhall SK7 ...... 36 A4
  Disley SK12 .... 38 B3
  Kidsgrove ST7 .... 195 E4
Hillside Cl CW8 .... 88 A1
Hillside Dr Crewe CW1 ...... 190 C3
  Ellesmere Port L66 .... 69 F4
  Macclesfield SK10 .... 88 A1
Hillside Gr WA5 .... 14 C2
Hillside La CW9 .... 126 C4
Hillside Pk WA16 .... 57 E1

Hollins Grange ST7 .... 210 B4
Hollins Hill CW6 .... 146 C
Hollins La Antrobus CW9 ...... 53 F
  Winwick WA2 .... 7 F
Hollins Rd SK11 .... 112 C
Hollins Terr SK11 .... 112 C
Hollins Way WA8 .... 22 A4
Hollinshead Cl ST7 .... 194 C
Hollinwood Cl ST7 .... 210 C
Hollinwood Rd Disley SK12 .. 38 B
  Kidsgrove ST7 .... 210 C
Hollow Dr WA4 .... 16 C
Hollow La Kingsley WA6 .... 75 D
  Knutsford WA16 .... 82 A
Hollow Oak La CW8 .... 101 E
Hollow The Gatley SK8 ...... 239 C
  Mount Pleasant ST7 .... 195 D
Holloway WA7 .... 23 F2
Hollowood Rd SY14 .... 213 D
Holly Ave Cheadle SK8 ...... 239 D
  Newton-le-W WA12 .... 2 B
Holly Bank M33 .... 242 C
Holly Bank Rd SK9 .... 34 A
Holly Bank Sch CH2 .... 237 D
Holly Bush La WA3 .... 10 B
Holly Cl Connah's Quay CH5 . 91 E
  Hale L24 .... 21 E
  Middle Trafford CH2 .... 119 F
Holly Ct Helsby WA6 .... 73 E
  Stockport SK5 .... 240 E
Holly Dr Sale M33 .... 242 A
  Winsford CW7 .... 149 E
Holly Gr Denton M34 .... 241 A
  Sale M33 .... 242 D
Tabley WA16 .... 56 A
  Warrington WA1 .... 17 D
Holly Grange WA14 .... 238 D
Holly Hedge La WA4 .... 25 E
Holly La Alsager ST7 .... 193 F
  Kidsgrove ST7 .... 195 F
  Styal SK9 .... 33 F
Holly Mount CW2 .... 206 C
Holly Rd Cheadle Hulme SK7 . 35 F
  Chester CH4 .... 140 C
  Ellesmere Port L65 .... 70 B
  Goldborne WA3 .... 3 E
  Haydock WA11 .... 1 A
  High Lane SK6 .... 37 F
  Lymm WA13 .... 19 D
  Macclesfield SK11 .... 112 A
  Newcastle-u-L ST5 .... 210 C
  Penketh WA5 .... 14 C
  Poynton SK12 .... 36 C
  Weaverham CW8 .... 102 B
Holly Rd N SK9 .... 60 A
Holly Rd S SK9 .... 60 A
Holly Terr Penketh WA5 ...... 14 C
  Tilston SY14 .... 198 B
Holly Tree Dr Biddulph ST6 .179 E
  Chester CW2 .... 190 B
Holly Wlk Northwich CW8 ... 103 E
  Partington M31 .... 11 E
Hollybank Audlem CW3 ...... 229 F
  Moore WA4 .... 25 D
Hollybank Rd WA7 .... 49 A
Hollybush Cres CW5 .... 205 E
Hollyfield Rd L65 .... 70 A
Hollyfields CW11 .... 191 F
Hollyheath Cl CW11 .... 175 E
Hollytree Rd WA7 .... 35 E
Hollytree Rd WA16 .... 80 C
Hollywood WA14 .... 238 D
Hollywood Way
  SK3 & SK4 .... 240 D
Holm Cl CH3 .... 142 C
Holm Dr CH2 .... 72 B
Holm Oak Way CH1 .... 94 C
Holme St Hyde SK14 .... 241 D
  Tarvin CH3 .... 120 C
Holmefield WA13 .... 242 B
Holmes Chapel Comp
  Sch CW4 .... 130 A
Holmes Chapel Prim
  Sch CW4 .... 130 A
Holmes Chapel Rd
  Allostock WA16 .... 106 A
  Brereton Green CW12 .... 154 B
  Congleton CW12 .... 155 E
  Lach Dennis CW9 .... 105 F
  Middlewich CW10 .... 128 C
  Ollerton WA16 .... 82 B
  Peover WA16 .... 82 B
  Sandbach CW11 .... 153 F
  Sproston Green CW4 .... 129 E
  Withington SK11 .... 109 D
Holmes Chapel Sta CW4 .. 130 B
Holmes Ct WA3 .... 3 E
Holmes St Cheadle SK8 .... 239 E
  Stockport SK2 & SK3 .... 240 E
Holmesville Ave CW12 ...... 156 A
Holmeswood Cl SK9 .... 60 B
Holmeswood Rd WA7 .... 23 E
Holmfield Cl SK4 .... 240 D
Holmfield Dr
  Cheadle Hulme SK8 .... 35 D
  Ellesmere Port L66 .... 69 E
Holmlea Dr CW1 .... 190 C
Holmes Way SK10 .... 96 B
Holmrook WA14 .... 238 B
Holmsfield Rd WA1 .... 16 B
Holmshaw La CW11 .... 192 A
Holmwood WA14 .... 238 A
Holmwood Dr L66 .... 70 A
Holt Hey L64 .... 67 D
Holt La WA7 .... 49 A
Holt St Altrincham WA14 .... 238 C
  Crewe CW1 .... 190 A
  Stockport SK1 .... 240 F

Holt's La SK9 .... 33 F2
Holy Family RC Jun & Inf
   Sch WA8 .... 12 B3
Holy Family RC Prim Sch
   M33 .... 242 E6
Holy Spirit RC Prim Sch
   The WA7 .... 49 E4
Holyhead Cl WA5 .... 7 E2
Holyoak Ave WA8 .... 13 D2
Holyrood Dr CW2 .... 205 F4
Holyrood Way CH1 .... 119 D1
Holywell Cl L64 .... 41 D1
Holywell La CH3 .... 182 B1
Home Farm Ave SK10 .... 86 C1
Home Pk CH1 .... 94 C1
Homecrofts L66 .... 66 C3
Homestead Ave WA11 .... 1 C3
Homestead Rd SK12 .... 38 B3
Homesteads The CW5 .... 172 A3
Homeway WA8 .... 73 D1
Honey Fields CW6 .... 103 D3
Honey Fields CW6 .... 146 B1
Honey Suckle Cl CH1 .... 94 C4
Honeysuckle Cl
   Broughton CH4 .... 139 E2
   Widnes WA8 .... 13 D2
Honeysuckle Dr SK15 .... 242 F2
Hong Kong Ave M90 .... 33 D4
Honister Ave WA2 .... 8 B1
Honiton Way
   Altrincham WA14 .... 238 B6
   Penketh WA5 .... 14 C2
   Widnes WA8 .... 15 E3
Hood La N WA5 .... 15 E3
Hood Manor Cty Prim Sch
   WA5 .... 15 E3
Hood Rd WA8 .... 12 C1
Hoofield La Duddon CH3 .... 145 D1
   Huxley CH3 .... 167 D4
Hoogreen La
   High Legh WA16 .... 29 F1
   Mere WA16 .... 29 F1
Hooker St CW8 .... 103 F4
Hookstone Dr L66 .... 69 E3
Hoole All Saints' CE Contr
   Inf Sch CH2 .... 119 D2
Hoole Cl WA8 .... 240 A1
Hoole Gdns CH2 .... 119 D2
Hoole La CH2 .... 119 D2
Hoole Rd CH2 .... 119 D2
Hoole Way CH2 .... 237 E3
Hooley Range SK4 .... 240 B7
Hooleyhey La
   Macclesfield Forest SK10 ... 89 E2
   Rainow SK10 .... 89 E2
Hoolpool La WA6 .... 72 C3
Hoosier St S SK3 .... 240 E5
Hooton La L66 .... 44 A1
Hooton La L66 .... 44 A1
Hooton Sta L66 .... 43 E1
Hooton Sta L66 .... 43 E1
Hooton Way Hooton L66 .... 44 A1
Hope Ave M22 .... 33 E4
Hope Ave SK9 .... 34 B2
Hope Croft L66 .... 69 F1
Hope Farm Prec L66 .... 69 F1
Hope Farm Rd L66 .... 69 F1
Hope Green Way SK12 .... 36 B1
Hope La Adlington SK12 ...... 36 C1
   Adlington, Hope Green SK10 .. 36 B1
Hope Rd Broughton CH4 .... 139 D2
   Sale M33 .... 242 A6
Hope St Ashton-u-L OL6 .... 242 A4
   Audley ST7 .... 209 F2
   Chester CH4 .... 140 C4
   Crewe CW2 .... 190 B1
   Macclesfield SK11 .... 112 C4
   Newton-le-W WA12 .... 2 A2
   Northwich CW8 .... 103 F4
   Sandbach CW11 .... 175 D3
   Stockport SK4 .... 240 D5
Hope St W SK11 .... 112 B4
Hope Terr SK11 .... 240 E4
Hopefield Rd WA13 .... 19 D2
Hopes Carr SK1 .... 240 F5
Hopkins Field WA14 .... 238 B1
Hopkins St SK14 .... 241 E8
Hopwood St WA1 .... 16 B3
Horace Black Gdns L65 ...... 70 B3
Horace Gr SK4 .... 240 E8
Horace Lawton Ct CW12 .. 156 B2
Horbury Gdns L66 .... 69 E3
Hornbeam Ave L66 .... 69 F1
Hornbeam CI WA7 .... 24 B1
Hornbeam Rd L26 .... 21 D4
Hornby Dr CW5 .... 205 D3
Hornby La WA2 .... 8 A3
Horncastle Cl WA12 .... 3 F4
Horridge Ave WA12 .... 2 B3
Horrocks La WA1 .... 16 A3
Horrocks Rd CW2 .... 118 C3
Horsemarket St WA1 .... 16 A3
Horseshoe Cl WA6 .... 75 D1
Horseshoe Cres WA2 .... 8 C2
Horseshoe La SK9 .... 60 A1
Horton La CW6 .... 167 F1
Horstone Cres L66 .... 69 F1
Horstone Gdns L65 .... 70 A1
Hospital La CW5 .... 203 F1
Hospital St Crewe CW1 ...... 190 B3
   Nantwich CW5 .... 204 C3
Hospital Way WA7 .... 49 F4
Hotel Rd M90 .... 33 E4
Hotel St WA12 .... 2 A2
Hothersall Cl CW11 .... 173 D1
Hough Cl SK10 .... 88 B3

Hough Gn Ashley WA15 .... 31 F3
   Chester CH4 .... 141 D4
Hough Green Rd WA8 .... 12 B2
Hough Green Rd WA8 .... 12 A1
Hough Hill Rd SK15 .... 242 D1
Hough La Alderley Edge SK9 .. 60 B2
   Barnton CW8 .... 78 A2
   Barnton CW8 .... 78 A2
   Norley WA6 .... 100 C3
   Wilmslow SK9 .... 60 B2
Hough's La WA4 .... 26 A3
Hougher Wall Rd ST7 ...... 209 E1
Houghley Cl SK10 .... 87 E1
Houghton Cft WA8 .... 12 B3
Houghton Cl Chester CH2 .. 118 C2
   Newton-le-W WA12 .... 2 A2
Houghton St
   Newton-le-W WA12 .... 2 A2
   Warrington WA2 .... 16 A3
   Widnes WA8 .... 13 E1
Houldsworth Ave WA14 .... 238 E7
Houndings La CW11 .... 175 D3
Housesteads Dr CH2 .... 118 C2
Housman Cl CH1 .... 118 A3
Hove Cl CW1 .... 190 A4
Hove The WA7 .... 50 B3
Howard Ave WA12 .... 2 A1
Howard Ave Bebington L62 .. 43 E4
   Lymm WA13 .... 19 D2
Howard Cl SK6 .... 241 A2
Howard Ct Neston L64 .... 41 F1
   Runcorn WA7 .... 24 B2
Howard Rd Broughton CH4 .. 68 B1
   Culcheth WA3 .... 5 D1
Howard St Crewe CW1 ..... 191 D3
   Stockport SK1 .... 240 F6
Howards Way L64 .... 67 D3
Howarth Ct WA2 .... 9 F1
Howbeck Cres CW5 .... 220 A4
Howbeck Wlk CW2 .... 206 B4
Howe Rd CH4 .... 141 D4
Howe St SK10 .... 87 F1
Howells Ave
   Ellesmere Port L66 .... 69 E2
   Sale M33 .... 242 B7
Howey Hill CW12 .... 156 B1
Howey La Congleton CW12 .. 156 B1
   Frodsham WA6 .... 74 A4
Howey Rise WA6 .... 74 A4
Howgill Cl L66 .... 68 C3
Howley La WA1 .... 16 C3
Howson Rd WA2 .... 8 B2
Howty Cl SK9 .... 34 B1
Hoxton Cl SK8 .... 241 A4
Hoylake Cl WA7 .... 50 B3
Hoylake Rd Sale M33 ...... 242 F5
   Stockport SK3 .... 240 B4
Hoyle St WA5 .... 15 F4
Hubert Dr CW10 .... 151 C4
Huddersfield Rd SK15 ...... 242 F2
Hudson Cl WA5 .... 15 E4
Hudson Gr WA3 .... 3 F4
Hugh St CH4 .... 141 E4
Hughes Ave WA2 .... 8 B1
Hughes Dr Crewe CW2 .... 189 F2
   Crewe, The Valley CW2 .... 190 A2
Hughes Pl WA2 .... 8 B1
Hughes St WA4 .... 16 B2
Hughley Pl SK10 .... 87 E1
Hulley Rd SK10 .... 87 F1
Hullock's Pool Rd ST7 ..... 209 F3
Hully St SK15 .... 242 C2
Hulme Ave SK8 .... 35 D4
Hulme Hall Cres SK8 .... 35 D4
Hulme Hall Jun Sch SK8 .... 35 D4
Hulme Hall La WA16 .... 106 A2
Hulme Hall Rd SK8 .... 35 D4
Hulme La Allostock WA16 .. 106 B4
Hulme Pl SK10 .... 87 E1
Hulme Sq SK11 .... 112 B3
Hulme St Ashton-u-L OL6 .. 242 A4
   Crewe CW1 .... 189 F3
Hulse La CW9 .... 105 E3
Hulsebank La WA16 .... 30 A2
Humber Cl WA8 .... 13 F2
Humber Dr ST6 .... 179 F1
Humber Rd
   Ellesmere Port L66 .... 69 F1
   Warrington WA2 .... 8 C1
Hume St WA1 .... 16 B3
Humphrey's Cl WA7 .... 50 B4
Hungerford Ave CW1 .... 190 C2
Hungerford Cty Prim Sch
   CW1 .... 190 C2
Hungerford Pl CW11 .... 175 D3
Hungerford Rd CW1 .... 190 C2
Hungerford Terr CW1 ...... 190 C2
Hunsterson Rd
   Bridgemere CW5 .... 231 E4
   Hatherton CW5 .... 220 E4
Hunt La WA5 .... 14 D4
Hunt Rd WA11 .... 1 C3
Hunter Ave
   Shavington CW2 .... 206 B4
   Warrington WA2 .... 8 A2
Hunter Cl CH1 .... 237 D3
Hunter's Cres CH3 .... 121 E1
Hunter's Dr CH3 .... 121 E1
Hunters CI Helsby WA6 ...... 73 E2
   Runcorn WA7 .... 49 F3
Hunters Field CW8 .... 103 E4
Hunters Hill Kingsley WA6 .. 75 E1
   Weaverham CW8 .... 77 E1
Hunters Mews Sale M33 .. 242 A7
   Wilmslow SK9 .... 60 B4

Hunters Rise CW7 .... 126 B1
Hunters Way L64 .... 66 B4
Hunters Wlk CH1 .... 237 D3
Huntersfield CW7 .... 126 A1
Huntingdon Cty Prim Sch
   CH3 .... 142 A3
Huntingdon Rd SK3 .... 240 B3
Huntley St WA5 .... 15 E2
Huntly Chase SK9 .... 60 B4
Hunts CI CH3 .... 119 D1
Hunts La WA4 .... 26 A3
Huntsbank Bsns Pk CW2 .. 205 F4
Huntsbank Dr ST5 .... 210 B1
Huntsham CI WA4 .... 238 B6
Huntsman Dr M44 .... 11 F4
Hurdsfield Cl CW10 .... 151 E4
Hurdsfield Cty Prim Sch
   SK10 .... 87 F1
Hurdsfield Gn SK10 .... 87 F1
Hurdsfield Ho SK10 .... 87 F1
Hurdsfield Ind Est SK10 .... 87 F2
Hurdsfield Rd SK10 .... 88 A1
Hurford Ave L65 .... 69 F2
Hurlbote Cl SK9 .... 34 B3
Hurlestone CI CH2 .... 96 C1
Hurley Cl WA5 .... 14 D4
Hurley Dr SK8 .... 239 E2
Hurn Cl CW1 .... 190 A4
Hurst Ave SK7 .... 35 E3
Hurst Bank Rd OL6 .... 242 B4
Hurst Cl SK7 .... 210 B3
Hurst Cl CW7 .... 185 F4
Hurst La Bollington SK10 .... 88 A4
   Glazebury WA3 .... 5 D4
Hurst Lea Rd SK22 .... 39 E4
Hurst Mews WA6 .... 75 E1
Hurst Mill La WA3 .... 5 E4
Hurst Rd ST6 .... 179 F1
Hurst St WA8 .... 23 D2
Hurst The WA6 .... 75 E1
Hursthead Cty Jun Sch
   SK7 .... 35 E4
Hursthead Inf Sch SK7 ...... 35 E4
Hursthead Rd SK8 .... 35 D4
Hurstvale Ave SK8 .... 239 B1
Hurstwood CH3 .... 143 D2
Hutchins' Cl CW10 .... 151 F3
Hutchinson St WA8 .... 23 D2
Huttfield Rd L24 .... 21 D2
Hutton Ave OL6 .... 242 B3
Hutton Cl Congleton CW12 .. 157 D1
   Culcheth WA3 .... 4 C3
Huxley Cl CH4 .... 141 A4
Huxley CE Contr Prim Sch
   CH3 .... 167 D4
Huxley Cl Bramhall SK7 .... 35 F4
   Macclesfield SK10 .... 87 D1
Huxley Ct L65 .... 69 F4
Huxley Dr SK7 .... 35 F4
Huxley La Huxley CH3 ..... 167 F3
   Tiverton CH3, CW6 .... 167 E3
Huxley St Altrincham WA14 .. 238 D7
   Northwich CW8 .... 103 F4
Hyacinth Cl Haydock WA11 .. 1 C3
   Stockport SK3 .... 240 D1
Hyde Bank Rd SK22 .... 39 E4
Hyde Central Sta SK14 .... 241 C6
Hyde Ellesmere Port L65 .... 69 F2
Hyde Fold SK14 .... 241 A7
Hyde Gr M33 .... 242 B6
Hyde Hospl SK14 .... 241 F5
Hyde Rd M34 & SK14 ...... 241 A7
Hyde St Paul's RC Prim
   Sch SK14 .... 241 F8
Hyde Tech Sch SK14 .... 241 D8
Hyde-Clarendon Coll
   SK14 .... 241 E8
Hyldavale Ave SK8 .... 239 B6
Hylton Cl L65 .... 70 C1
Hylton Ct SK7 .... 240 A3
Hylton Dr SK7 .... 210 B4
Ingle Rd SK8 .... 240 A2

Ian Rd ST7 .... 195 C3
Ikey La CW5 .... 202 C3
Ikins Dr ST7 .... 209 F1
Ilex Ave WA2 .... 8 A4
Ilford Gdns WA4 .... 26 B3
Illingworth Ave SK15 ...... 242 F2
Imperial Ave CH1 .... 117 E2
Imperial Mews L65 .... 70 A3
Ince Ave L66 .... 43 F2
Ince Cl SK4 .... 240 A8
Ince Dr CH2 .... 180 C1
Ince & Elton Sta CH2 .... 72 A2
Ince La Elton CH2 .... 72 A2
   Trafford CH2 .... 96 C3
Ince Orch CH2 .... 72 A2
Ince St CH1 .... 237 A4
Ingersley Rd SK10 .... 88 B4
Ingham Ave WA12 .... 2 B3
Ingham Cl CH3 .... 119 D1
Ingham Rd WA8 .... 22 C4
Ingleborough CI M20 .... 33 E4
Ingle Rd SK8 .... 240 A2
Inglegreen L60 .... 41 D4
Inglenook Rd WA5 .... 14 C2
Inglenook Rd WA5 .... 14 C2
Ingleton Cl Cheadle SK8 .. 239 C6
   Holmes Chapel CW4 .... 130 A2
Ingleton Gr WA7 .... 49 E3
Ingleton Rd SK3 .... 240 C3
Ingleton WA14 .... 238 C6
Inglewood Ave CW10 ...... 151 E3
Inglewood Cl WA3 .... 10 A3
Inglewood WA14 .... 241 D8
Inglis Rd L23 .... 1 A1
Inman Ave WA9 .... 1 C4
Innisfree CI L66 .... 69 E3
Insall Rd WA2 .... 9 D1

Intack La CW9 .... 28 A2
Intake Cl L24 .... 68 A4
International App M22 .... 33 E4
Inveresk Rd SY14 .... 198 B2
Inward Way L65 .... 70 A4
Ion Path CW7 .... 127 E1
Irby Cl L66 .... 69 E3
Ireland Rd Hale L24 .... 21 F1
   Haydock WA11 .... 1 B3
Ireland St Warrington WA2 .. 16 A4
   Widnes WA8 .... 13 E1
Irene Ave SK14 .... 241 A8
Iris Cl WA8 .... 12 B1
Iris Wlk M31 .... 11 F1
Irlam & Cadishead Comm
   High Sch M44 .... 11 F4
Irlam Rd M33 .... 242 A6
Irlam Rd WA8 .... 12 A4
Ironbridge Dr CW4 .... 130 B1
Irons La CH3 .... 120 C4
Irvine Dr M22 .... 34 A4
Irving's Cres CH4 .... 140 C3
Irwell Gr WA4 .... 16 A1
Irwell La WA7 .... 22 C2
Irwell Rd L65 .... 69 F2
Irwell Rise SK10 .... 87 F4
Irwell St WA8 .... 23 D2
Irwin Dr SK9 .... 34 B3
Irwin Rd WA12 .... 240 D6
Isabella Ct CW4 .... 140 C3
Isherwood Cl WA2 .... 8 C2
Isis Cl CW12 .... 156 C1
Islay Cl L65 .... 70 B1
Islington Ave WA14 .... 238 A6
Iveagh Cl WA7 .... 50 A4
Iver Cl Chester CH2 .... 118 C4
   Cronton WA8 .... 12 B3
Iver Rd CH2 .... 118 B4
Iver Bank Cty Prim Sch
   SK11 .... 112 A3
Ivy Ct CH4 .... 162 B1
Ivy Dr CW8 .... 102 A1
Ivy Farm Dr L24 .... 66 C3
Ivy Farm Gdns WA3 .... 4 B2
Ivy Farm Rd CW7 .... 149 F4
Ivy Gdns CW12 .... 156 B1
Ivy House Rd SK16 .... 179 E1
Ivy La Alsager ST7 .... 193 F1
   Macclesfield SK11 .... 112 A3
Join Rd M33 .... 242 D6
Jonathan's Way CH1 .... 117 F3
Jones Sq SK1 .... 240 F3
Jones's La CW10 .... 152 B3
Jonson Rd L64 .... 66 C4
Jordangate 5G SK11 .... 112 B4
Joseph Cres ST7 .... 193 F1
Joseph St WA8 .... 13 E3
Joules Ct SK1 .... 240 F5
Jowett St SK5 .... 240 F8
Joy La WA5 .... 6 C2
Joyce Ave CW7 .... 126 B1
Jubilee Ave Crewe CW2 .. 190 A2
   Penketh WA5 .... 14 C2
   Stalybridge SK16 .... 242 B1
   Warrington WA1 .... 16 C4
Jubilee Cres WA11 .... 1 C4
Jubilee Gdns
   Nantwich CW5 .... 204 C2
   New Mills SK22 .... 39 E4
Jubilee Gr WA13 .... 18 B2
Jubilee Rd CW12 .... 156 C1
Jubilee St SK16 .... 39 E4
Jubilee Terr CW5 .... 204 C2
Jubilee Villas CW11 .... 175 E1
Jubilee Way Widnes WA8 .. 12 C1
Jubits La WA8 .... 13 C3
Juddfield St WA11 .... 1 A4
Judy La SK11 .... 113 D2
Julian Way WA8 .... 12 C2
Jumper La SK10 .... 88 C4
Junction Eight Bsns Ctr
   L65 .... 70 A4
Junction La WA12 .... 2 A2
Junction Rd SK4 & SK2 ... 240 F3
June Ave Bebington L62 .... 43 F4
   Stockport SK4 .... 240 B6
Juniper Dr L66 .... 69 F1
Juniper Gr L66 .... 69 E1
Juniper La WA3 .... 18 A4
Juniper Rise SK10 .... 86 C1
Justice St SK9 .... 34 A2

K Edward Rd WA16 .... 57 D1
K.U.S. Ind Est CH5 .... 139 D3
Karen Cl WA5 .... 7 D3
Karen Way L66 .... 69 E2
Kay La WA13 .... 29 D4
Kay St SK15 .... 242 D1
Kaye Ave WA3 .... 4 C2
Keats Cl CH1 .... 94 C4
Keats Dr Macclesfield SK10 .. 86 C1
   Rode Heath ST7 .... 193 F4
Keats Gr WA2 .... 8 B1
Keats La CW9 .... 80 A3
Keats Terr CH1 .... 118 A3
Kebeck La WA8 .... 24 A4
Keckwick La Daresbury WA4 .. 25 D2
   Runcorn WA7 .... 24 C2
Keele Cres SK11 .... 112 A3
Keeper's La CW8 .... 102 C4
Keepers Cl WA8 .... 12 C2
Keepers La WA8 .... 12 C2
Keepers Wlk WA7 .... 23 F1
Keiths Ave WA5 .... 14 C3
Keith Dr Bebington L63 ..... 43 E3
   Cheadle SK8 .... 240 B3
Kelburn Ct WA3 .... 9 F3

Kelsall Ave L62 .... 43 F2
Kelsall Cl Bebington L62 ..... 43 F2
  Warrington WA3 .... 9 E1
  Widnes WA8 .... 12 B1
Kelsall Cres SK3 .... 240 D2
Kelsall Cty Prim Sch CW6 . 122 B2
Kelsall Rd Ashton CH3 ...... 121 F4
  Cheadle SK8 .... 240 A1
  Tarvin CH3 .... 121 E2
Kelsall St Congleton CW12 . 156 C2
  Sale M33 .... 242 C5
Kelsall Way Audley ST7 ..... 209 E1
  2 Wilmslow SK9 .... 60 A1
Kelsborrow Way CW6 .... 122 B2
Kelsterson Cl CH5 .... 91 E1
Kelsterton La CH6 .... 91 D1
Kelsterton Rd CH6, CH5 ..... 91 D1
Kelvin Ave M33 .... 242 B6
Kelvin Cl WA3 .... 9 E3
Kelvin Gr CH2 .... 118 C2
Kemberton Dr WA8 .... 13 D1
Kemble Cl CW2 .... 206 A4
Kemmel Ave WA4 .... 16 B2
Kemp St SK14 .... 241 E8
Kempsell Way L26 .... 21 D4
Kempton Ave CW1 .... 190 B4
Kempton Cl Chester CH1 ... 118 A1
  Newton-le-W WA12 .... 2 B3
  Runcorn WA7 .... 49 E3
Kempton Way SK10 .... 87 E2
Kendal Ave Denton M34 .... 241 A5
  Sale M33 .... 242 C5
  Warrington WA2 .... 8 D2
Kendal Cl Chester CH2 ...... 119 D3
  Ellesmere Port L66 .... 69 E1
  Macclesfield SK11 .... 111 F3
Kendal Ct CW12 .... 156 A1
Kendal Dr
  Cheadle Hulme SK7 .... 35 E3
  Ellesmere Port L66 .... 69 F1
  Gatley SK8 .... 239 C4
Kendal Gdns SK6 .... 241 B4
Kendal Rd
  Macclesfield SK11 .... 111 F3
  Widnes WA8 .... 12 B1
Kendal Rise WA7 .... 49 E3
Kendrick St WA1 .... 16 A3
Kenilworth Ave
  Knutsford WA16 .... 57 E1
  Runcorn WA7 .... 49 D4
  Wilmslow SK9 .... 34 B2
Kenilworth Cl
  Macclesfield SK11 .... 111 F3
  Wistaston CW2 .... 206 A4
Kenilworth Ct L65 .... 70 C1
Kenilworth Dr
  Hazel Grove SK7 .... 36 B4
  Warrington WA3 .... 16 C4
Kenilworth Gdns WA12 .... 2 B1
Kenilworth Gn SK11 .... 111 F3
Kenilworth Rd Cheadle SK8 239 F7
  Goldborne WA3 .... 3 F4
  Macclesfield SK11 .... 111 F3
  Neston L64 .... 66 C3
Kenley Ave WA8 .... 12 B3
Kenmare Bank CW9 .... 104 A3
Kenmore Gr M44 .... 11 E3
Kennard Pl WA14 .... 238 E6
Kennedy Ave SK10 .... 86 C1
Kennedy Cl CH2 .... 119 D3
Kennedy Way SK4 .... 240 C6
Kennel La CW8 .... 102 A1
Kennelwood Rd CW9 .... 78 B4
Kennerley's La SK9 .... 60 A4
Kennet Dr CW12 .... 156 C1
Kennet Rd WA11 .... 1 B3
Kennet Way WA11 .... 111 F4
Kenneth Rd WA8 .... 22 B4
Kenrick Cl CW3 .... 232 B1
Kensington Ave
  Ashton-u-L OL6 .... 242 B4
  Warrington WA4 .... 17 E1
Kensington Cl CH4 .... 141 D3
Kensington Ct Alsager ST7 192 C2
  Wilmslow SK9 .... 60 A3
  Winsford CW7 .... 149 E4
Kensington Gdns
  Altrincham WA15 .... 238 F1
  Hyde SK14 .... 241 F5
Kensington Gn CH4 .... 140 C3
Kensington Gr
  Altrincham WA14 .... 238 E8
  Stalybridge SK15 .... 242 D1
Kensington Rd Chester CH4 141 D3
  Ellesmere Port L65 .... 70 A3
  Stockport SK3 .... 240 B3
Kensington St SK14 .... 241 C5
Kensington Way CW9 .... 103 F2
Kent Ave Bollington SK10 ... 87 F3
  Cheadle SK8 .... 240 C1
Kent Cl L63 .... 43 D4
Kent Dr CW12 .... 156 B2
Kent Gdn CH2 .... 118 C3
Kent Gr WA7 .... 23 D1
Kent Rd Chester CH2 .... 118 C3
  Great Sankey WA5 .... 15 E2
  Irlam M44 .... 11 E3
  Partington M31 .... 11 F1
  Stockport SK3 .... 240 B4
Kent St Warrington WA4 ..... 16 B2
  Widnes WA8 .... 13 D1
Kent Wlk Macclesfield SK10 . 86 C1
  Newton-le-W WA12 .... 2 B1
Kent's Green La CW11 ...... 191 F4
Kent's La CW1 .... 173 E1

Kentmere Ave CW7 .... 126 B1
Kentmere CH SK8 .... 239 B3
Kenton Rd L26 .... 21 D4
Kentridge Dr L66 .... 69 E2
Kentwell Dr SK10 .... 87 E2
Kenview Cl WA8 .... 22 A2
Kenwick Cl L66 .... 69 E2
Kenwood Ave
  Altrincham WA15 .... 238 F2
  Cheadle Hulme SK7 .... 35 E3
  Gatley SK8 .... 239 A6
Kenworthy St SK15 .... 242 D1
Kenyon Ave WA5 .... 14 C3
Kenyon La WA3 .... 3 F2
Kenyon's La WA11 .... 1 C4
Kenyon's La N WA11 .... 1 C4
Kerfoot Bsns Pk WA2 .... 16 A4
Kerfoot St WA2 .... 16 A4
Keristal Ave CH3 .... 142 A4
Kerridge Cl CW10 .... 151 D4
Kerridge Rd SK10 .... 88 A2
Kerry Cft L66 .... 69 F1
Kershaw Gr SK11 .... 112 A4
Kershaw St WA8 .... 12 B1
Kestrel Ave WA16 .... 57 D2
Kestrel Cl Congleton CW12 . 156 C1
  Middlewich CW10 .... 151 E3
  Winsford CW7 .... 149 E3
Kestrel Dr CW1 .... 190 A4
Kestrel La WA3 .... 9 F2
Kestrel Rd Heswall L60 ...... 41 F4
  Northwich CW8 .... 103 E4
Kestrels Way WA7 .... 49 F3
Keswick Ave Bebington L63 . 43 E2
  Dukinfield SK14 .... 241 C8
  Gatley SK8 .... 239 B4
  Macclesfield SK11 .... 111 F3
  Warrington WA2 .... 8 B1
Keswick Cl Chester CH2 .... 119 D3
  Crewe CW2 .... 189 F2
  Irlam M44 .... 11 E3
  Macclesfield SK11 .... 111 F3
  Stalybridge SK15 .... 242 D4
  Widnes WA8 .... 12 B1
  Winsford CW7 .... 126 B1
Keswick Cres WA2 .... 8 B1
Keswick Ct CW7 .... 156 A1
Keswick Dr
  Cheadle Hulme SK7 .... 35 E3
  Frodsham WA6 .... 74 B4
  Keswick Rd SK6 .... 37 F4
Ketlan Ct CH4 .... 140 C4
Kettell Ave CW1 .... 190 A3
Kettle La WA3 .... 3 D3
Kettleshulme St James Sch
  SK23 .... 64 C2
Kettleshulme Way SK12 ..... 37 D2
Kettleshulme Wlk 7 SK9 ... 34 C1
Kew Dr SK8 .... 239 E2
Keyes Cl WA3 .... 9 F2
Keyes Gdns WA3 .... 16 C4
Keysbrook CW3 .... 166 B1
Keysbrook Ave CH3 .... 166 B1
Kidderton Cl CW5 .... 202 C4
Kidderton La Burland CW5 . 202 C4
  Faddiley CW5 .... 202 C4
Kidsgrove Bank ST7 .... 195 D1
Kidsgrove Sta ST7 .... 194 C1
Kilbuck La WA11 .... 2 A4
Kilburn Ave L62 .... 43 F3
Kilburn Cl SK8 .... 34 A4
Kilburn Rd SK3 .... 240 C3
Kildare Cl L24 .... 21 E1
Kildonnan Rd WA4 .... 17 D1
Kilford Cl WA5 .... 7 F1
Killingworth La WA3 .... 10 A3
Kilmorey Park Rd CH2 ...... 118 C2
Kilmorey Pk Ave CH2 .... 118 C2
Kilmorey Pk CH2 .... 237 F4
Kiln Croft La SK9 .... 34 C2
Kiln La CW5 .... 220 A4
Kilncroft WA7 .... 50 A3
Kilsby Dr WA8 .... 13 F1
Kilshaw Rd WA5 .... 6 C3
Kilsyth Cl WA2 .... 8 C2
Kimberley Ave SK6 .... 241 C2
Kimberley Dr WA4 .... 16 B1
Kimberley St Stockport SK3 240 E3
  Warrington WA5 .... 15 F3
Kimberley Terr CH2 .... 118 C1
Kinder Dr CW2 .... 189 E2
Kinder Gr SK6 .... 241 E2
Kinder St Stalybridge SK15 . 242 D2
  Stockport SK3 .... 240 E3
Kinder View SK22 .... 39 E4
Kinderton Cl WA16 .... 29 E2
Kinderton St CW10 .... 151 D4
King Arthur's Wlk WA7 ...... 24 A1
King Edward Rd 2 SK11 .. 112 B4
King Edward St
  Macclesfield SK11 .... 112 A4
  Middlewich CW10 .... 128 B1
  Warrington WA1 .... 16 C4
King George Ave CW9 ...... 104 A4
King George Cres WA1 ...... 16 C4
King George Rd WA11 .... 2 A3
King James Ct WA7 .... 49 F3
King Pl CW5 .... 204 C3
King St Audley ST7 .... 209 E1
  Chester CH1 .... 237 D3
  Congleton CW12 .... 156 C2
  Crewe CW1 .... 190 B2
  Ellesmere Port L65 .... 70 B3
  Hartford CW8 .... 103 D3
  Kidsgrove ST7 .... 241 D7
  Kidsgrove ST7 .... 195 D1
  Kidsgrove, Talke ST7 .... 210 B3
  Knutsford WA16 .... 57 D1

King St continued
  Lach Dennis CW9 .... 104 C3
  Macclesfield SK10 .... 112 C4
  Middlewich CW10 .... 128 A3
  Newton-le-W WA12 .... 2 A2
  Northwich CW9 .... 104 C3
  Runcorn WA7 .... 23 D2
  Sandbach CW11 .... 174 C4
  Stalybridge SK15 .... 242 D2
King St E SK1 .... 240 F6
King Street Trad Est
  CW10 .... 128 B1
  King's Ave WA3 .... 3 F4
King's Cres CW10 .... 128 B1
King's Cres E CH3 .... 119 D1
King's Cres W CH3 .... 119 D1
King's Dr WA3 .... 240 A7
King's La Cranage CW10 ... 106 B1
  Lach Dennis CW10 .... 105 D1
  Nantwich CW5 .... 204 B3
King's Rd Romiley SK6 ...... 241 A3
  Wilmslow SK9 .... 59 F4
King's Sch in Macclesfield
  The SK10 .... 87 C1
King's Sch The
  Chester CH4 .... 141 D2
  Macclesfield SK10 .... 112 C4
Kingfisher Cl
  Congleton CW12 .... 156 C1
  Crewe CW1 .... 189 F4
  Farndon CH3 .... 180 C1
  Nantwich CW5 .... 204 C4
  Runcorn WA7 .... 49 F3
  Warrington WA3 .... 9 F2
Kingfisher Ct CW9 .... 79 E1
Kingfisher Dr CW7 .... 149 E3
Kingfisher Gr CW7 .... 149 E3
Kingham Cl WA8 .... 13 E1
Kings Acre WA14 .... 238 A1
Kings Ave SK8 .... 239 A4
Kings Cl Chester CH4 .... 140 C3
  Wilmslow SK9 .... 60 A3
Kings Ct Nantwich CW5 .... 204 B3
  Stockport SK5 .... 240 F7
Kings Dr Helsby WA6 .... 73 D2
  Wistaston CW2 .... 205 F4
Kings Gate CW8 .... 42 A4
Kings Grove Cty High Sch
  CW2 .... 190 A2
Kings La CW6 .... 147 E2
Kings Meadow Runcorn WA7 50 B4
  Shavington CW2 .... 206 C1
Kings Mews L66 .... 69 E4
Kings Rd Connah's Quay CH5 . 91 E1
  Ellesmere Port L66 .... 69 E4
  Goldborne WA3 .... 3 D4
  Irlam M44 .... 11 F3
  Warrington WA2 .... 9 D1
Kingsbury Cl WA4 .... 26 B2
Kingsdale Rd WA5 .... 15 D2
Kingsfield Ct CH4 .... 141 E2
Kingshead Cl WA7 .... 24 A1
Kingsland Rd SK3 .... 240 A3
Kingsley Ave Bebington L62 . 43 F2
  Reddish SK4 .... 240 E8
  Wilmslow SK9 .... 34 B1
Kingsley Cl Hartford CW8 .. 103 E3
  Kidsgrove ST7 .... 210 B3
Kingsley Cres WA5 .... 23 D1
Kingsley Dr Appleton WA4 .. 26 B4
  Northwich CW9 .... 104 A3
Kingsley Gdns CH3 .... 142 A4
Kingsley Gn WA6 .... 74 C3
Kingsley & Newton Cty
  Prim Sch WA6 .... 74 C2
Kingsley Rd Chester CH3 .. 142 A4
  Congleton CW12 .... 157 D2
  Crowton CW8 .... 76 A1
  Ellesmere Port L65 .... 70 B3
  Frodsham WA6 .... 74 C2
  Haslington CW1 .... 191 E2
  Kingsley WA6 .... 74 C2
  Runcorn WA7 .... 23 D1
Kingsley St John's CE
  Aided Prim Sch WA6 .... 75 E1
Kingsmead Cl CW1 .... 126 A1
Kingsmead Chester CH2 ... 118 B4
  Davenham CW9 .... 103 F2
Kingsmead Ct WA3 .... 9 D4
Kingsmere
  Great Sankey WA5 .... 14 C3
  Macclesfield SK11 .... 112 C4
Kingston Cl WA7 .... 23 F1
Kingston Dr M33 .... 242 D7
Kingston Gdns SK14 .... 241 B7
Kingston Hill SK8 .... 239 D4
Kingston Pl Biddulph ST6 . 179 F1
  Cheadle SK8 .... 239 E2
Kingston Rd SK9 .... 34 B3
Kingston St SK4 .... 240 A5
Kingsway Altrincham WA14 . 238 D5
  Bollington SK10 .... 87 F4
  Cheadle M20 & SK8 .... 239 D6
  Chester CH2 .... 118 C3
  Crewe CW2 .... 190 A1
  Frodsham WA6 .... 74 A4
  Heswall L60 .... 41 E3
  Newton-le-W WA12 .... 2 B1
  Northwich CW9 .... 104 A4
  Widnes WA8 .... 12 C4
  Winsford CW7 .... 126 C1
Kingsway Cty High Sch
  CH2 .... 118 C3
Kingsway N WA1 .... 16 C3
Kingsway S WA4 .... 16 C2
Kingsway Sch SK8 .... 239 C4

Kingsway W CH2 .... 118 C2
Kingswood Kidsgrove ST7 .. 195 D1
  Poynton SK12 .... 36 C2
Kingswood Ave CH1 .... 94 B1
Kingswood Cres CW10 ..... 151 F3
Kingswood La CH1 .... 94 B1
Kingswood Rd WA5 .... 7 D1
Kingswood Wlk CW6 .... 122 B3
Kinloch Cl Crewe CW1 ..... 190 A3
  Halewood L26 .... 21 D4
Kinnerley Rd L65 .... 70 A3
Kinnersley Ave ST7 .... 210 C4
Kinnersley St ST7 .... 195 D1
Kinnerton Cl CH4 .... 140 C3
Kinnerton Hts CH4 .... 161 D4
Kinnerton La CH4 .... 161 D4
Kinnington Way CH1 .... 94 C4
Kinnock Parr WA5 .... 6 C3
Kinross Cl WA2 .... 8 C2
Kinsale Dr WA3 .... 9 E2
Kinsey Rd L65 .... 70 B1
Kinsey St CW12 .... 156 C1
Kinsey's La CH2 .... 71 F3
Kintore Cl L63 .... 43 E2
Kintore Dr WA5 .... 14 B3
Kipling Ave WA2 .... 8 C1
Kipling Cres WA8 .... 22 C4
Kipling Rd CH1 .... 117 F3
Kipling Way CW1 .... 190 C2
Kirby Cl CH2 .... 118 B3
Kircaldy Ave WA5 .... 14 B3
Kirkacre Ave WA12 .... 7 E4
Kirkby Rd WA3 .... 4 C2
Kirkfell Dr SK6 .... 22 D4
Kirkham Ave WA3 .... 3 F3
Kirkham Cl WA5 .... 15 D2
Kirkham Rd Cheadle SK8 ... 34 B4
  Widnes WA8 .... 13 E1
Kirkley St SK14 .... 241 E5
Kirkstall Cl SK10 .... 87 D1
Kirkstall Dr SK12 .... 36 B2
Kirkstead Rd SK7 .... 35 E3
Kirkstone Ave WA7 .... 48 B4
Kirkstone Cres WA7 .... 50 A2
Kirkstone Ct CW12 .... 156 A1
Kirkwall Dr WA5 .... 15 D2
Kirkwood Cl CH3 .... 119 D1
Kishfield La SK23 .... 65 D3
Kitchen St CH1 .... 118 A1
Kitchener Ave WA4 .... 11 E2
Kite Gr ST7 .... 195 A4
Kitfield Ave CW10 .... 151 E4
Kitt's Moss La SK7 .... 35 E3
Knap The L60 .... 41 D3
Knight Rd WA5 .... 6 C3
Knight St Hyde SK14 .... 241 E5
  Macclesfield SK11 .... 112 C4
  Warrington WA2 .... 16 A3
Knight's Cl SK11 .... 112 C4
Knight's Grange (Sports
  Complex) CW7 .... 126 B2
Knights La CW6 .... 123 F1
Knights Meadow CW7 ...... 126 B2
Knights Way CW2 .... 206 A2
Knightsbridge Ct SK3 ...... 240 F6
Knightsbridge Ave
  Davenham CW9 .... 103 F2
  Warrington WA4 .... 17 E1
Knightwake Rd SK22 .... 39 D4
Kniveton St SK14 .... 241 F7
Knole Ave SK12 .... 36 C4
Knoll St SK22 .... 39 D4
Knoll The Altrincham WA14 238 B5
  Runcorn WA7 .... 49 F4
Knott Fold SK14 .... 241 D5
Knottingley Dr L66 .... 69 E3
Knotty La CW12 .... 179 F4
Knowe The L64 .... 68 A4
Knowl Hey Rd L26 .... 21 D3
Knowl La CH3 .... 180 C3
Knowl St SK15 .... 242 E2
Knowl The CH3 .... 180 C3
Knowle Cl L66 .... 69 F2
Knowle Ave SK9 .... 34 B2
Knowle Pk SK9 .... 34 B2
Knowles Ind Est SK23 .... 39 E2
Knowles St WA8 .... 13 E1
Knowsley Ave WA3 .... 3 E4
Knowsley La ST7 .... 194 C2
Knowsley Rd Chester CH2 . 118 C2
  Hazel Grove SK7 .... 36 C4
  Macclesfield SK11 .... 112 B3
Knutsford Ave WA33 .... 242 E6
Knutsford Cty High Sch
  (Lower Sch) WA16 .... 56 C1
Knutsford Cty High Sch
  (Upper Sch) WA16 .... 56 C1
Knutsford L Ctr WA16 .... 56 C1
Knutsford Rd Antrobus CW9 . 53 E2
  Appleton WA4 .... 27 F4
  Chelford SK11 .... 84 A1
  Cranage CW4 .... 130 A3
  Great Budworth CW9 .... 54 A1
  Holmes Chapel CW4 .... 130 A3
  Lostock Green CW9 .... 78 C1
  Lawton-gate ST7 .... 193 F3
  Lindow End SK9, WA16 ...... 59 F2
  Mobberley WA16 .... 57 F2
  Mobberley Knolls Green WA16 58 C2
  Warrington WA4 .... 16 B2
  Wilmslow SK9, WA16 .... 59 F2
Knutsford Road Wlk 20
  SK11 .... 112 C4
Knutsford Service Area
  WA16 .... 56 B1
Knutsford Sta WA16 .... 57 D1
Knutsford Way CH1 .... 117 F1

Kohima Cres CH3 .... 142 A3
Kronsbec Ave L66 .... 69 E3
Kynaston Dr CH4 .... 140 A4

Labelia Wlk M31 .... 11 E3
Labernum Farm Cl L64 ...... 67 D2
Laburnam Cl
  Congleton CW12 .... 156 A2
  Kidsgrove ST7 .... 210 C4
Laburnum Ave
  Nantwich CW5 .... 204 C3
  Warrington WA1 .... 17 E4
  Wistaston CW2 .... 189 F4
Laburnum Cres ST7 .... 78 A3
Laburnum Gr
  Broughton CH4 .... 140 C3
  Crewe CW1 .... 190 B3
  Ellesmere Port CH1 .... 95 D4
  Runcorn WA7 .... 49 E1
  Weaverham CW8 .... 102 B3
Laburnum La
  Altrincham WA15 .... 31 F4
  Penketh WA5 .... 14 B4
Laburnum PI ST5 .... 210 B3
Laburnum Rd
  Davenham CW9 .... 103 F2
  Goldborne WA3 .... 3 F1
  Irlam M44 .... 11 E1
  Macclesfield SK11 .... 112 C4
  Northwich CW9 .... 104 B4
Laburnum Way Holt LL13 .. 180 B4
  Stockport SK3 .... 240 B6
Lacey Ave SK9 .... 34 A4
Lacey Ct Widnes WA8 .... 23 D4
  Wilmslow SK9 .... 34 A4
Lacey Gr SK9 .... 34 A4
Lacey Grn SK9 .... 34 A4
Lacey Green Cty Prim Sch
  SK9 .... 34 A4
Lacey St WA8 .... 23 D4
Lache Cty Inf & Jun Sch
  CH4 .... 141 D1
Lache Hall Cres CH4 .... 140 C1
Lache La Chester CH4 ...... 141 D1
  Dodleston CH4 .... 140 C1
Lache Park Ave CH4 .... 141 D1
Lacy St SK1 .... 240 F7
Ladies Wlk L64 .... 66 C4
Ladies Wlk L64 .... 66 C4
Ladram House Sch SK8 .... 239 D2
Lady Helen Wlk CW5 .... 204 C4
Lady Kelvin Rd WA14 .... 238 C1
Lady La Croft WA3 .... 9 A1
  Mobberley WA16 .... 58 B8
Ladybarn Ave WA3 .... 3 D4
Ladybarn Cr Sk7 .... 35 F1
Ladybrook Gr 10 SK9 .... 34 B1
Ladybrook Prim Sch SK7 ... 35 F1
Ladycroft Cl WA1 .... 17 F1
Ladyfield St SK9 .... 60 A4
Ladyfield Terr SK9 .... 60 A4
Ladypit Rd SK23 .... 39 F1
Ladypool L24 .... 21 E1
Ladys Cl SK12 .... 36 C1
Ladysmith Rd SK15 .... 242 D1
Ladysmith Sr SK3 .... 240 E8
Ladythorn Cres SK7 .... 35 F1
Ladythorn Gr SK7 .... 35 F1
Ladythorn Rd SK7 .... 35 F1
Ladywood Rd WA5 .... 7 F2
Lagos Gr CW7 .... 126 C1
Laira St WA2 .... 16 B4
Lake House Cl CW8 .... 77 E1
Lake La WA4 .... 52 C1
Lake Rd SK15 .... 242 C1
Lake View CW12 .... 156 A1
Lakelands Cl SK10 .... 112 C4
Lakeside CW8 .... 240 A7
Lakeside Dr Poynton SK12 . 36 C4
  Warrington WA1 .... 16 A4
Lakeside Rd WA13 .... 18 C1
Laleston Cl WA8 .... 22 C1
Lamb La WA14 .... 30 C3
Lamb St ST7 .... 195 D1
Lambert Cl WA8 .... 13 E1
Lambert Way CW8 .... 103 E1
Lambert's La CW12 .... 156 C1
Lamborne Gr CW10 .... 128 B2
Lambourn Ave WA8 .... 12 B1
Lambourn Cl SK12 .... 36 B4
Lambourn Dr CW1 .... 173 D1
Lambourne Cl
  Ellesmere Port CH1 .... 94 C4
  Wythenshawe M22 .... 33 E4
Lambourne Gr WA9 .... 1 A1
Lambs La WA1 .... 17 F2
Lambsickle Cl WA7 .... 48 C4
Lambsickle La WA7 .... 49 D4
Lampeter Cl WA5 .... 7 F1
Lampits La CH3 .... 120 C3
Lamport Cl WA8 .... 22 A4
Lanark Wlk SK10 .... 86 C1
Lancashire Hill
  SK1 & SK4 & SK5 .... 240 B8
Lancashire Rd M31 .... 11 F1
Lancaster Ave Goldborne WA3 3 E4
  Runcorn WA7 .... 48 B4
  Stalybridge SK15 .... 242 C1
  Widnes WA8 .... 12 C1
Lancaster Cl Hazel Grove SK7 36 B4
  Newton-le-W WA12 .... 1 C4
  Romiley SK6 .... 241 A3
  Winsford CW7 .... 149 D3
Lancaster Ct 5 SK10 .... 112 C4
Lancaster Dr CH3 .... 119 D2
Lancaster Fields CW1 ...... 191 C1
Lancaster Gdns L65 .... 70 B3

ncaster Pk CH4 .... 139 D2
ncaster Rd Denton M34 .... 241 A5
Irlam M44 .... 11 E3
Widnes WA8 .... 13 D2
Wilmslow SK9 .... 34 C1
ncaster St WA3 .... 15 F3
ncelyn Dr SK9 .... 60 B4
ncer Ct WA2 .... 23 F2
ncers Cft L66 .... 69 F1
ncing Ave 8 A2
ncing Rd L65 .... 70 B2
nd Cut La WA3 .... 9 E2
nd La SK9 .... 60 B3
ander Cl WA5 .... 15 E4
ander Cl WA3 .... 3 F4
ndscape Dean WA6 .... 73 E2
andsdowne St SK10 .... 87 F1
andseer Ave Neston L64 .... 66 C4
Warrington WA4 .... 16 A1
andseer Dr SK11 .... 111 F4
andswood Pk CW8 .... 103 D2
ane Ends SK6 .... 241 D3
ane Head Ave WA3 .... 3 F4
ane Head Rd SK23 .... 65 E3
ane The Whitewell SY14 .... 223 E2
Willington SY14 .... 223 E2
aneside Rd
Manchester M20 .... 239 C8
New Mills SK22 .... 39 F4
angcliffe Cl WA3 .... 4 C2
angdale Ave WA13 .... 18 C2
angdale Cl
Altrincham WA15 .... 238 E5
Gatley SK8 .... 239 C3
High Lane SK6 .... 37 F4
Macclesfield SK11 .... 111 F3
Warrington WA2 .... 8 C1
Widnes WA8 .... 22 B4
Winsford CW7 .... 126 B1
angdale Ct CW12 .... 156 A1
angdale Rd
Cheadle Hulme SK7 .... 35 E3
Partington M31 .... 11 F2
Romiley SK6 .... 241 B4
Runcorn WA7 .... 23 D1
Wistaston CW2 .... 189 E1
angdale Way WA6 .... 49 E1
angden Cl WA3 .... 4 B2
angfield WA3 .... 3 D5
angford Gr L62 .... 43 E3
angford L24 .... 21 E1
angford Ct CH3 .... 121 E1
angford Rd Lostock CW9 .... 80 A2
Manchester SK4 .... 240 C8
angford St 11 SK11 .... 112 B4
angham Rd
Altrincham WA14 .... 238 C2
Stockport SK4 .... 240 B5
angland Cl WA5 .... 7 F1
angley Ave WA12 .... 2 B1
angley Cl Gorstwood WA3 .... 3 F4
Newcastle-u-L ST5 .... 210 B1
Sandbach CW11 .... 175 E4
angley Ct L65 .... 70 C2
angley Dr SK9 .... 34 C2
angley Hall Cl SK11 .... 113 D2
angley Rd Northwich CW9 .... 104 A3
Sutton Lane Ends SK11 .... 113 D2
angport Dr CH3 .... 119 E1
angton Cl WA8 .... 12 A2
angton Gn WA1 .... 17 E4
angwell Cl WA3 .... 10 A3
anreath Cl SK10 .... 86 B1
ansdown Cl SK7 .... 35 E4
ansdowne CH4 .... 139 D2
ansdowne Culcheth WA3 .... 4 C2
Frodsham WA6 .... 74 B3
ansdowne Ave SK6 .... 241 D2
ansdowne Gr CH4 .... 141 D4
ansdowne Rd
Altrincham WA14 .... 238 D6
Connah's Quay CH5 .... 91 E1
Crewe CW1 .... 190 C3
Great Barrow CH3 .... 120 B2
Sale M33 .... 242 A8
apwing Cl
Newton-le-W WA12 .... 2 B2
Stalybridge SK15 .... 242 D4
Winsford CW7 .... 149 E3
apwing Gr WA7 .... 50 A3
apwing La Penketh WA4 .... 25 D4
Winnington SK11 .... 109 E3
apwing Rd ST7 .... 195 E2
arch Ave
Macclesfield SK11 .... 112 A3
Newton-le-W WA12 .... 2 B2
Penketh WA5 .... 14 C3
Shavington CW2 .... 206 C3
Widnes WA8 .... 13 D1
arch Cl Goldborne WA3 .... 3 F3
Poynton SK12 .... 36 C2
Sale M33 .... 49 E4
Weaverham CW8 .... 102 B4
arch Rd Denton M34 .... 241 A7
Haydock WA11 .... 1 C4
Partington M31 .... 11 F2
Runcorn WA7 .... 49 E4
Wistaston CW2 .... 189 E1
arch Rise SK10 .... 86 B3
arch Way CH4 .... 140 C3
archdale Cl CH1 .... 94 C4
archfields CH1 .... 117 D4
archtree Cl CW8 .... 78 A2
archway Cheadle Hulme SK7 .... 35 E4
High Lane SK6 .... 37 F4
archways WA4 .... 26 B3
archwood SK8 .... 239 D6
archwood Dr SK7 .... 60 C4

Lark Hall Cl SK10 .... 113 D4
Lark Hall Cres SK10 .... 113 D4
Lark Hall Rd SK10 .... 113 D4
Lark Hill SK15 .... 242 D4
Lark Hill Prim Sch SK3 .... 240 C4
Larkfield WA3 .... 240 C4
Larkfield ST7 .... 195 D1
Larkfield Ave WA1 .... 17 D3
Larkfield SK8 .... 240 C1
Larkhill View SK3 .... 240 C1
Larkspur Cl Chester CH4 .... 140 C2
Nantwich CW5 .... 204 C4
Runcorn WA7 .... 49 F2
Larkspur Cl WA4 .... 26 C3
Larkway L66 .... 41 D4
Larksway SK6 .... 241 A6
Larwood Ave SK4 .... 240 B3
Lasky La WA4 .... 17 F2
Latchford Rd L60 .... 41 D3
Latchford St WA4 .... 17 D2
Latham Ave Helsby WA6 .... 73 F1
Newton-le-W WA12 .... 2 B2
Runcorn WA7 .... 23 E1
Warrington WA2 .... 16 C4
Latham Rd SK11 .... 175 D3
Latham St CW7 .... 126 B1
Latham Gr M33 .... 242 C5
Lathom Rd M44 .... 11 F4
Lathom Way SK10 .... 87 F1
Latimer Dr CW2 .... 190 A2
Launceston Cl Runcorn WA7 .... 50 B3
Winsford CW7 .... 149 D4
Launceston Dr Bramhall SK7 .... 35 F4
Penketh WA5 .... 14 C2
Laura St CW2 .... 190 B1
Laurel Ave Cheadle SK8 .... 239 D5
Newton-le-W WA12 .... 2 B2
Warrington WA1 .... 17 E4
Laurel Bank Warrington WA4 .... 17 E1
Widnes WA8 .... 13 D2
Winsford CW7 .... 149 E4
Laurel Cl Barnton CW8 .... 78 A2
Saddleworth SK10 .... 128 A1
Sandbach CW11 .... 175 E3
Laurel Dr Ellesmere Port L65 .... 70 A1
Goldborne WA3 .... 3 F3
Kidsgrove ST7 .... 195 F2
Laurel End La SK4 .... 240 A7
Laurel Gn M34 .... 241 A6
Laurel Gr CW7 .... 119 D2
Laurel Pk CW6 .... 145 D3
Laurel Rd 6 SK4 .... 240 A8
Laurel St SK4 .... 240 E6
Laurel Wlk M31 .... 11 F1
Laurelwood Dr L66 .... 69 F1
Laureston Ave CW1 .... 190 C2
Lavender Cl WA7 .... 23 E1
Lavender Dr CW9 .... 104 C4
Lavender Wlk M31 .... 11 E1
Lavenders Brow 22 SK1 .... 240 F5
Lavenham Cl
Hazel Grove SK7 .... 36 C4
Macclesfield SK10 .... 87 D4
Lavington Ave SK8 .... 240 A2
Lavister Cl CW9 .... 103 F2
Lavister Wlks CH4 .... 162 B1
Law St CH2 .... 118 C2
Lawford Cl CW1 .... 189 F4
Lawford Dr L60 .... 41 E4
Lawn Ave WA1 .... 16 C4
Lawn Dr Altrincham WA15 .... 238 E6
Chester CH2 .... 118 B4
Lawnhurst Trad Est
SK3 & SK8 .... 240 B1
Lawns Ave L63 .... 43 D3
Lawnside CH2 .... 101 E3
Lawnswood Gr CH2 .... 72 A2
Lawrence Ave CW2 .... 126 C4
Lawrence Ave E CW10 .... 128 B1
Lawrence Ave W CW10 .... 128 B1
Lawrence Cl 4 CW11 .... 174 B3
Lawrence Rd WA14 .... 238 C6
Lawrence Rd Crewe CW1 .... 190 B2
Hawarden CH5 .... 116 A2
Newton-le-W WA12 .... 2 A2
Stockport SK1 .... 240 E5
Laws Gdns CH3 .... 142 A4
Lawson Ave CW2 .... 190 B4
Lawson Ave SK8 .... 239 B5
Lawson Cl WA1 .... 17 F4
Lawson M33 .... 242 A8
Lawton Ave Bramhall SK7 .... 35 F4
Lawton-gate ST7 .... 194 B2
Lawton Cl WA3 .... 4 C2
Lawton Coppice ST7 .... 194 B2
Lawton Heath Rd ST7 .... 193 F3
Lawton Rd Alsager ST7 .... 193 F2
Manchester SK4 .... 240 C8
Lawton Way CW11 .... 174 C4
Lawtongate Est ST7 .... 194 A2
Laxey Ave WA1 .... 17 E3
Laxton Cl L64 .... 94 C4
Laxton Way CW10 .... 128 B1
Layland Ave WA3 .... 4 C2
Layton Ave SK4 .... 241 C6
Layton Cl WA4 .... 9 F2
Le Dar Cw6 .... 241 C3
Lea Ave Crewe CW2 .... 190 C2
Lea Bank SK11 .... 112 A4

Lea Cl CW11 .... 175 E3
Lea Cross Gr WA8 .... 12 B2
Lea Ct SK4 .... 240 B8
Lea Dr Nantwich CW5 .... 204 B2
Wimboldsley CW10 .... 151 D2
Lea La CH3 .... 164 B2
Lea Rd Gatley SK8 .... 239 B1
Manchester SK4 .... 240 C8
Lea St SK22 .... 39 D4
Leacroft Rd WA3 .... 10 A3
Leadbeaters Cl SK11 .... 112 C4
Leadbeaters Rd SK11 .... 112 C4
Leadgate La CH3 .... 144 C1
Leadsmithy St CW10 .... 128 B1
Leadworks La CH2 .... 237 F3
Leaf La CW7 .... 127 D1
Leafield Dr SK8 .... 34 C3
Leafield Rd SK12 .... 38 B3
Leafy Way CW8 .... 102 B4
Leahurst Cl CH2 .... 118 C2
Leahurst University of
Liverpool Veterinary
Field La L64 .... 67 E4
Leam Dr OL6 .... 242 A4
Leamington Ave WA12 .... 2 B1
Leamington Cl
Great Sankey WA5 .... 15 D4
Neston L64 .... 66 C3
Leamington Rd
Congleton CW12 .... 155 F2
Macclesfield SK10 .... 88 A4
Lea Ct WA7 .... 205 F4
Leas Cl L66 .... 69 E3
Leaside WA7 .... 24 A1
Leaside Rd CH1 .... 117 F3
Leaside Way SK9 .... 60 B3
Leather La WA7 .... 24 A1
Leathers La CH 21 D4
Leawood Cl CW8 .... 103 D3
Ledbury Dr WA7 .... 206 A4
Ledge Ley SK8 .... 34 C4
Ledger Rd WA11 .... 1 A3
Ledsham Cl SK10 .... 87 F4
Ledsham Ct WA3 .... 9 E2
Ledsham Hall La L66 .... 68 C2
Ledsham La L66 .... 68 C2
Ledsham Park Dr L66 .... 69 D3
Ledsham Rd L66 .... 69 D3
Ledston Cl WA7 .... 24 B1
Ledward La WA4 .... 238 B2
Ledward St CW7 .... 127 D1
Ledyard Cl WA5 .... 15 E4
Lee Ave WA3 .... 238 C7
Lee Cl WA16 .... 56 C1
Lee Dale Cl M34 .... 241 A6
Lee Dr M34 .... 103 F4
Lee Rd WA5 .... 15 D3
Lee St Chester CH1 .... 94 C4
Lee Rd WA5 .... 15 D3
Leech Rd SK14 .... 213 D2
Leech St Hyde SK14 .... 241 F6
Stalybridge SK15 .... 242 D1
Leegate Gdns SK8 .... 240 A8
Leegate Rd SK4 .... 240 A8
Leek Old Rd SK11 .... 112 C1
Leek Rd CW12 .... 179 D4
Leen La CH1 .... 237 E2
Lees La Ellesmere Port L65 .... 70 C2
Mottram St Andrew SK10 .... 61 D4
Neston L64 .... 67 D4
Stanlow L65 .... 71 D2
Lees Rd SK6 .... 35 E3
Lees St SK15 .... 242 D2
Leeside SK4 .... 240 A5
Leesway Dr M34 .... 241 A6
Leftwich Cty Prim Sch
CW9 .... 104 A2
Legh Gdns WA16 .... 57 D1
Legh Rd Adlington SK10 .... 62 B3
Haydock WA11 .... 1 A3
Knutsford WA16 .... 56 C1
Prestbury SK10 .... 87 D4
Sale M33 .... 242 E5
Legh St Goldborne WA3 .... 3 D4
Lymm WA13 .... 18 C2
Newton-le-W WA12 .... 2 A2
Warrington WA1 .... 16 A3
Legh Vale Cty Prim Sch
ST7 .... 1 A3
Leicester Ave ST7 .... 193 E4
Leicester Rd
Altrincham WA15 .... 238 F2
Sale M33 .... 242 B7
Leicester St Northwich CW9 .... 79 D1
Warrington WA5 .... 15 F3
Widnes WA8 .... 13 D1
Leigh Ave Knutsford WA16 .... 57 E2
Widnes WA8 .... 13 D1
Leigh Golf Course WA3 .... 4 B3
Leigh Green Cl 4 WA8 .... 22 B4
Leigh La CW8 .... 77 E4
Leigh Rd Altrincham WA15 .... 238 E2
Congleton CW12 .... 157 D3
Disley SK12 .... 38 A3
Leigh St Hyde SK14 .... 241 E6
Macclesfield SK11 .... 112 C4
Leigh Street Prim Sch
SK14 .... 241 E6
Leigh's Brow CW8 .... 77 E1
Leigh's Chase L64 .... 41 E1
Leighton Chase L64 .... 41 E1
Leighton Dr WA3 .... 4 C2
Leighton Gr WA3 .... 4 C2
Leighton Hospl CW1 .... 172 C1
Leighton Park Cty Prim
Sch CW1 .... 189 F4

Leighton Pk L64 .... 66 B4
Leighton Rd L64 .... 41 E1
Leighton St CW1 .... 190 A3
Leighton View CW1 .... 190 A4
Leightons The L64 .... 66 B4
Leinster Cl WA7 .... 22 C2
Leinster St WA7 .... 22 C2
Leith Ave M33 .... 242 E6
Leith Rd M33 .... 242 E6
Lenfield Dr WA11 .... 1 A3
Lenham Wlk M22 .... 33 E4
Lenthall Ave CW12 .... 178 C4
Leon Cl WA5 .... 14 B4
Leonard St Blacon CH1 .... 117 F4
Runcorn WA7 .... 48 B4
Warrington WA4 .... 16 B4
Warrington, Stockton Heath
WA4 .... 16 B1
Leslie Rd CW7 .... 149 D4
Lessingham Rd WA8 .... 12 C2
Lester Cl ST7 .... 193 E2
Leven Ave CW7 .... 126 C1
Leven Wlk L65 .... 70 A4
Levens Cl SK8 .... 239 B4
Levens Way 3 WA8 .... 22 B4
Leverett Rd L24 .... 21 D2
Leverett Cl WA14 .... 238 A5
Levisham Gdns WA5 .... 15 F4
Lewin St CW10 .... 128 B1
Lewis Ave WA5 .... 7 F1
Lewis Cl CW5 .... 205 D3
Lewis Cres WA8 .... 23 D4
Lewis Gr WA8 .... 12 B1
Lewis St CW1 .... 190 B2
Lexden St WA5 .... 15 F3
Leyburn Gr SK6 .... 241 C2
Leycester Cl WA16 .... 82 B4
Leycester Rd
Knutsford WA16 .... 82 A4
Mobberley WA16 .... 58 F3
Leyfield Ave SK6 .... 241 C2
Leyfield Ct WA3 .... 140 C3
Leygate View SK22 .... 39 D4
Leyland Ave SK8 .... 239 B6
Leyland Dr CH4 .... 140 B3
Leyland Gr
Haslington CW1 .... 191 E2
Haydock WA11 .... 1 A3
Leyland St SK4 & WA4 .... 240 E5
Leyland Wlk CW7 .... 149 E3
Leys Rd WA14 .... 238 E8
Leyton Cl WA7 .... 49 D3
Lichdale Ave WA3 .... 3 E4
Lichfield Cl WA16 .... 82 A4
Lichfield St
3 Macclesfield SK10 .... 112 C4
Winsford CW7 .... 149 E4
Lichfield Dr CH1 .... 94 C4
Lichfield Rd Blacon CH1 .... 117 F3
Kidsgrove ST7 .... 210 B4
Lichfield St CW10 .... 128 B1
Lichfield Wlk SK6 .... 241 A1
Lidgetts La SK10 .... 88 B2
Liebig St WA1 .... 23 D4
Light Alders La SK12 .... 38 A3
Light Oaks Rd WA3 .... 5 E3
Lightburn St 7 WA7 .... 22 C1
Lightfoot Cl L60 .... 41 D4
Lightfoot La Eaton CW6 .... 147 D2
Lightfoot St CH2 .... 118 C1
Lighthorne Ave SK3 .... 239 F7
Lighthorne Gr SK3 .... 239 F7
Lighthorne Rd SK3 .... 239 F7
Lighthowne Rd L24 .... 47 F4
Lightley Cl WA11 .... 175 D2
Lightwood Green Ave
CW3 .... 229 D1
Lightwood Rd ST5 .... 210 B1
Lilac Ave Great Sankey WA5 .... 15 D3
Knutsford WA16 .... 56 C1
Widnes WA8 .... 13 D1
Lilac Cl Newcastle-u-L ST5 .... 210 B1
Tarvin CH4 .... 122 C1
Lilac Cres WA7 .... 49 E4
Lilac Dr CW8 .... 103 E3
Lilac Gr Ellesmere Port CH1 .... 95 D4
Warrington WA4 .... 16 C1
Lilac St SK3 .... 240 D3
Lily Cl SK3 .... 240 D1
Lily La Cranage CW10 .... 129 D3
Middlewich CW10 .... 129 D3
Lime Ave Frodsham WA6 .... 74 B3
Northwich CW8, CW9 .... 103 F4
Weaverham CW8 .... 102 B4
Lime Cl Hollins Green WA3 .... 11 A1
Middlewich CW10 .... 128 A1
Sandbach CW11 .... 175 D4
Tarporley CW6 .... 146 B1
Lime Ct CW9 .... 103 F3
Lime Gr Alsager ST7 .... 193 F1
Broughton CH4 .... 140 B3
Cheadle SK8 .... 239 D6
Chester CH2, CH4 .... 119 D2
Ellesmere Port CH1 .... 72 A2
Goldborne WA3 .... 3 F3
Macclesfield SK10 .... 112 C4
Runcorn WA7 .... 49 E4
Warrington WA1 .... 17 D1
Lime Kiln La ST7 .... 194 C1

Lime St Congleton CW12 .... 156 B1
Crewe CW1 .... 190 B3
Ellesmere Port L65 .... 70 B4
Lime Tree Ave
Congleton CW12 .... 156 A2
Crewe CW1 .... 190 C3
Lime Tree Ct CH1 .... 95 D4
Lime Tree Dr CH3 .... 180 C1
Lime Tree Gr L60 .... 41 E4
Lime Tree La WA16 .... 29 F3
Lime Trees Prim Sch
M33 .... 242 E5
Lime View WA11 .... 1 C4
Lime Wlk Partington M31 .... 11 E1
Wilmslow SK9 .... 34 B1
Limefield Ave WA13 .... 18 C1
Limehurst Gr L62 .... 43 E3
Limekiln La WA5 .... 6 C2
Limekiln Row WA7 .... 50 A4
Limes La WA4 .... 52 B3
Limes The WA3 .... 4 C2
Limetree Ave
Warrington, Paddington WA1 .... 17 D4
Warrington, Stockton Heath
WA4 .... 16 C1
Limeways WA4 .... 26 C3
Limewood Cres CW8 .... 78 A2
Limewood Gr CW8 .... 78 A2
Lincoln Ave Cheadle SK8 .... 14 A1
Lincoln Cl Goldborne WA3 .... 4 B4
Macclesfield SK10 .... 86 C1
Rainow SK10 .... 88 C3
Runcorn WA7 .... 49 D3
Warrington WA1 .... 17 F3
Lincoln Dr CW2 .... 119 D3
Lincoln Gr M33 .... 242 F6
Lincoln Pl SK10 .... 86 C1
Lincoln Rd Blacon CH1 .... 117 F3
Ellesmere Port L65 .... 69 F2
Kidsgrove ST7 .... 210 B4
Wilmslow SK9 .... 34 C1
Lincoln Sq WA8 .... 241 A1
Lincoln St L65 .... 13 D1
Lincoln Wlk 4 SK10 .... 190 A3
Lincoln Wlk SK10 .... 86 C1
Lincombe Hey SK10 .... 87 E4
Lincombe Rd M22 .... 33 E4
Lindale Cl CW12 .... 157 D3
Linden Ave WA15 .... 238 F5
Linden Cl
Congleton CW12 .... 179 D4
Denton M34 .... 241 A7
Ellesmere Port CH1 .... 94 C4
Warrington WA1 .... 17 E4
Linden Dr Biddulph ST6 .... 179 E1
Chester CW1 .... 190 C2
Helsby WA6 .... 73 D1
Mickle Trafford CH2 .... 96 C1
Linden Gr Broughton CH4 .... 140 B3
Cheadle Hulme SK7 .... 35 E2
Chester CH4 .... 119 D2
Linden Rd M34 .... 241 A7
Linden Road Prim Sch
M34 .... 241 A7
Linden Way High Lane SK6 .... 38 A4
Widnes WA8 .... 12 C2
Lindfield Cl WA4 .... 26 B3
Lindfield Est N SK9 .... 60 A3
Lindfield Est S SK9 .... 60 A3
Lindi Ave WA4 .... 17 E1
Lindisfarne Ave
Ellesmere Port L65 .... 70 B1
Goldborne WA3 .... 4 B4
Lindisfarne Cl SK12 .... 128 A1
Lindisfarne Dr SK12 .... 36 B2
Lindley Ave WA4 .... 16 C2
Lindop Cl WA16 .... 57 E1
Lindop Rd WA15 .... 238 F1
Lindow Cty Prim Sch
SK9 .... 59 E3
Lindow Fold Dr SK9 .... 59 E3
Lindow La SK9 .... 59 F4
Lindow Par SK9 .... 59 F4
Lindow Sq M33 .... 242 F5
Lindrick Cl SK10 .... 87 E2
Lindrum Ave SK11 .... 112 B1
Linds Worth Cl SK11 .... 15 E3
Lindsay St SK15 .... 242 E1
Lindsay Way ST7 .... 193 D2
Lindsay Wlk CW8 .... 102 A2
Lindsell Rd WA14 .... 238 C8
Linear View WA12 .... 2 B1
Linen Hall Pl CH1 .... 237 D2
Linen Rd WA11 .... 11 F4
Lingdale Rd SK8 .... 239 F2
Lingfield Cl WA13 .... 112 B3
Lingfield Rd WA7 .... 190 B4
Lingley Cl SK10 .... 87 E2
Lingley Green Ave WA5 .... 14 B4
Linglongs Ave SK23 .... 65 E3
Linglongs Rd SK23 .... 65 E3
Lingmell Gdns CW8 .... 78 A2
Lingmell Rd WA8 .... 12 B1
Lingwood Rd WA5 .... 14 C3
Link The SK9 .... 34 B2
Links Ave L66 .... 69 E4
Links Cl L63 .... 43 D3
Links Rd Romiley SK6 .... 241 D2
Wilmslow SK9 .... 59 F2

Linkside Ave WA2 ... 8 A3
Linkside Way CH1 ... 94 C4
Linksway Chester CH2 ... 118 B4
Congleton CW12 ... 156 C2
Gatley SK8 ... 239 A4
Linksway Cl CW12 ... 178 C4
Linkway WA7 ... 49 E4
Linley Gr Alsager ST7 ... 193 F2
Stockport SK3 ... 240 D1
Linley La ST7 ... 194 A1
Linley Rd Alsager ST7 ... 193 F1
Cheadle Hulme SK8 ... 35 D4
Kidsgrove ST7 ... 210 B4
Sale M33 ... 242 B7
Linley Trad Est ST7 ... 194 B1
Linnards La
Higher Wincham CW9, WA16 ... 80 A3
Plumley CW9, WA16 ... 80 A3
Linnet Cl Newton-le-W WA12 ... 2 B2
Warrington WA2 ... 8 A3
Winsford CW7 ... 150 A4
Linnet Gr Macclesfield SK10 ... 87 D1
Warrington WA3 ... 9 F2
Linnets Way L60 ... 40 C4
Linnett Cl CW11 ... 190 A4
Linton Cl WA16 ... 57 E1
Linton Gdns WA4 ... 26 B2
Linton Rd M33 ... 242 C8
Linwood Ave WA4 ... 26 B4
Linwood Cl WA7 ... 50 B3
Lion St CW12 ... 156 B1
Lisburn Ave M33 ... 242 A5
Liskeard Cl WA7 ... 50 A3
Liskeard Dr SK7 ... 35 F4
Lismore Ave SK3 ... 240 B4
Lismore Wlk M22 ... 33 F4
Lisson Gr WA15 ... 238 E2
Lister Rd WA7 ... 23 E2
Litherland Rd M33 ... 242 E5
Little La CW7 ... 125 F1
Little Abbey Gateway CH1 ... 237 D3
Little Aston Cl SK10 ... 87 E2
Little Bollington CE Contr
Prim Sch WA14 ... 20 A1
Little Budworth Ctry Pk
CW6 ... 147 E4
Little Delph WA11 ... 1 B4
Little Egerton St ⑤ SK1 ... 240 E6
Little Gn L66 ... 69 E2
Little Heath Cl CW3 ... 230 A3
Little Heath La WA14 ... 20 B3
Little Heath Rd
Chester CH3 ... 119 F1
Christleton CH3 ... 142 C4
Little La WA4 ... 41 D1
Little Leigh Cty Prim Sch
CW8 ... 77 E3
Little Meadow Cl SK10 ... 87 D4
Little Meadow Rd WA14 ... 238 B1
Little Moreton Hall CW12 ... 177 F1
Little Moss Cl ST7 ... 194 C3
Little Moss La ST7 ... 194 C3
Little Roodee CH5 ... 139 D4
Little St Congleton CW12 ... 156 B1
❸ Macclesfield SK11 ... 112 B4
Little St John St CH1 ... 237 E2
Little Stanney La CH2 ... 95 F4
Little Sutton CE Contr
Prim Sch L66 ... 69 D3
Little Sutton Sta L66 ... 69 E3
Little Underbank ❶ SK1 ... 240 F5
Little Wissage L66 ... 69 F1
Littlebourne WA7 ... 50 C4
Littlecote Ave WA4 ... 26 B2
Littledale Rd WA5 ... 14 B4
Littledales La CW8 ... 102 C2
Littler WA7 ... 49 F4
Littler Grange Ct CW7 ... 126 A1
Littler Rd WA3 ... 1 A3
Littlestone Cl WA8 ... 13 D2
Littleton CI Davenham CW9 ... 103 F2
Great Sankey WA5 ... 15 E2
Littleton La CH3 ... 119 F1
Littondale CI CW12 ... 157 D3
Liverpool Pl WA8 ... 12 B1
Liverpool Rd Backford CH1 ... 95 D2
Chester CH2 ... 118 B3
Great Sankey WA5 ... 15 E2
Haydock WA11 ... 1 D1
Irlam M44 ... 11 F3
Kidsgrove ST7 ... 195 D1
Neston L64 ... 41 F1
Newcastle-u-L ST5 ... 210 B1
Warrington WA5 ... 15 E2
Widnes WA8 ... 12 B1
Willaston L64 ... 41 F2
Liverpool Rd E
Kidsgrove ST7 ... 194 C1
Lawton-gate ST7 ... 194 C1
Liverpool Rd W ST7 ... 194 A2
Liverpool Row WA1 ... 7 E4
Liverpool St CW9 ... 104 B4
Livingstone Cl
Great Sankey WA5 ... 15 E4
Macclesfield SK11 ... 111 F4
Livingstone Rd L65 ... 70 B4
Livingstone Way CW10 ... 151 E3
Llanberis Rd SK8 ... 239 E1
Llandaff Cl L66 ... 69 F1
Llandovery Cl CW7 ... 149 D4
Llanfair Rd ❼ SK3 ... 240 C4
Lloyd Ave SK8 ... 239 A6
Lloyd Cl CH3 ... 180 C1
Lloyd Cres WA12 ... 1 C2
Lloyd Dr L65 ... 70 B1

Lloyd Gdns WA14 ... 238 D3
Lloyd Pl CH1 ... 117 F2
Lloyd Sq ❻ WA14 ... 238 D4
Lloyd St
Altrincham WA14 & WA15 ... 238 D4
Stockport SK4 ... 240 D7
Lloyd's Ct WA14 ... 238 D4
Llyndir La L12 ... 162 A1
Llys Caer CH4 ... 139 D2
Llys Derwen CH4 ... 161 D4
Loachbrook Ave CW12 ... 156 A1
Lobelia Gr WA7 ... 49 F3
Loch St WA7 ... 23 D2
Lochinvar Ave L66 ... 68 C3
Lochleven Rd CW2 ... 206 A4
Lochmaden Cl CW4 ... 130 A1
Lock La M31 ... 11 F2
Lock Rd Altrincham WA14 ... 238 C6
Bebington L62 ... 44 A4
Warrington WA1 ... 16 C3
Locker Ave WA2 ... 8 A1
Lockerbie Cl WA2 ... 8 C2
Lockett Rd WA8 ... 13 D2
Lockett St WA4 ... 16 C2
Lockgate East WA7 ... 24 B1
Lockgate West WA7 ... 24 A1
Locking Stumps Cty Prim
Sch WA3 ... 9 E2
Locking Stumps La WA3 ... 9 D2
Lockitt St CW2 ... 190 B2
Locksley Cl SK4 ... 240 C6
Lockton La WA5 ... 15 F4
Lodge Brow SK10 ... 63 D1
Lodge Cl WA13 ... 19 D2
Lodge Dr Moulton CW9 ... 126 C4
Winsford CW7 ... 127 D1
Lodge Hollow WA6 ... 73 D2
Lodge La Antrobus CW9 ... 54 A3
Crowton WA8 ... 12 A2
Dutton WA4 ... 76 B4
Hartford CW8 ... 103 D2
Hatherton CW5 ... 220 A2
Hyde SK14 ... 241 D8
Lostock CW9 ... 80 A1
Newton-le-W WA11 ... 2 A4
Runcorn WA7 ... 49 F4
Saughall CH1 ... 94 A1
Warrington WA5 ... 15 F4
Lodge Rd Alsager ST7 ... 193 E2
Kidsgrove ST7 ... 210 B3
Knutsford WA16 ... 57 E2
Sandbach CW11 ... 174 C3
Widnes WA8 ... 22 A4
Lodgefields Cty Prim Sch
CW2 ... 189 F2
Lodgefields Dr CW2 ... 189 F2
Lodmore La SY13 ... 233 E3
Lofthouse Gate WA8 ... 12 C2
Logwood Cl WA13 ... 18 C3
Lomas St SK5 ... 240 D3
Lomax Rd CW5 ... 205 E3
Lomond Gr L65 ... 70 A4
London Bridge WA7 ... 50 A1
London Rd Adlington SK10 ... 62 B3
Alderley Edge SK9 ... 60 A1
Allostock WA16 ... 107 D3
Appleton WA4 ... 26 B3
Blakenhall CW5 ... 220 B2
Brereton Green CW4 ... 130 B1
Bridgemere CW5 ... 232 A3
Davenham CW9 ... 104 A1
Davenham CW9 ... 104 A1
Frodsham WA6 ... 74 A4
Hatherton CW5 ... 220 B2
Holmes Chapel CW4 ... 130 B1
Macclesfield SK11 ... 112 B2
Nantwich CW5 ... 204 C3
Northwich CW9 ... 103 F4
Prestbury SK10 ... 62 A1
Sandbach CW11 ... 174 B4
Stapeley CW5 ... 205 D2
Sutton Lane Ends SK11 ... 112 B2
Warrington WA4 ... 26 B3
Woore CW5 ... 232 A3
London Rd S SK12 ... 36 B2
London Rd Terr SK11 ... 112 B3
London Row WA1 ... 7 E4
London Sq ⑩ SK1 ... 240 F5
Loney St SK11 ... 112 B4
Long Acre CW8 ... 77 E1
Long Acres Rd L64 ... 41 F1
Long Barn La WA1 ... 17 E4
Long Croft La SK8 ... 34 C4
Long Hill SK23 ... 65 E4
Long La Alpraham CW6 ... 169 F2
Bickerton SY14 ... 199 F2
Bollington SK10 ... 63 D1
Burland CW5 ... 203 D4
Chester CH2 ... 119 D3
Faddiley CW6 ... 186 B2
Hargrave CH3 ... 143 E1
Haughton Moss CW6 ... 186 B2
Huxley CH3 ... 166 B4
Kidsgrove ST7 ... 195 F2
Middlewich CW10 ... 151 E4
Peover WA16 ... 107 E4
Saughall CH1 ... 94 A1
Spurstow CW6 ... 186 B2
Tilston SY14 ... 198 A2
Warrington WA3 ... 9 E3
Waverton CH3 ... 143 E1
Wettenhall CW7 ... 170 B3
Whaley Bridge SK23 ... 65 F2
Long La S CW9 ... 151 E4
Long Lane Cty Prim Sch
WA2 ... 8 A1
Long Looms CH3 ... 120 C3
Long Marl Dr SK9 ... 34 C2

Long Meadow L60 ... 40 C3
Long Meadow Pas SK14 ... 241 D7
Long Row ST7 ... 195 D1
Long Shoot Rd SK11 ... 108 C1
Long Spinney WA7 ... 50 B4
Long Valley Rd ST6 ... 179 E1
Long Wlk WA31 ... 11 E1
Longacre St SK11 ... 112 B4
Longacres Rd WA15 ... 32 B4
Longbarn Bvd WA2 ... 9 E1
Longbarn Cty Prim Sch
WA2 ... 9 D1
Longbenton Way WA7 ... 24 A2
Longburgh Cl CH2 ... 118 C2
Longbutt La WA13 ... 18 C1
Longbutts La SK11 ... 111 F1
Longclough Rd ST5 ... 210 B1
Longcroft Dr WA14 ... 238 B4
Longdale Dr CH1 ... 117 E3
Longden Ct SK7 ... 35 F3
Longden La SK11 ... 113 D3
Longden St SK11 ... 112 C4
Longden St WA4 ... 16 C2
Longfield Ave Cheadle SK8 ... 34 B4
Chester CH2 ... 118 B4
Longfield Gdns M44 ... 11 E2
Longford St Crewe CW2 ... 190 B1
Warrington WA2 ... 16 A4
Longhill La CW3 ... 230 C3
Longhorn Cl CW10 ... 128 B1
Longlands Dr SK22 ... 39 D4
Longlands Rd SK22 ... 39 C4
Longley Ave CW6 ... 122 B3
Longlooms Rd L65 ... 70 B1
Longmeade Gdns SK9 ... 60 B3
Longmeadow
Cheadle Hulme SK7 ... 35 E4
Weaverham CW8 ... 102 B4
Longmoss Cl CW10 ... 151 D4
Longmynd Rise CW7 ... 149 D4
Longnor Rd Cheadle SK8 ... 34 B4
Hazel Grove SK7 ... 36 C4
Longridge WA16 ... 57 E2
Longridge Ave SK15 ... 242 D4
Longridge Trad Est WA16 ... 57 E2
Longsdon Cl ST5 ... 210 B1
Longshaw St WA5 ... 7 F1
Longshut La W WA1 ... 240 F3
Longshut La SK2 ... 240 F3
Longsides Rd WA15 ... 32 B4
Longsight La SK8 ... 34 C3
Longsight St SK4 ... 240 D6
Longster Trad Est WA6 ... 75 E2
Longstone Ave WA3 ... 3 E4
Longstone La CW6 ... 122 C4
Longview Ave WA7 ... 193 F2
Longwood Cl
Middlewich CW10 ... 151 E4
Romiley SK6 ... 241 E3
Longwood Rd Appleton WA4 ... 26 C3
Stretton WA4 ... 26 C3
Lonsdale Cl WA8 ... 22 B4
Looe Cl WA8 ... 12 C1
Loomes The L64 ... 41 D1
Loonies Ct ❽ SK1 ... 240 F4
Loont The CW7 ... 149 E4
Lord Nelson St WA1 ... 16 B3
Lord St Bollington SK10 ... 88 A4
Chester CH3 ... 118 C1
Crewe CW2 ... 190 B2
Croft WA3 ... 9 D4
Macclesfield SK11 ... 112 B4
Newton-le-W WA12 ... 2 A2
Runcorn WA7 ... 22 C2
Stockport SK1 ... 240 F5
Warrington WA4 ... 16 A2
Lord's St M44 ... 11 E3
Lords La WA3 ... 9 E2
Lords Mill Rd CW2 ... 206 A2
Lordship La WA6 ... 73 D4
Lordshire Pl ST7 ... 195 F1
Loreto Convent Gram Sch
WA4 ... 238 C5
Loreto Convent Prep Sch
WA4 ... 238 C5
Lorland Rd SK3 ... 240 C3
Lorgarth Ave CW9 ... 104 B4
Lorne St CH1 ... 237 D3
Lorraine St ST7 ... 195 F1
Lostock Ave Sale M33 ... 242 E6
Warrington WA5 ... 15 F4
Lostock Gralam CE Contr
Prim Sch CW9 ... 80 A1
Lostock Gralam Sta CW9 ... 80 A1
Lostock Hall Cty Prim Sch
SK12 ... 36 A2
Lostock Hall Rd SK12 ... 36 A2
Lostock Hollow CW9 ... 80 A1
Lostock Rd SK12 ... 36 B1
Lostock Way SK9 ... 34 B2
Lottery St SK3 ... 240 D5
Louise St CH1 ... 237 D3
Loushers La WA4 ... 16 B1
Loushers Lane Day Sch
WA4 ... 16 B1
Lovage Cl WA2 ... 9 E1
Lovat Dr WA16 ... 82 A4
Love La Hassall Green CW11 ... 176 B2
Nantwich CW5 ... 204 C3
Stockport SK4 ... 240 E6
Sun St CH ... 237 E2
Lovel Terr WA8 ... 22 A3
Lovell Dr SK14 ... 241 F8
Lovely La WA5 ... 15 F3
Low Hill WA6 ... 98 C4
Low Leighton Rd SK22 ... 39 E4
Low Meadow SK23 ... 65 E4

Lowcross La SY14 ... 198 B2
Lowe Ave Congleton CW12 ... 156 C1
Warrington WA4 ... 16 C2
Lowe Cres CW9 ... 53 E2
Lowe Dr WA16 ... 57 D1
Lowe St Denton M34 ... 241 B7
Goldborne WA3 ... 3 D4
Macclesfield SK11 ... 112 B4
⑮ Stockport SK1 ... 240 F5
Lower Ash Rd ST7 ... 194 C1
Lower Bank St WA16 ... 57 D1
Lower Beech Cotts SK10 ... 87 E1
Lower Bennett St SK14 ... 241 C8
Lower Bridge St CH4 ... 237 E1
Lower Brook St CH5 ... 91 E1
Lower Bury St SK4 ... 240 D6
Lower Carrs ㉑ SK1 ... 240 F5
Lower Church St WA8 ... 23 D2
Lower Cl L26 ... 21 D4
Lower Darwin St CW8 ... 103 F3
Lower Exchange St SK11 ... 112 B4
Lower Field Rd CH4 ... 141 D3
Lower Fold M34 ... 241 A6
Lower Greenhall La SK12 ... 38 C3
Lower Hague CH2 ... 38 C4
Lower Haigh St CW7 ... 149 E4
Lower Hall La CH3 ... 182 B1
Lower Hall Mews CH3 ... 182 B1
Lower Heath CW12 ... 156 C2
Lower Heath Ave CW12 ... 156 C2
Lower High St ST7 ... 195 E4
Lower Hillgate SK1 ... 240 F5
Lower House La WA8 ... 22 C2
Lower La CW6 ... 147 D2
Lower Macclesfield Rd SK23 ... 65 F3
Lower Meadow Rd SK9 ... 34 C2
Lower Mersey St L65 ... 70 B4
Lower Moat Cl SK4 ... 240 E7
Lower Park Cres SK12 ... 36 B3
Lower Park Cty Prim Sch
SK12 ... 36 B2
Lower Park Rd Chester CH4 ... 237 F2
Poynton SK12 ... 36 A3
Lower Peover CE Aided
Prim Sch WA16 ... 81 F1
Lower Rake La WA6 ... 73 D2
Lower Robin Hood La WA6 ... 73 D2
Lower Sandy La CH3 ... 199 E4
Lower Wash La WA4 ... 16 C2
Lowerfield Rd CW10 ... 87 F1
Lowerhouse SK10 ... 87 F4
Lowes La CW9 ... 80 B3
Lowes La SK11 ... 111 F1
Lowes The WA14 ... 238 B1
Loweswater Cl WA2 ... 8 A2
Loweswater Cres WA11 ... 1 A3
Loweswater Rd SK8 ... 239 B3
Lowfield Gdns WA3 ... 5 E4
Lowfield Gr SK2 ... 240 F3
Lowfields Ave L62 ... 43 F2
Lowfields Cl L62 ... 43 F2
Lowland Way WA16 ... 82 A4
Lowlands Rd ❸ WA7 ... 22 C1
Lowry Cl WA5 ... 15 E3
Lowther Ave WA3 ... 4 C2
Lowton Cl SK10 ... 88 B4
Lowton Gdns WA3 ... 3 E4
Lowton Jun & Inf Sch WA3 ... 4 A4
Lowton Rd WA3 ... 3 E4
Lowton Sch WA3 ... 4 A4
Lowton West Cty Prim Sch
WA3 ... 3 E4
Loxdale Dr L65 ... 69 F2
Loxley Cl Great Sankey WA5 ... 15 D4
Macclesfield SK11 ... 112 A4
Loyola Hey L35 ... 12 C4
Lucerne Cl CH3 ... 142 A3
Lucy St SK3 ... 240 E4
Ludford Cl ST5 ... 210 B1
Ludford St CW1 ... 190 B3
Ludlow Ave CW1 ... 190 C2
Ludlow Cl
Macclesfield SK10 ... 87 F1
Winsford CW7 ... 149 D4
Ludlow Cres WA7 ... 49 D4
Ludlow Rd L65 ... 70 C2
Ludlow Rd CH1 ... 118 A3
Ludwell Cl CH4 ... 141 D3
Lugsdale Rd WA8 ... 23 D4
Luke's Ave WA3 ... 3 E4
Lulworth Cl CW7 ... 149 D4
Lum Head Jun Sch SK8 ... 239 B3
Lumb Brook Rd WA4 ... 26 C4
Lumb Cl SK7 ... 35 F3
Lumb La SK7 ... 35 F3
Lumley Cl WA4 ... 26 C4
Lumley Pl CH1 ... 237 E2
Lumley Rd Chester CH2 ... 118 B2
Macclesfield SK11 ... 111 F4
Lumley Wlk L24 ... 21 F1
Lumn Hollow ④ SK14 ... 241 C6
Lumn Rd SK14 ... 241 C6
Lumn St CW12 ... 156 B2
Lundy Dr CW2 ... 95 E4
Lune Cl CW12 ... 157 D1
Lune Way WA8 ... 12 B1
Lunehurst WA3 ... 4 C1
Lunt Ave WA2 ... 190 B1
Lunts Heath Cty Prim Sch
WA8 ... 13 D3
Lupin Dr Haydock WA11 ... 1 C3
Huntington CH3 ... 142 A3
Lupus Way L66 ... 69 F2

Lurgan Ave M33 ... 242
Luscombe Cl L26 ... 21
Lutener St WA14 ... 238
Luther Gr WA1 ...
Luton Rd L65 ... 70
Luton St WA8 ... 23
Lutyens Cl SK11 ... 111
Luxton Cl CW1 ... 190
Lyceum Way CW1 ... 190
Lychgate WA4 ... 25
Lycroft Cl WA7 ... 49
Lydbury Cl WA5 ...
Lydden Rd L65 ... 70
Lydgate Cl Denton M34 ... 241
Wistaston CW2 ... 205
Lydiat La SK9 ... 60
Lydiate La Runcorn WA7 ... 48
Willaston L64 ... 42
Lydiate The L60 ... 40
Lydney Ave SK8 ... 34
Lydstep Ct WA5 ... 7
Lydyett La CW8 ... 78
Lymcote Dr CW8 ... 103
Lyme Ave Macclesfield SK11 ... 112
Wilmslow SK9 ... 34
Lyme Comm Inf Sch WA12 ... 1
Lyme Gr Altrincham WA14 ... 238
Lymm WA13 ... 18
Romiley SK6 ... 241
Stockport SK2 & SK3 ... 240
Lyme Green Bsns Pk SK11 ... 112
Lyme Green Settlement
SK11 ... 112
Lyme Hall SK12 ... 38
Lyme Park Ctry Pk SK12 ... 38
Lyme Rd Disley SK12 ... 38
Poynton SK12 ... 37
Lyme St Haydock WA11 ... 1
Newton-le-W WA12 ... 2
Lymewood Dr Disley SK12 ... 38
Wilmslow SK9 ... 60
Lymm Cherry Tree Cty
Prim Sch WA13 ... 18
Lymm Cl SK3 ... 240
Lymm High (VC) Sch WA13 ... 19
Lymm Rd
Little Bollington WA14 ... 20
Warrington WA1 ... 17
Lymm Statham Cty Prim
Sch WA13 ... 18
Lymmhay La WA13 ... 18
Lymmington Ave WA13 ... 18
Lynalls Cl CW9 ... 104
Lynbrook Rd CW1 ... 190
Lyncastle Rd WA4 ... 27
Lyncastle Way WA4 ... 27
Lyncombe Cl SK8 ... 35
Lyndale Ave Bebington L62 ... 43
Warrington WA2 ... 16
Lyndene Gdns SK8 ... 239
Lyndhurst Cl SK9 ... 59
Lyndon Gr WA7 ... 49
Lyngarth Ho ❶ WA14 ... 238
Lynham Ave WA5 ... 15
Lynn Ave Kidsgrove ST7 ... 210
Sale M33 ... 242
Lynn Cl WA7 ... 49
Lynn Gr SK11 ... 112
Lynndene L66 ... 69
Lynneal Ave L66 ... 69
Lynside Wlk M22 ... 33
Lynthorpe Ave M44 ... 11
Lynton Ave M44 ... 11
Lynton Cl Heswall L60 ... 41
Penketh WA5 ... 14
Lynton Cres WA8 ... 12
Lynton Gr
Altrincham WA15 ... 238
Haslington CW1 ... 191
Lynton La SK9 ... 60
Lynton Park Rd SK8 ... 34
Lynton Pl Alsager ST7 ... 193
Broughton CH4 ... 139
Lynton Way CW2 ... 206
Lyntonvale Ave SK8 ... 239
Lynwood Ave WA3 ... 3
Lynwood Gr M33 ... 242
Lynwood Rd CH1 ... 117
Lyon Ind Est WA14 ... 238
Lyon Rd WA14 ... 238
Lyon St Chester CH2 ... 237
Crewe CW1 ... 190
Lyons La Warrington WA4 ... 16
Lyon's La WA4 ... 16
Lyons Fold M33 ... 242
Lyons Rd WA5 ... 15
Lyster Cl WA7 ... 24
Lytham Cl SK7 ... 36
Lytham Rd SK9 ... 34
Lytham St SK3 ... 240
Lytherton Ave M44 ... 11
Lythgoes La WA2 ... 16

Mableden Cl SK8 ... 34
Mablins La CW1 ... 190
Mablins Lane Cty Prim
Sch CW1 ... 190
Mabs Ct DL6 ... 242
Macarthur Dr WA5 ... 15
Macclesfield Coll
Macclesfield SK11 ... 112
Macclesfield SK11 ... 112
Macclesfield District
General Hospl SK11 ... 112

Macclesfield Rd
Alderley Edge SK9 .... 85 E4
Congleton CW12 .... 156 C3
Eaton CW12 .... 134 A1
Hazel Grove SK7 .... 36 C4
Holmes Chapel CW4 .... 130 C2
Kettleshulme SK23, SK10 ... 64 B2
Nether Alderley SK9 .... 85 E4
Prestbury SK10 .... 86 C2
Rainow SK10 .... 89 D4
Whaley Bridge SK23 .... 65 E3
Wilmslow SK9 .... 60 B3
Macclesfield Sta SK11 ...... 112 B4
Macdermott Rd WA8 .... 22 C3
Macdonald Rd M44 .... 11 F4
Mackenzie Ind Pk
SK3 & SK8 .... 240 B2
Mackeson Dr OL6 .... 242 B4
Mackeson Rd OL6 .... 242 B4
Macon Ct CW1 .... 190 C2
Macon Ind Pk CW1 .... 190 C2
Macon Way CW1 .... 190 C2
Maddock St ST7 .... 209 E1
Maddocks Hill WA6 .... 100 C3
Madeley Cl Altrincham WA14 31 F4
Broughton CH4 .... 139 D2
Madeley St CW2 .... 190 B1
Madeline McKenna Ct
WA8 .... 12 B2
Madras Rd SK3 .... 240 C3
Madron Ave SK10 .... 86 B1
Maelor Cl L63 .... 43 E3
Mag La WA16 .... 28 C3
Magdala Pl CW9 .... 104 B4
Maggoty La SK11 .... 111 E1
Magnolia Cl
Ellesmere Port L66 .... 69 F1
Partington M31 .... 11 F2
Warrington WA1 .... 17 F2
Magnolia Dr WA7 .... 49 F2
Magnolia Rise SK10 .... 86 B3
Magpie Cres ST7 .... 195 D1
Mahood St SK3 .... 240 D3
Maidenhills CW10 .... 128 B1
Maidstone Cl SK10 .... 87 D1
Maidwell Cl CW7 .... 127 D2
Main Cl WA11 .... 1 A3
Main La WA3 .... 3 F2
Main Rd Broughton CH4 .... 139 D2
Goostrey SK4 .... 107 F1
Higher Kinnerton CH4 .... 161 F1
Langley SK11 .... 113 E2
Moulton CW9 .... 126 C4
Norton in Hales TF9 .... 236 B1
Shavington CW2 .... 206 A2
Weston CW2 .... 207 E4
Worleston CW5 .... 188 C3
Main St Frodsham WA6 ...... 220 A4
Great Barrow CH3 .... 120 C3
Hyde SK14 .... 241 D8
Runcorn WA7 .... 49 F4
Maintree Cres L24 .... 21 D2
Mainwaring Dr
Broughton CH4 .... 140 B4
Wilmslow SK9 .... 60 A4
Mainwaring Rd WA16 .... 108 A4
Mairesfield Ave WA4 .... 17 D1
Maisterson Ct CW5 .... 204 C3
Maitland Way CW1 .... 117 E2
Maitland Wood CW9 .... 104 B4
Majefield CI M33 .... 242 F6
Major Cross St 13 WA8 ..... 23 D4
Makepeace CI CW10 .... 119 E2
Malaga Ave WA9 .... 33 D4
Malakoff St SK15 .... 242 B1
Malam Dr CW9 .... 104 B3
Malbank CW5 .... 204 C3
Malbank Rd CW2 .... 189 F2
Malbank Sch SK5 .... 204 B3
Malcolm Ave WA2 .... 8 B1
Malcolm Cres L63 .... 43 E3
Malcolm St CW2 .... 190 C1
Malcolm Dr M20 .... 239 E8
Malhamdale Rd CW12 .... 157 D3
Malin Cl L24 .... 21 E1
Maliston Rd WA5 .... 15 D3
Mallaig Cl CW4 .... 130 A3
Mallard Cl Knutsford WA16 . 57 D1
Warrington WA3 .... 49 F3
Warrington WA2 .... 8 B2
Mallard Cres SK12 .... 36 A2
Mallard La WA3 .... 9 F2
Mallard Way CW7 .... 149 E3
Mallory Cl Altrincham WA14 338 D3
Congleton CW12 .... 155 F2
Mallory Rd L65 .... 70 A2
Mallory Wlk CH4 .... 162 A4
Mallow CI CH3 .... 142 A3
Mallow Wlk M31 .... 11 F1
Mallowdale CI L62 .... 43 F3
Malmesbury Ave SK8 .... 35 D3
Malmesbury CI
Middlewich CW10 .... 128 A1
Poynton SK12 .... 36 A2
Malmesbury Pk WA7 .... 24 B1
Malory Cl CW1 .... 190 C1
Malpas Aiport Endowed
Prim Sch SY14 .... 213 D2
Malpas Bishop Heber Cty
High Sch SY14 .... 213 E3
Malpas Cl Northwich CW9 .. 104 A4
Wilmslow SK9 .... 34 C1
Malpas Dr WA5 .... 15 E4
Malpas Rd Ellesmere Port L65 69 F2
Northwich CW9 .... 104 B4
Runcorn WA7 .... 49 E4

Malpas Way WA5 .... 15 E2
Malt Kiln Rd WA16 .... 80 C2
Malt St WA16 .... 57 D1
Malta Rd CH2 .... 95 D1
Maltmans Rd WA13 .... 18 B2
Malton Ave WA3 .... 3 F4
Malton Cl WA8 .... 12 B3
Malton Dr Altrincham WA14 238 A6
Hazel Grove SK7 .... 36 B4
Malton Rd SK4 .... 240 A8
Malvern Ave L65 .... 70 B2
Malvern Cl
Congleton CW12 .... 155 F2
Great Sankey WA5 .... 15 D4
Northwich CW9 .... 104 A4
Stockport SK4 .... 240 D7
Malvern Dr
Altrincham WA14 .... 238 B5
Macclesfield SK10 .... 87 F2
St Helens WA9 .... 1 A2
Malvern Way CW7 .... 149 D4
Manchester Airport M90 .... 33 D3
Manchester Airport Sta
M90 .... 33 D4
Manchester Bridge L .. 190 C2
Manchester Metr Univ,
Crewe & Alsager Faculty
CW1 .... 190 C2
Manchester Metr Univ,
Crewe & Alsager Faculty,
Alsager Campus ST7 ...... 193 D3
Manchester New Rd M31 ... 11 F2
Manchester Rd
Altrincham WA14 .... 238 D7
Cheadle M20 & SK8 .... 239 D7
Congleton CW12 .... 156 C3
Denton SK14 .... 241 C7
Hollins Green WA3 .... 11 D1
Knutsford WA16 .... 56 C2
Lostock CW9 .... 79 E1
Macclesfield SK10 .... 87 E2
Partington M31 .... 11 F2
Reddish SK4 .... 240 E8
Warrington WA1 .... 18 A4
Warrington, Bruche WA1 ... 16 C4
Warrington, Woolston WA1 . 17 E4
Wilmslow SK9 .... 34 B1
Manchester Row WA12 ..... 7 E4
Mancroft CI WA7 .... 50 A4
Mancunian Rd WA14 .... 241 A5
Mandarin Grn WA14 .... 238 B8
Manifold Cl CW11 .... 174 C4
Manifold Dr SK6 .... 37 F3
Manley Cl Antrobus CW9 ... 53 E2
Holmes Chapel CW4 .... 130 C2
Northwich CW9 .... 104 A3
Manley Cty Prim Sch WA6 . 99 D3
Manley Gdns SK7 .... 35 F3
Manley La
Dunham-on-t-H WA6 .... 97 F3
Manley WA6 .... 98 B2
Manley Rd Alvanley WA6 ... 98 C4
Frodsham WA6 .... 74 A2
Manley WA6 .... 99 D3
Warren SK11 .... 112 A2
Manley View WA6 .... 72 B2
Manna Dr CH2 .... 72 B2
Manners La L60 .... 40 C4
Manning La S CH2 .... 119 D3
Manning St CW7 .... 190 B1
Mannings La CH2 .... 119 D3
Manor Ave Crewe CW2 ...... 190 A1
Goldborne WA3 .... 3 F2
Goostrey SK4 .... 107 F1
Marston CW9 .... 79 D3
Newton-le-W WA12 .... 2 A2
Manor Cl Bramall SK7 .... 35 E4
Broughton CH5 .... 139 E4
Congleton CW12 .... 157 D1
Denton M34 .... 241 B6
Great Barrow CH3 .... 120 C3
Neston L64 .... 66 B4
Warrington WA1 .... 17 E4
Wilmslow SK9 .... 59 F4
Manor Cres Broughton CH4 . 139 E4
Knutsford WA16 .... 57 D1
Macclesfield SK10 .... 87 E2
Middlewich CW10 .... 151 E4
Manor Ct Crewe CW2 .... 190 A1
Goldborne WA3 .... 3 F2
Manor Dr Barnton CW8 ..... 78 A1
Chester CH3 .... 119 C2
Northwich, Rudheath CW9 . 104 B4
Manor Farm Cl CH2 .... 119 F3
Manor Farm Cres CH1 .... 94 A4
Manor Farm Ct CH5 .... 139 D4
Manor Farm Rd M22 .... 33 E4
Manor Fell WA7 .... 50 A4
Manor Fields CW10 .... 151 E4
Manor Gdns SK9 .... 60 B4
Manor Gr CW8 .... 103 E3
Manor La Broughton CH5 ... 139 D4
Davenham CW9 .... 104 B1
Ellesmere Port L66 .... 69 E2
Holmes Chapel CW4 .... 130 B2
Middlewich CW10 .... 151 E4
Ollerton WA16 .... 82 C3
Manor Park Ave WA7 .... 24 B1
Manor Park Cty Prim Sch
WA16 .... 57 E1
Manor Pk Great Barrow CH3 120 C4
Hawarden CH4 .... 139 D4
Manor Pk N WA16 .... 57 E1
Manor Pk S WA16 .... 57 E1

Manor Pl WA8 .... 12 A1
Manor Rd Altrincham WA15 238 E4
Bebington L63 .... 43 F3
Chester CH4 .... 141 D3
Cuddington CW8 .... 101 F1
Denton M34 .... 241 B5
Frodsham WA6 .... 49 E1
Haydock WA11 .... 1 C4
Lymm WA13 .... 18 C1
Mow Cop ST7 .... 195 D4
Nantwich CW5 .... 204 C3
Runcorn WA7 .... 23 E1
Sale M33 .... 242 B7
Sandbach CW11 .... 175 E3
Sealand CH5 .... 116 A3
Thornton Hough L63 .... 42 A4
Whaley Bridge SK23 .... 65 F3
Widnes WA8 .... 12 A1
Wilmslow SK9 .... 59 F4
Manor Rd N CW5 .... 204 C3
Manor Sq 5 CW7 .... 149 D4
Manor St CW8 .... 103 E3
Manor Way Crewe CW2 ..... 190 B1
Goldborne WA3 .... 3 F2
Manora Rd CW9 .... 104 A4
Manorfield Cl CH1 .... 69 D1
Manorial Rd S L64 .... 66 B4
Manse Field Rd WA6 .... 75 D1
Manse Gdns WA12 .... 2 B2
Mansell Cl WA8 .... 13 E3
Mansfield Cl WA3 .... 10 A2
Mansfield Cty Prim Sch
L65 .... 69 F2
Mansfield Rd
Ellesmere Port L65 .... 70 A1
Hyde SK14 .... 241 F5
Mansion Ct WA1 .... 204 C3
Mansion Dr WA16 .... 57 D1
Manston Rd WA5 .... 14 C2
Manuel Perez Rd WA5 ...... 15 D3
Manvers St SK5 .... 240 E7
Manx St WA4 .... 16 A4
Maori Dr WA6 .... 74 A4
Maple Ave Alsager ST7 ...... 193 F1
Cheadle SK8 .... 35 E3
Disley SK12 .... 39 D3
Ellesmere Port L66 .... 69 E3
Haydock WA11 .... 1 A4
Kidsgrove ST7 .... 210 B4
Macclesfield SK11 .... 112 B3
Newcastle-u-l ST5 .... 210 C1
Newton-le-W WA12 .... 2 B1
Poynton SK12 .... 36 C2
Runcorn WA7 .... 49 E4
Sutton WA7 .... 50 B4
Widnes WA8 .... 13 D1
Maple Cl
Brereton Green CW11 .... 153 F2
Congleton CW12 .... 155 F2
Holmes Chapel CW4 .... 130 B2
Sandbach CW11 .... 175 E3
Maple Cres WA5 .... 14 C2
Maple Gr Barnton CW8 ...... 78 A2
Bebington L62 .... 43 E4
Broughton CH4 .... 140 B3
Chester CH2 .... 119 D2
Crewe CW1 .... 190 C4
Ellesmere Port L65 .... 95 D4
Northwich, Greenbank
CW8 .... 103 E4
Warrington WA4 .... 16 B2
Winsford CW7 .... 127 D1
Maple La CW8 .... 101 E1
Maple PI ST7 .... 193 F4
Maple Rd Alderley Edge SK9 . 60 A2
Bramhall SK7 .... 35 F3
Partington M31 .... 11 F4
Warrington WA1 .... 17 F4
Winwick WA2 .... 8 B3
Mapleton Dr WA7 .... 49 F2
Maplewood Gr CH1 .... 117 D4
Maplewood Rd SK9 .... 60 A2
Mapplewell Cres WA5 ...... 15 D3
Marble Arch WA16 .... 57 D2
Marbury Dry Pk CW9 .... 78 C3
Marbury Gdns L65 .... 69 F3
Marbury La CW9 .... 78 C3
Marbury Rd Chester CH3 ... 119 C1
Comberbach CW9 .... 78 B3
Northwich CW9 .... 78 B3
Wilmslow SK9 .... 34 A1
Marbury St WA4 .... 16 B2
March Ave SK4 .... 240 B6
March St CW1 .... 190 D2
Marchbank Dr SK8 .... 239 C6
Marchwiel Rd L65 .... 70 B2
Marcien Way WA8 .... 12 C2
Marcliff Gr Knutsford WA16 . 57 D1
Stockport SK4 .... 240 A8
Marcross Cl WA5 .... 7 F1
Mardale Ave WA2 .... 8 B2
Mardale Cl Congleton CW12 157 D3
Stalybridge SK15 .... 242 D3
Mardale Cres WA13 .... 18 C2
Mardale Cl CW4 .... 130 A1
Mardale Dr SK8 .... 239 B6
Mardon Cl WA16 .... 57 E2
Marfields Cty Prim Sch
CW12 .... 156 B1
Marfords Ave L63 .... 43 E4
Margaret Ave WA1 .... 17 D4
Margaret Ct WA8 .... 23 D4
Margaret Danyers Coll
SK8 .... 239 F3
Margaret Rd M34 .... 241 A8
Margaret's La L66 .... 69 D4

Margery Ave ST7 .... 194 C4
Marian Dr CH3 .... 142 A4
Marian Rd WA11 .... 1 C4
Marie Cl CW4 .... 216 C2
Marie Dr WA4 .... 17 E1
Marigold Cl SK11 .... 111 F4
Marina Ave Denton M34 .... 241 A5
Great Sankey WA5 .... 15 E2
Marina Cl SK9 .... 34 B3
Marina Dr Chester CH2 ..... 118 C4
Ellesmere Port L65 .... 70 A3
Warrington WA2 .... 8 B1
Marina Gr WA7 .... 23 D1
Marina La WA7 .... 50 C4
Marina Village WA7 .... 50 C4
Marina Wlk L65 .... 70 A3
Marine Ave M31 .... 11 F2
Marine Dr L60 .... 40 B4
Mariner Cl WA7 .... 49 F4
Marion Dr WA7 .... 48 C3
Maritime Cl WA12 .... 2 B3
Mark Ave L66 .... 69 F2
Mark Cl CW2 .... 118 C1
Mark Rake L62 .... 43 E4
Market Cl CW7 .... 149 D4
Market Ctr The CW1 .... 190 B2
Market Gate WA1 .... 16 A3
Market PI Bollington SK10 . 88 A4
1 Hyde SK14 .... 241 D6
Macclesfield SK11 .... 112 B4
Stockport SK1 .... 240 F6
Market Sq Chester CH1 ..... 237 D2
Congleton CW12 .... 156 C1
Crewe CW1 .... 190 B2
Sandbach CW11 .... 175 D3
Market St
Altrincham WA14 .... 238 D4
Congleton CW12 .... 156 B1
Crewe CW1 .... 190 B3
Disley SK12 .... 38 B3
Hyde SK14 .... 241 D6
Kidsgrove ST7 .... 195 D1
Nantwich CW5 .... 204 C3
New Mills SK22 .... 39 D4
Newton-le-W WA12 .... 2 A2
Northwich CW9 .... 103 F4
Stalybridge SK15 .... 242 D2
Whaley Bridge SK23 .... 65 F4
Widnes WA8 .... 23 D2
Market Way CW9 .... 103 F4
Markland St L65 .... 241 E5
Marl Cl CH2 .... 142 A4
Marl Edge SK10 .... 87 D3
Marl Heys CW7 .... 118 C4
Marland Ave SK8 .... 239 F2
Marlborough
Alderley Edge SK9 .... 60 A1
Winsford CW7 .... 126 B2
Marlborough Cl
Knutsford WA16 .... 57 E2
Macclesfield SK10 .... 87 E2
Wistaston CW2 .... 205 F4
Marlborough Cres
Widnes WA8 .... 16 C1
Warrington WA2 .... 8 A1
Marlborough Wlk SK11 ..... 112 B4
Marlborough Cty Prim
Sch The SK10 .... 87 E2
Marlborough Dr
Helsby WA6 .... 73 D1
Macclesfield SK10 .... 87 E2
Reddish SK4 .... 240 D8
Marlborough Rd
Altrincham WA15 .... 32 B4
Ellesmere Port L65 .... 70 B2
Sale M33 .... 242 B6
Marlborough Wlk L65 .... 70 B2
Marlcroft Ave SK4 .... 240 B6
Marler Rd SK14 .... 241 E8
Marley Ave CW1 .... 190 A4
Marley Cl WA15 .... 238 F7
Marley Rd SK12 .... 36 C1
Marley Way CW4 .... 140 C4
Marlfield Rd
Altrincham WA15 .... 32 B4
Warrington WA1 .... 17 D1
Marline Ave L63 .... 43 E3
Marling Cl WA6 .... 74 B3
Marling Park WA8 .... 22 B1
Marlow Ave CH2 .... 118 B4
Marlow Cl Cheadle SK8 ..... 239 F2
10 Sandbach CW11 .... 174 B3
Warrington WA3 .... 9 F3
Marlow Dr Altrincham WA14 . 20 C1
Wilmslow SK9 .... 34 B3
Marlowe Cl Blacon CH1 .... 118 A2
Widnes WA8 .... 12 C1
Marlowe Ct SK11 .... 112 B3
Marlowe Dr CW5 .... 204 D3
Marlowe Rd Neston L64 .... 66 C4
Northwich CW9 .... 104 B3
Marlston Ave CH4 .... 141 B3
Marlston PI WA7 .... 49 D3
Marlston Rd SK9 .... 87 D2
Marple Cres CW2 .... 189 F2
Marple Rd CW9 .... 104 B4
Marquis Dr SK8 .... 34 B4
Marrick Ave SK8 .... 239 C5
Marritt Rd CW11 .... 174 C2
Marriott St SK1 .... 240 F4
Marron Ave WA2 .... 8 A1
Marsden Ave WA4 .... 17 D2
Marsden Rd SK6 .... 241 C3
Marsden Terr 16 SK11 ...... 112 B4
Marsh Ave ST7 .... 195 F1

Marsh Cl Alsager ST7 .... 193 D2
Stockport SK3 .... 240 D2
Marsh Gr ST6 .... 179 E2
Marsh Green Cl ST6 .... 179 E1
Marsh Green Rd
Biddulph ST6 .... 179 E1
Sandbach CW11 .... 174 C4
Marsh Hall Rd WA8 .... 13 D2
Marsh House La WA2 .... 16 B4
Marsh La Acton CW5 .... 204 A2
Alsager ST7 .... 193 D2
Churton CH3 .... 181 D3
Coddington CH3 .... 197 F2
Crowton CW8 .... 101 D4
Dutton WA4 .... 51 F2
Elton CW2 .... 72 A2
Frodsham WA6 .... 74 A4
Holmes Chapel CW4 .... 130 C1
Mere WA14 .... 30 C1
Nantwich CW5 .... 204 B3
New Mills SK22 .... 39 E3
Penketh WA5 .... 14 B1
Ravensmoor CW5 .... 203 F1
Runcorn WA7 .... 23 F2
Marsh Rd WA4 .... 27 D2
Marsh St Warrington WA1 . 16 B4
Widnes WA8 .... 23 D3
Marshall Ave WA5 .... 7 F1
Marshall Cl SK9 .... 60 A3
Marshall Cl WA8 .... 103 E3
Marshall Rd WA1 .... 17 E4
Marshfield Bank CW2 .... 189 E2
Marshfield La ST6 .... 179 E1
Marshfield Rd CW2 .... 189 E2
Marshgate WA8 .... 22 A3
Marshgate PI WA6 .... 49 F3
Marshlands Rd L64 .... 66 C3
Marsland Rd M33 .... 242 B5
Marsland St SK1 .... 240 F6
Marson St WA2 .... 16 A3
Marston Cl L62 .... 43 F2
Marston La CW9 .... 79 E3
Marten Ave L63 .... 43 E4
Martens Rd M44 .... 11 F3
Marthall La Chelford WA16 . 83 D4
Ollerton WA16 .... 82 C3
Marthall SK9 .... 84 C3
Martham Cl WA4 .... 17 D2
Martin Ave
Newton-le-W WA12 .... 2 B3
Newton-le-W, Newton Common
WA12 .... 1 C2
Warrington WA2 .... 8 C1
Martin Cl Chester CH2 ...... 118 B4
Culcheth WA3 .... 4 C2
Runcorn WA7 .... 50 A4
Martin St SK14 .... 241 E6
Martin's La CW3 .... 143 F2
Martindale Gr WA7 .... 49 E3
Martland Ave WA3 .... 3 E4
Martlet Ave SK12 .... 38 B3
Marton Cl Congleton CW12 . 156 C3
Hough Common CW2 .... 206 C2
Marton & District CE
Aided Prim Sch SK11 ..... 133 E3
Marton Grn SK3 .... 240 D1
Marton La Eaton SK11 ...... 134 A2
Marton SK11 .... 111 D1
Warren SK11 .... 111 D1
Marton PI WA3 .... 242 A6
Marton Rd CW4 .... 139 E2
Marton Way 4 SK8 .... 34 C3
Marwood Cl WA14 .... 238 B6
Mary Dendy Hospl SK9 ..... 83 F4
Mary St Cheadle SK8 .... 239 D6
Crewe CW1 .... 190 C3
Denton M34 .... 241 A8
Hyde SK14 .... 241 D7
Widnes WA8 .... 23 E4
Maryhill Cl ST7 .... 195 D2
Maryhill High & Prim Sch
ST7 .... 195 D2
Marys Gate CW7 .... 205 F4
Masefield Ave WA8 .... 22 C4
Masefield Dr Blacon CH1 ... 117 F2
Crewe CW1 .... 190 C2
Stockport SK4 .... 240 A6
Maskery PI CW12 .... 156 B2
Mason Ave Warrington WA1 . 16 C4
Widnes WA8 .... 13 D3
Mason Cl L66 .... 69 E1
Mason St Chester CH2 ...... 237 D3
Runcorn WA7 .... 23 E2
Warrington WA1 .... 16 B3
Masons La SK10 .... 87 D3
Masons St Hartford CW8 ... 103 D2
Lymm WA13 .... 18 A1
Warrington WA5 .... 7 F1
Winsford CW7 .... 126 C1
Massey Brook La WA13 ..... 18 A1
Massey Rd
Altrincham WA15 .... 238 E4
Sale M33 .... 242 E6
Massey St
Alderley Edge SK9 .... 60 A1
17 Stockport SK1 .... 240 F5
Masseyfield Rd WA7 .... 50 A3
Massie St SK8 .... 239 D6
Mates La SY14 .... 213 D3
Mather Ave Goldborne WA3 . 3 F3
Runcorn WA7 .... 48 B4
Mather Cl CW10 .... 151 E4

Mather Dr Comberbach CW9 . 78 B4
  Northwich CW9 .... 104 B4
Mathers CI WA2 .... 9 D2
Mathieson Rd WA8 .... 22 C3
Matlock CI
  Great Sankey WA5 .... 15 D4
  Sale M33 .... 242 C6
  Warrington WA5 .... 7 D1
Matlock Dr SK7 .... 36 C4
Matlock Rd SK8 .... 34 B4
Matterdale CI WA6 .... 74 B4
Matthew CI CH2 .... 118 C1
Matthews PI CW12 .... 157 D1
Matthews St WA1 .... 16 A4
Matty's La WA6 .... 74 A4
Mauldeth CI SK4 .... 240 A7
Mauldeth Rd SK4 & M19 . 240 A7
Mavor CI CW1 .... 190 A2
Maw Green Rd CW1 .... 190 C4
Maw La CW1 .... 191 E4
Mawdsley Ave WA1 .... 17 F4
Mawdsley CI ST7 .... 193 D2
Mawson CI WA5 .... 15 E4
Maxfield CI SK11 .... 111 F4
Maxwell CI L65 .... 70 A1
Maxwell Rd CW12 .... 179 D4
Maxwell St WA2 .... 190 B2
May Ave Cheadle Hulme SK8 . 35 D3
  Stockport SK4 .... 240 C6
May Rd Cheadle Hulme SK8 . 35 D3
  Heswall L60 .... 40 C4
May Wlk M31 .... 11 E1
Mayberry Gr WA2 .... 9 D1
Maybrook PI WA4 .... 16 C2
Mayhews Pas ⓶ SK11 .... 112 B4
Maydor Ave CH4 .... 140 B4
Mayfair CI
  Great Sankey WA5 .... 14 B4
  Poynton SK12 .... 36 C2
Mayfair Dr CW9 .... 103 F2
Mayfair Gr WA8 .... 12 B1
Mayfair L66 .... 69 F4
Mayfield Ave
  Macclesfield SK11 .... 112 B3
  Sale M33 .... 242 E6
  Widnes WA8 .... 12 A1
Mayfield CI CH4 .... 130 B2
Mayfield Dr Bebington L62 ... 44 A3
  Cuddington WA8 .... 102 A2
  Goldborne WA3 .... 4 B4
Mayfield Gdns L64 .... 41 F1
Mayfield Gr
  Cuddington WA8 .... 102 A2
  Wilmslow SK9 .... 59 F3
Mayfield Mews CW1 .... 189 F4
Mayfield Rd Blacon CH1 ... 117 E3
  Bramhall SK7 .... 35 F2
  Mobberley WA16 .... 60 F1
  Northwich CW9 .... 104 B4
  Warrington WA4 .... 17 D1
Mayfield View WA13 ...... 18 C1
Mayflower Rd CW5 .... 204 C2
Mayor's Rd WA15 .... 238 E4
Maythorn Ave WA3 .... 9 D4
Maytree Ave CH3 .... 119 D1
Maywood Ave M20 .... 239 B8
McCarthy CI WA3 .... 10 A2
McClellan PI WA8 .... 13 D1
McGarva Way L65 .... 70 B2
Mckee Ave WA1 .... 8 A1
Mckellin CI ST17 .... 209 F1
McLaren St CW1 .... 190 B4
McMinnis Ave WA9 .... 1 A1
McNeill Ave CW1 .... 190 A3
Mead Ave ST7 .... 194 C4
Mead CI WA16 .... 56 C1
Mead Rd WA1 .... 17 D4
Meade The SK9 .... 59 F1
Meadow Ave
  Congleton CW12 .... 156 B1
  Goostrey CW4 .... 107 E1
  Warrington WA4 .... 16 A1
  Weston CW2 .... 207 D3
Meadow Bank
  Adderley TF9 .... 235 D2
  Kelsall CW6 .... 122 B2
  Warrington WA4 .... 240 B6
Meadow Brow SK9 .... 60 A1
Meadow CI Cuddington CW8 . 102 A2
  Farndon CH3 .... 180 C1
  Goostrey CW4 .... 107 F1
  Helsby WA6 .... 73 D2
  High Lane SK6 .... 37 F4
  Neston L64 .... 66 C3
  Newton-le-W WA12 .... 1 C2
  Shavington CW2 .... 206 B3
  Tarvin CH3 .... 121 D1
  Whaley Bridge SK23 .... 65 E4
  Widnes WA8 .... 12 B2
  Willaston L64 .... 67 F4
  Wilmslow SK9 .... 59 F2
  Winsford CW7 .... 126 B2
Meadow Croft Alsager ST7 . 193 F1
  Willaston L64 .... 67 F4
Meadow Ct Mollington CH1 . 94 C1
  No Man's Heath SY14 ..... 214 A2
Meadow Cty Prim Sch
  L66 .... 69 F1
Meadow Dr Barnton CW8 .. 78 A2
  Prestbury SK10 .... 87 D4
  Wistaston CW2 .... 205 F4
Meadow Field Rd CH4 .... 141 D3
Meadow Gate CW9 .... 79 F3

Meadow Gr
  Northwich CW9 .... 104 A3
  Winsford CW7 .... 126 C3
Meadow Home Pk CW7 ... 126 B3
Meadow Ind Est SK5 ...... 240 F7
Meadow La Disley SK12 ... 38 B3
  Ellesmere Port L65 .... 70 B3
  Huntington CH3 .... 142 A3
  Moulton CW9 .... 126 C4
  Warrington WA2 .... 9 D1
  Willaston L64 .... 42 C1
Meadow Rd Broughton CH4 . 139 E2
  Weaverham CW8 .... 102 C4
Meadow Rise Clutton CH3 . 182 B1
  Winsford CW7 .... 126 A1
Meadow Row WA7 .... 24 A1
Meadow St Hyde SK14 .... 241 E5
  New Mills SK22 .... 39 E4
  Northwich CW9 .... 104 B3
Meadow View Elton CH2 .. 72 A2
  Middlewich CW10 .... 128 A1
  Sealand CH5 .... 116 A3
Meadow View Dr WA6 ..... 74 A4
Meadow Way
  Lawton-gate ST7 .... 194 A3
  Macclesfield SK10 .... 88 A3
  Wilmslow SK9 .... 59 F2
Meadow Wlk M31 .... 11 E1
Meadowbank Gdns WA3 .. 5 F4
Meadowcroft
  Higher Kinnerton CH4 ..... 161 D4
  Saughall CH1 .... 94 A1
Meadowfield
  Tarporley CW6 .... 146 B1
  Whaley Bridge SK23 .... 65 E4
Meadowfield Ct SK14 ..... 241 D8
Meadowgate CI CW7 ...... 149 D3
Meadows La Chester CH4 . 237 F1
  Saughall CH1 .... 117 D4
Meadows PI CH4 .... 141 F4
Meadows Rd Cheadle SK8 . 34 C4
  Gatley SK8 .... 239 B1
  Sale M33 .... 242 C6
Meadows The Ashton CH3 . 121 F4
  Congleton CW12 .... 156 C2
  Irlam M44 .... 11 F3
  Neston L64 .... 66 C3
Meadowside Adlington SK10 . 63 D4
  Disley SK12 .... 39 D3
  Northwich CW8 .... 103 E4
  Whaley Bridge SK23 .... 65 E4
Meadowside Ave ST7 ...... 209 E1
Meadowside Rd L62 .... 43 E4
Meadowsway CH2 .... 118 B4
Meadowsweet Rd WA16 .. 57 F2
Meadowvale CI CW5 .... 204 C4
Meads Rd ST7 .... 193 E2
Meadscroft Dr SK9 .... 59 F1
Meadway Bramhall SK7 ... 35 F3
  Ellesmere Port L66 .... 69 D4
  Goldborne WA3 .... 3 E4
  Heswall L60 .... 40 C3
  High Lane SK6 .... 37 F4
  Poynton SK12 .... 36 A2
  Prestbury SK12 .... 87 D3
  Runcorn WA7 .... 49 F4
  Widnes WA8 .... 12 A1
Meakin CI CW12 .... 157 F1
Meal St New Mills SK22 ... 39 E4
Mealhouse Brow ➋ SK1 .. 240 F5
Meddings CI SK8 .... 85 D4
Medina Ave CW7 .... 126 C1
Medina Way ST7 .... 195 D1
Medway CI Goldborne WA3 . 4 B4
  Warrington WA2 .... 8 C1
  Widnes WA8 .... 22 A1
Medway Cres WA16 .... 238 C6
Medway Dr ST6 .... 179 E1
Medway Rd WA3 .... 5 D1
Mee St SK11 .... 112 C3
Meeanee Rd CW5 .... 204 B2
Meerbrook Rd SK3 .... 240 A4
Meeting La WA5 .... 14 C4
Meg La Macclesfield SK11 . 111 F4
  Sutton Lane Ends SK11 ... 113 E1
Megacre ST7 .... 210 A1
Melbourne Ave M90 .... 33 D4
Melbourne Gr CW1 .... 191 E3
Melbourne Rd Blacon CH1 . 117 E2
  Bramhall SK7 .... 35 F3
Melbourne St SK15 .... 242 D1
Melbury CI WA3 .... 9 F3
Melbury Rd SK8 .... 35 D3
Melchett Cres CW9 .... 104 B4
Melford CI CW2 .... 206 B4
Melford Ct WA1 .... 17 E4
Melford Dr
  Macclesfield SK10 .... 87 E1
  Runcorn WA7 .... 23 E3
Meliden Gr WA6 .... 73 D1
Melkridge CI CH2 .... 119 D2
Melksham CI SK11 .... 112 A4
Mell La WA6 .... 98 C2
Mellard St ST7 .... 209 F1
Mellington Ave M20 .... 239 C8
Mellock CI L64 .... 66 C3
Mellock La L64 .... 66 C4
Mellor CI Ashton-u-L OL6 . 242 B2
  Runcorn WA7 .... 24 B1
Mellor Cres WA16 .... 57 F1
Mellor Rd
  Ashton-u-L OL6 .... 242 B3
  Cheadle SK8 .... 242 C4
Mellor St Crewe CW1 ...... 190 B3
  Packmoor ST7 .... 195 F1
Mellors Bank ST7 .... 195 E3

Melrose Ave Appleton WA4 . 26 B4
  Burtonwood WA5 .... 6 C4
  Cheadle SK3 .... 239 F7
  Chester CH3 .... 119 D1
  Sale M33 .... 242 B6
Melrose Cres SK12 .... 37 E3
Melrose Dr Crewe CW1 .... 190 A4
  Ellesmere Port L65 .... 94 C4
Melton Ave WA4 .... 26 A4
Melton CI CW12 .... 155 F2
Melton Dr CW12 .... 155 F2
Melton Rd WA7 .... 49 E4
Melton St SK5 .... 240 F8
Melverly Dr CH1 .... 117 E2
Melville CI Warrington WA2 . 16 A4
  Widnes WA8 .... 13 E1
Melville Rd M44 .... 11 E3
Menai Gr SK8 .... 240 A2
Menai Rd SK8 .... 240 E2
Mendell CI L62 .... 43 F4
Mendell Prim Sch L62 ..... 43 E4
Mendip Ave WA2 .... 8 A2
Mendip CI Cheadle SK8 ... 34 A4
  Ellesmere Port L66 .... 69 E1
  Stockport SK4 .... 240 E7
Mendip Ct SK4 .... 240 E7
Menin Ave WA4 .... 16 B2
Menlow CI WA4 .... 17 E1
Mentmore Gdns WA4 ...... 26 C3
Mentone Rd SK4 .... 240 C7
Meols CI Frodsham WA6 ... 74 A4
  Hale L24 .... 21 F1
Mercer CI SY14 .... 213 D2
Mercer Rd WA11 .... 1 B3
Mercer St Burtonwood WA5 . 6 C3
  Newton-le-W WA2 .... 2 B2
Mercer Way Chester CH4 .. 140 C3
Merchant Way SK5 .... 240 E3
Mercury Ct CH1 .... 117 F1
Mere Ave L63 .... 43 D3
Mere Bank CW9 .... 127 D4
Mere Brook Wlk CW2 ...... 190 B1
Mere CI Ellesmere Port L66 . 69 E1
  Haslington CW1 .... 191 E2
  Pickmere WA16 .... 80 A3
  Sale M33 .... 242 F5
Mere Cres CW8 .... 123 F3
Mere Ct ST7 .... 193 E2
Mere La Cuddington CW8 .. 102 A1
  Winsford CW9 .... 79 F4
  Pickmere WA16 .... 80 B3
Mere Rd Marston CW9 .... 79 D3
  Warrington WA2 .... 9 D1
  Weston CW2 .... 207 D3
Mere Side SK15 .... 242 C4
Mere St CW1 .... 191 E2
Merebank Rd CW2 .... 190 A1
Merebrook Rd SK11 .... 111 F4
Merecroft CH3 .... 119 D1
Meredith Ave WA4 .... 17 D1
Meredith St CW1 .... 190 B3
Merehaven CI WA16 .... 80 A4
Mereheath La
  Knutsford WA16 .... 56 C3
  Mere WA16 .... 56 C3
Mereheath Pk WA16 ...... 56 C2
Merelake Rd Alsager ST7 .. 210 A4
  Alsager ST7 .... 210 A4
Meremore Dr ST5 .... 210 B1
Mereside Ave CW12 .... 156 A2
Mereside CI Cheadle SK8 .. 239 F4
  Macclesfield SK10 .... 87 D1
Mereside Rd WA16 .... 80 B1
Merevale CI WA7 .... 49 F3
Merganser CI CW1 .... 189 F4
Meriton Rd SK9 .... 34 B2
Merlin Ave M33 .... 57 D2
Merlin CI Runcorn WA7 .... 24 A1
  Winsford CW7 .... 150 A4
Merlin Way CW1 .... 190 A4
Merlyn Ave M33 .... 242 C8
Merrick CI WA2 .... 8 C1
Merridale The WA15 .... 32 A4
Merriden Rd SK10 .... 87 D1
Merrill's Ave CW2 .... 189 F3
Merrivale Rd CW2 .... 206 A4
Merrydale CI SK10 .... 86 C1
Merryman's La SK9 .... 84 A4
Mersey PI CW7 .... 127 D1
Mersey Rd Runcorn WA7 .. 23 D2
  Sale M33 .... 242 B8
  Widnes WA8 .... 23 D2
Mersey Sq SK1 & SK4 ..... 240 F5
Mersey St Runcorn WA7 ... 23 D2
  St Helens WA9 .... 1 A2
  Warrington WA1 .... 16 A3
Mersey Vale Prim Sch SK4 . 240 A5
Mersey View WA7 .... 48 B4
Mersey View Rd WA8 ...... 22 A2
Mersey Wlk WA4 .... 16 C3
Merseyton Rd L65 .... 70 B4
Merseyway SK1 .... 240 F6
Merston Dr M20 .... 239 C8
Merton Ave CW9 .... 21 D4
Merton Ave Hazel Grove SK7 . 36 C4
  Romiley SK6 .... 241 A4
Merton CI L64 .... 66 C3
Merton Dr CH4 .... 141 D2
Merton House Sch CH2 ... 118 B3
Merton House St
  (Downswood) CH2 .... 237 D4
Merton Rd Bebington L62 .. 44 A2
  Ellesmere Port L66 .... 69 F2
  Sale M33 .... 242 A8
  ➑ Stockport SK3 .... 240 B4

Mertoun Rd WA4 .... 16 A1
Mervyn Rd CW8 .... 77 F1
Merwood Ave SK8 .... 34 B4
Message La CW12 .... 132 B2
Meteor Cres CW2 .... 8 B1
Mevagissey Rd WA7 .... 50 C1
Mevril Rd SK23 .... 65 F3
Mews The Barnton CW8 ... 78 A1
  Gatley SK8 .... 33 E2
  Styal SK9 .... 33 E2
Meyer CI CW9 .... 168 B4
Meyer St SK2 & SK3 .... 240 F2
Meynell CI CW7 .... 190 A1
Meynell PI CW1 .... 118 A3
Micawber Rd SK12 .... 36 C1
Mickle Trafford Cty Prim
  Sch CH2 .... 119 F4
Micklegate WA7 .... 50 B4
Micklewright Ave CW1 .... 190 B3
Mickly Hall La CW5 .... 218 A2
Mid Cheshire Coll
  (London Road Studios)
  CW9 .... 103 F3
Mid Cheshire Coll
  (Verdin Ctr) CW7 .... 126 B1
Mid-Cheshire Coll CW8 ... 103 E3
Middle Hillgate SK1 .... 240 F4
Middle La Adlington CH3 .. 163 F2
  Congleton CW12 .... 157 E2
  Kingsley WA6 .... 74 C1
  Partington M31 .... 11 E1
Middle Wlk Frodsham WA6 . 74 A4
  Knutsford WA16 .... 57 D1
Middlecroft CH3 .... 119 F3
Middlehills SK11 .... 113 D3
Middlehurst Ave WA8 ..... 102 C4
Middlehurst Rd WA4 ...... 17 D1
Middlewich Cty High Sch
  CW10 .... 151 E4
Middlewich Cty Inf & Jun
  Sch CW10 .... 151 D4
Middlewich Rd
  Allostock WA16 .... 106 A3
  Church Minshull CW1 ...... 172 C3
  Cranage CW4 .... 129 F2
  Cranage CW10 .... 129 F3
  Crewe CW1 .... 189 E2
  Holmes Chapel CW4 ...... 130 A2
  Nantwich CW5 .... 204 C4
  Northwich CW9 .... 104 B4
  Ollerton WA16 .... 82 A2
  Peover WA16 .... 106 B3
  Peover, Smithy Green WA16 . 81 F1
  Sandbach CW11 .... 174 C4
  Winsford CW10 .... 127 F1
  Worleston CW2 .... 189 D2
Middlewich Rd Ind Est
  CW10 .... 129 D3
Middlewich St CW1 .... 190 B3
Middlewood WA3 .... 3 F4
Middlewood Dr SK4 .... 240 A5
Middlewood Rd
  High Lane SK6 .... 37 E3
  Poynton SK12 .... 37 E3
Middlewood Sta (Lower)
  SK6 .... 37 E3
Middlewood View SK6 ..... 37 E4
Midfield CI ST6 .... 179 E1
Midgley Cres SK6 .... 242 B4
Midhurst CI SK8 .... 34 C4
Midland St WA8 .... 13 D1
Midland Terr SK22 .... 39 E4
Midland Way WA1 .... 16 A3
Midway SK8 .... 35 D3
Milborne CI CH2 .... 118 C3
Miles Bank Rd SY13 .... 226 B2
Miles St WA4 .... 16 A1
Miley CI SK4 .... 241 F6
Milford Ave SK8 .... 35 D3
Milk St Congleton CW12 .. 156 B2
  Sale SK8 .... 241 D6
Mill Ave WA5 .... 14 C4
Mill Bank L64 .... 67 D3
Mill Brow WA8 .... 13 E1
Mill CI Chester CH2 .... 118 B3
  Knutsford WA16 .... 57 D2
  Warrington WA3 .... 8 C2
Mill Cotts SK10 .... 88 A4
Mill Field CI CH3 .... 180 C1
Mill Green CI WA3 .... 5 D4
Mill Gr Bulkeley SY14 ..... 184 C1
  Kidsgrove ST7 .... 194 B1
Mill Green La WA13 .... 13 F3
Mill Green Sch WA12 ..... 2 C2
Mill Hill Ave SK7 .... 36 B4
Mill Hill Dr CW11 .... 175 D3
Mill Hollow
  Hazel Grove SK7 .... 36 B4
  Poynton SK12 .... 36 B4
Mill Hill La CW1 .... 175 D2
Mill La Adlington CH3 ..... 163 F2
  Audlem, Little Heath CW3 . 230 A2
  Audlem, Swanback CW3 .. 229 F1
  Bartholmley CW2 .... 208 B4
  Blakenhall CW5 .... 221 D2
  Bold Heath WA8 .... 13 E4
  Brereton Green CW4 ...... 153 F4
  Burton L64 .... 67 E1
  Cheadle SK8 .... 239 D6
  Chester CH2 .... 118 B3
  Congleton CW12 .... 179 E4
  Cronton WA8 .... 12 B3
  Crowton WA6 .... 75 F2
  Cuddington CW8 .... 101 F3
  Denton M34 & SK14 ...... 241 D6
  Duddon CW6 .... 145 D4
  Eaton CW6 .... 147 E1
  Ellesmere Port L66 .... 69 F3

Mill La continued
  Goostrey CW4 .... 107 F1
  Great Barrow CH3 .... 120 C1
  Hazel Grove SK7 .... 36 C1
  Heswall L60 .... 41 D1
  Higher Walton WA4 .... 25 F1
  Huxley CH3 .... 144 E2
  Kingsley WA6 .... 75 F1
  Lindow End SK9 .... 84 A1
  Little Budworth CW6 ..... 125 D1
  Lymm WA13 .... 19 E1
  Macclesfield SK11 .... 112 A4
  Middlewich CW10 .... 128 B3
  Middlewich, Newtonia CW10 128 A3
  Mobberley WA16 .... 58 A4
  Mottram St Andrew SK10 . 61 E1
  Neston L64 .... 67 E4
  News Bank CW12 .... 132 C2
  Norton-le-W WA12 .... 2 A2
  Peover WA16 .... 108 B3
  Prestbury SK10 .... 61 F1
  Sandbach CW11 .... 174 B4
  Siddington SK11 .... 109 A4
  Smallwood CW11 .... 175 F4
  Sutton WA6 .... 49 F1
  Tarvin, Sand Sands CH3 .. 121 F1
  Tarvin, Westwood Common
    CW6 .... 122 A4
  The Bank ST7 .... 195 D1
  Warrington WA2 .... 9 D1
  Warrington, Stockton Heath
    WA4 .... 26 A4
  Weston CW2 .... 207 D2
  Whitegate CW7 .... 149 A4
  Willaston L64 .... 42 C1
  Winwick WA2 .... 8 B4
  Winwick WA3 .... 3 C4
  Wythenshawe WA15 ...... 32 C4
Mill Park Dr L62 .... 43 F4
Mill Park Ind Sch L62 ..... 43 F4
Mill Park Jun Sch L62 ..... 43 F4
Mill Pool La CW5 .... 187 D1
Mill Rd SK11 .... 112 A4
Mill Rise ST7 .... 195 D1
Mill Row CW1 .... 175 D3
Mill St
  Altrincham WA14 & WA15 . 238 D6
  Chester CH4 .... 237 F1
  Congleton CW12 .... 156 B1
  Congleton CW12 .... 156 F2
  Crewe CW2 .... 190 B4
  Goldborne WA3 .... 3 D1
  Hyde SK14 .... 241 F5
  Macclesfield SK11 .... 112 B4
  Neston L64 .... 66 C3
  Stalybridge SK15 .... 242 D1
  Warrington WA1 .... 16 A4
  Wilmslow SK9 .... 60 A4
Mill View Nantwich CW5 .. 204 B4
  Waverton CH3 .... 143 A4
  Widnes WA8 .... 12 B2
Milland CI SK7 .... 36 A4
Millar CI SK7 .... 36 B4
Millards La Lymm WA13 .. 19 F1
Millbank CI SK10 .... 86 C1
Millbank Jun Sch M31 .... 11 E1
Millbeck CI CW2 .... 207 F2
Millbrook Cotts CH3 ...... 166 A4
Millbrook End CH3 .... 166 A4
Millbrook Gr ➌ SK9 .... 34 A4
Millbrook St SK1 .... 240 B4
Millbuck Way CW11 .... 174 C4
Milldale Rd WA3 .... 4 A4
Millend La ST7 .... 209 F4
Miller St WA4 .... 16 A1
Millers La Lymm WA13 .... 19 E1
  Meadow SK10 .... 88 B4
Millers View ST7 .... 195 E3
Millers Wharf ST7 .... 193 F1
Millersdale CI L62 .... 43 F4
Millersdale Gr WA7 .... 49 F4
Millfield La Haydock WA11 . 1 C1
  Saighton CH3 .... 142 C1
Millfield Rd WA8 .... 12 B1
Millfield Terr L66 .... 69 F2
Millfields CW5 .... 204 C2
Millfields Cty Prim Sch
  CW5 .... 204 C2
Millgate Cuddington CW8 . 101 F2
  Stockport SK1 .... 240 F6
Millgreen CW4 .... 130 A4
Millgreen La Runcorn WA7 . 49 D2
Millgreen The CW4 .... 130 A4
Millhouse La WA3 .... 9 D3
Millingford The CW4 ...... 130 A4
Millingford Ind Est WA3 .. 3 D1
Millington Hall La WA14 .. 30 A4
Millington La Runcorn WA7 . 49 D2
  Widnes WA8 .... 22 A1
Millington La WA14 .... 30 B1
Millington La
  Rostherne WA14 .... 30 C4
  Weaverham CW8 .... 102 A4
Millom PI SK8 .... 239 F3
Millrace Dr CW2 .... 206 A4
Mills Way CW1 .... 191 D4
Millstone Ave ST7 .... 194 C4
Millstone CI SK12 .... 36 A4
Millstone La CW5 .... 204 B4
Millstone Pas SK11 .... 112 B4
Millway
  Altrincham WA15 .... 32 A4
  Waverton CH3 .... 143 A4
Millway Rd L24 .... 21 F4
Millwood CI L24 .... 21 F4

Millwood Cty Prim Jun, Mix Sch L24 ... 21 D2
Millwood Terr 2 SK14 ... 241 D6
Milne CI CW2 ... 189 F1
Milner Ave WA14 ... 238 B7
Milner Cop L60 ... 41 D4
Milner Rd Heswall L60 ... 41 D4
　Northwich CW8 ... 103 E3
Milner St WA5 ... 15 F3
Milnthorpe Rd WA5 ... 6 C3
Milton Ave Irlam M44 ... 11 F3
　Newton-le-W WA12 ... 2 A2
　Widnes WA8 ... 22 C4
Milton CI
　Higher Wincham CW9 ... 80 A3
　Middlewich CW10 ... 151 E3
Milton Cres Cheadle SK8 ... 239 C5
　Kidsgrove ST7 ... 210 B4
Milton Dr Poynton SK12 ... 36 B2
　Sale M33 ... 242 B8
　Wistaston CW2 ... 206 A4
Milton Gr Helsby WA6 ... 73 D1
　Poynton SK12 ... 36 B2
　Sale M33 ... 242 A8
　Warrington WA4 ... 16 B2
Milton Rd Blacon CH1 ... 117 F3
　Bramhall SK7 ... 35 F4
　Ellesmere Port L65 ... 70 B2
　Goldborne WA3 ... 3 D4
　Widnes WA8 ... 23 D4
Milton Rough CW8 ... 76 C1
Milton St Chester CH2 ... 237 E3
　Hyde SK14 ... 241 D8
　Widnes WA8 ... 23 D3
Milvain Dr WA2 ... 8 B1
Milverton Dr SK8 ... 35 D3
Milne Way WA11 ... 1 C4
Miners Way Speke L24 ... 21 D2
　Widnes WA8 ... 23 D4
Minerva Ave WA11 ... 117 F1
Minerva CI WA13 ... 18 C1
Minshull La
　Church Minshull CW5 ... 171 E2
　Wettenhall CW7 ... 171 E2
Minshull New Rd CW1 ... 189 F4
Minshull St WA16 ... 57 D1
Minster Ct Runcorn WA7 ... 49 D4
Minster Ct Altrincham WA14 ... 31 D4
　Cheadle SK8 ... 240 A1
Minton CI CW12 ... 157 D1
Minton Way WA8 ... 13 D3
Mirfield Ave WA8 ... 240 B6
Mirfield CI WA3 ... 3 E4
Mirion St CW1 ... 190 B2
Misty CI WA8 ... 12 B1
Mitchell Ave
　Burtonwood WA5 ... 6 C3
　Kidsgrove ST7 ... 194 B1
Mitchell Dr ST7 ... 194 B1
Mitchell St Goldborne WA3 ... 3 D4
　Warrington WA4 ... 26 B4
Mithril CI WA8 ... 13 D3
Mitton CI WA8 ... 4 C3
Moadlock Sk6 ... 241 C4
Moat House Dr CW2 ... 190 A1
Moat La Audley ST7 ... 209 D2
　Hollins Green WA3 ... 10 C1
Mobberley CE Contr Prim Sch WA16 ... 58 B3
Mobberley CI WA4 ... 17 E2
Mobberley Rd Ashley WA14 ... 31 F2
　Knutsford WA16 ... 57 F2
　Wilmslow SK9 ... 33 E1
Mobberley Sta WA16 ... 57 F4
Moelfre Dr SK7 ... 35 F4
Mold Rd CH4 ... 139 D2
Mollets Wood M34 ... 241 A8
Mollington Cl CH1 ... 94 C1
Mollington Rd WA2 ... 33 F4
Molly Pitcher Way WA5 ... 15 D3
Molly Potts CI Hyde SK14 ... 82 A4
Molyneux Ave WA5 ... 15 F4
Mona Ave SK8 ... 239 D1
Mona St SK14 ... 241 E6
Monarch CI M44 ... 11 F3
Mond CI CW7 ... 149 D4
Mond St WA8 ... 78 A2
Money Ash Rd WA15 ... 238 E3
Monica Dr WA8 ... 13 D3
Monk St CW1 ... 190 A3
Monk's La CW3 ... 230 B3
Monks Coppenhall Cty Prim Sch CW1 ... 190 C4
Monks Gr L65 ... 70 A3
Monks La Acton CW5 ... 203 F4
　Crewe CW3 ... 189 F3
Nantwich CW5 ... 204 C3
Monks Orch CW5 ... 204 C3
Monks Way CW8 ... 103 D2
Monkswood CI WA5 ... 7 F1
Monmouth CI WA1 ... 17 F4
Monroe CI WA1 ... 17 D4
Monsall CI SK11 ... 112 C4
Monsall Dr SK11 ... 112 C4
Montague Rd
　Ashton-u-L OL6 ... 242 A3
　Sale M33 ... 242 B6
Montague Way SK15 ... 242 D2
Montclare Cres WA4 ... 16 C1
Montcliffe CI WA3 ... 9 E3

Montgomery CI WA16 ... 57 E2
Montgomery Rd WA8 ... 22 B4
Montgomery Way CW7 ... 149 D4
Montmorency Rd WA16 ... 57 E2
Montpelier Ave WA7 ... 48 C3
Montrose CI
　Macclesfield SK10 ... 87 D1
　Shavington CW2 ... 206 A2
　Warrington WA2 ... 8 C2
Montrose Ct Chester CH4 ... 140 C4
　Holmes Chapel CW4 ... 130 A1
Monument Bd ST7 ... 210 B3
Monument View ST7 ... 209 F1
Mood Gdns SK7 ... 22 C4
Moody St CW12 ... 156 B1
Moor CI WA8 ... 23 D4
Moor La ST5 ... 179 F1
Moor Cres WA8 ... 139 E1
Moor La Elton WA6 ... 72 C1
　Frodsham WA6 ... 74 A4
　Hawarden CH5 ... 116 A1
　Heswall L60 ... 40 C4
　Higher Kinnerton CH4 ... 161 E4
　Higher Kinnerton, Kinnerton Green CH4 ... 161 E3
　Waverton CH3 ... 143 D3
　Widnes WA8 ... 23 D4
　Wilmslow SK9 ... 59 F3
　Woodford SK7 ... 35 F2
Moor Lodge SK4 ... 240 B8
Moor Nook WA3 ... 242 D5
Moor Park Rd M20 ... 239 C8
Moor St CW12 ... 156 C1
Moor Top PI SK4 ... 240 B7
Moorcroft Ave CH3 ... 119 D1
Moorcroft Cres CH3 ... 119 E2
Moorcroft Mews CH4 ... 140 B3
Moordale Rd WA16 ... 57 D1
Moorditch La WA6 ... 48 B1
Moore Ave St Helens WA9 ... 1 A2
　Warrington WA4 ... 17 F2
Moore CI WA8 ... 13 E1
Moore Cty Prim Sch WA4 ... 25 D3
Moore Dr WA11 ... 1 C3
Moore Gr WA11 ... 19 D3
Moore La WA4 ... 25 E3
Moorfield Ave WA4 ... 241 A6
Moorfield Cres WA3 ... 4 A2
Moorfield Cty Prim Sch WA8 ... 13 E2
Moorfield Dr Neston L64 ... 41 E1
　Wilmslow SK9 ... 59 F3
Moorfield Rd WA8 ... 13 E2
Moorfields
　Willaston (nr Nantwich) CW5 ... 205 F3
　Wistaston CW5 ... 205 F3
Moorhead La CW11 ... 154 B2
Moorhill Rd SK11 ... 112 B2
Moorhouse Ave ST7 ... 193 D2
Moorhouse CI CH2 ... 118 B3
Mooring CI WA7 ... 49 F2
Moorings CW12 ... 156 C1
Moorings CI LL64 ... 41 D1
Moorings The Disley SK12 ... 38 E2
　Heswall L60 ... 40 B4
　Middlewich CW10 ... 128 B1
Moorland Ave M33 ... 242 C5
Moorland CI L60 ... 41 D4
Moorland Dr Cheadle SK8 ... 34 C4
　Runcorn WA7 ... 50 C4
Moorland Pk L60 ... 41 C4
Moorland Rd Biddulph ST6 ... 179 F1
　Ellesmere Port L65 ... 69 F4

Morland Ave Bebington L62 ... 43 E3
Neston L64 ... 66 C4
Moray CI CW7 ... 149 D4
Morley CI CH2 ... 119 F4
Morley Dr CW12 ... 157 D1
Morley Gn SK9 ... 33 E1
Morley Rd Runcorn WA7 ... 23 D3
　Warrington WA4 ... 16 A1
Morley St WA1 ... 16 B3
Mornant Ave CW8 ... 240 B6
Morningside Dr M20 ... 239 C8
Mornington Ave
　Cheadle SK8 ... 239 D4
　Ellesmere Port L65 ... 70 B2
Mornington CI 1 CW11 ... 174 B4
Mornington Rd
　Cheadle SK8 ... 239 D4
　Sale M33 ... 242 D7
Morphany La WA3 ... 51 F3
Morreys La CW6 ... 122 C4
Morris Ave WA4 ... 16 C2
Morris CI WA11 ... 1 A3
Morris Dr WA8 ... 77 E1
Morris Pk CW8 ... 103 D2
Morrison St WA5 ... 15 D3
Mort Ave WA4 ... 17 D2
Mortimer Ave WA2 ... 16 A4
Mortimer Dr CW11 ... 175 E3
Mortlake CI WA8 ... 12 B2
Mortlake Cres CH3 ... 119 D1
Morton Ave WA6 ... 73 D1
Morton CI WA5 ... 15 E4
Morton Dr Poynton SK12 ... 36 C2
　Sutton Lane Ends SK11 ... 112 C2
Morton Rd Blacon CH1 ... 117 F2
　Runcorn WA7 ... 50 B4
Morton St WA4 ... 240 E8
Morven CI WA2 ... 8 C2
Morven Dr SK3 ... 240 D3
Moscow Rd E SK3 ... 240 D3
Mosedale Gr WA7 ... 49 F3
Moseley Ave WA4 ... 17 D2
Moseley Grange SK8 ... 239 F3
Moseley Rd SK8 ... 239 F3
Mosley St 2 SK3 ... 240 E4
Mosley St WA1 ... 238 F7
Moss Bank
　Cheadle Hulme SK7 ... 35 E3
　Winsford CW7 ... 126 B1
Moss Bank Rd WA8 ... 23 E4
Moss Bower Rd SK11 ... 112 B2
Moss Brow WA6 ... 87 F4
Moss CI WA16 ... 58 A3
Moss CI Warrington WA4 ... 16 C1
　Willaston L64 ... 68 A4
Moss Croft SK11 ... 190 C4
Moss Dr Manley WA6 ... 98 C2
　Middlewich CW10 ... 151 E3
Moss Farm Recn Ctr CW8 ... 103 E4
Moss Gate WA3 ... 10 A3
Moss Gr Broughton CH4 ... 140 B3
　Lymm WA13 ... 19 D2
Moss Green Way WA9 ... 1 A1
Moss Hey Prim Sch SK7 ... 35 E3
Moss La Alderley Edge SK9 ... 60 A1
　Altrincham WA14 & WA15 ... 238 E4
　Altrincham, Timperley WA15 ... 238 F7
　Bollington SK10 ... 87 F4
　Brereton Green CW12 ... 154 C3
　Cheadle Hulme SK7 ... 35 E3
　Church Minshull CW1 ... 172 A1
　Congleton CW12 ... 156 C1
　Cranage CW10 ... 129 D4
　Crewe CW1 ... 173 D1
　Cuddington CW8 ... 102 A4
　Dunham Massey WA13 ... 20 A4
　Fowley Common WA3 ... 5 F3
　High Legh WA16 ... 29 F3
　High Legh, Sink Moss WA16 ... 28 B2
　Hollins Green WA3 ... 10 A3
　Irlam M44 ... 11 D3
　Knutsford WA16 ... 56 B3
　Lawton-gate ST7 ... 194 C2
　Lostock CW9 ... 105 E4
　Macclesfield SK11 ... 112 B2
　Manley WA6 ... 99 D2
　Middlewich CW10 ... 129 D4
　Mobberley WA16 ... 58 C2
　Moore WA4 ... 25 D3
　Mottram St Andrew SK10 ... 61 D1
　Norley WA6 ... 101 D3
　Northwich CW8 ... 103 E4
　Ollerton WA16 ... 83 E2
　Partington M31 ... 11 F1
　Partington M31 ... 11 F2
　Sandbach CW11 ... 174 B4
　Siddington SK11 ... 109 F1
　St Helens WA9 ... 1 A1
　Styal SK9 ... 33 F3
Moss PI ST7 ... 195 D2
Moss Rd Alderley Edge SK9 ... 60 B1
　Astbury CW12 ... 178 C4
　Congleton CW12 ... 178 C4
　Irlam M44 ... 11 E4
　Lostock SK14 ... 103 E4
　Warrington WA4 ... 17 D2
Moss Side L64 ... 60 A1
Moss Side La Antrobus CW9 ... 53 E4
　Hollins Green WA3 ... 10 C2
　Penketh WA4 ... 240 C4
Moss Side Rd M44 ... 11 F3
Moss Sq Crewe CW1 ... 190 A4
　Macclesfield SK11 ... 112 B2
Moss St Weaverham CW8 ... 77 E1
　Widnes WA8 ... 23 E4
Moss Terr Northwich CW8 ... 78 B1
　Warren SK11 ... 112 A3

Moss The CW9 ... 78 B4
Moss View Rd SK11 ... 112 A2
Moss Way ST7 ... 193 D2
Mossbank CI Crewe CW2 ... 189 F2
　Great Sankey WA5 ... 15 D4
Mossdale CI SK4 ... 240 B6
Mossfields ST7 ... 193 D2
Mossford Ave CW1 ... 190 A4
Mossgrove Rd WA15 ... 238 F6
Mosshall La WA4 ... 26 C1
Mosslands CI L66 ... 69 F1
Mossley Ave L62 ... 43 E4
Mossley CE Centr Prim Sch CW12 ... 179 D4
Mossley Rd OL6 ... 242 B4
Mossvale L66 ... 69 E4
Mosswood Pk M20 ... 239 B8
Mosswood Rd SK9 ... 34 C1
Moston Gr WA13 ... 18 B2
Moston Rd Chester CH2 ... 118 B4
　Sandbach CW11 ... 174 B3
Moston Way L66 ... 69 F2
Mostyn Ave Cheadle SK8 ... 239 E1
　Heswall L60 ... 40 B4
Mostyn Gdns L66 ... 41 E1
Mostyn House Sch L64 ... 66 B4
Mostyn PI CH1 ... 117 F3
Motcombe Farm Rd SK8 ... 239 B1
Motcombe Gr SK8 ... 239 A3
Motcombe Rd SK8 ... 239 A2
Motram CI WA4 ... 17 D2
Motterhead Rd WA8 ... 23 D4
Mottram CI Cheadle SK8 ... 240 A1
　Middlewich CW10 ... 151 E3
Mottram Fold SK1 ... 240 F6
Mottram Old Rd SK15 ... 242 F1
Mottram Rd
　Alderley Edge SK9 ... 60 B1
　Hyde SK14 ... 241 F6
　Sale M33 ... 242 F5
Mottram St 5 SK1 ... 240 F6
Mottram St Andrew GM Prim Sch SK10 ... 61 D1
Moughland La WA7 ... 49 D4
Moulders La WA1 ... 16 A2
Mouldsworth CH ... 103 F2
Mouldsworth Sta CH3 ... 99 D1
Moulton CI Davenham CW9 ... 103 F2
Runcorn WA7 ... 49 F2
Moulton Cty Prim Sch CW9 ... 126 C4
Mount Ave L60 ... 40 C4
Mount Carmel Sch SK9 ... 60 A1
Mount Farm Way L66 ... 69 E1
Mount Hall Mews L60 ... 40 C4
Mount PI CW2 ... 118 C1
Mount Pleasant
　Audlem CW3 ... 230 A2
　Bollington SK10 ... 88 A4
　Chester CH4 ... 140 C4
　Crewe CW1 ... 190 A3
　Elton CH2 ... 72 A2
　Haslington CW1 ... 191 E2
　Kidsgrove ST7 ... 195 D1
　Widnes WA8 ... 13 D1
　Wilmslow SK9 ... 60 B4
Mount Pleasant Ave WA5 ... 1 A2
Mount Pleasant Dr CW7 ... 149 D4
Mount Pleasant Rd
　Davenham CW9 ... 103 F1
　The Bank ST7 ... 195 D4
Mount Rd Kidsgrove ST7 ... 195 D1
　Runcorn WA7 ... 49 F4
　Stockport SK4 ... 240 C6
Mount St Hyde SK14 ... 241 E6
　Stalybridge SK15 ... 242 D2
　Widnes WA8 ... 13 D1
Mount Terr SK11 ... 112 C4
Mount The
　Altrincham WA14 ... 238 D5
　Altrincham, Halebarns WA15 ... 32 B4
　Chester CH3 ... 118 F1
　Congleton CW12 ... 156 A1
　Great Budworth CW9 ... 79 D4
　Heswall L60 ... 40 C4
　Kidsgrove ST7 ... 195 D1
　Scholar Green ST7 ... 194 C4
　Wilmslow SK9 ... 143 D2
Mountain View
　Broughton CH4 ... 140 C3
　Helsby WA6 ... 73 D3
Mountbatten Way CW12 ... 156 B2
Mountfield Rd Bramhall SK7 ... 35 F3
　Stockport SK3 ... 240 C3
Mourne CI L66 ... 69 E1
Mow Cop Rd ST7 ... 195 E3
Mow La Biddulph ST6 ... 179 F1
　Mount Pleasant ST7 ... 195 D3
Mowbray Ave WA3 ... 242 D5
Mowbray St 4 SK1 ... 240 F4
Mowcroft La WA4 ... 26 A1
Mowpen Brow WA16 ... 29 D3
Moxon Ave WA4 ... 16 C1
Moyles CI WA8 ... 12 B1
Mudhouse La L64 ... 67 F1
Mudhurst La SK12 ... 38 C1
Muir Rd CH1 ... 117 F2
Muirfield Ave SK6 ... 241 A4
Muirfield CI Northwich CW9 ... 104 A3
　Warrington WA2 ... 9 D2
　Wilmslow SK9 ... 60 B4
Muirfield Dr
　Macclesfield SK10 ... 87 E2
　Winsford CW7 ... 126 B1
Mulberry Ave WA3 ... 3 F4

Mulberry CI Cheadle SK8 ... 34 B4
Elton CH2 ... 72 B2
Warrington WA1 ... 17 F3
Mulberry Gdns CW11 ... 174 B4
Mulberry Mews SK4 ... 240 E6
Mulberry Mount St SK3 ... 240 E4
Mulberry Rd CW7 ... 189 F1
Mulberry Rise CW8 ... 103 E4
Mulcaster Ct CW1 ... 191 E3
Mull CI L65 ... 70 E1
Mullen CI WA5 ... 7 F1
Mullins Ave WA12 ... 2 B3
Mullion Dr WA15 ... 238 E6
Mullion Gr WA2 ... 9 D1
Mulsford La SY14 ... 222 A4
Murdishaw Ave WA7 ... 50 B3
Murdishaw West Cty Prim Sch WA7 ... 50 B3
Muriel CI WA5 ... 14 B3
Murieston Rd WA15 ... 238 E2
Murray CI SK10 ... 87 D1
Murrayfield SK10 ... 87 D3
Murrayfield Dr CW5 ... 205 E3
Museum St WA1 ... 16 A2
Music Hall Pass CH1 ... 237 E2
Myddleton La WA2 ... 8 B3
Myrica Gr CH2 ... 119 D2
Myrtle Ave Haydock WA11 ... 1 A4
　Higher Kinnerton CH4 ... 161 D4
　Newton-le-W WA12 ... 2 B1
Myrtle Gr Chester CH2 ... 119 D2
　Warrington WA4 ... 16 B2
　Widnes WA8 ... 22 B4
Myrtle Rd M31 ... 11 E2
Myrtle St Ellesmere Port L65 ... 70 B4
　Stockport SK3 ... 240 B4
Mythholme Ave M44 ... 11 E2

Nab CI SK10 ... 63 E1
Nab La SK10 ... 63 E1
Nabbswood Rd ST7 ... 195 D1
Nairn Ave CW4 ... 130 A1
Nairn CI Bebington L63 ... 43 E2
　Warrington WA2 ... 9 D2
Nancy View SK10 ... 63 E1
Nansen Rd SK8 ... 239 A4
Nansmoss La SK9 ... 33 E1
Nantwich Rd Audley ST7 ... 209 D1
　Barbridge CW5 ... 187 D4
　Betley ST7 ... 208 C1
　Broxton CH3 ... 183 E1
　Crewe CW2 ... 190 B1
　Ellesmere Port L66 ... 69 F2
　Middlewich CW10 ... 151 D4
　Tarporley CW6 ... 168 B4
　Tiverton CW6 ... 168 B4
　Wimboldsley CW10 ... 150 C3
　Winsford CW10 ... 151 D4
　Woore CW3 ... 232 A1
　Worleston CW7 ... 189 E1
　Wrenbury WA16 ... 217 D3
Nantwich Sta CW5 ... 204 C2
Naomi CI CH1 ... 117 E3
Napier Gdns ST7 ... 195 D1
Napier Rd Chester CH2 ... 118 B4
　Manchester SK4 ... 240 B7
Napier St Hyde SK14 ... 241 E5
　Warrington WA1 ... 16 B3
Napley Dr TF9 ... 236 B3
Napley Rd Muckelstone TF9 ... 236 B1
Napley Rd Hulse TF9 ... 236 B1
Nares CI WA5 ... 7 E1
Narrow La SK10 ... 37 D1
Naseby Rd CW12 ... 156 A2
Nasmyth Ave WA4 ... 241 A8
Nat La CW7 ... 126 C1
Nathan Dr WA11 ... 1 C3
Naughton Lea WA8 ... 12 B2
Naughton Rd WA8 ... 23 D4
Navigation Cty Prim Sch WA14 ... 238 D2
Navigation Prim Sch WA14 ... 238 D2
Navigation Rd
　Altrincham WA14 & WA15 ... 238 D6
　Northwich CW8 ... 103 F4
Navigation Road Sta WA14 ... 238 E6
Navigation St WA1 ... 16 B3
Naylor Ave WA3 ... 3 D4
Naylor Cres L66 ... 69 E4
Naylor Ct Crewe CW7 ... 103 F4
Naylor Rd WA8 ... 13 E1
Naylor St WA1 ... 16 A3
Neal Ave Ashton-u-L OL6 ... 242 A3
　Cheadle SK8 ... 34 A4
　Gatley SK8 ... 239 A4
Neath CI SK12 ... 36 B3
Needham Ave CW2 ... 23 E1
Needham Dr CW8 ... 103 D2
Needhams Wharf CI SK10 ... 88 A1
Neil St WA8 ... 13 D1
Neills Rd WA9 ... 6 A3
Nelson Ave SK12 ... 37 D2
Nelson CI SK12 ... 37 D2
Nelson Dr M44 ... 11 F3
Nelson Gr ST7 ... 193 F1
Nelson Ind Est ST7 ... 194 B1
Nelson Pit L66 ... 70 B4
Nelson St Chester CH2 ... 237 F3
　Congleton CW12 ... 156 B1
　Crewe CW2 ... 190 B1
　Hyde SK14 ... 241 E6
　Macclesfield SK11 ... 112 B4

Oak Rd continued
Partington M31 .... 11 E1
Penketh WA5 .... 14 C2
Sale M33 .... 242 D6
Oak St Crewe CW2 .... 190 B2
Croft WA3 .... 9 D4
Ellesmere Port L65 .... 70 B4
Hyde SK14 .... 241 E8
Northwich CW9 .... 79 D1
Rode Heath ST7 .... 193 F4
Sandbach CW11 .... 174 B4
Stockport SK3 .... 240 B4
Oak Tree Cl CW1 .... 190 C3
Oak Tree Dr CW1 .... 190 C3
Oak Tree Gate CW3 .... 229 F2
Oak Tree La CW4, CW10 .... 129 F4
Oak View Knutsford WA16 .... 57 E1
Marton SK11 .... 133 E3
Speke L24 .... 21 D2
Oak Wood Rd WA16 .... 29 F1
Oakdale Ave WA4 .... 16 B1
Oakdale Cl CH4 .... 139 D2
Oakdale Dr SK8 .... 239 B2
Oakdene Ave Cheadle SK8 .... 34 A4
Ellesmere Port L66 .... 69 E3
Warrington WA1 .... 17 E4
Oakdene Cl L62 .... 43 E3
Oakdene Way CW6 .... 168 B4
Oakenclough Cl SK9 .... 34 B1
Oakes Cnr CW5 .... 219 F2
Oakfield M33 .... 242 A7
Oakfield Ave Cheadle SK8 .... 239 E6
Chester CH2 .... 118 B4
Knutsford WA16 .... 57 E2
Wrenbury CW5 .... 216 C2
Oakfield Cl
Alderley Edge SK9 .... 60 A2
Wrenbury CW5 .... 216 C2
Oakfield Ct WA15 .... 238 F6
Oakfield Cty Inf & Jun Sch
WA8 .... 22 A4
Oakfield Dr Chester CH2 .... 118 B4
Widnes WA8 .... 22 A4
Oakfield Rd Alderley Edge SK9 60 A1
Altrincham WA15 .... 238 E4
Bebington L62 .... 43 E4
Blacon CH1 .... 117 E2
Ellesmere Port L66 .... 68 C4
Plumley WA16 .... 80 C2
Poynton SK12 .... 36 C2
Stockport SK3 .... 240 F1
Oakfield Rise CW4 .... 130 A2
Oakfield St WA15 .... 238 E5
Oakfield Trad Est WA15 .... 238 E5
Oakham Rd M34 .... 241 A5
Oakhill Cl SK10 .... 87 D2
Oakhurst Chase SK9 .... 60 A1
Oakhurst Dr
Cheadle SK3 & SK8 .... 240 B1
Wistaston CW2 .... 206 A4
Oakland Ave CW1 .... 191 E2
Oakland St
Warrington WA1 .... 16 C4
Widnes WA8 .... 23 D2
Oaklands CH3 .... 119 F2
Oaklands Ave CH3 .... 166 A1
Oaklands Cl SK9 .... 34 C1
Oaklands Cres CH3 .... 166 A1
Oaklands Cty Inf Sch SK9 .... 34 C1
Oaklands Dr Lymm WA13 .... 18 B1
Sale M33 .... 242 A7
Oaklands Rd Goldborne WA3 .... 3 F4
Ollerton WA16 .... 82 C3
Oaklands Sch CW7 .... 149 D4
Oaklea Ave CH2 .... 118 C2
Oakleigh Knutsford WA16 .... 82 B4
Manchester SK4 .... 240 B7
Oakleigh Ct CW12 .... 155 F2
Oakleigh Rise CW8 .... 78 C1
Oakley Cl CW11 .... 175 D4
Oakley St CW1 .... 190 B3
Oakley Villas SK4 .... 240 B7
Oakmere Cl CW11 .... 174 C4
Oakmere Dr Chester CH3 .... 142 A4
Ellesmere Port L66 .... 69 F1
Penketh WA5 .... 14 C2
Oakmere Rd Cheadle SK8 .... 239 F4
Wilmslow SK9 .... 34 B3
Winsford CW7 .... 125 F1
Oakmere St WA7 .... 23 D1
Oaks Dr The CH2 .... 118 B4
Oaks Pl WA8 .... 23 D4
Oaks The Bebington L62 .... 43 E4
Gatley SK8 .... 239 A2
Oaksdean Ct SK9 .... 34 A1
Oakside Cl SK8 .... 239 E6
Oaksway L60 .... 41 E3
Oaktree Cl Barnton CW8 .... 78 A2
Tarporley CW6 .... 146 B1
Oaktree Ct Cheadle SK8 .... 239 D5
Chester CH2 .... 119 D2
Oakway M20 .... 239 C8
Oakways WA4 .... 26 B3
Oakwood Av SK9 .... 59 F3
Oakwood Ave Gatley SK8 .... 239 B5
Warrington WA1 .... 16 C4
Oakwood Avenue Cty Prim Schs WA1 .... 16 B4
Oakwood Cl L66 .... 69 E1
Oakwood Cres Crewe CW2 .... 189 F2
Sandbach CW11 .... 175 F3
Oakwood Ct WA14 .... 31 D4
Oakwood Dr SK10 .... 87 E3
Oakwood Gate WA3 .... 9 E2
Oakwood La
Altrincham WA14 .... 238 B1
Barnton CW8 .... 78 A1
Sandbach CW11 .... 174 A4
Oakwood Rd Disley SK12 .... 38 B3
Rode Heath ST7 .... 193 F4
Romiley SK6 .... 241 C2
Oat Market CW5 .... 204 C3
Oathills SY14 .... 213 D3
Oathills Cl CW6 .... 146 B1
Oathills Dr CW6 .... 146 B1
Oatlands SK9 .... 85 D4
Oban Dr Heswall L60 .... 41 D4
Sale M33 .... 242 E5
Oban Gr WA2 .... 9 D2
Ocean St WA14 .... 238 B6
Ocean Street Trad Est
WA14 .... 238 B7
Off Ridge Hill La SK15 .... 242 C2
Offley Ave CW11 .... 175 D4
Offley Cty Inf & Jun Sch
CW11 .... 175 D4
Offley Rd CW11 .... 175 D4
Ogden Ct SK14 .... 241 E6
Ogden Rd SK7 .... 35 E3
Oglet La L24 .... 46 C4
Oil Sites Rd L65 .... 71 E3
Okell St WA7 .... 23 D1
Old Bank Cl SK6 .... 241 A3
Old Bedions Sports Ctr
M20 .... 239 A8
Old Boston WA11 .... 2 A4
Old Boston Trad Est WA11 .... 2 A4
Old Brickworks Ind Est
SK10 .... 63 F2
Old Butt La ST7 .... 194 B1
Old Chapel St SK3 .... 240 D3
Old Cherry La WA13 .... 28 A4
Old Chester Rd
Barbridge CW5 .... 187 E3
Ellesmere Port L66 .... 69 E2
Helsby WA6 .... 73 E2
Higher Walton WA4 .... 25 F4
Old Church Cl L65 .... 70 B4
Old Coach Rd
Broxton SY14 .... 199 D3
Edge Green SY14 .... 199 D3
Kelsall CW6 .... 122 B3
Old Farm Cl L64 .... 68 A4
Old Gardens St 3 SK1 .... 240 F4
Old Gate Cl CW10 .... 151 D4
Old Gorse Cl CW2 .... 189 F2
Old Hall Ave SK23 .... 65 F2
Old Hall Cl WA4 .... 26 A4
Old Hall Cres SK9 .... 34 C2
Old Hall Ct Ashton CH3 .... 121 F4
Malpas SY14 .... 213 D2
Old Hall Cty Prim Sch
WA5 .... 15 E4
Old Hall Dr L65 .... 70 A2
Old Hall Gdns CH2 .... 237 F4
Old Hall La Elton CH2 .... 72 A2
Knutsford WA16 .... 56 A2
Tabley WA16 .... 55 F2
Woodford SK7 .... 61 E4
Old Hall Pk CH3 .... 119 F3
Old Hall Pl CH1 .... 237 D2
Old Hall Rd Gatley SK8 .... 239 A6
Great Sankey WA5 .... 15 E4
Northwich CW9 .... 104 A3
Sale M33 .... 242 E6
Old Hall St SK10 .... 87 E1
Old Hey Wlk WA12 .... 2 B1
Old Higher Rd WA8 .... 21 E3
Old Hutte La L24 .... 21 D3
Old La Acton Bridge CW8 .... 76 C2
Antrobus CW9 .... 53 E2
Davenham CW9 .... 104 B1
Poulton CH4 .... 162 C1
Pulford CH4 .... 162 C1
Old Liverpool Rd WA5 .... 15 F2
Old Man of Mow The
ST7 .... 195 E4
Old Market Pl
Altrincham WA14 .... 238 D5
Knutsford WA16 .... 57 D1
Old Mill Cl L60 .... 41 D4
Old Mill Ct CH2 .... 118 B3
Old Mill La Hazel Grove SK7 .... 37 D4
Macclesfield SK11 .... 112 C3
Whitley WA4 .... 52 C2
Old Mill Rd CW11 .... 175 E3
Old Moss La Leigh WA3 .... 5 F3
Tarvin CH3 .... 144 B4
Old Oak Dr M34 .... 241 A7
Old Orchard Antrobus CW9 .... 53 E2
Wilmslow SK9 .... 60 A4
Old Orchard The CW8 .... 101 F2
Old Park Rd CW1 .... 207 E4
Old Pearl La CH3 .... 119 D1
Old Quay Cl L64 .... 66 B4
Old Quay La L64 .... 66 B4
Old Quay St WA7 .... 23 D2
Old Rd Anderton CW9 .... 78 B2
Audley ST7 .... 209 F2
Cheadle SK8 .... 239 F6
Hyde SK14 .... 241 D8
Stockport SK4 .... 240 E7
Warrington WA4 .... 16 A2
Whaley Bridge SK23 .... 65 F2
Whaley Bridge, Furness Vale
SK23 .... 39 E2
Whaley Bridge, New Horwich
SK23 .... 65 F3
Wilmslow SK9 .... 60 A4
Wilmslow, Handforth SK9 .... 34 B2
Old Rectory Gdns SK8 .... 239 D5
Old School Cl CH3 .... 180 C1
Old School House La
WA2 .... 8 A4
Old Smithy La WA13 .... 18 B1
Old St SK15 .... 242 D2
Old Stack Yd CH3 .... 120 C3
Old Upton La WA8 .... 12 C2
Old Vicarage Gdns CW3 .... 229 F2
Old Vicarage Rd L64 .... 68 A4
Old Wargrave Rd WA12 .... 2 B2
Old Warrington Rd CW9 .... 79 D1
Old Whint Rd WA11 .... 1 A3
Old Woman's La CH3 .... 142 B4
Old Wool La SK8 .... 239 F4
Old Wrexham Rd CH4 .... 141 E4
Oldfield Brow Prim Sch
WA14 .... 238 A5
Oldfield Cres CH4 .... 140 C3
Oldfield Cty Prim Sch
CH3 .... 119 E2
Oldfield Dr
Altrincham WA15 .... 238 F6
Chester CH3 .... 119 E1
Mobberley WA16 .... 58 A2
Oldfield Gr M33 .... 242 C7
Oldfield La WA14 .... 20 C2
Oldfield Mews WA14 .... 238 C5
Oldfield Rd
Altrincham WA14 .... 238 B5
Ellesmere Port L65 .... 70 A3
Lymm WA13 .... 18 B2
Sale M33 .... 242 C7
Sandbach CW11 .... 174 C2
Oldgate WA8 .... 22 B4
Oldhall St SY14 .... 213 D2
Oldham Dr SK6 .... 241 A4
Oldham St Bollington SK10 .... 88 A4
Hyde SK14 .... 241 D6
Warrington WA4 .... 16 B2
Oldham's Rise SK10 .... 87 E2
Oldhams Hill CW8 .... 78 C1
Oldhill Cl ST7 .... 210 C3
Olive Dr L64 .... 66 C4
Olive Gr ST5 .... 210 B1
Olive Rd L64 .... 66 C4
Oliver Cl SK10 .... 87 F4
Oliver La L66 .... 69 E2
Oliver St
Stockport SK1 & SK3 .... 240 F4
Warrington WA2 .... 16 A3
Ollerbarrow Rd WA15 .... 238 E2
Ollersett Ave SK22 .... 39 E4
Ollersett View Hospl SK22 .... 39 E4
Ollershaw La CW9 .... 79 E2
Ollerton Cl WA4 .... 17 D2
Ollerton Inf & Jun Sch
WA16 .... 83 D2
Ollerton Rd 14 SK9 .... 34 B3
Ollier St 13 WA8 .... 23 D4
One Oak La SK9 .... 60 C4
Onneley La CW3 .... 232 C2
Onslow Rd Blacon CH1 .... 117 E2
Stockport SK3 .... 240 C4
Onston La CW8 .... 101 F4
Onward St SK14 .... 241 D6
Openshaw La M44 .... 11 F3
Orange Gr WA2 .... 8 C1
Orange La CW9 .... 79 E1
Orchard Ave
Acton Bridge CW8 .... 76 C2
Lymm WA13 .... 18 C2
Partington M31 .... 11 F2
Whaley Bridge SK23 .... 65 E4
Orchard Brow WA3 .... 11 D1
Orchard Cl Barnton CW8 .... 78 A2
Cheadle Hulme SK7 .... 35 E4
Chester CH2 .... 118 B3
Ellesmere Port L66 .... 69 F1
Frodsham WA6 .... 74 A3
Goostrey CW4 .... 107 F1
Higher Wincham CW9 .... 80 A3
Macclesfield SK11 .... 112 A3
Middlewich CW10 .... 151 E4
Poynton SK12 .... 36 C2
Weaverham CW8 .... 77 E1
Wilmslow SK9 .... 59 F3
Winsford CW7 .... 149 E4
Orchard Cres
Kidsgrove ST7 .... 194 B1
Nantwich CW5 .... 204 C2
Nether Alderley SK10 .... 84 C3
Orchard Croft CH3 .... 119 F3
Orchard Ct Alsager ST7 .... 193 F2
Chester CH3 .... 119 D1
Haslington CW1 .... 191 E2
Orchard Dene CW8 .... 101 E3
Orchard Dr
Little Leigh CW8 .... 77 E3
Neston L64 .... 66 C3
Wilmslow SK9 .... 34 C1
Orchard Gn SK9 .... 60 A1
Orchard Gr CH3 .... 180 C1
Orchard Haven L66 .... 69 F1
Orchard La L66 .... 69 D4
Orchard Park La CH2 .... 72 B2
Orchard Pl WA6 .... 73 E2
Orchard Rd
Altrincham WA15 .... 238 E5
Ellesmere Port L65 .... 70 A1
Lymm WA13 .... 19 D3
Whaley Bridge SK23 .... 65 E4
Orchard Rise CW9 .... 126 C4
Orchard St Chester CH1 .... 237 D3
Crewe CW1 .... 190 B3
Hyde SK14 .... 241 E6
Northwich CW9 .... 104 A4
Stockport SK1 .... 240 F5
Warrington WA1 .... 16 B3
Warrington, Fearnhead WA2 .... 9 D1
Warrington, Hillcliffe WA4 .... 26 B4
Willaston (nr Nantwich)
CW5 .... 205 E3
Orchard Vale SK3 .... 240 C2
Orchard Way
Congleton CW12 .... 156 A2
Kelsall CW6 .... 122 B3
Widnes WA8 .... 12 A2
Orchards The
Broughton CH4 .... 140 B3
Pickmere WA16 .... 79 F3
Shavington CW2 .... 206 B2
Orchid Cl Huntington CH3 .... 142 A3
Irlam M44 .... 11 F4
Orchil Cl L66 .... 69 D3
Ordnance Ave WA3 .... 9 F2
Ordsall Cl CW11 .... 174 C2
Orford Ave Disley SK12 .... 38 B3
Warrington WA2 .... 16 B4
Orford Cl Hale L24 .... 21 E1
High Lane SK6 .... 37 F4
Orford Gn WA2 .... 8 B1
Orford La WA2 .... 16 A4
Orford Rd WA2 .... 16 C4
Orford St WA1 .... 16 A3
Oriel Bank High Sch SK3 .... 240 F1
Orkney Cl Ellesmere Port L65 .... 70 B1
Widnes WA8 .... 13 F2
Orme Cl Macclesfield SK10 .... 87 E2
Prestbury SK10 .... 87 D4
Orme Cres SK10 .... 87 E2
Ormerod Cl Romiley SK6 .... 241 A1
Sandbach CW11 .... 175 E3
Ormesby Gr L63 .... 43 D3
Ormond Cl WA8 .... 12 B1
Ormonde Rd CH2 .... 118 B2
Ormonde St CH2 .... 237 F3
Ormston Ave WA12 .... 2 A3
Orphanage St SK4 & SK5 .... 240 E7
Orrell Cl WA5 .... 15 D3
Orrishmere Rd SK8 .... 239 F3
Orton Cl CW7 .... 127 D2
Ortonbrook Prim Sch M31 .... 11 F1
Orwell Cl SK9 .... 34 B1
Osborne Ave WA2 .... 8 B1
Osborne Gr Gatley SK8 .... 239 A3
Shavington CW2 .... 206 B3
Osborne Rd
Altrincham WA15 .... 238 E5
Goldborne WA3 .... 3 F4
Hyde SK14 .... 241 E5
Stockport SK2 .... 240 F3
Warrington WA4 .... 16 A1
Osborne Terr M33 .... 242 B6
Osbourne Pl 7 WA14 .... 238 D4
Osier Cl CH2 .... 72 B2
Osmere Cl SY13 .... 226 A1
Osprey Ave CW7 .... 149 E3
Osprey Cl
Middlewich CW10 .... 151 E3
Runcorn WA7 .... 49 F3
Warrington WA2 .... 8 C2
Osprey Dr SK9 .... 60 B4
Osprey View ST7 .... 195 E2
Ossett Cl WA7 .... 50 B4
Ossmere Cl CW11 .... 174 C4
Ostler's La WA16 .... 58 C4
Otters Bank CW7 .... 126 A1
Otterspool Rd SK6 .... 241 B1
Oughtrington Cres WA13 .... 19 D2
Oughtrington Cty Prim Sch
WA13 .... 19 D2
Oughtrington La WA13 .... 19 D1
Oughtrington View WA13 .... 19 D2
Oulton Ave Chester CH2 .... 118 B4
Sale M33 .... 242 E7
Oulton Dr CW12 .... 155 F2
Oulton Mill La Eaton CW6 .... 147 D4
Utkinton CW6 .... 147 D4
Oulton Pl CH1 .... 237 E3
Our Lady of Lourdes RC Prim Sch M31 .... 11 F2
Our Lady of Perpetual Succour RC Aided Inf Sch
WA8 .... 12 A1
Our Lady of Perpetual Succour RC Aided Jun Sch
WA8 .... 22 A4
Our Lady's RC Aided Prim Sch Runcorn WA7 .... 50 A3
Warrington WA4 .... 16 C2
Our Lady's RC Inf & Jun Sch L65 .... 70 A2
Our Lady's RC Prim Sch
SK3 .... 240 E4
Out La CH3 .... 184 B3
Outwood Dr SK8 .... 34 A4
Outwood La M90 .... 33 D4
Outwood La W M90 .... 33 D4
Outwood Prim Sch SK8 .... 34 B4
Outwood Rd SK8 .... 34 A4
Oval The Cheadle SK8 .... 34 A4
Ellesmere Port L65 .... 70 B2
Ovenhouse La SK10 .... 87 F4
Over Hill Dr CW7 .... 149 E4
Over Rd CW5 .... 172 A4
Overdale La CW8 .... 101 E1
Overdale Rd Disley SK12 .... 38 C3
Romiley SK6 .... 241 A1
Willaston L64 .... 43 D1
Overdene Rd CW7 .... 149 E4
Overfields WA16 .... 57 E2
Overhill Dr SK9 .... 60 C4
Overhill La SK9 .... 60 C4
Overhill Rd SK9 .... 60 B4
Overleigh Ct CH4 .... 141 E4
Overleigh Rd CH4 .... 141 E4
Overleigh St Mary's CE Contr Prim Sch CH4 .... 141 E4
Overpool Gdns L66 .... 69 F2
Overpool Rd L65 .... 69 F3
Overpool Sta L66 .... 69 F3
Overton Cl
Congleton CW12 .... 156 B2
Middlewich CW10 .... 151 D4
Overton Dr WA6 .... 74 B3
Overton Rd ST6 .... 179 F3
Overton Way 4 SK9 .... 34 B3
Overway CW7 .... 126 C1
Overwood Ave CH1 .... 94 C1
Overwood La Blacon CH1 .... 117 E2
Mollington CH1 .... 94 B1
Ovington Cl WA7 .... 49 F2
Owen Cl CH1 .... 117 F3
Owen St Crewe CW2 .... 190 B1
Stockport SK3 .... 240 D5
Warrington WA2 .... 16 A4
Owley Wood Rd CW8 .... 77 F1
Ox-Hey Cres ST6 .... 179 E1
Ox-Hey Dr ST6 .... 179 E1
Oxborough Cl WA8 .... 12 C2
Oxenham Rd WA2 .... 8 A2
Oxford Cl CH1 .... 94 C4
Oxford Ct 4 SK10 .... 112 C4
Oxford Dr Halewood L26 .... 21 D4
Romiley SK6 .... 241 C4
Thornton Hough L63 .... 41 F3
Oxford Gr M44 .... 11 E3
Oxford Rd Altrincham WA14 .... 238 D3
Chester CH4 .... 140 C3
Macclesfield SK11 .... 112 A4
Runcorn WA7 .... 49 D4
Oxford St Crewe CW1 .... 190 A3
Newton-le-W WA12 .... 2 A2
Stalybridge SK15 .... 242 F1
Oxford St continued
Warrington WA4 .... 16 B2
Widnes WA8 .... 23 D4
Oxford Way SK4 .... 240 D7
Oxhey Fst Sch ST8 .... 179 F1
Oxheys WA7 .... 50 B4
Oxmead Cl WA2 .... 9 D1
Oxmoor Cl WA7 .... 50 A3
Oxney Cl SK11 .... 111 F4
Oxton Cl WA8 .... 12 B2
Oxton Gn L66 .... 69 E2

Pacific Rd WA14 .... 238 A6
Packmoor Prim Sch ST7 .... 195 F1
Packsaddle Pk SK10 .... 86 C3
Padarn Cl CH4 .... 140 B3
Padden Brook SK6 .... 241 B2
Padden Brook Mews SK6 .... 241 B2
Paddington Bank WA1 .... 16 C3
Paddock Brow SK10 .... 87 D3
Paddock Chase SK12 .... 36 C3
Paddock Dr L64 .... 41 E1
Paddock Hill WA16 .... 59 D1
Paddock La Audlem CW3 .... 230 A1
Dunham Town WA13 .... 20 A3
Kettleshulme SK23 .... 64 C2
Partington WA13 .... 19 E4
Whaley Bridge SK23 .... 65 F3
Paddock Rd CH4 .... 141 F1
Paddock Rise WA7 .... 49 F2
Paddock The Cheadle SK8 .... 239 E5
Chester CH4 .... 141 D4
Ellesmere Port L66 .... 69 E2
Elton CH2 .... 72 A2
Hartford CW8 .... 103 E2
Hassall Green CW11 .... 175 F1
Helsby WA6 .... 73 E1
Heswall L60 .... 41 E4
Lymm WA13 .... 19 E2
Tarporley CW6 .... 146 B1
Whaley Bridge SK23 .... 65 F3
Willaston (nr Nantwich)
CW5 .... 205 E2
Wilmslow SK9 .... 34 B2
Paddock Way CH4 .... 161 D4
Paddock Wlk CW8 .... 101 E3
Paddockhill La WA16 .... 59 D2
Paddocks Gn CW12 .... 178 C4
Paddocks The
Nova Scotia CW8 .... 125 D3
Prestbury SK10 .... 87 D3
Padgate Bsns Ctr WA1 .... 17 D4
Padgate Cty High Sch WA2 .... 8 C1
Padgate La WA1 .... 16 C4
Padgate Sta WA1 .... 9 D1
Padgbury Cl CW12 .... 156 A1
Padgbury La CW12 .... 156 A1
Padston Dr ST7 .... 193 D2
Padstow Cl Crewe CW1 .... 190 B4
Macclesfield SK10 .... 111 F4
Penketh WA5 .... 14 C2
Padstow Dr SK7 .... 35 F4
Padstow Sq WA7 .... 50 A3
Padworth Pl CW1 .... 173 D1
Page Gr CW2 .... 206 A2
Page La WA8 .... 13 E1
Paignton Cl WA5 .... 14 C2
Painswick Rd L66 .... 69 F1
Paisley Ave L62 .... 43 F2
Palace Fields Ave WA7 .... 50 A4
Palace Fields Local Ctr
WA7 .... 50 A3
Palace Hey L64 .... 67 D3
Palace Rd M33 .... 242 A7
Palacefields Cty Prim Sch
WA7 .... 50 A3
Palatine Cl CH1 .... 117 E3
Palgrave Cl CH1 .... 118 A3
Palin Dr WA5 .... 14 B4
Pall Mall CW5 .... 204 C3
Pallard Ave WA6 .... 74 B4
Palliser Cl WA3 .... 10 A2

Palm Gr L66 .... 70 A1
Palmer Ave SK8 .... 239 F6
Palmer Cres WA5 .... 15 E4
Palmer Rd CW11 .... 175 E3
Palmer St M33 .... 242 A6
Palmerston Cl CW1 .... 191 E3
Palmerston Rd SK11 .... 112 A4
Palmerston St SK10 .... 88 A4
Palmerston Way ST6 .... 179 E1
Palmerstone Cl CH1 .... 118 A2
Palmyra Sq N WA1 .... 16 A3
Palmyra Sq S WA1 .... 16 A3
Panda Way CW11 .... 175 D3

Pangbourne Cl
Appleton WA4 .... 26 C3
Stockport SK3 .... 240 C2
Panton Pl CH2 .... 118 C2
Panton Rd CH2 .... 118 C2
Parade Rd M90 .... 33 E4
Parade The Blacon CH1 .... 117 F7
Neston L64 .... 41 D1
Paradise CH4 .... 237 E1
Paradise La CW5 .... 171 F4
Paradise Mill (Mus) SK11 .. 112 B4
Paradise St SK11 .... 112 B4
Paragon Cl WA3 .... 13 D3
Parbold Ct WA8 .... 22 B4
Parchments The WA12 .... 2 B2
Parish Cl ST7 .... 193 D2
Park Ave Altrincham WA15 .. 238 F1
Altrincham, Timperley WA15 .. 238 F8
Broughton CH4 .... 140 C3
Cheadle SK8 .... 239 F1
Cheadle SK3 .... 239 F1
Cheadle Hulme SK7 .... 35 E3
Haydock WA11 .... 1 A3
Hyde SK14 .... 241 D8
Kidsgrove ST7 .... 210 C4
Poynton SK12 .... 36 C2
Romiley SK6 .... 241 C2
Sale M33 .... 242 A8
Saughall CH1 .... 94 A1
Tattenhall CH3 .... 166 A1
Warrington WA4 .... 16 B2
Weaverham CW8 .... 77 E1
Whaley Bridge SK23 .... 39 E2
Widnes WA8 .... 13 D1
Wilmslow SK9 .... 60 B4
Winsford CW7 .... 127 D2
Park Ave N WA12 .... 2 B1
Park Ave S WA12 .... 2 B1
Park Bank CW12 .... 156 C1
Park Brook Rd SK11 .... 112 A4
Park Bvd WA1 .... 16 A2
Park Cl Altrincham WA14 ...... 238 F8
Stalybridge SK15 .... 242 C3
Tarvin CH3 .... 121 D1
Park Court Mews SK8 .... 239 E4
Park Cres Appleton WA4 .... 26 B3
Ashton-u-L OL6 .... 242 B2
Cuddington CW8 .... 101 F2
Whaley Bridge SK23 .... 39 E2
Wilmslow SK9 .... 34 A1
Park Ct Chester CH2 .... 237 F2
Frodsham WA6 .... 74 A2
Runcorn WA7 .... 49 D4
Sale M33 .... 242 A8
Park Cty Prim Sch The
Runcorn WA7 .... 24 A1
Tattenhall CH3 .... 166 A1
Park Dr Altrincham WA15 ...... 238 F1
Chester CH2 .... 119 D2
Ellesmere Port L65 .... 70 A2
Hyde SK14 .... 241 D8
Stockport SK4 .... 240 A6
Wistaston CW2 .... 205 F4
Park Dr S CH2 .... 119 D2
Park Est CW2 .... 206 B3
Park Gn SK11 .... 112 B4
Park Ho SK4 .... 240 B8
Park House Dr
Prestbury SK10 .... 87 D4
Sandbach CW11 .... 175 E4
Park House La SK10 .... 87 D4
Park House Mews CW11 ...... 175 E4
Park La Appleton WA4 .... 26 A3
Audley ST7 .... 209 D2
Bate Heath WA16 .... 79 F4
Congleton CW12 .... 156 C1
Frodsham WA6 .... 74 A4
Hargrave CH3 .... 144 C2
Hartford CW8 .... 103 D2
Hatherton CW5 .... 219 F2
Higher Walton WA4 .... 25 F3
Little Bollington WA14 .... 20 A1
Macclesfield SK11 .... 112 B3
Moulton CW9 .... 126 C4
Pickmere WA16 .... 79 F4
Poynton SK12 .... 36 C2
Sandbach CW11 .... 174 C3
Park Lane Sch SK11 .... 112 A3
Park Lodge Cl SK8 .... 239 E4
Park Mount SK8 .... 239 A5
Park Mount Cl SK11 .... 112 A3
Park Mount Dr SK11 .... 112 A3
Park Rd
Altrincham WA15 .... 238 F1
Altrincham, Bowdon WA14 ...... 238 A2
Bebington L62 .... 43 F3
Cheadle SK8 .... 239 E6
Congleton CW12 .... 156 C2
Disley SK12 .... 38 A6
Eaton CW12 .... 134 C1
Ellesmere Port L65 .... 70 B2
Goldborne WA3 .... 3 D4

Park Rd continued
Great Sankey WA5 .... 14 B4
Haslington CW1 .... 191 E3
Heswall L60 .... 41 B1
High Lane SK6 .... 37 F3
Hyde SK14 .... 241 D8
Little Budworth CW6 .... 124 C1
Lymm WA13 .... 29 E4
Macclesfield SK11 .... 112 B3
Middlewich CW10 .... 128 B1
Nantwich CW5 .... 204 C2
New Mills SK22 .... 39 E4
Northwich CW8 .... 78 B1
Partington WA13 .... 19 E4
Romiley SK6 .... 241 C2
Runcorn WA7 .... 49 D4
Sale M33 .... 242 A8
Stalybridge SK15 & SK16 ...... 242 A2
Tarporley CW6 .... 146 B1
Thornton-le-M CH2 .... 71 F1
Warrington WA2 .... 8 B1
Whaley Bridge SK23 .... 65 E3
Widnes WA8 .... 13 D1
Willaston L64 .... 68 A4
Willaston (nr Nantwich)
CW5 .... 205 E3
Wilmslow SK9 .... 59 F4
Park Rd N WA12 .... 2 C2
Park Rd S WA12 .... 2 B1
Park Rd W CH4 .... 141 D4
Park Rise SK6 .... 241 C3
Park Road Cty Prim Sch
WA5 .... 14 C3
Park Road Prim Sch
Altrincham WA14 .... 238 EB
Sale M33 .... 242 A8
Park St Bollington SK10 .... 88 A4
Chester CH1 .... 237 E2
Congleton CW12 .... 156 C1
Haydock WA11 .... 1 A3
Macclesfield SK11 .... 112 B4
Neston L64 .... 66 C4
Northwich CW8 .... 103 F4
Stalybridge SK15 .... 242 E1
[6] Stockport SK1 .... 240 E6
Park The Christleton CH3 ...... 142 C4
Penketh WA5 .... 14 B2
Park Vale Rd SK11 .... 112 B3
Park View Audlem CW3 .... 230 B4
Bebington L62 .... 43 E4
Cheadle SK3 .... 239 F7
Gatley SK8 .... 239 A6
Little Bollington WA14 .... 20 A1
Park View Ct SK6 .... 241 C2
Park View Rd ST7 .... 195 D2
Park W CH1 .... 117 F1
Park Way CH1 .... 94 A2
Park West L60 .... 40 C4
Park Wlk CH2 .... 118 C2
Parkdale Ind Est WA4 .... 16 B2
Parkdale Rd WA1 .... 17 D4
Parker Ave CW8 .... 103 D3
Parker Dr CH3 .... 180 C1
Parker Dr S CH3 .... 180 C1
Parker St Macclesfield SK11 . 112 C4
Runcorn WA7 .... 23 D2
Warrington WA1 .... 16 A3
Parker's Rd CW1 .... 190 A4
Parker's Row CH3 .... 180 C3
Parkers Ct WA7 .... 49 F3
Parkett Heyes Rd SK11 .... 111 F4
Parkfield L65 .... 70 A1
Parkfield Ave WA4 .... 17 D2
Parkfield Ct WA14 .... 238 C4
Parkfield Dr
Ellesmere Port L65 .... 70 A2
Helsby WA6 .... 73 D2
Nantwich CW5 .... 204 C2
Parkfield Rd
Altrincham WA14 .... 238 C4
Broughton CH4 .... 139 E2
Cheadle SK8 .... 239 F1
Knutsford WA16 .... 82 A4
Northwich CW9 .... 104 B4
Parkfields La WA2 .... 8 C2
Parkgate Ave WA16 .... 108 A4
Parkgate Ct CH1 .... 118 A2
Parkgate Cty Prim Sch
L64 .... 41 E1
Parkgate La
Knutsford WA16 .... 57 E2
Thornton Hough L63 .... 41 F3
Parkgate Rd Chester CH1 .... 118 A2
Macclesfield SK11 .... 112 B2
Mollington CH1 .... 117 F4
Neston L64 .... 66 B4
Puddington L66 .... 68 A3
Saughall CH1 .... 94 B2
Shotwick CH1 .... 93 F4
Warrington WA4 .... 16 B1
Parkgate Trad Est WA16 .... 57 E2
Parkgate Way Runcorn WA7 . 50 D2
Willmslow SK9 .... 34 B2
Parkhill Ct WA13 .... 18 B4
Parkhouse Ind Est ST5 .... 210 C1
Parkhouse Rd E ST5 .... 210 C1
Parkhouse Rd W ST5 .... 210 C1
Parkland Cl WA4 .... 27 D2
Parkland Dr CH2 .... 118 C2
Parklands Ellesmere Port L66 . 69 E3
Kidsgrove ST7 .... 195 D1
Widnes WA8 .... 12 B2
Parklands Cty Prim Sch
L66 .... 69 E3
Parklands Dr Elton CH2 .... 72 B2
Heswall L60 .... 41 E3
Parklands Gdns L66 .... 69 E3

Parklands The
Congleton CW12 .... 157 D1
Macclesfield SK8 .... 240 EB
Parklands View L66 .... 69 E3
Parklands Way L66 .... 36 C2
Parklea CW5 .... 69 E3
Parkroyal Cty Prim Sch
SK11 .... 112 B4
Parkside SK6 .... 37 E4
Parkside Cl SK6 .... 37 E4
Parkside Hospl SK10 .... 112 A4
Parkside Rd
Newton-le-W WA3, WA12 .... 3 D1
Sale M33 .... 242 D5
Winwick WA3, WA12 .... 3 D1
Parkstone Dr CW1 .... 190 A4
Parksway WA1 .... 17 E4
Parkview Pk WA13 .... 29 E4
Parkway Cheadle SK3 .... 239 F7
Deeside Ind Est CH5 .... 92 C1
Wilmslow SK9 .... 60 A3
Parkwood Cl Bebington L62 .... 43 F4
Lymm WA13 .... 18 B1
Parliament St CW8 .... 103 F4
Parliament Way CH1 .... 94 C4
Parlington Cl WA8 .... 22 B4
Parnell Sq CW12 .... 157 D1
Parr Flat Comm Jun Sch
WA9 .... 1 A2
Parry Dr WA4 .... 26 B1
Parry Mead SK6 .... 241 A4
Parson St CW12 .... 156 B1
Parsonage Ct SK4 .... 240 B8
Parsonage Gn SK9 .... 60 A4
Parsonage Rd
Manchester SK4 .... 240 C8
Widnes WA8 .... 23 D2
Parsonage St Hyde SK14 ...... 241 D5
Macclesfield SK11 .... 112 B4
Stockport SK4 .... 240 E6
Parsonage Way
Cheadle SK8 .... 240 B1
Great Sankey WA5 .... 15 D3
Parsons La CH2 .... 118 A4
Partington Prim Sch M31 ... 11 F2
Partridge Cl
Congleton CW12 .... 156 C1
Warrington WA3 .... 9 F4
Partridge Way CW9 .... 79 F3
Parvey La SK11 .... 112 C2
Pastures Ct Kelsall CW6 .... 122 B2
Macclesfield SK10 .... 88 A4
Pasture Dr WA3 .... 9 D4
Pasture La WA2 .... 9 D1
Pasturefield Cl M33 .... 242 A6
Patch La SK7 .... 35 E3
Patmos La WA16 .... 105 F4
Patrivale Cl WA1 .... 16 C3
Patten La WA1 .... 16 A3
Patterdale Ave WA2 .... 8 B1
Patterdale Rd
Partington M31 .... 11 F2
Romiley SK6 .... 241 B4
Patterson Cl WA3 .... 2 A2
Patterson St WA12 .... 2 A2
Paul Cl WA5 .... 14 B3
Paul St WA2 .... 16 A3
Paulden Rd CW9 .... 80 A1
Pavement La WA16 .... 57 F2
Pavilions The
Davenham CW9 .... 103 F1
Eccleston CH4 .... 141 D2
Paxford PI SK9 .... 60 A3
Payne Cl WA5 .... 15 B3
Paythorne Cl WA3 .... 4 C2
Peach Field CH3 .... 142 A4
Peach Gr WA11 .... 1 C4
Peach Tree Cl L24 .... 21 F1
Peacock Ave Cheadle SK9 .... 34 A3
Warrington WA1 .... 16 C3
Winsford CW7 .... 149 E3
Peacock Cty Hay Rd ST7 ...... 210 C2
Peacock La WA16 .... 29 F3
Peacock Way SK9 .... 34 B3
Peak Rd SK22 .... 39 E4
Peakdale Ave SK8 .... 239 B1
Pear Tree Ave Crewe CW1 . 190 A4
Runcorn WA7 .... 49 E4
Pear Tree Cl Frodsham WA6 . 49 E1
Hale L24 .... 21 F1
Winsford CW7 .... 149 E4
Pear Tree Dr
Higher Wincham CW9 .... 80 A3
Stalybridge SK15 .... 242 E2
Pear Tree Farm Cotts
CW9 .... 104 C2
Pear Tree La
Aston Bridge CW8 .... 76 C2
Whitchurch SY13 .... 225 E1
Pear Tree Rd ST7 .... 209 F1
Pear Tree Way
Chester CH2 .... 118 C3
Ellesmere Port L66 .... 69 F2
Pearl La CH3 .... 119 D1
Pearl St SK10 .... 87 D4
Pearle St SK10 .... 87 E1
Pearlings The CH3 .... 119 D1
Pearson Ave WA4 .... 16 B1
Pearson St
[2] Macclesfield SK11 .... 112 C4
Reddish SK5 .... 240 F7
Peartree Cl CW11 .... 175 F3

Peartree SY13 .... 222 B1
Peartree PI WA4 .... 16 B2
Pearwood Cl CW6 .... 146 B1
Peasdale Cl SK6 .... 241 D2
Peasley Cl WA2 .... 9 D1
Pebble Brook Cty Prim
Sch 190 B1
Pebble Cl SK15 .... 242 D4
Peck Mill La WA6 .... 99 A4
Peckfield Cl WA7 .... 50 A3
Peckforton Castle CW6 .... 167 F1
Peckforton Cl Gatley M22 .. 239 A5
Sandbach CW11 .... 174 C4
Peckforton Dr
Ellesmere Port L66 .... 69 F2
Runcorn WA7 .... 49 F2
Peckforton Hall La
Peckforton CW6 .... 185 D3
Spurstow CW6 .... 185 D3
Peckforton Rd CW6 .... 168 A1
Peckforton Way
Chester CH2 .... 118 C3
Northwich CW8 .... 103 F4
Peckmill Cl SK9 .... 34 C1
Pedley Hill Adlington SK10 .. 62 C4
Rainow SK10 .... 88 D2
Pedley House La WA16 .... 58 C1
Pedley La Chelford WA16 ...... 83 E4
Congleton CW12 .... 157 F2
Pedley St CW2 .... 190 B1
Peebles Cl
Ellesmere Port L66 .... 68 C3
Holmes Chapel CW4 .... 130 A1
Peel Ave WA14 .... 238 D2
Peel Cres CH3 .... 121 F4
Peel Dr Astbury CW12 .... 178 A4
Sale M33 .... 242 E6
Peel Hall La CH3 .... 121 F4
Peel Hollow ST7 .... 209 D1
Peel La WA4 .... 13 D1
Peel Rd WA15 .... 238 E3
Peel Sq CW1 .... 190 A3
Peel St Crewe CW1 .... 190 A3
Hyde SK14 .... 241 F5
Macclesfield SK11 .... 112 B3
Newton-le-W WA12 .... 2 A3
Runcorn WA7 .... 22 C1
Stalybridge SK15 .... 242 C1
Stockport SK2 .... 240 F2
Peelgate Dr SK8 .... 239 A6
Peerglow Pk Est WA14 .... 238 EB
Peerswood Ct L64 .... 66 C3
Peewit Cl CW7 .... 149 E3
Peggie's La SK10 .... 62 B1
Pelham Cl CW1 .... 191 D3
Pelham Rd WA4 .... 17 E2
Pelican Cl CW1 .... 191 D3
Pemberton Cl L64 .... 68 A4
Pemberton Rd CH1 .... 237 D3
Pembridge Ct L65 .... 70 C2
Pembridge Gdns L65 .... 70 C2
Pembroke Cl CW4 .... 141 F3
Pembroke Ct WA7 .... 24 B3
Pembroke Dr L65 .... 70 A2
Pembroke Gdns WA1 .... 26 B2
Pembroke Gr M44 .... 11 E5
Pembroke Rd SK11 .... 111 F4
Pembroke Way CW7 .... 149 D4
Pemston Ct L66 .... 69 F2
Penare WA7 .... 50 B3
Penbrook Cl CW2 .... 189 E2
Pendennis Rd SK4 .... 240 C7
Pending Cl WA5 .... 7 F1
Pendle Cl CW1 .... 191 D3
Pendle Gdns WA3 .... 4 C1
Pendlebury Rd SK8 .... 239 B6
Pendlebury St WA4 .... 17 D2
Penfold Cl CH1 .... 94 A4
Penfold Hey CH2 .... 118 B4
Penfold Way M44 .... 162 A4
Penfold Wlk WA7 .... 23 E1
Penhale Mews SK7 .... 35 F4
Penistone Dr L66 .... 69 D3
Penketh's La WA7 .... 22 C2
Penketh Ave WA5 .... 15 F4
Penketh Ct WA7 .... 23 D1
Penketh Cty High Sch
WA5 .... 15 D3
Penketh Cty Prim Sch
WA5 .... 14 B2
Penketh Rd WA5 .... 15 D2
Penkford La WA5 .... 1 B1
Penkford Sch WA12 .... 1 C2
Penkford St WA12 .... 1 C2
Penkrih South Cty Prim
Sch WA5 .... 14 C2
Penlington Ct CW5 .... 204 C3
Penman Cres L65 .... 21 D4
Penmark Cl WA5 .... 7 F1
Penmon Cl CH1 .... 117 E2
Penn Gdns L65 .... 70 A3
Penn House Cl WA3 .... 4 C2
Penn La WA7 .... 22 C1
Pennant Cl WA3 .... 10 A2
Pennine Cl SK10 .... 87 F1
Pennine Dr
Altrincham WA14 .... 238 B5
Congleton CW12 .... 156 A4
Pennine Rd WA2 .... 8 B2
Pennine View SK15 .... 242 F4
Pennine Way Biddulph ST6 . 179 F1
Winsford CW7 .... 149 D4
Pennine Wlk L66 .... 69 D3
Pennington Cl WA6 .... 49 E1
Pennington Flash Ctry Pk
.... 4 A4
Pennington Gn L66 .... 69 E2

Pennington La WA5 .... 1 B1
Penninstons La SK11 .... 111 F3
Penny La Burtonwood WA5 ..... 1 B3
Cronton WA8 .... 12 A3
Haydock WA11 .... 2 A4
Rainow SK10 .... 88 B2
Stockport SK5 .... 240 F7
Penny's La
Lach Dennis CW9 .... 105 D3
Northwich CW9 .... 104 C4
Pennyfields Rd ST7 .... 195 E1
Pennymoor Dr WA14 .... 238 B6
Pennypleck La CW9 .... 28 A1
Penrhyn Ave SK8 .... 239 EB
Penrhyn Cres
Hazel Grove SK7 .... 36 B4
Runcorn WA7 .... 49 D4
Penrhyn Rd Northwich CW8 . 103 F4
Stockport SK3 .... 240 C4
Penrith Ave
Macclesfield SK11 .... 111 F5
Warrington WA2 .... 8 B1
Penrith Cl Frodsham WA6 ..... 49 E3
Partington M31 .... 11 F2
Penrose Gdns WA5 .... 14 B2
Penry Ave WA4 .... 11 C2
Penryn Cl WA5 .... 14 C2
Pensarn Gdns WA5 .... 7 F1
Pensarn Gr SK5 .... 240 F8
Pensby Ave CH2 .... 118 B3
Pensby Dr L66 .... 69 E2
Pensby Rd L60 .... 40 C4
Penshaw Ct WA7 .... 49 F4
Pentland Ave WA2 .... 8 B2
Pentland Cl Chester CH3 .... 119 D3
Winsford CW7 .... 149 D4
Pentland Pl WA2 .... 8 B2
Pentre Cl CH3 .... 121 F4
Pentre La CH3 .... 121 F4
Penzance Ct SK10 .... 111 F4
Peover Ave M33 .... 242 E6
Peover Hall WA16 .... 107 F4
Peover La Chelford SK11 .... 108 C4
Congleton CW12 .... 157 F2
Peover Rd 3 SK8 .... 34 C1
Peover Superior Endowed
Contr Prim Sch WA16 .... 108 A4
Pepper St Appleton WA4 .... 27 D2
Chelford SK11 .... 83 F1
Chester CH1 .... 237 E2
Christleton CH3 .... 142 C4
Hale L24 .... 21 E1
Henbury SK11 .... 111 D4
Lymm WA13 .... 18 C2
Middlewich CW10 .... 128 B3
Mobberley WA16 .... 31 F3
Nantwich CW5 .... 204 C1
Poppers The WA13 .... 218 C2
Percival Cl CW2 .... 118 B4
Percival La Ollerton WA16 .... 83 D2
Runcorn WA7 .... 22 C2
Percival Rd Chester CH2 .... 118 B4
Ellesmere Port L65 .... 70 A3
Percival St WA1 .... 16 B1
Percy James Cl ST7 .... 193 F2
Percy Rd CH4 .... 141 E4
Percy St Northwich CW9 ...... 104 A4
Stalybridge SK15 .... 242 C1
Stockport SK3 .... 240 F6
Warrington WA5 .... 15 F1
Peregrine Cl CW7 .... 149 E1
Perimeter Rd CW2 .... 72 B3
Periwood Cl WA7 .... 23 D1
Perrin Ave WA7 .... 48 C1
Perrin St WA14 .... 241 D6
Perrins Rd WA5 .... 6 C1
Perth Cl Bramhall SK7 .... 35 F1
Holmes Chapel CW4 .... 130 A1
Warrington WA2 .... 8 C1
Peter House Rd SK11 .... 112 C1
Peter PI CW1 .... 190 A1
Peter Salem Dr WA5 .... 15 D3
Peter St Altrincham WA14 ... 238 D2
Denton M34 .... 241 A1
Goldborne WA3 .... 3 D4
Macclesfield SK11 .... 112 B4
Northwich CW9 .... 103 F4
Peter St W SK11 .... 112 B4
Peterborough Cl SK10 .... 87 D3
Peterhouse Gdns SK6 .... 241 C1
Peters Cl SK10 .... 87 D3
Petersburg Rd SK3 .... 240 D3
Petersfield Gdns WA3 .... 4 C2
Petersgate SK4 .... 50 B3
Petersham Dr WA4 .... 26 C2
Peterstone Cl WA5 .... 7 E1
Petrel Ave SK12 .... 36 A4
Petrel Cl CW7 .... 149 E1
Petunia Cl SK11 .... 112 A4
Petworth Ave WA2 .... 8 A1
Petworth Cl CW2 .... 206 A4
Pevensey Dr WA16 .... 82 A4
Peverel Cl WA4 .... 26 C1
Peveril Dr SK7 .... 36 C1
Peveril Gdns SK12 .... 39 D3
Peveril Mews SK12 .... 39 D3
Peveril Rd WA14 .... 238 C2
Peveril Wlk SK11 .... 111 F5
Peveril's La CW5 .... 231 D3
Pewithall Cty Jun Sch WA7 . 49 F4
Pewterspear La WA4 .... 26 C1
Pexhall Rd CW4 .... 130 C3
Pexhill Ct SK4 .... 240 A6
Pexhill Dr SK10 .... 87 D1
Pexhill Rd Henbury SK11 ..... 111 F5
Macclesfield SK11 .... 111 E5
Siddington SK11 .... 110 B1
Warren SK10, SK11 .... 111 E5

Pheasant Cl WA3 ... 9 F2
Pheasant Dr CW9 ... 79 F3
Pheasant Field L24 ... 21 E1
Pheasant Rise WA14 ... 238 D1
Pheasant Way CW7 ... 149 E3
Pheasant Wlk WA16 ... 29 E2
Philip Rd WA8 ... 22 A4
Philip St CH5 ... 116 A1
Philips La WA5 ... 14 B4
Philips La L65 ... 69 E2
Phillip St CH2 ... 118 C2
Phillips Rd CH1 ... 117 E2
Phillips Way L60 ... 40 C4
Phipps' La WA5 ... 6 C4
Phoenix Ave WA5 ... 7 F1
Phoenix St CH5 ... 116 A2
Phythian Cres WA5 ... 14 C2
Piccadilly WA3 ... 240 F5
Pichael Nook WA4 ... 17 D2
Pickenham Cl SK11 ... 111 F3
Pickering Cres WA4 ... 17 E2
Pickering Rd WA8 ... 22 A3
Pickering St CH2 ... 237 F4
Pickering's Pasture WA8 ... 22 A2
Pickerings Cl WA7 ... 49 E3
Pickford St SK11 ... 112 B4
Pickford's Brow 3 SK1 ... 240 F5
Pickmere Cl
  Sandbach CW11 ... 174 C4
  Stockport SK3 ... 240 C2
Pickmere Dr Bebington L62 ... 43 F2
  Chester CH3 ... 142 A4
  Runcorn WA7 ... 50 B3
Pickmere Gdns SK8 ... 239 F4
Pickmere La
  Higher Wincham CW9 ... 79 F3
  Pickmere WA16 ... 55 E1
  Tabley WA16 ... 55 E1
Pickmere Rd SK9 ... 34 B3
Pickmere St WA5 ... 15 F3
Pickwick Cl CW11 ... 175 E4
Pickwick Pl ST7 ... 194 B1
Pickwick Rd SK12 ... 36 B2
Picow Farm Rd WA7 ... 22 C1
Picow St WA7 ... 23 D1
Picton Ave
  Ellesmere Port L65 ... 70 B3
  Runcorn WA7 ... 23 D1
Picton Cl Bebington L62 ... 43 F2
  Davenham CW9 ... 103 F2
  Warrington WA3 ... 9 E2
Picton Dr Wilmslow SK9 ... 34 C1
  Winsford CW7 ... 126 A1
Picton Gorse La
  Chester CH2 ... 119 D4
  Picton CH2 ... 119 D4
Picton La Mickle Trafford CH2 96 B2
  Picton CH2 ... 96 B2
  Stoak CH2 ... 96 B2
Picton Sq CW4 ... 130 B2
Piele Rd WA11 ... 1 C4
Pierce St SK11 ... 112 B4
Pierpoint La CH1 ... 237 E2
Pierpoint St Goldborne WA3 ... 3 D4
  Warrington WA5 ... 15 F4
Pigot Pl WA4 ... 16 A4
Pike La WA6 ... 75 D2
Pike Rd SK10 ... 89 D3
Pike St WA4 ... 16 B1
Pike The CW5 ... 204 C2
Pikemere Rd ST7 ... 193 D3
Pikemore Cty Prim Sch
  ST7 ... 193 D3
Pikenall La CW8 ... 76 B2
Pilgrim Cl WA1 ... 8 A3
Pillmoss La WA4 ... 52 A4
Pilmoor Cl WA4 ... 26 B3
Pimblett Rd WA11 ... 1 C4
Pimblett St WA3 ... 3 D4
Pimmcroft Way M33 ... 242 F5
Pincot Rd SK22 ... 39 E4
Pine Ave Newton-le-W WA12 ... 2 B1
  Widnes WA8 ... 13 D1
Pine Cl Haydock WA11 ... 1 B3
  Macclesfield SK10 ... 87 F1
Pine Ct ST7 ... 193 F2
Pine Gdns CH2 ... 118 B3
Pine Gr Chester CH2 ... 119 D2
  Denton M34 ... 241 A7
  Ellesmere Port L66 ... 70 A1
  Goldborne WA3 ... 3 E4
  Sandbach CW11 ... 175 E3
  Warrington WA1 ... 17 D4
  Winsford CW7 ... 127 D1
Pine Rd Bramhall SK7 ... 35 F4
  Heswall L60 ... 41 E4
  Macclesfield SK10 ... 87 F1
  Poynton SK12 ... 36 A2
  Runcorn WA7 ... 49 E4
Pine St SK3 ... 240 D4
Pine Tree Cl CH4 ... 139 E2
Pine Trees WA16 ... 57 F4
Pine Wlk CW5 ... 204 C2
Pinedale Cl CH1 ... 95 D4
Pinehey L64 ... 41 E1
Pinehurst SK10 ... 86 C3
Pinellas WA7 ... 23 D2
Pinetree Cl CW8 ... 78 A2
Pineways WA4 ... 26 B3
Pinewood WA14 ... 238 A2
Pinewood Ave WA16 ... 16 C4
Pinewood Cl Elton CH2 ... 72 B2
  Manchester SK4 ... 240 A7

Pinewood Dr L60 ... 41 D4
Pinewood Gr ST5 ... 210 C1
Pinewood Rd
  Burtonwood WA5 ... 7 D4
  Wilmslow SK9 ... 60 C4
Pinfold Ct CH4 ... 141 F3
Pinfold La Chelford WA16 ... 83 E3
  Chester CH4 ... 141 F4
  Little Budworth CW6 ... 147 F4
  Middlewich CW10 ... 128 A1
  Plumley WA16 ... 81 D2
  Romiley SK6 ... 241 E4
  Wythenshawe M90 ... 32 C3
Pinfold St 5 SK11 ... 112 B4
Pinfold Way CW8 ... 77 E1
Pingard's La CW8 ... 101 E3
Pingate Dr SK8 ... 35 D3
Pingate La SK8 ... 35 D3
Pingate La S SK8 ... 35 D3
Pingot Croft CH3 ... 142 A4
Pinmill Brow WA6 ... 74 A4
Pinmill Cl WA6 ... 74 B4
Pinners Brow WA2 ... 16 A3
Pinsley Green Rd CW5 ... 216 C1
Pinsley View CW5 ... 216 C2
Pintail Pl CW7 ... 149 E3
Pipe La WA1 ... 9 E1
Piper's Cl L60 ... 40 B4
Piper's End L60 ... 40 B4
Piper's La L60 ... 40 B4
Pipers Ash CW7 ... 126 A1
Pipers Ct CH2 ... 119 D2
Pipers La Chester CH2 ... 119 D2
  Puddington L64 ... 93 D4
Pipers The WA3 ... 3 F4
Pipit Ave WA12 ... 2 B2
Pipit La WA3 ... 9 F2
Pippin Cl CW10 ... 151 E4
Pippits Row WA7 ... 49 F2
Pirie Cl CW12 ... 157 D2
Pirie Rd CW12 ... 157 D2
Pit La
  Hough Common CW2 ... 206 C1
  Kingsgrove ST7 ... 210 B3
  Widnes WA8 ... 13 D2
Pitt St Hyde SK14 ... 241 D7
  Macclesfield SK11 ... 112 B3
  Stockport SK3 ... 240 D4
  Warrington WA5 ... 15 F4
Pitts Cl CH3 ... 121 E1
Pitts Heath La WA7 ... 24 C2
Pitville Terr WA8 ... 22 B4
Pius XII RC Aided Prim Sch
  L66 ... 69 E3
Place Rd WA14 ... 238 C6
Plaistow Ct WA7 ... 49 F4
Plane Gr ST5 ... 210 C1
Plane Tree Dr CW1 ... 190 C3
Plane Tree Gr WA11 ... 2 A4
Plane Tree Rd M31 ... 11 E2
Plant Cl M33 ... 242 A7
Plant La CW11 ... 174 A4
Plant St CW11 ... 175 D4
Plantagenet Cl CW7 ... 149 E3
Plantation Cl WA7 ... 24 A1
Plantation Dr L66 ... 69 F4
Plantation St OL6 & SK16 ... 242 A2
Plas Newton La CH2 ... 118 C3
Platt Ave CW11 ... 175 D4
Platt St SK8 ... 239 B5
Platt's La CH3 ... 164 C3
Platts La Christleton CH3 ... 143 E4
  Tarvin CH3 ... 121 D1
  Tarvin, Broom Bank CH3 ... 144 A4
  Tattenhall CH3 ... 183 F4
Platts St WA11 ... 1 A3
Play St SK6 ... 240 F4
Pleasance Way WA12 ... 2 B2
Pleasant St
  Macclesfield SK10 ... 87 F1
  Northwich CW9 ... 103 F1
Pleasant Way SK7 ... 35 E3
Pleck Rd L65 ... 70 A1
Plemstall Cl CH2 ... 119 F4
Plemstall La CH2 ... 97 D1
Plemstall Way CH2 ... 96 C1
Plex The ST7 ... 193 E2
Plinston Ave WA4 ... 16 C2
Plough La CH3 ... 143 D4
Ploughmans Cl CH1 ... 94 C4
Ploughmans Way
  Ellesmere Port CH66 ... 94 C4
  Macclesfield SK10 ... 87 D2
Plover Ave CW7 ... 149 E3
Plover Cl Farndon CH3 ... 180 C1
  Newton-le-W WA12 ... 2 B2
Plover Dr
  Altrincham WA14 ... 238 B8
  Runcorn WA7 ... 50 A4
Plovers La WA6 ... 73 E3
Plum Terr CH1 ... 237 D3
Plumbs Fold CW8 ... 78 A1
Plumley Cl Chester CH3 ... 119 E1
  Stockport SK3 ... 240 F1
Plumley Moor Rd WA16 ... 81 E1
Plumley Rd SK9 ... 34 B3
Plumley Sta WA16 ... 81 D2
Plumpstons La WA6 ... 49 D1
Plumtre Ave WA5 ... 15 F4
Plymouth Cl WA7 ... 50 C3
Plymouth Dr SK7 ... 35 F4
Plymouth Gr SK3 ... 240 F1
Plymyard Ave L62 ... 43 E3
Plymyard Cl L62 ... 43 E3
Plymyard Copse L62 ... 43 E3
Poachers La WA4 ... 16 C2
Pochard Ave CW7 ... 149 E3

Pochard Dr
  Altrincham WA14 ... 238 B7
  Poynton SK12 ... 36 A2
Pochard Rise WA7 ... 50 A4
Pochin Way CW10 ... 128 C1
Pocket Nook La WA3 ... 4 A4
Pocklington Ct WA2 ... 8 C1
Pole La CW9 ... 53 F1
Poleacre Dr WA8 ... 12 B1
Police St 1 WA14 ... 238 D5
Pollen Rd WA14 ... 238 C6
Polperro Cl
  Macclesfield SK10 ... 86 B1
  Warrington WA5 ... 14 C2
Pond St WA3 ... 4 A4
Pond View Cl L60 ... 41 E4
Pond Wlk WA9 ... 1 A1
Pool End Cl SK10 ... 87 E2
Pool End Rd SK10 ... 87 E2
Pool Hall Ind Est L65 ... 70 A4
Pool House Rd SK12 ... 37 E3
Pool La Elton CH2 ... 71 F2
  Haslington CW11 ... 192 A4
  Lymm WA13 ... 18 A2
  Runcorn WA7 ... 48 C4
  Tarvin CH3 ... 121 E2
  Warrington WA4 ... 16 A1
Pool Rd WA3 ... 11 D2
Pool Side ST7 ... 194 A4
Pool St Macclesfield SK11 ... 112 C3
  Widnes WA8 ... 23 D4
Poolcroft M33 ... 242 F5
Poole Ave WA2 ... 8 A1
Poole Cres WA2 ... 8 A1
Poole Hall La L65 ... 69 F4
Poole Hall Rd L65 ... 69 F4
Poole La CH2 ... 71 F1
Poolford La CW4 ... 129 E1
Pools La CW11 ... 177 D3
Pools Platt La CW9 ... 53 F3
Poolside CH ST7 ... 193 F2
Poolside Rd WA7 ... 23 D1
Pooltown Cty Jun Sch
  L65 ... 69 F3
Pooltown Rd L65 ... 69 F3
Poplar Ave
  Altrincham WA14 ... 238 B6
  Culcheth WA3 ... 4 C1
  Moulton CW9 ... 126 C4
  Newton-le-W WA12 ... 2 B2
  Penketh WA5 ... 14 C2
  Warrington WA1 ... 17 D4
  Wilmslow SK9 ... 59 F3
Poplar Cl Congleton CW12 ... 156 A2
  Cuddington CW8 ... 102 A2
  Gatley SK8 ... 239 B5
  Runcorn WA7 ... 49 E4
  Winsford CW7 ... 149 D4
Poplar Dr Alsager ST7 ... 193 F1
  Kidsgrove ST7 ... 195 D1
  Middlewich CW10 ... 151 E4
Poplar Gr Bollington SK10 ... 88 A4
  Crewe CW1 ... 190 C3
  Elton CH2 ... 72 A2
  Haydock WA11 ... 1 B3
  Sale M33 ... 242 B5
  Liga TF9 ... 236 C3
Poplar Rd Chester CH4 ... 140 C3
  Haydock WA11 ... 1 B3
  Macclesfield SK11 ... 112 B3
  Weaverham CW8 ... 102 B2
Poplar Way SK6 ... 38 A4
Poplars Ave WA2 ... 8 B2
Poplars The WA7 ... 4 B4
Poplar Weint L64 ... 66 C4
Popular Gr M44 ... 11 E3
Popular Wlk M31 ... 11 E3
Porlock Cl Heswall L60 ... 41 D3
  Penketh WA5 ... 14 C2
Port St M1 ... 240 E6
Portal Gr M34 ... 241 B5
Porter Ave WA12 ... 2 B3
Porter Dr CW9 ... 104 B3
Porter St WA7 ... 23 E1
Porter Way CW9 ... 104 B3
Porters Croft CH3 ... 119 F3
Portford CH SK10 ... 86 C1
Porthcawl Cl WA8 ... 12 B2
Portland Dr Biddulph ST6 ... 179 E1
  Scholar Green ST7 ... 194 C3
Portland Gr Haslington CW1 191 E3
  5 Manchester SK4 ... 240 B8
Portland Pl WA6 ... 73 E2
Portland St WA14 ... 238 D3
Portland St
  Newton-le-W WA12 ... 1 C2
  Runcorn WA7 ... 22 C2
Portland Wlk SK11 ... 111 F4
Portleven Rd WA7 ... 50 A3
Portloe Rd SK8 ... 34 A4
Portman Pl 1 CW7 ... 149 D4
Portmarnock Cl SK10 ... 87 D2
Portola Cl WA4 ... 17 E1
Portrea Cl SK12 ... 240 F1
Portree Ave L63 ... 43 E3
Portree Dr CW4 ... 130 A1
Portrush Dr SK10 ... 87 E2
Portside WA7 ... 50 C4
Portsmouth Pl WA7 ... 50 C3
Portwood Pl SK1 ... 240 F6
Posnett St SK3 ... 240 C4
Post Office La Betley CW2 ... 207 F1
  Hampton SY14 ... 213 E4
  Norley WA6 ... 100 C4
  Runcorn WA7 ... 48 B4
Post Office Pl CW9 ... 79 D1
Post Office St WA14 ... 238 D5
Postles Pl CW9 ... 103 F3

Pott Shrigley Church Sch
  SK10 ... 63 E2
Potters End ST6 ... 179 E1
Potters La WA8 ... 21 F3
Poulton Cres WA1 ... 17 E4
Poulton Dr WA8 ... 22 B4
Poulton Hall Rd L63 ... 43 D4
Poulton Rd L63 ... 43 D4
Poulton Rd L66 ... 69 E4
Povey Rd WA2 ... 8 B1
Powell Ave Hyde SK14 ... 241 E7
  Warrington WA9 ... 9 F2
Powell St WA4 ... 16 C2
Powell's Orch CH4 ... 141 E4
Powey La Mollington CH1 ... 94 A3
  Saughall CH1 ... 94 A3
Powicke Wlk SK6 ... 241 A1
Pownall Ave SK7 ... 35 F4
Pownall Cl SK7 ... 59 F4
Pownall Green Cty Prim
  Sch SK7 ... 35 F4
Pownall Hall Sch SK9 ... 59 F4
Pownall Rd
  Altrincham WA14 ... 238 D3
  Wilmslow SK9 ... 59 F4
Pownall Sq SK1 ... 112 A4
Pownall St SK7 ... 87 E1
Powy Dr ST7 ... 195 D1
Powys Sch SY14 ... 222 A4
Powys St WA5 ... 15 F3
Poynton Cl WA4 ... 17 D2
Poynton Cty High Sch
  SK12 ... 36 C1
Poynton St 9 SK11 ... 112 B4
Poynton Sta SK12 ... 36 B2
Pratchitts Row CW5 ... 204 C3
Preece Cl WA8 ... 12 B2
Preece Ct CW1 ... 190 A3
Preesall Ave SK8 ... 34 A4
Prenton Cl CH4 ... 141 F4
Prescot Rd
  Altrincham WA15 ... 238 F2
  Widnes WA8 ... 12 B1
Prescot Cl CH2 ... 118 C2
Prescot Rd SK9 ... 34 A1
Prescott St WA4 ... 16 C2
Prescott Wlk M34 ... 241 B5
Prestbury Ave WA5 ... 14 B4
Prestbury CE Aided Prim
  Sch SK10 ... 86 C4
Prestbury Dr WA4 ... 17 E2
Prestbury La SK10 ... 87 D4
Prestbury Rd
  Macclesfield SK11 ... 112 B4
  Nether Alderley SK10 ... 86 A3
  Nether Alderley, Adder's Moss
    SK10 ... 85 F3
  Wilmslow SK9 ... 60 C3
Prestbury Sta SK10 ... 87 D4
Preston Ave M44 ... 11 E4
Preston On The Hill WA4 ... 50 C3
Preston St W SK11 ... 112 A3
Prestwich Ave WA3 ... 4 C2
Prestwick Cl
  Macclesfield SK10 ... 87 E3
  Winsford CW7 ... 126 B1
Prestwood Ct WA3 ... 10 A4
Pretoria St CH4 ... 141 E4
Price Ave CW11 ... 175 D3
Price Gr WA9 ... 1 A1
Priest Ave SK8 ... 239 A4
Priest La SK10 ... 61 D1
Priest St SK1 ... 240 F3
Priestfield Rd L65 ... 70 B3
Priestley Coll WA1 ... 16 B2
Priestley St WA5 ... 15 F3
Priestner Dr WA6 ... 73 D2
Priestway La CW7 ... 67 F1
Priesty Ct CW12 ... 156 B1
Priesty Fields CW12 ... 156 B1
Primitive St ST7 ... 195 E4
Primrose Ave
  Haslington CW1 ... 191 E3
  Macclesfield SK11 ... 112 A3
  Warrington WA8 ... 22 C1
Primrose Cotts WA14 ... 238 C1
Primrose Cl WA11 ... 1 C4
Primrose Hill Crewe CW2 ... 189 F3
  Cuddington CW8 ... 101 F2
  Kelsall CW6 ... 122 C3
Primrose La WA6 ... 73 D1
Primrose Way CW9 ... 79 D1
Prince Albert St CW2 ... 190 B1
Prince Edward St CW5 ... 204 C3
Prince Henry Sq WA1 ... 16 A3
Prince Rd SK12 ... 37 E3
Prince William Ave CH5 ... 116 A2
Prince's Ave WA6 ... 74 A4
Prince's Rd SK6 ... 241 A3
Prince's St 4 Stockport SK1 240 E6
  Widnes WA8 ... 23 D4
Princes Ave Bebington L62 ... 43 F2
  Chester CH2 ... 237 F3
  Northwich CW9 ... 104 A4
Princes Cl WA7 ... 23 F1
Princes Dr M33 ... 242 D5
Princes Pk WA8 ... 78 A1
Princes Pk WA8 ... 12 C1
Princes Rd
  Altrincham WA14 ... 238 D6
  Ellesmere Port L65 ... 70 A3
  Manchester SK4 ... 240 A8
  Sale M33 ... 242 D5

Princes St WA12 ... 2 A2
Princes Way SK11 ... 111 F4
Princess Ave Audley ST7 ... 209 E1
  Great Sankey WA5 ... 14 C4
  Haydock WA11 ... 1 A4
  Warrington WA1 ... 16 C3
  Warrington, Paddington WA1 ... 17 D4
Princess Cl CW2 ... 205 F4
Princess Cres
  Middlewich CW10 ... 151 E3
  Warrington WA1 ... 16 C3
Princess Ct ST7 ... 210 B3
Princess Dr Bollington SK10 ... 87 F4
  Nantwich CW5 ... 205 D3
  Sandbach CW11 ... 175 D4
  Wistaston CW2 ... 205 F4
Princess Gr CW2 ... 205 F4
Princess Rd Lymm WA13 ... 18 B2
  Wilmslow SK9 ... 59 F3
Princess St
  Altrincham WA14 ... 238 C8
  Ashton-u-L OL6 ... 242 A4
  Bollington SK10 ... 87 F4
  Chester CH1 ... 237 D2
  Congleton CW12 ... 156 B2
  Crewe CW1 ... 190 B3
  Hyde SK14 ... 241 E6
  Kidsgrove ST7 ... 210 B3
  Knutsford WA16 ... 57 D1
  Northwich CW9 ... 79 F1
  Runcorn WA7 ... 23 D2
  Warrington WA5 ... 15 C2
  Winsford CW7 ... 127 D1
Princess Wlk SK7 ... 36 A4
Princeway WA6 ... 74 A4
Printworks Rd SK15 ... 242 F3
Prior Cl CW2 ... 189 F1
Priory Ave CW9 ... 103 F2
Priory Cl Chester CH2 ... 118 B2
  Congleton CW12 ... 179 D4
  Crewe CW1 ... 190 A4
  Runcorn WA7 ... 24 A1
  Sale M33 ... 242 D8
  Winsford CW7 ... 126 B2
Priory Ct SK10 ... 86 C1
Priory La SK10 ... 86 C1
Priory Pl Chester CH1 ... 237 E2
  Kidsgrove ST7 ... 195 E2
Priory Rd Altrincham WA14 ... 31 D4
  Cheadle SK8 ... 240 A1
  Runcorn WA7 ... 24 B1
  Sale M33 ... 242 D7
  Wilmslow SK9 ... 59 F3
Priory St M33 ... 242 A6
Priory St Altrincham WA14 ... 238 C1
  Northwich CW9 ... 104 A4
  Warrington WA4 ... 16 A2
Priory The WA2 ... 8 B2
Priory Way CW8 ... 103 D2
Priscilla St CW1 ... 190 C2
Pritchard Dr CW9 ... 103 F1
Probert Cl CW2 ... 190 A2
Proctor Cl WA8 ... 13 E1
Proctors La CW11 ... 174 C3
Proffits La WA6 ... 73 F2
Promised Land La CH3 ... 142 C3
Prospect Ave M44 ... 11 F3
Prospect Dr
  Altrincham WA15 ... 32 B4
  Daventham CW9 ... 103 F1
Prospect La WA3 ... 10 B2
Prospect Rd M44 ... 11 F3
Prospect St CW12 ... 156 B1
Prospect Vale Prim Sch
  SK8 ... 239 B1
Prosperity Way CW10 ... 128 B1
Prosser Rd CH2 ... 95 E1
Provan Way CH1 ... 117 E3
Providence St OL6 ... 242 A4
Provident St WA9 ... 1 A2
Prunus Rd CW1 ... 190 C3
Pryors The CH3 ... 121 E2
Ptarmigan Pl CW7 ... 149 E3
Public Hall St WA7 ... 23 D2
Pudding La CH6 ... 168 A4
Puddington La Neston L64 ... 92 C4
  Puddington L64 ... 93 D4
Puffin Ave SK12 ... 36 A2
Pulford Cl Davenham CW9 ... 103 F2
  Runcorn WA7 ... 49 F3
Pulford Ct CH4 ... 162 B1
Pulford La CH4 ... 162 A3
Pulford Rd Blacon CH1 ... 117 F3
  Ellesmere Port L65 ... 69 F1
  Winsford CW7 ... 126 B1
Pullman Cl L60 ... 41 E4
Pullman Dr CH4 ... 104 B4
Pump La Churton CH3 ... 181 D3
  Runcorn WA7 ... 49 F4
Pumptree Mews SK11 ... 111 F4
Purdy Cl WA5 ... 7 F1
Purley Dr M44 ... 11 E3
Purser La SY14 ... 211 F2
Puss Bank Cty Inf & Jun
  Sch SK10 ... 112 C4
Putney Ct WA7 ... 49 F4
Pye Cl WA11 ... 2 A4
Pye Rd L60 ... 41 D4
Pyecroft Cl WA5 ... 14 B3
Pyecroft St CH4 ... 141 E4
Pym's La CW1 ... 189 F3
Pymgate Dr SK8 ... 239 A2
Pymgate La SK8 ... 239 A2

Pyrus Ave CW1 .... 190 C3
Pyrus Gr WA6 .... 73 E2
Pytcheley Hollow WA6 ...... 100 C3

Quad The CH1 .... 117 F1
Quadrant Cl WA7 .... 50 B3
Quadrant The Blacon CH1 . 117 F1
　Romiley SK6 .... 241 A2
Quail Cl WA2 .... 8 B2
Quakers Coppice CW1 ...... 191 D1
Quakers Way LL13 .... 180 C1
Quantock Cl
　Ellesmere Port L66 .... 69 D3
　Stockport SK4 .... 240 E6
　Winsford CW7 .... 149 D4
Quarry Ave CH3 .... 180 C1
Quarry Bank CW6 .... 146 B4
Quarry Bank Mill SK9 .... 33 F1
Quarry Bank Rd SK9 .... 33 F2
Quarry Cl Chester CH4 ..... 141 E4
　Runcorn WA7 .... 23 E1
Quarry Hill CH3 .... 180 C1
Quarry La Appleton WA4 .. 26 B3
　Christleton CH3 .... 142 C4
　Kelsall CW6 .... 122 B3
Quarry Rd New Mills SK22 . 39 E4
　Romiley SK6 .... 241 B2
　Wilmslow L64 .... 42 B1
Quarry St SK15 .... 242 C1
Quarry Terr ST7 .... 195 D1
Quay Fold WA5 .... 15 F3
Quay Pl WA7 .... 50 C4
Quay Side WA6 .... 49 E1
Quay The WA6 .... 49 E1
Quayle Cl WA11 .... 1 A3
Quayside Congleton CW12 . 156 C1
　Neston L64 .... 66 C3
Quayside Mews WA13 ...... 18 C2
Quayside Way WA13 .... 112 C4
Queasteybirch La WA4 ...... 26 A1
Quebec Rd WA2 .... 16 B4
Queen Anne Ct SK9 .... 60 B3
Queen Sq OL6 .... 242 A4
Queen St Audley ST7 .... 209 E1
　Bollington SK10 .... 88 A4
　Bunbury CW6 .... 185 F4
　Cheadle SK8 .... 239 F6
　Chester CH1 .... 237 E2
　Congleton CW12 .... 156 B1
　Congleton CW12 .... 156 C2
　Crewe CW1 .... 190 C3
　Ellesmere Port L65 .... 70 B4
　Goldborne WA3 .... 3 D4
　Hyde SK14 .... 241 E6
　Kidsgrove ST7 .... 195 D1
　Macclesfield SK11 .... 112 B4
　Middlewich CW10 .... 128 B1
　Nantwich CW5 .... 204 C3
　Newton-le-W WA12 .... 2 A2
　Northwich CW9 .... 103 F4
　Shavington CW2 .... 206 B2
　Stalybridge SK15 .... 242 D2
Queen Victoria St 図 SK11 112 B4
Queen's Ave Chester CH2 .. 237 F3
　Connah's Quay CH5 .... 5 E1
　Glazebury WA3 .... 5 D1
　Hawarden CH5 .... 116 A2
　Macclesfield SK10 .... 87 F1
　Romiley SK6 .... 241 A3
　Widnes WA8 .... 22 B4
Queen's Cl Macclesfield SK10 87 F1
　Runcorn WA7 .... 22 C1
Queen's Dr Chester CH4 ... 237 F1
　Manchester SK4 .... 240 A6
　Middlewich CW10 .... 151 E4
　Nantwich CW5 .... 204 B2
　Sandbach CW11 .... 175 D4
Queen's Gdns SK8 .... 239 F6
Queen's Par CW1 .... 190 B3
Queen's Park Gdns CW2 . 189 F2
Queen's Park Ho CW4 ..... 237 E1
Queen's Park Rd CW4 ...... 237 E1
Queen's Rd SK8 .... 238 F3
Queen's Rd OL6 .... 242 A4
Queen's Rd Cheadle SK8 . 239 F4
　Chester CH2 .... 237 F3
　Romiley SK6 .... 241 A3
　Runcorn WA7 .... 22 C1
　Wilmslow SK9 .... 60 A3

Queen's Sch (Jun Dept)
　The CH1 .... 118 B2
Queen's Sch The CH1 ...... 237 D2
Queen's Way CW4 .... 139 D2

Queens Ave
　Ellesmere Port L65 .... 70 A2
　Warrington WA1 .... 16 C4
Queens Cl Bollington SK10 . 87 F3
　Manchester SK4 .... 240 A6
Queens Cres Chester CH2 . 118 C4
　Warrington WA1 .... 17 D4
Queens Ct Manchester SK4 . 240 A7
　Winsford CW7 .... 126 B1
Queens Dr Goldborne WA3 . 3 E4
　Helsby WA6 .... 73 D2
　Heswall L60 .... 40 C4
　Newton-le-W WA12 .... 2 B3
　Warrington WA4 .... 17 D1
Queens Gdns
　Ellesmere Port L65 .... 70 A3
　Kidsgrove ST7 .... 195 D1
Queens Park Cty High Sch
　CH4 .... 237 E1
Queens Park Golf Course
　CW2 .... 189 F2

Queens Pl CH1 .... 237 E3
Queens Rd
　Chester CH1, CH3 .... 119 D2
　Ellesmere Port L66 .... 69 E4
　Haydock WA11 .... 2 A4
Queensbury Way WA8 ..... 12 B2
Queensgate Bramhall SK7 ... 35 F3
　Northwich CW8 .... 103 F4
Queensgate Prim Sch SK7 . 35 F2
Queensway Alsager ST7 ... 193 D3
　Cheadle SK8 .... 240 A4
　Chester CH2 .... 118 C3
　Crewe CW1 .... 190 B2
　Frodsham WA6 .... 74 A4
　Heswall L60 .... 40 B4
　Knutsford WA16 .... 56 C2
　Poynton SK12 .... 36 B2
　Runcorn WA7 .... 22 C2
　Widnes WA8 .... 22 C3
　Winsford CW7 .... 149 E4
Quillet The L64 .... 66 C4
Quinn St WA8 .... 23 D2
Quinta Cty Prim Sch The
　CW12 .... 156 A1
Quinta Rd CW12 .... 156 A2

Raby Ave L63 .... 43 D3
Raby Cl Bebington L63 ...... 43 D4
Raby Dr L63 .... 43 D3
Raby Gdns L64 .... 66 C4
Raby Hall Rd Bebington L63 . 43 D3
　Thornton Hough L63 .... 42 C3
Raby Mere Rd Bebington L63 . 42 B3
　Thornton Hough L63 ...... 42 B3
Raby Park Cl L64 .... 66 C4
Raby Park Rd L64 .... 41 F1
Raby Rd Neston L64 .... 66 C4
　Thornton Hough L63 .... 42 B3
Race The SK9 .... 34 B1
Racecourse La CW6 .... 124 A1
Racecourse Pk SK9 .... 59 F3
Racecourse Rd SK9 .... 59 F3
Racefield Cl WA13 .... 18 C2
Racefield Rd
　Altrincham WA14 .... 238 C4
　Knutsford WA16 .... 56 C1
Radcliffe Ave WA3 .... 4 C2
Radcliffe Rd
　Sandbach CW11 .... 174 C2
　Sutton Lane Ends SK11 . 135 E4
Raddel La WA4 .... 52 B3
Raddle Wharf L65 .... 70 B4
Radford Cl WA8 .... 22 B4
Radford Cl WA5 .... 14 C2
Radley Dr L63 .... 41 F3
Radley La WA2 .... 9 A2
Radnor Cl Congleton CW12 . 156 A2
　Sandbach CW11 .... 174 C4
Radnor Dr Chester CH4 ... 141 D2
　Widnes WA8 .... 12 B1
Radnor Park Trad Est
　CW12 .... 156 A2
Radway Gn L66 .... 69 F3
Radway Green Rd CW2 .... 208 C4
Rae St SK3 .... 240 C4
Raeburn Ave Bebington L62 . 43 F3
　Neston L64 .... 66 C4
Raeburn Prim Sch L62 ..... 43 E3
Raglan Ct WA3 .... 9 F2
Raglan Dr WA14 .... 238 E8
Raglan Rd Macclesfield SK10 . 87 F1
　Sale M33 .... 242 A5
Raglan St SK14 .... 241 C6
Ragley Cl SK12 .... 36 C2
Railbrook Ct CW2 .... 190 B1
Railton Ave CW1 ....
Railway Age Ex Ctr The
　CW1 .... 190 B2
Railway Bank SK14 .... 241 C6
Railway Cotts CW12 .... 157 D1
Railway Rd SK1 & SK3 ..... 240 E4
Railway St
　Altrincham WA14 .... 238 D4
　Crewe CW2 .... 190 B1
　Newton-le-W WA12 .... 2 A2
　Stockport SK4 .... 240 E6
Railway Terr CH5 .... 116 A2
Railway View WA1 .... 1 B1
Rainbow Cl WA8 .... 12 B2
Rainbow St CW1 .... 190 B2
Rainford Cl ST7 .... 195 F1
Rainow Cl WD10 .... 151 D4
Rainow Cty Prim Sch SK10 . 88 B2
Rainow Rd
　Macclesfield SK10 .... 88 A3
　Disley SK10 .... 88 A1
　Stockport SK3 .... 240 C2
Rainow View SK10 .... 63 D3
Rainow Way
　図 Wilmslow SK9 .... 34 B1
　図 Wilmslow SK9 .... 34 B1
Rake La Backford CH2 .... 95 E3
　Christleton CH3 .... 143 D4
　Dunham-on-t-H CH2 .... 97 D4
　Dunham-on-t-H WA6 .... 97 F4
　Eccleston CH4 .... 141 E1
　Frodsham WA6 .... 72 C3
　Hawarden CH5 .... 139 D4
　Helsby WA6 .... 73 B4
　Helsby, Helsby Marsh WA6 . 73 D3
　Stoak CH2 .... 95 E3
Rake The Bebington L62 .... 43 F4
　Burton L64 .... 67 E1
Rake Way CH1 .... 94 A1
Raleigh Cl WA5 .... 7 E1

Raleigh Rd L64 .... 41 F1
Raleigh St SK5 .... 240 E8
Ramp Rd E M90 .... 33 E4
Ramp Rd S M90 .... 33 E4
Ramp Rd W M90 .... 33 D4
Rampit Cl WA11 .... 1 A3
Ramsbottom St CW1 .... 190 A3
Ramsbrook La Hale L24 .... 21 E2
　Widnes L24 .... 21 E2
Ramsdale Rd SK7 .... 35 F4
Ramsden Ct CH4 .... 140 C2
Ramsey Cl Warrington WA3 . 9 F2
　Widnes WA8 .... 13 F2
Ramsfield Rd L24 .... 21 D2
Randle Bennett Cl CW11 . 174 C4
Randle Meadow L66 .... 69 F1
Randolph Pl SK3 .... 240 E3
Range Rd SK3 .... 240 E3
Rangemoor Cl WA3 .... 10 A3
Rannoch Cl L65 .... 70 C4
Ranworth Rd WA5 .... 14 C3
Rappax Rd WA15 .... 32 A4
Rassbottom Brow SK15 .. 242 C2
Rassbottom St SK15 .... 242 C2
Rassbottom St SK15 .... 242 C2
Ratcliffe St 図 SK1 .... 240 F4
Rathbone Pk CW6 .... 146 B1
Rathbone St WA12 .... 2 A2
Rathlin Cl WA11 .... 13 F2
Rathmell Cl WA3 .... 4 C2
Raven Cl CW11 .... 175 D4
Raven's La ST7 .... 209 F2
Ravenbank Cty Prim Sch
　WA13 .... 18 C2
Ravenfield Dr WA8 .... 12 B2
Ravenho La SK10 .... 88 B2
Ravenoak Park Rd SK8 ..... 35 D4
Ravenoak Rd SK8 .... 35 D4
Ravens Cl ST7 .... 209 F2
Ravens La Acton CW5 ...... 203 F3
　Swaney CW5 .... 203 F3
Ravenscliffe Rd ST7 .... 195 D1
Ravenscroft CW4 .... 130 A2
Ravenscroft Cl CW11 ..... 175 E4
Ravenscroft Rd CW7 ...... 189 F2
Ravensdale Cl WA2 .... 8 B2
Ravensdale Rd L12 .... 66 C4
Ravensholme Cl CH3 ...... 166 A1
Ravensholme La CH3 ...... 166 A1
Ravensmead Prim Sch
　ST7 .... 209 F2
Ravenstone Cl WA8 .... 22 A3
Ravenswood CW8 .... 103 D2
Ravenswood Ave WA4 ..... 240 A5
Ravenswood Dr SK8 .... 35 D4
Ravenswood Rd SK9 .... 59 F2
Ravenwood Dr WA15 .... 32 B4
Rawcliffe Cl WA8 .... 12 C2
Rawdon Cl WA7 .... 50 A4
Rawlings Cl WA3 .... 9 F2
Rawlinson Cres L26 .... 21 D4
Rawson Rd L61 .... 22 A4
Ray Ave CW5 .... 204 C4
Rayleigh Ave CW9 .... 127 D4
Rayleigh Way SK10 .... 86 C1
Raymond Ave WA4 .... 16 B1
Raymond St CH1 .... 237 D3
Raymond Way L64 .... 67 D4
Rays Brow CW8 .... 78 A1
Read St SK14 .... 241 C7
Reades La CW12 .... 179 E4
Reades La CW12 .... 179 E4
Reasedale Ave CW2 .... 189 F1
Reading Room La CH3 ..... 199 E4
Reaper Cl WA5 .... 15 E3
Reaseheath Coll CW5 ..... 188 B1
Reay St WA8 .... 13 E1
Record Bsns Pk WA2 .... 16 A4
Rectory Ave WA3 .... 3 E4
Rectory Cl Denton SK14 .. 241 A6
　Farndon CH3 .... 180 C1
　Heswall L60 .... 40 C4
　Nantwich CW5 .... 204 C3
　Wistaston CW2 .... 205 F4
Rectory La Adderley TF9 . 235 D3
　Capenhurst CH1 .... 94 A4
　Heswall L60 .... 40 C4
　Ledsham L66 .... 68 C1
　Nantwich CW5 .... 204 C3
　Waverton CH3 .... 143 C2
Rectory View ST7 .... 210 B3
Red Bank Ave WA12 .... 2 C1
Red Brow La
　Preston on the Hill WA7, WA4 50 C4
　Runcorn, WA4 .... 50 C4
Red Cow Yd WA16 .... 57 A2
Red Ct L66 .... 69 E4
Red House La WA4 .... 26 B4
Red La Appleton WA4 .... 26 B4
　Disley SK12 .... 38 B3
　Frodsham WA6 .... 74 B4
　Huxley CH3 .... 166 B3
　Sandbach CW11 .... 174 B3
　Warrington WA4 .... 26 B4
　Whitley WA4 .... 52 B1
Red Lane Ct SK14 .... 210 B4
Red Lion La
　Ellesmere Port L66 .... 69 E4
　Nantwich CW5 .... 204 B3
Red Pike L66 .... 69 E4
Red Stone Hill WA4 .... 73 F2
Redacre SK12 .... 36 C3
Redbourne Dr WA8 .... 12 A2
Redbrook Cl L62 .... 43 E3
Redbrook Gr 図 SK9 .... 34 B1
Redbrook Rd M31 .... 11 F1
Redbrook Way SK10 .... 62 B3
Redcar Dr L62 .... 43 E3
Reddish Ave SK23 .... 65 E3

Reddish Cres WA13 .... 18 C2
Reddish La Lymm WA13 ... 19 D3
　Whaley Bridge SK23 .... 65 E3
Reddish Rd SK23 .... 65 E3
Reddish Vale La WA4 .... 30 A4
Redesdale Cl
　Sandbach CW11 .... 174 C4
　Warrington WA2 .... 8 C2
Redesmere Cl CW9 .... 104 A3
Redesmere Dr
　Alderley Edge SK9 .... 60 A1
　Cheadle SK8 .... 239 F4
Redesmere La SK11 .... 110 A2
Redesmere Rd SK9 .... 34 B3
Redfern Ave WA3 .... 240 C5
Redfern Dr CW12 .... 156 C2
Redgate CW8 .... 103 E4
Redhill Rd Chester CH4 ... 140 C3
　Kelsall CW6 .... 122 B3
Redhills Mews L65 .... 70 C4
Redhouse La Disley SK12 . 38 C3
　Romiley SK6 .... 241 A4
Redland CH4 .... 141 D4
Redmayne Cl WA12 .... 2 A2
Redmere Dr L60 .... 41 E4
Redmoor La Disley SK12 ... 39 D2
　New Mills SK22 .... 39 D3
Redpoll La WA3 .... 9 F2
Redruth Ave SK10 .... 86 C1
Redruth Cl WA7 .... 50 B3
Redshank Ave CW7 .... 149 E3
Redshank Cl WA12 .... 2 B2
Redshank La WA3 .... 9 E2
Redstone Dr CW7 .... 126 A1
Redvales Ct WA3 .... 9 F2
Redvers Ave L66 .... 44 C1
Redway La SK10 .... 88 A4
Redwood Cl Barnton CW8 . 78 A2
　Broughton CH4 .... 140 C3
　Warrington WA1 .... 17 F4
Redwood Dr
　Ellesmere Port L66 .... 69 F1
　Elton CH2 .... 72 B2
Reece Cl CW2 .... 219 F4
Reed La CW9 .... 53 E3
Reedgate La CW9 .... 27 F1
Reedham Cl L60 .... 66 C4
Reedsmere Wlk CW9 .... 78 B4
Reel Cl WA1 .... 17 E3
Reeman Ct SK6 .... 241 A4
Reeman Ct SK6 .... 34 A1
Rees Cres CW4 .... 130 B2
Reeve St WA3 .... 4 A3
Reeves Rd CH3 .... 142 A4
Regal Cl SK6 .... 241 A2
Regal Cres WA8 .... 22 A4
Regency Ct CW7 .... 149 E4
Regency Dr SK7 .... 35 F3
Regency Pk SK9 .... 59 F3
Regency Prep Sch SK11 . 112 A4
Regency Way Haydock WA11 . 1 A4
　Macclesfield SK11 .... 112 A3
　Warrington WA1 .... 17 D4
Regent Bk SK9 .... 59 F3
Regent Cl Bramhall SK7 .... 35 E2
　Shavington CW2 .... 206 A2
　Wilmslow SK9 .... 59 F3
Regent Ct WA14 .... 238 D4
Regent Rd
　Altrincham WA14 .... 238 D4
　Widnes WA8 .... 13 D1
Regent St
　Ellesmere Port L65 .... 70 A3
　Moulton CW9 .... 126 C4
　Newton-le-W WA12 .... 2 A2
　Runcorn WA7 .... 23 A3
　Warrington WA1 .... 16 A3
Regent Theological Coll
　CW5 .... 205 D3
Regents Cl CH1 .... 119 D1
Regents Gate CW5 .... 205 D3
Regents Pk CW7 .... 149 D4
Regents Way ST7 .... 194 B1
Reginald Mitchell Prim
　Sch The ST7 .... 194 B1
Reid Ave WA5 .... 15 F4
Reid St CW1 .... 190 B3
Remer St CW1 .... 190 B4
Rena Cl SK4 .... 240 D7
Rena Dr SK4 .... 240 D7
Renaissance Ct CW1 .... 191 D2
Renaissance Way CW1 .... 191 D2
Rendel Cl WA12 .... 2 B1
Rendlesham Cl WA3 .... 10 A3
Renfrew Cl WA7 .... 43 F3
Renfrew Cl SK10 .... 86 C1
Renown Cl WA3 .... 9 F2
Renshaw Rd CW9 .... 79 E1
Renshaw St WA14 .... 238 E5
Rensherds Pl WA16 .... 79 F2
Renton Ave WA7 .... 23 E1
Repton Ave SK14 .... 241 E7
Repton Cl WA16 .... 29 E2
Repton Dr CW1 .... 191 E3
Repton Rd L65 .... 70 A2
Reservoir Rd
　Stockport SK3 .... 240 D3
　Whaley Bridge SK23 .... 65 E4
Reservoir Terr CH2 .... 118 C1
Retreat The Crewe CW1 .. 190 B3
　Romiley SK6 .... 241 C1
Reuben St SK4 .... 240 E8
Revesby Cl WA8 .... 12 B1
Rex Bldgs SK9 .... 60 A3
Reynard St SK14 .... 241 D7
Reyner St OL6 .... 242 B3
Reynold St SK14 .... 241 D6

Reynold's La CW11 .... 175 F3
Reynolds Ave WA9 .... 1 A1
Reynolds Mews SK9 .... 60 C4
Reynolds St WA4 .... 16 C2
Rhoden St CW1 .... 191 D3
Rhodes Cl CW1 .... 191 D3
Rhodes St Denton SK14 . 241 C7
　Warrington WA2 .... 16 B4
Rhodes St N SK14 .... 241 C7
Rhodesway L60 .... 41 D4
Rhona Cl L63 .... 43 E2
Rhona Dr WA3 .... 14 C3
Rhos Ave SK8 .... 239 E1
Rhuddlan Cl L65 .... 70 B1
Rhuddlan Rd CH1 .... 117 E2
Rhum Cl L65 .... 70 B1
Rhyl St WA8 .... 22 C4
Ribble Ave CW7 .... 127 D1
Ribble Cl Culcheth WA3 ...... 4 C2
　Widnes WA8 .... 13 F2
Ribble Dr ST6 .... 179 F1
Ribble Pl CW7 .... 127 D1
Ribblesdale L65 .... 70 B4
Ribblesdale Ave CW12 ... 157 D3
Ribblesdale Cl L62 .... 43 F3
Richbester Gdns L63 .... 43 F3
Richard Cl WA7 .... 24 A1
Richard Evans Comm Prim
　Sch WA11 .... 1 A3
Richard Moon St CW1 ..... 190 A2
Richard St Crewe CW1 .... 190 A3
　Northwich CW9 .... 104 B4
　図 Stockport SK3 .... 240 F6
Richards Croft CH3 .... 142 A4
Richardson Cl 図
　Sandbach CW11 .... 174 B3
　Warrington WA2 .... 206 B3
Richardson St WA2 .... 16 B4
Richmond Ave Haydock WA11 . 1 A4
　Runcorn WA7 .... 23 F3
　Warrington WA4 .... 17 D2
　Warrington, Thelwall WA4 . 17 E2
　Wilmslow SK9 .... 34 B2
Richmond Cl Culcheth WA3 . 4 B2
　Lymm WA13 .... 19 D2
　Sale M33 .... 242 F5
　Sandbach CW11 .... 174 C4
　Warrington WA1 .... 17 E2
Richmond Cres WA13 ..... 119 C1
Richmond Ct
　Altrincham WA14 .... 238 B2
　Cheadle SK8 .... 239 F6
　Ellesmere Port L65 .... 70 B2
Richmond Dr Lymm WA13 . 19 D2
　Northwich CW9 .... 104 A2
Richmond Gn WA14 .... 238 B2
Richmond Gr SK8 .... 239 F1
Richmond Hill
　Knutsford WA16 .... 57 D1
　Macclesfield SK11 .... 112 A4
Richmond Hill Rd SK8 .... 239 C6
Richmond Pl SK11 .... 112 C3
Richmond Rd
　Altrincham WA14 .... 238 D5
　Altrincham, Rosehill WA14 . 238 C4
　Crewe CW1 .... 190 C3
　Romiley SK6 .... 241 C4
Richmond St 図 Hyde SK14 . 241 E6
　Stalybridge SK15 .... 242 F2
　Warrington WA1 .... 17 D2
　Widnes WA8 .... 13 E1
Rickaby Cl L63 .... 43 E4
Ridding La WA7 .... 50 A3
Riddings Cl WA15 .... 238 F8
Riddings La Hartford CW8 . 103 D2
　Wybunbury CW5 .... 220 A4
Riddings Rd WA15 .... 238 F2
Ridge Cl SK6 .... 241 F2
Ridge Hill
　Sutton Lane Ends SK11 . 113 D1
　Utkinton CH3 .... 146 A3
Ridge Hill La SK15 .... 242 D3
Ridge Pk SK7 .... 35 E3
Ridge The CW8 .... 123 D4
Ridge View SK11 .... 112 B3
Ridgeborne Cl WA5 .... 7 E1
Ridgemont Ave WA4 ...... 240 B6
Ridgeway Alvanley WA6 .... 74 A1
　Goldborne WA3 .... 3 D4
　Wilmslow SK9 .... 60 C4
Ridgeway Gdns WA13 .... 18 B2
Ridgeway The Cronton WA8 . 12 B3
　Disley SK12 .... 38 B3
　Heswall L60 .... 41 D4
　Runcorn WA7 .... 50 B3
　Tarvin CH3 .... 121 F2
Ridgewell Ave WA3 .... 3 F3
Ridgmont Rd SK7 .... 35 F1
Ridgway St Crewe CW1 .. 190 B3
　Warrington WA2 .... 16 B4
Ridgway The SK6 .... 241 A2
Ridings Cty Inf Sch The
　CH1 .... 94 A3
Ridings The CH1 .... 117 D4
Ridley Cl CW2 .... 206 C2
Ridley Dr WA5 .... 15 E2
Ridley Gr WA13 .... 242 F5
Ridley Rd SK10 .... 87 F4
Ridley Wood Rd LL13 ...... 196 A2
Ridsdale L63 .... 43 E4
Rifle Rd M21 & M33 .... 242 F7
Rigby Ave CW7 .... 190 A4
Rigby Rd ST7 .... 195 D2
Rigby St Altrincham WA14 . 238 D6
　Goldborne WA3 .... 3 D4
Rigby's Row CW5 .... 204 C3
Rigg St CW1 .... 190 A3

ley Bank Mews WA6 ...... 74 A1
ley Cl CW11 .... 174 C3
ley Dr WA7 .... 49 D4
leys Way ST7 .... 209 F1
lshaw La CW7 .... 150 A4
lston Ave WA3 .... 4 E2
mington Cl WA3 .... 4 B2
msdale Cl Gatley SK8 .... 239 A3
Wistaston CW2 .... 206 A4
ng Rd CH3 .... 119 E2
ng-o'-Bells La SK12 ...... 38 A8
ngsfield Rd L24 .... 21 D1
ngstead Cl SK9 .... 34 B1
ngstead Dr SK9 .... 34 B1
ngstone Way SK23 .... 65 E4
ngway Ellesmere Port L66 . 69 F2
Neston L64 .... 41 F1
Waverton CH3 .... 143 D3
ngway Golf Course
WA15 .... 32 B4
ngway Rd Runcorn WA7 .. 23 E1
Wythenshawe M22, M90 .. 33 E4
ngway Rd W M90 .... 33 E4
ngwood Cl WA3 .... 10 A3
pley Ave SK8 .... 35 D3
pley Cl SK7 .... 36 C4
pley St WA5 .... 15 F3
pon Ave
Ellesmere Port L66 ...... 69 E3
Goldborne WA3 .... 3 E4
pon Cl WA12 .... 2 B3
pon Dr CW7 .... 206 A4
pon Rd WA7 .... 49 E3
pon Wlk SK6 .... 241 A1
se The SK23 .... 65 E3
seley St SK11 .... 112 B4
seley's Pas 88 SK11 .... 112 B4
sing Sun Cl SK11 ...... 112 A3
sing Sun Rd SK11 ...... 112 A2
sley Moss Ctry Pk WA3 . 10 A2
sley Rd WA3 .... 9 F3
vacre Brow L66 .... 69 E4
vacre Rd Bebington L62 .. 44 A2
Ellesmere Port L66 ...... 44 B1
vacre Valley Ctry Pk
L66 .... 69 E4
vacre Valley Ctry Prim
Sch L66 .... 69 E4
ver La Broughton CH4 ... 140 C4
Chester CH4 .... 141 E4
Farndon CH3 .... 180 C1
vington Rd M31 .... 11 F2
ver Rd WA4 .... 16 A2
ver St Congleton CW12 .. 156 B2
Macclesfield SK11 ...... 112 C3
Wilmslow SK9 .... 60 A4
ver View CW7 .... 126 C1
verbank Cl
Bollington SK10 .... 87 F4
Heswall L60 .... 40 C3
Nantwich CW5 .... 204 C4
verbank Rd L60 .... 40 C3
verdane Rd CW12 ...... 156 C2
vermead Ave WA15 ...... 32 B4
Warrington WA1 .... 16 D1
verdale Rd
Cheadle SK8 .... 239 C5
Runcorn WA7 .... 49 E4
vershill WA13 .... 242 A8
vershill Gdns WA15 ..... 32 B3
verside Nantwich CW5 .. 204 B3
verside Bsns Pk SK9 .... 60 A4
verside Cl WA1 .... 16 D2
verside Cres CW4 ...... 130 B2
verside Ct Chester CH4 .. 141 E4
Langley SL11 .... 113 E2
verside Dr CW8 .... 103 F3
verside Gr WA7 .... 189 E2
verside Pk CH5 .... 116 A4
verside Ret Pk WA4 .... 16 B2
verside Wlk L66 .... 66 B3
versmead CH3 .... 142 A3
verton Rd M20 .... 239 B8
verview Rd L64 .... 66 C3
vington Ct WA1 .... 17 D1
vington Gr M44 .... 11 E3
vington Rd
Altrincham WA15 .... 238 F2
Ellesmere Port L65 ..... 70 C4
Runcorn WA7 .... 50 C2
ixton Ave WA5 .... 15 C2
oaches The SK11 ...... 112 A3
oachill Cl WA14 .... 238 B5
oad Beta CW7 .... 151 E4
oad Four CW7 .... 127 E1
oad One CW7 .... 127 D2
oad Six CW6 .... 146 A2
oad Three CW7 .... 127 E1
oad Two CW7 .... 127 D2
oadside CH3 .... 3 E4
oan Ct SK11 .... 112 C4
oan House Way SK11 .. 112 C4
oan Mews SK11 .... 112 C4
ob Rd WA12 .... 2 E3
obert Moffat WA16 ..... 29 E3
obert St Hyde SK14 .... 241 C7
Macclesfield SK11 ...... 103 F3
Runcorn WA7 .... 23 E1
Sale M33 .... 242 E6
Warrington WA5 .... 15 F3
Widnes WA8 .... 13 D1
obert's Terr CW1 .... 190 B4
oberts Ave WA11 .... 1 A3
oberts Ct WA7 .... 49 F3
oberts Dr CW7 .... 104 B3

Roberts Rd CW9 .... 80 A1
Robin Cl Rainow SK10 .... 88 C3
Runcorn WA7 .... 50 B4
Sandbach CW11 .... 175 D4
Robin Cres SK11 .... 112 B1
Robin Hood Ave SK11 ... 112 B3
Robin Hood La WA6 ..... 73 D1
Robin La Chelford SK11 .. 84 A2
Sutton Lane Ends SK11 . 112 B1
Robin's La Bramhall SK7 . 35 F4
Cheadle Hulme SK7 ...... 35 F4
Robins Cft L66 .... 69 F1
Robins Cl SK7 .... 35 F4
Robins La WA3 .... 4 B1
Robinson St Hyde SK14 . 241 F7
Stalybridge SK15 .... 242 C1
Stockport SK3 .... 240 D3
Robinsons Croft CH3 .... 142 A4
Robinsway WA14 .... 238 C1
Robson St WA1 .... 16 B3
Roby Gr WA5 .... 15 D3
Roche Gdns SK8 .... 35 D3
Rochester Cl Goldborne WA3 . 3 D4
Great Sankey WA5 .... 15 A2
Rochester Cres CW1 .... 190 C3
Rochester Dr SK5 .... 70 B2
Rochford Ave M22 ...... 33 E4
Rock Bank Sch SK8 ..... 65 F3
Rock Dr WA6 .... 49 E1
Rock Farm Cl L64 .... 67 D3
Rock Farm Dr L64 ...... 67 D3
Rock Farm Gr L64 ...... 67 D3
Rock La Burwardsley CW6 . 184 B3
Chester CH2 .... 237 D4
Rock Rd WA3 .... 4 B1
Rock St SK22 .... 39 E4
Rock The WA6 .... 73 E1
Rockfield Cl WA8 .... 12 B1
Rockfield Dr WA6 .... 73 E1
Rockford Lodge WA16 .. 57 E1
Rockhouse La ST7 ..... 210 B4
Rockingham Cl WA3 .... 4 B3
Rocklands La L63 ...... 42 B4
Rocklee Gdns L64 ...... 67 D3
Rocklife La CH6 .... 91 D2
Rocklynes SK6 .... 241 B2
Rocksavage Expressway
WA7 .... 49 F3
Rockside ST7 .... 195 E3
Rockwood Ave CW2 .... 190 A2
Rocky La Heswall L60 ... 40 B2
Tattenhall CH3 .... 182 C4
Rocky La S L60 .... 41 D4
Roddy La WA6 .... 75 F1
Rode Hall ST7 .... 194 A4
Rode Heath Cty Prim Sch
ST7 .... 193 F4
Rode House Cl ST7 .... 193 F4
Rode The ST7 .... 193 E2
Rodeheath Cl SK9 ...... 60 B4
Rodepool Cl SK9 .... 34 B1
Rodgers Cl WA6 .... 49 D2
Rodmill Dr SK8 .... 239 A4
Rodney St
Ashton-u-L OL6 .... 242 A4
Macclesfield SK11 ..... 112 B4
Roe Pk CW12 .... 178 C1
Roe St Congleton CW12 . 156 C1
Roebuck Gdns WA3 .... 242 A6
Roebuck La WA3 ...... 242 A6
Roebuck St CW1 ...... 190 B3
Roeburn Way WA5 ..... 14 B2
Roeden Wlk CW1 ...... 190 B3
Roehampton Dr WA7 .... 49 F4
Roehurst La CW7 ...... 126 B1
Roemarsh Ct WA7 ..... 49 F3
Roewood La
Macclesfield SK10 ...... 88 A1
Macclesfield, Higherfence
SK10 .... 113 D4
Roften Ind Est L66 ..... 68 C4
Rokeby Ct WA7 .... 24 B3
Rokeden WA12 .... 2 B2
Roland Ave WA7 .... 22 C1
Rolands Wlk WA7 ...... 23 F1
Rolleston St WA2 .... 16 B3
Rolls Ave CW1 .... 190 A4
Rolt Cres CW10 .... 151 D4
Roman Cl WA7 .... 23 F1
Roman Ct L64 .... 66 C2
Roman Dr CH1 .... 117 E3
Roman Rd Stockport SK4 . 240 E6
Warrington WA4 .... 16 B1
Widnes WA8 .... 12 C4
Roman Rise CW8 .... 78 A3
Roman Way CW11 ..... 174 C4
Romanes St CW8 ...... 103 F4
Romford Ave M34 ..... 241 A8
Romiley Prec SK6 ...... 241 C2
Romiley Prim Sch SK6 . 241 C2
Romiley Sta SK6 .... 241 C2
Romley Rd L66 .... 69 F3
Romley Sta SK6 .... 241 C2
Romney Cl L64 .... 66 C4
Romney Croft L64 ...... 66 C4
Romney Way L64 ...... 66 C4
Romney Rd SK3 .... 35 E3
Romsey Dr SK7 .... 35 E3
Ronald Dr WA2 .... 9 D1
Ronaldshay WA8 .... 13 F1
Ronaldsway Halewood L26 . 21 D4
.... 40 C3
Rood Hill CW12 .... 156 B2
Rood La CW12 .... 156 C2
Rook Rd WA4 .... 16 C2

Rook St CW12 .... 190 B1
Rookery Cl Nantwich CW5 . 204 C3
Sandbach CW11 .... 174 B3
Rookery Dr Nantwich CW5 . 204 C2
Tattenhall CH3 .... 166 A1
Rookery Rd Kidsgrove ST7 . 195 E2
Tilston SY14 .... 198 A2
Rookery Rise CW7 ..... 127 D1
Rookery The Broughton CH4 139 D2
Newton-le-W WA12 .... 2 B2
Rookerypool Cl SK9 .... 34 B1
Rookfield Ave M33 ..... 242 C7
Rooks Way L60 .... 40 C4
Roome St WA7 .... 16 B4
Roscoe St SK1 .... 240 D6
Rope Bank Ave CW2 ... 206 A3
Rope La Shavington CW2 . 206 A3
Wistaston CW2 .... 206 A3
Rope Wlk CW12 .... 156 B2
Ropewalk The L64 ...... 66 C2
Rosam Ct WA7 .... 49 F3
Roscoe Ave
Newton-le-W WA12 .... 2 C2
Warrington WA4 .... 26 C3
Roscoe Pk Est WA14 ... 238 E8
Roscoe Rd M44 .... 11 E4
Roscote The L60 .... 40 C4
Roscote Cl L60 .... 40 C4
Rose Ave Haydock WA11 .. 1 C3
Irlam M44 .... 11 F4
Rose Bank WA3 .... 18 C2
Rose Cl WA8 .... 12 B1
Rose Cres CW8 .... 22 C4
Rose Gdns L64 .... 66 C3
Rose La CW8 .... 13 D2
Rose St Reddish SK5 ... 240 A8
.... 22 C4
Rose Terr Crewe CW1 .. 190 B3
Stalybridge SK15 ...... 242 D1
Rose Vale CW8 .... 34 B4
Rose View Ave WA8 .... 13 D1
Rose Wlk M31 .... 11 E1
Roseacre Dr Cheadle SK8 . 34 B4
Gatley SK8 .... 239 C1
Rosebank Cl CW7 ..... 149 F4
Rosebank Rd M44 ..... 11 E2
Rosebank Sch CW8 .... 78 A2
Rosebank Wlk CW8 .... 78 A2
Roseberry Way CW1 ... 191 E2
Rosedale Ave Golborne WA3 . 3 E4
Rosedale Rd Warrington WA4 . 17 E4
Rose Wst WA1 .... 16 A3
Rowland Cl WA2 .... 16 C4
Rowley Bank La WA16 . 29 D1
Rowley Rd SK7 .... 36 C4
Rowley Way WA16 ..... 82 A4
Rowson Dr M44 .... 11 E3
Rowthorn Cl WA8 ..... 22 C4
Rowton Bridge Rd CH3 . 142 C4
Rowton Cl CW9 .... 103 F2
Rowton La CH3 .... 142 C3
Rowton Rd CW2 ...... 189 E2
Roxbo Rough Cl WA5 .... 7 D3
Roxburgh Cl SK10 .... 87 F1
Roxburgh Rd L66 ...... 69 E2
Roxby Way WA16 ...... 82 A4
Roxholme Wlk M22 .... 33 E4
Royal Ave WA8 .... 12 B1
Royal Gdns
Altrincham WA14 ...... 20 C1
Northwich CW9 .... 103 F2
Royal George St SK1 & SK3 240 F4
Royal La CW6 .... 147 D2
Royal Meadows SK10 .. 87 D1
Royal Mews CW9 ...... 103 F2
Royal Mount CW1 ..... 173 D1
Royal Oak Yd 1 SK1 .. 240 F5
Royal Pl WA8 .... 22 A4
Royal Rd SK12 .... 38 B3
Royal Sch for the Deaf The
.... 34 B3
Royce Ave WA15 ...... 238 E5
Royce Cl CW1 .... 190 A4
Royden Ave Irlam M44 .. 11 F4
Runcorn WA7 .... 49 D4
Royds Cl CW8 .... 103 D2
Roylands Dr CW10 .... 151 E4
Royle St Congleton CW12 . 156 B2
Northwich CW9 .... 104 A4
Stockport SK1 .... 240 F3
Rudheath Cl WA3 .... 4 B4
Rudheath Cty High Sch
CW9 .... 104 B4
Rudheath Cty Prim Sch
CW9 .... 104 B4
Rudheath L Ctr CW9 ... 104 B4
Rudloe Ct WA12 .... 2 C2
Rudstone Cl L66 .... 69 D3
Rudyard Cl SK11 ..... 112 A3
Rue De Bohars CW6 ... 168 A4
Rufford Ave SK14 .... 241 F6
Rufford Cl CW2 ...... 206 A4
Rufford Dr WA4 ...... 17 F4
Rufus Ct CH1 .... 237 D3
Rugby Cl SK10 .... 87 F2
Rugby Dr SK10 .... 87 F2

Rugby House SK10 ...... 87 E2
Rugby Rd L65 .... 70 B2
Ruislip Cl WA2 .... 8 C1
Runcorn Docks Rd WA7 . 22 C1
Runcorn East Sta WA7 .. 50 B4
Runcorn Rd Barnton CW8 . 78 A1
Little Leigh CW8 .... 77 E3
Moore WA4 .... 25 E3
Runcorn Spur Rd WA7 .. 49 E4
Runcorn Sta WA7 ...... 22 C1
Runger La WA15 .... 32 C4
Runnell The L64 .... 42 C4
Runnymede WA1 ...... 17 F4
Runnymede Cl WA5 ... 240 C2
Runnymede Dr WA11 .... 1 A3
Runnymede Gdns
Warrington WA5 .... 240 C2
Rushey Cl WA15 .... 32 B4
Rushfield Cres SK6 .... 241 D3
Rushfield Rd
Cheadle Hulme SK8 .... 35 D3
Chester CH4 .... 141 D3
Rushgreen Rd WA13 ... 19 D2
Rushmere La CH3 ..... 163 F2
Rushmore Gr WA1 ..... 17 D4
Rusholme Cl L26 ...... 21 D3
Rushside Rd SK8 .... 35 D3
Rushton Ave WA12 ...... 2 A2
Rushton CE Contr Prim
Sch 159 D1
Rushton Cl Northwich CW9 . 104 B4
Widnes WA8 .... 12 C2
Rushton Dr Chester CH2 . 118 B4
Hough Common CW2 .... 206 C1
Middlewich CW10 ...... 151 E4
Romiley SK6 .... 241 C3
Rushton Fold SK10 ..... 61 D1
Rushton La Little Budworth CW6 . 147 E3
Little Budworth CW6 ... 147 E3
Rushton Rd
Cheadle Hulme SK8 .... 35 D3
Stockport SK3 .... 240 B3
Rushy View WA12 .... 2 A2
Rushyfield Cres SK6 ... 241 D3
Ruskin Ave
Newton-le-W WA12 ...... 2 B2
Warrington WA2 .... 8 B1
Ruskin Cl SK6 .... 241 A3
Ruskin Cty High Sch The
CW2 .... 190 B1
Ruskin Dr L65 .... 70 A3
Ruskin Gdns SK6 ..... 241 A3
Ruskin Gr CW12 ...... 156 B1
Ruskin Rd
Congleton CW12 ...... 156 B1
Crewe CW2 .... 190 B1
Ruskin Way WA16 ..... 57 D2
Russell Ave Alsager ST7 . 193 E3
High Lane SK6 .... 37 F4
Sale M33 .... 242 D7
Russell Cl WA12 ...... 179 D4
Russell Ct WA8 .... 13 D2
Russell Dr WA5 .... 15 A2
Russell Gdns Dr CW1 .. 240 B5
Russell Rd Runcorn WA7 . 48 C4
Winsford CW7 .... 149 E4
Russell St
Ashton-u-L OL6 .... 242 A4
Chester CH2 .... 237 F3
Hyde SK14 .... 241 C8
Russet Cl CW10 ...... 128 A1
Russet Rd L64 .... 102 B4
Russett Sch The CW8 .. 102 C4
Rutherford Cl WA14 ... 241 D6
Ruthin Ave SK8 .... 239 E2
Ruthin Cl L65 .... 70 B2
Ruthin Wlk SK3 ...... 73 D1
Rutland Ave Denton M34 . 241 B6
Goldborne WA3 .... 3 E4
Handforth SK9 .... 21 D4
Warrington WA4 .... 26 A4
Rutland Cl
Ashton-u-L OL6 .... 242 A2
Congleton CW12 ...... 156 C2
Gatley SK8 .... 239 B6
1 Sandbach CW11 ..... 174 B3
Rutland Dr
Middlewich CW10 ..... 151 E4
Weaverham CW8 .... 77 E1
Rutland La M33 .... 242 A6
Rutland Pl CW2 .... 119 D3
Rutland Rd
Altrincham WA14 ..... 238 D6
Hazel Grove SK7 ..... 36 C4
Irlam M44 .... 11 E4
Kidsgrove ST7 .... 195 D1
Macclesfield SK11 .... 112 B2
Partington M31 .... 11 F1
Rutland St
Ashton-u-L OL6 .... 242 A2
Runcorn WA7 .... 22 C1
Gatley SK8 .... 239 B6
1 Sandbach CW11 ..... 174 B3
Ryburn Rd SK11 ...... 112 A3
Rydal Ave High Lane SK6 . 37 F4
Warrington WA4 .... 16 A1
Rydal Cl Ellesmere Port L65 . 70 B2
Gatley SK8 .... 239 B4
Holmes Chapel CW4 ... 130 A1
Neston L64 .... 66 C3
Winsford CW7 .... 126 B2
Rydal Ct CW12 .... 156 A1
Rydal Gr Chester CH4 .. 141 D3
Helsby WA6 .... 73 D1
Runcorn WA7 .... 49 D4

Rydal Pl SK11 .... 112 A3
Rydal St WA2 .... 2 B2
Rydal Way Alsager ST7 ...... 193 E3
Widnes WA8 .... 12 B1
Ryde Ave SK4 .... 240 B6
Ryde Cl CW1 .... 190 A4
Ryder Ave WA14 .... 238 E7
Ryder Rd Warrington WA1 .... 17 E4
Widnes WA8 .... 13 D3
Ryders St CW8 .... 103 F4
Rye Cl ST7 .... 193 D2
Ryebank Ave CW1 .... 190 A4
Ryebank Way SK10 .... 87 E2
Ryecroft CH2 .... 72 A2
Ryecroft Cl CW10 .... 151 D4
Ryecroft La Duddon CW6 ... 144 B3
Mobberley WA16 .... 57 F2
Ryecroft Rd L60 .... 41 E4
Ryedale Cl SK4 .... 240 B7
Ryehills ST7 .... 209 F1

Rylands St
Warrington WA1 .... 16 A3
🔟 Widnes WA8 .... 23 D4
Ryle St SK11 .... 112 B3
Ryle's Park Rd SK11 .... 112 B3
Ryles Cl SK11 .... 112 B3
Ryles Cres SK11 .... 112 B3
Ryles Park Cty High Sch
SK11 .... 112 A3
Ryleys La SK9 .... 59 F1
Ryleys Sch The SK9 .... 59 F1

Sabre Cl WA7 .... 50 B4
Sack La CW9 .... 54 C3
Sacred Heart Rc Aided
Prim Sch WA5 .... 15 F3
Saddleback Dr SK10 .... 86 C4
Saddlers Rise WA7 .... 50 B4
Sadler Cl CW7 .... 126 B1
Sadler Rd CW7 .... 126 B1
Sadler St WA8 .... 13 E1
Sadler's Cl CW4 .... 130 A2
Sadlers La CW6 .... 124 A1
Sadlers Wells CW6 .... 185 F4
Safferon Cl WA2 .... 9 D1
Saffron Wlk M31 .... 11 F1
Sagars Rd SK9 .... 34 B2
Sage Cl WA2 .... 9 D1
Saighton CE Aided Prim
Sch CH3 .... 142 C1
Saighton La Saighton CH3 .. 142 C1
Waverton CH3 .... 142 C1
SS Peter & Paul RC Aided
High Sch WA8 .... 22 C4
SS Peter & Paul RC High
Sch WA8 .... 12 C1
St Aelred's RC High Sch
WA12 .... 2 B2
St Alban Rd WA5 .... 15 F3
St Alban's RC Aided Prim
Sch SK10 .... 86 C1
St Alban's RC Aided Sch
WA5 .... 15 F3
St Albans Cl WA11 .... 2 A4
St Albans Cres WA14 .... 238 C8
St Albans Dr CW5 .... 204 C2
St Albans Pl SK22 .... 39 E4
St Albans St SK22 .... 39 E4
St Ambrose Coll WA15 ...... 32 A4
St Ambrose Rc Jun Mix Inf
Sch L24 .... 21 D1
St Ambrose RC Prim Sch
SK3 .... 240 E1
St Ambrose Rd WA8 .... 13 E1
St Andrew's Ave WA15 ..... 238 F7
St Andrew's CE Prim Sch
WA2 .... 9 D2
St Andrew's Cl SK6 .... 241 B1
St Andrew's Gdns ST7 ..... 193 F1
St Andrew's Rd
Ellesmere Port L65 .... 70 C2
Macclesfield SK11 .... 112 A4
St Andrews Cl
Northwich CW9 .... 104 C4
Warrington WA2 .... 9 D2
St Andrews Ct WA15 .... 238 F3
St Andrews Dr
Holmes Chapel CW4 .... 130 A1
Kidsgrove ST7 .... 195 E2
St Andrews Rd
Gatley SK8 .... 239 C1
Manchester SK4 .... 240 B8
St Andrews Sch (Special
Needs) CW4 .... 141 E4
St Andrews Wlk
Mickle Trafford CW2 .... 96 C1
New Mills SK22 .... 39 E4
St Ann's Ave CW10 .... 151 E4
St Ann's CE Aided Prim
Sch WA2 .... 8 B1
St Ann's Rd CW10 .... 151 E4
St Ann's Rd N SK8 .... 239 B2
St Ann's Rd S SK8 .... 34 B4
St Ann's Sq SK8 .... 34 B4
St Anne St CH2 .... 237 E3
St Anne's CE Prim Sch
M33 .... 242 D6
St Anne's Ct M33 .... 242 C6
St Anne's Cty Prim Sch
M34 .... 241 A8
St Anne's Dr M34 .... 241 A8
St Anne's Hospl WA14 ..... 238 C2
St Anne's La CW5 .... 204 B3
St Anne's RC Prim Sch
CW5 .... 204 C2

St Anne's Rd
Dukinfield M34 .... 241 A8
Widnes WA8 .... 13 D1
St Annes Ave SK4 .... 240 A4
St Annes Ave E WA4 .... 17 D1
St Annes Ave W WA4 .... 17 D1
St Annes RC High Sch
SK4 .... 240 D8
St Anns St M33 .... 242 F5
St Anthony's Prim Sch
CH4 .... 140 C3
St Asaph Dr WA5 .... 7 F2
St Asaph Rd CH1 .... 94 C4
St Augustine's Ave WA4 ... 16 C2
St Augustine's RC Aided
Prim Sch WA4 .... 16 C2
St Augustine's RC Aided
Sch WA4 .... 16 C2
St Augustine's Rd SK3 .... 240 B4
St Austel Cl WA5 .... 14 C2
St Austell Ave SK10 .... 86 C1
St Austell Cl
Macclesfield SK10 .... 86 C1
Runcorn WA7 .... 50 A3
St Austell Dr SK8 .... 34 A4
St Austins La WA1 .... 16 A2
St Barnabas CE Aided Prim
Sch WA5 .... 15 F3
St Barnabas CE Contr Prim
Sch SK11 .... 112 B3
St Barnabas Ct SK11 .... 112 B3
St Barnabas Pl WA5 .... 15 F3
St Basil's RC Aided Prim
Sch WA4 .... 26 B3
St Bede's Ave CW8 .... 77 E1
St Bede's RC Aided Inf &
Jun Sch WA8 .... 13 D1
St Bede's RC Prim Sch
CW8 .... 102 C4
St Bees Cl SK8 .... 239 B3
St Benedicts Cl WA4 .... 16 B4
St Benedicts RC Aided Prim
Sch Warrington WA2 .... 16 B4
Wilmslow SK9 .... 34 C2
St Bernard's RC Aided Prim
Sch L65 .... 70 B2
St Berteline's CE Aided
Prim Sch WA7 .... 50 B4
St Brannocks Rd SK8 .... 35 D4
St Brides Cl WA5 .... 14 C2
St Bridget's RC Aided Prim
Sch WA2 .... 8 C2
St Bridgets Cl WA2 .... 8 C2
St Bridgets Ct CH4 .... 141 D3
St Catherine's RC Prim Sch
WA3 .... 3 F4
St Catherines Dr CW8 ..... 103 D2
St Chad's Ave SK6 .... 241 C2
St Chad's CE Prim Sch
ST5 .... 210 B1
St Chad's Gr SK6 .... 241 C2
St Chad's RC Aided Comp
Sch WA7 .... 49 F4
St Chad's Rd CH1 .... 117 F2
St Chads Cl CW5 .... 220 A4
St Chads Way TF9 .... 236 B1
St Christopher's Dr SK6 .. 241 A2
St Christopher's RC Prim
Sch SK6 .... 241 A2
St Christophers Cl CH2 ... 118 B4
St Clairs St CW2 .... 190 B1
St Clare's RC Aided Prim
Sch CH4 .... 141 D3
St Clement's RC Aided Prim
Sch WA7 .... 49 D4
St David Rd L62 .... 44 A3
St David's Ave SK6 .... 241 B2
St David's High Sch CH4 . 140 B3
St David's Terr CH4 .... 140 B3
St Davids Cl M33 .... 242 A5
St Davids Dr
Ellesmere Port CH1 .... 94 C4
Warrington WA5 .... 7 F1
St Edward's RC Aided Prim
Sch Macclesfield SK11 ...... 112 B3
Runcorn WA7 .... 23 D2
St Edwards Cl SK11 .... 112 B3
St Elmo Pk SK12 .... 37 E2
St Elphins Cl WA1 .... 16 B3
St Gabriel's RC Aided Prim
Sch ST7 .... 193 E2
St George's CE Inf Sch
SK2 .... 240 F2
St George's CE Jun Sch
SK2 .... 240 F2
St George's CE (VA) Prim
Sch SK4 .... 241 D5
St George's Cres
Chester CH4 .... 237 F1
Waverton CH3 .... 143 D3
St George's Ct
Altrincham WA14 .... 238 B7
Widnes WA8 .... 22 B4
St George's Gdns M34 ..... 241 A5
St George's Pl SK11 .... 112 B4
St George's Rd CW7 .... 149 E4
St George's St
Macclesfield SK11 .... 112 B3
Stalybridge SK15 .... 242 D3
St George's Way L63 .... 42 A3
St Georges Ave CH1 .... 94 C4
St Georges Ct WA4 .... 26 C2
St Georges Ct 🔟 SK14 .... 241 E6
St Georges Dr SK14 .... 241 D5
St Georges Rd SK22 .... 39 E4
St Giles Ct SK14 .... 241 F6
St Gregory's RC Aided High
Sch WA5 .... 15 E3

St Gregory's RC Aided Prim
Sch SK10 .... 87 F4
St Helen's Coll Newton
Campus WA12 .... 2 A2
St Helens CE Prim Sch
WA3 .... 11 D1
St Helens Cl WA3 .... 11 D2
St Helens Rd
Goldborne WA3, WN7 .... 4 A4
Northwich CW9 .... 104 A4
St Hilary's Sch SK9 .... 85 D4
St Hilary's Sch for Girls
SK9 .... 60 A1
St Hilda's Dr WA6 .... 49 E1
St Hugh's Cl WA14 .... 238 E8
St Hugh's RC Prim Sch
WA15 .... 238 F8
St Ives Ave SK8 .... 240 A2
St Ives Cl SK10 .... 86 C1
St Ives Pk CH5 .... 116 A2
St James Ave Chester CH2 . 118 C4
Congleton CW12 .... 156 B1
Warren SK11 .... 111 F1
St James CE Inf Sch WA11 ... 1 C3
St James CE Jun Sch WA11 . 1 C3
St James Cl Audlem CW3 . 230 A2
Frodsham WA6 .... 49 E1
St James Ct
Altrincham WA15 .... 238 E4
Manchester M20 .... 239 B8
St James' Dr M33 .... 242 A5
St James' Dr SK9 .... 60 A3
St James' RC High Sch
SK8 .... 34 C3
St James' Sq SK22 .... 39 E4
St James St OL6 .... 242 A2
St James Terr 🔟 CW7 ..... 149 D4
St James' Way SK8 .... 34 C3
St James Wlk CW8 .... 103 F4
St James's CE Contr Jun
Sch CH2 .... 119 F3
St John Ave WA4 .... 16 A1
St John Fisher RC Aided
Prim Sch WA8 .... 13 E1
St John Fisher RC Prim
Sch M34 .... 241 B5
St John St Chester CH1 ... 237 E2
Newton-le-W WA12 .... 2 A2
St John The Evangelist RC
Prim Sch ST7 .... 195 D2
St John The Evangelist RC
Prim Sch (Annexe) ST7 . 194 C1
St John Vianney Lower
Sch SK4 .... 240 B6
St John's Ave
Knutsford WA16 .... 56 C1
Warrington WA1 .... 16 B4
St John's CE Aided Prim
Sch Bollington SK10 .... 88 A4
Macclesfield SK11 .... 112 A4
Sandbach CW11 .... 175 F3
St John's Cl
Northwich CW9 .... 104 C4
Romiley SK6 .... 241 B2
St John's Dr SK14 .... 241 F7
St John's Dr SK14 .... 241 F7
St John's La SK9 .... 59 F2
St John's RC Sch WA4 ...... 16 C3
St John's Rd
Altrincham WA14 .... 238 D3
Bebington L62 .... 44 A3
Chester CH4 .... 237 F1
Congleton CW12 .... 156 C3
Knutsford WA16 .... 57 D1
🔟 Macclesfield SK11 .... 112 B4
Wilmslow SK9 .... 59 F2
St John's Rear Rd CH4 .... 237 F1
St John's St WA7 .... 23 D2
St John's the Evangelist
RC Prim Sch ST7 .... 194 C1
St John's Way
Cuddington CW8 .... 102 A1
Sandbach CW11 .... 175 F3
St John's Wood ST7 .... 194 C1
St John's Wood Cty Prim
Sch WA16 .... 57 E1
St Johns Dr CW7 .... 149 D4
St Joseph's Cl WA5 .... 14 C3
St Joseph's RC Aided Prim
Sch WA5 .... 14 C3
St Joseph's RC Prim Sch
M33 .... 242 B6
St Joseph's RC Sch SK1 . 240 F5
St Josephs Way WA1 .... 16 B4
St Katherines Way WA1 ... 16 B3
St Lawrence Cl WA5 .... 204 C3
St Lawrence Rd
Denton M34 & M16 .... 241 A7
Frodsham WA6 .... 74 A4
St Leonard's Way CW3 ... 232 B1
St Leonards Dr WA15 ...... 238 F6
St Lesmo Ct SK3 .... 240 C3
St Lesmo Rd SK3 .... 240 C3
St Lewis RC Prim Sch
WA3 .... 4 A1
St Luke's CE Prim Sch
WA3 .... 3 F2
St Luke's Cres WA8 .... 13 D2
St Luke's RC Aided Prim
Sch WA6 .... 49 E1
St Luke's Way WA6 .... 49 D1
St Lukes Cl CW4 .... 130 B2
St Margaret's Ave WA2 ...... 8 B1
St Margaret's CE Aided Jun
Sch WA7 .... 8 B1
St Margaret's Cl WA14 .... 238 C4

St Margaret's Rd
Altrincham WA14 .... 238 C4
Cheadle SK8 .... 240 A2
St Mark's Ave WA14 .... 238 A5
St Mark's RC Prim Sch
SK6 .... 241 A4
L26 .... 21 D4
St Mark's St Haydock WA11 . 1 A3
Romiley SK6 .... 241 A4
St Marks Cres CH1 .... 94 C4
St Marks Rd CH4 .... 140 C3
St Martin's Ave WA4 .... 16 A1
St Martin's Cl SK14 .... 241 F6
St Martin's Rd ST7 .... 210 C3
St Martin's Way CH1 .... 237 D3
St Martins Dr L66 .... 69 E1
St Martins La WA7 .... 50 B4
St Martins RC Aided Prim
Sch WA7 .... 50 B4
St Mary's Ave CW8 .... 77 E1
St Mary's CE Contr Sch
SK11 .... 158 B4
St Mary's CE Prim Sch
Bebington L62 .... 44 A3
Goldborne WA3 .... 4 A4
Irlam M44 .... 11 E3
Sale M33 .... 242 A6
St Mary's Cl Alsager ST7 .. 193 E3
Appleton WA4 .... 26 B3
St Mary's Dr SK8 .... 239 F6
St Mary's Hill CH4 .... 237 E2
St Mary's Inf Sch CH1 .... 237 D3
St Mary's RC Aided Prim
Sch Congleton CW12 .... 156 B2
Crewe CW2 .... 190 A1
St Mary's RC Inf Sch WA12 . 2 B2
St Mary's RC Prim Sch
Ashton-u-L OL6 .... 242 A4
New Mills SK22 .... 39 D4
Stockport SK4 .... 240 E6
St Mary's Rd
Altrincham WA14 .... 238 C3
Disley SK12 .... 38 B3
Dodleston CH4 .... 162 A4
Nantwich CW5 .... 204 C4
Northwich CW9 .... 104 A4
Penketh WA5 .... 14 C3
Runcorn WA8 .... 23 F1
St Mary's Rd M33 .... 242 A6
St Mary's Way WA7 .... 23 D2
St Mary's St Crewe CW1 . 190 B2
Warrington WA4 .... 16 B2
St Marys Cl L24 .... 21 F1
St Marys Ct CW5 .... 204 A4
St Matthew's CE Prim Sch
SK3 .... 240 E4
St Matthew's Rd L24 .... 240 E4
St Matthew's Terr SK3 .... 240 D4
St Matthews CE Aided
Prim Sch WA4 .... 26 C1
St Matthews Cl
Appleton WA4 .... 26 B4
Haslington CW1 .... 191 E2
St Mawes Cl WA8 .... 12 C1
St Mawgan Ct WA2 .... 8 C1
St Michael's Ave SK7 .... 35 F4
St Michael's Cl
Little Leigh CW8 .... 77 E3
Widnes WA8 .... 22 B4
St Michael's Ind Est WA8 . 22 B4
St Michael's RC Prim Sch
WA8 .... 22 B4
St Michael's Rd WA8 .... 22 B4
St Michael's View CW1 .... 190 B3
St Michael's Way CW10 .. 128 B3
St Monicas Cl WA4 .... 26 B4
St Nicholas Ct CW5 .... 204 C3
St Nicholas RC (Aided)
High Sch CW8 .... 103 E3
St Nicholas Rd WA3 .... 4 A2
St Olave St CH4 .... 237 E1
St Oliver Plunkett RC
Aided Prim Sch WA3 .... 9 F2
St Oswald's CE Aided Prim
Sch CH1 .... 94 C1
St Oswald's Cres CW11 ... 153 F3
St Oswald's RC Prim Sch
WA1 .... 16 B4
St Oswalds Cl
Malpas SY14 .... 213 D2
Winwick WA2 .... 8 A4
St Oswalds Way CH1 .... 237 E3
St Paul of the Cross RC
Aided Prim Sch WA5 .... 15 D2
St Paul's Cl CW1 .... 190 B2
St Paul's Hill Rd SK14 .... 241 F6
St Paul's Pl CW9 .... 79 D1
St Paul's RC Prim Sch SK15 . 242 F2
St Paul's Rd
🔟 Macclesfield SK11 ...... 112 C4
Manchester SK4 .... 240 A8
Widnes WA8 .... 23 D4
St Paul's St
Crewe CW1 .... 190 B2
Hyde SK14 .... 241 E7
Stalybridge SK15 .... 242 F2
St Pauls Gdns L66 .... 69 E1
St Pauls Rd Aided Prim Sch
SK12 .... 36 C1
St Pauls Trad Est SK15 ... 242 F2
St Peter's Ave WA16 .... 56 C1
St Peter's CE Prim Sch
Heswall L60 .... 40 C4
Newton-le-W WA12 .... 2 C2
St Peter's Cl Heswall L60 . 40 C4
Lymm WA13 .... 19 D2

St Peter's Dr Hyde SK14 241
Little Budworth CW6 .... 147ᵃ
St Peter's RC Aided Prim
Sch WA1 17
St Peter's RC Prim Sch
SK15 242
St Peter's Rise CW11 174
St Peter's Sq SK1 .... 240ᵃ
St Peter's Way WA1 17
St Peters Rd CW12 156
St Peters Way CW2 .... 119ᵃ
St Petersgate SK1 & SK3 .. 240ᵃ
St Philips Church & Comm
Prim Sch WA5 7
St Saviour's CE Contr Prim
Sch ST7 194
St Saviour's RC Aided Inf
& Jun Sch L66 .... 69ᵃ
St Saviour's St ST7 194
St Stephen Rd WA5 14
St Stephen's Ave WA2 8
St Stephen's Prim Sch
WA2 8
St Stephens Cl L60 41
St Stephens Ct CW11 174
St Teresa's RC Prim Sch
M44 11
St Theresa's RC Aided
Prim Sch CH1 .... 117ᵃ
St Thomas' CE Prim Sch
ST7 195
St Thomas' Cl WA5 .... 240ᵃ
St Thomas Cl SK1 240
St Thomas St WA8 12
St Thomas Hospl SK3 ..... 240ᵃ
St Thomas More RC
(Aided) High Sch CW2 ... 190
St Thomas of Canterbury
CE Aided Jun Sch
CH1 237
St Thomas St ST7 195
St Thomas's CE Aided Prim
Sch WA1 17
St Thomas's Pathway CH1 . 237
St Thomas's Pl SK1 .... 240ᵃ
St Vincent Dr CW8 102
St Vincent Rd WA5 14
St Vincent St WA15 238
St Vincent's RC Aided Prim
Sch WA15 57
St Vincent's RC Inf Sch
WA15 238
St Vincent's RC Jun Sch
WA15 238
St Vincent's RC Prim Sch
Penketh WA5 14
Widnes WA8 1
St Wenefredes Gn SY14 .. 214
St Werburgh CE Aided
Prim Sch WA1 16
St Werburgh St CH1 237
St Werburgh's & St
Columba's RC Aided
Prim Sch CH2 118
St Wilfred's Dr WA4 17
St Wilfrid's RC Prim Sch
CW8 103
St Winefride's RC Aided
Prim Sch L64 66
St Winefride's RC Prim Sch
L64 66
St Winifred's RC Prim Sch
SK4 240
Salander Cres CW2 206
Sale Gram Sch M33 242
Sale Sta M33 242
Sale Water Pk M33 242
Salerno Rd CW7 242
Salesbrook La CW5 228
Salford CW3 232
Salford Pl CW12 156
Salisbury Ave
Broughton CH4 .... 190ᵃ
Crewe CW2 .... 190ᵃ
Salisbury Cl Crewe CW2 .. 190
Ellesmere Port CH1 94
Salisbury Ct 🔟 SK10 112
Salisbury Pl SK10 87
Salisbury Rd
Altrincham WA14 238
Haydock WA11 1
Salisbury St Blacon CH1 .. 118
Goldborne WA3 3
Runcorn WA7 23
🔟 Widnes WA8 22
Salkeld St CW9 104
Salop Pl ST7 195
Salop Rd ST7 195
Salt Line Way CW11 174
Salt Mus The CW8 103
Saltash Cl WA7 50
Salter's La Bickerton SY14 . 199
Fuller's Moor CH3 183
Picton CH2 119
Salters La Siddington SK11 . 109ᵃ
Withington SK11 132
Saltersbrook Gr 🔟 SK9 .. 34
Saltersgate L66 69
Saltings Cl WA6 .... 49ᵃ
Saltney Ferry Cty Prim Sch
CH4 140
Saltney Ferry Rd CH4 140
Salton Gdns WA5 15
Saltwood Dr WA7 50
Samuel Laycock Spec Sch
SK15 242

amuel St Chester CH2 ...... 237 F3
Crewe CW1 .... 190 A3
Manchester SK11 .... 112 B4
Packmoor ST7 .... 195 F1
Stockport SK4 .... 240 D7
Warrington WA5 .... 15 F2
anbec Gdns WA8 .... 12 B3
and La SK10 .... 84 C3
andwood Cl WA2 .... 8 B1
andbach Cty High Sch
CW11 .... 175 D4
andbach Cty Prim Sch
CW11 .... 175 D3
andbach Golf Course
CW11 .... 174 C4
andbach Rd
Congleton CW12 .... 156 A2
Hassall Green CW11 .... 176 B1
Sanders Hey Cl WA7 .... 193 F3
Node Heath ST7 .... 193 F4
Sale M33 .... 242 F5
andbach Rd N ST7 .... 193 E2
andbach Rd S ST7 .... 193 E2
andbach Sch - (Ind)
(Boys) CW11 .... 175 D3
andbach Service Sta
CW11 .... 175 F3
andbach St WA11 .... 174 B4
anderling Rd WA12 .... 2 B2
Sanders Hey Cl WA7 .... 50 A3
Sanders Sq SK11 .... 112 B3
anderson Cl Crewe CW2 .... 206 B4
Great Sankey WA5 .... 14 B3
andfield Ave CW5 .... 216 C2
andfield Cl WA3 .... 3 F4
andfield Cres WA3 .... 3 F4
andfield Ct Frodsham WA6 .. 74 A4
Wrenbury CW5 .... 216 C2
andfield La
Acton Bridge CW8 .... 76 C1
Hartford CW8 .... 103 E2
andfield Pk L60 .... 40 B4
andfield Rd WA6 .... 74 A4
andford Rd Nantwich CW5 . 204 C4
Sale M33 .... 242 F5
andgate Rd SK10 .... 87 F1
andham Rd L24 .... 41 E4
andham Rd L24 .... 21 D2
andheys WA8 .... 41 E1
andhill St SK14 .... 241 F8
andiway Ct Handforth WA16 . 83 E2
Crowton CW8 .... 101 D4
andhurst Ave CW2 .... 190 A1
andhurst Dr SK9 .... 34 B1
andhurst Rd L24 .... 21 D3
andhurst St WA4 .... 16 C2
andicroft Cl WA3 .... 9 E3
andiford Rd CW4 .... 130 B2
andileigh Ct WA2 .... 118 C2
andileigh Ave
Altrincham WA15 .... 238 F3
Cheadle SK8 .... 240 A2
Knutsford WA16 .... 56 C1
andileigh Dr WA15 .... 238 F3
andiway Bebington L63 ..... 43 E3
Knutsford WA16 .... 57 D1
andiway Ave WA8 .... 12 A1
andiway Cl WA8 .... 102 A1
andiway Cty Prim Sch
CW8 .... 102 A2
andiway Golf Course
CW8 .... 102 B1
andiway La CW9 .... 53 D1
andiway Pk CW8 .... 102 C2
andiway Pl WA14 .... 238 D5
andiway Rd
Cheadle SK8 .... 238 D6
Crewe CW1 .... 190 A4
Wilmslow SK9 .... 34 B3
andle Bridge La WA14 .... 83 F3
andle Bridge Rise WA16 .... 83 F3
andon Cres L46 .... 66 C3
andon Park Gdns CW2 ..... 189 E2
andon Pl WA8 .... 13 E1
andon Rd CH2 .... 118 C2
andon St WA1 .... 190 B2
andown Cl Culcheth WA3 .. 4 C2
Middlewich CW10 .... 151 E4
Runcorn WA7 .... 49 E3
Wilmslow SK9 .... 60 A6
andown Cres CW8 .... 102 A2
andown Dr WA15 .... 32 B3
andown Pl SK11 .... 111 F4
andown Rd Crewe CW1 .... 190 B4
Stockport SK3 .... 240 B6
andpiper Cl Crewe CW1 .... 189 F4
Newton-le-W WA12 .... 2 B2
andpiper Dr SK3 .... 240 D2
andringham Ave
Chester CH2 .... 119 D1
Helsby WA6 .... 73 D2
Stalybridge SK15 .... 242 D3
andringham Cl
Altrincham WA14 .... 238 D1
Davenham CW9 .... 103 F2
Winsford CW7 .... 126 B2
andringham Dr
Great Sankey WA5 .... 15 E2
Poynton SK12 .... 36 B2
Stockport SK4 .... 240 A5
Wistaston CW2 .... 205 F4
andringham Gdns L65 ..... 70 B3
androck Rd WA8 .... 13 D2
androck Rd CH3 .... 142 C4
ands Rd ST7 .... 195 F3
andsdown Cl ST6 .... 179 E1
andside Rd ST7 .... 193 D2

Sandstone Wlk L60 .... 41 D4
Sandwell Dr M33 .... 242 B8
Sandwich Dr SK10 .... 87 E2
Sandwood Ave CH4 .... 139 D2
Sandy Brow La WA3 .... 3 F1
Sandy Cl SK10 .... 87 F4
Sandy Gr ST7 .... 193 E2
Sandy La Allostock WA16 .. 106 C3
Astbury CW12 .... 177 F3
Aston CW5 .... 217 E1
Bold Heath WA8 .... 14 A3
Broughton CH4 .... 140 B3
Brown Knowl CH3 .... 199 E4
Bulkeley SY14 .... 188 B1
Chester CH3 .... 119 D1
Congleton CW12 .... 155 E2
Congleton, Astbury Marsh
CW12 .... 156 A1
Croft WA3 .... 9 D4
Cronton WA8 .... 12 B3
Goldborne WA3 .... 2 C4
Goldborne, Wash End WA3 . 4 A4
Goostrey CW4 .... 107 E1
Haslington CW11 .... 192 A4
Hatherton CW5 .... 219 F3
Higher Kinnerton CH4 .... 161 D3
Huntington CH3 .... 142 B2
Lymm WA13 .... 19 D2
Macclesfield SK10 .... 86 B1
Neston L64 .... 67 D3
Nova Scotia CW8 .... 125 E3
Penketh WA5 .... 15 D2
Romiley SK6 .... 241 D3
Runcorn, Preston Brook WA7 . 50 C3
Runcorn, Weston Point WA7 . 48 C4
Sandbach CW11 .... 174 B3
Stalybridge SK15 .... 242 B1
Stockport SK4 & SK5 .... 240 E7
Swettenham CW12 .... 131 F2
Tarvin CH3 .... 121 E2
Threapwood SY14 .... 222 C4
Warrington WA2 .... 8 A2
Warrington, Cobbs WA4 .... 26 B4
Weaverham CW8 .... 77 E1
Widnes WA8 .... 12 B3
Wilmslow SK9 .... 59 F4
Sandy La W WA2 .... 8 A2
Sandy Moor La WA7 .... 49 E4
Sandyhill Pl CW7 .... 149 E3
Sandyhill Rd CW7 .... 149 E3
Sandylands Pk CW2 .... 205 E4
Sankey St Goldborne WA3 . 3 D4
Newton-le-W WA12 .... 2 A2
Widnes WA8 .... 22 D3
Sankey Sta WA1 .... 15 D3
Sankey Valley Ind Est
WA12 .... 2 A1
Sankey Valley Park WA12 .. 1 B2
Sankey Way
Great Sankey WA5 .... 15 E3
Warrington WA5 .... 43 D3
Sanky La WA4 .... 25 F1
Santon Dr WA3 .... 3 E4
Sapling La CW6 .... 146 C2
Sarra La CH3 .... 184 A3
Sarsfield Ave WA3 .... 3 E4
Saughall Cl CW9 .... 103 F2
Saughall Hey CH1 .... 94 A1
Saughall Rd CH1 .... 117 F3
Saunders St CW1 .... 190 A2
Saundersfoot Cl WA5 .... 7 F1
Saunderton Cl WA11 .... 1 B4
Saville Ave WA5 .... 14 C2
Saville St SK8 .... 239 B6
Saville St SK11 .... 112 C3
Savoy Rd CW1 .... 207 D4
Sawley Cl Culcheth WA3 ... 4 B2
Runcorn WA7 .... 50 C4
Sawley Dr SK7 .... 35 E3
Sawpit St WA13 .... 20 A3
Sawyer Brow SK14 .... 241 F8
Sawyer Dr ST6 .... 179 E1
Saxon Crossway CW7 .... 126 A1
Saxon Rd WA7 .... 23 A3
Saxon Terr WA8 .... 13 D1
Saxon Way Blacon CH1 .... 117 F3
Ellesmere Port CH1 .... 94 C4
Sandbach CW11 .... 175 E3
Saxons La Northwich CW8 . 103 F3
Northwich, Greenbank CW8 . 103 E4
Sayce St WA8 .... 13 D1
Scafell Ave WA2 .... 8 B2
Scafell Cl Bebington L63 ... 43 E2
High Lane SK6 .... 37 F4
Scaife Rd CW5 .... 204 C3
Scaliot Cl SK22 .... 39 D4
Scar La SY14 .... 198 C1
Sceptre Cl WA12 .... 2 B2
Scholar Green Cty Prim
Sch ST7 .... 194 C3
Scholar's Cl L64 .... 66 C4
Scholars' Green La WA13 .. 18 C1
School Ave L46 .... 66 B3
School Bank WA6 .... 101 D3
School Brow Romiley SK6 . 241 A2
Warrington WA1 .... 16 B1
School Cl Audley ST7 .... 210 A1
Knutsford WA16 .... 56 C1
Marbury SY13 .... 226 C4
Poynton SK12 .... 36 C2
School Cres Crewe CW1 .... 190 C2
Stalybridge SK15 .... 242 D4
School Dr SK3 .... 240 F2

School Gn CH3 .... 182 B1
School Hill L60 .... 40 C4
School La Alsford CH3 ...... 163 F1
Antrobus CW9 .... 53 B3
Astbury CW12 .... 178 A4
Audlem CW3 .... 230 A2
Bold Heath WA8 .... 13 F4
Brereton Green CW11 .... 153 F3
Bunbury CW6 .... 168 C1
Burwardsley CH3 .... 184 A3
Cheadle Hulme SK8 .... 35 D4
Cuddington CW8 .... 102 A1
Dunham Town WA14 .... 20 B3
Eaton (nr Congleton) CW12 . 156 C4
Ellesmere Port L66 .... 69 D4
Elton CH2 .... 72 A2
Frodsham WA6 .... 74 B4
Great Budworth CW9 .... 79 D4
Guilden Sutton CH3 .... 119 F3
Hartford CW8 .... 103 E2
Henbury SK11 .... 111 D3
Hollins Green WA3 .... 11 D1
Irlam M44 .... 11 E3
Lostock CW9 .... 80 A1
Marbury SY13 .... 215 F1
Marton SK11 .... 133 E3
Mickle Trafford CH2 .... 119 F4
Moulton CW9 .... 126 C4
Nantwich CW5 .... 204 C3
Neston L64 .... 66 C3
Neston, Parkgate L64 .... 41 D1
Nether Alderley SK10 .... 86 A3
Norley WA6 .... 100 B3
Ollerton WA16 .... 83 D2
Poynton SK12 .... 36 C2
Runcorn WA7 .... 49 F4
Sandbach, Betchton CW11 . 175 F3
Sandbach, Ettiley Heath
CW11 .... 174 C4
Southwald CW11 .... 176 C3
Warmingham CW11 .... 173 F4
Warrington WA3 .... 10 B3
Whitley WA4 .... 52 C3
Willaston L64 .... 42 A1
School Mews SK7 .... 35 F4
School Rd Altrincham WA15 . 238 F3
Ellesmere Port L65 .... 70 A3
Lach Dennis CW9 .... 104 D3
Sale M33 .... 242 A7
Sale M33 .... 242 B7
Warrington WA3 .... 8 B1
Wilmslow SK9 .... 34 A3
Winsford CW7 .... 127 D1
Winsford, Meadowbank CW7 126 C3
School Sq CW6 .... 104 C3
School Rd S CW9 .... 104 C3
School St Chester CH2 ...... 118 C2
Goldborne WA3 .... 3 D4
Haslington CW11 .... 191 E3
Warrington WA4 .... 16 A2
School Way Northwich CW9 104 A4
Widnes WA8 .... 23 D3
Schools Hill SK8 .... 239 D3
Schooner Cl WA7 .... 50 B3
Scilly Cl L65 .... 70 B1
Scotch Hall La CW9 .... 53 D2
Scotland Rd WA1 .... 16 A3
Scott Ave Crewe CW1 .... 190 C2
Widnes WA8 .... 22 C4
Scott Cl Macclesfield SK10 . 113 D4
Reddish SK5 .... 240 F8
Rode Heath ST7 .... 193 F4
Sandbach CW11 .... 174 B3
Scott Rd SK10 .... 87 D4
Scott St WA2 .... 16 B3
Scott Wlk WA12 .... 2 B1
Scotthorpe Cl SK11 .... 111 F3
Scotton Ave L65 .... 69 D3
Scretton Green Distribution
Pk WA4 .... 27 E2
Scroggins La M31 .... 11 F2
Sea Bank CW10 .... 128 B1
Sea La WA7 .... 23 E1
Sea View L64 .... 66 C2
Seabank Rd L60 .... 40 A3
Seabury St WA4 .... 17 D2
Seacombe Dr L66 .... 69 F2
Seacombe Gr SK3 .... 240 B4
Seaford Ave L62 .... 44 A3
Seafield Ave L60 .... 40 C3
Seaford Cl WA7 .... 24 A3
Seaford Pl WA2 .... 8 A2
Seaford Cl WA5 .... 190 C3
Seahill Rd CH1 .... 116 C4
Seal Rd SK7 .... 35 F4
Sealand Cl WA2 .... 8 C1
Sealand Ind Est CH1 .... 117 F1
Sealand Rd Blacon CH1 .... 117 E2
Chester CH1 .... 118 A1
Sealand CH5 .... 116 B3
Sealand Way ■ SK9 .... 34 B2
Seamon's Dr WA14 .... 238 A6
Seamon's Rd WA14 .... 238 A6
Seamons Wlk WA14 .... 238 B5
Seathwaite Cl WA7 .... 49 F3
Seaton Cl WA1 .... 190 A4
Seaton Pk WA7 .... 24 A2
Seaton St ST7 .... 127 E1
Seaview Ave L62 .... 44 A3
Seaville St CH2 .... 237 F3
Secker Ave WA4 .... 16 B1
Secker Cl WA4 .... 16 B1
Second Ave Adington SK10 . 36 B1
Crewe CW1 .... 190 C1
Deeside Ind Est CH5 .... 92 F2
Kidsgrove ST7 .... 194 C1
Runcorn WA7 .... 49 F4
Sandbach CW11 .... 175 D3

Second Dig La CW5 .... 219 E4
Second Wood St CW5 .... 204 B3
Sedburgh Cl WA7 .... 49 F3
Sedbergh Gr WA7 .... 49 F3
Sedbury La WA14 .... 130 A2
Seddon Rd WA14 .... 238 D2
Seddon St Middlewich CW10 128 B1
Seddon St CW10 .... 128 B1
Sedgefield Cl SK9 .... 34 B1
Sedgefield Rd CH1 .... 118 A1
Sedgwick Cres WA5 .... 6 C3
Sedgmere Ave CW1 .... 190 A4
Sedum Cl CH3 .... 142 A3
Sefton Ave Congleton CW12 157 D1
Widnes WA8 .... 13 D2
Sefton Cres M33 .... 242 B8
Sefton Dr SK9 .... 34 B1
Sefton Rd Chester CH2 ..... 119 D1
Sale M33 .... 242 B7
Sefton St L64 .... 1 C2
Seftons The SK9 .... 34 B1
Selby Cl Poynton SK12 ..... 36 B3
Runcorn WA7 .... 24 C2
Selby Gdns SK7 .... 35 E3
Selby La L66 .... 69 D3
Selby St Reddish SK4 .... 240 D8
Warrington WA5 .... 15 F3
Selkirk Ave Bebington L62 . 43 F2
Warrington WA4 .... 17 D2
Selkirk Cl Ellesmere Port L66 . 68 C3
Macclesfield SK10 .... 86 C1
Selkirk Dr Chester CH4 ..... 141 D4
Holmes Chapel CW4 .... 130 A1
Selkirk Rd CH4 .... 141 D4
Seller St CH2 .... 237 F3
Selsdon Ct CH4 .... 141 E4
Selsey Ave SK3 .... 239 F7
Selsey Cl CW1 .... 190 A4
Selsey Dr M20 .... 239 C8
Selworth Ave M33 .... 242 E6
Selworth Cl WA15 .... 238 E6
Selworthy Dr Crewe CW1 .. 190 A4
Warrington WA4 .... 17 E2
Selwyn Cl WA8 .... 13 E2
Selwyn Dr
Cheadle Hulme SK7 .... 35 E4
Sutton Lane Ends SK11 .... 112 C2
Semper Cl CW2 .... 157 D2
Seneschal Ct WA7 .... 49 F3
Senna La Antrobus CW9 ... 53 D1
Comberbach CW9 .... 78 B4
Sennen Cl WA7 .... 50 B3
Sephton Ave WA3 .... 4 C2
Sergeant York Loop WA5 .. 15 D3
Serin Cl WA12 .... 2 B2
Serpentine The CH4 .... 141 D4
Service St SK3 .... 240 B4
Service Cl L65 .... 69 F3
Set St SK15 .... 242 C1
Sett Cl SK22 .... 39 D4
Seven Sisters La WA16 ..... 82 C3
Sevenoaks Cl SK10 .... 87 D1
Sevenoaks Rd SK8 .... 239 B6
Severn Cl Altrincham WA14 238 C6
Biddulph ST6 .... 179 E1
Congleton CW12 .... 156 C1
Macclesfield SK10 .... 86 C1
Warrington WA2 .... 8 B1
Widnes WA8 .... 13 F2
Severn Dr SK7 .... 35 E3
Severn Rd WA3 .... 4 C1
Severn Wlk CW7 .... 127 D1
Severnvale L65 .... 70 A2
Severn St WA7 .... 23 D1
Sextant Cl WA7 .... 50 B3
Sexton Ave WA9 .... 1 A1
Seymour Chase WA16 ...... 82 A4
Seymour Ct WA2 .... 24 B2
Seymour Dr
Ellesmere Port L66 .... 69 F3
Poynton SK12 .... 36 C4
Seymour Gr M33 .... 242 B6
Shackleton Cl WA5 .... 15 E4
Shackleton Cl WA5 .... 15 E4
Shadewood Cres WA4 ...... 17 D1
Shadewood Rd SK11 .... 112 A3
Shadowmoss Rd M22 .... 33 F4
Shady Brook La CW8 .... 77 F1
Shaftesbury Ave
Chester CH3 .... 119 E1
Warrington WA5 .... 14 C1
Shaftesbury Rd SK3 .... 240 B2
Shaftesbury Way WA5 ...... 6 C4
Shaftway Cl WA11 .... 1 C4
Shakerley Ave CW12 .... 156 C2
Shakespeare Cl CW9 .... 104 B4
Shakespeare Dr
Cheadle SK8 .... 239 F6
Crewe CW1 .... 191 D2
Shakespeare Gr WA2 .... 8 B1
Shakespeare Rd
Neston L64 .... 41 F1
Widnes WA8 .... 13 D1
Shalcombe Cl L26 .... 21 D4
Shalford Dr M22 .... 33 E4
Shall Acres L65 .... 69 F3
Shallcross Ave SK23 .... 65 F2
Shallcross Cres SK23 .... 65 F2
Shallcross Rd SK23 .... 65 F2
Shalmarsh Rd L63 .... 43 D3
Shanklin Cl Sale M33 .... 14 B3
Shannon Cl Chester CH4 .. 140 C3
(nr Nantwich)
CW5 .... 205 E3
Shargate Cl CW4 .... 107 F1
Sharnbrook Dr CW2 .... 189 E2
Sharon Park Cl WA4 .... 17 E1
Sharp St Warrington WA1 .. 16 B3
Warrington WA2 .... 16 B3
Sharples St SK4 .... 240 E7

Sharpley St SK11 .... 112 B4
Sharston Cres WA16 .... 57 D1
Shavington Ave CW2 .... 118 C2
Shavington Cty High Sch
CW2 .... 206 A3
Shavington Cty Prim Sch
CW2 .... 206 B2
Shavington Way CW9 .... 103 F2
Shaw Dr WA16 .... 57 E2
Shaw Entry WA8 .... 12 A4
Shaw Heath SK2 & SK3 .... 240 E3
Shaw Moor Ave SK15 ...... 242 F1
Shaw Rd S WA3 .... 240 E2
Shaw St Ashton-u-L OL6 .. 242 A3
Culcheth WA3 .... 5 D2
Haydock WA11 .... 1 C3
Macclesfield SK11 .... 112 B4
Runcorn WA7 .... 22 C1
Warrington WA3 .... 4 B1
Shaw's Ave WA2 .... 16 B4
Shaw's Rd WA14 .... 238 D4
Shawcross Fold ⑤ SK1 ..... 240 F6
Shawell Ct WA8 .... 13 F1
Shaws Fold SK9 .... 33 F2
Shaws La
Mottram St Andrew SK10 .. 86 B4
Winsford CW7 .... 126 C2
Winsford CW7 .... 127 D2
Shay La Ashton CH3 .... 122 A4
Hampton SY14 .... 200 A1
Tarvin CH3 .... 121 F2
Shay's La CW6 .... 124 C2
Sheaf Cl CH3 .... 121 E1
Shearbrook La CW4 .... 107 F1
Sheardhall Ave SK12 .... 38 C3
Sheath St CW9 .... 104 A4
Shed La CH3 .... 119 D1
Sheepfield Cl L66 .... 69 E4
Sheerwater Cl WA1 .... 16 C4
Sheffield Rd WA5 .... 15 E3
Sheffield Rd SK14 .... 241 F8
Sheffield Row WA12 .... 7 E4
Sheffield St SK4 .... 240 E7
Sheiling Cl WA14 .... 238 C4
Sheilings The WA3 .... 4 B4
Shelagh Ave WA8 .... 13 D1
Shelburne Dr WA7 .... 191 E3
Shelbourne Ave Chester CH3 . 119 D1
Congleton CW12 .... 157 D1
Sheldon Rd SK7 .... 36 C4
Sheldon Dr L64 .... 66 C3
Sheldrake Rd WA14 .... 238 B8
Shellbrook Gr ■ SK9 .... 34 B1
Shelley Ave CW9 .... 103 F2
Shelley Cl Crewe CW1 ...... 190 C2
Rode Heath ST7 .... 193 F4
Shelley St ☑ CW11 .... 174 B3
Shelley Dr CW7 .... 189 F1
Shelley Gr WA4 .... 16 C2
Shelley Rd Blacon CH1 ..... 117 F3
Widnes WA8 .... 13 D1
Shellow La SK11 .... 134 B3
Shellway Rd L65 .... 71 D2
Shelton Cl WA8 .... 13 F2
Shelton Rd SK4 .... 241 C8
Shepcroft La WA4 .... 26 B2
Shepherd's Brow WA14 .... 238 A3
Shepherd's La CW7 .... 118 B3
Shepherds Fold Dr CW7 ... 126 B2
Shepherds Row WA7 .... 23 F1
Shepley Ct WA9 .... 1 C4
Shepley St ■ Hyde SK14 . 241 E6
Stalybridge SK15 .... 242 D2
Sheppard Cl CW1 .... 190 B3
Sheppenhall Gr CW5 .... 217 E1
Sheppenhall La
Newhall CW5 .... 228 B3
Royal's Green CW5 .... 228 B3
Shepperton Cl WA4 .... 26 C3
Shepsides Cl L66 .... 69 E1
Shepton Rd L66 .... 69 F1
Sherborne Cl WA7 .... 24 C2
Sherborne Rd
Cheadle SK3 .... 240 A3
Crewe CW1 .... 190 B3
Sherborne Ave CH4 .... 141 D3
Sherborne Cl SK3 .... 35 D3
Sherbourne Rd
Ellesmere Port L66 .... 70 B2
Macclesfield SK11 .... 111 F4
Sherbourne Way WA5 ...... 6 C4
Sherbrook Rise SK9 .... 60 B3
Sherbrooke Rd SK12 .... 38 B3
Sheri Dr WA12 .... 2 B1
Sheridan Ave WA3 .... 3 E4
Sheridan Cl CW1 .... 173 D2
Sheringham Cl CH4 .... 140 C3
Sheringham Dr WA5 .... 190 A4
Sheringham Dr WA5 .... 14 C3
Sherlock Ave WA11 .... 1 C4
Sherratt Cl CW12 .... 156 C1
Sherrington's La CH3 .... 199 E4
Sherwin St CW2 .... 190 B1
Sherwood Ave
Cheadle SK8 .... 239 F2
Sale M33 .... 242 D7
Sherwood Cl WA5 .... 240 A5
Sherwood Cl WA8 .... 12 B1
Sherwood Cres WA5 .... 6 C3
Sherwood Gr WA6 .... 73 D2
Sherwood Rd SK11 .... 112 B3

Shetland Cl Warrington WA2 .. 8 C2
Widnes WA8 .... 13 F2
Shetland Dr Bebington L62 .... 43 F4
Ellesmere Port L65 .... 70 B1
Shevington Cl WA8 .... 13 F2
Shevington Wlk WA8 .... 13 F2
Shield St SK3 .... 240 E4
Shiers Dr SK8 .... 239 E4
Shiggins Cl WA3 .... 15 E3
Shillingford Cl WA4 .... 26 C3
Shilton Cl CW10 .... 151 F3
Ship St WA6 .... 49 E1
Shipbrook Rd Chester CH2 .. 118 C3
  Lach Dennis CW9 .... 104 A2
  Northwich CW9 .... 104 B3
Shipgate St CH4 .... 237 C1
Shipton Cl
  Great Sankey WA5 .... 15 D4
  Widnes WA8 .... 34 B3
Shirley Ave SK8 .... 34 B3
Shirley Dr WA4 .... 17 D1
Shirley Gr SK7 .... 240 E2
Shirleys Cl SK10 .... 87 D3
Shirleys Dr SK10 .... 87 D3
Shocklach Oviatt CE Contr
  Prim Sch SY14 .... 211 E4
Shocklach Rd CH2 .... 118 C3
Shones Croft L64 .... 67 D3
Shop La CW6 .... 124 C1
Shopping Precinct The
  CH2 .... 72 A2
Shoreham Dr CH3 .... 15 D2
Shores Green Dr CW9 .... 79 F3
Shores La CW5 .... 203 E4
Shorewell Cl WA5 .... 14 B4
Short Cl WA12 .... 1 C2
Short St Haydock WA11 ..... 1 C3
  Macclesfield SK11 .... 112 B4
  Newton-le-w WA12 .... 1 C2
  Stockport SK4 .... 240 E7
  Widnes WA8 .... 23 D3
Short St E SK4 .... 240 E7
Shorthorn Cl CW10 .... 128 B1
Shotwick La CH1 .... 93 F3
Shotwick Rd CH1 .... 93 D2
Shrewsbury Cres CW5 ...... 204 C2
Shrewsbury Rd CW5 .... 204 B2
Shrewsbury Dr ST5 .... 210 C1
Shrewsbury Gdns SK7 ...... 35 E3
Shrewsbury Rd L65 .... 70 B3
Shrewsbury St WA4 .... 16 C2
Shrewsbury Way CH4 ...... 140 E1
Shrigley Cl SK9 .... 34 B1
Shrigley Rd Bollington SK10 . 63 D3
  Pott Shrigley SK10 .... 63 D3
  Poynton SK12 .... 37 E2
Shrigley Rd N SK12 .... 37 E2
Shrigley Rise SK10 .... 63 E1
Shropshire Cl
  Middlewich CW10 .... 151 D4
  Warrington WA1 .... 17 F3
Shropshire La
  Newhall SY13 .... 227 F1
  Old Woodhouse SY13 ...... 227 F1
Shropshire Rd L65 .... 70 C2
Shropshire St CW3 .... 229 F2
Shurlach Rd CW9 .... 104 B3
Shutley La CW3 .... 77 E3
Sibbersfield La CH3 ...... 180 C2
Sibell St CH2 .... 237 F3
Sibley Rd SK4 .... 240 B7
Sibson Rd M33 .... 242 B6
Siddall St CW9 .... 104 A4
Siddeley Cl CH4 .... 139 E2
Siddeley Dr WA12 .... 1 C2
Siddington Ave
  Northwich CW9 .... 104 A2
  Stockport SK3 .... 240 D2
Siddington Bank SK11 ..... 109 F2
Siddington Rd Poynton SK12 . 36 C1
  Wilmslow SK9 .... 34 B3
Siddon St CW7 .... 126 C1
Side Ave WA14 .... 238 C1
Side End La SK23 .... 64 C2
Sidebottom St SK15 ...... 242 C2
Sidlaw Cl L66 .... 69 D3
Sidley Pl SK14 .... 241 F7
Sidley St SK14 .... 241 F7
Sidmouth Cl WA5 .... 14 C2
Sidmouth Gr SK8 .... 34 C4
Sidney Rd L64 .... 41 F1
Siemens Rd WA4 .... 11 F3
Silcock St WA3 .... 3 D4
Silk Hill SK23 .... 65 F4
Silk Mill St WA16 ...... 57 D1
Silk Mus & Heritage Ctr
  SK11 .... 112 B4
Silk Rd The Bollington SK10 . 87 F2
  Macclesfield SK10 .... 87 F2
Silk St CW12 .... 156 B1
Silkstone Cres WA7 ..... 50 A4
Silsden Ave WA3 .... 4 A4
Silvan Ct WA10 .... 87 D1
Silver Ave WA11 .... 1 A3
Silver Hill Rd SK14 .... 241 E5
Silver La Croft WA3 .... 9 F4
  Warrington WA3 .... 10 B3
Silver St Bollington SK10 . 88 A4
  Congleton CW12 .... 156 C1
  Warrington WA3 .... 16 A3
Silverbeech Ave WA8 .... 22 C3
Silverbirch Croft CH4 ... 139 D2
Silverbirch Way CH1 .... 94 C4
Silverdale Altrincham WA14 238 D4
  Northwich CW8 .... 103 E4

Silverdale Ave M34 .... 241 A6
Silverdale Cl Frodsham WA6 . 74 B4
  High Lane SK6 .... 37 F4
Silverdale Dr SK9 .... 60 A2
Silverdale Rd Gatley SK8 . 239 B4
  Manchester SK4 .... 240 D8
  Newton-le-W WA12 .... 2 A2
Silvergate Ct CW12 ..... 178 C4
Silvermine Cl ST7 ...... 195 D1
Silverthorne Cl SK15 ... 242 D1
Silverwood ST7 .... 195 D1
Simms Cross Cty Prim Sch
  WA8 .... 23 D4
Simon Cl M33 .... 242 A5
Simons La WA6 .... 74 A3
Simonside WA8 .... 12 B1
Simonstone Rd CH4 ..... 139 E2
Simonswood Cl CW10 .... 151 D4
Simpkin Ave WA4 .... 16 C2
Simpson Cl CW1 .... 95 E1
Simpson Ct CW1 .... 173 D1
Simpson La SK10 .... 63 E4
Simpson Rd CW2 .... 95 E1
Simpson St Hyde SK14 .. 241 D6
  [7] Stockport SK3 ..... 240 E4
Simpsons Way CH4 ...... 139 D2
Sinclair Ave Alsager ST7 . 193 D2
  Warrington WA2 .... 8 A1
  Widnes WA8 .... 23 D4
Sinderland La WA14 .... 20 C4
Sinderland Rd WA14 ... 238 C8
Singapore Ave M90 ..... 33 D4
Singleton Ave CW1 ..... 190 B3
Singleton Rd
  Ellesmere Port L65 .... 69 F2
  [2] Manchester SK4 .... 240 B8
Sir John Deane's Sixth
  Form Coll CW9 .... 103 F3
Sir Thomas Boteler Cty
  High Sch The WA4 ..... 16 C2
Siskin Cl WA12 .... 2 B2
Six Acre Gdns WA4 .... 25 D3
Six Acre La WA4 .... 25 D3
Sixpenny Wlk WA1 ..... 16 B3
Sixth Ave CH5 .... 92 C1
Skaife Rd M33 .... 242 E6
Skeath Cl CW11 .... 175 F3
Skellern St ST7 ...... 194 B1
Skelton Rd WA4 .... 238 E7
Skiddaw Cl WA7 .... 50 A3
Skip's La CH3 .... 142 C4
Skipton Cl SK7 .... 36 B4
Skipton Dr L66 .... 69 E3
Skye Cl Ellesmere Port L65 . 70 B1
  Widnes WA8 .... 13 F2
Skye Croft SK6 .... 241 D3
Skylark Cl CW1 .... 189 F4
Slack St Hyde SK14 ... 241 F8
  Macclesfield SK11 .... 112 C3
Slacken La ST7 .... 194 B1
Slade La Mobberley WA16 . 58 A4
  Nether Alderley SK10 .. 85 F3
Slade St CW9 .... 104 A4
Slag La Golborne WA3 .. 3 E4
  Haydock WA11 .... 1 B4
Slater St Macclesfield SK11 . 112 B3
  Warrington WA4 .... 16 A2
Slindon Cl ST5 .... 210 B1
Sloane St CW5 .... 242 D1
Slutchers La WA1 ..... 16 A2
Small Ave WA2 .... 8 B1
Small Cres WA2 .... 8 B1
Small La WA16 .... 58 A4
Smallbrook Wlk CW2 .. 206 B4
Smallman Rd CW2 ..... 190 B1
Smallwood CE Contr Prim
  Sch CW11 .... 176 C3
Smallwood Cl
  Middlewich CW10 ..... 151 E4
  Newcastle-u-L ST5 .... 210 B1
Smethurst Cl SK9 .... 59 F2
Smethwick La
  CW11, CW12 .... 154 C2
Smith Cl ST7 .... 193 D2
Smith Cres WA2 .... 16 B4
Smith Dr WA2 .... 16 B4
Smith Gr CW1 .... 190 A3
Smith La Mobberley WA16 . 59 F1
  Rainow SK10 .... 89 D3
Smith Rd WA8 .... 22 C4
Smith St Cheadle SK8 . 239 F6
  Macclesfield SK11 .... 112 B3
  Warrington WA1 .... 16 A3

Smithy La continued
  Cronton WA8 .... 12 B3
  Cuddington CW8 .... 102 A3
  Dunham Town WA14 ..... 20 B2
  Ellesmere Port L66 .... 69 E3
  Fuller's Moor CH3 ..... 183 E1
  Great Budworth CW9 .... 79 D4
  Helsby WA6 .... 73 E3
  Hulse SK14 .... 241 E5
  Kingsley WA6 .... 75 D1
  Little Leigh CW8 ...... 77 D3
  Lostock CW9 .... 80 A1
  Malpas SY14 .... 213 D2
  Mottram St Andrew SK10 . 61 E1
  Mouldsworth CH3 .... 98 C1
  Partington M31 .... 11 F2
  Utkinton CH6 .... 146 B3
  Weston CW2 .... 207 E3
  Willaston L64 .... 68 A4
Smithy Pathway CH4 .... 140 C2
Smithy The CH2 .... 118 B4
Smithy Vale SK10 ...... 87 F4
Smithy Wlk [1] CW1 .... 174 C2
Smokehall La CW7, CW9 . 126 C3
Smokehall Lane Ind Est
  CW7 .... 127 D3
Smokey La SY13 .... 224 A1
Smokies Way ST6 ...... 179 E1
Smyth Rd WA8 .... 13 E1
Snab La L64 .... 66 C3
Snabwood Cl L64 ...... 66 C3
Snaefell Rise WA4 .... 26 B4
Snape Hollow CW2 ..... 207 F2
Snape La CW2 .... 207 E2
Snape Rd Crewe CW2 .. 206 B4
  Macclesfield SK10 .... 87 F1
Snapebrook Gr [6] SK9 . 34 C1
Snelson La
  Chelford SK11 .... 108 C1
  Chelford, Marthall WA16 . 83 C2
Snipe Cl SK12 .... 36 A2
Snow Hill SK11 .... 112 C3
Snowberry Cl WA8 ..... 13 F2
Snowberry Wlk M31 .... 11 E1
Snowdon Cl
  Ellesmere Port L66 ... 69 D3
  Great Sankey WA5 .... 14 B4
Snowdon Cres CH4 .... 141 D3
Snowdon Dr CW2 ...... 189 E2
Snowdrop Cl WA7 ..... 49 F2
Solly Cres CW12 ..... 156 A1
Solway Cl WA2 .... 8 C2
Solway Gr WA7 .... 49 E3
Solway Rd CW8 .... 78 B1
Somerford Ave CW2 ... 190 A2
Somerford Cl CW11 ... 175 E4
Somerford Rd CW4 ... 130 B3
Somerford Wlk WA8 .. 13 F2
Somerley Cl CW1 .... 190 A4
Somerset Ave ST7 ... 194 C1
Somerset Cl
  Congleton CW12 ..... 156 B2
  Irlam M44 .... 11 E3
Somerset Pl M33 .... 242 B8
Somerset Rd
  Altrincham WA14 .... 238 D6
  Chester CH2 .... 118 C3
Somerset St CW7 .... 237 E4
Somerset Way WA1 ... 17 D4
Somerton Ave M33 ... 242 C5
Somerton St CW1 .... 111 F4
Somerton Rd SK11 ... 111 F4
Somerville Cl
  Bebington L63 .... 43 D3
  High Legh WA16 ...... 29 E2
Somerville Cres L65 . 70 B2
Somerville Gdns WA15 238 F7
Somerville St WA4 .. 190 A1
Soot Hill CW9 ...... 78 B2
Sorbus Cl CW7 ...... 72 B2
Sorbus Dr CW1 ...... 190 C3
Sorby Rd M44 .... 11 F4
Sorrel Cl Huntington CH3 . 142 A3
  Warrington WA2 ..... 9 E1
Soss Moss Hospl SK10 . 84 B3
Sossmoss La SK10 ... 84 B3
Sound Cty Prim Sch CW5 . 217 F3
Sound La Ravensmoor CW5 . 203 F1
  Sound CW5 .... 217 E4
Sourace Fold SK15 ... 242 D3
Souter's La CH1 .... 237 E2
South Acre Dr
  Macclesfield SK11 ... 113 D4
  Wilmslow SK9 .... 34 B2
South Ave Chester CH2 . 237 F4
  Haslington CW1 ..... 191 E2
  Warrington WA2 ..... 16 A4
  Warrington, Stockton Heath
   WA4 .... 16 B1
South Bank CW2 ..... 206 A3
South Bank Gr CW12 . 156 C1
South Bank Terr WA7 . 22 C2
South Back St CH1 .. 237 A3
South Blk SK9 ...... 60 A1
South Cft CW6 ...... 185 E3
South Cheshire Coll CW1 . 190 B2
South Cheshire Coll
  (Annexe) CW1 .... 190 B2
South Cl Tarporley CW6 . 146 B1
  Wilmslow SK9 .... 59 F3
South Crescent Rd CH4 . 237 B2
South Crofts CW5 ... 204 C3
South Dale WA5 ..... 14 C3
South Downs WA16 ... 57 E1
South Downs Dr WA14 . 238 D1

South Downs Rd WA14 .. 238 D1
South Dr Gatley SK8 ... 239 A4
Heswall L60 .... 40 C4
Northwich CW9 .... 104 B3
Plumley WA16 .... 80 C2
South Gn CH5 .... 116 A3
South Gr Alderley Edge SK9 . 60 A1
  Sale M33 .... 242 B5
South La WA8 .... 13 F3
South Lane Entry WA8 . 13 F3
South Mead SK12 ..... 36 A3
South Meadway SK6 ... 37 F4
South Oak La SK9 .... 59 F3
South Par WA7 .... 48 B4
South Park Dr SK12 .. 36 C1
South Park Rd Gatley SK8 . 239 B6
  Macclesfield SK11 ... 112 B4
South Pier Rd L65 ... 70 B4
South Rd
  Altrincham, Ashley Heath
   WA14 .... 31 F4
  Altrincham, Rosehill WA14 . 238 C2
  Ellesmere Port L65 .. 70 B2
  Runcorn WA7 .... 48 B4
  St Helens L34 .... 21 D3
  Stanlow L65 .... 70 C2
South St Alderley Edge SK9 . 60 A1
  Chester CH3 .... 119 D1
  Congleton CW12 ..... 156 B2
  Crewe CW2 .... 190 B1
  Mount Pleasant ST7 . 195 D3
  [2] Widnes WA8 ..... 23 D2
South Trafford Coll of
  F Ed WA14 .... 238 D8
South Vale Cres WA15 . 238 F5
South View SK11 .. 113 E1
South View Rd CH1 .. 118 A1
South View WA7 ..... 50 A3
South Way CH1 ...... 117 F2
South West Ave SK10 . 87 F3
South Wirral High Sch L62 . 43 E2
Southampton Way WA7 . 50 C3
Southbank CW9 ..... 79 D4
Southbank Ave CW2 . 206 B3
Southdale Rd WA1 .. 17 D4
Southdown Cl
  Macclesfield SK10 .. 87 E2
  Warrington WA5 .... 14 C1
Southern St WA4 ... 16 B1
Southey Cl [3]
  Sandbach CW11 ..... 174 B3
  Widnes WA8 .... 22 C4
Southfield Cl SK9 .. 34 B2
Southfield Rd L66 .. 69 E3
Southfield St SK9 .. 34 B2
Southfields Ave WA5 . 14 C3
Southfields Cl CW5 . 220 A4
Southlands CW4 .... 130 B1
Southlands Ave WA5 . 14 C2
Southlands Mews CW7 . 22 C1
Southlands Rd CW12 . 179 D4
Southlands View WA4 . 107 F1
Southpoint SK4 .... 240 A6
Southport St WA9 .. 1 A2
Southward Rd WA11 . 2 A4
Southwark Pl [8] CW7 . 149 D4
Southway
  Altrincham WA14 ... 238 E6
  Runcorn WA7 .... 49 E1
  Widnes WA8 .... 22 B4
Southway Ave WA4 . 26 B4
Southwell Cl Goldborne WA3 . 3 E4
  Romiley SK6 .... 241 A1
Southwood Ave WA7 . 24 B1
Southworth Ave WA5 . 15 F4
Southworth La
  Croft WA3, WA2 .... 8 C4
  Winwick WA3, WA2 .. 8 C4
Southworth Rd WA12 . 2 C2
Sovereign Cl
  Northwich CW9 ..... 104 C3
  Warrington WA3 .... 50 B4
Sovereign Cn WA3 . 9 E2
Sovereign Way CH1 . 117 F1
Spark Hall Cl WA4 . 26 C1
Spark La Runcorn WA7 . 23 F1
  Smallwood CW11 .... 154 B1
Sparks Cl CH3 ..... 142 A4
Sparrow La WA16 ... 57 D1
Sparrowbutts Gr ST7 . 195 E1
Sparrowhawk Cl WA7 . 50 A4
Sparth Cl SK4 ..... 240 D7
Sparth La SK4 ..... 240 D7
Sparthfield Rd SK4 . 240 D7
Spawell Cl WA3 .... 3 F4
Speakman Ave WA12 . 2 B3
Speakman St WA7 .. 22 C2
Speed's Way CH4 .. 180 C1
Speedwell Cl Heswall L60 . 41 E4
  Huntington CH3 .... 142 A3
Speedwell Dr L60 . 41 E4
Speedwell Rd ST5 . 210 C1
Speke Bvd Halewood L24 . 21 D2
  Speke L24 .... 21 D2
Speke Hall Ave L24 . 21 D1
Speke Rd WA8 ..... 22 B4
Spencer Brook SK10 . 86 C3

Spencer Cl Alsager ST7 .. 192
  Widnes WA8 12
  Wistaston CW2 206
Spencer Rd L64 41
Spencer St CW7 78
Spendmore Ct WA7 . 49
Spennymoor Ct WA7 . 49
Spey Cl Altrincham WA14 . 238
  Winsford CW7 126
Spey Dr ST7 195
Spike Island WA8 .. 23
Spindle Ave SK15 .. 242
Spindle St CW12 ... 156
Spink La WA16 60
Spinnaker Cl WA7 . 50
Spinner Cres CW9 . 78
Spinney CW8 101
Spinney Ave Goostrey CW4 . 107
Spinney Cl
  Chester CH3 142
Spinney End CH3 .. 166
Spinney La WA16 .. 56
Spinney Mead SK10 . 87
Spinney The Cheadle SK8 . 239
  Heswall L60 41
  Lawton-gate ST7 .. 194
  Neston L64 41
  Norley WA6 100
  [1] Sandbach CW11 . 175
  Willaston (nr Nantwich)
   CW5 205
Spinney Wlk WA7 . 24
Spirewood Gdns SK6 . 241
Spital Wlk CH2 ... 118
Spodegreen La WA14 . 30
Spout La WA16 ... 58
Spragg St CW12 .. 156
Spring Ave L66 ... 69
Spring Bank
  Altrincham WA14 . 238
  Stalybridge SK15 . 242
Spring Bank La
  Adlington SK10 ... 63
  Stalybridge SK15 . 242
Spring Bank Pl SK1 & SK3 . 240
Spring Bank Rd SK22 . 39
Spring Cl ST7 193
Spring Ct WA7 ... 24
Spring Gdns Crewe CW1 . 190
  Ellesmere Port L65 . 69
  Hyde SK14 241
  Macclesfield SK10
Spring Hill CW6 . 168
Spring La Coddington CH3 . 181
  Croft WA3 9
  Lymm WA13 19
Spring Meadow CW8 . 78
Spring Mount SK22 . 39
Spring Rd Altrincham WA14 . 238
  Poynton SK12 36
Spring St Congleton CW12 . 156
  Stalybridge SK15 . 242
  Widnes WA8 23
  Wilmslow SK9 60
Springbank SK10 . 87
Springbank Cl WA7 . 49
Springbank Cres CW7 . 149
Springbourne WA6 . 74
Springcroft L64 . 41
Springe La CW5 .. 203
Springfield Ave
  Goldborne WA3 ... 3
  Helsby WA6 73
  Lymm WA13 19
  Malpas SY14 213
  Warrington WA4 .. 17
  Warrington, Paddington WA1 . 17
Springfield Cl CW8 . 161
Springfield Dr Chester CH2 . 118
  Wilmslow SK9 59
  Wistaston CW2 ... 205
Springfield Pk WA11 . 1
Springfield Prim Sch M33 . 242
Springfield Rd
  Altrincham WA14 . 238
  Gatley SK8 239
  Macclesfield SK11 . 113
  Malpas SY14 213
  Mobberley WA16 . 57
  Sale M33 242
  Widnes WA8 22
Springfield Sch CW7 . 190
Springfield St WA1 . 16
Springfields
  Cuddington CW8 . 101
  Knutsford WA16 . 57
  Mickle Trafford CH2 . 119
  Prestbury SK10
Springfields Dr CW12 . 156
Springhead Cl ST7 . 195
Springhead Dr CW7 . 210
Springhill Prim Sch ST7 . 210
Springhill SK10 . 88
Springhill Ave L62 . 43
Springholm Dr WA4 . 26
Springmount WA3 . 3
Springs La CW5 .. 242
Springs The WA14 . 238
Springs Wood Gr WA3 . 3
Springwood Ave WA10 . 1
Springwood Cl WA10 . 1
Springwood Cres SK6 . 241
Springwood La WA6 . 100
Sprink La CW12 .. 157

aroston Way CW9 .... 103 F2
ruce Ave CW8 .... 102 A2
ruce Cl Goldborne WA3 .... 3 F4
Warrington WA1 .... 17 F4
ruce Gr ST7 .... 193 F4
ruce Lodge SK8 .... 239 D6
ouley La Pott Shrigley SK10 .. 63 E1
Rainow SK10 .... 63 E1
ounhill Ave L66 .... 69 E1
ourlong Rd WA5 .... 6 C3
ourston Cl WA16 .... 29 E2
quare St SK11 .... 112 C3
quare The
Altrincham WA15 .... 32 B4
Audlem CW3 .... 229 F2
Christleton CH3 .... 142 C4
Hyde SK14 .... 241 D6
Ince CH2 .... 71 F3
Manchester SK4 .... 240 C7
Neston L64 .... 41 A4
Woore CW3 .... 232 B1
quires Ave WA8 .... 23 D4
quires Cl WA11 .... 1 A3
quirrel Cl WA8 .... 103 E4
quirrel Ct WA14 .... 238 C8
quirrel's Jump SK9 .... 60 B1
quirrels Chase SK10 .... 86 C3
table La CH3 .... 99 D2
ablings The SK9 .... 60 A3
adium Ind Est CW11 .... 118 A2
adium Way CH1 .... 118 A2
admocslow La ST7 .... 195 F2
afford Cl SK10 .... 86 C1
afford Gdns L65 .... 70 A3
afford Rd WA4 .... 16 B1
afford St Audlem CW3 .... 230 A2
Crewe CW1 .... 190 B3
afford Wlk SK10 .... 86 C1
ag Ind Est WA14 .... 238 B6
age La WA13 .... 19 E2
ainer Cl WA4 .... 26 C3
ainmore Cl WA3 .... 10 A3
aithes Rd WA22 .... 33 E4
albridge Rd CW2 .... 190 B1
alybridge Cl L65 .... 242 F2
allard Way CW10 .... 151 A4
almine Ave SK4 .... 34 A4
aly Hall Rd SK15 .... 242 F2
alybridge Ridge Hill Cty
Inf Sch SK15 .... 242 C3
alybridge Ridge Hill Jun
Sch SK15 .... 242 C3
alybridge SK15 .... 242 C2
amford Ave
Altrincham WA14 .... 238 A5
Ashton-u-L SK15 .... 242 B2
Crewe CW2 .... 190 B2
amford Cl
amford Ct Chester CH2 ... 119 E1
Lymm WA13 .... 18 C2
Macclesfield SK11 .... 112 B3
amford Dr SK15 .... 242 C2
amford Gr SK15 .... 242 C2
amford Grange ■ WA14 238 C4
amford High Sch L60 .... 242 B4
amford La CH1 .... 120 B1
amford New Rd WA14 .. 238 D4
amford Park Inf Sch
WA15 .... 238 E3
amford Park Jun Sch
WA15 .... 238 E3
amford Rd WA15 .... 238 E3
amford Pl M33 .... 242 C6
Alderley Edge SK9 .... 60 A1
Altrincham WA14 .... 238 A5
Blacon CH1 .... 117 F3
Little Bollington WA14 .... 20 A1
Macclesfield SK11 .... 112 B2
Wilmslow SK9 .... 34 A1
amford Sq
■ Altrincham WA14 .... 238 D5
Ashton-u-L OL6 .... 242 A2
amford St
Altrincham WA14 .... 238 D5
Ellesmere Port L65 .... 70 A3
Sale M33 .... 242 A8
Stalybridge OL6 & SK15 ..... 242 C2
amford St E OL6 .... 242 A2
amford Way ■ WA14 .... 238 D5
amore Rd WA7 .... 23 E1
amp Ave CW1 .... 190 B3
anbank St SK4 .... 240 E6
anbridge Ct SK4 .... 240 E6
andford Dr CW9 .... 104 A3
anhope Ave CW1 .... 190 C2
anhope Cl SK9 .... 60 B4
anhope Rd WA14 .... 238 C6
anhope St OL6 .... 242 A4
anier Cl CW1 .... 191 D2
anlaw Rd L65 .... 70 B2
anley Ave
Great Sankey WA5 .... 14 B4
Hyde SK14 .... 241 E8
Warrington WA4 .... 16 C1
anley Cl Hartford CW8 ..... 103 D2
Widnes WA8 .... 13 E1
anley Ct ST7 .... 193 E2
anley Dr ST5 .... 210 B1
anley Gr Manchester SK4 .. 240 B8
Northwich CW9 .... 79 F1
anley Green Ind Est
SK8 .... 34 C3
anley Green Ret Pk
SK8 .... 34 C3

Stanley Hall La SK12 .... 38 B3
Stanley La L62 .... 43 F2
Stanley Mount M33 .... 242 A5
Stanley Park Ct CW4 ..... 140 C3
Stanley Park Dr CW4 ..... 140 C3
Stanley Pl Chester CH1 .... 237 D2
Warrington WA4 .... 16 C1
Stanley Rd Biddulph ST6 .. 179 F1
Cheadle SK8 .... 34 C3
Cheadle Hulme SK8 .... 34 C3
Ellesmere Port L65 .... 70 A3
Knutsford WA16 .... 56 C1
Runcorn WA7 .... 22 C1
Stanley Rd Ind Est WA16 .. 57 D1
Stanley St Chester CH1 .... 237 D2
Crewe CW1 .... 190 B2
Newton-le-W WA12 .... 2 A2
Northwich CW9 .... 104 B4
Runcorn WA7 .... 23 D2
Stalybridge SK15 .... 242 C1
Warrington WA1 .... 16 A2
Stanley Woods Ave CH2 .... 95 E4
Stanlow Abbey Cty Prim
Sch L65 .... 70 C1
Stanlow & Thornton Sta
Stannage La CH3 .... 180 C3
Stanner Cl WA5 .... 7 E1
Stannerhouse La CW11 .. 175 F2
Stanney Cl Bebington L62 ... 43 F2
Neston L64 .... 66 C4
Stanney Cty High Sch L65 .. 70 B1
Stanney Grange Cty Prim
Sch L65 .... 70 B2
Stanney Grange Sports
Complex The L65 .... 70 C2
Stanney La Ellesmere Port L65 70 B2
Stoak L65 .... 70 C4
Stanney Mill La
Ellesmere Port L65 .... 70 C1
Stanlow L65 .... 70 C1
Stanney Mill Rd L65 .... 70 C1
Stanney Ten Ind Est L65 .. 70 C1
Stanney Woods Ave L65 .. 70 B1
Stanney Woods Cty Prk
L66 .... 70 A1
Stanneybrook Cl WA6 .. 101 D3
Stanneylands Cl SK9 .... 34 B1
Stanneylands Dr SK9 .... 34 A1
Stanneylands Rd SK9 .... 34 A2
Stansfield Ave WA1 .... 16 C3
Stansfield Rd SK14 .... 241 E8
Stanstead Ave WA5 .... 14 C2
Stanthorne Ave CW2 .... 190 A2
Stanton Cl WA11 .... 1 B3
Stanton Ct L64 .... 66 C4
Stanton Dr CH2 .... 118 B3
Stanton Gdns SK4 .... 240 B5
Stanton Rd WA4 .... 17 E2
Stanway Dr WA15 .... 238 F5
Stapeley Broad Lane CE
Contr Prim Sch CW5 .. 205 D1
Stapeley Terr CW5 .... 205 D1
Stapeley Water Gdns
CW5 .... 205 D2
Stapleford Cl M33 .... 242 E7
Stapleford Ct L66 .... 69 F4
Stapleford Rd WA4 .... 16 B4
Stapleton Rd SK10 .... 87 E2
Stapleton Way WA8 .... 22 C1
Stapley Cl WA7 .... 22 C1
Star La Lymm WA13 .... 18 B2
Macclesfield SK11 .... 112 B2
Starbeck Dr L66 .... 69 D3
Starkey Gr WA4 .... 16 C3
Starling Cl Farndon CH3 .. 180 C1
Runcorn WA7 .... 50 B4
Start La SK23 .... 65 D4
Statham Ave Lymm WA13 .. 18 B2
Warrington WA2 .... 8 A1
Statham Cl Denton M34 .. 241 A7
Lymm WA13 .... 18 B2
Statham La WA13 .... 18 B2
Statham La WA13 .... 18 A3
Statham St
Station Ave
Ellesmere Port L66 .... 69 E4
Helsby WA6 .... 73 D2
Station Cl Hyde SK14 .... 241 D6
Neston L64 .... 66 C4
Station Gn L66 .... 69 E4
Station Hill CW8 .... 76 C1
Station La CW8 .... 77 F2
Station Rd Acton Bridge CW8 77 D1
Adderley TF9 .... 235 D3
Alpraham CW6 .... 169 F1
Alsager ST7 .... 193 E2
Astbury ST7 .... 178 A1
Backford CW5 .... 95 D2
Biddulph ST6 .... 179 E1
Chelford SK11 .... 84 A1
Chester CH2 .... 237 F4
Crowton CW8 .... 76 B1
Cuddington & Sandiway CW8 . 102 A3
Dunham Town WA14 .... 20 A3
Eaton SK11 .... 135 D1
Ellesmere Port, Little Sutton
L66 .... 69 E4
Elton CH2 .... 72 A3
Goostrey CW4 .... 131 D4
Great Sankey WA5 .... 14 B4
Hawarden CH5 .... 116 A1
Haydock WA11 .... 1 B4
Heswall L60 .... 40 C3
Holmes Chapel CW4 .... 130 B1
Irlam M44 .... 11 F4
Kidsgrove ST7 .... 194 C1

Station Rd continued
Kidsgrove, Newchapel ST7 .. 195 F1
Lostock CW9 .... 80 A1
Mobberley WA16 .... 57 F4
Mouldsworth CH3 .... 99 D2
Mow Cop ST7 .... 195 E4
Nantwich CW5 .... 204 C3
Neston L64 .... 66 C4
Neston L64 .... 66 C4
Neston, Burton L64 .... 67 D1
New Mills SK22 .... 39 D3
Northwich CW9 .... 79 D1
Runcorn WA7 .... 22 C1
Sandbach CW11 .... 174 B4
Scholar Green ST7 .... 195 D4
Styal SK9 .... 34 A2
Sutton WA7 .... 50 A2
Warrington WA4 .... 17 D1
Warrington, Fearnhead WA2 ... 9 D1
Weaverham CW8 .... 77 D1
Whaley Bridge SK23 .... 39 E2
Wilmslow SK9 .... 60 A4
Wilmslow, Handforth SK9 .... 34 B2
Winsford CW7 .... 127 D1
Worleston CW5 .... 188 C3
Station Rd N WA2 .... 9 D1
Station Rd S WA2 .... 9 D1
Station St SK10 .... 87 E1
Station View Chester CH2 .. 118 C1
Northwich CW9 .... 204 C2
Staveley Ave SK15 .... 242 D3
Staveley Dr CW7 .... 126 B1
Stayley Dr SK15 .... 242 D3
Steam Mill St CH2 .... 237 F3
Stearns Cl CH1 .... 118 A3
Steel St WA1 .... 16 C4
Steele Rd CW10 .... 151 E3
Steele St CH1 .... 237 E2
Steeles Ave SK14 .... 241 E7
Steeple Cl L64 .... 66 C4
Steeple St SK10 .... 87 F1
Stein Ave WA3 .... 4 A1
Stenhills Cres WA7 .... 23 E1
Step Hill ■ SK11 .... 112 B4
Stephen La SK13 .... 16 B3
Stephen's Gr WA6 .... 73 D1
Stephens Gdns L66 .... 69 D3
Stephens Rd SK15 .... 242 C4
Stephens Terr L66 .... 69 D3
Stephens Way ST7 .... 209 F1
Stephenson Dr CW1 .... 191 D2
Stephenson Wlk CW7 .... 149 D4
Sterndale Rd Romiley SK6 . 241 B1
Stockport SK3 .... 240 E1
Sterne Cl ■ CW11 .... 174 B3
Stetchworth Rd WA4 .... 16 A1
Steven Ct CH2 .... 118 C4
Stevenage Cl SK11 .... 112 A4
Stevenage Dr SK11 .... 112 A4
Stevens Rd L60 .... 41 E4
Stevens St SK9 .... 60 A1
Steventon WA7 .... 24 C2
Steward's Ave WA8 .... 22 C4
Stewart St CW7 .... 190 A2
Stile End CH2 .... 119 F4
Stiles The CW8 .... 101 E3
Stiperstones Cl L66 .... 68 C3
Stirling Cl Chester CH1 .. 119 D1
Macclesfield SK10 .... 86 C1
Stockport SK3 .... 240 C2
Stirling Ct Ellesmere Port L65 70 B2
Holmes Chapel CW4 .... 130 A1
Stirling Dr SK15 .... 242 D3
Stirrup Cl WA2 .... 8 C2
Stitch La SK4 .... 240 D7
Stock La
Hough Common CW5 .... 206 A1
Shavington CW5 .... 206 A1
Stockdale Ave SK4 .... 240 F1
Stockham Cl WA7 .... 50 A4
Stockham La WA7 .... 50 A4
Stockholm Rd SK3 .... 240 E4
Stockley Farm CW9 .... 54 C4
Stockley La WA4 .... 52 C4
Stockport Coll of F & H Ed
SK3 .... 240 F2
Stockport SK3 .... 240 F4
Stockport Infmy SK3 .... 240 F4
Stockport Rd
Altrincham WA15 .... 238 F5
Cheadle SK8 .... 239 E6
Cheadle, Cheadle Heath SK3 240 A3
Romiley SK6 .... 241 B2
Warrington WA4 .... 17 F2
Stockport Rd E SK6 .... 241 A4
Stockport Rd W SK6 .... 240 E5
Stockport Trad Est SK4 .. 240 E5
Stocks Ave CH3 .... 119 D3
Stocks Gdns SK15 .... 242 F1
Stocks Hill CW7 .... 149 F4
Stocks La Chester CH3 .... 119 D3
Penketh WA5 .... 14 B3
Ellesmere Port L65 .... 82 C1
Stalybridge SK15 .... 242 F1
Stockswell Rd L35 .... 12 A2
Stockton Ave ■ SK3 ..... 240 B4
Stockton Heath Cty Prim
Sch WA4 .... 16 B1
Stockton La WA4 .... 16 C1
Stockton St WA7 .... 59 F2
Stoke Abbott Cl SK7 .... 35 F4
Stoke Cl ST7 .... 210 A1
Stoke Gdns L65 .... 70 B2
Stokehall La
Barbridge CW5 .... 187 F3
Cholmondeston CW5 ..... 187 F3

Stokesay Ct L65 .... 70 C2
Stokoe Ave WA14 .... 238 A6
Stone Barn La WA7 .... 50 A3
Stone Chair La ST7 .... 194 C4
Stone Croft CH3 .... 142 A4
Stone Cross La WA3 .... 3 E4
Stone Heyes La CW8 .... 77 E4
Stone House La CW6 .... 184 C3
Stone Mead Ave WA15 .. 241 E3
Stone Mead Ave WA15 .. 32 B4
Stone Pit La WA3 .... 3 F1
Stone Pl CH2 .... 118 C2
Stoneacre Gdns WA4 .... 26 C2
Stonebank Dr L64 .... 67 D3
Stonebridge Rd CW5 .... 204 C2
Stonechat Cl Crewe CW1 .. 189 F4
Runcorn WA7 .... 49 F3
Stonecliffe Ave SK15 .... 242 D2
Stonecliffe Terr SK15 .... 242 D3
Stonecrop Cl Runcorn WA7 . 49 F2
Warrington WA3 .... 9 E2
Stonehaven Dr WA4 .... 9 D2
Stoneheads Rise SK23 .... 65 E4
Stonehill Cl WA4 .... 26 B2
Stonehills La WA7 .... 23 E1
Stonehouse Gn CW12 .... 156 C1
Stonelea WA7 .... 24 A1
Stoneleigh Cl SK10 .... 87 E1
Stoneleigh Gdns WA4 .... 17 E1
Stoneleigh Gr CW1 .... 190 B4
Stoneley Rd CW1 .... 190 B4
Stonemill Terr SK5 .... 240 F7
Stonepail Rd M22 & SK8 .. 239 A5
Stones Manor La CW8 .... 103 E3
Stoney Holt WA7 .... 50 B4
Stoney La Delamere CW6 .. 123 E3
Warrington WA5 .... 59 F3
Stoneyfield SK15 .... 242 D4
Stoneyfold La SK11 .... 113 D3
Stoneyhurst Cres WA3 .... 4 B3
Stoneyland Dr SK22 .... 39 D4
Stony La CW12 .... 179 D4
Stonyford Rd SK33 .... 194 C6
Stopford St SK3 .... 240 D4
Stopford Sq SK8 .... 34 B4
Storeton Rd SK11 .... 112 B3
Straight Length WA6 .... 73 F4
Straight Mile
Eccleston CH4 .... 162 C3
Poulton CH4 .... 163 D2
Straker Ave L65 .... 69 F3
Stratford Rd Blacon CH1 .. 117 F2
Neston L64 .... 66 B3
Stratford Sq SK8 .... 34 B4
Stratford Way SK11 .... 112 B3
Strathaven Rd CW1 .... 205 F4
Strathclyde Cl CW4 .... 130 A1
Strathearn Rd L60 .... 40 C4
Strathmore Ave M34 .... 241 B6
Stratton Cl WA7 .... 50 A3
Stratton Pk WA8 .... 12 C3
Stratton Rd WA5 .... 15 D3
Strawberry Cl
Altrincham WA14 .... 238 B7
Warrington WA3 .... 9 E2
Strawberry Dr CH1 .... 95 D4
Strawberry Fields L64 .... 142 A4
Strawberry Gn CH1 .... 95 D4
Strawberry La
Acton Bridge CW8 .... 76 C2
Mollington CH1 .... 94 B2
Wilmslow SK9 .... 59 F3
Street Hey La WA8 .... 43 D1
Street La Adlington SK10 .. 62 B4
Rode Heath ST7 .... 176 C4
Warrington WA8 .... 52 B2
Street The Buxton SK17 .... 90 B3
Chester CH2 .... 119 E4
Mickle Trafford CH2 .... 119 E4
Stretton Ave WA3 .... 3 E4
Stretton Cl L62 .... 43 F2
Stretton Mill SY14 .... 198 A3
Stretton Rd WA4 .... 26 C1
Stretton Way ■ SK9 .... 34 B3
Stretton Wlk SK9 .... 103 F2
Stringer Ave CW1 .... 191 D3
Stringer Cres WA4 .... 16 C2
Stringer's La LL12, CH4 ... 161 D2
Strumness Cl WA2 .... 9 D2
Stuart Cl Chester CH3 .... 119 F2
Winsford CW7 .... 149 E3
Stuart Ct SK10 .... 87 D1
Stuart Dr WA4 .... 16 C1
Stuart Pl CH2 .... 237 E3
Stuart Rd WA4 .... 16 A2
Stubbs La Lostock CW9 .... 80 A1
Mobberley WA16 .... 58 C2
Stubbs Pl CH1 .... 117 C4
Stubbs Terr SK11 .... 112 C4
Styal Cl CW9 .... 103 F2
Styal City Pfk SK9 .... 33 F2
Styal Cty Prim Sch SK9 .. 33 F2
Styal Gr SK8 .... 239 A3
Styal Rd
Gatley M22 & SK8 & M90 &
SK9 .... 239 A3
Wilmslow SK9 .... 34 A1
Wythenshawe M22 .... 33 F4
Styal View SK9 .... 34 A1
Sudbrook Cl WA3 .... 3 F4
Sudbury Cl SK7 .... 36 C4
Sudbury Dr SK7 .... 36 C4
Sudlow La Knutsford WA16 .. 56 B1
Plumley WA16 .... 81 E4

Suez St Newton-le-W WA12 ...... 2 A2
Warrington WA1 .... 16 A3
Suffolk Ave L65 .... 69 F3
Suffolk Cl Congleton CW12 .. 156 B2
Macclesfield SK10 .... 86 C1
Warrington WA1 .... 17 F3
Suffolk Dr SK9 .... 34 B1
Suffolk Pl WA8 .... 22 B4
Suffolk Rd WA14 .... 238 B5
Suffolk St WA7 .... 23 D2
Sugar La Adlington SK10 .. 63 D1
Manley WA6 .... 98 C3
Rainow SK10 .... 88 B3
Sugar Pit La WA16 .... 56 C2
Sugden St OL6 .... 242 A3
Sulby Ave WA4 .... 16 A2
Sulgrave Ave SK10 .... 36 C2
Summer Cl WA7 .... 23 F1
Summer La Daresbury WA4 .. 51 E4
Runcorn WA7 .... 23 F1
Summerfield ST7 .... 195 D1
Summerfield Ave WA5 .... 7 F1
Summerfield Dr CW9 .... 126 C4
Summerfield Pl WA7 .... 60 A3
Summerfield Rd
Guilden Sutton CH3 .... 119 F3
Mobberley WA16 .... 57 F2
Summerfields WA16 .... 57 E2
Summerhill Dr ST5 .... 210 B1
Summerhill Rd SK10 .... 86 C4
Summerlea SK8 .... 35 D4
Summers Cl SK9 .... 242 F2
Summers Cl WA16 .... 82 A4
Summers Way WA16 .... 82 A4
Summertrees Rd L66 .... 69 F2
Summertime Gdns WA4 .. 26 C1
Summerville Rd SK9 .... 4 B3
Sumner Cl WA14 .... 26 C1
Sumner Rd CH1 .... 117 F2
Sumner St WA1 .... 1 A3
Sumpter Pathway CH2 .. 118 C2
Sunart Cl CW2 .... 206 A3
Sunbank La WA15 .... 32 C2
Sunbeam St WA12 .... 2 B2
Sunbury Cl SK9 .... 34 C1
Sunbury Cres CH4 .... 140 C3
Sunbury Gdns WA4 .... 26 C4
Suncroft Cl WA4 .... 17 E4
Suncroft Rd L60 .... 41 E4
Sundale Dr CW2 .... 189 E2
Sunderland St SK11 .... 112 B4
Sundown Cl SK22 .... 39 D4
Sunfield L66 .... 40 C1
Sunfield Cl L66 .... 69 E2
Sunningdale Ave Sale M33 242 C5
Widnes WA8 .... 12 A1
Sunningdale Cl
Burtonwood WA5 .... 6 C4
Northwich CW9 .... 104 C4
Sunningdale Dr
Bebington L63 .... 43 D3
Bramhall SK7 .... 36 A4
Sunningdale Rd
Cheadle Hulme SK8 .... 35 D4
Denton M34 .... 241 B5
Macclesfield SK11 .... 112 A3
Sunningdale Way L64 .... 66 C2
Sunninghey Ct SK9 .... 59 F2
Sunny Bank Wilmslow SK9 .. 60 A3
Wilmslow, Lindow SK9 .... 59 E2
Sunny Bank Rd SK11 .... 112 B3
Sunny Bank Rd WA14 .... 31 E4
Sunnybank Cl WA12 .... 2 B2
Sunnybank Rd CW2 .... 189 F2
Sunnyside Alsager ST7 .. 193 D2
Great Sankey WA5 .... 14 B4
Sunnyside Cres OL6 .... 242 A2
Sunnyside Gr OL6 .... 242 A2
Surrey Dr CW12 .... 156 C3
Surrey Rd Chester CH2 .... 119 D3
Kidsgrove ST7 .... 195 D1
Warren SK11 .... 112 A2
Surrey St Crewe CW1 .... 190 C2
Runcorn WA7 .... 23 D1
Warrington WA1 .... 16 B2
Surridge WA3 .... 29 E3
Susan Dr WA5 .... 14 B3
Susan St WA8 .... 13 E1
Sussex Ave SK11 .... 112 A3
Sussex Dr ST7 .... 194 C1
Sussex Rd Chester CH2 .... 118 C2
Irlam M44 .... 11 E3
Partington M31 .... 11 F1
Stockport SK3 .... 240 B4
Sussex Way WA14 .... 13 E1
Sussex Way CH1 .... 118 C2
Sutherland Ct WA3 .... 23 D1
Sutherland Dr Bebington L62 43 E2
Macclesfield SK10 .... 87 D1
Sutherland St OL6 .... 242 A3
Sutherland Way CW3 .... 119 D2
Sutton Ave Culcheth WA3 .... 4 C2
Neston L64 .... 66 C4
Sutton Causeway WA6 .... 49 F1
Sutton Cl Bebington L62 .... 43 F2
Higher Wincham CW9 .... 79 F3
Macclesfield SK11 .... 112 B3
Mickle Trafford CH2 .... 119 F4
Sutton Cty High Sch L66 .. 69 F3
Sutton Dr CH2 .... 118 C3
Sutton Green Cty Prim Sch
L66 .... 69 E3
Sutton Hall Dr L66 .... 69 D3
Sutton Hall Gdns L66 .... 69 D3

Sutton La CW10 .... 151 E4
Sutton Rd Alderley Edge SK9 .. 59 F1
Manchester SK4 .... 240 C7
Poynton SK12 .... 37 D1
Sutton St Runcorn WA7 .... 23 D1
Warrington WA1 .... 16 B2
Sutton Way
Ellesmere Port L66 .... 69 F2
■ Wilmslow SK8 .... 34 C3
Sutton Way Cty Jun Sch
.... 69 F2
Sutton's La WA8 .... 22 C3
Swaine St WA3 .... 240 E5
Swale Dr WA14 .... 238 C6
Swale Rd L65 .... 70 A4
Swaledale Ave CW12 .... 157 D3
Swaledale Cl Bebington L62 .. 43 F3
Great Sankey WA5 .... 14 B4
Swallow Cl Kidsgrove ST7 .... 195 D1
Macclesfield SK10 .... 113 D4
Warrington WA3 .... 9 C5
Swallow Ct CW7 .... 149 E3
Swallow Dr CW11 .... 175 C4
Swallow St WA1 .... 240 F3
Swallowfield Cl CW2 .... 206 A4
Swallowfield Gdns WA4 .... 26 C3
Swan Ave WA1 .... 1 A1
Swan Bank Congleton CW12 156 B1
Kidsgrove ST7 .... 210 B4
Swan Cl Ellesmere Port L66 .. 69 F2
Kidsgrove ST7 .... 210 B4
Poynton SK12 .... 36 A2
Swan Ct CW8 .... 101 F4
Swan Farm La CW3 .... 232 A1
Swan Gr WA16 .... 106 B4
Swan La Bunbury CW6 .... 185 F4
Cheadle Hulme SK8 .... 35 D4
Swan Rd WA12 .... 1 C2
Swan St Congleton CW12 ...... 156 B1
Wilmslow SK9 .... 60 A4
Swanage Cl WA4 .... 16 C1
Swanage Ct CW7 .... 149 E3
Swanborne Gdns SK3 .... 240 C7
Swanley La CW5 .... 203 E2
Swanlow Ave CW7 .... 149 E3
Swanlow Dr CW7 .... 149 E3
Swanlow La CW7 .... 149 F3
Swanscoe Av SK10 .... 88 A3
Swanscoe Cl CW10 .... 151 D4
Swanscoe La SK10 .... 88 A2
Swanwick Cl CW4 .... 107 E1
Sweet Briar Cres CW2 .... 189 F2
Sweet Brier Cl CW8 .... 78 A2
Sweetenham Cl ST7 .... 193 E2
Sweetfield Gdns L66 .... 69 E4
Sweetfield Rd L66 .... 69 E4
Sweettooth La CW11 .... 175 E4
Swettenham Rd
Swettenham CW12 .... 132 A1
Wilmslow SK9 .... 34 B3
Swettenham St WA1 .... 240 F3
Swift Cl Kidsgrove ST7 .... 195 D1
Warrington WA2 .... 8 C2
Wistaston CW2 .... 205 F4
Swinburne Dr CW1 .... 190 C2
Swindale Ave WA2 .... 8 A2
Swinden Cl WA7 .... 24 B1
Swine Market CW5 .... 204 C3
Swineyard La WA16 .... 28 B2
Swinford Ave WA8 .... 13 F1
Swinley Chase SK9 .... 34 C1
Swinleys Hey CH3 .... 142 A4
Swinnerton St CW2 .... 190 B1
Swinton Sq WA16 .... 57 D1
Swireford Rd WA6 .... 73 D1
Swiss Cott SK10 .... 87 D1
Swiss Hill SK9 .... 60 A1
Swithin Rd WA7 .... 33 F4
Swynnerton Way WA8 .... 13 D3
Swythamley Cl SK3 .... 240 A4
Swythamley Rd SK3 .... 240 A4
Sycamore Ave Alsager ST7 .. 193 F1
Altrincham WA14 .... 238 A5
Congleton CW12 .... 155 F2
Crewe CW1 .... 190 B3
Haydock WA11 .... 1 A3
Newton-le-W WA12 .... 2 A2
Rode Heath ST7 .... 193 F4
Widnes WA8 .... 13 D1
Winsford CW7 .... 149 E4
Sycamore Cl
Ashton-u-L OL6 .... 242 B2
Audlem CW3 .... 230 A2
Biddulph ST6 .... 179 F1
Holmes Chapel CW4 .... 130 B2
Kidsgrove ST7 .... 210 C4
Wilmslow SK9 .... 34 A1
Sycamore Cres
Barnton CW8 .... 78 A2
Hollins Green WA3 .... 11 D1
Macclesfield SK11 .... 112 A4
Sycamore Ct CW5 .... 204 C4
Sycamore Dr Chester CH4 .. 140 C3
Ellesmere Port L66 .... 70 A1
Lymm WA13 .... 18 B2
Middlewich CW10 .... 151 F3
Sutton WA7 .... 50 A2
Sycamore Farm Cl SK10 ...... 87 D1
Sycamore Gr
Broughton CH4 .... 139 D2
Sandbach CW11 .... 175 D4
Sycamore La WA5 .... 15 D3
Sycamore Lane Cty Prim
Sch WA5 .... 15 D3

Sycamore Rd Partington M31 11 F2
Romiley SK6 .... 241 A4
Runcorn WA7 .... 49 F4
Sycamore Rise SK11 .... 112 A3
Sycamore St Sale M33 .... 242 E6
Stockport SK3 .... 240 B8
Sycamore Wlk SK8 .... 239 D6
Syddal Cr SK7 .... 35 D1
Syddal Gn SK7 .... 35 E3
Syddal Rd SK7 .... 35 E3
Syddall Ave SK8 .... 34 B4
Syddall St SK14 .... 241 D6
Sydney Ave M90 .... 33 D4
Sydney Rd Blacon CH1 .... 118 A2
Bramhall SK7 .... 35 F3
Crewe CW1 .... 190 C3
Sydney St Northwich CW8 .. 103 E4
Runcorn WA7 .... 48 B4
Sykes Meadow SK3 .... 240 D2
Sykes St WA14 .... 241 F5
Sylvan Ave Altrincham WA15 238 F8
Sale M33 .... 242 C5
Wilmslow SK9 .... 59 F3
Sylvan Cl CW8 .... 103 E4
Sylvan Gr WA14 .... 238 D5
Symondley Rd SK11 .... 112 C1
Symons Rd M33 .... 242 B7
Synge St WA2 .... 16 B4
Sytch Croft L64 .... 66 C4

T
Tabley Ave WA8 .... 12 B1
Tabley Cl Knutsford WA16 .... 56 C2
Sandbach CW11 .... 174 C4
Tabley Gr WA16 .... 56 C1
Tabley Hill La
Knutsford WA16 .... 56 A1
Tabley WA16 .... 56 A1
Tabley Ho WA16 .... 81 D4
Tabley Mere Gdns SK8 .... 239 F3
Tabley Rd Crewe CW2 .... 189 F2
Knutsford WA16 .... 56 C2
Wilmslow SK9 .... 34 B3
Tabor St CW9 .... 79 D1
Tabor St SK11 .... 112 C3
Tadgers La WA6 .... 73 E4
Tadman Gr WA14 .... 238 A6
Talbot Ave L64 .... 66 C3
Talbot Cl Neston L64 .... 66 C3
Shavington CW2 .... 206 A2
Warrington WA3 .... 9 F2
Talbot Gdns L64 .... 66 C3
Talbot Rd
Alderley Edge SK9 .... 60 A1
Altrincham WA14 .... 238 B2
Dunham-on-t-H WA6 .... 97 F4
Ellesmere Port L66 .... 69 F2
Sale M33 .... 242 E6
Talbot St Chester CH2 .... 237 E4
Goldborne WA3 .... 3 D4
Stockport SK1 & SK3 .... 240 E5
Talfryn Cl CH5 .... 91 E1
Talisman CW7 .... 149 D4
Talke Rd Alsager ST7 .... 193 F2
Audley ST5 .... 210 D1
Tall Ash Ave CW12 .... 157 D2
Tall Trees Cl CW8 .... 103 E3
Talvern Green Prim Sch
SY14 .... 222 C3
Tamar Cl Congleton CW12 .. 156 C1
Macclesfield SK10 .... 86 C1
Tamar Rd WA11 .... 1 B3
Kidsgrove ST7 .... 195 D1
Tamar Wlk CW7 .... 127 D1
Tame Cl Biddulph ST6 .... 179 F1
Sandbach CW11 .... 174 C4
Stalybridge SK15 .... 242 F3
Tame St SK15 .... 242 B1
Tame Wlk SK9 .... 34 E1
Tameside Coll of Tech
Ashton-u-L OL6 .... 242 A3
Hyde SK14 .... 241 E6
Tameside General Hospl
OL6 .... 242 B4
Tameside L Pk SK14 .... 241 F6
Tamworth Cl SK7 .... 36 A4
Tamworth St WA12 .... 2 A2
Tan House La
Widnes WA8 .... 22 B4
Tanfield Rd M20 .... 239 B8
Tanhouse Ind Est WA8 .... 23 E4
Tankersley Gr WA5 .... 15 D3
Tanner St
Congleton CW12 .... 156 C1
Hyde SK14 .... 241 D7
Tanner's La WA3 .... 3 C4
Tanners La WA3 .... 16 A3
Tannery La Neston L64 .... 66 C4
Penketh WA5 .... 14 B2
Tannery Way WA14 .... 238 E7
Tanyard Dr WA15 .... 32 B4
Tanyard La WA15 .... 32 B3
Tapley Ave SK12 .... 36 C1
Taplow Cl WA4 .... 26 C3
Taplow Gr SK8 .... 239 A4
Target Cl ST7 .... 210 C3
Target Rd L60 .... 40 B4
Tarn Cl CW7 .... 126 C1
Tarn Ct WA1 .... 17 F4
Tarn Mount SK11 .... 112 A3
Tarnbeck WA7 .... 50 B4
Tarns The SK8 .... 239 B3
Tarnway WA3 .... 3 F4
Tarporley Wlk ■ SK9 .... 34 C1
Tarporley CE Contr Prim
Sch CW6 .... 146 B1
Tarporley Cty High Sch
CW6 .... 146 B1

Tarporley Rd
Common Side CW6, CW8 ...... 124 B3
Duddon 145 D3
Ellesmere Port L66 .... 69 F2
Little Leigh WA4 .... 52 A1
Stretton WA4 .... 52 B4
Tarvin CH3 .... 121 E1
Utkinton CW6 .... 146 C3
Whitchurch SY13 .... 225 F2
Whitley WA4 .... 52 B2
Tarran Gr WA4 .... 241 B5
Tarran Pl WA14 .... 238 E6
Tarr Cl CW11 .... 94 C1
Tarvin Ave CW2 .... 189 E2
Tarvin Cl Ellesmere Port L65 .. 70 A2
Goldborne WA3 .... 3 F4
Macclesfield SK11 .... 112 C3
Middlewich CW10 .... 151 E3
Widnes WA8 .... 13 D2
Tarvin Cty Prim Sch CH3 .. 121 D1
Tarvin Rd Alvanley WA6 ...... 73 F2
Bebington L62 .... 43 F2
Chester, Boughton CH3 .... 119 D1
Chester, Vicarscross CH3 .... 119 F1
Christleton CH3 .... 120 B2
Frodsham WA6 .... 73 F2
Manley WA6 .... 99 D2
Tarvin CH3 .... 120 C2
Tarvin Sands Industries
CH3 .... 121 D2
Tarvin Way SK9 .... 34 B3
Tasman Cl WA5 .... 15 E4
Tate Cl WA8 .... 12 B1
Tate Ct WA1 .... 191 E2
Tattenhall La Beeston CH3 .. 167 D1
Beeston CW6 .... 167 F1
Tattenhall CH3 .... 167 D1
Tattenhall Rd CH3 .... 166 B2
Tatton CI Alsager ST7 .... 193 E2
Chester CW9 .... 140 C3
Davenham CW9 .... 103 F2
Winsford CW7 .... 126 B1
Tatton Ct SK4 .... 240 C8
Tatton Dr CW11 .... 175 E4
Tatton Hall WA16 .... 56 D1
Tatton Lodge WA16 .... 57 D1
Tatton Park WA16 .... 57 D4
Tatton Pl M33 .... 242 B7
Tatton Rd Crewe CW2 .... 189 F1
Denton M34 .... 241 A5
Sale M33 .... 242 B7
Wythenshawe SK8 .... 34 C3
Tatton Rd S SK4 .... 240 C8
Tatton St Knutsford WA16 .. 57 D1
Widnes WA8 .... 13 D1
■ Stockport SK1 & SK3 .... 240 E5
Tatton Stile WA16 .... 58 A2
Tavener Cl L63 .... 43 E3
Tavistock Rd WA5 .... 14 C2
Tavlin Ave WA5 .... 7 F1
Tawney Cl ST7 .... 195 D1
Taxal & Fernilee CE Contr
Prim Sch SK23 .... 65 E3
Taxal Lodge Sch SK23 .... 65 E3
Taxal Moor Rd SK23 .... 65 E2
Taxi Rd M90 .... 33 D4
Taxmere Cl CW11 .... 174 C4
Tay Cl SY16 .... 179 F1
Taylor Ind Est WA3 .... 4 C1
Taylor Rd Altrincham WA14 238 A5
Haydock WA11 .... 1 C4
Taylor St Hyde SK14 .... 241 F7
Stalybridge SK15 .... 242 C1
Warrington WA4 .... 16 B1
Widnes WA8 .... 13 E1
Taylor's La CW1 .... 192 B1
Taylors La CW1 .... 192 B1
Taylors Row WA7 .... 23 E1
Teal Ave WA11 .... 1 A4
Teal Cl Altrincham WA14 .... 238 B8
Warrington WA3 .... 8 C2
Tearall Gr WA1 .... 16 C1
Warrington, Oakwood WA3 .. 9 F2
Winsford CW7 .... 149 E3
Teals Way L60 .... 40 C4
Tebay Rd L62 .... 43 F4
Tedder Dr M22 .... 33 E4
Tedder Sq WA8 .... 22 B4
Teddington Cl WA4 .... 26 C3
Tees Ct L65 .... 70 A4
Teesdale Cl WA5 .... 14 C4
Teesdale Rd WA11 .... 1 A3
Tefler Ct CW10 .... 151 F3
Tegg's Nose Ctry Pk SK11 .. 113 E3
Teggsnose La SK11 .... 113 E3
Tegid Way CH4 .... 140 F6
Tegsnose Mt SK11 .... 113 E2
Telegraph Rd L60 .... 41 D4
Telford Cl Congleton CW12 . 157 D1
Kidsgrove ST7 .... 210 C4
Macclesfield SK10 .... 88 A1
Widnes WA8 .... 12 B2
Telford Gdns ■ CW11 .... 174 C2
Telford Pl CW5 .... 204 B3
Telford Rd L65 .... 70 C2
Telford Way Audlem CW3 .. 229 F2
Chester CH4 .... 140 C3
Middlewich CW10 .... 128 C1
Telford's Quay CH1 .... 94 A1
Temple Moor Inf Sch
M33 .... 242 E6
Temple Rd M33 .... 242 D6
Templeton Cl WA14 .... 238 B6
Tenbury Cl WA5 .... 15 F3
Tenby Cl WA5 .... 15 F3
Tenby Dr WA7 .... 50 A3
Tenby Rd Macclesfield SK11 . 111 F3
Stockport SK3 .... 240 B3
Tennyson Ave CW1 .... 190 C2

Tennyson Cl
Macclesfield SK11 .... 111 F3
Rode Heath ST7 .... 193 F4
Stockport SK4 .... 240 A7
Wistaston CW2 .... 190 A1
Tennyson Dr WA2 .... 8 B1
Tennyson Rd Cheadle SK8 .. 239 F6
Ellesmere Port L65 .... 70 A2
Widnes WA8 .... 13 D1
Tennyson Wlk CH1 .... 118 A3
Tensing Cl WA5 .... 15 D4
Terence Ave WA1 .... 16 C3
Terminal Rd E M90 .... 33 D4
Terminal Rd N M22 .... 33 E4
Terminal Rd S M90 .... 33 D4
Tern Ave ST7 .... 195 E1
Tern Cl Altrincham WA14 .... 238 B8
Widnes WA8 .... 13 D2
Tern Dr SK12 .... 36 A2
Terra Nova Sch CW8 .... 108 B1
Terrace Rd WA8 .... 23 D3
Terrick Rd SY13 .... 226 A1
Tetchill Cl Ellesmere Port L66 69 E1
Runcorn WA7 .... 50 B4
Tetton La CW10 .... 151 F2
Tewkesbury Cl
Cheadle Hulme SK8 .... 35 D3
Chester CH2 .... 118 B4
Ellesmere Port CH1 .... 94 C4
Middlewich CW10 .... 128 A1
Poynton SK12 .... 36 B2
Tewkesbury Dr SK10 .... 87 F2
Tewkesbury Rd
Cheadle SK3 .... 240 B2
Goldborne WA3 .... 3 D4
Thackeray Dr CH3 .... 119 D1
Thames Cl Congleton CW12 . 156 C1
Warrington WA2 .... 8 B1
Thames Dr ST6 .... 179 E1
Thames Gales L65 .... 70 A2
Thames Rd WA1 .... 41 C1
Thames Side L65 .... 70 A2
Thamesdale L65 .... 70 A2
Thaxted Wlk M22 .... 33 E4
Theatre Ct CW9 .... 103 F4
Theatre St ■ WA15 .... 238 E6
Thelwall Cty Inf Sch WA4 .. 17 E2
Thelwall Cty Jun Sch WA4 . 17 E2
Thelwall La East WA4 .... 17 E2
Thelwall La West WA4 .... 17 D2
Thelwall Massey Hall Sch
WA4 .... 17 F1
Thelwall New Rd WA4 .... 17 E2
Thelwall Rd
Ellesmere Port L66 .... 69 F2
Sale M33 .... 242 E5
Theobald Rd WA14 .... 238 D1
Thetford Cl SK10 .... 87 E2
Thetford Rd WA5 .... 14 C3
Thewlis St WA5 .... 15 F3
Third Ave Adlington SK10 .. 36 B1
Crewe CW1 .... 190 C1
Deeside Ind Est CH5 .... 92 C1
Kidsgrove ST7 .... 195 E1
Runcorn WA7 .... 49 F4
Sandbach CW11 .... 175 D3
Thirlmere WA11 .... 1 B2
Thirlmere Ave CW1 .... 191 B2
Thirlmere Cl
Alderley Edge SK9 .... 59 F1
Frodsham WA6 .... 49 E1
Holmes Chapel CW4 .... 130 A2
Thirlmere Ct CW12 .... 156 A1
Thirlmere Dr WA13 .... 18 C2
Thirlmere Rd Chester CH2 .. 119 D3
Ellesmere Port L65 .... 70 A1
Neston L64 .... 66 C3
Partington M31 .... 11 F2
Wistaston CW2 .... 190 A1
Thirlmere Way ■ WA8 .... 22 B4
Thirsk Cl WA7 .... 49 E3
Thistle Sq M31 .... 11 F1
Thistle Wlk M31 .... 11 F1
Thistleton Cl SK11 .... 112 B3
Thistlewood Dr SK9 .... 60 B4
Thomas Cl Alsager ST7 .... 193 F2
Blacon CH1 .... 117 F3
Denton M34 .... 241 A8
Ellesmere Port L65 .... 70 A1
Mickle Trafford CH2 .... 119 F4
Thomas Pl CW7 .... 127 D1
Thomas St
Altrincham WA15 .... 238 E6
Biddulph ST6 .... 179 E1
Congleton CW12 .... 156 C2
Crewe CW1 .... 190 B2
Goldborne WA3 .... 3 D4
Kidsgrove ST7 .... 210 B4
Packmoor ST7 .... 195 F1
Romiley SK6 .... 241 A3
Stockport SK1 .... 240 F3
Thomas St W SK1 & SK2 .... 240 F3
Thomas Trad Ctr WA4 .... 16 C1
Thomas Wedge CE Contr
Jun Sch The CH1 .... 94 A1
Thomasons Bridge La
.... 38 F3
Thompson Ave WA3 .... 4 C2
Thompson Cl WA12 .... 2 B1
Thompson St WA3 .... 3 D3
Thomson St SK3 .... 240 E4
Thoresway Rd SK9 .... 59 F3
Thorley Cl SK9 .... 60 A4
Thorley Gr CW2 .... 190 A1
Thorley La M90 .... 33 D4
Thorley Mews SK7 .... 35 F4

Thorn Cl Penketh WA5 .... 14 ...
Runcorn WA7 49
Thorn Dr SK8 .... 34 ...
Thorn Gr Altrincham WA15 .. 238?
Cheadle Hulme SK8 35
Sale M33 .... 242 ...
Thorn La CW8 .... 103 ...
Thorn Rd Cheadle Hulme SK7 . 35?
Runcorn WA7 49
Thorn Wlk M31 .... 11 ...
Thornberry Cl CH1 .... 117 ...
Thornbury Ave WA3 .... 3 ...
Thornbush Cl WA3 .... 3 ...
Thorncliffe Cl SK10 87
Thorne Dr L66 .... 69 ...
Thorney Dr SK7 .... 35 ...
Thorneyholme Dr WA16 57
Thornfield Cl WA3 .... 3 ...
Thornfield Hey SK9 60
Thornfield Rd SK9 .... 60 ...
Thornfield Sch WA4 .... 240 ...
Thorngrove Dr SK9 .... 60?
Thorngrove Hill SK9 .... 60?
Thorngrove Rd SK9 .... 60?
Thornhills WA8 .... 12 ...
Thornleigh Ave L66 .... 43 ...
Thornleigh Dr L66 .... 69 ...
Thornley Rd Dukinfield M34 . 241 ...
Lymm WA13 .... 18?
Thornley St SK14 .... 241 ...
Thornsgreen Rd M22 33
Thornton WA8 .... 22 ...
Thornton Ave SK11 .... 112 ...
Thornton Bank CW6 .... 169?
Thornton Common Rd
Bebington L63 .... 43 ...
Thornton Hough L63 .... 42 ...
Thornton Cres L60 .... 41 ...
Thornton Dr Chester CH2 .. 118 ...
Wilmslow M22 .... 34 ...
Wistaston CW2 .... 206 ...
Thornton Gate SK8 .... 239?
Thornton Green La CH2 ...... 96 ...
Thornton Hough Cty Prim
Sch L63 .... 42 ...
Thornton Mews L66 .... 69 ...
Thornton Pl ■ SK4 .... 240 ...
Thornton Rd Cheadle SK8 .. 34 ...
Ellesmere Port L65 .... 70?
Great Sankey WA5 .... 15 ...
Thornton Sq SK11 .... 112 ...
Thorntondale Dr WA5 .... 14 ...
Thorntree Gr WA4 .... 27 ...
Thornway Bollington SK10 .. 88?
Cheadle Hulme SK7 .... 35 ...
High Lane SK6 .... 37 ...
Thornwythe Gr L66 .... 69 ...
Thornycroft CW7 .... 126 ...
Thornycroft Cl WA1 .... 17 ...
Thornycroft St ■ SK11 .... 112 ...
Thorold Gr M33 .... 242 ...
Thorpe St SK10 .... 112 ...
Thorpe Cl CW1 .... 189 ...
Thorsby Cl WA16 .... 56 ...
Thorsby Rd WA15 .... 241 ...
Thowler La WA14 .... 30 ...
Threaphurst La SK7 .... 37 ...
Three Fields Cl CW12 .... 156?
Threeways CW8 .... 101 ...
Thresher Cl M33 .... 242 ...
Throstle Bank St SK14 .... 241 ...
Thurlestone Rd WA14 .... 238?
Thurlow WA3 .... 3 ...
Thursfield Ave ST7 .... 195?
Thursfield Prim Sch ST7 .... 195?
Thurstaston Rd L60 .... 40 ...
Thurston Cl WA5 .... 15?
Thurston Gn SK9 .... 60 ...
Thurston Rd CH4 .... 140?
Thyme St WA1 .... 16?
Tib St SK14 .... 241 ...
Tibb St ST7 .... 209?
Tibbs Cross La WA8 .... 13 ...
Tidal La WA1 .... 16?
Tideswell Cl SK7 .... 34 ...
Tideswell Rd SK7 .... 36 ...
Tidnock Ave CW12 .... 156?
Tiffild Ct CW7 .... 127 ...
Tilbury Pl WA7 .... 50 ...
Tidsley Cres WA7 .... 48?
Tile La WA8 .... 12 ...
Tilestone Paddocks CW6 . 168 ...
Tilewright Cl ST7 .... 195 ...
Tillard Ave SK3 .... 240 ...
Tilley St WA1 .... 16 ...
Tilman Cl WA5 .... 15 ...
Tilston Ave WA4 .... 16?
Tilston Parochial CE Contr
Prim Sch SY14 .... 213 ...
Tilston Rd Edge Green SY14 213?
Malpas SY14 .... 213 ...
Tilston Wlk ■ SK9 .... 34?
Tilstone Cl
Hough Common CW2 .... 206?
Northwich CW9 .... 104 ...
Timber Cl WA8 .... 13?
Timber St SK10 .... 87 ...
Timberfields Rd CH1 .... 117?
Timberley Ave WA4 .... 17 ...
Timberscombe Gdns WA1 . 17 ...
Timbrell Ave CW1 .... 9 ...
Timmis Cl WA2 .... 9?
Timmis Cres WA8 .... 13?
Timperley St WA8 .... 23?

mperley Sta WA15 .... 238 F8
nkwood La SY14 .... 211 F1
nsley St WA4 .... 16 C2
ntagel Cl
  Macclesfield SK10 .... 111 F4
  Runcorn WA7 .... 50 A3
ntagel Ct SK15 .... 242 C2
ntern Ave CW2 .... 118 C3
ntern Cl WA5 .... 7 F1
ntern Rd SK8 .... 35 D3
pping St WA14 .... 238 D3
rley La CW6 .... 123 D1
he Barn Prim Sch SK4 . 240 A7
cheban CI L60 .... 40 C4
cheban Cl L44 .... 41 D1
cheban Rd WA15 .... 32 B4
things The WA7 .... 23 F1
verton Cl Chester CH2 .. 118 C3
  Sandbach CW11 .... 175 E4
verton WA8 .... 12 B2
verton Sq WA5 .... 14 C2
viot Dale SK1 .... 240 F6
viot Way SK1 & SK4 & SK5 240 F7
bermorry Cl WA11 .... 1 A3
bermorry Rd SK8 .... 239 C1
brook Cl SK23 .... 65 E3
aft Cl Chester CH4 .... 140 C3
  Widnes WA8 .... 12 C1
oft Rd WA16 .... 82 A4
oft Way SK9 .... 34 C2
oll Bar Ave SK11 .... 112 A2
oll Bar Rd Christleton CH3 . 142 B4
  Macclesfield SK11 .... 111 F4
  Warrington WA2 .... 8 A2
ollamd La WA15 .... 31 F4
ollard Cl SK8 .... 35 D3
ollbar St SK3 .... 240 F4
ollemache Dr CW1 .... 190 C1
ollemache Terr CH2 ...... 118 C1
ollgate Cl ST7 .... 210 B4
ollgate Dr CW3 .... 229 F2
ollitt St CW1 .... 190 B2
om Fields ST7 .... 209 F1
om La WA14 .... 30 C3
om Shepley St SK14 .... 241 E6
omlinson St CW2 .... 237 F4
omlins Terr CH1 .... 117 F3
omlinson Ave WA2 .... 16 B4
ommy's La
  Congleton CW12 .... 156 C2
  Crewe CW1 .... 190 C1
onbridge Cl SK10 .... 87 D1
oogood Cl CW2 .... 119 F4
op Farm La CW7 .... 170 C1
op Rd Frodsham WA6 ...... 74 B3
  Kingsley WA6 .... 75 D1
op Station Rd ST7 .... 195 E4
oppgate Cl L60 .... 41 D4
opping Ct WA3 .... 9 D2
oppings The SK9 .... 241 A3
orbrook Gr **7** SK9 .... 34 B1
orkington Rd Gatley SK8 . 239 B5
  Wilmslow SK9 .... 60 A8
orkington St SK3 .... 240 D4
oronto Ave M90 .... 33 D4
orr Rd SK11 .... 112 B2
orr Rise CW6 .... 146 B1
orr Top St SK22 .... 39 E4
orridon Gr L65 .... 69 F2
orrin Cl SK21 .... 240 F1
orrvale Rd SK22 .... 39 D4
otland Gr CH2 .... 118 C2
otton Cl WA1 .... 9 E1
ourney Gn WA5 .... 7 D1
ower Hill SK10 .... 88 B2
ower Hill Rd ST7 .... 195 F4
Weaverham CW8 .... 77 D1
ower Rd CH1 .... 118 A1
ower St Hyde SK14 .... 241 D5
  Stalybridge SK16 .... 242 A1
ower Way CW1 .... 190 B2
owers Ct Poynton SK12 ... 36 C3
  Wistaston CW2 .... 206 A4
owers Ct WA5 .... 14 A6
owers Rd SK1 .... 36 C3
owfield La WA13 .... 19 D4
own Farm La WA6 .... 100 C4
own Hill WA1 .... 16 A3
own Mobberley WA16 ...... 58 A2
ownfield View WA7 .... 24 B1
ownfields Knutsford WA16 . 57 E1
  Sandbach CW11 .... 175 D3
ownfields Cres CW7 ..... 149 E4

Townfields Dr CW7 .... 149 E4
Townfields Gdns CW7 ..... 149 E4
Townfields Rd CW7 .... 149 E4
Townfields Pl **22** SK11 . 112 B4
Townley St WA1 .... 112 B4
Townsend La ST1 .... 194 A4
Townsend Rd CW12 .... 156 C1
Townshend Dr CW6 .... 147 F4
Townshend Rd CW1 .... 82 A3
Township Cl CH1 .... 182 B1
Townwell Ct CW5 .... 204 B3
Tracy Dr WA12 .... 2 C2
Trafalgar Ave SK12 .... 37 D2
Trafalgar Cl SK12 .... 37 D2
Trafalgar Ct WA8 .... 23 D3
Trafalgar Rd WA3 .... 242 C8
Trafford Ave WA5 .... 15 F4
Trafford Cres WA7 .... 49 E3
Trafford Rd
  Alderley Edge SK9 .... 60 A1
  Wilmslow SK9 .... 34 A1
Trafford St CH2 .... 237 E3
Tragan Dr WA5 .... 14 B2
Tramway Ave M44 .... 11 F4
Tramway St CW2 .... 237 F3
Tranmere Dr SK9 .... 34 C1
Tranmere Rd **1** SK3 ...... 240 B4
Trap Rd CW12 .... 132 B2
Trap St SK11 .... 132 A3
Traver's Entry WA9 .... 6 A4
Travis Brow SK4 .... 240 D5
Travis St Hyde SK14 .... 241 E6
  10 Widnes WA8 .... 23 D4
Treborth Rd CH1 .... 117 E2
Tree Bank Cl WA7 .... 49 D4
Tree Tops L64 .... 66 C2
Tree Way WA16 .... 82 A4
Treen Cl WA10 .... 86 B1
Treetops Cl WA1 .... 16 C4
Trefoil Cl Huntington CH3 . 142 A3
  Warrington WA3 .... 9 E3
Tregele Cl CH1 .... 117 E2
Trenance Cl WA7 .... 50 A4
Trenchard Dr M22 .... 33 F4
Trent Ave CW7 .... 127 D1
Trent Cl Cheadle Hulme SK7 .. 35 E3
  Widnes WA8 .... 13 D2
  Winsford CW7 .... 127 D1
Trent Way L60 .... 41 D3
Trentdale L65 .... 70 A2
Trentham Cl WA8 .... 13 D2
Trentham St WA7 .... 22 C2
Trevithick Cl CW1 .... 191 D2
Trevone Cl CW1 .... 57 D1
Tribune Ave WA14 .... 238 B7
Tricketts La CW5 .... 205 F3
Tricketts Mews CW5 ...... 205 F3
Trinity Ave M33 .... 242 D6
Trinity Cl CW2 .... 190 A1
Trinity Ct WA3 .... 9 F3
Trinity La SK11 .... 112 C2
Trinity Pl Congleton CW12 . 179 D4
  13 Widnes WA8 .... 23 D3
Trinity Rd M33 .... 242 D6
Trinity Sch SK5 .... 242 C1
Trinity Sq SK10 .... 87 F3
Trinity St Chester CH1 .... 237 D2
  Runcorn WA7 .... 23 D2
  Stalybridge SK16 .... 242 D1
Trinity Terr CW8 .... 78 A1
Troon Cl Bebington L63 ..... 43 E3
  Bramhall SK7 .... 36 A4
  Haydock WA11 .... 1 A3
Troon Dr SK8 .... 239 C1
Trossach Cl WA7 .... 8 C1
Troutbeck Ave
  Congleton CW12 .... 156 A1
  Warrington WA2 .... 8 B2
Troutbeck Cres CW7 ...... 119 D3
Troutbeck Gr CW7 .... 126 B1
Troutbeck Rd SK8 .... 239 D2
Trouthall La WA16 .... 81 D1
Trowbridge Rd M34 .... 241 A5
Trubshaw Ct ST7 .... 195 E2
Trubshaw Pl ST7 .... 195 D2
Trumans La L66 .... 69 E4
Truro Cl Bramhall SK7 ...... 35 F4
  Congleton CW12 .... 178 C4
  Runcorn WA7 .... 50 B3
  Warrington WA5 .... 14 C1
Tudor Cl
  Ellesmere Port CH1 .... 94 C4
  Northwich CW9 .... 104 C4
  Warrington WA1 .... 17 D1
  Winsford CW7 .... 149 E3
Tudor Gn Blacon CH1 ...... 117 F3
  Wilmslow SK9 .... 34 C1
Tudor Rd Altrincham WA14 . 238 B7
  Runcorn WA7 .... 24 A2
  Wilmslow SK9 .... 34 C1
Tudor Way Chester CH3 . 142 A4
  Congleton CW12 .... 156 B1
  Nantwich CW5 .... 204 C2
Tudorway L60 .... 41 D4
Tulip Cl SK3 .... 240 D1
Tulip Dr Haydock WA11 ...... 1 C3
  Partington M31 .... 11 F1
Tully Ave WA12 .... 1 C2
Tumblewood Dr SK8 ...... 239 E4
Tunbridge Cl
  Warrington WA5 .... 15 D4
  Wistaston CW2 .... 206 A4
Tunnel Rd CW8 .... 78 A1
Tunnicliffe Rd SK11 .... 112 C2
Tunnicliffe St **1** SK11 . 112 B4

Tunstall Rd Bosley SK11 . 158 B4
  Congleton CW12 .... 157 F1
  Woodhouse Green
    SK11, CW12 .... 158 B4
Tunstall St SK4 .... 240 E6
Turf La SK11 .... 112 B2
Turnall Rd WA8 .... 22 A4
Turnberry Cl Lymm WA13 . 18 B2
  Macclesfield SK10 .... 87 E2
  Northwich CW9 .... 104 C4
  Winsford CW7 .... 126 B1
Turnberry Dr SK9 .... 60 B4
Turnberry Rd SK8 .... 239 C1
Turnbury Cl M33 .... 242 B8
Turner Ave ST7 .... 210 A1
Turner Cl Goldborne WA3 . 3 E4
Turner Gdns SK14 .... 241 E8
Turner La SK14 .... 241 F8
Turner St Bollington SK10 . 88 A4
Nantwich CW5 .... 204 C3
Turnfield Rd SK8 .... 239 D3
Turnhurst Rd ST7 .... 195 F1
Turnock St SK11 .... 112 C4
Turnstone Ave WA12 .... 2 B2
Turret Hall Dr WA3 .... 4 C1
Turriff Dr L63 .... 43 E2
Turrocks Cl L64 .... 66 C3
Turrocks Croft L64 .... 66 C3
Turton Cl Hale L24 .... 21 F1
  Warrington WA3 .... 9 E3
Turton St WA3 .... 3 D4
Turves Rd SK8 .... 239 F1
Tuscan Cl M20 .... 13 D3
Tuscan Way SK10 .... 86 F1
Tushingham Ct Contr
  Prim Sch SY13 .... 214 B1
Tushingham Cl CH3 .... 142 A4
Tuson Dr WA8 .... 12 C3
Tutor Bank Dr WA12 .... 2 B2
Tweed Cl WA4 .... 238 C6
Tweedsmuir Cl WA2 .... 9 D2
Twemlow Ave CW11 .... 175 D4
Twemlow La CW4 .... 130 B3
Twenty Acre Rd WA5 .... 15 F4
Twinnies Cl SK9 .... 34 A1
Twinnies Rd SK9 .... 34 A1
Twiss Green Dr WA3 .... 4 C2
Twiss Green La WA3 .... 4 C2
Twiss Green Sch WA3 .... 4 C2
Twist Ave WA3 .... 3 E4
Two Acre Gr L66 .... 69 F1
Two Trees High Sch M34 . 241 A5
Two Trees La M34 .... 241 A5
Twyford Cl WA8 .... 13 D3
Twyford La WA8 .... 13 E3
Tyler St SK9 .... 60 A1
Tyne Cl WA2 .... 8 C1
Tynedale Ave CW2 .... 190 B1
Tynwald Cres WA8 .... 12 C3
Tynwald Dr WA4 .... 26 B4
Tyrer Rd WA12 .... 2 A1
Tytherington Bsns Pk
  SK10 .... 87 E3
Tytherington Cty High Sch
  SK10 .... 87 E1
Tytherington Dr SK10 ...... 87 E1
Tytherington La SK10 .... 87 D2
Tytherington Park Rd SK10 87 E2
Tytherington Sh Ctr SK10 . 87 E2

Ullapool Cl L66 .... 68 C3
Ullswater SK11 .... 111 F3
Ullswater Ave Crewe CW2 . 189 F2
  Warrington WA2 .... 8 B2
Ullswater Cres CW7 .... 119 D3
Ullswater Gr WA7 .... 49 E3
Ullswater Rd
  Congleton CW12 .... 156 A1
  Ellesmere Port L65 .... 70 B1
  Wilmslow SK9 .... 34 B2
Ullswater Terr SK15 .... 242 D4
Ulverston Ave WA2 .... 8 A2
Ulverston Cl WA11 .... 1 A3
Ulverston Ct WA11 .... 1 A3
Ulverston La L61 .... 4 C2
Ulwet Gate WA16 .... 29 E2
Under Rainow Rd CW12 . 157 F1
Underbridge La WA4 .... 25 E3
Underhill Sk6 .... 241 C2
Underhill Way WA7 .... 49 F4
Underwood Cl SK10 .... 86 C1
Underwood Ho PK CW1 . 190 A3
Underwood La CW1 .... 190 A3
Underwood Rd SK10 .... 60 B1
Underwood West Cty Inf
  & Jun Sch CW1 .... 190 A3
Unicorn Gateway SK11 .. 112 B4
Union Cl CW12 .... 156 D3
Union Rd Macclesfield SK11 112 C4
  New Mills SK22 .... 39 F2
Union St Chester CH1 .... 237 F2
  Congleton CW12 .... 156 D2
  Crewe CW2 .... 190 B2
  Hyde SK14 .... 241 E6
  Macclesfield SK11 .... 112 B4
  Runcorn WA7 .... 23 A2
  Stockport SK1 .... 240 F4
  Warrington WA1 .... 16 A3
Union Terr CH1 .... 237 E3
Union Wlk CH1 .... 237 E2
Unir of Liverpool Botanic
  Gdns The L66 .... 67 D2
University Coll Chester
  CH2 .... 237 D4
Upcast La SK9 .... 59 F2

Uplands CW8 .... 101 E2
Uplands Rd CW9 .... 78 C2
Uplands The Biddulph ST6 . 179 F1
  Runcorn WA7 .... 50 A4
Upper Cambrian Rd CH1 . 118 A1
Upper Downs WA14 .... 238 C3
Upper Haigh St CW7 .... 149 E4
Upper Mersey Rd WA8 ..... 23 D3
Upper Mersey St L65 .... 70 B4
Upper Northgate St CH1 . 237 D3
Upper Rd L64 .... 42 A1
Upton Acresfield Cty Prim
  Sch CH2 .... 118 C4
Upton Sale 35 D4
Upton Bridle Path WA8 ... 12 C2
Upton Cl Goldborne WA3 .. 3 E4
  Winsford CW7 .... 126 C2
Upton Dr Altrincham WA14 . 238 E8
  Chester CH2 .... 118 C4
  Penketh WA5 .... 14 C3
Upton Grange WA8 .... 12 C2
Upton La CH2 .... 118 B4
Upton Manor Cty Jun Sch
  CH2 .... 118 C4
Upton Mill View Cty Prim
  Sch CH2 .... 118 C4
Upton Pk CH2 .... 118 B4
Upton St Mary's Inf Sch
  CH2 .... 69 E2
Upton St
  Stockport SK1 .... 240 E7
Upton Way Chester CH2 . 118 C4
  10 SK9 .... 34 B3
Upton Westlea Cty Prim
  Sch CH2 .... 118 C4
Upton-by-Chester Cty
  High Sch CH2 .... 118 C3
Upwood Rd WA3 .... 9 D3
Urban Ave WA15 .... 238 E4
Urban Dr WA15 .... 238 E4
Urban Rd Altrincham WA15 . 238 E4
  Sale M33 .... 242 A6
Ure Ct L65 .... 70 A4
Urwick Rd SK6 .... 241 C2
Utkinton CE Contr Prim
  Sch CW6 .... 146 A4
Utkinton La CW6 .... 146 A4
Utkinton Rd Tarporley CW6 . 146 B3
  Utkinton CW6 .... 146 B3

Vahler Terr WA7 .... 23 E1
Vale Ave Sale M33 .... 242 E7
  Warrington WA2 .... 16 A4
Vale Cl Broughton CH4 ... 139 E2
  Romiley SK6 .... 241 F2
Vale Cres WA8 .... 12 B4
Vale Ct WA4 .... 51 D2
Vale Gdns
  Ellesmere Port L65 .... 70 B2
  Helsby WA6 .... 73 D2
Vale Head SK9 .... 34 B1
Vale Owen Rd WA2 .... 8 B1
Vale Rd Alpraham CW6 ... 169 D2
  Altrincham WA14 .... 238 B1
  Ellesmere Port L65 .... 70 B2
  Hartford CW8 .... 103 E2
  Marston CW9 .... 79 D3
  Romiley SK6 .... 241 B1
  Tiverton CW6 .... 168 C3
Vale Royal Dr CW8 .... 126 A4
Vale View CW9 .... 79 E1
Valebrook Dr CW5 .... 220 A4
Valentine Rd
  Kidsgrove ST7 .... 195 D1
  Newton-le-W WA12 .... 1 C2
Valewood Ave SK14 .... 240 A5
Valiant Cl WA2 .... 8 C1
Valley Cl Alsager ST7 .... 192 C2
  Cheadle SK8 .... 239 E3
  Knutsford WA16 .... 82 A4
Valley Ct WA2 .... 8 C1
Valley Dr Chester CH2 ... 118 B3
Valley La WA6 .... 99 E2
Valley Rd Bebington L62 ... 43 E4
  Bramhall SK7 .... 35 F4
  Cheadle SK8 .... 239 E3
  Crewe CW2 .... 190 A1
  Macclesfield SK11 .... 112 A3
  Stockport SK4 .... 240 A5
  Weaverham CW8 .... 77 E1
  Wistaston CW2 .... 189 F1
Valley View
  Ellesmere Port L66 .... 69 E3
  Newton-le-W WA12 .... 2 A1
  Northwich CW9 .... 104 B4
Valley Way Knutsford WA16 . 82 A4
  Stalybridge SK15 .... 242 F1
Vanguard Ct WA3 .... 9 E2
Varden Gr SK3 .... 240 D1
Vardon Dr SK9 .... 60 B3
Varey Rd CW12 .... 156 C2
Vaudrey Cres CW12 .... 156 C2
Vaudrey La M34 .... 241 A6
Vaudrey St SK15 .... 242 D1
Vaughan Rd
  Stockport SK4 .... 240 D7
  Whaley Bridge SK23 .... 65 F3
Vaughans La CH3 .... 142 A4
Vauxhall Cl WA5 .... 14 B3
Vauxhall Rd CW5 .... 205 D6
Vauxhall Way CW7 .... 149 E3
Vearows Pl CW8 .... 103 F4
Venable's Rd CH1 .... 117 F2

Venables Rd CW9 .... 79 D1
Venables Way
  High Legh WA16 .... 29 E2
  Middlewich CW10 .... 151 F3
Venns Rd WA2 .... 16 B4
Ventnor Ave M33 .... 242 B8
Ventnor Cl
  Great Sankey WA5 .... 14 B4
  Middlewich CW10 .... 151 E4
Ventnor Rd SK4 .... 240 A6
Verbena Cl M31 .... 11 F2
Verbena Cl WA7 .... 49 F2
Verdin Cl WA8 .... 78 C1
Verdin Cl Moulton CW9 .. 126 C4
  Winsford CW7 .... 126 B1
Verdin Ct WA1 .... 190 A4
Verdin City High Sch
  CW7 .... 126 B1
Verdin St CW9 .... 104 B4
Vere St CW1 .... 190 B3
Verity Cl CW1 .... 191 E2
Vernay Gn CH4 .... 141 D3
Vernon Ave Audley ST7 . 209 E1
  Congleton CW12 .... 178 C4
  Hooton L66 .... 44 A1
Vernon Cl Audley ST7 ..... 209 F1
  Cheadle SK8 .... 239 E1
  Poynton SK12 .... 36 B1
  Saughall CH1 .... 117 D4
Vernon Cty Inf Sch The
  SK12 .... 36 C2
Vernon Dr CW3 .... 230 C2
Vernon Gr M33 .... 242 E5
Vernon Rd Chester CH1 . 118 A2
  Poynton SK12 .... 36 C1
Vernon St Crewe CW1 .... 190 A3
  Hyde SK14 .... 241 E6
  Macclesfield SK10 .... 112 C4
  4 Stockport SK1 .... 240 F6
  Warrington WA1 .... 16 A2
Vernon Way CW1 .... 190 B2
Vernon Wlk SK1 .... 240 F6
Veronica Way L66 .... 69 E4
Vetch Cl WA3 .... 11 D3
Vetches The CH3 .... 119 F3
Viaduct Rd WA14 .... 238 D7
Viaduct St
  Newton-le-W WA12 .... 2 A2
  Stockport SK3 .... 240 E5
Vicar's La CH1 .... 237 E2
Vicarage Ave SK8 .... 35 D4
Vicarage Cl
  Guilden Sutton CH3 .... 119 F3
  Hale L24 .... 21 F1
Vicarage Ct LL13 .... 196 C4
Vicarage Dr WA11 .... 1 A4
Vicarage Gdns Hyde SK14 . 241 F6
  Sandbach CW11 .... 174 C4
Vicarage Gr CW7 .... 149 E3
Vicarage Hill WA6 .... 73 C2
Vicarage La
  Altrincham WA14 .... 238 C1
  Audern CW3 .... 230 A2
  Bunbury CW6 .... 168 C1
  Burton L64 .... 67 E1
  Frodsham WA6 .... 74 B4
  Hassall Green CW11 .... 175 F3
  Helsby WA6 .... 73 E2
  Little Budworth CW6 .... 147 F4
  Poynton SK12 .... 36 C3
  Sandbach CW11 .... 174 C4
Vicarage Rd Chester CH2 . 118 C2
  Haslington CW1 .... 191 E3
  Northwich CW9 .... 104 A4
  Stockport SK3 .... 240 E2
  Widnes WA8 .... 23 D4
Vicarage Row L62 .... 44 A3
Vicarage Wlk CW9 .... 104 B4
Vicars Cross Rd CH3 ...... 119 F3
Vicker's Cl CH3 .... 121 F4
Vickers Rd WA8 .... 22 C2
Vickers Way CW9 .... 104 A4
Victoria Ave
  Altrincham WA15 .... 238 F7
  Crewe CW1, CW2, CW4 . 190 A2
  Great Sankey WA5 .... 14 B3
  Haslington CW1 .... 191 E2
  Heswall L60 .... 41 D3
  Holmes Chapel CW4 .... 130 B1
  Kidsgrove ST7 .... 194 C1
  Widnes WA8 .... 13 D2
Victoria Cl
  Cheadle Hulme SK7 .... 35 E3
  Stockport SK3 .... 240 E3
Victoria Com Cty High Sch
  CW1 .... 190 B3
Victoria Cres Chester CH2 . 237 D4
  Chester, Handbridge CH4 . 237 F1
Victoria Ct Chester CH2 . 237 D4
  Haslington CW1 .... 191 E2
Victoria Ctr CW1 .... 190 B4
Victoria Dr WA11 .... 1 C4
Victoria Inf Sch CH2 .... 237 D4
Victoria Jr Sch WA11 .... 1 C4
Victoria Gall CW5 .... 204 C3
Victoria Gdns SK14 .... 241 F8
Victoria La CH2 .... 237 D4
Victoria Mkt SK15 .... 242 D1
Victoria Pathway CH4 .... 237 F1
Victoria Pk CW8 .... 78 C1
Victoria Pl Chester CH1 . 237 D3
  Warrington WA4 .... 16 B1

Victoria Rd
Altrincham WA15 .... 238 D3
Broughton CH4 .... 140 B3
Chester CH1 .... 237 D3
Chester CH2 .... 237 D4
Ellesmere Port L65 .... 70 B3
Great Sankey WA5 .... 15 D2
Macclesfield SK10 .... 87 D1
Neston L64 .... 67 D3
Newton-le-W WA12 .... 2 B2
Northwich CW9 .... 104 A4
Penketh WA5 .... 14 B2
Runcorn WA7 .... 23 D1
Sale M33 .... 242 D5
Warrington WA4 .... 16 C1
Warrington, Stockton Heath
WA4 .... 16 B1
Widnes WA8 .... 23 D3
Wilmslow SK9 .... 60 A3
**Victoria Road Cty Prim
Sch** Northwich CW9 ..... 104 A4
Warrington WA7 .... 23 D1
Victoria Sq
Warrington WA1 .... 16 B1
6 Winsford CW7 .... 149 D4
Victoria St
Altrincham WA14 .... 238 D5
Crewe CW1 .... 190 B2
Hyde SK14 .... 241 F8
Knutsford WA16 .... 56 C1
New Mills SK22 .... 39 D3
Northwich CW9 .... 79 F1
Sandbach CW11 .... 175 D4
Stalybridge SK15 .... 242 C2
Warrington WA1 .... 16 B3
Widnes WA8 .... 23 D4
Victoria Way SK7 .... 35 E3
Victoria Wlk 2 SK10 .. 112 C4
Victory Rd WA4 .... 11 E2
Vienna Rd SK3 .... 240 D2
Vienna Rd E SK3 .... 240 E2
Viewlands Dr SK3 .... 34 B1
Villa Rd CW5 .... 116 A4
Villagate La WA4 .... 27 E3
Village Cl Lostock CW9 145 D4
Runcorn WA7 .... 50 A4
Warrington WA4 .... 17 F2
Village Ct WA3 .... 34 B1
Village La WA4 .... 52 B2
Village Rd Christleton CH3 .. 142 C4
Great Barrow CH7 .... 120 C3
Heswall L60 .... 40 C4
Village The Astbury CW12 .. 178 A4
Burton L64 .... 67 E1
Prestbury SK10 .... 86 C3
Village Way SK9 .... 34 B1
Villars St WA1 .... 16 B3
Villiers Russell Cl CW1 190 B3
Villiers St
Ashton-u-L OL6 .... 242 A2
Hyde SK14 .... 241 F6
Vincent Cl WA5 .... 15 E4
Vincent Dr CH4 .... 141 E3
Vincent St Crewe CW1 190 C2
Macclesfield SK11 .... 112 B4
Vine Bank Rd ST7 ...... 195 D1
Vine Cl SK11 .... 112 A3
Vine Cres WA5 .... 14 B4
Vine Rd L66 .... 69 F1
Vine St Bollington SK10 .. 88 A4
Runcorn WA7 .... 23 D1
Widnes WA8 .... 23 D3
Vine Tree Ave Crewe CW2 190 A1
Shavington CW2 .... 206 A2
Vine Tree Cty Prim Sch
CW2 .... 190 A1
Violet Cl WA3 .... 9 E3
Violet St Stockport SK2 240 F2
Widnes WA8 .... 23 D4
Virginia Chase SK8 ...... 34 C4
Virginia Dr CH1 .... 117 E2
Viscount Dr Cheadle SK8 .. 34 A4
Wythenshawe WA15 ...... 32 C4
Vista Ave WA12 .... 2 A2
Vista Rd Haydock WA12 .. 2 A3
Newton-le-W WA12 .... 2 A3
Runcorn WA7 .... 49 D4
Vista The WA1 .... 11 E2
Vista Way WA12 .... 2 A2
Volunteer Ave CW5 ..... 204 C3
Volunteer Fields CW5 .. 204 C3
Volunteer St Chester CH1 .. 237 E2
Frodsham WA6 .... 49 E1
Vose Cl WA5 .... 15 E3
Vulcan Cl Newton-le-W WA12 .. 2 B1
Warrington WA2 .... 8 C1
Vyrnwy Rd CH4 .... 140 B3

Waddington Cl
Goldborne WA3 .... 3 F4
Warrington WA2 .... 8 C1
Wade Cess CH4 .... 78 A2
Wade Deacon Cty High Sch
WA8 .... 13 D1
Wade Cl CW9 .... 79 D1
Wadebrook Gr 15 SK9 . 34 B1
Wades La CW7 .... 126 B2
Wadeson Way WA3 .... 9 D4
Wadham Gdns SK6 ..... 241 C4
Wadham Way WA11 .... 238 F1
Wadsworth Cl SK9 .... 34 C2
Wagg Cl CW12 .... 156 B3
Waggs St CW12 .... 156 B1
Wagon La WA11 .... 1 A3
Waine St CW1 .... 190 B3

Wainwright Rd WA14 ... 238 C5
Wainwright St SK16 .... 242 A1
Waitney Croft SK10 .... 113 E4
Wakefield Cres SK14 ... 241 A1

Wakefield Rd
Ellesmere Port L66 .... 69 F1
Stalybridge SK15 .... 242 E3
Wakefield St WA3 .... 3 D4
Wakefield Wlk M34 .... 241 A5
Wakeham Cl SK11 ...... 111 F4
Wakes Meadow CW6 .. 185 F4
Walden Cl WA4 .... 17 E2
Walden Dr CH1 .... 93 E4
Walden Ave SK8 .... 239 D5
Walden Rd SK11 .... 112 A3
Waldron Gdns CW2 .... 189 F1
Waldron Rd CW1 .... 191 E2
Walfield Ave CW12 ..... 156 B3
Walford Ave CW2 .... 190 A2
Walgrove Cl CW12 ...... 156 A2
Walker Ave SK15 .... 242 F2
Walker Cl Haslington CW1 .. 191 E2
Hyde SK14 .... 241 F6
Walker Dr CW10 .... 151 E4
Walker Fold SK14 .... 241 F6
Walker La Hyde SK14 .. 241 F6
Sutton Lane Ends SK11 . 112 C1
Walker St Chester CH2 . 237 F4
Crewe CW1 .... 190 A3
7 Macclesfield SK11 .. 112 B4
Stockport SK1 .... 240 E5
Warrington WA2 .... 16 A3
Walkers La
Ellesmere Port L66 .... 69 E3
Penketh WA5 .... 14 C2
Scholar Green ST7 .... 177 D1
Tarporley CW6 .... 146 B1
Walkersgreen Rd ST5 . 210 B1
Wall Fields Rd CW5 .... 204 C4
Wall Hill Way CW6 ...... 76 C2
Wall La CW5 .... 204 C3
Wallace Ct CW7 .... 127 E1
Wallace St Northwich CW8 .. 103 F4
Wallcroft L64 .... 68 A4
Waller St SK11 .... 112 C3
Wallerscote Cty Prim Sch
CW8 .... 102 C4
Wallerscote Rd CW8 ... 102 C4
Walleys La CW5 .... 203 E4
Wallfields Cl CW5 .... 204 C4
Wallhill La CW11 .... 177 E4
Wallingford Rd SK9 ..... 34 B3
Wallis St Crewe CW1 ... 190 B3
Warrington WA4 .... 16 A2
Wallrake L60 .... 40 C4
Walls Ave CH1 .... 118 A1
Wallsend Ct WA8 .... 12 C2
Wallworth's Bank CW12 .. 156 C1
Walmer Pl CW7 .... 149 E3
Walmoor Pk CH3 .... 119 D1
Walmsley St
Newton-le-W WA12 .... 2 B2
Reddish SK5 .... 240 F7
Widnes WA8 .... 23 E4
Walnut Ave CW6 .... 102 B4
Walnut Cl Chester CH2 118 A3
Warrington WA1 .... 17 F4
Wilmslow SK9 .... 60 C4
Walnut Croft CH3 .... 180 C3
Walnut Dr CW7 .... 127 D1
Walnut Gr
Ellesmere Port L66 .... 70 A1
Sale M33 .... 242 A6
Walnut La CW8 .... 103 D3
Walnut Rd M31 .... 11 E2
Walnut Rise CW12 ..... 156 A1
Walnut Tree La CW10 . 153 D2
Walnut Tree Rd SK3 ... 240 A4
Walpole Cl CW1 .... 191 E3
Walpole Gr WA2 .... 8 B1
Walpole Rd WA7 .... 49 F2
Walpole St CW7 .... 237 D4
Walsh Cl WA22 .... 2 B3
Walsingham Dr WA7 ... 24 B1
Walsingham Rd WA5 .. 14 C3
Walter St Chester CH2 237 E4
Warrington WA1 .... 16 C4
Widnes WA8 .... 13 E1
Walthall St CW2 .... 190 B1
Waltham Ave WA3 .... 5 E4
Waltham Cl WA4 .... 24 C2
Waltham Dr SK8 .... 35 D3
Waltham Pl CH4 .... 141 D3
Walton Ave WA5 .... 14 C3
Walton Gr ST7 .... 210 B4
Walton Hall WA4 .... 25 F3
Walton Heath Dr SK10 .. 87 E2
Walton Heath Rd WA4 . 16 A1
Walton Lea Rd
Higher Walton WA4 .... 25 F4
Warrington WA4 .... 26 A4
Walton New Rd WA4 .... 26 A4
Walton Pl CH1 .... 117 F2
Walton Rd
Altrincham WA14 .... 238 B5
Culcheth WA3 .... 4 C1
Warrington WA4 .... 26 A4
Walton St Runcorn WA7 23 D1
8 Stockport SK1 .... 240 F3
Walton Way Denton M34 .. 241 A5
Kidsgrove ST7 .... 210 B4
Waltons The CH4 .... 141 F3
Wanshill Pl WA2 .... 8 A2
War Memorial Hospl CW6 146 B1
Warbeck Gr M33 .... 242 D5
Warburton Bridge Rd WA3 .. 11 D1

Warburton Cl
Altrincham WA15 .... 32 B3
Lymm WA13 .... 19 D2
Romiley SK6 .... 241 A1
Warburton Dr WA15 ..... 32 B3
Warburton La WA1, WA13 .. 11 F1
Warburton St WA4 ...... 16 B1
Warburton View WA3 .. 11 D1
Ward Ave SK10 .... 88 A4
Ward Cl WA5 .... 7 D1
Ward La SK7 .... 38 C2
Ward St SK14 .... 241 E6
Ward's La CW11 .... 153 E3
Ward's Terr CH2 .... 118 C2
Wardle Ave CW5 .... 187 E4
Wardle Cres SK11 ...... 111 F1
Wardle Ind Est CW5 ... 187 D4
Wardle Mews CW10 .... 151 E4
Wardle Rd M33 .... 242 C6
Wardley Rd WA4 .... 16 A1
Wardour Cl SK11 .... 111 F4
Wardour St WA5 .... 15 F3
Wards La CW12 .... 179 E4
Wareham Cl WA1 .... 17 E4
Wareham Dr CW1 .... 190 A4
Warford Ave WA16 ...... 37 D1
Warford Cres SK9 .... 84 A4
**Warford Hall (Mary Dendy
Hospl)** SK9 .... 84 A3
Warford La WA16 .... 59 D1
Warford Cty Prim Sch
WA12 .... 2 B1
Wargrave House Sch
WA12 .... 2 B1
Wargrave Mews WA12 .. 2 B1
Wargrave Rd
Newton-le-W WA12 .... 2 B1
Newton-le-W, Wargrave WA12 2 A2
Warham St SK9 .... 60 A4
Waring Ave St Helens WA9 . 1 A1
Warrington WA4 .... 16 C2
Warkworth Cl WA8 ...... 12 B2
Warkworth Ct L65 .... 70 C2
Warley Cl SK8 .... 239 E6
**Warmingham CE Aided
Prim Sch** CW11 .... 173 F4
Warmingham La
Middlewich CW10 .... 151 E3
Sandbach CW11 .... 174 A4
Warmingham Rd
Crewe CW1 .... 173 E2
Sandbach CW11 .... 173 E2
Warmley Cl WA8 .... 12 B2
Warren Ave Cheadle SK8 .. 239 D5
Heswall L60 .... 40 B4
Knutsford WA16 .... 56 C2
Lostock CW9 .... 80 A2
Warren Ct Knutsford WA16 .. 56 C1
Middlewich CW10 .... 151 D4
Poynton SK12 .... 36 A2
Warren Croft WA7 .... 50 B4
Warren Ct Ellesmere Port L66 .. 69 E2
Frodsham WA6 .... 74 B3
Warren Dr Altrincham WA15 .. 32 B4
Appleton WA4 .... 26 B4
Broughton CH4 .... 139 D2
Ellesmere Port L66 .... 69 F4
Newton-le-W WA12 .... 2 C2
Warren SK11 .... 111 E1
Warren Gr SK11 .... 111 E1
Warren La Hartford CW8 .. 103 D2
Warrington WA1 .... 17 E4
Warren Lea SK12 .... 36 C3
Warren Rd Appleton WA4 .. 26 B4
Stockport SK2 .... 240 E2
Warrington WA4 .... 26 B4
Warren St SK1 .... 240 F6
Warren The CW8 .... 101 E3
Warren Way Tarporley CW6 .. 168 B4
Wilmslow SK9 .... 60 C4
Warrener St WA2 .... 242 D6
Warrilow Heath Rd ST5 210 B1
Warrington Ave
Crewe CW1 .... 190 B3
Ellesmere Port L65 .... 70 A1
Warrington Bank Quay Sta
WA5 .... 15 F2
Warrington Bsns Pk WA2 .. 8 B1
Warrington Central Sta
WA2 .... 16 A3
**Warrington Collegiate Inst
Padgate Campus** WA1 .. 9 D2
**Warrington District General
Hospl** WA5 .... 15 F3
Warrington La WA13 .... 19 F2
Warrington Rd
Bold Heath WA8 .... 13 E4
Comberbach CW9 .... 78 B4
Croft WA3 .... 9 F4
Cronton L35 .... 12 C4
Cuddington CW8 .... 102 A3
Dunham-on-t-H WA6 ..... 97 E3
Glazebury WA3 .... 5 E3
Goldborne WA12 .... 3 D3
Hatton WA4 .... 25 F2
Little Leigh CW8 .... 77 D3
Lymm WA13 .... 19 E4
Mere WA16 .... 56 B4
Mickle Trafford CH2 ..... 119 F4
Penketh WA5 .... 14 C2
Runcorn, Castlefields WA7 .. 23 F1
Runcorn, Manor Park WA7 .. 24 A2
Warrington WA3 .... 9 F4
Warrington, Locking Stumps
WA3 .... 9 F4
Widnes WA8 .... 13 E1
Widnes, Moss Bank WA8 .. 23 E4

**Warrington Road Cty Prim
Sch** WA8 .... 13 E1
Warrington St SK15 .... 242 E1
**Warrington Tech Coll
North Campus**
WA2 .... 8 A1
Warton Cl Bramhall SK7 .. 36 A4
Penketh WA5 .... 15 D2
Warwick Ave
Great Sankey WA5 .... 14 B4
Newton-le-W WA12 .... 2 B1
Warrington WA5 .... 15 F4
Warwick Cl Kidsgrove ST7 .. 195 D2
Knutsford WA16 .... 57 E1
Macclesfield SK11 .... 111 F3
Manchester SK4 .... 240 D8
Neston L64 .... 66 C4
Warwick Ct
Ellesmere Port L65 .... 70 C1
Manchester SK4 .... 240 C7
Warwick Cty Prim Sch
SK11 .... 111 F3
Warwick Dr
Altrincham WA15 .... 238 F1
Hazel Grove SK7 .... 36 B4
Sale M33 .... 242 B6
Warwick Mall SK8 ...... 239 D6
Warwick Pl CW7 .... 149 E3
Warwick Rd
Altrincham WA15 .... 238 E1
Blacon CH1 .... 117 E1
Irlam M44 .... 11 E3
Macclesfield SK11 .... 111 F3
Manchester SK4 .... 240 C7
Romiley SK6 .... 241 A4
Warwick Wlk SK11 ...... 111 F3
Wasdale Dr SK8 .... 239 B3
Wasdale Gr CW1 .... 173 D1
Wasdale Terr SK15 ..... 242 D4
Wash La Allostock WA16 .. 106 C2
Warrington WA4 .... 16 C2
Washington Cl SK11 ... 179 E1
Washington Dr WA5 .... 15 D3
Washway Rd M33 .... 242 A6
Wasley Cl WA2 .... 8 C2
Waste La Cuddington CW8 .. 101 F2
Kelsall CW6 .... 122 C2
Watch La CW11 .... 174 A3
Water La SK9 .... 60 A4
Water Lode CW5 .... 204 C3
Water Rd SK15 .... 242 C2
Water St Bollington SK10 .. 88 A4
Hyde SK14 .... 241 D6
Macclesfield SK11 .... 112 C4
Water St continued
Newcastle-u-L ST5 .... 210 B1
Newton-le-W WA12 .... 2 B2
Northwich CW9 .... 104 A4
Runcorn WA7 .... 23 D2
Stalybridge SK15 .... 242 D2
Stockport SK1 .... 240 F5
Widnes WA8 .... 23 D3
Water Tower (Mus) CH1 118 A1
Water Tower Rd L64 .... 41 F1
Water Tower St CH1 ... 237 D3
Waterbank Row WA3 .. 103 F4
Waterbridge Ct WA4 .... 26 B4
Waterfoot La SK23 .... 65 E3
Waterford Dr Ashton SK6 .. 241 F2
Waterford Dr L64 .... 67 D4
Waterford Pl SK8 .... 34 A4
Waterford Way WA7 .... 50 B3
Watergate Row WA1 ... 237 D2
Watergate Sq CH1 ...... 237 D2
Watergate St CH1 .... 237 D2
Waterhouse Ave SK10 .. 87 F4
Waterloo Cl L65 .... 70 B3
Waterloo Gr ST7 .... 195 D1
Waterloo La WA6 .... 74 C1
Waterloo Rd Bramhall SK7 .. 35 F4
Chester CH2 .... 118 B2
Haslington CW1 .... 191 E2
Northwich CW8 .... 103 F4
Poynton SK12 .... 37 D1
Romiley SK6 .... 241 E2
Waterloo St W SK11 .... 112 B4
Watermeetings La SK6 .. 241 F1
Watermill Dr SK11 ...... 112 C4
Waters Edge CW9 .... 79 E2
Waters Gn SK11 .... 112 B4
Waters Reach SK12 ..... 36 C3
Watersedge Rd WA6 .... 49 E1
Watersfield Cl SK8 ...... 34 C4
Waterside Appleton WA4 .. 26 B4
Disley SK12 .... 38 C4
Waterside La WA8 .... 22 C4
Waterside Mews 3 CW5 .. 174 C2
Waterside Rd Disley SK12 .. 38 C4
New Mills SK22 .... 39 D3
Waterside View CW9 ... 104 C1
Waterside Way CW10 . 128 A1
Watertower View CW1 .. 118 C1
Waterway CH3 .... 143 D3
Waterways WA5 .... 15 E3
Waterworks La
Ellesmere Port L66 .... 68 C4
Winwick WA2 .... 8 A4
Watery La Astbury CW12 .. 178 A3
Winwick WA2 .... 7 F3

Watkin St Hawarden CH5 .. 116
Warrington WA2 16
Watking Ave WA12 1
Watkinson Way WA8 13
Watlands Rd ST7 209
Watling Cres CW4 141
Watling Ct CH3 118
Watling Dr CW6 123
Watling St CW9 103
Watson Sq 20 SK1 240
Watson St Crewe CW1 .. 190
Watson's Cl CW4 139
Watt St CH4 17
Wavell Ave WA8 13
Wavells Way CH3 142
Waveney Dr WA12 2
Waverley Ave WA4 26
Waverley Cl SK10 113
Waverley Dr SK8 39
Waverley Rd Sale M33 . 242
Stockport SK3 240
Waverley Terr CH2 118
Waverton Cl
Davenham CW9 103
Hough Common CW2 206
Waverton Cty Prim Sch
CH3 143
Waverton Mill Quays CH3 143
Waverton Rd L66 69
Wavertree Ave
Scholar Green ST7 194
Widnes WA8 23
Wavertree Ct L66 69
Wavertree Dr CW10 151
Wavertree Rd CH1 117
Way's Gn CW7 126
Waybutt La Betley CW2 . 221
Hough Common CW2 221
Wayfarers Dr WA12 2
Wayford Cl WA6 49
Wayside ST7 193
Wayside Cl WA3 3
Wayside Ct CW2 119
Wayside Dr SK12 36
Wayside Rd SK10 112
Waywell Cl WA2 8
Weal Stone La CH2 118
Weald Dr L66 69
Wealstone Ct CW2 118
Wearhead Cl WA3 2
Weaste La WA4 17
Weates Cl WA8 4
Weathercock La CW12 . 157
Weaver Cl Alsager ST7 .. 193
Biddulph ST6 179
Sandbach CW11 174
Weaver Cres WA6 49
Weaver Ct SK11 112
Weaver Cty Prim Sch The
CW5 204
Weaver Gr
Mickle Trafford CH2 119
St Helens WA9 1
Weaver Grange CW9 ... 126
Weaver La WA6 49
Weaver Park Ind Est WA6 .. 49
Weaver Rd Culcheth WA3 .. 5
Ellesmere Port L65 70
Frodsham WA6 49
Moulton CW9 126
Nantwich CW5 204
Northwich CW8 103
Runcorn WA7 49
Weaver St Chester CH1 . 237
Winsford CW7 126
Weaver Vale Cty Prim Sch
WA6 49
Weaver View Audlem CW3 .. 229
Church Minshull CW5 ... 172
Northwich CW8 103
Weaverham CW8 77
Weaver's Way WA8 78
Weaver's La SK7 35
Weaverhall La CW7 126
Weaverham Cty High Sch
CW8 102
**Weaverham Forest Cty
Prim Sch** CW8 77
Weaverham Rd
Cuddington CW8 102
Weaverham CW8 102
Weaverham Way 4 SK9 34
Weaverside WA5 15
Weaverside Ave WA7 49
Webb Dr WA5 6
Webb's La CW10 128
Webster Cl CW4 130
Websters La L66 69
Weddell Cl WA5 14
Wedge Ave WA11 1
Wedgewood Ave ST7 ... 210
Wedgwood Dr WA8 13
Wedgwood La ST6 179
Wedgwood Rd WA3 2
Wednesbury Dr WA5 15
Weedon Ave WA12 2
Weighbridge Rd CH5 92
Weir Gr ST7 195
Weir La WA1 17
Weir St Northwich CW9 . 103
Warrington WA4 16
Welbeck Cl CW10 128
Welbeck Rd SK14 241
Welch Rd SK14 241
Welcroft St 2 SK1 240
Weldon Rd WA14 238
Welford Ave WA3 3
Welford Cl SK9 60

ell Ave SY14 .... 213 D2
ell Bank CW11 .... 175 D3
ell Bank La WA16 ..... 108 B4
ell Cl L64 .... 67 E3
ell Farm CI SY14 .... 213 D2
ell Field CI WA16 .... 80 A4
ell La Alsager ST7 ..... 193 E2
  Antrobus CW9 .... 53 D2
  Biddulph ST6 .... 179 E2
  Winsford CW7 .... 126 B1
  Heswall L60 .... 41 D3
  Kingsley WA6 .... 75 E1
  Little Budworth CW6 ... 147 F4
  Manley WA6 .... 98 C2
  Mollington CH1 .... 94 C1
  Neston L64 .... 66 C3
  Penketh WA5 .... 14 C2
  Prestbury SK10 .... 87 E4
  Stretton WA4 .... 52 C4
  Weaverham CW8 .... 77 E1
ell Meadow SK14 ...... 241 D8
ell St Malpas SY14 .... 213 D2
  Mow Cop ST7 .... 195 E4
  New Mills SK22 .... 39 D4
  Winsford CW7 .... 126 B1
elland CI 🔟 CW11 .... 174 B3
ellbrook CI WA7 .... 50 B3
ellcroft CI CW2 .... 206 A4
eller Ave SK12 .... 36 B1
eller La SK12 .... 36 B1
elles St SY11 .... 175 D3
ellesbourne CI
  Macclesfield SK10 ..... 86 C1
  Neston L64 .... 66 B3
elfield
  Preston on the Hill WA7 . 50 C3
  Romiley SK6 .... 241 C4
  Winsford CW7 .... 50 C3
  Widnes WA8 .... 13 D2
  Winsford CW7 .... 127 D1
ellfield Rd WA3 .... 4 C2
ell St WA5 .... 15 F3
ellington Ave L62 ..... 43 F2
ellington CI
  Ellesmere Port L65 .... 70 B3
  Knutsford WA16 .... 57 E2
  Sale M33 .... 242 C8
ellington Gdns WA12 . 2 A2
ellington Gr SK2 ...... 240 A2
ellington Mill SK3 ..... 240 E5
ellington PI
  Altrincham WA14 ...... 238 D4
  Chester CH2 .... 237 E3
ellington Rd
  Altrincham WA15 ...... 238 F6
  Bollington SK10 .... 87 F4
  Broughton CH4 .... 139 D2
  Ellesmere Port L65 .... 70 B2
  Ellesmere Port L65 .... 70 B3
  Hazel Grove SK7 .... 37 D4
  Kidsgrove ST7 .... 195 D1
  Nantwich CW5 .... 204 C2
ellington Rd N
  Ellesmere Port L65 .... 70 B3
  Stockport M19 & SK3 & SK4 240 D7
ellington Rd S SK1 & SK2 240 F6
ellington St Denton SK14 241 C7
  Macclesfield SK11 ..... 112 B4
  Newton-le-W WA12 .... 2 A2
  Northwich CW8 .... 103 F4
  Runcorn WA7 .... 23 D2
  Stockport SK3 & SK4 .. 240 F5
  Warrington WA1 .... 16 B3
  Widnes WA8 .... 23 D3
ells Ave CW1 .... 191 E3
ells CI Cheadle SK8 ... 34 B4
  Ellesmere Port CH1 .... 94 C4
  Mickle Trafford CH2 ... 119 F4
  Warrington WA1 .... 17 D4
ellswood Dr CW7 ..... 205 F4
ellwood Rd L66 .... 69 F4
elsby Cl WA2 .... 8 C2
elsh La CW7 .... 149 E3
elsh Rd Ellesmere Port L66 . 68 C2
  Ledsham L66 .... 68 C2
  Puddington CH1 .... 93 E3
  Shotwick CH1 .... 93 E3
elsh Row Nantwich CW5 204 B3
  Nether Alderley SK10 . 84 C3
elshampton CI L66 ... 69 E1
elshmen's La CW5 .... 204 B4
elshpool CI WA5 ...... 7 E1
elton CI SK9 .... 59 F2
elton Dr SK9 .... 59 F2
elton Gr SK9 .... 59 F2
elwyn CI WA4 .... 17 E2
emyss Rd CH1 .... 117 E2
endover CI WA11 ..... 1 B4
enger Rd WA8 .... 13 D3
enlock CI
  Macclesfield SK10 ..... 87 D1
  Newcastle-u-L ST5 .... 210 C1
enlock Gdns L66 ...... 69 F1
enlock La L66 .... 69 F1
enlock Rd WA7 .... 50 A2
enlock Way CW4 ..... 140 C3
ensley Dr SK7 .... 36 B4
ensley Rd Cheadle SK8 . 239 C6
  Goldborne WA3 .... 3 F4
enslydale
  🔟 Reddish SK5 ..... 240 F8
ensleydale Ave
  Bebington L62 .... 43 F3
  Cheadle SK8 .... 239 C6
  Congleton CW12 .... 157 D3

Wensleydale CI WA5 ... 14 C4
Wentworth Ave
  Macclesfield SK11 ..... 111 F3
  Warrington WA1 .... 17 D4
Wentworth CI
  Northwich CW9 .... 104 C4
  Widnes WA8 .... 13 D3
Wentworth Dr Bebington L63 43 E3
  Bramhall SK7 .... 36 A4
  Kidsgrove ST7 .... 195 E2
Wereton Rd ST7 .... 209 E1
Werneth Ct SK14 ...... 241 E5
Werneth Low Rd SK6 . 241 D4
Werneth Rd SK14 ..... 241 F6
Werneth Sch SK6 ..... 241 A2
Wervin Rd Chester CH2 . 96 A2
  Stoak CH2 .... 96 A2
Wesley Ave Alsager ST7 . 193 E2
  Haydock WA11 .... 1 C4
  Sandbach CW11 .... 175 D3
Wesley C CW12 .... 156 B1
Wesley Ct Nantwich CW5 . 204 C3
  Neston L64 .... 66 B4
Wesley Ct CW7 .... 126 C1
Wesley Gdns ST7 ..... 195 D1
Wesley PI Crewe CW2 . 190 B1
  Northwich CW9 .... 104 A4
Wesley St Audley ST7 . 210 A1
  🔟 Stockport SK1 ..... 240 F5
Wessex CS Shavington CW2 . 206 B2
  Warrington WA1 .... 17 F4
Wessex Dr CW9 .... 104 B3
West Ave Altrincham WA14 . 238 A5
  Crewe CW1, CW2 ...... 190 A2
  Gatley SK8 .... 239 C1
  Kidsgrove ST7 .... 194 B3
  Middlewich CW10 ..... 128 B1
  Northwich CW9 .... 104 B4
  Stalybridge SK15 ..... 242 D3
  Warrington WA2 ...... 16 A4
  Weston CW2 .... 207 D3
West Bank
  Alderley Edge SK9 .... 85 D4
  Chester CH2 .... 118 B2
West Bank Cty Prim Sch
  WA8 .... 23 D2
West Bank Dock Est WA8 . 22 C3
West Bank Rd SK10 ... 87 D1
West Bank St WA8 .... 23 D3
West Bond St SK11 ... 112 D8
West Cheshire Coll
  Handbridge Ctr CH4 .. 141 E4
  West Cl SK10 .... 87 F4
West Downs Rd SK8 .. 239 F3
West Dr Gatley M22 & SK8 . 239 A4
  Great Sankey WA5 .... 15 D2
  Heswall L60 .... 41 D4
  Neston L64 .... 66 C3
  Winsford CW7 .... 127 D1
West Dudley St CW7 . 126 C1
West End CH3 .... 121 F4
West End Ave SK8 .... 239 A6
West End Cotts CW12 . 156 B1
West End Gr WA11 ... 1 A3
West End Rd WA11 ... 1 A3
West Gate WA8 .... 22 A4
West Gr Alsager ST7 . 193 F2
West Heath Ave WA1 . 18 B2
West Heath Sh Ctr CW12 . 156 A2
West Hill Sch SK15 ... 242 C2
West House Ct SK10 .. 66 C1
West Hyde WA13 ..... 18 B2
West La Cuddington CW8 . 101 F2
  High Legh WA16 ...... 29 E3
  Runcorn WA7 .... 49 F4
West Lea WA14 .... 241 A6
West Lorne St CW1 ... 237 D3
West Mains L24 .... 21 D2
West Oak PI SK8 ..... 239 F1
West Over SK6 .... 241 A1
West Park Ave Denton SK14 . 241 B6
  Poynton SK12 .... 36 A2
West Park Dr CH1 .... 94 C4
West Quay Rd WA2 .. 7 F2
West Rd Altrincham WA14 . 238 C2
  Congleton CW12 ...... 156 B2
  Ellesmere Port L65 ... 70 B2
  Runcorn WA7 .... 48 B4
  Weaverham CW8 ..... 77 D1
West Side Ave WA11 . 1 A3
West St Alderley Edge SK9 . 60 A1
  Chester CH2 .... 237 F4
  Congleton CW12 ...... 156 B2
  Crewe CW1 .... 190 A3
  Haslington CW1 ...... 191 E3
  Macclesfield SK11 .... 112 A4
  Middlewich CW10 .... 128 B1
  Mount Pleasant ST7 . 195 D3
  Stalybridge SK15 .... 242 C2
  Stockport SK3 .... 240 D5
  Warrington WA2 ..... 16 A4
West Vale L64 .... 66 C3
West Vale Rd WA15 . 238 F6
West View WA2 ...... 9 D1
West Way
  Holmes Chapel CW4 . 130 A2
  Sandbach CW11 ..... 174 C2
  Shavington CW2 ..... 206 B3
  Great Budworth CW9 . 79 D4

Westbourne Ave CW1 . 190 A3
Westbourne Gr M33 .. 242 A6
Westbourne Rd Blacon CH1 118 A2
  Warrington WA4 ...... 26 A4
Westbrook Ave WA4 . 26 A4
Westbrook Cres
  Great Sankey WA5 .... 7 D1
  Warrington WA5 ...... 7 D1
Westbrook Ctr WA5 .. 7 D1
Westbrook Dr SK10 .. 87 E1
Westbrook Rd WA5 .. 75 D1
Westbrook Way WA5 . 7 D1
Westbury CI
  Middlewich CW10 .... 151 D4
  Shavington CW2 ..... 206 B4
Westbury Dr SK11 ... 112 A4
Westbury Way WA5 . 140 C3
Westby CI SK7 .... 36 A4
Westcourt Rd SK10 .. 242 A8
Westdale Rd WA1 ... 17 D4
Westerham St CW13 . 196 B4
Westenra Ave L65 ... 69 F3
Western App CH2 ... 118 C2
Western Ave Blacon CH1 117 E2
  Ellesmere Port L65 .. 70 B3
  Macclesfield SK11 ... 112 B3
  Milton Green CH3 ... 165 E1
  Nantwich CW5 ...... 204 C2
Western Ct CH2 ..... 118 C2
Western Ct SK10 ... 87 E1
Western Dr L65 ..... 69 F3
Westfield Ave Audley ST7 . 209 E1
Westfield CI CH4 ... 141 D4
Westfield Cres WA7 . 22 C1
Westfield Cty Prim Sch
  WA7 .... 22 C1
Westfield Dr
  Knutsford WA16 .... 56 C1
  Runcorn WA7 .... 22 C1
Westfield Gr CW8 ... 77 F2
Westfield Mews WA7 . 22 C1
Westfield Rd Cheadle SK8 . 34 A4
  Mow Cop ST7 .... 195 E4
  Northwich CW9 .... 104 A4
  Runcorn WA7 ...... 22 C1
Westfields WA15 ... 31 F4
Westfields Rise CW3 . 232 B1
Westford Rd WA4 ... 16 A1
Westgate Altrincham WA15 238 E2
  Sale M33 .... 242 A6
  Wilmslow SK9 ...... 60 A3
Westgate Ave CW7 . 126 A1
Westholme CI WA4 . 26 A4
Westhouse CI L63 ... 43 E3
Westlands L7 .... 209 F1
Westlands CI L64 ... 41 F1
Westlands Cty High Sch
  CW12 .... 156 A2
Westlands Rd CW10 . 128 A1
Westlands The CW7 . 156 B1
Westmere Ct CW7 . 207 D3
Westmere Dr CW1 . 190 C1
Westminster Ave CW4 . 141 D3
Westminster CI
  Middlewich CW10 ... 128 A1
  Warrington WA4 ... 17 E1
  Widnes WA8 .... 22 A4
Westminster Dr
  Bebington L63 ..... 43 E4
  Cheadle Hulme SK8 . 35 D3
  Chester CH4 .... 141 B4
  Wilmslow SK9 ..... 60 A2
Westminster Gr
  Chester CH4 .... 141 E4
  Ellesmere Port L65 . 70 B3
  🔟 Winsford CW7 ..... 149 D4
Westminster Ind Pk L65 . 69 F3
Westminster PI WA1 . 16 A3
Westminster Rd
  Broughton CH4 .... 139 D2
  Chester CH2 .... 118 C2
  Ellesmere Port L65 . 70 B3
  🔟 Macclesfield SK11 . 87 E1
  Macclesfield SK11 . 112 B4
Westminster St
  Crewe CW2 .... 190 B1
  🔟 Macclesfield SK11 . 112 B4
Westminster Terr CH4 . 141 E4
Westmoor Gables SK4 . 240 A8
Westmoreland CI WA14 . 31 D4
Westmorland Ave
  Kidsgrove ST7 ..... 210 C4
  Widnes WA8 .... 13 D1
Westmorland CI SK10 . 86 C1
Westmorland Rd M31 . 11 F1
Westmorland Terr CW4 . 130 A2
Weston CI Crewe CW1 . 190 C1
  Middlewich CW10 . 151 D5
Weston Cres WA7 . 49 D3
Weston Ct WA7 .... 48 C4
Weston Cty Prim Sch
  Runcorn WA7 ..... 49 D3
Weston Dr M34 ... 241 A7
Weston La CW2 ... 118 B4
Weston La CW2 ... 206 C3
Weston Point Cty Prim Sch
  WA7 .... 48 C4
Weston Point Expressway
  WA7 ....
Weston Rd Crewe CW1 . 190 C1
  Runcorn WA7 ..... 48 C4
  Weston CW1 ...... 207 D4
  Wilmslow SK9 .... 60 C3
Weston St SK5 .... 240 E8
Westover Rd WA1 . 16 C4

Westrees CW8 .... 101 E3
Westville Dr CW12 ... 156 A1
Westward Rd Chester CH3 142 A4
  Wilmslow SK9 .... 59 F3
Westway L60 .... 40 C3
Westway Cres WA3 . 10 A3
Westwood WA7 .... 24 B1
Westwood Ave WA15 238 F7
Westwood Ct L64 .. 34 A4
Westwood Rd SK8 . 34 A4
Westy La WA4 ..... 16 C2
Wetgate La WA13 . 19 E2
Wetheral Rd SK10 . 87 D1
Wetherby CI Chester CH1 118 A1
  Newton-le-W WA12 . 2 B3
Wetherby Way L66 . 69 E3
Wetreins La Barton SY14 197 E3
  Farndon SY14 ..... 197 E3
Wexford Ave L24 .. 21 E1
Wey Gates Dr WA15 32 B4
Weybridge CI WA4 . 26 C4
Weybridge Dr SK10 87 D2
Weymouth CI WA7 . 50 C3
Weymouth Rd WA5 . 6 C3
Whaddon Dr CH4 .. 140 C2
Whaley Bridge Prim Sch
  SK23 .... 65 F4
Whaley Bridge Sta SK23 65 F4
Whaley La SK23 ... 65 F4
Whalley Ave Glazebury WA3 5 F4
  Sale M33 .... 242 C7
Whalley CI WA15 .. 238 F8
Whalley Dr CW6 ... 147 D2
Whalley Gr WA8 ... 13 E2
Whalley Hayes SK11 112 B4
Whalley Rd CW9 .. 104 A4
Whalley St WA1 ... 16 B3
Wharams Bank CW11 176 C3
Wharfdale Ave WA14 238 D7
Wharfdale CI WA5 . 178 A2
Wharf Rd
  Altrincham WA14 . 238 D7
  Newton-le-W WA12 . 1 C1
Wharf St
  Stockport SK4 & SK5 240 E7
  Warrington WA1 .. 16 B2
Wharf The WA7 ... 50 C3
Wharfdale CI L62 . 43 F3
Wharfdale Dr L62 . 43 F3
Wharfdale Rd
  Congleton CW12 . 157 D3
  Crewe CW1 ..... 173 D1
Wharfe CI CW12 . 156 C1
Wharfe La L65 ... 70 A4
Wharfedale WA7 . 50 A3
Wharford La WA7 . 24 C2
Wharmby Rd WA11 . 1 C3
Wharton (Donefields) Ind
  Est CW7 .... 127 D2
Wharton Gdns CW7 127 D2
Wharton Park Rd CW7 126 C1
Wharton Rd CW7 . 127 D1
Whatcroft CI WA7 . 49 E3
Whatcroft La
  Davenham CW9 . 104 C1
  Lach Dennis CW9 104 C1
Wheat Croft SK3 . 240 F1
Wheat Moss SK11 . 84 A2
Wheatcroft CI WA5 . 15 E3
Wheatfield CI Barnton CW8 . 78 A2
  Ellesmere Port L66 . 69 E2
  Macclesfield SK10 . 88 A8
  Romiley SK6 ..... 241 A4
Wheatfield Rd WA8 . 22 A4
Wheatland CI WA8 . 22 B3
Wheatland Rd L60 . 41 E4
Wheatlands WA7 . 23 F1
Wheatley Ave WA12 . 2 B3
Wheatley Rd CW1 . 190 C3
Wheatsheaf La WA13 . 28 B3
Wheatsheaf Rd SK23 . 65 F3
Wheelman Rd CW1 . 190 A4
Wheelock Cl Alsager ST7 . 193 D2
  Wilmslow SK9 .... 34 B1
Wheelock Cty Prim Sch
  CW11 .... 175 D2
Wheelock Dr CW7 . 126 A1
Wheelock St CW10 . 128 B1
Wheelock Way ST7 . 195 D1
Wheldon Cl CH2 .. 118 B4
Wheldrake CI L66 . 69 E4
Whernside WA8 .. 12 B2
Whernside CI SK4 . 240 E7
Whetstone Hey L66 . 69 E3
Whetstone Rd ST6 . 179 E1
Whickham CI WA4 . 26 C4
Whimbrel Ave WA12 . 2 B2
Whimbrel CI WA7 . 49 F3
Whinberry Rd WA14 . 238 B7
Whinchat Ave WA12 . 2 B2
Whinchat Dr WA3 . 9 F2
Whinfell Gr WA7 .. 50 C4
Whipcord La CH1 . 118 A1
Whirley Cty Prim Sch
  SK10 .... 86 B1
Whirley La SK10 .. 85 F1
Whirley Rd SK10 . 86 B1
Whirlow Rd WA7 . 206 A4
Whisterfield La SK11 . 109 F2
Whiston St SK11 .. 112 B4
Whitbarrow Rd WA13 . 18 B2
Whitburn Cl WA3 . 3 E1
Whitby CI Cheadle SK8 . 239 C6
  Crewe CW1 ..... 190 A4
  Poynton SK12 ... 36 B2

Whitby Cty High Sch The
  L66 .... 70 A1
Whitby Heath Cty Prim Sch
  L65 .... 70 A2
Whitby La CH1 ...... 95 D3
Whitby Rd
  Ellesmere Port L65 . 70 B3
  Runcorn WA7 ..... 23 D1
Whitby's La CW7 .. 126 A1
Whitchurch CI WA1 . 17 D4
Whitchurch Gr ST5 . 210 C1
Whitchurch Rd
  Audlem SY14 ..... 229 E2
  Broxton SY14 .... 199 D2
  Chester CH3 ..... 119 D1
  Chowley CH3 .... 183 D2
  Christleton CH3 .. 142 C4
  Hunger Hill CH3 . 199 D2
  Milton Green CH3 165 E2
  Nantwich CW5 .. 229 E2
  Royal's Green SY13 228 B1
  Sound CW5 ..... 218 A4
  Sound, Newtown CW5 217 F2
  Waverton CH3 .. 143 A4
Whitchurch Way WA7 49 E4
White Ave SK7 ... 189 F2
White Broom WA13 19 D2
White Field Ave WA12 . 2 C1
White Friars CH1 . 237 D2
White Hall La CW11 . 173 F4
White Hall Rd ST7 . 194 C1
White Hart Gdns CW8 . 102 C2
White Hart La CW2 . 205 F4
White Hart St SK14 . 241 D8
White House CI WA11 . 1 A3
White House Dr WA1 . 17 F4
White La CH3 ..... 162 B4
White Lodge Cl L62 . 43 E3
White Lodge Mews CW8 . 102 A2
White Park Cl SK10 . 128 B1
White St Macclesfield SK1 . 112 B3
  Warrington WA1 . 16 A3
  Warrington, Stockton Heath
  WA4 .... 16 B1
  Widnes WA8 .... 23 D3
Whiteacre Rd OL6 . 242 A4
Whitebarn Rd SK9 . 85 B4
Whitebeam Ave L66 . 69 F1
Whitebeam CI
  Newcastle-u-L ST5 . 210 B1
  Runcorn WA7 ... 24 B1
Whitecroft Rd L66 . 69 F1
Whitecross Rd WA5 . 15 F3
Whitefield L64 ... 240 D7
Whitefield Ave WA1 . 16 C4
Whitefield CI Goldborne WA3 . 3 D4
  Lymm WA13 .... 19 D3
Whitefield Ct WA3 . 4 C1
Whitefield Rd Sale M33 . 242 A7
  Warrington WA4 . 26 A4
Whitefields CH2 . 72 A2
Whitefriars WIk M22 . 33 E4
Whitegate CH3 ... 121 F4
Whitegate CE Aided Prim
  Sch CW8 .... 125 F4
Whitegate Fields L13 . 108 B1
Whitegate Rd CW7 . 125 E2
Whitegates SK8 . 239 D5
Whitegates CI L64 . 42 C1
Whitegates Cres L64 . 67 F4
Whitegates Rd SK8 . 239 D5
Whitehall CI Barnton CW8 . 78 A2
  Wilmslow SK9 ... 60 A3
Whitehall CI CW5 . 204 B3
Whitehall Dr Hartford CW8 . 103 E3
  Shavington CW2 . 206 A2
Whitehall Gr L66 . 124 C1
Whitehall PI WA6 . 74 A4
Whitehall Rd M33 . 242 B5
Whitehaven La CW5 . 203 D4
Whitehaven Rd SK7 . 35 E3
Whitehill Prim Sch SK4 . 240 E8
Whitehill Rd ST7 . 195 D1
Whitehill St W SK4 . 240 E8
Whitehouse Dr WA15 . 32 A4
Whitehouse Expressway
  WA7 .... 50 A3
Whitehouse La
  Dunham Town WA14 . 20 B4
  Nantwich CW5 . 204 C4
  Plumley WA16 .. 80 C3
Whitehouse Rd WA16 . 30 A2
Whitehouse Vale Ind Est
  WA7 .... 50 C2
Whitelands Rd
  OL6 & SK15 & SK16 . 242 A4
Whiteland St SK3 . 240 D1
Whiteleas Rd SK23 . 65 E2
Whitelegg PI WA14 . 238 D6
Whitelow Rd SK4 . 240 A7
Whitemere Ct SK11 . 96 F4
Whitemoor Rd CW10 . 151 E3
Whiteridge Rd ST7 . 195 D1
Whites La CW2 ... 207 D3
Whites Meadow CH3 . 142 A4
Whiteshands Rd WA13 . 18 B2
Whiteside Rd WA11 . 1 A3
Whitethorn Ave WA5 . 14 B4
Whitethorn Way ST5 . 210 C1
Whitewood La SY14 . 212 B4
Whitfield Gr WA11 . 1 A3

Whitfield Rd ST7 ....195 D1
Whitfields The SK10 ....87 D1
Whitley Ave Barnton CW8 ....78 A2
Warrington WA4 ....17 D2
Whitley Cl
Middlewich CW10 ....151 D4
Runcorn WA7 ....48 C4
Whitley Cty Comp Sch
WA4 ....52 B2
Whitley Dr CW8 ....103 D2
Whitley La WA16 ....55 D4
Whitley Rd SK4 ....240 B7
Whitlow Ave
Altrincham WA14 ....238 B8
Nantwich CW5 ....204 C2
Whittaker Ave WA2 ....8 B1
Whittington Gdns CW9 ....104 A1
Whittle Ave
Great Sankey WA5 ....15 D4
Haydock WA11 ....1 A3
Whittle Cl CH5 ....116 A2
Whittle Hall La WA5 ....14 B4
Whittles Ave M34 ....241 A6
Whittles Wlk M34 ....241 A6
Whittlewood Cl WA3 ....10 A3
Whitton Dr CH2 ....118 C3
Wickenby Dr M33 ....242 A6
Wicker La Altrincham WA15 ....32 B4
Guilden Sutton CH3 ....120 A2
Wicklow Ave SK3 ....240 B3
Wicklow Cl L66 ....69 D3
Wickson La Ch3, CW6 ....167 E2
Wicksten Dr WA7 ....23 E1
Widdale Cl WA5 ....14 C4
Widgeon Cl SK12 ....36 A2
Widgeon Cl WA3 ....10 A3
Widgeons Covert L63 ....41 F3
Widnes North Sta WA8 ....13 D2
Widnes Rd WA8 ....23 D4
Widnes Sixth Form Coll
WA8 ....12 C3
Wiend The CW2 ....118 B2
Wight Cl L65 ....70 B1
Wightman Ave WA12 ....2 A2
Wigmore Cl WA3 ....10 A3
Wigmore St OL6 ....242 A4
Wigsey La WA13 ....19 D4
Wigshaw La WA3 ....4 C2
Wilbraham Cl CW5 ....204 A4
Wilbraham Rd Acton CW5 ....204 A4
Congleton CW12 ....156 C2
Weaverham CW8 ....77 F1
Wilbraham's Wlk ST7 ....209 E1
Wilbrahams Way ST7 ....193 E2
Wilcott Dr SK9 ....59 F2
Wilcott Rd M22 ....239 A5
Wild Clough SK14 ....241 F5
Wild Goose Ave ST7 ....195 E2
Wild St SK6 ....241 A2
Wildcote Cl WA8 ....13 E2
Wilderhope Cl CW2 ....206 B4
Widerspool Cswy WA4 ....16 A1
Widerspool Cswy WA4 ....16 B2
Wilding Ave WA7 ....23 D1
Wilding St CW1 ....190 C2
Wildings Old La WA3 ....9 F4
Wildwood Gr WA11 ....17 D4
Wilkin Croft SK8 ....239 E1
Wilkins La SK9 ....33 F3
Wilkinson Ave WA1 ....16 C3
Wilkinson Cl WA8 ....23 D3
Wilkinson Rd SK4 ....240 E6
Wilkinson St
Ellesmere Port L65 ....70 B3
Sale M33 ....242 D6
Warrington WA2 ....16 B4
Wilkinson St N L65 ....70 B3
Willan Rd CH1 ....117 E2
Willaston CE Contr Prim Sch
L64 ....67 F4
Willaston Cty Prim Sch
CW5 ....205 E3
Willaston Dr L24 ....21 D3
Willaston Hall Gdns CW5 ....205 E3
Willaston Rd L63 ....42 B3
Willaston Way SK9 ....34 B3
Willbank La CW5 ....202 B3
Willcock Rd WA11 ....2 A4
Willdor Gr SK3 ....240 B2
Willeymoor La SY13 ....225 E4
William Beamont Cty
High Sch WA2 ....8 A1
William Johnson Gdns L65 ....70 B3
William Penn Cl WA5 ....14 C3
William Rd Haydock WA11 ....1 A3
Kidsgrove ST7 ....195 D1
William St Chester CH1 ....237 E3
Chester, Hoole Park CH2 ....118 C2
Congleton CW12 ....156 D2
Macclesfield SK10 ....112 C4
Northwich CW9 ....104 A4
Widnes WA8 ....13 E1
Winsford CW7 ....126 C1
William Stockton Cty Prim
Sch L65 ....70 A3
William Wlk 2 WA14 ....238 D3
Williams Ave CW1 ....191 D3
Williams Cl CH2 ....118 B2
Williams Way CW11 ....111 E4
Williams Ave SK6 ....241 A4
Williamson Cres SK23 ....65 E4
Williamson Rd SK15 ....243 E4
Willington La Duddon CW6 ....145 F4
Kelsall CW6 ....122 B2

Willington Rd Duddon CW6 ....145 D4
Kelsall CW6 ....122 B2
Tarvin CW6 ....122 B1
Willis Rd SK3 ....240 E2
Willis St WA1 ....16 B3
Willmer Cres ST7 ....195 D3
Willotts Hill Rd ST5 ....210 B1
Willoughby Cl Sale M33 ....242 A7
Warrington WA5 ....7 E1
Willow Ave Cheadle SK8 ....239 F2
Newton-le-W WA12 ....2 C2
Reddish SK5 ....240 F8
Widnes WA8 ....13 D1
Willow Bank SK8 ....35 D3
Willow Bank CM20 ....239 B8
Willow Bank Est WA12 ....2 C2
Willow Cl Chester CH2 ....118 B4
Lymm WA13 ....18 C4
Newcastle-u-L ST5 ....210 B1
Northwich CW9 ....79 E2
Runcorn WA7 ....49 E4
Winsford CW7 ....126 B2
Willow Cres Chester CH2 ....119 D2
Warrington WA1 ....17 D4
Wilstaston CW7 ....189 F1
Willow Ct Alsager ST7 ....193 F2
Gatley SK8 ....239 A6
Higher Kinnerton CH4 ....161 E4
Macclesfield SK10 ....87 D1
Middlewich CW10 ....128 B1
Sale M33 ....242 E7
Willow Dr Blacon CH1 ....117 E3
Bunbury CW6 ....185 F4
Sandbach CW11 ....175 F4
Wilmslow SK9 ....60 A2
Willow Gn Knutsford WA16 ....56 C2
Weaverham CW8 ....102 B4
Willow Gr Barnton CW8 ....78 A2
Chester CH2 ....119 D2
Ellesmere Port CH1 ....95 D4
Elton CH2 ....72 A2
Willow Hayes CH3 ....121 F4
Willow La Appleton WA4 ....26 B2
Goostrey CW4 ....107 F1
Thornton Hough L63 ....42 B2
Willow Lea L61 ....94 C1
Willow Mews SK10 ....86 C1
Willow Rd Chester CH4 ....140 C3
Haydock WA11 ....1 C4
Newton-le-W WA12 ....2 C2
Newton-le-W WA12 ....2 C2
Partington M31 ....11 F1
Willow Sq CW7 ....127 D1
Willow Tree Cl CW12 ....156 C2
Willow Tree Gn ST7 ....193 F4
Willow Tree Mews SK8 ....239 B1
Willow Tree Rd WA14 ....238 D3
Willow Way Broughton CH4 ....139 D2
Cheadle Hulme SK7 ....35 E4
Prestbury SK10 ....87 D3
Willow Wood Cl OL6 ....242 B3
Willoway Rd CH3 ....119 D1
Willowbank Dr SK10 ....88 B4
Willowbrow Rd L63, L64 ....42 B2
Willowdale Ave SK8 ....239 B2
Willowgreen La CW1 ....94 C4
Willowgreen La CW8 ....77 D3
Willowherb Cl CH3 ....142 A3
Willowmead Dr SK10 ....87 D3
Willows Cl CW2 ....206 A4
Willows The Frodsham WA6 ....74 B4
Higher Wincham CW9 ....79 F3
Manchester SK4 ....240 A6
Partington M31 ....11 F2
Wilmere La WA8 ....13 D3
Wilmot Ave WA5 ....14 B4
Wilmot Dr WA3 ....2 C4
Wilmslow Ave L66 ....69 F3
Wilmslow Cres WA4 ....17 F2
Wilmslow Cty High Sch
SK9 ....60 A3
Wilmslow Dr L66 ....69 F3
Wilmslow Golf Course
WA16 ....59 D1
Wilmslow Grange Cty Prim
Sch SK9 ....34 B2
Wilmslow Old Rd
Mottram St Andrew SK10 ....61 D1
Wythenshawe M90 ....32 C3
Wilmslow Park Rd SK9 ....60 B4
Wilmslow Prep Sch SK9 ....60 A4
Wilmslow Rd
Alderley Edge SK9 ....60 A2
Cheadle SK8 ....239 D3
Cheadle SK8 ....239 D5
Cheadle, Handforth SK9 ....34 B3
Mottram St Andrew SK10 ....61 D2
Mottram St Andrew SK10 ....61 D2
Mottram St Andrew, Greendale
SK10 ....86 A4
Prestbury SK10 ....61 E3
Wilmslow SK10 ....34 B3
Woodford SK7 ....35 E1
Wythenshawe WA15 ....32 C3
Wilmslow Sta SK9 ....60 A4
Wilmslow Wlk 2 SK11 ....112 C4
Wilsden Rd WA8 ....12 A1
Wilson Cl WA4 ....17 E2
Wilson Cres
Ashton-u-L OL6 ....242 B4
Lostock CW9 ....80 A2
Wilson Dr CW9 ....126 C4
Wilson Patten St WA1 ....16 A3
Wilson Rd SK14 ....240 B8
Wilson St Hyde SK14 ....241 E6
Sale M33 ....242 B7
Warrington WA2 ....16 A4

Wilsons La L65 ....70 A2
Wilton Ave SK8 ....34 B4
Wilton Cres
Alderley Edge SK9 ....59 F1
Macclesfield SK11 ....111 F3
Wilton Dr WA15 ....32 B4
Wilton La WA3 ....4 A3
Wiltshire Cl
Macclesfield SK10 ....86 C1
Warrington WA5 ....17 E4
Wiltshire Dr CW12 ....156 C2
Wiltshire Rd M31 ....11 F1
Wiltshire Wlk SK10 ....86 C1
Winwick La L61 ....11 F4
Wimberry Dr ST5 ....210 B1
Wimbledon Cl SK5 ....240 C3
Wimboldsley Cty Prim Sch
CW10 ....150 C2
Wincham Ave CW9 ....79 E2
Wincham Bsns Pk CW9 ....79 F2
Wincham Cty Prim Sch
CW9 ....79 F3
Wincham La CW9 ....79 E2
Winchester Ave
Ellesmere Port L65 ....70 B2
Great Sankey WA5 ....15 E3
Winchester Cl
Shavington CW2 ....206 A2
Wilmslow SK9 ....59 F3
Winchester Ct 2 WA8 ....22 C4
Winchester Dr SK4 ....240 B6
Winchester Pl WA8 ....22 C4
Winchester Sq CH4 ....140 C3
Wincle Ave SK7 ....36 C1
Wincle CE Aided Prim Sch
SK11 ....136 C1
Wincroft Cl WA8 ....22 B4
Wincroft Rd WA8 ....22 B4
Windermere Ave CH2 ....119 D3
Windermere Dr CW12 ....156 A1
Windermere Ave
Warrington WA2 ....8 B2
Widnes WA8 ....13 D2
Windermere Cl L64 ....66 C4
Windermere Dr SK9 ....59 F1
Windermere Rd
Ellesmere Port L65 ....70 B1
Haydock WA11 ....1 A3
High Lane SK6 ....37 F4
Stalybridge SK15 ....242 D4
Wilmslow SK9 ....34 B2
Winsford CW7 ....126 B1
Wistaston CW2 ....189 F1
Windermere St WA8 ....13 D2
Windfield Gdns L66 ....69 E4
Windings The CW10 ....128 A1
Windle Ct Neston L64 ....41 F1
Warrington WA3 ....9 E2
Windlehurst Rd SK6 ....37 E4
Windmill Cl Appleton WA4 ....26 B3
Windmill La WA8 ....23 D2
Windmill Dr CW3 ....229 F2
Windmill Hill Ave N WA7 ....24 B1
Windmill Hill Ave E WA7 ....24 B1
Windmill Hill Ave N WA7 ....24 B2
Windmill Hill Ave S WA7 ....24 B2
Windmill Hill Ave W WA7 ....24 B1
Windmill Hill Cty Prim Sch
WA7 ....24 B1
Windmill La
Appleton WA4 ....26 B3
Bollington SK10 ....88 A3
Buerton CW3 ....230 C2
Christleton CH3 ....142 B4
Penketh WA5 ....14 C3
Preston on the Hill WA4 ....51 D3
Windmill Rise CW2 ....118 B4
Windmill St
Macclesfield SK11 ....112 C3
Runcorn WA7 ....23 D1
Windscale Rd WA7 ....50 A1
Windsor Ave Crewe CW1 ....190 A3
Gatley M22 ....239 A5
Manchester SK4 ....240 A7
Nantwich CW5 ....204 C2
Newton-le-W WA12 ....2 B1
Tarporley CW6 ....146 B1
Wilmslow SK9 ....59 F4
Windsor Cl Bollington SK10 ....87 F3
Cuddington CW8 ....101 F2
Poynton SK12 ....36 A2
Windsor Dr Alsager ST7 ....192 C2
Altrincham WA14 ....238 F8
Broughton CH4 ....139 D2
Ellesmere Port L65 ....70 A2
Faddiley CW5 ....202 C4
Helsby WA6 ....73 D1
Stalybridge SK15 ....242 D3
Warrington WA4 ....17 D2
Winsford CW7 ....149 E3
Windsor Gr Cheadle SK8 ....34 C4
Romiley SK6 ....241 E2
Runcorn WA7 ....49 D4
Windsor Pl CW2 ....156 C1
Windsor Rd Chester CH4 ....140 C3
Cheadle SK8 ....239 B4
Widnes WA8 ....13 D2
Wistaston CW2 ....205 F4
Windsor Sq SK11 ....112 B2
Windsor Way WA16 ....56 C1
Windsor Wlk SK2 ....240 F2
Windways L66 ....69 E4
Windy Bank Ave WA3 ....3 F4
Winfield St SK14 ....241 F6

Winfield Way WA8 ....23 D4
Winfrith Rd WA2 ....9 D1
Wingate Rd
Bebington L62 ....43 F2
Manchester SK4 ....240 C8
Wingfield Ave SK9 ....59 F3
Wingfield Dr SK9 ....59 F3
Wingfield Pl CW7 ....149 D3
Winghay Rd ST7 ....195 D2
Winifred St WA2 ....16 B4
Winkwell Dr CW4 ....141 D3
Winmarith Dr WA15 ....32 B4
Winmarleigh St WA1 ....16 A2
Winnington Ave CW8 ....103 E4
Winnington Park Cty Prim
Sch CW8 ....103 E4
Winnington St
Northwich CW8 ....78 B1
Winsford CW7 ....126 C1
Winnows The WA7 ....23 E1
Winnwick Psychiatric Hospl
....8 A3
Winscombe Dr CH3 ....119 E1
Winsfield Rd SK7 ....36 C4
Winsford Ave WA2 ....8 B2
Winsford Cl WA11 ....1 C4
Winsford Darnhall Cty
Prim Sch CW7 ....149 E3
Winsford Dr WA5 ....6 C4
Winsford Gr L66 ....69 E2
Winsford Grange Cty Prim
Sch CW7 ....126 A1
Winsford Greenfields Cty
Prim Sch CW7 ....126 A1
Winsford Handley Hill Cty
Prim Sch CW7 ....149 D4
Winsford High Street Cty
Prim Sch CW7 ....126 B1
Winsford Ind Est CW7 ....127 E2
Winsford Over Hall Cty
Prim Sch CW7 ....149 A4
Winsford Over St John's
CE Contr Prim Sch CW7 ....126 A1
Winsford Rd
Cholmondeston CW7 ....171 D1
Wettenhall CW7 ....170 C3
Winsford St Chad's CE
Contr Prim Sch CW7 ....149 F4
Winsford St Joseph's RC
Aided Prim Sch CW7 ....149 D4
Winsford Sta CW7 ....127 E1
Winsford Way CH1 ....117 F1
Winsford Wharton CE
Contr Jun Sch CW7 ....127 D1
Winsford Wharton Leaf
Lane Cty Inf Sch CW7 ....127 D1
Winsford Wharton Willow
Wood Cty Inf & Jun Sch
CW7 ....127 D1
Winsford Woodford Lodge
Cty High Sch CW7 ....149 D4
Winslow Cl WA7 ....50 B4
Winsley's CI WA5 ....15 E3
Winstanley Ind Est WA2 ....8 A1
Winstanley Rd Neston L64 ....66 C3
Sale M33 ....242 C7
Winston Ave Alsager ST7 ....193 E3
Newton-le-W WA12 ....2 B1
St Helens WA9 ....1 A1
Winston Ct CW2 ....119 D3
Winter Gr WA9 ....1 A2
Winter La SY14 ....198 A2
Winterbottom La WA16 ....55 F4
Winterford La CW6 ....147 D1
Wintergreen Wlk M31 ....11 F1
Winterside Cl ST5 ....210 B1
Winterton Way SK11 ....112 B2
Winton CI WA14 ....238 C2
Winton Rd
Altrincham WA14 ....238 C2
Goldborne WA3 ....3 F3
Winton St SK15 ....242 E1
Winwick CE Aided Prim Sch
....8 A3
Winwick La Croft WA3 ....3 F2
Goldborne WA3 ....3 F2
Winwick Link Rd WA2 ....8 B3
Winwick Rd
Newton-le-W WA12 ....2 C1
Warrington WA2 ....8 A1
Winwick St WA2 ....16 A3
Winwick View WA5 ....1 B1
Winwood Rd M20 ....239 C8
Wirral CI WA3 ....4 C2
Wirral Cres Neston L64 ....66 C3
Stockport SK3 ....240 A4
Wirral City Pk Neston L64 ....67 E4
Wirral Cty Pk WA6 ....67 E4
Wirral City Pk The
Heswall L64 ....41 D2
Neston L64 ....41 D2
Wirral Ed Ctr L62 ....43 E4
Wirswall Rd SY13 ....226 A4
Wisenholme Cl WA7 ....49 F3
Wistaston Ave CW2 ....189 F4
Wistaston Berkeley Cty
Prim Sch CW2 ....206 A4
Wistaston Church Jun Sch
CW2 ....205 F4
Wistaston Green Cl CW2 ....189 F1
Wistaston Green Inf &
Jun Sch CW2 ....189 F1
Wistaston Green Rd CW2 ....189 F1
Wistaston Pk CW2 ....189 E1
Wistaston Rd Crewe CW2 ....190 B2
Wistaston Rd Bsns Ctr
CW2 ....190 B2
Wistaston CW5 ....205 F3

Wistaston Road Bsns Ctr
CW2 190
Wistaston Westfield Cty
Inf Sch CW2 205
Wisterdale Cl CW2 206
Witchcroft Heath Rd
SK11 109
Witham Cl CW2 206
Witham St OL6 242
Witham Way ST6 179
Withens Cl CW8 102
Withens La CW8 102
Withens La SK11 136
Wither's Ave WA16 28
Withers Ave WA2 16
Within Way L24 47
Withington Ave WA3 5
Withington Cl
Northwich CW9 104
Sandbach CW11 175
Withinlee Rd SK10 86
Withins Rd Culcheth WA3 4
Haydock WA11 1
Withy Cft CH3 142
Withy Cl WA3 10
Withy Tree CE 1 M34 241
Withycombe Rd WA5 14
Withyfold Dr SK10 87
Witney La SY14 213
Witt Rd WA8 23
Wittenbury Rd SK4 240
Witter Pl CH2 237
Wittering La L60 40
Witterings The L64 41
Witton Church Walk CE
Special Agreement Sch
CW9 104
Witton St CW9 79
Witton Wlk CW9 103
Wivern Pl WA7 23
Woburn Ave WA12 2
Woburn Cl Haydock WA11 1
Macclesfield SK10 87
Woburn Ct SK12 36
Woburn Dr Chester CH2 118
Cronton WA8 12
Woburn Rd WA2 8
Woking Rd SK8 35
Wolfe Cl WA16 57
Wolseley Rd M33 242
Wolsey Dr WA14 238
Wolstanholme Cl CW12 156
Wolverham Cty Prim Sch
L65 70
Wolverham Rd L65 70
Wolverton Dr Runcorn WA7 24
Wilmslow SK9 34
Wolvesey Pl CH4 141
Wood Croft CH3 119
Wood End La L64 42
Wood Hey Gr 2 M34 241
Wood La Appleton WA4 26
Bradwall Green
CW10, CW11 152
Broughton CH4 139
Burton L64 67
Cheadle SK8 239
Goostrey CW4 107
Mobberley WA16 58
Neston L64 42
Partington M31 11
Runcorn WA7 49
Runcorn, Brookvale WA7 50
Tattenhall CH3 167
Utkinton CW6 146
Weaverham CW8 102
Willaston L64 43
Wood La E SK10 63
Wood La S SK10 63
Wood La W SK10 63
Wood Lane Ends SK7 210
Wood Memorial Sch CH4 139
Wood Orchard La CW3 230
Wood St Altrincham WA14 238
Audley ST7 209
Cheadle SK8 239
Congleton CW12 156
Crewe CW2 190
Goldborne WA3 3
Hawarden CH5 116
Hyde SK14 241
Macclesfield SK11 112
Mow Cop ST7 195
New Mills SK22 39
Stalybridge SK15 242
Stockport SK3 240
Warrington WA1 16
Widnes WA8 13
Wood View ST7 210
Wood's La CW8 101
Woodacre Gr L66 69
Woodacre Rd WA5 14
Woodall Cl SK23 242
Woodall Dr WA7 23
Woodavens Gr CW3 229
Woodbank Cl CW2 189
Woodbank La CH1 93
Woodbank Rd
Ellesmere Port L65 70
Penketh WA5 15
Woodbine Ave M44 11
Woodbine Cres SK22 240
Woodbine Rd WA13 18
Woodbourne Rd SK22 39
Woodbridge SK23 65
Woodbrook SK23 65

oodbrook Ave SK14 ...... 241 F6
oodbrook Ct SK23 .... 65 F4
oodbrook Rd SK9 .... 60 B1
oodburn Dr L60 .... 40 C3
oodbury Rd SK3 .... 240 B3
oodchurch La L66 .... 69 F3
ooddose L66 .... 44 A1
oodcock La ST7 .... 195 E3
oodcocks' Well CE Contr
Prim Sch ST7 .... 195 E3
oodcote Ave L65 .... 70 A1
oodcote Cl WA2 .... 8 B1
oodcotes View SK9 .... 34 C1
oodcotes The L62 .... 43 E3
oodcott Ave CW7 .... 126 A1
oodcott Cl CW2 .... 206 C1
oodcott Gr 8 SK9 .... 34 C1
oodcotthill La CW15 ...... 238 E5
oodcroft ST7 .... 210 A1
oodend WA7 .... 50 C4
oodend Cl CW10 .... 151 E3
oodend La
Hollins Green WA3 .... 10 B1
Hyde SK14 .... 241 D5
Wobberley WA16 .... 58 C4
oodend Rd L65 .... 69 F3
oodfall Cl L64 .... 67 D3
L64 .... 67 D3
oodfall Gr L64 .... 67 D3
oodfall La L64 .... 67 D3
oodfield Ave SK6 .... 241 A4
oodfield Cty Prim Sch
CH2 .... 119 D3
oodfield Gr Chester CH2 . 119 D3
Sale M33 .... 242 A8
oodfield Rd
Altrincham WA14 .... 238 C6
Cheadle Hulme SK8 .... 35 D4
Ellesmere Port L65 .... 70 B3
oodfield Rd N L65 .... 70 B3
oodfields CH3 .... 142 C4
oodfin Croft SK11 .... 84 A2
oodford Ave
Duknifield M34 .... 241 A8
Goldborne WA3 .... 3 E4
oodford Cl Crewe CW2 . 189 F1
Helsby WA6 .... 73 D1
Runcorn WA7 .... 49 D3
Warrington WA4 .... 17 E2
oodford Court Ind Est
CW7 .... 149 D4
oodford La Prestbury SK10 34 B4
Winsford CW7 .... 149 D4
oodford La W CW7 ...... 149 D4
oodford Park Ind Est
CW7 .... 148 C4
oodford Rd Bramhall SK7 .. 35 F2
Poynton SK12 .... 36 A3
Wilmslow SK9 .... 61 D4
Woodford SK7 .... 35 F2
oodform Ct CW7 .... 149 D4
oodgate Ave CW7 .... 194 A3
oodgreen La CW5 .... 171 E3
oodhall Cl
Great Sankey WA5 .... 15 D4
Winsford SK7 .... 35 F2
oodhall Rd Kidsgrove ST7 195 E2
Reddish SK5 .... 240 F8
oodham Cl CW8 .... 103 E3
oodham Gr L64 .... 66 C3
oodhatch Rd WA7 .... 50 A3
oodhead Rd WA15 .... 238 F1
oodhey La CW5 .... 202 B3
oodhouse Cl WA3 .... 9 F2
oodhouse End Rd SK11 . 135 D4
oodhouse La
Biddulph ST6 .... 179 F1
Buerton CW3 .... 235 E4
Dunham Town WA14 .... 20 B2
Warren SK11 .... 111 F1
Wythenshawe M90 .... 33 E4
oodhouse Mid Sch ST8 . 179 F1
oodhouse Park Prim Sch
M22 .... 33 E4
oodhouse Rd M22 .... 33 E4
oodhouse Ave Crewe CW1 190 C2
Lymm WA13 .... 19 D1
Nantwich CW5 .... 205 D3
Newton-le-W WA12 .... 2 C1
Widnes WA8 .... 12 C1
oodland Bank CH2 .... 96 C1

Woodland Cl SK11 .... 84 A2
Woodland Ct ST7 .... 193 E2
Woodland Dr WA13 .... 19 D1
Woodland End SK11 .... 84 A2
Woodland Gdns CW1 .... 190 B3
Woodland Rd
Ellesmere Port L65 .... 70 A1
Rode Heath ST7 .... 193 F4
Woodland Wlk Bebington L62 43 E4
Runcorn WA7 .... 24 A1
Woodlands Ave
Chester CH1 .... 118 A2
Congleton CW12 .... 156 B2
Kidsgrove ST7 .... 194 B1
Woodlands Cl Neston L64 66 B4
Utkinton CW6 .... 147 D4
Woodlands Cres WA16 .... 29 E2
Woodlands Ct WA15 ..... 238 E5
Woodlands Cty Inf & Jun
Sch L66 .... 69 F1
Woodlands Dr Chester CH2 118 C2
Goostrey WA4 .... 107 F1
Knutsford WA16 .... 57 D1
Warrington WA4 .... 17 F2
Woodlands Gr CW8 .... 77 F2
Woodlands Ind Est WA12 .. 2 B3
Woodlands Inf Sch M31 .... 11 E2
Woodlands La
Altrincham WA15 .... 238 E5
Chester CH3 .... 119 D1
Woodlands Parkway
WA15 .... 238 E6
Woodlands Rd
Altrincham WA14 & WA15 238 E5
Disley SK12 .... 38 A3
Hartford CW8 .... 103 D3
Huntington CH3 .... 142 A3
Macclesfield SK11 .... 112 B3
Neston L64 .... 66 B4
New Mills SK22 .... 39 D4
Sale M33 .... 242 C6
Wilmslow SK9 .... 33 F1
Wilmslow, Handforth SK9 . 34 C2
Woodlands Rd E CW8 ... 103 E3
Woodlands The
Higher Wincham CW9 ...... 80 A3
Northwich CW8 .... 78 C1
Woodlands Way CW6 .... 146 B1
Woodlark CW7 .... 150 A4
Woodlea Ave CW6 .... 118 B4
Woodlea Cl L61 .... 43 E3
Woodlea Ct CW8 .... 103 E4
Woodlea Dr SK10 .... 87 F4
Woodley Fold WA5 .... 14 C2
Woodmans Cl WA5 .... 240 E6
Woodmount CL L64 ...... 241 F2
Woodnoth Dr CW2 .... 206 B3
Woodpecker Cl WA3 .... 9 F2
Woodpecker Dr CW9 .... 103 F2
Woodridge WA7 .... 24 B1
Woodridings WA14 ...... 238 B3
Woodrow Way WA4 .... 11 F4
Woodruff Cl ST7 .... 195 F1
Woodruff Wlk WA13 .... 11 F1
Woods Gr SK8 .... 35 D4
Woods La SK8 .... 35 D4
Woods Rd M44 .... 11 F4
Woods The WA14 .... 238 E6
Woodsfin La CW5 .... 183 F4
Woodshutt's St ST7 ...... 194 C1
Woodside
Ellesmere Port L65 .... 70 B1
Knutsford WA16 .... 57 D1
Lawton-gate ST7 .... 194 C2
Siddington SK11 .... 110 A2
Woodside Ave Alsager ST7 . 193 F2
Frodsham WA6 .... 74 B4
Kidsgrove ST7 .... 195 D1
Wistaston CW2 .... 189 F1
Woodside Ct CH2 .... 118 B2
Woodside Cty Jun Sch WA7 49 E4
Woodside Dr High Lane SK6 . 37 F4
Hyde SK14 .... 241 A8
Sandbach CW11 .... 175 E3
Woodside La Poynton SK12 36 C2
Wistaston CW2 .... 189 F1
Woodside Rd Blacon CH1 . 117 E3
Great Sankey WA5 .... 14 B4
Haydock WA11 .... 1 A3
Lymm WA13 .... 19 D1
Woodside St SK22 .... 39 D3
Woodside Terr CW9 ...... 103 D3
Woodslands Rd CH4 .... 141 D4

Woodsome Cl L65 .... 70 A1
Woodsome Dr L65 .... 70 A1
Woodstock Ave
Cheadle Hulme SK8 .... 35 D4
Newton-le-W WA12 .... 2 B1
Woodstock Cl SK10 .... 87 D1
Woodstock Dr CW10 .... 151 F3
Woodstock Gr WA8 .... 12 B1
Woodstock Rd WA14 .... 238 C8
Woodvale WA14 .... 238 C2
Woodvale Cl WA2 .... 8 C1
Woodvale Rd
Ellesmere Port L66 .... 69 E3
Knutsford WA16 .... 82 A4
Woodview Rd WA8 .... 22 A4
Woodville Dr M33 .... 242 A7
Woodville Pl WA8 .... 12 B1
Woodville Rd
Altrincham WA14 .... 238 C3
Sale M33 .... 242 A7
Woodward St CW8 .... 77 E1
Woodward Wlk CH3 ...... 121 E2
Woolacombe Cl WA4 ...... 16 B1
Woolaston Dr ST7 .... 193 E2
Woolden Rd M44 .... 11 D4
Woollam Dr L66 .... 69 E4
Woolley Ave SK12 .... 36 B1
Woolley Cl WA6 .... 49 E1
Woolmer Cl WA3 .... 10 A3
Woolston Ave CW12 ..... 157 D1
Woolston CE Aided Prim
Sch WA1 .... 17 E4
Woolston Cty High Sch
WA1 .... 17 D4
Woolston Cty Prim Sch
WA1 .... 17 E4
Woolston Grange Ave WA1 .. 9 F1
Woolston Rd WA11 .... 1 B4
Woolton Ct L66 .... 69 F4
Woore Cty Prim Sch CW3 232 A1
Woore Rd Audlem CW3 .. 230 B2
Buerton CW3 .... 230 B2
Wootton St SK14 .... 241 D8
Worcester Ave
Denton M34 .... 241 A5
Goldborne WA3 .... 3 D4
Worcester Cl
Great Sankey WA5 .... 15 D3
Kidsgrove ST7 .... 210 B4
Romiley SK6 .... 241 A1
Worcester Pl CH1 .... 118 A2
Worcester St L65 .... 70 B3
Worcester Wlk L65 .... 70 B3
Wordsworth Ave
Warrington WA4 .... 16 A1
Widnes WA8 .... 22 C4
Wordsworth Cl
8 Sandbach CW11 ...... 174 B3
Wistaston CW2 .... 189 F1
Wordsworth Cres CH1 ... 118 A3
Wordsworth Ct CW1 .... 190 C2
Wordsworth Mews CH1 .. 118 A3
Wordsworth Sq CH1 ..... 118 A3
Wordsworth Way
Alsager ST7 .... 193 E2
Ellesmere Port L66 .... 69 F1
Works La CW9 .... 79 D4
World Way M90 .... 33 D4
Worleston Ce Contr Prim
Sch CW5 .... 188 C4
Worleston Cl CW10 ...... 151 E3
Worrall St Congleton CW12 156 D2
Stockport SK3 .... 240 E3
Worsborough Ave WA5 ... 15 D3
Worsley Ave Saughall CH1 . 117 D4
Warrington WA4 .... 16 C2
Worsley Dr CW12 .... 157 D1
Worsley Rd WA4 .... 16 A1
Worsley St Goldborne WA3 .. 3 F4
Warrington WA5 .... 15 F4
Worth Cty Prim Sch SK12 . 36 C1
Worthing St CW9 .... 104 B4
Worthington Ave M31 ..... 11 F2
Worthington Prim Sch
M33 .... 242 F6
Worthington Rd
Denton M34 .... 241 B5
Sale M33 .... 242 F6

Worthington St SK15 ..... 242 C1
Wrekin Way CH4 .... 140 C3
Wren Ave CW4 .... 129 E1
Wren Cl Crewe CW1 ...... 189 F4
Macclesfield SK10 .... 87 D1
Runcorn WA7 .... 50 A3
Warrington WA3 .... 9 F2
Wrenbury Cl CT5 .... 210 B1
Wrenbury Cres SK3 ...... 240 C2
Wrenbury Cty Prim Sch
CW5 .... 216 C2
Wrenbury Dr SK8 .... 239 E6
Wrenbury Hall Dr CW5 .. 217 D3
Wrenbury Heath Rd CW5 . 217 E3
Wrenbury Ind Est CW5 .. 217 D2
Wrenbury Rd CW5 .... 217 D2
Wrenbury Sta CW5 .... 217 D2
Wrenmere Cl CW11 ...... 174 C4
Wrenshot La WA16 .... 29 E3
Wrexham Cl Biddulph ST6 . 179 E1
Warrington WA5 .... 7 E1
Wrexham Ind Est (Ystad
Ddiwdiannol Wrecsam)
LL13 .... 196 A1
Wrexham Rd Bickerton SY14 200 A4
Bulkeley SY14 .... 184 C1
Burland CW5 .... 203 E4
Chester CH4 .... 141 D2
Dodleston CH4 .... 141 D2
Eccleston CH4 .... 162 C3
Faddiley CW5 .... 202 B3
Holt LL13 .... 196 A4
Malpas SY14 .... 212 C1
Pulford CH4 .... 162 C3
Ridley CW6 .... 185 E1
Wright Ave CW9 .... 104 B3
Wright Cres WA8 .... 23 D3
Wright St Altrincham WA14 238 D7
Ashton-u-L OL6 .... 242 A4
Kidsgrove ST7 .... 194 B1
Wright Tree Villas M44 .... 11 E3
Wright's La Burtonwood WA5 . 6 C2
Sandbach CW11 .... 175 E3
Wrights La WA5 .... 14 A1
Wrigley La SK10 .... 86 A2
Wrigley Rd WA11 .... 1 C3
Wrinehill Rd
Blakenhall CW5 .... 220 C4
Wybunbury CW5 .... 220 C4
Wroxham Cl Chester CH2 . 237 E4
Helsby WA6 .... 73 D2
Wroxham Rd WA5 .... 14 B4
Wrynose Rd L62 .... 43 F4
Wt Bear Yd WA16 .... 57 D1
Wyatt St SK4 .... 240 E6
Wybersley Rd SK6 .... 38 A4
Wybunbury La
Haymoor Green CW5 .... 205 F2
Wybunbury CW5 .... 220 A4
Wybunbury Rd CW5 ..... 205 E3
Wych House La CW10 .. 128 B1
Wych La SK10 .... 62 B3
Wyche Ave CW5 .... 204 B3
Wyche Cl CW9 .... 104 C3
Wyche Cty Prim Sch CW5 204 C3
Wyche La CW6 .... 185 F4
Wyche Rd CW6 .... 185 F4
Wychelm Rd M31 .... 11 F2
Wychwood Ave WA13 ..... 18 B2
Wychwood Ave WA13 ..... 18 B2
Wycliffe Ave SK9 .... 60 A4
Wycliffe Rd
Ellesmere Port L65 .... 69 F2
Ellesmere Port L65 .... 70 B3
Wycliffe St SK4 .... 240 D6
Wyedale L65 .... 70 A2
Wyedale Rd WA11 .... 1 B3
Wykroft Cl L65 .... 70 A2
Wynd The CW6 .... 122 B2
Wyndham Cl SK7 .... 35 F4
Wyndham Cres L66 .... 69 F1
Wyndham Rd CH1 .... 117 E2
Wynfield Ave M22 .... 33 E4
Wyngate Rd
Altrincham WA15 .... 31 F4
Cheadle SK8 .... 239 F1
Wynnstay Rd
Broughton CH4 .... 139 E2
Sale M33 .... 242 B7
Wynter Cl SY14 .... 198 A2
Wythburn Gr WA7 .... 49 F3

Wythens Rd SK8 .... 34 A4
Wythenshawe Rd M33 .. 242 F6

Yagol Gynradd Holt City
Prim Sch LL13 .... 196 B4
Yardley Ave WA5 .... 15 F4
Yarmouth Rd WA5 .... 14 C3
Yarrow Cl CH4 .... 139 E2
Yarwood St WA14 .... 238 D3
Yarwoodheath La WA14 .. 30 C4
Yatehouse La
Lach Dennis CW10 .... 128 B4
Middlewich CW10 .... 128 B4
Yates Cl WA5 .... 15 E3
Yates Rd New Mills SK22 . 39 E4
Thornton-le-M CH2 .... 71 F1
Yates St CW7 .... 190 B1
Yealand Ave SK4 .... 240 D7
Yeald Brow WA13 .... 18 A2
Yeardsley Ave SK23 .... 39 E2
Yeardsley Grn SK23 ...... 65 E4
Yeardsley La SK23 .... 39 E2
Yeld La CW6 .... 122 C4
Yeoford Dr WA14 .... 238 B6
Yeoman Way L66 .... 69 F1
Yeovil Cl WA1 .... 17 E4
Yerburgh St CH2 .... 118 B2
Yew St SK4 .... 240 C5
Yew Tree Ave WA12 .... 2 A2
Yew Tree Bank CW6 ..... 145 D3
Yew Tree Cl Broughton CH4 139 E2
Bulkeley SY14 .... 184 B1
Little Budworth CW6 .... 147 F4
Macclesfield SK11 .... 112 A3
Middlewich CW10 .... 128 A1
Prestbury SK10 .... 87 D4
Thornton-le-M CH2 .... 71 F1
Wilmslow SK9 .... 60 B4
Yew Tree Ct ST7 .... 193 F1
Yew Tree Dr Barnton CW8 . 78 A2
Neston L64 .... 204 B3
Sale M33 .... 242 E6
Yew Tree Gr SK8 .... 239 A3
Yew Tree La Appleton WA4 . 27 E3
Astbury CW12 .... 178 B2
Yew Tree Park Rd SK8 .... 35 D3
Yew Tree Rd Adlington SK10 . 37 D1
Wistaston CW2 .... 206 A4
Yew Tree Way SK10 .... 87 E3
Yew Wlk M31 .... 11 E1
Yewdale Dr L66 .... 69 F1
Yewlands CH8 .... 101 E3
Yewlands Dr WA16 .... 57 C1
Yewtree La SK12 .... 36 C2
Yewtree Rd WA10 .... 80 C2
York PI WA7 .... 23 D1
York Rd Altrincham WA14 . 238 C1
Connah's Quay CH5 ...... 91 E1
Ellesmere Port L65 .... 70 B3
Sale M33 .... 242 A7
Warrington WA4 .... 17 D1
York St Altrincham WA15 . 238 E3
Chester CH1 .... 237 E3
Macclesfield SK10 .... 112 C4
Stockport SK3 .... 240 E4
Warrington WA4 .... 16 B2
Yorkshire Rd M31 .... 11 F1
Yule St SK3 .... 240 D4

Zan Dr CW11 .... 175 D2
Zan Ind Pk CW11 .... 175 D2
Zinnia Dr M44 .... 11 F4
Zion St CW8 .... 103 F4

STREET ATLASES ORDER FORM

The Street Atlases are available from all good bookshops or by mail order direct from the publisher. Orders can be made in the following ways. **By phone** Ring our special Credit Card Hotline on **01933 443863** during office hours (9am to 5pm) or leave a message on the answering machine, quoting your full credit card number plus expiry date and your full name and address. **By post or fax** Fill out the order form below (you may photocopy it) and post it to: **Philip's Direct, 27 Sanders Road, Wellingborough, Northants NN8 4NL** or fax it to: **01933 443849.** Before placing an order by post, fax or on the answering machine, please telephone to check availability and prices.

COLOUR LOCAL ATLASES	PAPERBACK	Quantity @ £3.50 each	£ Total
CANNOCK, LICHFIELD, RUGELEY		☐ 0 540 07625 2 ➤	
DERBY AND BELPER		☐ 0 540 07608 2 ➤	
NORTHWICH, WINSFORD, MIDDLEWICH		☐ 0 540 07589 2 ➤	
PEAK DISTRICT TOWNS		☐ 0 540 07609 0 ➤	
STAFFORD, STONE, UTTOXETER		☐ 0 540 07626 0 ➤	
WARRINGTON, WIDNES, RUNCORN		☐ 0 540 07588 4 ➤	

COLOUR REGIONAL ATLASES				
	HARDBACK	SPIRAL	POCKET	
	Quantity @ £10.99 each	Quantity @ £8.99 each	Quantity @ £4.99 each	£ Total
MERSEYSIDE	☐ 0 540 06480 7	☐ 0 540 06481 5	☐ 0 540 06482 3 ➤	
	Quantity @ £12.99 each	Quantity @ £8.99 each	Quantity @ £5.99 each	£ Total
BERKSHIRE	☐ 0 540 06170 0	☐ 0 540 06172 7	☐ 0 540 06173 5 ➤	
	Quantity @ £12.99 each	Quantity @ £9.99 each	Quantity @ £4.99 each	£ Total
DURHAM	☐ 0 540 06365 7	☐ 0 540 06366 5	☐ 0 540 06367 3 ➤	
	Quantity @ £12.99 each	Quantity @ £9.99 each	Quantity @ £5.50 each	£ Total
GREATER MANCHESTER	☐ 0 540 06485 8	☐ 0 540 06486 6	☐ 0 540 06487 4 ➤	
TYNE AND WEAR	☐ 0 540 06370 3	☐ 0 540 06371 1	☐ 0 540 06372 X ➤	
	Quantity @ £12.99 each	Quantity @ £9.99 each	Quantity @ £5.99 each	£ Total
BEDFORDSHIRE	☐ 0 540 07801 8	☐ 0 540 07802 6	☐ 0 540 07803 4 ➤	
BIRMINGHAM & WEST MIDLANDS	☐ 0 540 07603 1	☐ 0 540 07604 X	☐ 0 540 07605 8 ➤	
BUCKINGHAMSHIRE	☐ 0 540 07466 7	☐ 0 540 07467 5	☐ 0 540 07468 3 ➤	
CHESHIRE	☐ 0 540 07507 8	☐ 0 540 07508 6	☐ 0 540 07509 4 ➤	
DERBYSHIRE	☐ 0 540 07531 0	☐ 0 540 07532 9	☐ 0 540 07533 7 ➤	
EDINBURGH & East Central Scotland	☐ 0 540 07653 8	☐ 0 540 07654 6	☐ 0 540 07656 2 ➤	
NORTH ESSEX	☐ 0 540 07289 3	☐ 0 540 07290 7	☐ 0 540 07292 3 ➤	
SOUTH ESSEX	☐ 0 540 07294 X	☐ 0 540 07295 8	☐ 0 540 07297 4 ➤	
GLASGOW & West Central Scotland	☐ 0 540 07648 1	☐ 0 540 07649 X	☐ 0 540 07651 1 ➤	
NORTH HAMPSHIRE	☐ 0 540 07471 3	☐ 0 540 07472 1	☐ 0 540 07473 X ➤	

COLOUR REGIONAL ATLASES

	HARDBACK	SPIRAL	POCKET	
	Quantity @ £12.99 each	Quantity @ £9.99 each	Quantity @ £5.99 each	£ Total
SOUTH HAMPSHIRE	☐ 0 540 07476 4	☐ 0 540 07477 2	☐ 0 540 07478 0 ➤	
HERTFORDSHIRE	☐ 0 540 06174 3	☐ 0 540 06175 1	☐ 0 540 06176 X ➤	
EAST KENT	☐ 0 540 07483 7	☐ 0 540 07276 1	☐ 0 540 07287 7 ➤	
WEST KENT	☐ 0 540 07366 0	☐ 0 540 07367 9	☐ 0 540 07369 5 ➤	
LEICESTERSHIRE	☐ 0 540 07854 9	☐ 0 540 07855 7	☐ 0 540 07856 5 ➤	
NORTHAMPTONSHIRE	☐ 0 540 07745 3	☐ 0 540 07746 1	☐ 0 540 07748 8 ➤	
OXFORDSHIRE	☐ 0 540 07512 4	☐ 0 540 07513 2	☐ 0 540 07514 0 ➤	
SURREY	☐ 0 540 07794 1	☐ 0 540 07795 X	☐ 0 540 07796 8 ➤	
EAST SUSSEX	☐ 0 540 07306 7	☐ 0 540 07307 5	☐ 0 540 07312 1 ➤	
WEST SUSSEX	☐ 0 540 07319 9	☐ 0 540 07323 7	☐ 0 540 07327 X ➤	
WARWICKSHIRE	☐ 0 540 07560 4	☐ 0 540 07561 2	☐ 0 540 07562 0 ➤	
SOUTH YORKSHIRE	☐ 0 540 06330 4	☐ 0 540 07667 8	☐ 0 540 07669 4 ➤	
WEST YORKSHIRE	☐ 0 540 07671 6	☐ 0 540 07672 4	☐ 0 540 07674 0 ➤	
	Quantity @ £14.99 each	Quantity @ £9.99 each	Quantity @ £5.99 each	£ Total
LANCASHIRE	☐ 0 540 06440 8	☐ 0 540 06441 6	☐ 0 540 06443 2 ➤	
NOTTINGHAMSHIRE	☐ 0 540 07541 8	☐ 0 540 07542 6	☐ 0 540 07543 4 ➤	
	Quantity @ £14.99 each	Quantity @ £10.99 each	Quantity @ £5.99 each	£ Total
STAFFORDSHIRE	☐ 0 540 07549 3	☐ 0 540 07550 7	☐ 0 540 07551 5 ➤	

BLACK AND WHITE REGIONAL ATLASES

	HARDBACK	SOFTBACK	POCKET	
	Quantity @ £11.99 each	Quantity @ £8.99 each	Quantity @ £3.99 each	£ Total
BRISTOL & AVON	☐ 0 540 06140 9	☐ 0 540 06141 7	☐ 0 540 06142 5 ➤	
	Quantity @ £12.99 each	Quantity @ £9.99 each	Quantity @ £4.99 each	£ Total
CARDIFF, SWANSEA & GLAMORGAN	☐ 0 540 06186 7	☐ 0 540 06187 5	☐ 0 540 06207 3 ➤	

Name..

Address..

....

....

..............................Postcode.................

◆ Add £2 postage and packing per order

◆ All available titles will normally be dispatched within 5 working days of receipt of order but please allow up to 28 days for delivery

☐ Please tick this box if you do not wish your name to be used by other carefully selected organisations that may wish to send you information about other products and services

Registered Office: 2-4 Heron Quays, London E14 4JP
Registered in England number: 3597451

Total price of order £☐
(including postage and packing at £2 per order)

I enclose a cheque/postal order, for £☐
made payable to *Octopus Publishing Group Ltd,*

or please debit my ☐ Mastercard ☐ American Express

☐ Visa   account by £☐

Account no
☐☐☐☐ ☐☐☐☐ ☐☐☐☐ ☐☐☐☐

Expiry date ☐☐ ☐☐

Signature..

Post to: Philip's Direct, 27 Sanders Road, Wellingborough, Northants NN8 4NL

Ordnance Survey
MOTORING ATLAS
Britain

Updated annually

The best-selling *OS Motoring Atlas Britain* uses unrivalled and up-to-date mapping from the Ordnance Survey digital database. The exceptionally clear mapping is at a large scale of 3 miles to 1 inch (Orkney/Shetland Islands at 5 miles to 1 inch).

A special feature of the atlas is its wealth of tourist and leisure information. It contains comprehensive directories, including descriptions and location details, of the properties of the National Trust in England and Wales, the National Trust for Scotland, English Heritage and

Historic Scotland. There is also a useful diary of British Tourist Authority Events listing more than 300 days out around Britain during the year.

Available from all good bookshops or direct from the publisher:
Tel: 01933 443863

The atlas includes:

- ◆ 112 pages of fully updated mapping
- ◆ 45 city and town plans
- ◆ 8 extra-detailed city approach maps
- ◆ route-planning maps
- ◆ restricted motorway junctions
- ◆ local radio information
- ◆ distances chart
- ◆ county boundaries map
- ◆ multi-language legend